# Microsoft

# WORD

## 6 for Windows™

**NITA HEWITT RUTKOSKY**

Pierce College at Puyallup
Puyallup, Washington

# PARADIGM

| | |
|---|---|
| Developmental Editor | Sonja Brown |
| Editorial Consultant | Carol McGonagill |
| Project Manager | Laura Beaudoin |
| Copy Editor | Rosemary Wallner |
| Proofreaders | Nancy Sauro, Joy McComb |
| Indexer | Mona Reese |
| Cover Designer | Queue Publishing Services |
| Text Designer | Joan Silver |
| Desktop Publisher | Brad Olsen |

Microsoft, Word, and Windows are registered trademarks of Microsoft Corporation. IBM is a registered trademark of IBM Corporation.

Material for selected documents has been excerpted from *Telecommunications: Systems and Applications* by Robert Hendricks, Leonard Sterry, and William Mitchell, published by Paradigm Publishing Inc., 1993.

## Acknowledgments

The publishing of a book requires the support, encouragement, and assistance of many people. We wish to acknowledge and thank the following reviewers for their time, dedication, and excellent suggestions: Mary Kelly McWaters, Palm Beach Community College; Rosalyn Culver, Washtenaw Community College; Sally Visci, Lorain County Community College.

## Dedication

To Laura Beaudoin, for her talent, patience, and professionalism and for always remaining the calm in the eye of the storm.

— *Nita Rutkosky*

## Library of Congress Cataloging-in-Publication Data

Rutkosky, Nita Hewitt.
    Microsoft Word 6.0 for Windows / Nita Hewitt Rutkosky.
       p.  cm.
    Includes index.
    ISBN 1-56118-732-1 (with 3.5" disk) : -- ISBN
1-56118-738-0 (text alone) :
      1. Microsoft Word for Windows.  2. Word processing.   I. Title.
II. Title: Microsoft Word six point zero for Windows.
Z52.5.M523R89 1995
652.5'536--dc20
                           94-5236
                           CIP

Text + 3.5" Disk: ISBN 1-56118-732-1

Order number: 01190

Text + 5.25" Disk: ISBN 1-56118-733-X

Order number: 04190

# Contents

* This feature appears in each chapter.

# Preface

When students prepare for a successful business career, they need to acquire the necessary skills and qualifications essential to becoming a productive member of the business community. Microcomputer systems are prevalent in most business offices, and students will encounter employment opportunities that require a working knowledge of computers and computer software.

Microcomputers, with the appropriate software, are used by businesses in a variety of capacities. One of the most popular uses of a microcomputer system is word processing—the creation of documents.

Word processing certainly belongs in the business office, but it is also a popular application for home computer use. People will want to learn word processing to write personal correspondence, keep personal records, provide support for a home-based business or cottage industry, write term papers and reports, and much more.

This text provides students with the opportunity to learn word processing for employment purposes or home use and to utilize a microcomputer as a word processor. The Word for Windows, Version 6, program and an IBM or IBM-compatible microcomputer system must be available for students to practice the features of the program. Word for Windows, Version 6, needs to be installed on a hard-drive or network system. To properly install the program, please refer to the Word for Windows User's Guide provided by Microsoft.

This textbook instructs students in the theories and practical applications of one of the most popular word processing software programs—Word for Windows. The text is designed to be used in beginning and advanced word processing classes and provides approximately 80 to 120 hours of instruction.

The book is divided into six units. Chapters within units each contain a performance objective, material introducing and explaining new concepts and commands, a chapter summary, and a knowledge self-check. At the Computer exercises illustrate new commands step by step. Skill Assessments reinforce acquired skills while providing practice in decision making and problem solving. In addition, a Performance Assessment is included at the end of each unit.

The performance objective identifies what the student should be able to do upon completion of the chapter. Each chapter introduces a new theory, including features and procedures, and provides examples and explanations to assist learning. A summary highlights the main points of the chapter. A section called Check Your Understanding helps students determine if they understood the material presented in the chapter.

Each chapter includes guided exercises called At the Computer. These exercises can be completed while the students are working through a chapter or after they have completed reading the chapter. After a feature or features have been presented, a computer disk icon displays with a computer exercise number keyed to the exercise at the end of the chapter.

The final chapter exercises, called Skill Assessments, require that students prepare documents without step-by-step instructions. In addition, simulation exercises at the end of each unit require students to make decisions about document preparation and formatting. These practical exercises provide ample opportunity to practice new functions and commands as well as previously learned material. Optional Composing Activities are presented at the end of each unit providing students with the opportunity to compose and format business documents. Research Activities are also included at the end of each unit. These activities help students learn how to use the Word for Windows User's Guide provided by Microsoft Corporation.

By the time students have completed the textbook, they have mastered most of the features and commands of Word for Windows, Version 6, and are ready to perform on the job as a word processing specialist.

# Basic Character and Line Formatting

UNIT

1

*In this unit, you will learn to adjust characters and lines in the creation of simple office documents, such as memoranda and letters.*

# Starting Word for Windows 1

Upon completion of chapter 1, you will be able to operate a word processing system; maintain storage devices; and create, save, close, and open a Word document.

This textbook provides you with instructions for a word processing program using a microcomputer system. The program you will learn to operate is the *software*. Software is the program of instructions that tells the computer what to do. The computer equipment you will use is the *hardware*.

You will be learning to operate a software program called Word for Windows, Version 6, on a microcomputer system. Word for Windows operates within the Windows program.

## Identifying Computer Hardware

As you work your way through this textbook, you will learn functions and commands for Word for Windows, Version 6. To do this, you will need an IBM PC or an IBM-compatible computer. This computer system should consist of the CPU, monitor, keyboard, printer, disk drive, and mouse. If you are not sure what equipment you will be operating, check with your instructor.

The computer system displayed in figure 1.1 consists of six components. Each component is discussed separately in the material that follows.

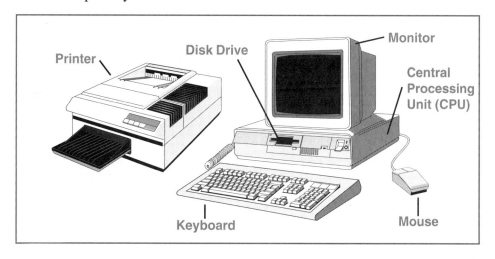

*Figure 1.1*
*IBM Personal*
*Computer System*

## CPU

CPU stands for Central Processing Unit. The CPU is the intelligence of the computer. All the processing occurs in the CPU. Silicon chips, which contain miniaturized circuitry, are placed on boards that are plugged into slots within the CPU. Whenever an instruction is given to the computer, that instruction is processed through circuitry in the CPU.

## Monitor

The monitor is a piece of equipment that looks like a television screen. It displays the information of a program and what is being input at the keyboard.

The quality of display for monitors varies depending on the type of monitor and the type of resolution. Monitors can also vary in the display color. Some monitors are monochrome, displaying only one color, while other monitors display many colors. More than likely, the monitor that you are using is a color monitor.

## Keyboard

The keyboard is used to input information into the computer. Keyboards for microcomputers vary in the number and location of the keys. Microcomputers have the alphabetic and numeric keys in the same location as the keys on a typewriter. The symbol keys, however, may be placed in a variety of locations, depending on the manufacturer.

In addition to letters, numbers, and symbols, most microcomputer keyboards contain function keys, arrow keys, and a numeric keypad. Figure 1.2 shows an enhanced keyboard.

*Figure 1.2*
*Microcomputer*
*Enhanced Keyboard*

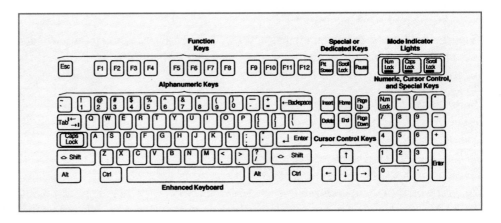

The 12 keys at the top of the enhanced keyboard, labeled with the letter F followed by a number, are called *function keys*. These keys can be used to perform Word functions.

To the right of the regular keys is a group of *special*, or *dedicated*, *keys*. These keys are labeled with specific functions that will be performed when you press the key. Below the special keys are arrow keys. These keys are used to move the insertion point in the document screen.

In the upper right corner of the keyboard are three mode indicator lights. When certain modes have been selected, a light appears on the keyboard. For example, if you press the Caps Lock key, which disables the lowercase alphabet, a light appears next to Caps Lock. Similarly, pressing the Num Lock key will disable the special functions on the numeric keypad, which is located at the right side of the keyboard.

## Disk Drive

Depending on the computer system you are using, the Word program is saved on a hard drive or saved as part of a network system. Whether you are using Word on a hard-drive or network system, you will need to have a disk drive available for inserting a disk, on which you will save and open documents.

A disk drive spins a disk and reads information from the disk. There are two sizes of disks—5.25 inches and 3.5 inches. Generally, more information can be saved on a 3.5-inch disk than on a 5.25-inch disk. A 3.5-inch student data disk accompanies this text.

The memory capacity for disks varies depending on the size and the density of the disk. Disk memory is measured in kilobytes (thousands) and megabytes (millions). Figure 1.3 shows the memory capacity for various disks.

| 5.25-inch, Double Density (DD) | 360,000 bytes (360 Kilobytes; written as 360Kb) |
| 5.25-inch, High Density (HD) | 1,200,000 bytes (1.2 Megabytes; written as 1.2Mb) |
| 3.5-inch, Double Density (DD) | 720,000 bytes (720 Kilobytes; written as 720Kb) |
| 3.5-inch, High Density (HD) | 1,440,000 bytes (1.44 Megabytes; written as 1.44Mb) |

*Figure 1.3*
*Disk Memory Capacity*

## Printer

When you create a document at the document screen, it is considered *soft copy*. If you want a *hard copy* of a document, you need to have it printed on paper. To print documents you will need to access a printer.

Printers are either *impact* or *nonimpact*. Impact printers have a mechanism that strikes the paper to create text. Nonimpact printers use a variety of methods—heat, ink jet, laser—to print characters. These printers are much quieter and faster than impact printers; they are generally also more expensive than impact printers.

## Mouse

Some Word functions are designed to operate more efficiently with a *mouse*. A mouse is a piece of equipment that sits on a flat surface next to the computer. A mouse can be operated with the left or the right hand. Figure 1.1 shows an illustration of a mouse.

The display of the mouse pointer changes depending on where the mouse is positioned in the Word screen. When the mouse pointer is positioned in the document screen, it appears in the shape of an I-beam (Ι). This is referred to as the *I-beam pointer*. When the mouse pointer is moved to the Menu bar, toolbars at the top of the Word screen, or to the scroll bars at the right side and bottom of the screen, the mouse pointer displays as an arrow. This is referred to as the *arrow pointer*. For specific instructions on how to use a mouse, please refer to appendix A at the end of this textbook.

## ■ *Properly Maintaining Disks*

A 3.5-inch student data disk containing a variety of documents accompanies this textbook. You will be saving and opening documents on this student data disk. To ensure that you will be able to retrieve information from the disk, you need to follow certain rules of disk maintenance. To properly maintain a 3.5-inch disk, follow these rules:

1. Do not expose the disk to extreme heat or cold.
2. Keep the disk away from magnets and magnetic fields. They can erase the information saved on the disk.
3. Do not wipe or clean the magnetic surface of the disk.
4. Keep the disk away from food, liquids, and smoke.
5. Never remove the disk from the disk drive when the drive light is on.

If you have an opportunity to use a 5.25-inch disk, you would follow these additional rules:

1. Do not touch the exposed surfaces of the disk.
2. Do not use paper clips or rubber bands on the disk.
3. Always keep the disk in the protective envelope when it is not in use.
4. Do not write on the disk with a pencil or ballpoint pen. If you need to write on the disk label, use a felt-tip pen.
5. Store the disk in an upright position when it is not being used.

The disk that you will be using for saving and opening documents has been formatted and includes a number of documents. If you use Word with a blank disk, that disk must be formatted. Formatting is a process that establishes tracks and sectors on which information is stored and prepares the disk to accept data from the disk operating system. The procedure for formatting a disk is presented in appendix B. (Your student data disk has already been formatted—do not format it again.)

## Using the Word Keyboard Template

Microsoft Corporation includes a keyboard template with the Word program that identifies WordPerfect keys and the equivalent Word keys, identifies Word shortcut commands, and identifies Word function keys. This template can be folded and placed next to your computer as a quick reference guide.

A keyboard template is included with this textbook designed by Paradigm Publishing Company. Use this template as a visual aid to Word functions.

## Creating a Word Document

Eight basic steps are completed when working with the Word program to create a document. The steps are:

1. Load the program.
2. Key (type) the information to create the document.
3. Save the document on the disk.
4. Bring the document back to the document screen.
5. Make any necessary edits (changes).
6. Save the revised document on the disk.
7. Print a hard copy of the document.
8. Exit the program.

In this chapter, you will be provided with the information necessary to complete all the steps except 5 and 7. You will complete several exercises to practice the steps.

### Loading Word

The steps to load Word may vary depending on your system setup. Generally, to load Word on a hard-drive system, you would complete the following steps:

1. Turn on the computer. (This may include turning on the CPU, the monitor, and possibly the printer.)
2. At the DOS prompt, load the Windows program by keying **win** (either uppercase or lowercase is acceptable), then pressing Enter.
3. When the Windows program is loaded, you will see a screen that may resemble the one shown in figure 1.4 (your screen display may vary).
4. If you are using a mouse, position the mouse arrow pointer on the Word program group icon, then double-click the left mouse button. If you are using the keyboard, press the Alt key, the letter F for File, then the letter O for Open.

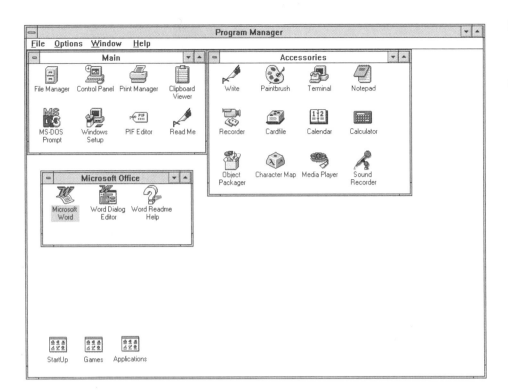

*Figure 1.4*
*Windows Program*
*Manager Screen*

When Word is first loaded, a Tip of the Day dialog box displays in the document screen with a tip about Word for Windows. After reading the tip, choose OK or press Enter. If you do not want the tip to display when you load Word, choose Show Tips at Startup in the lower left side of the Tip of the Day dialog box.

Operating Word on your computer system may vary from these instructions. If necessary, ask your instructor for specific steps to load Word, then write the steps here:

_____

_____

_____

_____

_____

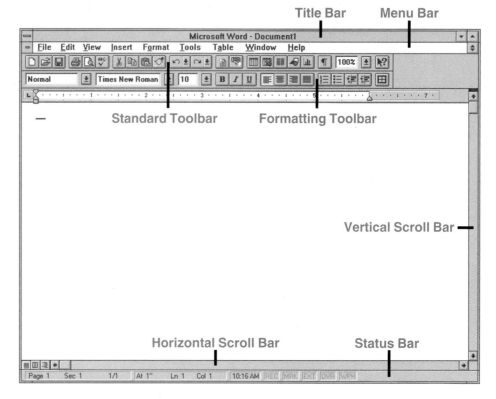

**Figure 1.5**
*Word Screen*

## Identifying the Parts of the Word Screen

When you load Word, you will be presented with a screen that looks similar to the one shown in figure 1.5. This is referred to as the Word screen.

### Title Bar

The top line of the Word screen is referred to as the *Title bar*. When you load Word, you are provided with a new document with the name Document1. When a document is completed, it can be saved with a new name. If you open a previously saved document to the Word screen, the document name is displayed in the Title bar.

### Menu Bar

The second line of the Word screen is called the *Menu bar*. The Menu bar contains a list of options that are used to customize a Word document. Word functions and features are grouped into menu options located on the Menu bar. For example, functions to save, close, or open a new document are contained in the File option from the Menu bar.

### Toolbars

The Word screen displays two toolbars with buttons containing common Word functions. The toolbar directly below the Menu bar is called the *Standard toolbar*. The toolbar below the Standard toolbar is called the *Formatting toolbar*.

The icons on the toolbars represent functions. For example, the button to print a document contains an icon of a printer. The button containing the icon of a pair of scissors is used to cut selected text from the document.

Word provides a *ToolTip* that shows what the button on the toolbar will perform. To view the ToolTip, position the arrow pointer on a button on the Standard or Formatting toolbar. After approximately one second, the ToolTip displays. For example, to display the ToolTip for the Save button on the Standard toolbar as shown in figure 1.6, position the arrow pointer on the Save button and wait approximately one second.

The display of the toolbars is on by default. You can turn off the display of the toolbars using a shortcut menu or with an option from the Menu bar.

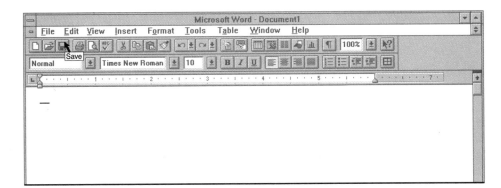

Figure 1.6
Save ToolTip

To turn off the display of the Standard toolbar using the shortcut menu, you would complete the following steps:

1. Position the arrow pointer anywhere in the Standard toolbar or the Formatting toolbar.
2. Click the *right* mouse button.
3. At the drop-down menu that displays, position the arrow pointer on Standard, then click the left mouse button.

Complete similar steps to turn off the display of the Formatting toolbar.

To turn off the display of the Standard and Formatting toolbars using an option from the Menu bar, you would complete the following steps:

1. Click on View, then Toolbars or press the Alt key, then press V for View, then T for Toolbars.
2. At the Toolbars dialog box shown in figure 1.7, remove the X from the Standard check box. To do this with the mouse, position the tip of the arrow pointer in the check box, then click the left mouse button. If you are using the keyboard, make sure Standard is selected in the Toolbars list box, then press the space bar.
3. Remove the X from the Formatting check box.
4. Choose OK or press Enter.

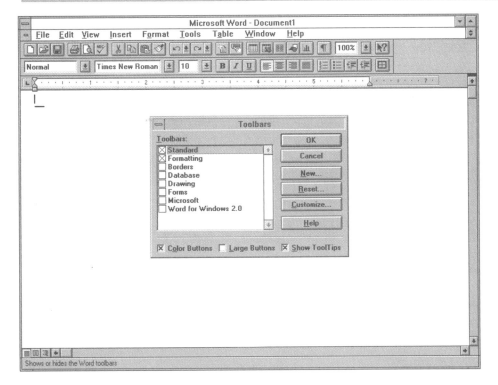

Figure 1.7
Toolbars Dialog Box

You would complete similar steps to turn on the display of the Standard and Formatting toolbars.

At the Toolbars dialog box you can also enlarge the display of the buttons on the Standard and Formatting toolbars. To do this, choose Large Buttons. To return the buttons to their default size, remove the X from the Large Buttons option at the Toolbars dialog box.

In addition to the Standard and Formatting toolbars, Word provides five other toolbars that can be displayed. The toolbars are shown in appendix F at the end of this textbook.

### Insertion Point

The blinking vertical bar, located below the Formatting toolbar at the left side of the screen, is called the *insertion point*. The insertion point indicates the location where the next character entered at the keyboard will appear.

The insertion point is positioned in the portion of the Word screen called the *document screen*. The document screen is the portion of the screen where text is entered, edited, and formatted.

The underline symbol immediately right of the insertion point is the *end of document* marker and indicates the end of the document.

In addition to the insertion point, a mouse pointer will also display in the document screen. When the mouse pointer is positioned in the document screen, it displays as an I-beam ( I ). This is referred to as the *I-beam pointer*. When the mouse pointer is positioned anywhere else in the Word screen, it displays as an arrow pointing up and to the left. This is referred to as the *arrow pointer*. For more information on how to use the mouse, please refer to appendix A.

### Scroll Bars

The gray shaded bars along the right and bottom of the Word screen are called *scroll bars*. The scroll bar at the right side of the Word screen is called the *vertical scroll bar*. The scroll bar at the bottom of the Word screen is called the *horizontal scroll bar*. Use the scroll bars to view various parts of the document. Additional information on the scroll bars is presented in chapter 2.

### Status Bar

The gray bar at the bottom of the Word screen is called the *Status bar*. The Status bar displays information about the text in the document and whether certain working modes are active.

The Status bar displays the current location of the insertion point by page number, section number, line measurement, line count, and column position. The current time is also displayed in the Status bar.

At the right side of the Status bar, working modes are displayed. When the working mode is dimmed it is not active. When the working mode is active, it displays in black. For example, if you want to change from the insert mode to the Overtype mode, press the Insert key on the keyboard or double-click on the OVR mode in the Status bar. This causes the OVR mode to display in black. This indicates that the Overtype mode is active. To turn off the Overtype mode, press the Insert key again or double-click on OVR.

The Status bar will also display a brief description of the currently selected command or toolbar button. For example, if you position the arrow pointer on the Print icon on the Standard toolbar, the message *Prints the active document using the current defaults* displays at the left side of the Status bar.

### Word Wrap

As you key (type) text, you do not need to press the Enter key at the end of each line. Word wraps text to the next line. A word is wrapped to the next line if it begins before the right margin and continues past the right margin. The only times you need to press Enter are to end a paragraph, create a blank line, or end a short line.

## AutoCorrect

Word contains a feature called AutoCorrect that automatically corrects certain words as they are being keyed (typed). For example, if you key the word *adn* instead of *and*, AutoCorrect automatically corrects it when you press the space bar after the word. There are several other automatic corrections. If you key the text shown in figure 1.8, then press the space bar, it will be corrected as indicated.

| Key | Corrected as |
|-----|--------------|
| adn | and |
| don;t | don't |
| i | I |
| incl | include |
| occurence | occurrence |
| recieve | receive |
| seperate | separate |
| teh | the |

*Figure 1.8*
*AutoCorrect Text*

In a later chapter, you will learn how to create and edit AutoCorrect entries.

## Completing Computer Exercises

You will be completing hands-on exercises at the end of each chapter or at the end of sections within chapters. These exercises will provide you with the opportunity to practice the functions and commands presented. After one or more features have been presented in a chapter, an icon of a computer disk will display directing you to a particular exercise. The computer exercise can be completed at this point or after you have read the entire chapter. Check with your instructor to find out when to complete exercises.

Exercises in the beginning chapters present text in arranged form. Exercises in later chapters include unarranged text. This provides you with decision-making opportunities. The skill assessment exercises at the end of each chapter include general directions. If you do not remember how to perform a particular function, refer to the text in the chapter.

In the exercises at the end of this chapter, you will be creating and saving several short documents. Press Enter only to end a paragraph or to create a blank line between paragraphs. Otherwise, let the word wrap feature wrap text to the next line within paragraphs.

The document screen displays somewhere between 16 and 19 lines of text at one time. When more lines than this are entered, the text scrolls off the top of the document screen. The text is not lost or deleted. When the document is saved, all the text is saved, not just the lines visible in the document screen.

## Keying and Saving a Word Document

At a clear document screen, you can begin keying information to create a document. A document is any information you choose; for instance, a letter, a memo, a report, a term paper, or a table.

### Saving a Document

When you have created a document, the information will need to be saved on your disk. When a document is keyed (typed) for the first time and is displayed in the document screen, it is temporary. If you turn off the computer or if the power goes off, you will lose the information and have to rekey it. Only when you save a document on the disk is it saved permanently. Every time you load Word you will be able to bring a saved document back to the document screen.

A variety of methods can be used to save a document. You can save by clicking on the Save button on the Standard toolbar; by choosing File, then Save; or with the shortcut command, Ctrl + S.

Figure 1.9
Save As Dialog Box

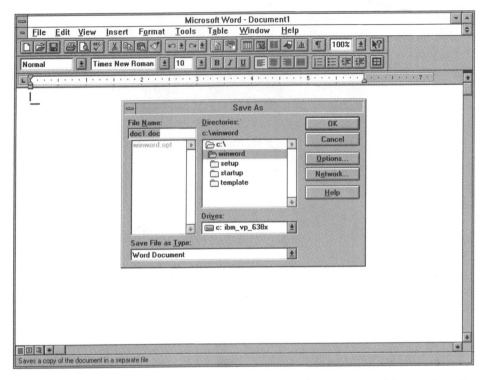

To save a document with the Save button on the Standard toolbar, you would complete the following steps:

1. Position the arrow pointer on the Save button (the third button from the left) on the Standard toolbar, then click the left mouse button.
2. At the Save As dialog box shown in figure 1.9, key the name of the document.
3. Click on OK.

In addition to the Save button on the Standard toolbar, a document can be saved by executing a command. There are three methods that can be used. One method uses the Menu bar with the mouse, one uses the Menu bar with the keyboard, and the other method uses a shortcut command.

To save a document using the Menu bar with the mouse, you would complete the following steps:

1. Click on File, then Save.
2. At the Save As dialog box, key the name of the document.
3. Click on OK.

To save a document using the Menu bar with the keyboard, you would complete the following steps:

1. Press the Alt key, the letter F for File, then the letter S for Save.
2. At the Save As dialog box, key the name of the document.
3. Press the Enter key.

To save a document using the shortcut command, you would complete the following steps:

1. Press Ctrl + S.
2. At the Save As dialog box, key the name of the document.
3. Press the Enter key.

In this text, the steps to execute a command with the Menu bar and the mouse or keyboard, the toolbar (if applicable), and the shortcut command are combined. For example, the steps to save a document are written as follows:

1.  Choose File, then Save; click on the Save button on the Standard toolbar; or press Ctrl + S.
2.  At the Save As dialog box, key the name of the document.
3.  Choose OK or press Enter.

The first part of the step, "Choose File, then Save," identifies what is selected from the Menu bar and the drop-down menu using either the mouse or the keyboard. The second part of the first step, "click on the Save button on the Standard toolbar," identifies the button on the toolbar. The third part of the first step, "press Ctrl + S," identifies the shortcut command. The last step for saving a document identifies the option that is selected to complete the function.

If you are using the mouse, the word *choose* means to position the arrow pointer on the option, then click the left mouse button. If you are using the keyboard, the word *choose* means to press the Alt key, press the underlined letter of the desired menu from the Menu bar, then press the letter of the desired option from the drop-down menu.

For more information on choosing commands, please refer to appendix C at the end of this text.

## Changing the Default Directory

At the end of this and the remaining chapters in the textbook, you will be saving documents. More than likely, you will want to save documents onto your student data disk. Also, beginning with chapter 2, you will be opening documents that have been saved on your student data disk.

To save documents on and open documents from your data disk, you will need to specify the drive where your disk is located as the default directory. Unless your computer system has been customized, Word defaults to the hard drive (usually c:) or the network drive. Once you specify the drive where your data disk is located, Word uses this as the default directory until you exit the Word program. The next time you load Word, you will need to specify the drive where your data disk is located.

You can change the default directory at the Open dialog box or the Save As dialog box. To change the directory at the Open dialog box using the mouse, you would complete the following steps:

1.  Click on the Open button on the Standard toolbar (the second button from the left); or click on File, Open.
2.  At the Open dialog box, position the arrow pointer on the down-pointing arrow at the right side of the Drives text box, hold down the left mouse button, drag the arrow pointer to *a:* or *b:* (depending on where your data disk is located), then release the mouse button.
3.  Click on the Cancel button at the right side of the dialog box.

To change the default drive to *a:* or *b:* using the keyboard, you would complete the following steps:

1.  Press the Alt key, the letter F, then the letter O; or press Ctrl + O.
2.  At the Open dialog box, press Alt + V for Drives.
3.  Press the up or down arrow key to select *a:* or *b:*.
4.  With the drive selected, press Enter.
5.  Press the Tab key until the marquee surrounds the Cancel button at the right side of the dialog box, then press Enter.

You only need to change the default directory once each time you enter the Word program.

## Changing the Default Typeface

By default, Word uses a proportional typeface (usually Times New Roman) in a 10-point size. (You will learn more about typefaces in chapter 5.) The text shown in the exercises at the end of this and other chapters will generally display in a monospaced typeface named Courier. If you want to change the default typeface to Courier, you would complete the following steps:

1. Choose Format, then Font.
2. At the Font dialog box, select the Courier typeface in the Font list box. To do this with the mouse, position the arrow pointer on the up arrow in the scroll bar at the right side of the Font list box, then click the left mouse button until Courier is displayed. Click on Courier to select it. If you are using the keyboard, press the up arrow key on the keyboard until Courier is selected.
3. Choose Size, then key **12**.
4. Choose the Default command button at the right side of the dialog box.
5. At the box containing a question mark (called a *query* box), choose Yes.

Once the default typeface has been changed in this manner, the new typeface will be in effect each time you load the Word program. The exercises in this textbook assume that the default font is 12-point Courier.

## Naming a Document

A Word document name can be from one to eight characters in length. It can contain letters, numbers, or both. You can use either uppercase or lowercase letters. Whichever case you use when keying the document name, Word uses only lowercase letters. The document name cannot contain spaces.

You can extend your document name past eight characters by adding a period to the end of the name. This is called an extension. After the period, you can add up to three more characters.

The following are examples of valid document names:

| | |
|---|---|
| mathdept.ltr | wilson.doc |
| chapter1 | 34522 |
| memo.294 | report.wp |
| 3412.888 | document.32 |

The following are examples of invalid document names:

| | |
|---|---|
| chapter 2 | manuscript |
| collins.memo | letter* 3 |

The first document name, *chapter 2*, is invalid because of the space. The *manuscript* name is invalid because it is more than eight characters in length. The *collins.memo* document name is invalid because there are more than three characters after the period. The *letter*3* document name is invalid because the asterisk symbol is used.

If you do not include an extension to a document name, Word automatically adds the extension *.doc* to the name.

## Canceling a Command

If a drop-down menu is displayed in the document screen, it can be removed with the mouse or the keyboard. If you are using the mouse, position the I-beam pointer in the document screen (outside the drop-down menu), then click the left mouse button. If you are using the keyboard, press the Alt key. You can also press the Esc key twice. The first time you press Esc, the drop-down menu is removed but the menu option on the Menu bar is still selected. The second time you press Esc, the option on the Menu bar is no longer selected.

Several methods can be used to remove a dialog box from the document screen. To remove a dialog box with the mouse, position the arrow pointer on the Cancel command button, then click the left mouse button. A dialog box can be removed from the document screen with the keyboard by pressing the Esc key. You can also remove a dialog box that contains a Cancel button from the document screen with the keyboard by pressing the Tab key until the Cancel command button is selected, then pressing the Enter key.

## Closing a Document

When a document is saved with the Save or Save As options from the File drop-down menu, the document is saved on the disk and remains in the document screen. To remove the document from the screen, choose File, then Close.

When you close a document, the document is removed from the screen and a blank screen is displayed. At this screen, you can open a previously saved document, create a new document, or exit the Word program.

## Opening a Document

When a document has been saved, it can be opened with the Open option from the File drop-down menu; the Open button on the Standard toolbar; or the shortcut command, Ctrl + O. To open a previously saved document, you would complete the following steps:

1. Choose File, Open; click on the Open button on the Standard toolbar; or press Ctrl +O.
2. At the Open dialog box, key the name of the document to be opened.
3. Choose OK or press Enter.

You can also open a document at the Open dialog box with the mouse by double-clicking on the document name. For example, to open a document named *letter01* using the mouse, you would complete the following steps:

1. At a clear editing window, click on the Open button on the Standard toolbar.
2. At the Open dialog box, position the arrow pointer on the document named *letter01*, then double-click the left mouse button.

When a document is opened it is displayed in the document screen where you can make changes. Whenever changes are made to a document, save the document again to save the changes.

## Opening a New Document

When you close a document, a blank screen is displayed. If you want to create a new document, you must open a new document. Click on the New button on the Standard toolbar (the first one) to open a new document, or complete the following steps:

1. Choose File, New.
2. At the New dialog box shown in figure 1.10, choose OK or press Enter.

## Exiting Word and Windows

When you are finished working with Word and have saved all necessary information, exit Word by choosing File, then Exit.

After exiting Word for Windows, you must exit the Windows program. When you exit Word, the Program Manager appears on the screen. To exit Windows, you would complete the following steps:

1. Choose File, then Exit Windows.
2. At the Exit Windows dialog box, choose OK or press Enter.

Figure 1.10
New Dialog Box

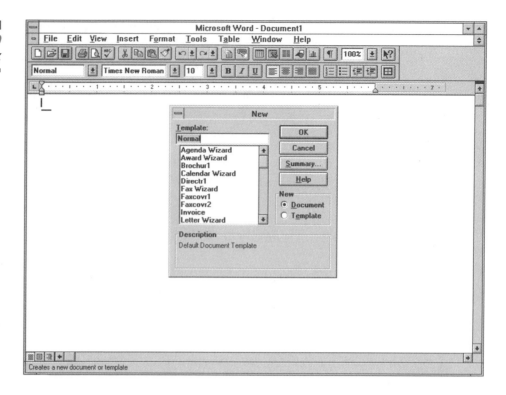

## CHAPTER SUMMARY

- Computer equipment is called the hardware. The program used to operate the computer is called the software.
- A computer system generally consists of six items: Central Processing Unit, monitor, keyboard, printer, disk drive, and mouse.
- Disks need to be handled carefully to ensure that the saved documents can be read by the disk drive. A blank disk must be formatted before saving documents on it.
- Microsoft Corporation includes a template with Word for Windows, Version 6, that identifies the six levels of each function key. The template also identifies WordPerfect keys and the equivalent Word keys; the template also includes Word shortcut commands.
- Seven basic steps are followed when creating a Word document: load the program, key the data, save the document on disk, open the document, make any necessary edits, save the revised document on disk, and print a hard copy of the document.
- The Title bar is the top line of the Word screen. The Title bar displays the name of the current document.
- The Menu bar is the second line on the screen. It contains a list of options that are used to customize a Word document.
- Word provides two toolbars with buttons containing common Word functions. By default, the Standard toolbar appears below the Menu bar and the Formatting toolbar displays below the Standard toolbar.
- The icon on each button on the toolbars represents the function each button performs. More information about each button is provided in the ToolTip that appears when the arrow pointer is positioned on a button.
- The blinking vertical bar is called the insertion point and indicates the position of the next character to be entered at the document screen. The underline symbol immediately right of the insertion point is the end of document marker and indicates the end of the document.
- If a mouse is being used, the mouse pointer will display as an I-beam or an arrow pointing up and to the left called an arrow pointer.

- The scroll bars appear as gray shaded bars along the right and bottom of the document screen and are used to view various parts of a document.
- The Status bar appears as a gray bar at the bottom of the Word screen. It displays such information as the current location of the insertion point, whether certain modes are active, and the current time.
- Word automatically wraps text to the next line as you key information. Press the Enter key only to end a paragraph, create a blank line, or end a short line. When the arrow pointer is positioned on a button on the Standard or Formatting toolbar, information about the button is displayed in the Status bar.
- Word contains a feature called AutoCorrect that automatically corrects certain words as they are keyed. For example, the error *adn* will automatically be replaced with *and*.
- In order to save on and open documents from your data disk, the default directory should be changed. Change the default directory at the Open File dialog box or the Save As dialog box.
- By default, Word uses a proportional typeface, usually 10-point Times New Roman. The text in the exercises at the end of chapters will generally display in a monospaced typeface named Courier. The default typeface can be changed at the Font dialog box.
- Document names can be from one to eight characters and can contain letters, numbers, or both but no spaces. By adding a period, you can extend the document name by three characters. If you do not key an extension for a document name, Word adds the extension *.doc*.
- Drop-down menus and dialog boxes can be removed from the editing window with the mouse or the keyboard.
- When a document is saved on the disk using the Save or Save As options, the document still remains in the document screen. To remove the document from the screen, choose File, then Close.
- Be sure to save all needed documents before exiting Word and Windows.

## Loading Word for Windows

1. Turn on the computer.
2. At the DOS prompt, key **win**, then press Enter to load the Windows program.
3. Position the arrow pointer on the Word program group icon, then double-click the left mouse button.

## Saving a Document

### Using the Standard Toolbar with the Mouse

1. Click on the Save button on the Standard toolbar.
2. At the Save As dialog box, key the name of the document.
3. Click on OK.

### Using the Menu Bar with the Mouse

1. Click on File, then Save.
2. At the Save As dialog box, key the name of the document.
3. Click on OK.

### Using the Menu Bar with the Keyboard

1. Press the Alt key, press F for File, then press S for Save.
2. At the Save As dialog box, key the name of the document.
3. Press the Enter key.

### Using the Shortcut Command

1. Press Ctrl + S.
2. At the Save As dialog box, key the name of the document.
3. Press the Enter key.

## Changing the Default Directory

### At the Open Dialog Box Using the Mouse

1. Click on the Open button on the Standard toolbar, or click on File, Open.
2. Position the arrow pointer on the down-pointing arrow at the right side of the Drives text box, hold down the left mouse button, drag the arrow pointer to a: or b:, then release the mouse button.
3. Click on the Cancel button on the right side of the dialog box.

### At the Open Dialog Box Using the Keyboard

1. Press the Alt key, key the letter **F** for File, then the letter **O** for Open; or press Ctrl + O.
2. At the Open dialog box, press Alt + V for Drives.
3. Press the up or down arrow key to select a: or b:.
4. With the drive selected, press Enter.
5. Press the Tab key until the marquee surrounds the Cancel button at the right side of the dialog box, then press Enter.

## Changing the Default Typeface Using the Mouse

1. Click on Format, then Font.
2. Select the Courier typeface in the Font list box by positioning the arrow pointer on the up arrow in the scroll bar at the right side of the Font list box, then clicking the left mouse button until Courier is displayed. Click on Courier to select it.
3. Select the number in the Size text box, then key **12**.
4. Choose the Default command button at the right side of the dialog box.
5. At the box containing a question mark, choose Yes.

## Changing the Default Typeface Using the Keyboard

1. Choose Format, then Font by pressing the Alt key, then keying the letter **O** for Format, then the letter **F** for Font.
2. Select the Courier typeface in the Font list box by pressing the up arrow key on the keyboard until Courier is selected.
3. Choose Size by holding down the Alt key, then pressing S for Size. Key **12**.
4. Choose the Default command button at the right side of the dialog box.
5. At the box containing a question mark, choose Yes.

## Closing a Document Using the Mouse or the Keyboard

1. Choose File, then Close.

## Opening a Document

1. Choose File, then Open; click on the Open Button on the Standard toolbar; or press Ctrl + O.
2. At the Open dialog box, key the name of the document to be opened or double-click on the document name.
3. Choose OK or press Enter.

## Exiting Word

1. Be sure all needed documents have been saved.
2. Choose File, then Exit.

## Exiting Windows

1. Choose File, then Exit Windows.
2. At the Exit Windows dialog box, choose OK or press Enter.

## CHECK YOUR UNDERSTANDING

**True/False:** Circle the letter T if the statement is true; circle the letter F if the statement is false.

| | | | |
|---|---|---|---|
| T | F | 1. | The insertion point appears in the document screen as an underline. |
| T | F | 2. | Software is the list of instructions that tells the computer how to operate. |
| T | F | 3. | CPU stands for Central Processing Unit. |
| T | F | 4. | Text displayed in the document screen is soft copy. |
| T | F | 5. | A blank disk must be formatted before documents can be saved on it. |
| T | F | 6. | The Word template identifies WordPerfect keys and the equivalent Word keys. |
| T | F | 7. | The mouse pointer appears as a vertical bar. |
| T | F | 8. | The document name *letter.march1* is a valid name. |
| T | F | 9. | The document name *report 6* is a valid name. |
| T | F | 10. | The document name *medical.doc* is a valid name. |

**Completion:** In the space provided at the right, indicate the correct term.

1. The default typeface for Word for Windows, Version 6. _____
2. The intelligence of the computer. _____
3. The feature that automatically corrects certain keyboarding errors. _____
4. Produces a hard copy of a document. _____
5. Used to input information into the program. _____
6. Among other things, this bar displays the current location of the insertion point. _____
7. This bar is located at the top of the Word screen and displays the name of the current document. _____
8. This bar is the second line on the Word screen and is used to customize a document. _____
9. By default, this bar is the third line on the Word screen. _____
10. The name of the gray bars along the right and bottom of the document screen. _____

## Exercise 1

1. Follow the instructions in this chapter to load Windows and Word for Windows.
2. At the clear document screen, change the default directory to the drive where your student data disk is located using the mouse by completing the following steps. (Depending on the your system configuration, this may not be necessary. Check with your instructor before changing the default directory.)
   a. Click on the Open button on the Standard toolbar.
   b. At the Open dialog box, position the arrow pointer on the down-pointing arrow on the scroll bar at the right side of the Dri<u>v</u>es text box, hold down the left mouse button, drag the arrow pointer to *a:* or *b:* (depending on where your data disk is located), then release the mouse button.
   c. Click on the Cancel command button at the right side of the dialog box.
3. At the document screen, key (type) the text in figure 1.11. Do not worry about mistakes. You will learn how to correct errors in chapter 2.
4. When you are done keying the text, save the document and name it c01ex01 (for chapter 1, exercise 1) by completing the following steps:
   a. Click on the Save button on the Standard toolbar.
   b. At the Save As dialog box, key **c01ex01**. (Key a zero when naming documents, not the letter O. In this textbook, the zero, 0, displays thinner and taller than the letter O.)
   c. Click on the OK command button.
5. Close c01ex01 by clicking on <u>F</u>ile, then <u>C</u>lose.

### Figure 1.11

Imagine the business office of the year 2,000 as presented in a textbook by William Mitchell, Robert Hendricks, and Leonard Sterry. Upon your arrival at work, you seat yourself at the ergonomically designed work station where most of your activities are conducted. (Ergonomics is the science of helping individuals interface with their immediate office environments so they can function at their highest levels.)  Features that contribute to productivity are chairs that are comfortable and that offer good back support, sufficient lighting to minimize eye strain, panels that provide visual privacy, and sufficient space to do the jobs required.

Another component of your work station is a multifunction display terminal that can generate, store, transmit, and receive voice, data, work image and video information.  This terminal has a filter to eliminate glare from windows or lighting systems and is positioned so that the top of the screen is at eye level.

## Exercise 2

1. At the blank screen, open the document named c01ex01 by completing the following steps:
   a. Click on the Open button on the Standard toolbar.
   b. At the Open dialog box, position the arrow pointer on *c01ex01* in the File Name list box, then double-click the left mouse button.
2. Close c01ex01 by clicking on File, then Close.

## Exercise 3

1. At the blank screen, open a new document by clicking on the New button on the Standard toolbar (the first button).
2. At the clear document screen, key the information shown in figure 1.12.
3. Save the document and name it c01ex03 by completing the following steps:
   a. Choose File, then Save; click on the Save button on the Standard toolbar; or press Ctrl + S.
   b. At the Save As dialog box, key **c01ex03**.
   c. Choose OK or press Enter.
4. Close the document by choosing File, then Close.

**Figure 1.12**

In the office of the next century, documents and information you create are dictated to your voice-actuated display terminal. Words appear on your terminal display for editing and revision. This activity can be done on your keyboard or with an electronic pointer device that allows you to make changes orally. Once the document is completed, you direct the system to check for spelling, grammar, and syntax errors.

The completed document can now be distributed via electronic mail to one or more individuals anywhere in the world. An electronic copy of what you created is automatically stored in the optical digital disk storage system.

## Exercise 4

1. Open c01ex03 by completing the following steps:
   a. Choose File, Open; click on the Open button on the Standard toolbar; or press Ctrl + O.
   b. At the Open dialog box, key **c01ex03**.
   c. Choose OK or press Enter.
2. Close c01ex03.
3. Exit Word for Windows and Windows by completing the following steps:
   a. Choose File, then Exit.
   b. At the Windows Program Manager, choose File, then Exit Windows.
   c. At the Exit Windows dialog box, choose OK or press Enter.

## Assessment 1

1. Load Windows and Word for Windows.
2. At the clear document screen, change the default directory to the drive where your student data disk is located. (Check with your instructor to determine if this step is necessary.)
3. At the document screen, key the text in figure 1.13.
4. Save the document and name it c01sa01.
5. Close c01sa01.

### Figure 1.13

Managing telecommunications properly in the Information Age is essential. The larger the organization, the more likely you will find telecommunications professionals. These are individuals who have earned college degrees or completed in-service programs with an emphasis in some aspect of telecommunications. In smaller organizations, telecommunications becomes one of many responsibilities attached to the manager's job.

Whether the source is voice, data, or video, transmission technology differences are minimized with the migration to digital transmission, since everything is converted to digitized data. The first step is to bring all forms of telecommunications under one unit such as a person, department, or division. The organization's size and strategic plan are key factors in establishing and managing telecommunications responsibilities.

Once the responsibilities for telecommunications have been assigned, the company can address changing, upgrading, redesigning, administering, and maintaining the telecommunications system.

## Assessment 2

1. Open c01sa01.
2. Close c01sa01.
3. Exit Word for Windows and Windows.

# Editing a Document

Upon successful completion of chapter 2, you will be able to edit and print a Word document.

Many documents that are created need to have changes made to them. These changes may include adding text, called *inserting*, or removing text, called *deleting*. To insert or delete text, you need to be able to move the insertion point to certain locations in a document without erasing the text it passes through. For example, if you key three paragraphs and then notice an error in the first paragraph, you need to move the insertion point through lines of text to the location of the error without deleting the lines.

To move the insertion point without interfering with text, you can use the mouse, the keyboard, or the mouse combined with the keyboard.

## Moving the Insertion Point with the Mouse

The mouse can be used to move the insertion point quickly to specific locations in the document. To move the insertion point, position the I-beam pointer at the location where you want the insertion point, then click the left mouse button.

### Scrolling with the Mouse

In addition to moving the insertion point to a specific location, the mouse can be used to move the display of text in the document screen. Scrolling in a document changes the text displayed but does not move the insertion point. If you want to move the insertion point to a new location in a document, scroll to the location, position the I-beam pointer in the desired location, then click the left mouse button.

You can use the mouse with the *horizontal scroll bar* and/or the *vertical scroll bar* to scroll through text in a document. The horizontal scroll bar displays at the bottom of the Word screen and the vertical scroll bar displays at the right side. Figure 2.1 displays the Word screen with the scroll bars and scroll boxes identified.

### Scrolling with the Vertical Scroll Bar

An up-pointing arrow displays at the top of the vertical scroll bar. This up-pointing arrow is called the *up scroll arrow*. You can scroll up a line in the document by positioning the arrow pointer on the up scroll arrow and clicking the left button. To scroll through the document continuously, position the arrow pointer on the up scroll arrow, then hold down the left button.

Figure 2.1
Scroll Bars

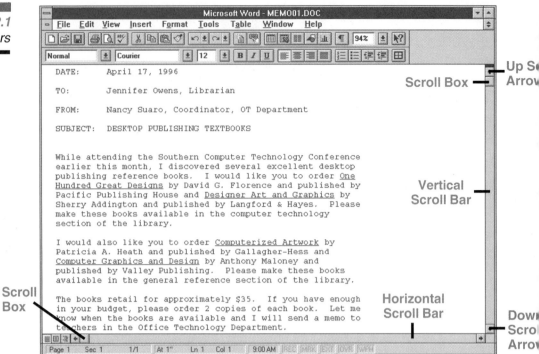

The down-pointing arrow at the bottom of the vertical scroll bar is the *down scroll arrow*. Scroll down a line in the document by positioning the arrow pointer on the down scroll arrow, then clicking the left button. Hold down the left button if you want continuous action.

When you begin working in longer documents, the scroll bars will be useful for scrolling to certain areas in a document. The small gray box located in the vertical scroll bar is called the *scroll box*. This scroll box indicates the location of the text in the document screen in relation to the remainder of the document. The scroll box moves along the vertical scroll bar as you scroll through the document. You can scroll up or down through a document one screen at a time by using the arrow pointer on the scroll bar. To scroll up one screen, position the arrow pointer above the scroll box (but below the up scroll arrow) and click the left button. Position the arrow pointer below the scroll box and click the left button to scroll down a screen. If you hold the left button down, the action becomes continuous. You can also position the arrow pointer on the scroll box, hold down the left mouse button, then drag the scroll box along the scroll bar to reposition text in the document screen. For example, if you want to scroll to the beginning of the document, position the arrow pointer on the scroll box in the vertical scroll bar, hold down the left mouse button, drag the scroll box to the beginning of the scroll bar, then release the mouse button.

## Scrolling with the Horizontal Scroll Bar

A left-pointing arrow called the *left scroll arrow* displays at the left side of the horizontal scroll bar (after three buttons containing icons). The *right scroll arrow* displays at the right side of the horizontal scroll bar. These scroll arrows operate in the same manner as the up and down scroll arrows. Click on the left scroll arrow to scroll the text to the right in the document screen. Click on the right scroll arrow to scroll the text to the left in the document screen.

If you position the arrow pointer to the right of the scroll box but before the right scroll arrow, then click the left mouse button, the text scrolls an entire screenful to the left. If you position the arrow pointer to the left of the scroll box but before the left scroll arrow, then click the left mouse button, the text scrolls an entire screenful to the right.

You can reposition text in the document screen by positioning the arrow pointer on the scroll box, holding down the left mouse button, then dragging the scroll box along the horizontal scroll bar.

# ■ Moving the Insertion Point with the Keyboard

To move the insertion point with the keyboard, use the arrow keys located to the right of the regular keyboard. (You can also use the arrow keys on the numeric keypad. If you use these keys, make sure Num Lock is off.) The illustration in figure 2.2 shows arrow keys marked with left, right, up, and down arrows.

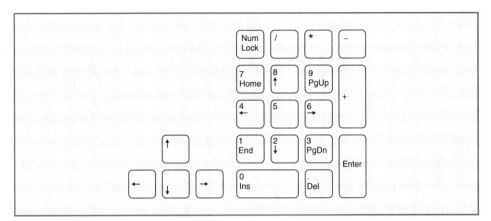

**Figure 2.2**
*Insertion Point
Movement Keys*

Use the arrow keys together with other keys to move the insertion point to various locations in the document as shown in figure 2.3.

| To move insertion point | Press |
|---|---|
| One character left | ← |
| One character right | → |
| One line up | ↑ |
| One line down | ↓ |
| One word to the left | CTRL + ← |
| One word to the right | CTRL + → |
| To end of a line | END |
| To beginning of a line | HOME |
| To beginning of current paragraph | CTRL + ↑ |
| To beginning of previous paragraph | CTRL + ↑ ↑ |
| To beginning of next paragraph | CTRL + ↓ |
| Up one screen | PG UP |
| Down one screen | PG DN |
| To top of screen | CTRL + PG UP |
| To bottom of screen | CTRL + PG DN |
| To top of previous page | ALT + CTRL + PG UP |
| To top of next page | ALT + CTRL + PG DN |
| To beginning of document | CTRL + HOME |
| To end of document | CTRL + END |

**Figure 2.3**
*Insertion Movement
Commands*

When moving the insertion point, Word considers a word to be any series of characters between spaces. A paragraph is any text that is followed by a stroke of the Enter key. A page is text that is separated by a soft or hard page break.

## Moving the Insertion Point to a Specific Page

Word includes a Go To option that you can use to move the insertion point to a specific page within a document. To move the insertion point to a specific page, you would complete the following steps:

1. Choose Edit, Go To; press Ctrl + G; or double-click on the page number at the left side of the Status bar.
2. At the Go To dialog box, key the page number.
3. Choose Go To or press Enter.
4. Choose Close to close the Go To dialog box. To do this with the mouse, position the arrow pointer on the Close command button, then click the left mouse button. If you are using the keyboard, press the Tab key until the Close command button is selected, then press Enter.

If you open a previously saved document, you can move the insertion point to where the insertion point was last located when the document was closed by pressing Shift + F5.

## Inserting Text

Once you have created a document, you may want to insert information you forgot or have since decided to include. At the default document screen, Word moves existing characters to the right as you key text.

If you want to key over something, switch to the Overtype mode. You can do this by pressing the Insert key or by double-clicking on the OVR mode button on the Status bar. When Overtype is on, the OVR mode button displays in black. To turn off Overtype, press the Insert key or double-click on the OVR mode button.

## Deleting Text

When you edit a document, you may want to delete (remove) text. Commands for deleting text are presented in figure 2.4.

*Figure 2.4*
*Deletion Commands*

| To delete | Press |
|---|---|
| Character right of insertion point | DEL |
| Character left of insertion point | BACK SPACE |
| Word before insertion point | CTRL + BACK SPACE |
| Word after insertion point | CTRL + DEL |

## Splitting and Joining Paragraphs

By inserting or deleting, paragraphs of text can be split or joined. To split a large paragraph into two smaller paragraphs, position the insertion point on the first character that will begin the new paragraph, then press the Enter key twice. The first time you press Enter, the text is moved to the next line. The second time you press Enter, a blank line is inserted between the paragraphs.

To join two paragraphs into one, you need to delete the spaces between them. To do this, position the insertion point on the first character of the second paragraph then press the Backspace key until the paragraphs join. More than likely, you will then need to press the space bar twice to separate the sentences. You can also join two paragraphs together by positioning the insertion point two spaces past the period at the end of the first paragraph and then pressing the Delete key until the paragraphs join. When you join the two paragraphs, the new paragraph will be automatically adjusted.

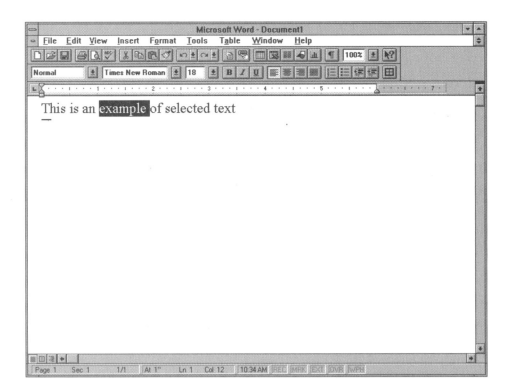

Figure 2.5
Selected Text

## ■ *Selecting Text*

The mouse and/or keyboard can be used to select a specific amount of text. Once selected, you can delete the text or perform other Word functions involving the selected text.

### Selecting Text with the Mouse

The mouse can be used to select varying amounts of text. When text is selected it displays in reverse video in the document screen as shown in figure 2.5. For example, if the document screen displays with a white background and black characters, selected text will display as white characters on a black background.

You can use the mouse to select a word, line, sentence, paragraph, or the entire document. Figure 2.6 indicates the steps to follow to select various amounts of text. To select certain amounts of text such as a line, the instructions in the figure tell you to click in the selection bar. The selection bar is the space at the left side of the document screen between the left edge of the screen and the text. When the arrow pointer is positioned in the selection bar, the pointer turns into an arrow pointing up and to the right (instead of to the left).

| To select | complete these steps using the mouse |
|---|---|
| A word | Double-click on word. |
| A line of text | Click in selection bar to left of line. |
| Multiple lines of text | Drag in selection bar to left of lines. |
| A sentence | Hold down Ctrl key, then click anywhere in sentence. |
| A paragraph | Double-click in selection bar next to paragraph or triple-click anywhere in paragraph. |
| Multiple paragraphs | Drag in selection bar. |
| An entire document | Triple-click in selection bar. |

Figure 2.6
Selecting with the
Mouse

To select an amount of text other than a word, sentence, or paragraph, position the I-beam pointer on the first character of the text to be selected, hold down the left mouse button, drag the I-beam pointer to the last character of the text to be selected, then release the mouse button. You can also select all text between the current insertion point and the I-beam pointer. To do this, position the insertion point where you want the selection to begin, hold down the Shift key, click the I-beam pointer at the end of the selection, then release the Shift key.

To cancel a selection using the mouse, click anywhere outside the selected text in the document screen.

### Selecting Text with the Keyboard

To select a specific amount of text using the keyboard, use the Extend Selection key, F8, along with the arrow keys. When you press F8, the extend selection mode is turned on and the EXT mode button on the Status bar displays in black letters. As you move the insertion point through text, the text is selected. If you want to cancel the selection, press the Esc key, then press any arrow key.

You can also select text with the commands shown in figure 2.7.

*Figure 2.7*
*Selecting with the Keyboard*

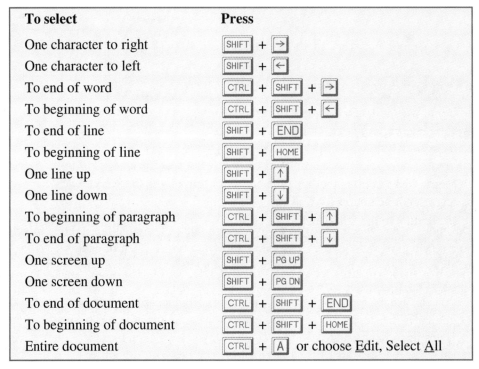

| To select | Press |
|---|---|
| One character to right | SHIFT + → |
| One character to left | SHIFT + ← |
| To end of word | CTRL + SHIFT + → |
| To beginning of word | CTRL + SHIFT + ← |
| To end of line | SHIFT + END |
| To beginning of line | SHIFT + HOME |
| One line up | SHIFT + ↑ |
| One line down | SHIFT + ↓ |
| To beginning of paragraph | CTRL + SHIFT + ↑ |
| To end of paragraph | CTRL + SHIFT + ↓ |
| One screen up | SHIFT + PG UP |
| One screen down | SHIFT + PG DN |
| To end of document | CTRL + SHIFT + END |
| To beginning of document | CTRL + SHIFT + HOME |
| Entire document | CTRL + A or choose Edit, Select All |

If you use one of the commands in figure 2.7 to select text and then decide to cancel the selection, press any arrow key.

With text selected, press the Delete key to remove the selected text from the document, or press Shift + Delete to remove it from the document and save it in temporary memory. If you want to insert the saved text in the document, move the insertion point to the desired location, then press Shift + Insert.

## ■ Using the Undo and Redo Buttons

If you make a mistake and delete text that you did not intend to delete, or if you change your mind after deleting text and want to retrieve it, you can use the Undo or Redo buttons on the Standard toolbar. The Undo button is the eleventh button from the left on the Standard toolbar and the Redo button is the twelfth. If you click on the Undo button, text you just keyed will be removed. Word removes text to the beginning of the document or up to the point where text had been previously deleted.

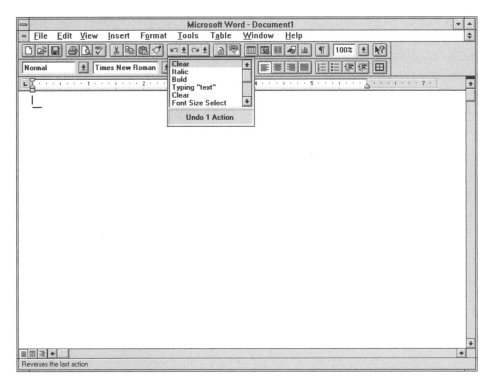

Figure 2.8
*Undo Drop-Down List*

If you use the Undo button and then decide you do not want to reverse the original action, click on the Redo button. For example, if you select underlined text, then decide to remove underlining, click on the Undo button. If you then decide you want the underlining back on, click on the Redo button.

Many Word actions can be undone or redone. Some actions, however, such as printing and saving cannot be undone or redone.

In addition to the Undo and Redo buttons on the Standard toolbar, you can use options from the Edit drop-down menu to undo and redo actions. The first two options at the Edit drop-down menu will vary depending on the last action completed. For example, if you just clicked on the Numbering button on the Formatting toolbar, then displayed the Edit drop-down menu, the first option displays as Undo Number Default. The second option displays as Repeat Number Default.

If you decide you do not want the numbering option, choose Edit, then Undo Number Default. You can also just click on the Undo button on the Standard toolbar. You can also use a shortcut command to undo or redo an action. Press Ctrl + Z to undo an action or press Ctrl + Y to redo an action.

Word maintains actions in temporary memory. If you want to undo an action performed earlier, click on the down-pointing arrow to the right of the Undo button. This causes a drop-down list to display as shown in figure 2.8.

To make a selection from this drop-down list, double-click on the desired action. You can do the same with the actions in the Redo drop-down list. To display the Redo drop-down list, click on the down-pointing arrow to the right of the Redo button. To redo an action, double-click on the desired action. Multiple actions should be undone or redone in sequence.

## Saving Documents

In chapter 1, you learned to save a document with the Save button on the Standard toolbar or the Save option from the File drop-down menu. The File drop-down menu also contains a Save As option. The Save As option is used to save a previously created document with a new name.

For example, suppose you created and saved a document named *memo*, then later open it. If you save the document again with the Save button on the Standard toolbar or the Save option from the File drop-down menu, Word will save the document with the same name. You will not be prompted to key a name for the document. This is because Word assumes that when you use the <u>S</u>ave option on a previously saved document, you want to save it with the same name. If you open the document named *memo* to the document screen, make some changes to it, then want to save it with a new name, you must use the Save <u>A</u>s option. When you use the Save <u>A</u>s option, Word displays the Save As dialog box where you can key a new name for the document.

To save a document with Save As, you would complete the following steps:

1. Choose <u>F</u>ile, Save <u>A</u>s.
2. At the Save As dialog box, key the document name.
3. Choose OK or press Enter.

In many of the computer exercises in this textbook, you will be asked to open a document from your student data disk, then save it with a new name. You will be instructed to use the Save <u>A</u>s option to do this.

## ■ *Printing a Document*

The computer exercises you will be completing require that you make a hard copy of the document. (Soft copy is a document displayed in the document screen and hard copy is a document printed on paper.) There are several methods for printing a document. To immediately print the document displayed in the document screen, click on the Print button on the Standard toolbar. You can also print from the Print dialog box. To print the current document through the Print dialog box, you would complete the following steps:

1. Open the document to be printed.
2. Choose <u>F</u>ile, then <u>P</u>rint; or press Ctrl + P.
3. At the Print dialog box, choose OK or press Enter.

When you choose OK or press Enter at the Print dialog box, the document is sent to the printer. Before displaying the dialog box, check to make sure the printer is turned on.

## CHAPTER SUMMARY

- The insertion point can be moved throughout the document without interfering with text by using the mouse, the keyboard, or the mouse combined with the keyboard.
- The insertion point can be moved by character, word, screen, or page and from the first to the last character in a document.
- Switch to the Overtype mode if you want to key over something. When Overtype is on, the OVR mode button in the Status bar displays in black.
- Text can be deleted by character, word, line, several lines, or partial page using specific keys or by selecting text using the mouse or the keyboard.
- The horizontal/vertical scroll bars and the mouse can be used to scroll through a document. The scroll box indicates the location of the text in the document screen in relation to the remainder of the document.
- To split a paragraph into two, position the insertion point on the first letter that will begin the new paragraph, then press Enter twice. To join two paragraphs into one, position the insertion point on the first character of the second paragraph, then press the Backspace key twice.
- A specific amount of text can be selected using the mouse or the keyboard. That text can then be deleted or manipulated in other ways using Word functions.
- The selection bar can be used to select specific units of text such as a line. The selection bar is the space at the left side of the document screen between the left edge of the screen and the text.

- Use the Undo or Redo buttons on the Standard toolbar if you change your mind after deleting text and want to retrieve it. Also, if you click on the Undo button, text you just keyed will be removed back to the beginning of the document or up to the point where text had been previously deleted.
- The Save <u>A</u>s option is used to save a previously created document with a new name.
- To print a document, open the document to be printed, then click on the Print button on the Standard toolbar.

## COMMANDS REVIEW

### Scrolling Review

#### Using the Mouse and the Vertical Scroll Bar

| | |
|---|---|
| Up one line | Click on the up scroll arrow of the vertical scroll bar |
| Up several lines | Position arrow pointer as above, then hold down left button |
| Down one line | Click on the down scroll arrow of the vertical scroll bar |
| Down several lines | Position arrow pointer as above, then hold down left mouse button |
| Up one screen | Click with arrow pointer above the scroll box on the vertical scroll bar |
| Up several screens | Position the arrow pointer as above, then hold down left mouse button |
| Down one screen | Click with arrow pointer below the scroll box on the vertical scroll bar |
| Down several screens | Position the arrow pointer as above, then hold down left mouse button |
| To beginning of document | Position the arrow pointer on the scroll box, hold down left mouse button, drag the scroll box to the beginning of the scroll bar, then release the mouse button |
| To end of document | Position the arrow pointer on the scroll box, hold down left mouse button, drag the scroll box to the end of the scroll bar, then release the mouse button |

#### Using the Mouse and the Horizontal Scroll Bar

| | |
|---|---|
| One screenful to the left | Position the arrow pointer to the right of the scroll box on the horizontal scroll bar, then click the left mouse button |
| One screenful to the right | Position the arrow pointer to the left of the scroll box on the horizontal scroll bar, then click the left mouse button |
| Reposition text horizontally in the document screen | Position the arrow pointer on the scroll box on the horizontal scroll bar, hold down the left mouse button, then drag the scroll box along the scroll bar |

### Insertion Point Movement Review

#### Using the Mouse

| | |
|---|---|
| To move to a specific location | Move arrow pointer to desired location, then click left mouse button |
| To move to a specific page | 1. Choose <u>E</u>dit, <u>G</u>o To; or double-click on the page number at the left side of the Status bar. |
| | 2. Key the page number. |
| | 3. Choose Go <u>T</u>o or press Enter. |
| | 4. Click on the Close command button. |

## *Using the Keyboard*

| *To move insertion point* | *Press* |
|---|---|
| One character left | ← |
| One character right | → |
| One line up | ↑ |
| One line down | ↓ |
| One word to the left | CTRL + ← |
| One word to the right | CTRL + → |
| To end of line | END |
| To beginning of line | HOME |
| To beginning of current paragraph | CTRL + ↑ |
| To beginning of previous paragraph | CTRL + ↑ ↑ |
| To beginning of next paragraph | CTRL + ↓ |
| Up one screen | PG UP |
| Down one screen | PG DN |
| To top of screen | CTRL + PG UP |
| To bottom of screen | CTRL + PG DN |
| To top of previous page | ALT + CTRL + PG UP |
| To top of next page | ALT + CTRL + PG DN |
| To beginning of document | CTRL + HOME |
| To end of document | CTRL + END |
| To a specific page | 1. CTRL + G |

2. Key the page number.
3. Choose Go To or press Enter.
4. Click on the Close command button.

| | |
|---|---|
| To last location when document was closed | SHIFT + F5 |

## Deletion Commands Review

| *To delete* | *Press* |
|---|---|
| Character right of insertion point | DEL |
| Character left of insertion point | BACK SPACE |
| Word before insertion point | CTRL + BACK SPACE |
| Word after insertion point | CTRL + DEL |

## Selecting Text Review

### *Using the Mouse*

| | |
|---|---|
| To select text | Position I-beam pointer at the beginning of text to be selected, hold down left mouse button, drag the I-beam pointer to end of text to be selected, then release the mouse button |

| *To select* | *Complete these steps* |
|---|---|
| A word | Double-click on the word |
| A line of text | Click in selection bar to the left of line |
| Multiple lines of text | Drag in selection bar to left of lines |
| A sentence | Hold down Ctrl key then click anywhere in sentence |
| A paragraph | Double-click in selection bar next to paragraph or triple-click anywhere in paragraph |
| Multiple paragraphs | Drag in selection bar |
| An entire document | Triple-click in selection bar |
| To cancel a selection | Click anywhere outside the selected text in the document screen |

## Using the Keyboard

| *To select* | *Press* |
|---|---|
| One character to right | SHIFT + → |
| One character to left | SHIFT + ← |
| To end of word | CTRL + SHIFT + → |
| To beginning of word | CTRL + SHIFT + ← |
| To end of line | SHIFT + END |
| To beginning of line | SHIFT + HOME |
| One line up | SHIFT + ↑ |
| One line down | SHIFT + ↓ |
| To beginning of paragraph | CTRL + SHIFT + ↑ |
| To end of paragraph | CTRL + SHIFT + ↓ |
| One screen up | SHIFT + PG UP |
| One screen down | SHIFT + PG DN |
| To end of document | CTRL + SHIFT + END |
| To beginning of document | CTRL + SHIFT + HOME |
| Entire document | CTRL + A or choose Edit, Select All |
| To cancel a selection | Press any arrow key |

## Deleting Selected Text

| | |
|---|---|
| Select, then permanently delete selected text | Select text, press DEL |
| Select, then remove text to temporary memory | Select text, press SHIFT + DEL |
| Insert text from temporary memory into document | Position insertion point, press SHIFT + INS |

## Other Commands Review

| | |
|---|---|
| Turn on Overtype | Double-click on the OVR mode button on the Status bar, or press the Insert key |
| Undo option | Click on the eleventh button from the left on the Standard toolbar; or click on the down-pointing arrow to the right of the Undo button; or choose Undo from the Edit drop-down menu; or press Ctrl + Z |

| Redo option | Click on the twelfth button from the left on the Standard toolbar; or click on the down-pointing arrow to the right of the Redo button; or choose Redo from the Edit drop-down menu; or press Ctrl + Y |
|---|---|
| Save As | 1. Choose File, then Save As. |
| | 2. At the Save As dialog box, key the document name. |
| | 3. Choose OK or press Enter. |
| Print | 1. Open the document. |
| | 2. Click on the Print button on the Standard toolbar |
| | or |
| | 1. Open the document. |
| | 2. Choose File, then Print or press Ctrl + P. |
| | 3. At the Print dialog box, choose OK or press Enter. |

## CHECK YOUR UNDERSTANDING

**True/False:** Circle the letter T if the statement is true; circle the letter F if the statement is false.

T F 1. By default, Word replaces old text with new characters that are keyed over the old text.

T F 2. Scrolling in a document changes the text displayed but does not move the insertion point.

T F 3. Text in the document screen can be adjusted to the right or left using the vertical scroll bar.

T F 4. When moving the insertion point, Word considers a paragraph to be any text followed by two strokes of the Enter key.

T F 5. To split one paragraph into two, position the insertion point on the first letter that will begin a new paragraph, then press Enter twice.

T F 6. Select text only if you plan to delete it.

T F 7. Many Word actions can be undone or redone with the Undo or Redo buttons.

T F 8. The Save As option is used to save a previously created document with a new name.

T F 9. The printer produces a soft copy of a document.

T F 10. Use the Go To command to place the insertion point at a specific position on the current page.

**Completion:** In the space provided at the right, indicate the correct term, command, or number.

1. Use this keyboard command to move the insertion point to the beginning of the previous page. _____

2. When Overtype is on, this mode button displays black. _____

3. To delete the word after the insertion point, use this keyboard command. _____

4. To join two paragraphs into one, position the insertion point on the first character of the second paragraph, then press this key until the paragraphs join. _____

5. Complete these steps using the mouse to select one word. _____

6. Use this keyboard command to select text to the end of the line. _____

7. If you click on this button on the Standard toolbar, text you just keyed will be removed. _____

8. Use this keyboard command to move the insertion point to the end of the document. _____

9. Use this keyboard command to select text to the end of the paragraph. _____

10. To select various amounts of text using the mouse, you can click on this bar. _____

## Exercise 1

1. Load Word following the instructions in chapter 1.
2. Open report01. This document is located on your student data disk.
3. Practice moving the insertion point and scrolling through the document using the mouse by completing the following steps:
   a. Position the I-beam pointer at the beginning of the first paragraph, then click the left mouse button. This moves the insertion point to the location of the I-beam pointer.
   b. Position the arrow pointer on the down scroll arrow on the vertical scroll bar, then click the left mouse button several times. This scrolls down lines of text in the document. With the arrow pointer on the down scroll arrow, hold down the left mouse button and keep it down until the end of the document is displayed.
   c. Position the arrow pointer on the up scroll arrow and hold down the left mouse button until the beginning of the document is displayed.
4. Position the arrow pointer below the scroll box, then click the left mouse button. Continue clicking the mouse button below the scroll box until the end of the document is displayed.
5. Position the arrow pointer on the scroll box in the vertical scroll bar. Hold down the left mouse button, drag the scroll box to the top of the vertical scroll bar, then release the mouse button.
6. Close report01.

## Exercise 2

1. Open report01. This document is located on your student data disk.
2. Practice moving the insertion point with the keyboard by completing the following steps:
   a. Press the right arrow key to move the insertion point to the next character to the right. Continue pressing the right arrow key until the insertion point is located at the end of the first paragraph.
   b. Press Ctrl + right arrow key to move the insertion point to the next word to the right. Continue pressing Ctrl + right arrow until the insertion point is located on the last word of the second paragraph.
   c. Press Ctrl + left arrow key until the insertion point is positioned at the beginning of the document.
   d. Press the End key to move the insertion point to the end of the title.
   e. Press the Home key to move the insertion point to the beginning of the title.
   f. Press Ctrl + Page Down to move the insertion point to the bottom of the document screen.
   g. Press Ctrl + Page Up to move the insertion point to the top of the document screen.
   h. Press Alt + Ctrl + Page Down to position the insertion point at the beginning of page 2. Press Alt + Ctrl + Page Down again to position the insertion point at the beginning of page 3.
   i. Press Alt + Ctrl + Page Up to position the insertion point at the beginning of page 2.
   j. Press Alt + Ctrl + Page Up to position the insertion point at the beginning of the document.
   k. Position the insertion point at the beginning of page 3 using the Go To option by completing the following steps:
      (1) Choose Edit, Go To; press Ctrl + G; or double-click on the page number at the left side of the Status bar.
      (2) At the Go To dialog box, key **3.**
      (3) Choose Go To or press Enter.

(4) When the insertion point is positioned at the beginning of page 3, choose Close to close the Go To dialog box. To do this with the mouse, click on the Close command button. If you are using the keyboard, press the Tab key until the Close command button is selected, then press Enter.

   l.  Press Ctrl + End to move the insertion point to the end of the document.

   m. Press Ctrl + Home to move the insertion point to the beginning of the document.

3. Close report01.

## Exercise 3

1. Open c02ex03. This document is located on your student data disk.
2. Make the changes indicated by the proofreaders' marks in figure 2.9. (Proofreaders' marks are listed and described in appendix E at the end of this textbook.)
3. Save the document with the same name (c02ex03) by using the Save option from the File menu or clicking on the Save button on the Standard toolbar.
4. Close c02ex03.

---

**Figure 2.9**

In a ~~text~~book on telecommunications written by William Mitchell, Robert Hendricks, and Leonard Sterry, the authors ~~describe~~ *define* telecommunications technology as "the electronic communication of information over distance." This definition contains ~~several~~ key words. First, "electronic" refers to the present-day use of *three* telecommunications ~~which involves the use of technology for signaling purposes.~~

*The* A second ~~critical~~ *important* word in the definition is "communication." This word ~~denotes~~ *indicates* that the receiver of the information ~~understands~~ *comprehends* what has been transmitted. ~~In other words,~~ information becomes knowledge only after it has been communicated and understood.

*The third* ~~Another~~ key word is "information." Information comes in ~~many~~ *several* forms, including text, sound, graphics, animation, and video images. ~~You are probably already familiar with specific examples of these forms without being aware that they are products of telecommunications technology.~~

---

## Exercise 4

1. Open c02ex04. This document is located on your student data disk.
2. Delete the name, *Dr. Lillian Stanford*, and the department, *Office Technology Department*, using the mouse by completing the following steps:
   a. Position the I-beam pointer on the *D* in *Dr.* (in the address).
   b. Hold down the left mouse button, then drag the mouse down until *Dr. Lillian Stanford* and *Office Technology Department* are selected.
   c. Release the left mouse button.
   d. Press the Delete key.
3. Position the insertion point at the left margin on the line above *Knoxville Community College*, then key the name **Mrs. Lisa Kissinger**.
4. Delete the reference line, *Re: Desktop Publishing Course*, using the Extend Selection key, F8, by completing the following steps:
   a. Position the insertion point on the *R* in *Re:*.
   b. Press F8 to turn on select.

    c. Press the down arrow key twice. (This selects the reference line and the blank line below it.)

    d. Press the Delete key.

5. Delete the first sentence in the first paragraph using the mouse by completing the following steps:

    a. Position the I-beam pointer anywhere in the sentence, *The Southern Computer Technology conference we attended last week was very educational for me.*

    b. Hold down the Ctrl key, then click the left mouse button.

    c. Press the Delete key.

6. Delete the first sentence in the second paragraph (the sentence that reads *The interest in the class has been phenomenal.*) using the keyboard by completing the following steps:

    a. Position the insertion point on the first letter of the sentence (the *T* in *The*).

    b. Hold down the Shift key, then press the right arrow key until the sentence is selected. Be sure to include the period at the end of the sentence and the two spaces after the period.

    c. Press the Delete key.

7. Delete the third paragraph in the letter using the mouse by completing the following steps:

    a. Position the I-beam pointer anywhere in the third paragraph (the paragraph that begins *The instructor for the course...*).

    b. Triple-click the left mouse button.

    c. Press the Delete key.

    d. Press the Delete key to delete the blank line before the last paragraph.

8. Save the document with the same name (c02ex04) by using the Save option from the File menu or clicking on the Save button on the Standard toolbar.

9. Close c02ex04.

## Exercise 5

1. Open para01. This document is located on your student data disk.

2. Move the insertion point to the end of the document. Press the Backspace key until the last three words of the document (*cluttering your desk.*) are deleted. Be sure to delete the space before the word *cluttering*.

3. Undo the deletion by clicking on the Undo button on the Standard toolbar.

4. Redo the deletion by clicking on the Redo button on the Standard toolbar.

5. Key a period after the word *papers* to end the sentence.

6. Select the first sentence in the first paragraph, then delete it.

7. Select the second paragraph in the document, then delete it.

8. Undo the two deletions by completing the following steps:

    a. Click on the down-pointing arrow to the right of the Undo button.

    b. Click on the first Clear listed in the drop-down menu. (This redisplays the paragraph that was deleted, and the paragraph is selected.)

    c. Click on the down-pointing arrow to the right of the Undo button.

    d. Click on the only Clear. (This redisplays the sentence.)

    e. Deselect the sentence.

9. Save the document with the same name (para01) by using the Save option from the File menu or clicking on the Save button on the Standard toolbar.

10. Close para01.

## Exercise 6

1. Open para02. This document is located on your student data disk.

2. Save the document with the name c02ex06 using Save As by completing the following steps:

    a. Choose File, Save As.

    b. At the Save As dialog box, key **c02ex06**.

    c. Choose OK or press Enter.

3. Make the changes indicated by the proofreaders' marks in figure 2.10.
4. Save the document again with the same name (c02ex06). To do this, choose File, then Save; click on the Save button on the Standard toolbar; or press Ctrl + S.
5. Close c02ex06.

**Figure 2.10**

Telecommunications plays a^n ~~vital~~ *important* role in our personal and business lives. ~~Because of these versatile systems,~~ we can watch ~~rock~~ concerts broadcast via satellite; use paging devices that display telephone numbers and print messages ~~as well~~; ~~view live telecasts of championship boxing matches,~~ transmit and receive information via facsimile (FAX) machines; listen to compact laser discs of our favorite music; call clients on cellular phones; and send computer data ~~via~~ modems.
^ *by way of*

The technologies that make these activities possible are remarkable in themselves. They become even more impressive when you consider that most have been developed in only the past one or two decades. # Telecommunications technology is expected to continue growing at *an* ~~this~~ astounding rate. A telecommunications magazine *editor* has projected that worldwide annual spending on telecommunications ~~products and services~~ will reach 1 trillion dollars by the year 2001.

## Exercise 7

1. Print c02ex03 by completing the following steps:
   a. Open c02ex03.
   b. Choose File, then Print; or press Ctrl + P.
   c. At the Print dialog box, choose OK or press Enter.
2. Close c02ex03.
3. Open c02ex04.
4. Print c02ex04 by clicking on the Print button on the Standard toolbar.
5. Close c02ex04.

## SKILL ASSESSMENTS

## Assessment 1

1. Open para03. This document is located on your student data disk.
2. Save the document with Save As and name it c02sa01.
3. Make the changes indicated by the proofreaders' marks in figure 2.11.
4. Save the document again with the same name (c02sa01). To do this, choose File, then Save; click on the Save button on the Standard toolbar; or press Ctrl + S.
5. Print c02sa01.
6. Close c02sa01.

**Figure 2.11**

You have just been hired as an assistant manager of a fourteen-location pizza delivery ~~firm~~ company. Your first ~~big~~ assignment is to evaluate operations and recommend changes that will improve service to customers, increase sales, reduce operating costs, and help develop your company's image as a leader in applying state-of-the-art technology.

The ~~Your~~ company's top management is concerned about problems ~~that have surfaced~~ with the current order-taking and processing system. Customers now must read through a list of fourteen delivery systems in the Yellow Pages to find the store closest to their homes. Quite often ~~Oftentimes,~~ customers dial the wrong store ~~because they are unaware of the company's system of carving the city into smaller, more manageable delivery areas.~~

No #
Once the customer reaches the correct store, a worker at the store writes down the order, including the customer's name, address, telephone number, time called, type of pizza requested, cost, and in some cases, directions to the customer's home. ~~Frequently, employees have to answer questions about ingredients used and preparation methods.~~

## Assessment 2

1. Open para04. This document is located on your student data disk.
2. Save the document with Save As and name it c02sa02.
3. Make the changes indicated by the proofreaders' marks in figure 2.12.
4. Save the document again with the same name (c02sa02).
5. Print c02sa02.
6. Close c02sa02.

**Figure 2.12**

Every time a customer calls, the information-gathering process ~~must~~ be repeated. Each store needs one or more phone lines for ~~incoming~~ _taking_ ~~orders, and someone must be available at each store to take~~ telephone orders. ~~In addition,~~ since the stores do not keep permanent records of incoming calls ~~and orders,~~ management has no way to target repeat customers for promotional advertisements and mailings.

Having studied telecommunications, you know that there are more efficient ways to handle customer orders. After ~~carefully~~ assessing the company's current telephone and order-filling system, you examine the alternatives.

_No #_

When you deliver your recommendation to the ~~pizza corporation~~ _company_ executives, you must be able to prove that the initial cost of a new ordering system will be recovered in reduced labor and communication costs and an increased customer base. The new ordering system should promise more efficient handling of calls and dispatching of information. A high-quality system will ensure ~~rapid and~~ accurate filling of new orders, personalized service, and a recordkeeping system for repeat customers. ~~The new system must also be simple to use.~~

## Assessment 3

1. Open para01.
2. Print para01.
3. Close para01.

# Formatting Characters

Upon successful completion of chapter 3, you will be able to enhance single-page business documents and reports with character formatting including all caps, bold, italics, underlining, double underlining, and changing the case of letters. You will also learn to use Word's Help feature.

As you work with Word, you will learn a number of commands and procedures that affect how the document appears when printed. The appearance of a document in the document screen and how it looks when printed is called the *format*. Formatting may include such elements as all caps, line spacing, indenting, even or uneven margins, tabs, bolding, underlining, and much more.

## Creating Text in All Caps

To key text in all uppercase letters, activate the Caps Lock feature by pressing the Caps Lock key. Press Caps Lock again to deactivate the uppercase feature. When Caps Lock is activated, a green mode indicator light appears at the upper right side of the keyboard.

## Using the Tab Key

The Word program contains a variety of default settings. A *default* is a preset standard or value that is established by the program.

One default setting in Word is a tab line that contains tab stops every 0.5 inches. In a later chapter, you will learn how to change the default tab stops. For now, use the default tab stops to indent text from the left margin. To indent text, press Tab. The Tab key on a microcomputer keyboard is generally located above the Caps Lock key.

## Formatting Text

Text can be formatted to accentuate text, elicit a particular feeling from the text, or draw the reader's eyes to a particular word or words. There are a variety of ways that text can be accentuated such as bolding, italicizing, and underlining. Text can be bolded, italicized, or underlined with buttons on the Formatting toolbar or shortcut commands.

## Bolding Text

The Bold button on the Formatting toolbar or the shortcut command, Ctrl + B, can be used to bold text. When text is bolded, it appears darker than surrounding text in the document screen and also on the printed page. Text can be bolded as it is being keyed, or existing text can be bolded.

To bold text as it is being keyed using the Bold button on the Formatting toolbar, you would complete the following steps:

1. Click on the Bold button on the Formatting toolbar.
2. Key the text to be bolded.
3. Click on the Bold button on the Formatting toolbar.

The first time you click on the Bold button the button becomes active and displays with a lighter gray background than the other buttons. To bold text as it is being keyed using the shortcut command, you would complete the following steps:

1. Press Ctrl + B.
2. Key the text.
3. Press Ctrl + B.

Text that has already been keyed in a document can be identified as bold text by selecting the text first, then using the Bold button on the Formatting toolbar or the shortcut command, Ctrl + B. For example, to bold the words *ST. FRANCIS MEDICAL CENTER*, you would complete the following steps:

1. Key **ST. FRANCIS MEDICAL CENTER**.
2. Use the mouse or the keyboard to select *ST. FRANCIS MEDICAL CENTER*.
3. Click on the Bold button on the Formatting toolbar or press Ctrl + B.

You can bold a single word by positioning the insertion point on any letter of the word, then clicking on the Bold button on the Formatting toolbar.

To remove bolding from text, select the text containing the bold formatting, then click on the Bold button on the Formatting toolbar, or press Ctrl + B. You can remove all character formatting from selected text by pressing Ctrl + space bar.

## Italicizing Text

Word's italics feature can be used in documents to emphasize specific text such as the names of published works. Text can be italicized using the Italic button on the Formatting toolbar or the shortcut command, Ctrl + I.

To italicize text with the Italic button on the Formatting toolbar as it is being keyed, you would complete the following steps:

1. Click on the Italic button on the Formatting toolbar.
2. Key the text.
3. Click on the Italic button on the Formatting toolbar.

To italicize text as it is being keyed using the shortcut command, you would complete the following steps:

1. Press Ctrl + I.
2. Key the text.
3. Press Ctrl + I.

Text identified with italics will appear in italics in the document screen.

Text that has already been keyed in a document can be italicized by selecting the text first. For example, to italicize the title *Desktop Publishing Theory and Applications*, you would complete the following steps:

1. Key **Desktop Publishing Theory and Applications**.
2. Select *Desktop Publishing Theory and Applications*.
3. Click on the Italic button on the Formatting toolbar or press Ctrl + I.

You can italicize a single word by positioning the insertion point on any letter of the word, then clicking on the Italic button on the Formatting toolbar.

## Underlining Text

Text can be underlined using the Underline button on the Formatting toolbar or the shortcut command, Ctrl + U. To underline text as it is being keyed using the Underline button on the Formatting toolbar, you would complete the following steps:

1. Click on the Underline button on the Formatting toolbar.
2. Key the text.
3. Click on the Underline button on the Formatting toolbar.

To underline text as it is being keyed using the shortcut command, you would complete the following steps:

1. Press Ctrl + U.
2. Key the text.
3. Press Ctrl + U.

Text that has already been keyed in a document can be underlined by selecting the text first, then using the Underline button on the Formatting toolbar or the shortcut command Ctrl + U. For example, to underline the name *Word for Windows*, you would complete the following steps:

1. Key **Word for Windows**.
2. Select *Word for Windows*.
3. Click on the Underline button on the Formatting toolbar or press Ctrl + U.

You can underline a single word by positioning the insertion point on any letter of the word, then clicking on the Underline button on the Formatting toolbar.

The Underline button on the Formatting toolbar and the shortcut command, Ctrl + U, underline words, spaces between words, and spaces created with the Tab key. If you want just words underlined, use the shortcut command, Ctrl + Shift + W. Use this command either as you are keying text or on selected text.

## Double Underlining

Text can be formatted with double underlining. To double underline text use the shortcut command, Ctrl + Shift + D. There is no button on the Formatting toolbar for double underlining.

To double underline text as it is being keyed, you would complete the following steps:

1. Press Ctrl + Shift + D.
2. Key the text to be double underlined.
3. Press Ctrl + Shift + D.

To double underline existing text, you would complete the following steps:

1. Select the text to be double underlined.
2. Press Ctrl + Shift + D.

Figure 3.1
Change Case
Dialog Box

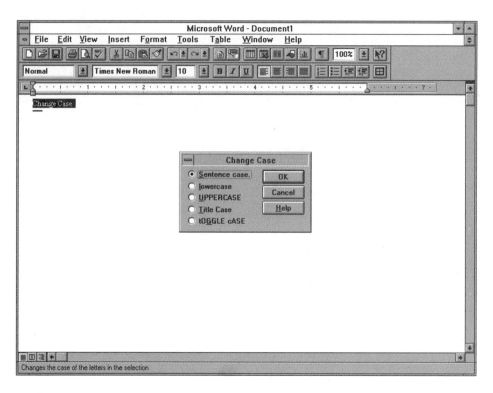

## Changing the Case of Letters

With Word's Change Case option, you can change the case of selected text. Change the case of selected text at the Change Case dialog box or with the shortcut command, Shift + F3.

To change the case of selected text at the Change Case dialog box, you would complete the following steps:

1. Select the text you want changed.
2. Choose Format, Change Case.
3. At the Change Case dialog box shown in figure 3.1, choose the desired style of case.
4. Choose OK or press Enter.

If you choose the Sentence case. option from the Change Case dialog box, selected text will display with the first letter of the sentence in an uppercase letter and the remaining letters in lowercase.

The lowercase option will change selected text to all lowercase letters. Choose UPPERCASE if you want all selected letters to change to uppercase. The Title Case will change the first letter of each selected word to uppercase. The last option, tOGGLE cASE, will cause selected lowercase letters to change to uppercase and selected uppercase letters to change to lowercase.

The shortcut command, Shift + F3, can also be used to change the case of selected text. Each time you press Shift + F3, the selected text reflects the changes. The changes match the options at the Change Case dialog box. Continue pressing Shift + F3 until the selected text displays with the desired cases, then deselect the text.

## Using Help

Word's Help feature is an on-screen reference manual containing information about all Word functions and commands. To display the Word Help dialog box shown in figure 3.2, press the F1 function key or choose Help, then Contents.

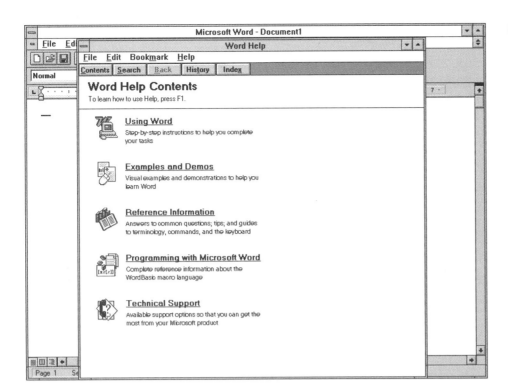

Figure 3.2
Word Help Dialog
Box

The Word Help dialog box displays with five categories: Using Word, Examples and Demos, Reference Information, Programming with Microsoft Word, and Technical Support. To view information from one of these categories using the mouse, position the arrow pointer on the desired category until the pointer turns into a hand with a pointing index finger, then click the left mouse button. If you are using the keyboard, press the Tab key until the desired category displays with purple letters on a black background, then press Enter.

If you choose Search for Help on from the Help drop-down menu, the Search dialog box shown in figure 3.3 displays. You can also display the dialog box by double-clicking on the Help button on the Standard toolbar. The Help button is the last button at the right side of the Standard toolbar that contains an arrow and a question mark. At the Search dialog box, key the topic name you want help with, then choose Show Topics. Choose the desired topic in the topic list, then choose Go To.

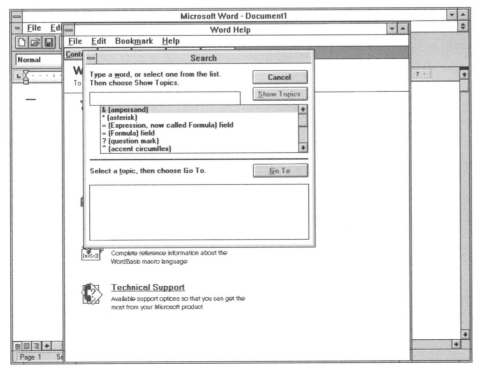

Figure 3.3
Search Dialog Box

As an example of how to use the Search dialog box, you would complete the following steps to display information about the Bold feature:

1. Choose <u>H</u>elp, then <u>S</u>earch for Help on; or double-click on the Help button on the Standard toolbar.
2. At the Search dialog box, key **bold**.
3. Choose <u>S</u>how Topics.
4. With the option *Applying or removing character formats* selected in the topics list, choose <u>G</u>o To.
5. Read the information on the Bold feature. (Press the down arrow key to view all the information.)
6. After reading the information on Bold, click on the Close button.
7. At the Word Help dialog box, choose <u>F</u>ile, E<u>x</u>it.

Choosing <u>I</u>ndex from the <u>H</u>elp drop-down menu causes an index to display as shown in figure 3.4. Use the index to display topics that begin with a particular letter. For example, to display topics that begin with the letter I, you would complete the following steps:

1. Choose <u>H</u>elp, <u>I</u>ndex.
2. Position the arrow pointer on the letter I at the top of the dialog box until it turns into a hand with a pointing index finger, then click the left mouse button.

To view all topics that begin with the letter I, click on the down scroll arrow in the vertical scroll bar or press the down arrow key on the keyboard. If you want to view information about a particular topic, position the arrow pointer on the topic until it turns into a hand with a pointing index finger, then click the left mouse button. If you are using the keyboard, press the Tab key until the topic is selected, then press Enter.

With the <u>Q</u>uick Preview option from the <u>H</u>elp drop-down menu, you can view information about new Word features. When you choose <u>H</u>elp, then <u>Q</u>uick Preview, a Quick Preview screen displays with the following options: <u>G</u>ETTING STARTED, <u>W</u>HAT'S NEW? and <u>T</u>IPS FOR WordPerfect

*Figure 3.4*
*Help Index*

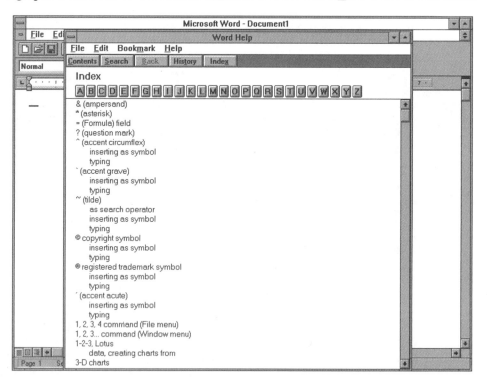

USERS. Choose one of these options, then read the information on the screen. After viewing a screen and reading any information displayed, choose <u>N</u>ext. Continue in this manner until the preview is over.

The <u>E</u>xamples and Demos option from the <u>H</u>elp drop-down menu provides step-by-step instructions on how to perform certain Word functions. You are shown on the screen how to perform the required steps to accomplish a task.

As an example of how to use this option, you would complete the following steps to see a demonstration on how to copy character formatting:

1. Choose <u>H</u>elp, <u>E</u>xamples and Demos.
2. At the Word Examples and Demos screen, click on *Formatting Text*.
3. Click on *Copying character formatting*.
4. At the next screen, click on <u>D</u>emo.
5. At the next screen, read the information, then choose <u>S</u>tart.
6. Read the information displayed on the screen, then choose <u>N</u>ext. Continue reading and choosing <u>N</u>ext.
7. When the demonstration is completed, click on <u>C</u>lose. Continue clicking on Close until the Word Help screen is displayed.
8. At the Word Help screen, choose <u>F</u>ile, then E<u>x</u>it.

Word provides a variety of helpful tips on using Word. A tip is displayed each time you load Word (unless the program has been customized). To view the tips offered by Word, choose <u>H</u>elp, Ti<u>p</u> of the Day. At the Tip of the Day screen, read the tip, then choose <u>N</u>ext Tip. You can view a list of tip contents by choosing <u>M</u>ore Tips.

If you have been a WordPerfect user and would like information on how to carry out a command in Word, choose <u>H</u>elp, <u>W</u>ordPerfect Help.

For information on Microsoft's technical support, choose <u>H</u>elp, <u>T</u>echnical Support.

The last option, <u>A</u>bout Microsoft Word, displays information about the Word program including such information as the release date, license number, and system information.

## CHAPTER SUMMARY

- To key text in all uppercase letters, press the Caps Lock key. Press Caps Lock again to deactivate the uppercase feature.
- The default or preset tab stops are set every 0.5 inches from the left margin. Press the Tab key to indent text 0.5 inches.
- Text can be bolded, italicized, and underlined with buttons on the Formatting toolbar or with shortcut commands. Do this as text is keyed or apply the features later by selecting the text, then choosing the desired feature.
- Text can be underlined without underlining the spaces between the words or double underlined using shortcut commands.
- You can remove all character formatting from selected text by pressing Ctrl + space bar.
- Change the case of selected text at the Change Case dialog box or with a shortcut command. You can choose to change text from/to uppercase/lowercase or to Sentence, Title, or other choices.
- Word's Help feature is an on-screen reference manual containing information about all Word functions and commands. The Word Help dialog box displays with five categories: Using Word, Examples and Demos, Reference Information, Programming with Microsoft Word, and Technical Support.
- If you have been a WordPerfect user and would like information on how to carry out a command in Word, choose <u>H</u>elp, <u>W</u>ordPerfect Help.

| | Mouse (Formatting Toolbar) | Keyboard |
|---|---|---|
| Bold | Click on the Bold button | CTRL + B |
| Italics | Click on the Italic button | CTRL + I |
| Underline (including spaces) | Click on the Underline button | CTRL + U |
| Underline (not including spaces) | | CTRL + SHIFT + W |
| Double underline | | CTRL + SHIFT + D |

| | Mouse (Menu bar) | Keyboard |
|---|---|---|
| Remove all character formatting from selected text | | CTRL + space bar |
| Change Case | Choose Format, Change Case | SHIFT + F3 |
| Uppercase function | | CAPS LOCK |
| Help | Choose Help, Contents | F1 |

## CHECK YOUR UNDERSTANDING

**True/False:** Circle the letter T if the statement is true; circle the letter F if the statement is false.

**T F** 1. The default tab stops are set 1 inch apart.

**T F** 2. Before italicizing existing text, the text must first be selected.

**T F** 3. Text that has been formatted with italics will only appear in italics when the document is printed.

**T F** 4. To double underline text, click on the Double Underline button on the Formatting toolbar.

**T F** 5. If you choose the Sentence case. option from the Change Case dialog box, selected text will display with the first letter of the sentence in uppercase and the remaining letters in lowercase.

**T F** 6. With the Quick Preview option from the Help drop-down menu, you can view information about new Word features.

**T F** 7. Press Ctrl to key text in all uppercase letters.

**T F** 8. The shortcut command to underline text is Alt + U.

**T F** 9. Use the Help index to display topics that begin with a particular letter.

**T F** 10. The appearance of a document in the document screen and how it looks when printed is called the *format*.

**Completion:** In the space provided at the right, indicate the correct term, command, or number.

1. The shortcut command to bold text. _____
2. The shortcut command to underline text. _____
3. The shortcut command to double underline text. _____
4. The command to remove all character formatting from selected text. _____
5. Change the case of selected text at the Change Case dialog box or with this shortcut command. _____
6. Remove Underline only from selected text with this shortcut command. _____
7. Press this key to indent text to the next tab stop. _____
8. Press this function key to access Word's Help feature. _____
9. Display the Search for Help On dialog box from the Help drop-down menu or here. _____
10. This choice from the Help drop-down menu provides step-by-step instructions on how to perform certain Word functions. _____

## Exercise 1

*Note: In this exercise and other exercises in the text, you will be required to create memoranda. Please refer to appendix D at the end of this text for the correct placement and spacing of a traditional-style memorandum. Unless otherwise instructed by your teacher, use this format when creating memoranda. The initials of the person keying the memo usually appear at the end of a memorandum. In this text, the initials will appear in the exercises as xx. Key your initials where you see the xx. Identifying document names in correspondence is a good idea because it lets you find and open the document quickly and easily at a future date. In this text, the document name is identified after the reference initials.*

1. At a clear document screen, key the memorandum shown in figure 3.5 in the traditional memorandum format. Use Caps Lock to key the memorandum headings—*DATE, TO, FROM,* and *SUBJECT*. To align the information after *DATE:*, key **DATE:**, press Tab, then key **February 8, 1996**. (Press Tab after the other headings to align them properly. You will need to press Tab twice after *TO:*.) Bold the populations as shown in the memorandum as it is being keyed by completing the following steps:
   a. Press Ctrl + B.
   b. Key the population number.
   c. Press Ctrl + B.
2. Save the memorandum and name it c03ex01.
3. Print c03ex01.
4. Close c03ex01.

**Figure 3.5**

```
DATE:     February 8, 1996

TO:       Kim How, President

FROM:     Shari Reeves, Development Coordinator

SUBJECT:  HILLTOP PROJECT


The Hilltop region you are interested in is characterized by a
series of rivers, valleys, and forested palisades which create a
distinctive natural landscape.  Settlement in the region has been
in small, compact villages which are linked together with a system
of farm to market roads.  Green Valley was incorporated in 1890 and
has 24,000 residents; Kamas in 1949 with 7,500 residents; Eastland
in 1891 with 6,300 residents; Cortez in 1889 with 2,100 people; and
Grover in 1909 with 700 residents.

Development expansion has been on the increase with new large
communities underway near Moore.  Northwest Manufacturing is
planning an operation nearby.  Kamas and Eastland have recently
extended their municipal boundaries through annexation.  The Tahoma
Development Corporation is situated to play a major role in the
future development and expansion of this region.

xx:c03ex01
```

## Exercise 2

1. Open c03ex01.
2. Save the memorandum with Save As and name it c03ex02.
3. With c03ex02 displayed in the document screen, bold the words *Green Valley* in the first paragraph by completing the following steps:
   a. Select *Green Valley*. (Do this with either the mouse or the keyboard.)
   b. Click on the Bold button on the Formatting toolbar.
4. Bold *Kamas* in the memorandum by positioning the insertion point on any letter in *Kamas*, then clicking on the Bold button on the Formatting toolbar.
5. Bold the following text in the memorandum:
   a. *Eastland*
   b. *Cortez*
   c. *Grover*
   d. the heading *DATE:*
   e. the heading *TO:*
   f. the heading *FROM:*
   g. the heading *SUBJECT:*
6. Change the document name after your initials from c03ex01 to c03ex02.
7. Save the memorandum again with the same name (c03ex02).
8. Print c03ex02.
9. Close c03ex02.

## Exercise 3

1. Open c03ex02.
2. Save the memorandum with Save As and name it c03ex03.
3. Remove bold from the heading *DATE:* by completing the following steps:
   a. Select *DATE:*.
   b. Click on the Bold button on the Formatting toolbar or press Ctrl + B.
4. Complete steps similar to those in 3a and 3b to remove bold from the headings *TO:*, *FROM:*, and *SUBJECT:*.
5. Change the document name after your initials from c03ex02 to c03ex03.
6. Save the memorandum again with the same name (c03ex03).
7. Print c03ex03.
8. Close c03ex03.

## Exercise 4

1. At a clear document screen, key the text shown in figure 3.6. Italicize the text shown as it is being keyed by completing the following steps:
   a. Press Ctrl + I.
   b. Key the text.
   c. Press Ctrl + I.
2. Save the document and name it c03ex04.
3. Print c03ex04.
4. Close c03ex04.

Figure 3.6

Bennett, Darnell E. (1994) *Administrative Management* (pp. 126-132). Salt Lake City, UT: Monticello Press.

Levesque, Corinne A. (1996) *Organizational Systems and Designs* (3rd ed.). Toronto, Ontario, Canada: Vancouver, British Columbia, Canada: Scarborough Publishing International.

Olafson, Connan L. (1995) *Theory and Application of Quality Management*. Coeur d'Alene, ID: Ponderay Publishing House.

Vezina, Marcia M. (1995) *Supervisory Skills and Techniques* (pp. 31-44). Calgary, Alberta, Canada: Widman/Suttles Publishing House.

## Exercise 5

1. Open biblio01. This document is located on your student data disk.
2. Save the document with Save As and name it c03ex05.
3. Select and italicize the title *The Art of Desktop Publishing* by completing the following steps:
   a. Select *The Art of Desktop Publishing*.
   b. Click on the Italic button on the Formatting toolbar.
4. Select and italicize the following titles in the document:
   a. *Practical Desktop Publishing Designs* in the second paragraph.
   b. *A Resource Guide to Desktop Publishing* in the third paragraph.
   c. *Desktop Publishing Projects* in the fourth paragraph.
5. Save the document again with the same name (c03ex05).
6. Print c03ex05.
7. Close c03ex05.

## Exercise 6

1. At a clear document screen, key the text shown in figure 3.7. Underline the text shown as it is being keyed by completing the following steps:
   a. Press Ctrl + U.
   b. Key the text.
   c. Press Ctrl + U.
2. Save the document and name it c03ex06.
3. Print c03ex06.
4. Close c03ex06.

Figure 3.7

Addington, Sherry. (1995) <u>Designer Art and Graphics</u>. New York, NY: Langford & Hayes.

Florence, David G. (1994) <u>One Hundred Great Designs</u>. Los Angeles, CA: Pacific Publishing House.

Heath, Patricia A. (1996) <u>Computerized Artwork</u>. Memphis, TN: Gallagher-Hess.

Maloney, Anthony. (1995) <u>Computer Graphics and Design</u>. San Francisco, CA: Valley Publishing.

## Exercise 7

1. Open c03ex05.
2. Save the document with Save As and name it c03ex07.
3. Remove the italics from the titles.
4. Select and underline the title *The Art of Desktop Publishing* by completing the following steps:
    a. Select *The Art of Desktop Publishing*.
    b. Click on the Underline button on the Formatting toolbar.
5. Select and underline the following titles in the document:
    a. *Practical Desktop Publishing Designs* in the second paragraph.
    b. *A Resource Guide to Desktop Publishing* in the third paragraph.
    c. *Desktop Publishing Projects* in the fourth paragraph.
6. Save the document again with the same name (c03ex07).
7. Print c03ex07.
8. Close c03ex07.

## Exercise 8

1. Open notice01. This document is located on your student data disk.
2. Save the document with Save As and name it c03ex08.
3. Select and underline the words *as soon as possible* in the first paragraph by completing the following steps:
    a. Select *as soon as possible* in the first paragraph (do not include the exclamation point at the end of the sentence).
    b. Press Ctrl + Shift + W.
4. Select and underline the following text in the document using Ctrl + Shift + W:
    a. *a thousand toys* in the second paragraph;
    b. *Bring your appetite* in the third paragraph;
    c. *fun-filled evening with your family* in the fourth paragraph.
5. Save the document again with the same name (c03ex08).
6. Print c03ex08.
7. Close c03ex08.

## Exercise 9

1. Open number01. This document is located on your student data disk.
2. Save the document with Save As and name it c03ex09.
3. Select and underline the number *214.98* in the first column.
4. Select and underline the number *159.88* in the second column.
5. Select and double underline the total *744.76* by completing the following steps:
    a. Select *744.76*.
    b. Press Ctrl + Shift + D.
6. Save the document again with the same name (c03ex09).
7. Print c03ex09.
8. Close c03ex09.

## Exercise 10

1. Open report01. This document is located on your student data disk.
2. Save the document with Save As and name it c03ex10.
3. Select and bold the title, *TYPE SPECIFICATION*.
4. Select the heading *Type Measurement* and change the case to uppercase letters by completing the following steps:
   a. Select *Type Measurement*.
   b. Choose Format, Change Case.
   c. At the Change Case dialog box, choose UPPERCASE.
   d. Choose OK or press Enter.
5. Select the heading *Type Size* and change the case to uppercase letters by completing the following steps:
   a. Select *Type Size*.
   b. Press Shift + F3 (until the heading displays in all uppercase letters).
6. Select the heading *Type Style* and change to all uppercase letters.
7. Save the document again with the same name (c03ex10).
8. Print c03ex10.
9. Close c03ex10.

## Exercise 11

1. Use Word's Help feature to read information about selecting text by completing the following steps:
   a. At a clear document, screen double-click on the Help button on the Standard toolbar.
   b. At the Search dialog box, key **selecting text**.
   c. Click on Show Topics.
   d. Click on *Selecting text and graphics by using the mouse* in the topics list (the bottom list box).
   e. Click on Go To.
   f. Read the information about selecting text with the mouse. (You may not be able to see all of the text. To expand the viewing area, position the arrow pointer on the button in the upper right corner of the dialog box containing the up-pointing triangle, then click the left mouse button. This is the Maximize button and causes the viewing area to expand to fill the entire document screen. After reading the information on selecting text, return the viewing area to the original size by clicking on the button in the upper right corner of the document screen containing the up- and down-pointing triangles. This is called the Restore button and restores the size of the viewing area to its original size before being maximized.)
   g. After reading the information on selecting text, click on the Close button.
   h. At the Word Help dialog box, choose File, Exit.

## Exercise 12

1. Use Word's Help feature to read about new Word features by completing the following steps:
   a. At a clear document screen, click on Help, Quick Preview.
   b. At the Quick Preview screen, click on WHAT'S NEW?
   c. After Word loads the demonstration, read the information on the screen, then click on the Next button at the bottom right side of the screen.
   d. Continue reading and watching the demonstrations, then clicking on the Next button.
   e. After reading and watching demonstrations on several Word features, click on the Cancel button at the bottom right side of the screen. (These demonstrations can take quite some time. For this exercise, read and watch three or four demonstrations on Word features before clicking on Cancel.)
   f. At the Quick Preview screen, click on Return to Word.

## Exercise 13

1. Use Word's Help feature to see a demonstration of how to apply character formatting by completing the following steps:
   a. At a clear document screen, choose Help, Examples and Demos.
   b. At the Word Examples and Demos screen, click on *Formatting Text*.
   c. Click on *Applying or removing character formats*.
   d. At the next screen, click on Demo.
   e. At the next screen, read the information, then choose Start.
   f. Read the information displayed on the screen, then choose Next. Continue reading and choosing Next.
   g. When the demonstration is completed, click on Close. Continue clicking on Close until the Word Help screen is displayed.
   h. At the Word Help screen, choose File, then Exit.

## Exercise 14

1. Use Word's Help feature to read information on helpful tips by completing the following steps:
   a. At a clear document screen, choose Help, Tip of the Day.
   b. At the Tip of the Day screen, read the tip.
   c. Choose Next Tip.
   d. Continue reading tips, then choosing Next Tip.
   e. After reading about five or six tips, choose OK or press Enter.
2. Display information about the version of Word you are using by completing the following steps:
   a. Choose Help, About Microsoft Word.
   b. At the About Microsoft Word dialog box, read the information in the dialog box, then choose System Info.
   c. Read the information in the Microsoft System Information dialog box, then choose Close.
   d. At the About Microsoft Word dialog box, choose OK or press Enter.

## SKILL ASSESSMENTS

### Assessment 1

1. At a clear document screen, key the memorandum shown in figure 3.8. Bold and underline the text as shown.
2. Save the memorandum and name it c03sa01.
3. Print c03sa01.
4. Close c03sa01.

Figure 3.8

**DATE:**     November 13, 1995

**TO:**        Nancy Suaro

**FROM:**     Elena Kemp

**SUBJECT:**  DESKTOP PUBLISHING


After reviewing a number of desktop publishing textbooks, I have chosen <u>Desktop Publishing Theory and Applications</u> for use in **OT 233, Desktop Publishing.**   The bookstore manager has ordered the book for next quarter.

The class was to be held in **Room 226.**   Due to computer requirements, the class has been moved to **Room 301.**   The classroom can accommodate 25 people.   Therefore, the class enrollment has been changed from 30 to 25.

xx:c03sa01

## Assessment 2

1. Open memo01. This document is located on your student data disk.
2. Save the memorandum with Save As and name it c03sa02.
3. Make the following changes:
   a. Select the book title *One Hundred Great Designs*; remove the underlining then add italics.
   b. Select the book title *Designer Art and Graphics*; remove the underlining then add italics.
   c. Select the book title *Computerized Artwork*; remove the underlining then add italics.
   d. Select the book title *Computer Graphics and Design*; remove the underlining then add italics.
   e. Select and bold the headings *DATE:*, *TO:*, *FROM:*, and *SUBJECT:* (just the headings, not the text after the headings).
   f. Insert your initials at the end of the document where you see the *xx*. Change the document name after your initials from memo01 to c03sa02.
4. Save the document again with the same name (c03sa02).
5. Print c03sa02.
6. Close c03sa02.

## Assessment 3

1. Open c03sa01.
2. Save the memorandum with Save As and name it c03sa03.
3. Make the following changes:
   a. Remove the bold and underline formatting from the text.
   b. Select and italicize the book title, *Desktop Publishing Theory and Applications*.
   c. Select and double underline *Room 226* and *Room 301*.
   d. Select and bold the two occurrences of the number 25 in the second paragraph and the number 30 in the second paragraph.
   e. Change the document name after your initials from c03sa01 to c03sa03.
4. Save the document again with the same name (c03sa03).
5. Print c03sa03.
6. Close c03sa03.

## Assessment 4

1. Open notice01. This document is located on your student data disk.
2. Save the document with Save As and name it c03sa04.
3. Make the following changes:
   a. Select the title, RIDGWAY ELEMENTARY SCHOOL CARNIVAL, then change the case to Title Case at the Change Case dialog box.
   b. Select *Friday, May* (in the first paragraph) and change the case to uppercase.
   c. Select *a thousand toys* (in the second paragraph) and change the case to uppercase.
   d. Select *Bring your appetite* (in the third paragraph) and change the case to uppercase.
4. Save the document again with the same name (c03sa04).
5. Print c03sa04.
6. Close c03sa04.

# Formatting Paragraphs 4

Upon successful completion of chapter 4, you will be able to enhance business memoranda and letters by changing the alignment, indents, and line spacing of paragraphs.

In Word, a paragraph is any amount of text followed by a paragraph mark. A paragraph mark is inserted in a document each time the Enter key is pressed. By default, this paragraph mark is not visible. When changes are made to a paragraph, the formatting changes are inserted in the paragraph mark. If the paragraph mark is deleted, the formatting in the mark is eliminated and the text returns to the default.

## Displaying Nonprinting Characters

When you begin formatting text by paragraph, you may find it useful to display some nonprinting characters. As mentioned above, Word inserts paragraph formatting into the paragraph mark. If you want to remove paragraph formatting from text, delete the paragraph mark.

To display the paragraph mark and other nonprinting characters, use the Show/Hide button on the Standard toolbar, a shortcut command, or options from the Options dialog box.

To display nonprinting characters using the Standard toolbar, click on the Show/Hide button. The Show/Hide button is the third button from the right on the Standard toolbar containing an image of a paragraph mark. You can also display nonprinting characters by pressing Shift + Ctrl + *. This causes nonprinting characters to display as shown in the document in figure 4.1.

To turn off the display of nonprinting characters, click on the Show/Hide button on the Standard toolbar or press Shift + Ctrl + *.

The Show/Hide button on the Standard toolbar and Shift + Ctrl + * turns on the display of all nonprinting characters. To control which nonprinting characters display, use the Options dialog box shown in figure 4.2. To display this dialog box, choose Tools, then Options. (Make sure the View tab is selected. If not, click on the View tab.)

Choose options from the Nonprinting Characters section of the Options dialog box to determine what nonprinting characters you want displayed in the document. Choose the All option if you want all nonprinting characters displayed. After making changes to the Options dialog box, choose OK or press Enter.

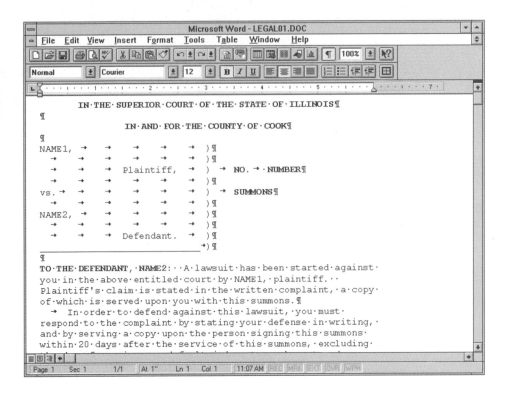

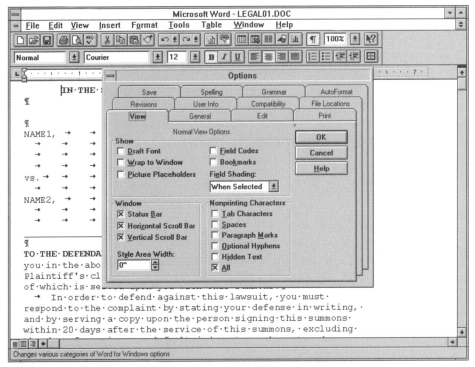

## ■ *Changing the Alignment of Text in Paragraphs*

By default, paragraphs in a Word document are aligned at the left margin and ragged at the right margin. This default alignment can be changed with buttons on the Formatting toolbar or with shortcut commands. Text in a paragraph can be aligned at the left margin, between margins, right margin, or to the left and right margins. Figure 4.3 illustrates the different paragraph alignments.

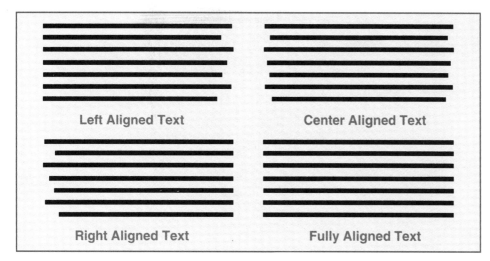

Figure 4.3
Paragraph
Alignments

Left Aligned Text                Center Aligned Text

Right Aligned Text                Fully Aligned Text

Use the buttons on the Formatting toolbar or the shortcut commands shown in figure 4.4 to change the alignment of text in paragraphs.

| To align text | Button | Shortcut Command |
|---|---|---|
| at left margin | | CTRL + L |
| between margins | | CTRL + E |
| at right margin | | CTRL + R |
| at left and right margins | | CTRL + J |

*Figure 4.4*
*Paragraph*
*Alignment Buttons*
*and Commands*

You can change the alignment of text in paragraphs before you key the text or you can change the alignment of existing text. If you change the alignment before keying text, the alignment formatting is inserted in the paragraph mark. As you key text and press Enter, the paragraph formatting is continued. For example, if you press Ctrl + E to turn on center aligning, key text for the first paragraph, then press Enter, the center alignment formatting is still active and the insertion point displays in the middle of the margins.

To return paragraph alignment to normal (left aligned), click on the Left Align button on the Formatting toolbar or press Ctrl + L. You can also return all paragraph formatting to normal by pressing Ctrl + Q. This shortcut command returns all paragraph formatting (not just alignment) to the normal settings.

To change the alignment of existing text in a paragraph, position the insertion point anywhere within the paragraph. The entire paragraph does not have to be selected.

To change the alignment of several adjacent paragraphs in a document, select a portion of the first paragraph through a portion of the last paragraph. Only a portion of the first and last paragraphs needs to be selected.

If you want to apply paragraph formatting to several paragraphs that are not adjacent, you can use the Repeat key, F4, the shortcut command, Ctrl + Y, or the Repeat option from the Edit drop-down menu. For example, if you apply center alignment to a paragraph and then want to repeat it for another paragraph, position the insertion point anywhere in the next paragraph, then press F4; press Ctrl + Y; or choose Edit, Repeat Paragraph Alignment.

*Figure 4.5*
*Paragraph Dialog*
*Box with Indents*
*and Spacing Tab*
*Selected*

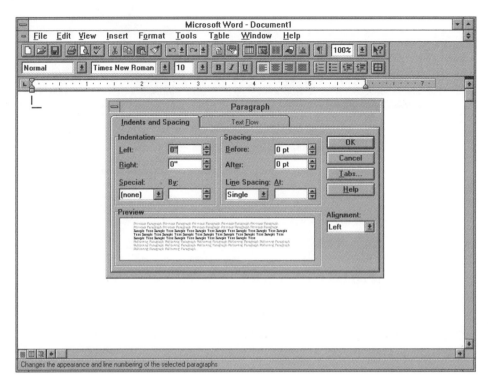

## Changing Alignment at the Paragraph Dialog Box

Paragraph alignment can also be changed at the Paragraph dialog box shown in figure 4.5.

To change the alignment of text in a paragraph, you would complete the following steps:

1. Choose Format, Paragraph.
2. At the Paragraph dialog box, choose Alignment. To do this with the mouse, click on the down-pointing arrow in the Alignment text box. If you are using the keyboard, press Alt + G.
3. At the drop-down menu, choose an alignment option.
4. Choose OK or press Enter.

## Using Shortcut Menus

Word provides shortcut menus that can be used to display commands related to the text or item of selected text or where the insertion point is positioned. Use shortcut menus to format documents. You learned to use a shortcut menu in chapter 1 to turn on and/or off the display of toolbars.

You can use a shortcut menu to display the Paragraph dialog box shown in figure 4.5. To do this, you would complete the following steps:

1. Position the insertion point in the text that you want formatted with an option from the Paragraph dialog box.
2. Click the *right* button on the mouse. This causes a drop-down menu to display at the location of the insertion point as shown in figure 4.6.
3. Click on Paragraph to display the Paragraph dialog box.
4. Make changes to the Paragraph dialog box as needed, then choose OK or press Enter.

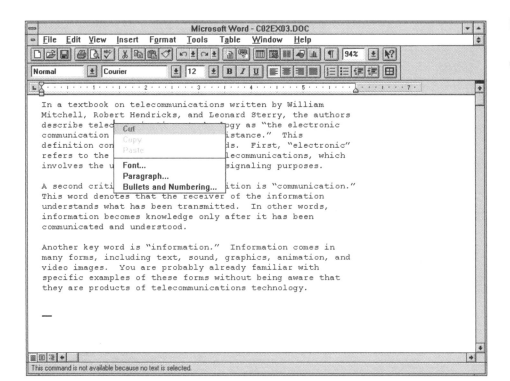

Figure 4.6
Shortcut Menu

## ■ *Indenting Text in Paragraphs*

By now you are familiar with the word wrap feature of Word which ends lines and wraps the insertion point to the next line. To indent text from the left margin, the left and right margin, or create numbered items, use indent buttons from the Formatting toolbar, shortcut commands, options from the Paragraph dialog box, or markers on the Ruler.

With markers on the Ruler you can indent text in a paragraph. To display the Ruler, choose View, then Ruler. The Ruler displays below the Formatting toolbar as shown in figure 4.7. The indent markers on the Ruler are identified in figure 4.7. In addition to the indent markers shown in figure 4.7, the small box below the left indent marker can be used to move both the first-line and left indent markers at the same time.

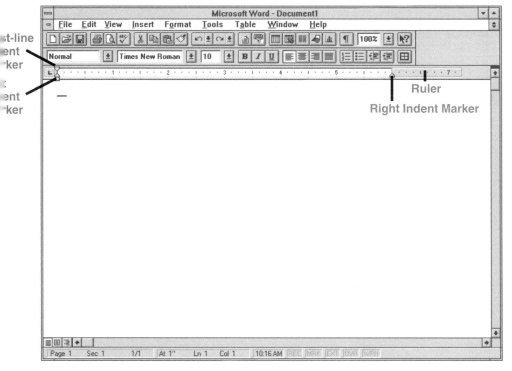

Figure 4.7
Ruler and Indent
Markers

## Indenting the First Line of Text in a Paragraph

When creating certain documents, you may want to indent the first line of a paragraph to identify where a new paragraph begins. You can indent the first line of a paragraph by pressing the Tab key, with an option from the Paragraph Format dialog box, or with the first-line indent marker on the Ruler.

If you use the Tab key to indent the first line of a paragraph, the insertion point is indented to the first tab stop. By default, Word contains a tab stop every 0.5 inches. Therefore, if the insertion point is positioned at the left margin and you press the Tab key, the insertion point is moved 0.5 inches from the left margin.

You can also indent the first line of text in a paragraph with an option from the Paragraph dialog box shown in figure 4.5. To display this dialog box, choose Format, then Paragraph. At the Paragraph dialog box, you can specify a measurement you want text indented. Additionally, if you indent the first line of text in a paragraph with the Paragraph dialog box, each paragraph you key will have the first line of text indented.

To indent the first line of text in a paragraph using the Paragraph dialog box, you would complete the following steps:

1. Choose Format, Paragraph.
2. At the Paragraph dialog box, choose Special. To do this with the mouse, position the arrow pointer on the down-pointing arrow to the right of the Special text box, then click the left mouse button. If you are using the keyboard, press Alt + S.
3. From the drop-down menu that displays, choose First Line. To do this with the mouse, click on First Line. If you are using the keyboard, press the down arrow key until First Line is selected.
4. Choose OK or press Enter.

By default, Word indents the text in the first line of the paragraph 0.5 inches. At the Paragraph dialog box, you can change the first indent measurement. To change the indent measurement, enter the desired measurement in the By text box in the Paragraph dialog box.

The first line of text in a paragraph can also be indented with the first-line indent marker on the Ruler. The first-line indent marker is identified in figure 4.7. As an example of how to use the Ruler to indent the first line of text in a document 0.5 inches, you would complete the following steps:

1. Select the paragraphs with text that you want indented.
2. Position the arrow pointer on the first-line indent marker on the Ruler.
3. Hold down the left mouse button, then drag the first-line indent marker to the 0.5-inch mark on the Ruler.
4. Release the mouse button.

## Indenting Text from the Left Margin

All lines of text in a paragraph can be indented to a tab stop or to a specific measurement from the left margin. All lines of text in a paragraph can be indented using a shortcut command, a button on the Formatting toolbar, an option from the Paragraph dialog box, or the left indent marker on the Ruler.

To indent all lines of text in a paragraph or selected paragraphs with a shortcut command, you would complete the following steps:

> 1. Position the insertion point in the paragraph to be indented or select the paragraphs to be indented.
> 2. Press Ctrl + M.

When you press Ctrl + M, text is indented to the first tab stop from the left margin. By default, this tab stop is 0.5 inches from the left margin. If you press Ctrl + M again, the text is indented to the next tab stop, which is 1 inch from the left margin by default.

You can also indent all lines of text in a paragraph or selected paragraphs by clicking on the Increase Indent button on the Formatting toolbar. The Increase Indent button is the second button from the right on the Formatting toolbar.

All lines of text in a paragraph can be indented to a specific measurement from the left margin using an option from the Paragraph dialog box. For example, to indent all lines of text in a paragraph or selected paragraphs 0.8 inches from the left margin using the Paragraph dialog box, you would complete the following steps:

> 1. Position the insertion point in the paragraph to be indented or select the paragraphs to be indented.
> 2. Choose Format, Paragraph.
> 3. At the Paragraph dialog box, key **0.8** in the Left text box. (The *0"* measurement in the Left text box is automatically selected when you first display the Paragraph dialog box.)
> 4. Choose OK or press Enter.

You can key a measurement in the Left text box, or you can click on the up- or down-pointing triangles to the right of the Left text box to increase or decrease the left indent measurement.

To indent all lines of text in a paragraph or selected paragraphs with the Ruler, you would complete the following steps:

> 1. Position the insertion point in the paragraph to be indented or select the paragraphs to be indented.
> 2. Position the arrow pointer on the small box below the left indent marker on the Ruler, hold down the left mouse button, drag the small box to the desired position on the Ruler, then release the mouse button.

Go To
Exercise
8

## Decreasing the Indent

You can decrease the indent of text in a paragraph with the shortcut command, Ctrl + Shift + M, or with the Decrease Indent button on the Formatting toolbar. The Decrease Indent button is the third button from the right on the Formatting toolbar.

When you press Ctrl + Shift + M or click on the Decrease Indent button on the Formatting toolbar, the lines of text in the paragraph or selected paragraphs are moved to the previous tab stop or the left margin. To decrease the indent using the Ruler, drag the small box below the left indent marker to the left on the Ruler. You can also decrease the left margin indent by decreasing the number in the Left text box at the Paragraph dialog box.

## Indenting Text from the Left and Right Margins

Text in paragraphs can be indented from the left and the right margins with options at the Paragraph dialog box or with markers on the Ruler. Indent text from the left and right margins for text that you want set off from other text in a document such as a quotation.

As an example of how to indent text from the left and right margins, you would complete the following steps to indent text 0.5 inches from the left and right margins using the Paragraph dialog box:

1. Position the insertion point in the paragraph to be indented or select paragraphs to be indented.
2. Choose Format, Paragraph.
3. Key **0.5** in the Left text box.
4. Choose Right. To do this with the mouse, select the current measurement in the Right text box. If you are using the keyboard, press Alt + R.
5. Key **0.5** in the Right text box.
6. Choose OK or press Enter.

To indent text from the left and right margins using the Ruler, drag the small box below the left indent marker and the right-indent marker to the desired measurements on the Ruler.

## Creating a Hanging Paragraph

Hanging paragraphs such as bibliographic references shown in figure 4.8 can be created in a document. Hanging paragraphs are also useful when creating enumerated items or any text you want flagged or marked with a specific character.

*Figure 4.8*
*Hanging*
*Paragraphs*

```
Bodhaine, Anke.   (1995)   The Art of Desktop Publishing
     (3rd ed.).   Montreal, Quebec, Canada:   St. Nicolas
     Press.

Fischer, Heidi L.   (1995)   Practical Desktop Publishing
     Designs (pp. 63-75).  Albuquerque, NM:  Morley-
     Childers Publications.
```

In a hanging paragraph, the first line of the paragraph remains at the left margin, while the remaining lines are indented to the first tab stop. Hanging paragraphs can be created with the shortcut command, Ctrl + T, or with options from the Paragraph dialog box. To create a hanging paragraph or paragraphs using the shortcut command, Ctrl + T, you would complete the following steps:

1. Position the insertion point in the paragraph to be hanging indented or select the paragraphs to be hanging indented.
2. Press Ctrl + T.

To create a hanging paragraph or paragraphs using options from the Paragraph dialog box, you would complete the following steps:

1. Position the insertion point in the paragraph to be hanging indented or select the paragraphs to be hanging indented.
2. Choose Format, Paragraph.
3. At the Paragraph dialog box, choose Special. To do this with the mouse, position the arrow pointer on the down-pointing arrow to the right of the Special text box, then click the left mouse button. If you are using the keyboard, press Alt + S.
4. Choose *Hanging* from the Special drop-down menu.
5. Choose OK or press Enter.

You can also use the hanging paragraph feature to create enumerated (numbered) paragraphs such as the paragraphs shown in figure 4.9.

```
1.  You can use hanging paragraphs to create numbered
    paragraphs such as the ones in this figure.

2.  This is the second numbered paragraph.  You can
    create a numbered paragraph like this with a shortcut
    command, with markers on the Ruler, or with options
    from the Paragraph dialog box.
```

**Figure 4.9**
*Numbered
Paragraphs*

As an example of how to create hanging paragraphs, you would complete the following steps to create the numbered paragraphs in figure 4.9:

1. Key **1.**
2. Press the Tab key.
3. Key the paragraph.
4. Press Enter twice.
5. Key **2.**
6. Press the Tab key.
7. Key the paragraph.
8. Select the paragraphs.
9. Press Ctrl + T.

You could also create the hanging numbered paragraphs with markers on the Ruler or with options from the Paragraph dialog box.

## Creating Numbered and Bulleted Paragraphs

You can automate the creation of numbered paragraphs with a button on the Formatting toolbar or options from the Bullets and Numbering dialog box. The advantage to doing it this way is if you insert or delete paragraphs, Word automatically renumbers the paragraphs.

In addition to automatically creating numbered paragraphs, you can also create bulleted paragraphs. Bulleted paragraphs are preceded by a bullet as shown in figure 4.10.

```
•   This is a paragraph preceded by a bullet.  A bullet
    is used to indicate a list of items or topics.

•   This is another paragraph preceded by a bullet.
    Bulleted paragraphs can be easily created with the
    Bullets button on the Formatting toolbar.
```

**Figure 4.10**
*Bulleted
Paragraphs*

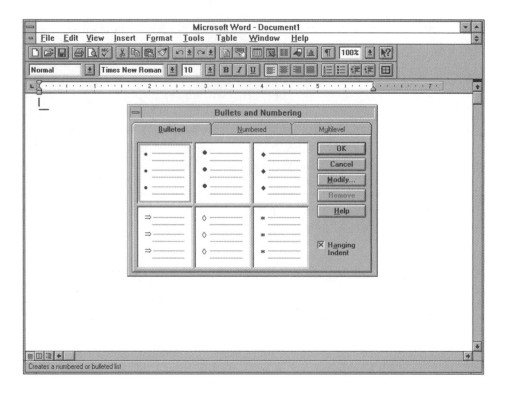

To create numbered paragraphs using the Numbering button on the Formatting toolbar, you would complete the following steps:

1. Key the text you want numbered at the left margin.
2. Select the paragraphs you want numbered.
3. Position the arrow pointer on the Numbering button on the Formatting toolbar, then click the left mouse button.

You would follow similar steps to create bulleted paragraphs. When creating bulleted paragraphs, select the paragraphs, then click on the Bullets button on the Formatting toolbar.

The Numbering and Bullets buttons on the Formatting toolbar indent the text 0.25 inches from the left margin. If you want to increase the space between the numbers or the bullets and the text, select the paragraphs then press Ctrl + T. In addition to buttons on the Formatting toolbar, you can also use options from the Bullets and Numbering dialog box shown in figure 4.11 to number paragraphs or insert bullets. To display this dialog box, choose Format, then Bullets and Numbering.

The Bullets and Numbering dialog box contains three tabs: Bulleted, Numbered, and Multilevel. Display the Bulleted tab if you want to insert bullets before selected paragraphs. Display the Numbered tab if you want to insert numbers before selected paragraphs. When you choose Multilevel, the dialog box displays as shown in figure 4.12.

With the options at the Bullets and Numbering dialog box with the Multilevel tab selected, you can specify the numbering type for paragraphs at the left margin, first tab stop, second tab stop, etc.

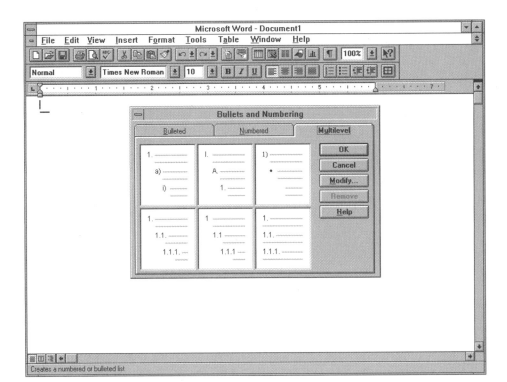

**Figure 4.12**
*Bullets and
Numbering Dialog
Box with Multilevel
Tab Selected*

As an example of how to use the Bullets and Numbering dialog box to number paragraphs, you would complete the followings steps to number multilevel paragraphs with 1., a), and i):

1. Key the paragraphs. Key paragraphs you want numbered with 1. at the left margin; key paragraphs you want lettered (a), b), c), etc.) at the first tab stop; and key paragraphs you want lettered with lowercase Roman numerals (i), ii), iii), etc.) at the second tab stop.
2. Select the paragraphs.
3. Choose Format, Bullets and Numbering.
4. At the Bullets and Numbering dialog box, choose the Multilevel tab.
5. Select the first numbering option box. To do this with the mouse, position the arrow pointer somewhere in the first option box, then click the left mouse button. If you are using the keyboard, press the Tab key until the marquee surrounds the first option box.
6. Choose OK or press Enter.

## ■ *Changing Line Spacing*

By default, Word's word wrap feature single spaces text. There may be occasions when you want to change to another spacing, such as line and a half or double. Line spacing can be changed with shortcut commands or options from the Paragraph dialog box. Figure 4.13 illustrates the shortcut commands to change line spacing.

| Press | to change line spacing to |
|-------|---------------------------|
| CTRL + 1 | single spacing |
| CTRL + 2 | double spacing |
| CTRL + 5 | 1.5 line spacing |

**Figure 4.13**
*Line Spacing
Shortcut
Commands*

Line spacing can also be changed at the Paragraph dialog box. At the Paragraph dialog box, you change line spacing with the Line Spacing option or the At option. For example, to change line spacing to double using the Paragraph dialog box and the At option, you would complete the following steps:

1. Position the insertion point in the paragraph or select the paragraphs for which you want the line spacing changed.
2. Choose Format, Paragraph.
3. At the Paragraph dialog box, make sure the Indents and Spacing tab is selected, then click on the up-pointing triangle to the right of the At text box until 2 displays in the At text box. If you are using the keyboard, press Alt + A, then key 2 in the At text box.
4. Choose OK or press Enter.

To change line spacing with the Line Spacing option, you would complete the following steps:

1. Position the insertion point in the paragraph or select the paragraphs for which you want to change the line spacing.
2. Choose Format, Paragraph.
3. At the Paragraph dialog box, make sure the Indents and Spacing tab is selected, then choose Line Spacing. To do this with the mouse, click on the down-pointing arrow to the right of the Line Spacing text box. If you are using the keyboard, press Alt + N.
4. Choose *Double* from the Line Spacing drop-down list.
5. Choose OK or press Enter.

## CHAPTER SUMMARY

- In Word, a paragraph is any amount of text followed by a paragraph mark (press of the Enter key).
- Word inserts into the paragraph mark any paragraph formatting that is turned on before the text is keyed. If you want to remove paragraph formatting from text, delete the paragraph mark. You can also use the shortcut command Ctrl + Q to remove all formatting from a paragraph.
- To turn on or off the display of nonprinting characters such as paragraph marks, click on the Show/Hide button on the Standard toolbar.
- By default, paragraphs in a Word document are aligned at the left margin and ragged at the right margin. This default alignment can be changed at the Formatting toolbar, at the Paragraph dialog box, or with shortcut commands to left, center, right, or fully aligned.
- You can change the alignment of text in paragraphs before you key the text or you can change the alignment of existing text. To change the alignment of existing text in a paragraph, just position the insertion point anywhere within the paragraph, then choose the desired alignment.
- If you want to apply paragraph formatting to several paragraphs that are not adjacent, you can use the Repeat key, F4, the shortcut command, Ctrl + Y; or the Repeat option from the Edit drop-down menu.
- The first line of text in a paragraph can be indented by pressing the Tab key, with an option from the Paragraph Format dialog box, or with the first-line indent marker on the Ruler.
- All lines of text in a paragraph can be indented to a tab stop or to a specific measurement from the left margin using a shortcut command, an option from the Paragraph dialog box, or the left indent marker on the Ruler.

- Text in paragraphs can be indented from the left and the right margins with options at the Paragraph dialog box or with the left and right indent markers on the Ruler.
- In a hanging paragraph, the first line of the paragraph remains at the left margin, while the remaining lines are indented to the first tab stop. Hanging paragraphs can be created with a shortcut command or with options from the Paragraph dialog box.
- Create numbered paragraphs using the hanging paragraph feature by keying the number and the paragraph, then selecting the paragraph and changing it to hanging indented.
- You can automate the creation of numbered paragraphs with a button on the Formatting toolbar or options from the Bullets and Numbering dialog box.
- Line spacing can be changed with shortcut commands or options from the Paragraph dialog box.

## COMMANDS REVIEW

| | Mouse | Keyboard |
|---|---|---|
| Turn on/off display of nonprinting characters | Choose Tools, Options; or click on Show/Hide button on the Standard toolbar | Tools, Options; or press `SHIFT` + `CTRL` + `✳` |
| *To align text...* | *Click on these Formatting toolbar buttons* | |
| at left margin | ▤ | `CTRL` + `L` |
| between margins | ▤ | `CTRL` + `E` |
| at right margin | ▤ | `CTRL` + `R` |
| at left and right margins | ▤ | `CTRL` + `J` |
| Return paragraph alignment to normal (left aligned) | ▤ | `CTRL` + `L` |
| Return all paragraph formatting to normal | | `CTRL` + `Q` |
| Repeat formatting command for several paragraphs | Position insertion point in paragraph, choose Edit, Repeat Paragraph Alignment | `F4` ; or `CTRL` + `Y` |
| Paragraph dialog box | Format, Paragraph; or position insertion point in paragraph, click *right* mouse button, click on Paragraph | Format, Paragraph |
| Display the Ruler | View, Ruler | View, Ruler |
| Indent first line of a paragraph | At the Paragraph dialog box, choose Special, then First Line; or with arrow pointer on the Ruler, hold down the left mouse button and drag the first-line indent marker to desired measurement | ⬓ |

|  | **Mouse** | **Keyboard** |
|---|---|---|
| Indent left margin of all lines of text in a paragraph or selected paragraphs | At the Paragraph dialog box, key indent measurement in the <u>L</u>eft text box; or with arrow pointer on the Ruler, hold down the left mouse button and drag the first-line indent marker and then the left-indent marker to desired measurements; or click on the Increase Indent button on Formatting toolbar | CTRL + M |
| Decrease indent of text in a paragraph | Decrease number in the <u>L</u>eft text box at the Paragraph dialog box; or drag the first-line indent marker and the left indent marker to desired measurements; or click on the Decrease Indent button on the Formatting toolbar | CTRL + SHIFT + M |
| Indent left and right margins of paragraph | At the Paragraph dialog box, key indent measurement in the <u>L</u>eft and <u>R</u>ight text boxes; or with the arrow pointer on the Ruler, hold down the left mouse button and drag the first-line, left-indent, and right-indent markers to the desired measurements | |
| Create a hanging paragraph | At the Paragraph dialog box, key the desired indent measurement in the <u>L</u>eft text box, choose <u>S</u>pecial, Hanging | CTRL + T |
| Create numbered/bulleted paragraphs | Select paragraphs, click on Numbering/Bullets button on Formatting toolbar; or access the Bullets and Numbering dialog box | |
| Bullets and Numbering dialog box | F<u>o</u>rmat, Bullets and <u>N</u>umbering | F<u>o</u>rmat, Bullets and <u>N</u>umbering |
| Change to single spacing | | CTRL + 1 |
| Change to double spacing | | CTRL + 2 |
| Change to 1.5 line spacing | | CTRL + 5 |
| Change line spacing at Paragraph dialog box | Click on the up/down pointing triangle to right of <u>A</u>t box; or choose Li<u>n</u>e Spacing | |

**True/False:** Circle the letter T if the statement is true; circle the letter F if the statement is false.

**T  F**  1.  In Word, the default alignment for paragraphs is fully aligned.

**T  F**  2.  To change the alignment of an existing paragraph, the insertion point must be on the first character.

**T  F**  3.  The Repeat key is F4.

**T  F**  4.  To align text between margins, use the shortcut command Ctrl + E.

**T  F**  5.  To use a shortcut menu to display the Paragraph dialog box, position the insertion point in the text to be formatted, then click the left button on the mouse.

**T  F**  6.  If the insertion point is positioned at the left margin and the tab stops are at the default setting, the insertion point is moved 1.0 inch from the left margin when you press the Tab key one time.

**T  F**  7.  To indent text from the left and right margins using the Ruler, drag the first-line, left-indent, and the right-indent markers to the desired measurements.

**T  F**  8.  Hanging paragraphs are often used for bibliographic references.

**T  F**  9.  You can use the hanging paragraph feature or options from the Bullets and Numbering dialog box to create numbered paragraphs.

**T  F**  10.  By default, Word uses 1.5 line spacing.

**Completion:**  In the space provided at the right, indicate the correct term, command, or number.

1.  Word inserts paragraph formatting into this mark.  _____

2.  To turn on or off the display of nonprinting characters, click on this button on the Standard toolbar.  _____

3.  You can return all paragraph formatting to normal with this keyboard command.  _____

4.  To indent right and left margins in a paragraph, display this dialog box.  _____

5.  Indent the left margin of a paragraph with this shortcut command.  _____

6.  In this kind of paragraph, the first line remains at the left margin and the remaining lines are indented to the first tab stop.  _____

7.  Automate the creation of bulleted paragraphs with a button on this toolbar.  _____

8.  The Bullets and Numbering dialog box contains three tab options: Bulleted, Numbered, and this.  _____

9.  At the Paragraph dialog box, change line spacing with the Line Spacing option or this.  _____

10.  This is the shortcut command to change line spacing to 2.  _____

## AT THE COMPUTER

### Exercise 1

1.  Open report01. This document is located on your student data disk.

2.  Turn on the display of nonprinting characters by clicking on the Show/Hide button on the Standard toolbar. (The Show/Hide button is the third button from the right on the Standard toolbar containing an image of a paragraph mark.)

3.  Scroll through the document to see how the document appears with nonprinting characters displayed.

4.  Move the insertion point back to the beginning of the document, then turn off the display of nonprinting characters by clicking on the Show/Hide button on the Standard toolbar.

5.  Turn on the display of only tab and paragraphs marks by completing the following steps:

    a.  Choose Tools, Options.

b. At the Options dialog box, make sure the View tab is selected.

c. Choose Tab Characters, then Paragraph Marks from the Nonprinting Characters section of the Options dialog box.

d. Choose OK or press Enter.

6. Scroll through the document to see how the document appears with tab and paragraph marks visible.

7. Turn off the display of tab and paragraph marks by completing steps 5a through 5d.

8. Close report01 without saving it.

## Exercise 2

1. At a clear document screen, key the text shown in figure 4.14.

2. After keying the text, select all the text, then turn on bold. (Hint: You can quickly select the entire document with Ctrl + A.)

3. With the entire document still selected, change the alignment of paragraphs to center by pressing Ctrl + E.

4. Save the document and name it c04ex02.

5. Print c04ex02.

6. Close c04ex02.

---

**Figure 4.14**

OT 233, DESKTOP PUBLISHING

Monday through Friday

8:30 a.m. to 9:20 a.m.

Room 301

---

## Exercise 3

1. Open para02. This document is located on your student data disk.

2. Save the document with Save As and name it c04ex03.

3. Change the alignment of the text in paragraphs to justified by completing the following steps:

a. Select the entire document.

b. Click on the Justify button on the Formatting toolbar.

4. Save the document again with the same name (c04ex03).

5. Print c04ex03.

6. Close c04ex03.

## Exercise 4

1. Open para04. This document is located on your student data disk.

2. Save the document with Save As and name it c04ex04.

3. Change the alignment of text in paragraphs to justified using the Paragraph dialog box by completing the following steps:

a. Select the entire document.

b. Choose Format, Paragraph.

c. At the Paragraph dialog box, choose Alignment. To do this with the mouse, click on the down-pointing arrow at the right of the Alignment text box. If you are using the keyboard, press Alt + G.

d. At the drop-down menu, choose Justified.

e. Choose OK or press Enter.

4. Save the document again with the same name (c04ex04).
5. Print c04ex04.
6. Close c04ex04.

## Exercise 5

1. At a clear document screen, turn on the display of nonprinting characters.
2. Change the alignment of text to Right by completing the following steps:
   a. Position the I-beam pointer anywhere in the document screen, then click the *right* mouse button.
   b. At the drop-down menu that displays, click on Paragraph.
   c. At the Paragraph dialog box, change the Alignment to Right.
   d. Choose OK or press Enter.
3. Key the first line of text shown in figure 4.15, then press Enter.
4. Key the remaining lines of text. (Each time you press Enter, the formatting from the previous paragraph is carried to the next paragraph.)
5. Select then bold the entire document.
6. Save the document and name it c04ex05.
7. Print c04ex05.
8. Turn off the display of nonprinting characters.
9. Close c04ex05.

**Figure 4.15**

```
          ST. FRANCIS MEDICAL CENTER
             300 Blue Ridge Boulevard
               Kansas City, MO 63009
                   (816) 555-2000
```

## Exercise 6

1. Open para03. This document is located on your student data disk.
2. Save the document with Save As and name it c04ex06.
3. Indent the first line of each paragraph 0.3 inches by completing the following steps:
   a. Select the entire document.
   b. Choose Format, Paragraph.
   c. At the Paragraph dialog box, choose Special. To do this with the mouse, position the arrow pointer on the down-pointing arrow to the right of the Special text box, then click the left mouse button. If you are using the keyboard, press Alt + S.
   d. From the drop-down menu that displays, choose First Line.
   e. Change the number in the By text box to 0.3. To do this with the mouse, click on the down-pointing arrow to the right of the By text box until 0.3 displays. If you are using the keyboard, press Alt + Y, then key **0.3**.
   f. Choose OK or press Enter.
4. Save the document again with the same name (c04ex06).
5. Print c04ex06.
6. Close c04ex06.

## Exercise 7

1. Open para04. This document is located on your student data disk.
2. Save the document with Save As and name it c04ex07.
3. Indent the first line of all paragraphs in the document approximately 0.5 inches by completing the following steps:
   a. Display the Ruler by choosing View, then Ruler. (If the Ruler is already displayed, skip this step.)
   b. Select the entire document.

    c.  Position the arrow pointer on the first-line indent marker on the Ruler.

    d.  Hold down the left mouse button, drag the first-line indent marker to the 0.5-inch mark on the Ruler, then release the mouse button.

4.   With the document still selected, change the paragraph alignment to justified.

5.   Save the document again with the same name (c04ex07).

6.   Print c04ex07.

7.   Close c04ex07.

## Exercise 8

1.   Open memo02. This document is located on your student data disk.

2.   Save the document with Save As and name it c04ex08.

3.   Indent the second paragraph in the document (containing the book title) to the first tab setting by completing the following steps:

    a.  Position the insertion point anywhere in the second paragraph.

    b.  Press Ctrl + M.

4.   Indent the third paragraph by completing the following steps:

    a.  Position the insertion point anywhere in the third paragraph.

    b.  Click on the Increase Indent button on the Formatting toolbar.

5.   Indent the fourth paragraph by completing the following steps:

    a.  Position the insertion point anywhere in the fourth paragraph.

    b.  Choose Format, Paragraph.

    c.  At the Paragraph dialog box, key **0.5** in the Left text box. (The *0"* measurement in the Left text box is automatically selected when you first display the Paragraph dialog box.)

    d.  Choose OK or press Enter.

6.   Indent the fifth paragraph in the document by completing the following steps:

    a.  Make sure the Ruler is displayed. (If not, choose View, Ruler.)

    b.  Position the insertion point anywhere in the fifth paragraph.

    c.  Position the arrow pointer on the small box below the left indent marker on the Ruler, hold down the left mouse button, drag the small box to the 0.5-inch mark on the Ruler, then release the mouse button.

7.   Save the document again with the same name (c04ex08).

8.   Print c04ex08.

9.   Close c04ex08.

## Exercise 9

1.   At a clear document screen, key the document shown in figure 4.16. Bold and center align the title as indicated.

2.   After keying the document, indent the third paragraph of the document from the left and right margins by completing the following steps:

    a.  Make sure the Ruler is displayed. (If not, choose View, Ruler.)

    b.  Position the insertion point anywhere in the third paragraph.

    c.  Position the arrow pointer on the small box below the left indent marker on the Ruler, hold down the left mouse button, drag the small box to the 0.5-inch mark on the Ruler, then release the mouse button.

    d.  Position the arrow pointer on the right-indent marker on the Ruler, hold down the left mouse button, drag the right-indent marker to the 5.5-inch mark on the Ruler, then release the mouse button.

3.   Indent the fifth paragraph in the document from the left and right margins by completing the following steps:

    a.  Position the insertion point anywhere within the fifth paragraph.

    b.  Choose Format, Paragraph.

    c.  At the Paragraph dialog box, key **0.5** in the Left text box.

    d. Choose <u>Right</u>. To do this with the mouse, select the current measurement in the <u>Right</u> text box. If you are using the keyboard, press Alt + R.

    e. Key **0.5** in the <u>Right</u> text box.

    f. Choose OK or press Enter.

4. Select all the paragraphs in the document (excluding the title), then change the paragraph alignment to justified.

5. Save the document and name it c04ex09.

6. Print c04ex09.

7. Close c04ex09.

**Figure 4.16**

### DESKTOP PUBLISHING

Desktop publishing is the use of a microcomputer-based system to produce publication materials, typeset or near-typeset quality text and graphics integrated on a page. These materials include memos, correspondence, notices, flyers, posters, certificates, office forms, brochures, schedules, catalogs, reports, manuals, newsletters, newspapers, magazines, books, anything that is made up of words and pictures.

In her book, *Desktop Publishing Technology and Design*, Holly Yasui states:

What makes desktop publishing different from traditional publishing is that equipment small enough to fit on a person's desktop can provide all the resources needed to prepare and assemble pages.

In a later section of her book, Holly Yasui makes the following statement about desktop publishing technology:

In the graphic arts world, desktop publishing is considered a **prepress** technology, that is, the desktop publishing system itself is generally not used to produce the final multiple copies of a publication, but rather to produce masters for reproduction.

## Exercise 10

1. Open biblio01. This document is located on your student data disk.
2. Save the document with Save As and name it c04ex10.
3. Create a hanging indent for the first two paragraphs by completing the following steps:
   a. Select at least a portion of the first and second paragraphs.
   b. Press Ctrl + T.
4. Create a hanging indent for the third and fourth paragraphs by completing the following steps:
   a. Select at least a portion of the third and fourth paragraphs.
   b. Choose Format, Paragraph.
   c. At the Paragraph dialog box, choose Special. To do this with the mouse, position the arrow pointer on the down-pointing arrow to the right of the Special text box, then click the left mouse button. If you are using the keyboard, press Alt + S.
   d. Choose *Hanging* from the Special drop-down menu.
   e. Choose OK or press Enter.
5. Save the document again with the same name (c04ex10).
6. Print c04ex10.
7. Close c04ex10.

## Exercise 11

*Note: In this exercise and other exercises in the text, you will be required to create business letters. Please refer to appendix D at the end of this text for the correct placement and spacing of a block-style and modified block-style business letter.*

1. At a clear document screen, key the text shown in figure 4.17 in an appropriate business letter format. Bold the text in the paragraphs as indicated. When keying the numbered paragraphs, key the number, the period, then press the Tab key.
2. After all text has been keyed, indent the numbered paragraphs by completing the following steps:
   a. Select the numbered paragraphs.
   b. Press Ctrl + T.
3. Select all paragraphs in the body of the letter (excluding the date, inside address, salutation, complimentary close, and reference initials and document name), then change the paragraph alignment to justified.
4. Save the letter and name it c04ex11.
5. Print c04ex11.
6. Close c04ex11.

**Figure 4.17**

May 8, 1996


Dr. Lillian Stanford
Knoxville Community College
550 Academy Drive
Knoxville, TN 33506

Dear Lillian:

I was happy to hear that you will be offering a desktop publishing
course at Knoxville Community College during fall quarter.  In
answer to your question about word processing terminology, I
include the following information about features common to all word
processing programs:

1.  A flexible text entry tool, called an **insertion point** or a
**cursor**.

2.  The elimination of the need for a manual carriage return at the
end of lines within paragraphs by means of **word wrapping**.

3.  The display of text on the screen and the ability to view
different portions of a document on the screen by means of
**scrolling**.

4.  The ability to **select** blocks of text for deletion, copying, or
moving from one part of the document to another.

5.  The ability to **search and replace** strings of characters--parts
of words, whole words, and phrases.

Relating word processing terms to desktop publishing gives the
students a perspective to begin to understand desktop publishing.

Sincerely,


Nancy Suaro

xx:c04ex11

## Exercise 12

1. At a clear document screen, key the text shown in figure 4.18. Bold and center the text in uppercase letters as indicated. Press the Enter key twice after each paragraph.
2. After keying the document, insert bullets before the two paragraphs of text below *GRAPHICS FUNCTIONS AVAILABLE IN ALL GRAPHICS PROGRAMS* by completing the following steps:
   a. Select the two paragraphs of text below *GRAPHICS FUNCTIONS AVAILABLE IN ALL GRAPHICS PROGRAMS*.
   b. Click on the Bullets button on the Formatting toolbar.
3. Follow steps similar to those in 2a and 2b to insert bullets before the four paragraphs of text below *BIT-MAPPED FUNCTIONS SPECIFIC TO PAINT PROGRAMS*.
4. Follow steps similar to those in 2a and 2b to insert bullets before the five paragraphs of text below *OBJECT-ORIENTED FUNCTIONS SPECIFIC TO DRAW PROGRAMS*.
5. Save the document and name it c04ex12.
6. Print c04ex12.
7. Close c04ex12.

---

**Figure 4.18**

**GRAPHICS FUNCTIONS AVAILABLE IN ALL GRAPHICS PROGRAMS**

rotations and reflections

duplication of areas/objects

**BIT-MAPPED FUNCTIONS SPECIFIC TO PAINT PROGRAMS**

bit-by-bit detail editing

bit-by-bit speckling and shading

creation of custom fill patterns and pouring of fills into selected areas

bit-wise functions:  inverting, making outlines, etc.

**OBJECT-ORIENTED FUNCTIONS SPECIFIC TO DRAW PROGRAMS**

positioning of objects and editing of attributes

variable grouping and layering of objects

aligning objects, including type

reshaping and smoothing of objects

drawing of smooth curves

# Exercise 13

1. Open quiz01. This document is located on your student data disk.
2. Save the document with Save As and name it c04ex13.
3. Insert paragraph numbering before all paragraphs in the document (except the title) and create hanging indented paragraphs by completing the following steps:
   a. Select all paragraphs in the document (except the title).
   b. Click on the Numbering button on the Formatting toolbar.
   c. With the paragraphs still selected, press Ctrl + T.
4. Add the paragraph shown in figure 4.19 between paragraphs 3 and 4 by completing the following steps:
   a. Position the insertion point immediately to the right of the question mark at the end of the third paragraph.
   b. Press Enter.
   c. Key the paragraph shown in figure 4.19.
5. Delete the second paragraph by completing the following steps:
   a. Select the text of the second paragraph (you will not be able to select the number).
   b. Press the Delete key.
6. Save the document again with the same name (c04ex13).
7. Print c04ex13.
8. Close c04ex13.

**Figure 4.19**

What has happened technologically to make the picture phone a realistic alternative to the voice-only telephone?

# Exercise 14

1. Open outln01. This document is located on your student data disk.
2. Save the document with Save As and name it c04ex14.
3. Number the paragraphs in the agenda using the Bullets and Numbering dialog box by completing the following steps:
   a. Select the paragraphs in the document (excluding the title and the blank lines below the title).
   b. Choose Format, Bullets and Numbering.
   c. At the Bullets and Numbering dialog box, choose the Multilevel tab.
   d. Click on the second numbering option box.
   e. Choose OK or press Enter.
4. Add *Emergency Room* between *Coronary Care Unit* and *Pediatrics* by completing the following steps:
   a. Position the insertion point immediately right of the *t* in *Coronary Care Unit*.
   b. Press Enter.
   c. Key **Emergency Room**.
5. Select then delete *Customer Survey*.
6. Add *Contractors* between *Timelines* and *Costs*.
7. Save the document again with the same name (c04ex14).
8. Print c04ex14.
9. Close c04ex14.

# Exercise 15

1. Open para02. This document is located on your student data disk.
2. Save the document with Save As and name it c04ex15.
3. Change the line spacing for all paragraphs to 1.5 line spacing by completing the following steps:

a. Select the entire document.

b. Press Ctrl + 5.

4. Change the alignment of all paragraphs to justified.

5. Save the document again with the same name (c04ex15).

6. Print c04ex15.

7. Close c04ex15.

## Exercise 16

1. Open c04ex13.

2. Save the document with Save As and name it c04ex16.

3. Change the line spacing to double using the Paragraph dialog box by completing the following steps:

   a. Select the paragraphs in the document (excluding the title and the blank lines below the title).

   b. Choose Format, Paragraph.

   c. At the Paragraph dialog box, make sure the Indents and Spacing tab is selected, then click on the up-pointing triangle to the right of the At text box until 2 displays in the At text box. If you are using the keyboard, press Alt + A, then key 2 in the At text box.

   d. Choose OK or press Enter.

4. Save the document again with the same name (c04ex16).

5. Print c04ex16.

6. Close c04ex16.

## SKILL ASSESSMENTS

## Assessment 1

1. Open memo01. This document is located on your student data disk.

2. Save the document with Save As and name it c04sa01.

3. Turn on the display of nonprinting characters.

4. Make the following changes to the memo:

   a. Bold the headings, DATE:, TO:, FROM:, and SUBJECT:.

   b. Change the line spacing to 1.5 for the three paragraphs in the body of the memo.

   c. Change the paragraph alignment to justified for the three paragraphs in the body of the memo.

5. Turn off the display of the nonprinting characters.

6. Save the document again with the same name (c04sa01).

7. Print c04sa01.

8. Close c04sa01.

## Assessment 2

1. At a clear document screen, key the memo shown in figure 4.20 with the following specifications:

   a. Bold text as indicated.

   b. Center text as indicated.

   c. Change the alignment of paragraphs in the body of the memo to justified.

2. Save the memo and name it c04sa02.

3. Print c04sa02.

4. Close c04sa02.

Figure 4.20

```
DATE:      April 15, 1996

TO:        Administrative Support Staff

FROM:      Edward Goldberg, Training and Education

SUBJECT:   DESKTOP PUBLISHING CLASSES


Mountain Community College administrative support staff will have
the opportunity to complete training on desktop publishing using
Word for Windows, version 6.  This training is designed for current
users of Word who want to become familiar with advanced desktop
publishing features.

The desktop publishing classes will be held in Room 301 from 3:30
p.m. to 5:30 p.m. on the following days:

                    Monday, May 6
                  Wednesday, May 8
                  Tuesday, May 14
                  Thursday, May 16


There are 25 computers in Room 301.  For this reason, each training
session is limited to 25 employees.  Preregistration is required.
To register, please call Training and Education at extension 244.

xx:c04sa02
```

## Assessment 3

1. At a clear document screen, key the memo shown in figure 4.21. Indent the second paragraph in the body of the memo 0.5 inches from the left and right margins.
2. Save the memo and name it c04sa03.
3. Print c04sa03.
4. Close c04sa03.

Figure 4.21

DATE:        March 5, 1996

TO:          Jean Orcutt, College Relations

FROM:        Nancy Suaro, OT Department

SUBJECT:     DESKTOP PUBLISHING COURSE


The desktop publishing course, OT 133, has been a great success this quarter.  Because of the interest in the course, we have decided to offer it spring quarter.  Please include the following description for the course in the spring schedule:

Students in Desktop Publishing, OT 133, will learn formatting features of Word for Windows, Version 6, to prepare documents including newsletters, flyers, brochures, advertisements, announcements, and business forms.

I would like to see the course advertised not only in the spring schedule but also in the school newspaper.  Would you help me write an advertisement for the newspaper?  You can contact me at extension 208.

xx:c04sa03

## Assessment 4

1. At a clear document screen, create the document shown in figure 4.22 with the following specifications:
   a. Change the line spacing to double.
   b. Center, bold, and italicize text as indicated.
   c. Create hanging paragraphs as indicated.
   d. Change the alignment of paragraphs to justified.
2. Save the document and name it c04sa04.
3. Print c04sa04.
4. Close c04sa04

Figure 4.22

**BIBLIOGRAPHY**

Abernathy, Richard M.    (1996)   *One Hundred Attention-Getting*

*Ideas* (pp. 45-66).   St. Louis, MO:   Independence Press.

Damain, Christine.   (1995)   *Computer Designing and Artwork* (pp.

47-56).   Charlotte, NC:   Horton Press.

Kimmel, Roseanne A.   (1995)   *Graphic Design and Publication* (pp.

87-98).   Baton Rouge, LA:   Lafontaine-Meyers.

Neubauer, Eric G.   (1995)   *Creative Letterheads* (pp. 10-15).

Boston, MA:   Ivory Tower Publishing.

## Assessment 5

1. Open memo02. This document is located on your student data disk.
2. Save the document with Save As and name it c04sa05.
3. Insert bullets before paragraphs two through five (the paragraphs containing the book titles).
4. Change the alignment of paragraphs in the body of the memo to justified.
5. Save the document again with the same name (c04sa05).
6. Print c04sa05.
7. Close c04sa05.

## Assessment 6

1. Open jobdes01. This document is located on your student data disk.
2. Save the document with Save As and name it c04sa06.
3. Bold and center the title, JOB DESCRIPTION, and subtitle, REGISTERED NURSE.
4. Select the text paragraphs in the document, then make the following changes:
   a. Change the line spacing to double.
   b. Change the alignment to justified.
   c. Insert numbers at the beginning of each paragraph. (Hint: Use the Numbering button on the Formatting toolbar.)
   d. Hanging indent the paragraphs. (Hint: Use the shortcut command, Ctrl + T.)
5. Delete the fifth paragraph.
6. Add the paragraph shown in figure 4.23 between the fourth and fifth paragraphs. (This paragraph will be numbered 5.)
7. Save the document again with the same name (c04sa06).
8. Print c04sa06.
9. Close c04sa06.

Figure 4.23

Supervises, trains, and monitors licensed practical nurses and nurses' aides.

# Assessment 7

1. At a clear document screen, create the document shown in figure 4.24.
2. After keying the document, insert multilevel numbering before each paragraph in the document (excluding the title, subtitle, and blank lines below the subtitle). (Choose the numbering option that inserts Roman numerals at the left margin, uppercase letters at the first tab stop, and Arabic numbers at the second tab stop.)
3. Save the document and name it c04sa07.
4. Print c04sa07.
5. Close c04sa07.

**Figure 4.24**

```
                    ST. FRANCIS MEDICAL CENTER

                      Quality Care Program

INTRODUCTION

      Policy Statement
      Goals of the Plan

COMMITTEES

      Safety
      Infection Control
      Patient Care

MEDICAL CENTER OPERATIONS

      Administration
            Regulatory Agency Review
            Risk Management and Litigations
            Infection Surveillance
      Governing Board

EVALUATION

      Assignment of Authority
      Evidence of Solution
      Impact on Care
```

# Changing Fonts 5

Upon successful completion of chapter 5, you will be able to adjust the style and size of type as well as the appearance of characters in standard business documents.

By default, Word uses a font that prints text with varying amounts of space. In chapter 1, you learned how to change the default font to a Courier font that prints text with uniform appearance and spacing. Other fonts may be available depending on the printer you are using. The number of fonts available ranges from a few to several hundred. A font consists of three parts: typeface, type size, and type style.

## Choosing a Typeface

A *typeface* is a set of characters with a common design and shape. Typefaces may be decorative, blocked, or plain. Typefaces are either *monospaced* or *proportional*. Word refers to typeface as font. A monospaced typeface allots the same amount of horizontal space for each character. Courier is an example of a monospaced typeface. Proportional typefaces allot a varying amount of space for each character. The space allotted is based on the width of the character. For example, the lowercase *i* will take up less space than the uppercase *M*.

Proportional typefaces are divided into two main categories: *serif* and *sans serif*. A serif is a small line at the end of a character stroke. Traditionally, a serif typeface is used with documents that are text intensive (documents that are mainly text) because the serifs help move the reader's eyes across the page.

A sans serif typeface does not have serifs (*sans* is French for *without*). Sans serif typefaces are often used for headlines and advertisements that are not text intensive. Examples of serif typefaces are shown in figure 5.1.

| | |
|---|---|
| **Figure 5.1**<br>*Serif Typefaces* | Bookman Light<br>New Century Schoolbook<br>Palatino<br>Times New Roman<br>*Zapf Chancery Medium Italic*<br>Times New Roman (TT) |

Examples of sans serif typefaces are shown in figure 5.2.

| | |
|---|---|
| **Figure 5.2**<br>*Sans Serif Type-*<br>*faces* | Avant Garde Gothic Book<br>Helvetica<br>Century Gothic<br>Arial (TT) |

## ■ Choosing a Type Size

Type size is divided into two categories: *pitch* and *point size*. Pitch is a measurement used for monospaced typefaces; it reflects the number of characters that can be printed in 1 horizontal inch. (For some printers, the pitch is referred to as *cpi*, or *characters per inch*. For example, the font Courier 10 cpi is the same as 10-pitch Courier.) Pitch measurement can be changed to increase or decrease the size of the characters. The higher the pitch measurement, the smaller the characters. The lower the pitch number, the larger the characters.

Examples of different pitch sizes in Courier typeface are shown in figure 5.3.

| | |
|---|---|
| **Figure 5.3**<br>*Different Pitch Sizes*<br>*in Courier* | ```
12-pitch Courier
10-pitch Courier
8-pitch Courier
``` |

Proportional typefaces can be set in different sizes. The size of proportional type is measured vertically in units called *points*. A point is approximately 1/72 of an inch. The higher the point size, the larger the characters. Examples of different point sizes in the Arial typeface are shown in figure 5.4.

| | |
|---|---|
| **Figure 5.4**<br>*Different Point*<br>*Sizes in Arial* | 8-point Arial<br>12-point Arial<br>18-point Arial<br>24-point Arial |
```

# ■ Choosing a Type Style

Within a typeface, characters may have a varying style. There are four main categories of type styles:

1. normal (for some typefaces, this may be referred to as *light*, *black*, *regular*, or *roman*)
2. bold
3. italic
4. bold italic

The four main type styles in 12 points are shown in figure 5.5.

Helvetica regular
**Helvetica bold**
*Helvetica italic*
***Helvetica bold italic***

Times New Roman regular
**Times New Roman bold**
*Times New Roman italic*
***Times New Roman bold italic***

The term *font* describes a particular typeface in a specific style and size. Examples of fonts are *10-pitch Courier*, *10-point Arial*, *12-point Times New Roman Bold*, *12-point Palatino Italic*, and *14-point Century Gothic*.

# ■ Choosing a Font

The printer you are using has built-in fonts. These fonts can be supplemented with cartridges and/or soft fonts. The types of fonts you have available with your printer depend on the type of printer you are using, the amount of memory installed with the printer, and what supplemental fonts you have.

A font cartridge is inserted directly into the printer and lets you add fonts. To install a font cartridge, refer to the documentation that comes with the cartridge.

Soft fonts are available as software on disk. When soft fonts are installed, specify a directory in Word for the soft fonts. The Word for Windows, Version 6, program comes with additional fonts that were loaded during installation.

## Using the Font Dialog Box

The fonts available with your printer are displayed in the Font list box at the Font dialog box. To display the Font dialog box, shown in figure 5.6, choose Format, then Font; or press Ctrl + D. You can also display the Font dialog box with a shortcut menu. To do this, you would complete the following steps:

1. Position the I-beam pointer anywhere within the document screen.
2. Click the right mouse button.
3. From the drop-down menu that displays, click on Font.

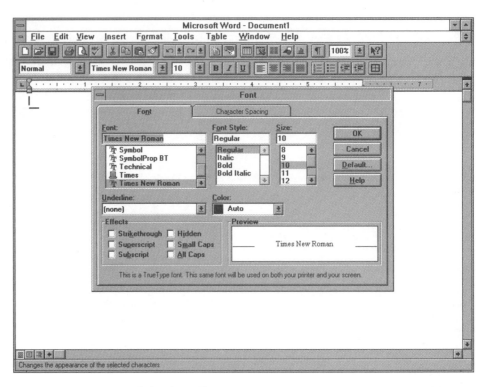

**Figure 5.6**
**Font Dialog Box**

**Font:** The Font list box at the Font dialog box displays the typefaces (fonts) available with your printer. Figure 5.6 shows the typefaces available with a popular PostScript printer (the fonts displayed with your printer may vary from those shown).

An icon displays before the typefaces in the Font list box. The printer icon identifies a built-in font. These are fonts provided with your printer. The TT icon identifies soft fonts. Word for Windows, Version 6 provides a number of True Type soft fonts that are identified with the TT icon. The True Type fonts are graphically generated while printer fonts are printer generated. Graphically generated fonts take longer to print than printer generated fonts.

To select a typeface, select the desired typeface (font), then choose OK or press Enter. For example, to choose the True Type typeface Times New Roman, you would complete the following steps:

1. Display the Font dialog box. To do this, choose one of the following methods:
   - Choose Format, Font.
   - Press Ctrl + D.
   - Position the I-beam pointer anywhere in the document screen, click the right mouse button, then click on Font.
2. At the Font dialog box, select Times New Roman. To do this with the mouse, click on the down-pointing arrow in the Font list scroll bar until Times New Roman displays, then click on it. If you are using the keyboard, press the down arrow key until Times New Roman is selected.
3. Choose OK or press Enter.

When different typefaces are selected, the Preview Box in the lower right corner of the dialog box displays the appearance of the selected font.

In addition to using the Font dialog box to select a typeface, you can use the Font option on the Formatting toolbar. The Font option displays a font name followed by a down-pointing arrow. For example, if your default typeface is Courier, the name Courier displays in a box on the Formatting toolbar followed by a down-pointing arrow. Only the mouse, not the keyboard, can be used to change the font with the Font option on the Formatting toolbar. When you position the arrow pointer on the down-pointing arrow after the Font option, a drop-down menu displays as shown in figure 5.7 (your drop-down menu may vary).

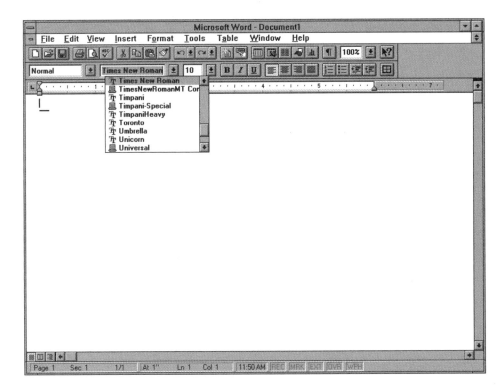

Figure 5.7
Font Drop-Down
Menu

To select a typeface, position the arrow pointer on the desired typeface, then click the left mouse  button.

**Size:** The Size list box at the Font dialog box displays a variety of common type sizes. Decrease point size to make text smaller or increase point size to make text larger. To select a point size with the mouse, click on the desired point size. To view more point sizes, click on the down-pointing arrow in the Size scroll bar. If you are using the keyboard, press Alt + S for Size, then press the down arrow key until the desired point size is selected.

You can also key a specific point size. To do this with the mouse, select the number in the Size text box, then key the desired point size. If you are using the keyboard, press Alt + S, then key the desired point size.

Word also provides shortcut commands that can be used to increase or decrease the point size of  selected text. To increase the point size of text, select the text, then press Ctrl + ]. To decrease the point size of text, select the text, then press Ctrl + [.

In addition to the Font dialog box, you can use the Font Size option on the Formatting toolbar to change type size. The Font Size option is a box containing the current point size followed by a down-pointing arrow. Only the mouse, not the keyboard, can be used to change the size with the Font Size option on the Formatting toolbar. To change the type size with the Font Size option, position the arrow pointer on the down-pointing arrow after the box containing the current point  size, then click the left mouse button. From the drop-down menu that displays, click on the desired type size.

**Font Style:** The Font Style list box displays the styles available with the selected typeface. As you select different typefaces at the Font dialog box, the list of styles changes in the Font Style list box. For example, to change the typeface to Times New Roman and the type style to Bold Italic, you would complete the following steps:

1. Display the Font dialog box.
2. At the Font dialog box, select Times New Roman. To do this with the mouse, click on the down-pointing arrow in the scroll bar at the right side of the Font list box until Times New Roman displays, then click on it. If you are using the keyboard, press the down arrow key until Times New Roman is selected.

Go To Exercise 5

3. Change the Font Style to Bold Italic. To do this with the mouse, click on Bold Italic in the Font Style list box. If you are using the keyboard, press Alt + O, then press the down arrow key until Bold Italic is selected.
4. Choose OK or press Enter.

**Underline Options:** When underlining is turned on, Word will underline words and spaces between words with a single line. With Underline options, you can underline words and spaces between words with a single line, a double line, or a dotted line. You can also tell Word to underline words only and not the spaces between words. As an example of how to use this feature, you would complete the following steps to underline words with a dotted line:

1. Select the text to be underlined with a dotted line.
2. Display the Font dialog box.
3. Choose Underline, then Dotted. To do this with the mouse, click on the down-pointing arrow at the right side of the Underline text box, then click on Dotted. If you are using the keyboard, press Alt + U, then press the down arrow key until Dotted is selected.
4. Choose OK or press Enter.

Go To Exercise 6

**Color Options**: With Color options from the Font dialog box, you can specify a color for text or selected text. If you do not have access to a color printer, text identified with color will print in shades of gray. As an example of how to use the Color options, you would complete the following steps to change the color of selected text to Blue:

1. Select the text.
2. Display the Font dialog box.
3. Choose Color, then Blue. To do this with the mouse, click on the down-pointing arrow at the right side of the Color text box, then click on Blue. If you are using the keyboard, press Alt + C, then press the down arrow key until Blue is selected.
4. Choose OK or press Enter.

Go To Exercise 7

**Effects**: The Effects section of the Font dialog box contains a variety of options that can be used to create different character styles.

The Strikethrough option lets you show text that needs to be deleted from a document. Strikethrough prints text with a line of hyphens running through it. This feature has practical application for some legal documents in which deleted text must be retained in the document. The hyphens indicate that the text has been deleted. Strikethrough text looks like this:

Go To Exercise 8

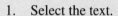
This is Strikethrough text.

With the Superscript option, you can create text that is raised slightly above the line. Some mathematical expressions are written with superscripted numbers. For example, the mathematical expression 4 to the second power is written as $4^2$. You can create superscripted text as you key text or you can superscript selected text.

To create a superscripted character as you key the text, you would complete the following steps:

1. Key text to the point where superscripted text is to appear.
2. Display the Font dialog box.
3. At the Font dialog box, choose Superscript.
4. Choose OK or press Enter.
5. Key the superscripted text.
6. Repeat steps 2 through 4 to turn off superscript.

To superscript an existing character, you would complete the following steps:

1. Select the character.
2. Display the Font dialog box.
3. At the Font dialog box, choose Superscript.
4. Choose OK or press Enter.

Text can be superscripted at the keyboard with Ctrl + Shift + = (equal sign). Press Ctrl + Shift + = to turn on superscript, key the text to be superscripted, then press Ctrl + Shift + = to turn off superscript. To superscript existing text, select the text, then press Ctrl + Shift + =.

With the Subscript option from the Font dialog box, you can create text that is lowered slightly below the line. Some chemical formulas require the use of subscripted characters. For example, the formula for water is written as $H_2O$. You can create a subscripted character as you are keying text or you can subscript a selected character or characters.

Text can be subscripted at the keyboard with Ctrl + =. Press Ctrl + = to turn on subscript, key the text to be subscripted, then press Ctrl + = to turn off subscript. To subscript existing text, select the text, then press Ctrl + =.

With the Hidden option from the Font dialog box, you can include such items as comments, personal messages, or questions in a document. These items can be displayed, printed, or hidden.

To create Hidden text, you would complete the following steps:

1. Display the Font dialog box.
2. At the Font dialog box, choose Hidden.
3. Choose OK or press Enter.
4. Key the text to be hidden.
5. Repeat steps 1 through 3 to turn off the feature.

Hidden text will display in the document screen only if the display of nonprinting characters has been turned on. Hidden text displays on the screen with a dotted underline below. To turn the display of nonprinting characters on or off, click on the Show/Hide button on the Standard toolbar.

To create hidden text with the keyboard, press Ctrl + Shift + H, key the text, then press Ctrl + Shift + H.

By default, hidden text does not print. If you want to print hidden text, you would complete the following steps:

1. Display the Print dialog box.
2. Choose Options.
3. At the Options dialog box, choose Hidden Text.
4. Choose OK or press Enter.
5. At the Print dialog box, choose OK or press Enter.

If you decide that you do not want hidden text to print, complete the steps above to remove the X from the Hidden Text check box at the Options dialog box.

From the Font dialog box, the Small Caps option lets you print small capital letters. This works for some printers, but not all. When text is identified as small caps, it will look like this:

THIS IS TEXT IN SMALL CAPS.

To create small caps with the keyboard, press Ctrl + Shift + K, key the text to be set in small caps, then press Ctrl + Shift + K to turn off small caps. To set existing text in small caps, select the text, then press Ctrl + Shift + K.

There are several methods for keying or setting text in uppercase letters. You can press the Caps Lock key on the keyboard, then key text in all uppercase letters; or, you can choose the All Caps option at the Font dialog box or the command Ctrl + Shift + A, then key text.

## Spacing Punctuation

Standard practice when keying a document is to space twice after end-of-sentence punctuation such as a period, question mark, or exclamation point, and after a colon. If you change to a proportional typeface, space only once after end-of-sentence punctuation and after a colon. Proportional type is set closer and extra white space at the end of a sentence or after a colon is not needed. If the extra white space is added, the text will appear blotchy.

## Formatting with Format Painter

Word for Windows, Version 6, contains a button on the Standard toolbar that you can use to copy character formatting already applied to text to different locations in the document. This button is called the Format Painter and displays on the Standard toolbar as a paintbrush.

To use the Format Painter button, position the insertion point on a character containing the desired character formatting, click on the Format Painter button, then select text to which you want the character formatting applied. When you click on the Format Painter button, the I-beam point displays with a paint brush attached.

For example, suppose you have changed the font for some text to 14-point Arial and want to apply this formatting to other text in the document. To do this, you would complete the following steps:

1. Position the insertion point on a character that has been changed to 14-point Arial.
2. Click on the Format Painter button on the Standard toolbar.
3. Select text in the document you want to apply 14-point Arial.

When you select text, then release the mouse button, the selected text changes to 14-point Arial.

If you want to apply character formatting to other text in the document only once, click on the Format Painter button once. If, however, you want to apply the character formatting in more than one location in the document, double-click on the Format Painter button.

If you have double-clicked on the Format Painter button, turn off the feature by clicking once on the Format Painter button.

The keyboard can also be used to apply formatting to text. To do this, select the text containing the formatting to be applied to other text, then press Ctrl + Shift + C. Select the text to which you want to apply the formatting, then press Ctrl + Shift + V.

## Inserting Symbols

Many of the typefaces (fonts) include special symbols such as bullets, publishing symbols, and letters with special punctuation (such as É, ö, and ñ). To insert a symbol, you would complete the following steps:

1. Choose Insert, then Symbol.
2. At the Symbol dialog box shown in figure 5.8, double-click on the desired symbol.
3. Choose Close.

At the Symbol dialog box you can also use the keyboard to insert a symbol in a document. To do this, display the Symbol dialog box, then move to the desired symbol with the up, down, left, or right arrow keys. When the desired symbol is selected, press Alt + I to insert the symbol in the document. To close the Symbol dialog box, press Enter. (The Close button should be automatically selected. If it is not, press the Tab key until the Close button is selected, then press Enter.)

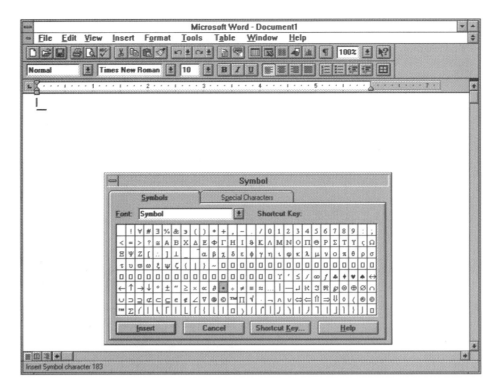

Figure 5.8
*Symbol Dialog Box*

## Changing the Font for Symbols

At the Symbol dialog box, you can change the font with the Font option. When you change the font, different symbols display in the dialog box. To change the font, you would complete the following steps:

1. Choose Insert, Symbol to display the Symbol dialog box.
2. Choose Font, then select the desired font. To do this with the mouse, click on the down-pointing arrow at the right side of the Font text box, then click on the desired font. If you are using the keyboard, press Alt + F, press the down arrow key until the desired font is selected, then press Enter.
3. Select a symbol, then choose Insert.
4. Choose Close to close the Symbol dialog box.

## Inserting Special Characters

At the Symbol dialog box, special characters can be inserted in a document. To do this, display the Symbol dialog box, then choose the Special Characters tab. The dialog box displays as shown in figure 5.9.

Figure 5.9
Symbol Dialog Box
with Special
Characters Tab
Selected

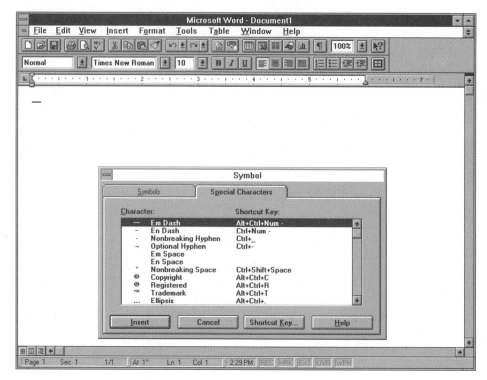

Special characters can be inserted in a document from the Symbol dialog box using the mouse or the keyboard. If you are using the mouse, double-click on the desired character, then click on the Close button. If you are using the keyboard, press the up or down arrow key until the desired character is selected, then press Alt + I. Press Enter to close the Symbol dialog box.

Special characters can also be inserted using shortcut keys. The shortcut keys are listed in the Symbol dialog box. For example, to insert a copyright symbol in a document, you would press Alt + Ctrl + C.

## ■ Displaying Formatting

When formatting is applied to a document, such as paragraph or character formatting, the text in the document displays in the document screen as it will appear when printed. Word provides a feature that lets you view what formatting has been applied to text. To view formatting, you would complete the following steps:

1. Click once on the Help button on the Standard toolbar; or press Shift + F1.
2. Position the arrow pointer (displays with a question mark) on the text containing formatting you want to view, then click the left mouse button.
3. After viewing the formatting information, click once on the Help button on the Standard toolbar.

Figure 5.10 displays the formatting information for the title of the legal01 document located on your student data disk.

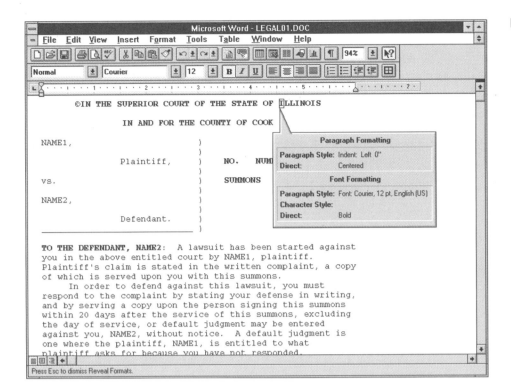

Figure 5.10
Formatting
Information

# CHAPTER SUMMARY

- A font consists of three parts: typeface, type size, and type style.
- A typeface is a set of characters with a common design and shape. Typefaces are either monospaced or proportional. A monospaced typeface, such as Courier, allots the same amount of horizontal space for each character. A proportional typeface, such as Arial, allots a varying amount of space for each character.
- Type size is measured in pitch or point size. Pitch is the number of characters per inch—the higher the pitch, the smaller the characters. Point size is a vertical measurement—the higher the point size, the larger the characters.
- A type style is a variation of style within a certain typeface. There are four main kinds of type styles: normal, bold, italic, and bold italic.
- The kinds of fonts you have available with your printer depend on the type of printer you are using, the amount of memory installed with the printer, and what supplemental fonts you have.
- Change the font at the Font dialog box or use the Font option on the Formatting toolbar. To use the Font option, click on the down-pointing arrow next to the font name on the Formatting toolbar, then click on your font choice.
- The fonts available with your printer are displayed in the Font list box at the Font dialog box. Changes can also be made at this dialog box to the type size, font style, underline options, and text color.
- The Effects section of the Font dialog box contains the following options that can be used to create different character styles: Strikethrough, Superscript, Subscript, Hidden text, and Small Caps.
- Space only once after end-of-sentence punctuation and after a colon when using proportional typefaces.
- The Format Painter button (displays on the Standard toolbar as a paintbrush) lets you copy character formatting already applied to text to different locations in the document.
- Many of the typefaces (fonts) include special symbols such as bullets and publishing symbols. Insert a symbol in a document at the Symbol dialog box.

| | Mouse | Keyboard |
|---|---|---|
| Font dialog box | Format, Font; or with I-beam in document screen, click right mouse button, then click on Font in drop-down menu | CTRL + D |
| Increase point size of selected text | | CTRL + ] |
| Decrease point size of selected text | | CTRL + [ |
| Superscript text | | CTRL + SHIFT + = |
| Subscript text | | CTRL + = |
| Hidden text | | CTRL + SHIFT + H |
| Small caps | | CTRL + SHIFT + K |
| All caps | | CTRL + SHIFT + A |
| To use Format Painter button | Position insertion point on a character with desired formatting, click on Format Painter button, with the mouse select text you want the formatting applied to, release mouse button | |
| Copy formatting | | CTRL + SHIFT + C |
| Insert formatting | | CTRL + SHIFT + V |
| Symbol dialog box | Insert, Symbol | Insert, Symbol |

## CHECK YOUR UNDERSTANDING

**True/False:** Circle the letter T if the statement is true; circle the letter F if the statement is false.

T   F   1.   Always space twice after end-of-sentence punctuation.

T   F   2.   The hidden text option appears in the Font dialog box.

T   F   3.   The strikethrough option lets you show text that needs to be deleted from a document.

T   F   4.   To use Format Painter to apply formatting to several locations in a document, double-click on the Format Painter button.

T   F   5.   You can probably insert this symbol ♥ from the Symbol dialog box.

T   F   6.   In French, the word *sans* means *without*.

T   F   7.   Printer generated fonts take longer to print than graphically generated fonts.

T   F   8.   The TT icon identifies True Type soft fonts.

T   F   9.   In addition to the Font dialog box, you can change the font at the Font toolbar.

T   F   10.   Change from continuous single underline to double underline at the Font dialog box.

**Matching:** In the space provided at the left, indicate the correct letter *or letters* that match each description.

| | | | |
|---|---|---|---|
| A. | Courier | J. | sans serif |
| B. | typeface | K. | pitch |
| C. | type style | L. | Times New Roman |
| D. | type size | M. | font |
| E. | bold | N. | italic |
| F. | proportional | O. | superscript |
| G. | serif | P. | point |
| H. | subscript | Q. | normal |
| I. | bold italic | | |

1. Kinds of type styles. _____
2. Typeface that allots the same amount of horizontal space for each character. _____
3. This kind of typeface does not have a small line at the end of each character stroke. _____
4. A particular typeface in a specific style and size. _____
5. A set of characters with a common design and shape. _____
6. Text that is lowered slightly below the regular line of text. _____
7. With this type of measurement, the higher the number, the larger the characters. _____
8. Examples of different typefaces. _____
9. A measure of the number of characters that can be printed in 1 horizontal inch. _____
10. With this type of measurement, the lower the number, the larger the characters. _____

## AT THE COMPUTER

### Exercise 1

1. Open para02. This document is located on your student data disk.
2. Save the document with Save As and name it c05ex01.
3. Change the typeface to Times New Roman by completing the following steps:
   a. Select the entire document.
   b. Display the Font dialog box by choosing one of the following options:
      - Choose Format, Font.
      - Press Ctrl + D.
      - Position the arrow pointer anywhere in the document screen, click the *right* mouse button, then click on Font.
   c. At the Font dialog box, select Times New Roman. To do this with the mouse, click on the down-pointing arrow at the right side of the Font list box until Times New Roman displays, then click on it. If you are using the keyboard, press the down arrow key until Times New Roman is selected.
   d. Choose OK or press Enter.
4. Save the document again with the same name (c05ex01).
5. Print c05ex01.
6. Close c05ex01.

## Exercise 2

1. Open para03. This document is located on your student data disk.
2. Save the document with Save As and name it c05ex02.
3. Change the typeface to Arial using the Font option on the Formatting toolbar by completing the following steps:
   a. Select the entire document.
   b. Click on the down-pointing arrow to the right of the Font option.
   c. From the drop-down menu that displays, click on Arial. (You may need to click on the up or down arrow in the scroll bar to display Arial.)
4. Save the document again with the same name (c05ex02).
5. Print c05ex02.
6. Close c05ex02.

## Exercise 3

1. Open para04. This document is located on your student data disk.
2. Save the document with Save As and name it c05ex03.
3. Change the font to 10-point Century Gothic using the Font dialog box by completing the following steps:
   a. Select the entire document.
   b. Display the Font dialog box.
   c. At the Font dialog box, select Century Gothic. To do this with the mouse, click on the up- or down-pointing arrow at the right side of the Font list box until Century Gothic displays, then click on it. If you are using the keyboard, press the up or down arrow key until Century Gothic is selected.
   d. Change the Size option to 10. To do this with the mouse, click on the 10 in the Size list box. If you are using the keyboard, press Alt + S, then press the up arrow key until 10 is selected.
   e. Choose OK or press Enter.
4. With the document still selected, change the alignment of paragraphs to justified.
5. Save the document again with the same name (c05ex03).
6. Print c05ex03.
7. Close c05ex03.

## Exercise 4

1. Open para02. This document is located on your student data disk.
2. Save the document with Save As and name it c05ex04.
3. Change the font to 10-point Colonna MT using the Formatting toolbar by completing the following steps:
   a. Select the entire document.
   b. Click on the down-pointing arrow to the right of the Font option on the Formatting toolbar.
   c. From the drop-down menu that displays, click on Colonna MT.
   d. Click on the down-pointing arrow to the right of the Size option on the Formatting toolbar.
   e. From the drop-down menu that displays, click on 10.
4. Save the document again with the same name (c05ex04).
5. Print c05ex04.
6. Close c05ex04.

## Exercise 5

1. Open para03. This document is located on your student data disk.
2. Save the document with Save As and name it c05ex05.
3. Change the typeface to Bookman Old Style and the style to Bold Italic by completing the following steps:
   a. Select the entire document.
   b. Display the Font dialog box.
   c. At the Font dialog box, select Bookman Old Style in the Font list box.
   d. Change the Font Style to Bold Italic. To do this with the mouse, click on Bold Italic in the Font Style list box. If you are using the keyboard, press Alt + O, then press the down arrow key until Bold Italic is selected.
   e. Choose OK or press Enter.
4. Save the document again with the same name (c05ex05).
5. Print c05ex05.
6. Close c05ex05.

## Exercise 6

1. Open notice01. This document is located on your student data disk.
2. Save the document with Save As and name it c05ex06.
3. Underline the words *Friday, May 10, 1996* in the first paragraph with a dotted line by completing the following steps:
   a. Select *Friday, May 10, 1996*.
   b. Display the Font dialog box.
   c. Choose Underline, then Dotted. To do this with the mouse, click on the down-pointing arrow at the right side of the Underline text box, then click on Dotted. If you are using the keyboard, press Alt + U, then press the down arrow key until Dotted is selected.
   d. Choose OK or press Enter.
4. Select the words *6:00 p.m.* in the first paragraph, then underline with a Dotted line.
5. Select the words *9:30 p.m.* in the first paragraph, then underline with a Dotted line.
6. Select the words *20 new gadgets* in the second paragraph, then underline with a Dotted line.
7. Select the words *in advance* in the third paragraph, then underline with a Dotted line.
8. Select the words *exciting and fun-filled evening* in the last paragraph, then underline with a Dotted line.
9. Save the document again with the same name (c05ex06).
10. Print c05ex06.
11. Close c05ex06.

## Exercise 7

1. Open notice02. This document is located on your student data disk.
2. Save the document with Save As and name it c05ex07.
3. Select the entire document, then change the font to 12-point Times New Roman.
4. Change the text color to Magenta by completing the following steps:
   a. Select the entire document.
   b. Display the Font dialog box.
   c. Choose Color, then Magenta. To do this with the mouse, click on the down-pointing arrow at the right side of the Color text box, then click on Magenta. If you are using the keyboard, press Alt + C, then press the down arrow key until Magenta is selected.
   d. Choose OK or press Enter.
5. Save the document again with the same name (c05ex07).
6. Print c05ex07.
7. Close c05ex07.

## Exercise 8

1. Open legal01. This document is located on your student data disk.
2. Save the document with Save As and name it c05ex08.
3. Select the entire document, then change the font to 10-point Century Gothic.
4. Deselect the text.
5. If necessary, add Tabs to realign the right parentheses in the heading and lengthen the line below *Defendant* so it almost reaches the right parenthesis.
6. Select the last sentence in the second paragraph (the one that begins *A default judgment is one where the plaintiff...*), and identify it for strikethrough by completing the following steps:
   a. Select the sentence.
   b. Display the Font dialog box.
   c. Choose Strikethrough.
   d. Choose OK or press Enter.
7. Select the last paragraph (one sentence) that begins *This Summons is issued pursuant...*, then identify it for strikethrough.
8. Save the document again with the same name (c05ex08).
9. Print c05ex08.
10. Close c05ex08.

## Exercise 9

1. At a clear document screen, key the memorandum shown in figure 5.11 in an appropriate memorandum format with the following specifications:
   a. Change the font to 12-point Times New Roman.
   b. Indent and italicize text as indicated.
   c. Create the superscripted numbers in the memorandum by completing the following steps:
      (1) Key text to the point where superscripted text is to appear.
      (2) Display the Font dialog box.
      (3) At the Font dialog box, choose Superscript.
      (4) Choose OK or press Enter.
      (5) Key the superscripted text.
      (6) Repeat steps (2) through (4) to turn off superscript.
   d. Create the subscripted numbers in the memorandum by completing the following steps:
      (1) Key text to the point where subscripted text is to appear.
      (2) Press Ctrl + =.
      (3) Key the subscripted text.
      (4) Press Ctrl + =.
2. Save the memorandum and name it c05ex09.
3. Print c05ex09.
4. Close c05ex09.

Figure 5.11

DATE: April 3, 1996; TO: Nicole Kreitinger; FROM: Chris Walden; SUBJECT: STATISTICAL ANALYSIS

The research and analysis you are conducting on medical health care is very important to the project planning. As you complete your analysis, please address the following areas:

1.  What is the relationship between the indices $C$, $D$, and $I$ to both $r^1$ and $r^2$?

2.  What is the improvement when $r^1 = .55$ and $r^2$ is nearly .79?

3.  What is the main effect on the scores of $X_1$, $X_2$, and $X_3$?

When these areas have been addressed, please give me a copy of the analysis.

xx:c05ex09

## Exercise 10

1.  Open memo01. This document is located on your student data disk.
2.  Save the document with Save As and name it c05ex10.
3.  Create hidden text at the end of the document by completing the following steps:
    a.  Move the insertion point to the end of the document.
    b.  Key (**Check the availability of these books before sending the memo.**).
    c.  Select the sentence (**Check the availability of these books before sending the memo.**).
    d.  Display the Font dialog box.
    e.  At the Font dialog box, choose Hidden.
    f.  Choose OK or press Enter.
4.  Save the document again with the same name (c05ex10).
5.  Print the memo and the hidden text by completing the following steps:
    a.  Display the Print dialog box.
    b.  Choose Options.
    c.  At the Options dialog box, choose Hidden Text.
    d.  Choose OK or press Enter.
    e.  At the Print dialog box, choose OK or press Enter.
6.  After the memo is printed, remove the X from the Hidden Text option at the Options dialog box by completing the following steps:
    a.  Display the Print dialog box.
    b.  Choose Options.
    c.  At the Options dialog box, choose Hidden Text.
    d.  Choose OK or press Enter.
    e.  At the Print dialog box, choose Close.
7.  Close c05ex10.

## Exercise 11

1.  Open memo01. This document is located on your student data disk.
2.  Save the document with Save As and name it c05ex11.
3.  Select the entire document, then change the font to 12-point Century Gothic.
4.  With the document still selected, change the text in the document to Small Caps by completing the following steps:
    a.  Display the Font dialog box.
    b.  Choose Small Caps.

      c. Choose OK or press Enter.

   5. Align the text properly after DATE: at the beginning of the memorandum by pressing the Tab key between the heading and the text.

   6. Save the document again with the same name (c05ex11).

   7. Print c05ex11.

   8. Close c05ex11.

## Exercise 12

   1. At a clear document screen, key the memorandum shown in figure 5.12 in an appropriate memorandum format with the following specifications:

      a. Change the font to 12-point Times New Roman.

      b. Space only once after end-of-sentence punctuation.

      c. Center the unit and department names as indicated.

   2. After keying the memorandum, change the color of the centered unit and department names to Red.

   3. Save the document and name it c05ex12.

   4. Print c05ex12.

   5. Close c05ex12.

**Figure 5.12**

DATE: March 12, 1996; TO: Leah Aversen; FROM: Mariah Jackson;
SUBJECT: CONTINUING EDUCATION CLASSES

The nursing staff in the medical center departments are required to attend continuing education classes. In the past, the classes have been scheduled by the director of each department. The Training Coordination Committee has determined that it would be more efficient to have the classes scheduled by one department. After interviewing the directors of various departments, a decision was made to have the classes scheduled by the Training and Education Department.

The following areas of the hospital require continuing education classes for nurses:

Intensive Care Unit
Labor and Delivery Unit
Coronary Care Unit
Surgical Unit
Pediatric Unit
Medical Services
Emergency Room

Please contact the director of each unit or department to determine immediate and future educational requirements. If you need additional support staff to coordinate these classes, please contact me.

xx:c05ex12

## Exercise 13

1. Open biblio01. This document is located on your student data disk.
2. Save the document, with Save As and name it c05ex13.
3. Select the entire document then change the font to 12-point Times New Roman.
4. Select the book title, *The Art of Desktop Publishing*, then click on the Italics button on the Formatting toolbar.
5. Use the Format Painter to change the other book titles to italics by completing the following steps:
   a. Position the cursor on any character in the italicized book title, *The Art of Desktop Publishing*.
   b. Double-click on the Format Painter button on the Standard toolbar.
   c. Select the book title *Practical Desktop Publishing Designs*. (This applies the italics formatting.)
   d. Select the book title *A Resource Guide to Desktop Publishing*. (This applies the italics formatting.)
   e. Select the book title *Desktop Publishing Projects*. (This applies the italics formatting.)
   f. Click once on the Format Painter button on the Standard toolbar.
6. Save the document again with the same name (c05ex13).
7. Print c05ex13.
8. Close c05ex13.

## Exercise 14

1. Open report01. This document is located on your student data disk.
2. Save the document with Save As and name it c05ex14.
3. Select the entire document, then change the font to 12-point Times New Roman.
4. Select the title, *TYPE SPECIFICATION*, then change the font to 14-point Times New Roman Bold.
5. Use the Format Painter button to change the three headings in the report to 14-point Times New Roman Bold by completing the following steps:
   a. Position the insertion point on any character in the title, *TYPE SPECIFICATION*.
   b. Double-click on the Format Painter button on the Standard toolbar.
   c. Select the heading *Type Measurement*.
   d. Select the heading *Type Size*.
   e. Select the heading *Type Style*.
   f. Click once on the Format Painter button on the Standard toolbar.
6. Select the last four paragraphs (lines of text) in the report, then click on the Bullets button on the Formatting toolbar.
7. Save the document again with the same name (c05ex14).
8. Print c05ex14.
9. Close c05ex14.

## Exercise 15

1. At a clear document screen, key the memorandum shown in figure 5.13 in an appropriate memorandum format. Complete the following steps to create the ë, ô, °, and ■ special symbols:
   a. Choose Insert, then Symbol.
   b. At the Symbol dialog box, change the Font to MS Line Draw. To do this with the mouse, click on the down-pointing arrow at the right side of the Font text box, click on the down scroll arrow until MS Line Draw is displayed, then click on it. If you are using the keyboard, press Alt + F, press the down arrow key until MS Line Draw is selected, then press Enter.

c. Double-click on the desired symbol. (If you click once on a symbol it will display larger. Do this if you need to find the correct symbol.)

d. Choose Close.

2. Press Alt + Ctrl + R to create the registered trademark symbol (®).

3. Save the memorandum and name it c05ex15.

4. Print c05ex15.

5. Close c05ex15.

---

**Figure 5.13**

```
DATE:   April 9, 1996; TO:  Edward Raphaël; FROM:  Lindsay Carrick;
SUBJECT:   DISTRICT NEWSLETTER

The layout for the May newsletter looks great!   Jolene Pacôme said
that the image on the second page can be rotated either 90° or
270°.  What would you prefer?

Jolene plans to offer an informal workshop on some of the graphic
capabilities of Word for Windows®.   She plans to address the
following topics:

     ■     adding borders
     ■     inserting pictures
     ■     drawing shapes
     ■     creating graphs

If you want her to address any other topics, please give me a call
by the end of this week.

xx:c05ex15
```

## Exercise 16

1. Open c05ex14.

2. View formatting information by completing the following steps:

   a. Click once on the Help button on the Standard toolbar; or press Shift + F1.

   b. Position the arrow pointer (displays with a question mark) on the title, *TYPE SPECIFICATION*, then click the left mouse button.

   c. After viewing the formatting information for the title, click once on the Help button on the Standard toolbar.

3. View formatting information for the heading *Type Measurement* by completing steps similar to those in 2a through 2c.

4. View formatting information about the text in the first paragraph by completing steps similar to those in 2a through 2c.

5. Close c05ex14.

---

## SKILL ASSESSMENTS

## Assessment 1

1. Open report01. This document is located on your student data disk.

2. Save the document with Save As and name it c05sa01.

3. Make the following changes to the document:

a. Select the entire document, then change the font to 12-point Times New Roman.

b. Select the title, *TYPE SPECIFICATION*, then change the font to 18-point Arial Bold.

c. Select the heading *Type Measurement*, then change the font to 14-point Arial Bold.

d. Use Format Painter to change the formatting to 14-point Arial Bold for the headings *Type Size* and *Type Style*.

e. Select the last four paragraph (lines of text) in the document, then click on the Bullets button on the Formatting toolbar to add bullets before each selected paragraph.

4. Save the document again with the same name (c05sa01).

5. Print c05sa01.

6. Close c05sa01.

## Assessment 2

1. Open legal02. This document is located on your student data disk.

2. Save the document with Save As and name it c05sa02.

3. Make the following changes to the document:

a. Select the entire document, then change the font to 12-point Times New Roman.

b. Adjust the right parentheses and the line below *Defendant*.

c. Select the title, *IN DISTRICT COURT NO. 4, COOK COUNTY, STATE OF ILLINOIS*, then change the font to 14-point Times New Roman Bold.

d. Select the words *the Sixty-Day Rule* toward the end of the first paragraph and identify them as strikethrough text.

e. Select the punctuation and words *, if any, and a copy of the alcohol influence report form* at the end of the second numbered paragraph and identify them as strikethrough text.

f. Select the words *upon the satisfactory examination of the inspection data heretofore requested* at the end of the fourth numbered paragraph and identify them as strikethrough text.

4. Save the document again with the same name (c05sa02).

5. Print c05sa02.

6. Close c05sa02.

## Assessment 3

1. At a clear document screen, create the document shown in figure 5.14 with the following specifications:

a. Center the text as indicated.

b. Indent the paragraph below *General Description* and indent the paragraph below *Distinguishing Features*.

c. Insert the first diamond symbol by completing the following steps:

(1) Choose Insert, then Symbol.

(2) At the Symbol dialog box, change the font to Symbol.

(3) Double-click on the diamond symbol (in the fifth row from the top and fourth from the right side).

(4) Choose Close.

d. Repeat steps (1) through (4) above to insert the other diamond symbols.

2. Select the entire document, then change the font to 12-point Arial.

3. Select the title *TECHNICAL SUPPORT PARTNER,* then change the font to 14-point Arial Bold.

4. Use Format Painter to change the font to 14-point Arial Bold for the headings *General Description*, *Distinguishing Features*, *Principal Accountabilities*, and *Minimum Qualifications*.

5. Save the document and name it c05sa03.

6. Print c05sa03.

7. Close c05sa03.

Figure 5.14

# TECHNICAL SUPPORT PARTNER

## General Description

The Technical Support Partner is a team member working under the direction of a Registered Nurse to provide quality care that is focused on the comfort and well-being of the patient and family.

## Distinguishing Features

This position requires a service oriented-individual with strong interpersonal skills for the purpose of delivering care and services to patients from diverse ethnic and social groups. Independent decision making is expected in the execution of daily routine duties.

## Principal Accountabilities

- Performs direct patient care activities

- Maintains a clean and comfortable environment in assigned patient rooms

- Obtains blood specimens using approved procedures for venipuncture and capillary collection

- Performs simple respiratory therapy functions

- Assists the Clinical Partner in providing patient care as needed

- Assembles and disassembles specialty equipment

## Minimum Qualifications

- High school graduate or equivalent

- Previous work experience in a health care environment as an Aide, Housekeeper, or Transporter preferred

- Previous experience in phlebotomy preferred and/or willingness to train

- Basic knowledge and ability to perform specified tasks

- Knowledge of medical terminology

## Assessment 4

1. At a clear document screen, key the memorandum shown in figure 5.15 in an appropriate memorandum format with the following specifications:
   a. Space once after end-of-sentence punctuation.
   b. Indent, italicize, superscript, and subscript text as indicated.
   c. After keying the document, select the entire document, then change the font to 12-point Times New Roman.

2. Save the memorandum and name it c05sa04.
3. Print c05sa04.
4. Close c05sa04.

*Figure 5.15*

DATE: April 10, 1996; TO: Chris Walden; FROM: Nicole Krietinger; SUBJECT: STATISTICAL ANALYSIS

I have been running an analysis on the areas mentioned in your April 3 memo. Completing the computations has brought up the following questions:

1. With smaller section ratios of $r^1$ and $r^2$ (.10 to .25)[1], what will be the yield increase?

2. What is the interaction effect on the scores of $X_1$, $X_2$, and $X_3$?

I will try to report on the findings to these questions by the end of next week.

xx:c05sa04

## Assessment 5

1. At a clear document screen, key the memorandum shown in figure 5.16 in an appropriate memorandum format with the following specifications:
   a. Space once after end-of-sentence punctuation.
   b. Use the Symbol dialog box to insert the right-pointing arrow before the paragraphs as indicated. (The right-pointing arrow can be found in the Symbol font.)
   c. After keying the document, select the entire document, then change the font to 12-point Times New Roman.
2. Save the memorandum and name it c05sa05.
3. Print c05sa05.
4. Close c05sa05.

*Figure 5.16*

DATE: April 10, 1996; TO: Edward Raphaël; FROM: Leslie Greerson; SUBJECT: POSITION DESCRIPTION

At the end of last week, I sent you a position description to be included in the May newsletter. Since that time, the department manager has decided to add the following responsibilities to the list:

→ Skill in interpersonal relationships with emphasis on reaching out and being friendly.

→ Ability to be sensitive and show positive regard for fellow employees, patients, and families.

→ Ability to set priorities and use good judgment.

→ Ability to willingly accept responsibilities.

I hope these additional responsibilities can be included in the May newsletter. Please contact me to let me know if you receive this memorandum before the newsletter deadline.

xx:c05sa05

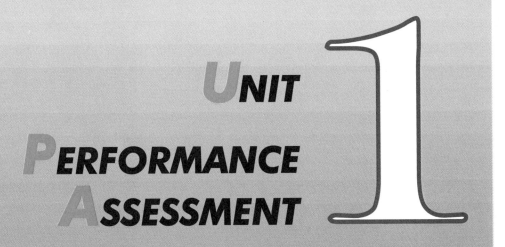

# UNIT 1
## PERFORMANCE ASSESSMENT

In this unit, you have learned to adjust characters and lines in the creation of simple office documents, such as memoranda and letters.

*Note: By now, you have saved a considerable number of documents on your student data disk. The amount of space available for saving documents is limited. In order to conserve space on your disk you may want to delete all documents created in unit 1. This includes documents from chapters 1-5, as well as unit 1 Performance Assessment documents. Check with your instructor before deleting documents. For the steps for deleting documents, either check with your instructor or refer to the "Deleting Documents" section in chapter 15.*

### Assessment 1

1. At a clear document screen, key the text shown in figure U1.1 in an appropriate memorandum format. Indent the second paragraph as indicated.
2. Change the alignment of the paragraphs in the body of the memorandum to justified.
3. Save the document and name it u01pa01.
4. Print u01pa01.
5. Close u01pa01.

**Figure U1.1**

DATE:       April 23, 1996
TO:          All Employees
FROM:      Leslie Greerson
SUBJECT:  DISTINGUISHED EMPLOYEE AWARD

The tenth annual Distinguished Employee Award will be presented to an employee of the Center on Wednesday, June 5, 1996. The Center has a large number of talented employees who are worthy of special recognition. Allison St. Germaine, president of St. Francis Medical Center, stated at a recent meeting:

> The success of St. Francis Medical Center is due in large part to the hard work and dedication of all employees. The Distinguished Employee Award provides the opportunity to call attention to the special talents and efforts of an exemplary employee of the Center.

Please nominate an employee on the attached nomination form. Be sure to include the reasons why you feel your nominee should be the recipient of the Distinguished Employee Award.

xx:u01pa01
Attachment

## Assessment 2

1. At a clear document screen, key the document shown in figure U1.2. Center, indent, and underline the text as indicated. Use the Numbering button on the Formatting toolbar to number the paragraphs as indicated. (Indent the text after the numbers to the first tab stop with Ctrl + T.)
2. After keying the document, complete the following steps:
   a. Select the entire document, then change the font to 12-point Arial.
   b. Select the title, *DISTINGUISHED EMPLOYEE AWARD*, then change the font to 18-point Arial Bold.
   c. Select the subtitle, *NOMINEE FORM*, then change the font to 14-point Arial Bold.
3. Save the document and name it u01pa02.
4. Print u01pa02.
5. Close u01pa02.

---

**Figure U1.2**

DISTINGUISHED EMPLOYEE AWARD

NOMINEE FORM

The person you nominate for the Distinguished Employee Award should meet the following criteria:

1. The nominee should be an employee who has consistently displayed excellence in performing required duties.

2. The nominee should have made significant contributions to the Center in the areas of quality patient care, teamwork, and productivity.

3. The nominee should be an employee in good standing who has worked for the Center for at least two years.

The Distinguished Employee Award committee will base its selection on nomination forms and interviews.

If you wish to nominate someone for this award, please complete the Distinguished Employee Award nomination form at the bottom of this sheet.  Please include several comments in support of your nominee. Each nominee will be asked to provide information about themselves to allow the committee to adequately judge the nominations.  The deadline for submitting the nomination form is May 15, 1996.  Please return the form to Leslie Greerson in the Human Resources Department.

Name of Nominee:

Title of Nominee:

Department:

I nominate this person for the following reasons:

## Assessment 3

1. At a clear document screen, key the text shown in figure U1.3 in an appropriate business letter format. Center and bold text as indicated. Space once after end-of-sentence punctuation.
2. After keying the document, select the entire document, then change the font to 12-point Times New Roman.
3. Save the document and name it u01pa03.
4. Print u01pa03.
5. Close u01pa03.

**Figure U1.3**

April 18, 1996

Mr. William Renner
2102 Mountain View Drive
Enumclaw, WA 98002

Dear Mr. Renner:

As another tax season ends, we want to thank you for making 1995 the best year yet for *Tax Advantage*. With the almost constant changes in tax laws, however, there are sure to be many additional challenges and opportunities in the coming year. So we've taken your suggestions, added some ideas and innovations of our own, and already started working to make 1996's *Tax Advantage* even better.

**Mr. Renner, here's your chance to get a jump on next year's taxes. Become a priority Tax Advantage customer now!**

As a priority *Tax Advantage* customer, you will get the final version of *Tax Advantage* (for Windows), "first to ship" priority status when we begin shipping the 750,000 orders we expect to fulfill next January, and shipment via U.S. Priority Mail.

**Next year's Tax Advantage will prepare your return the same dependable way you have come to rely on!**

Because these are truly remarkable savings, this nontransferable offer is for *Tax Advantage* customers only. We must receive the enclosed order form by June 30, 1996!  Order today so you don't have to worry about placing your order during next year's busy tax season.

Sincerely,

Carol Wyman
President

xx:u01pa03

## Assessment 4

1. At a clear document screen, key the text shown in figure U1.4 with the following specifications:
   a. Change the font to 24-point Brush Script.
   b. Change the line spacing to 1.5.
2. Save the document and name it u01pa04.
3. Print u01pa04.
4. Close u01pa04.

Figure U1.4

*Distinguished Employee Award*

*Wednesday, June 5, 1996*

*Rochelle Theater*

*1320 Rialto Drive, Kansas City*

*6:30 p.m. to 10:00 p.m.*

## Assessment 5

1. At a clear document screen, create the document shown in figure U1.5 with the following specifications:
   a. Change the line spacing to double.
   b. Center text as indicated.
   c. Insert bullets using the Bullets button on the Formatting toolbar.
   d. After keying the document, select the document, then change the font to 12-point Century Gothic.
   e. Select the title, *ST. FRANCIS MEDICAL CENTER*, then change the font to 18-point Century Gothic Bold.
   f. Use Format Painter to apply the 18-point Century Gothic Bold font to the subtitle, *INSTRUCTIONS TO PERSONNEL*.
   g. Select the heading *On-Duty* then change the font to 14-point Century Gothic Bold.
   h. Use Format Painter to apply the 14-point Century Gothic Bold font to the other headings: *Off-Duty* and *If Called to Duty*.
2. Save the document and name it u01pa05.
3. Print u01pa05.
4. Select the bulleted paragraphs and change to numbers (use the Numbering button on the Formatting toolbar.)
5. Save the document again with the same name (u01pa05).
6. Print u01pa05.
7. Close u01pa05.

```
                    ST. FRANCIS MEDICAL CENTER

                    INSTRUCTIONS TO PERSONNEL

On-Duty

  •  Remain at your post-of-duty until reassigned or requested to

     report elsewhere.

  •  Keep ALL switchboard lines open for emergency use.

  •  Accept transfer of station or change of duties without

     question.

  •  Remain on duty until relieved.

Off-Duty

  •  Keep your phone free. Do NOT call the hospital.

  •  If you are not called, REPORT on duty at your REGULAR scheduled

     time or as determined by your unit-specific plan.

If Called to Duty

  •  Carry and present name tag, I.D. card, or other form of

     identification for admission to that area.

  •  Park in employee parking lot.

  •  Enter hospital through any hospital entrance other than

     Emergency Department entrance.

  •  Report to preassigned unit as SOON as possible.  If not needed

     there, or if without preassigned service area, report to

     manpower pool in Emergency Department waiting room.
```

## COMPOSING ACTIVITIES

The following activities give you the opportunity to practice your writing skills along with demonstrating an understanding of some of the important Word features you have mastered in this unit. In planning the documents, remember to shape the information according to the writing purpose and the audience. Use correct grammar, appropriate word choices, and clear sentence constructions.

## Activity 1

**Situation:** You are Leslie Greerson, director of the Human Resources Department of St. Francis Medical Center. Compose a memo to Scott Sideres, administrative assistant in the Training and Education Department, that includes the following information:

- He has been nominated for the Distinguished Employee Award.
- You would like to schedule an interview with him in your office on either of the following dates and times: Wednesday, May 22, 1996, at 2:00 p.m. or Thursday, May 23, 1996, at 10:30 a.m.

Save the memorandum and name it u01act01. Print and then close u01act01.

## Activity 2

**Situation:** You are Angela Leon of Management Consultants, Inc. Compose a letter to Brenda Hogue, director of the Training and Education Department at St. Francis Medical Center, that includes the following information:

- Confirmation of a two-day employee training on team building to be held on Monday, April 25, 1996, from 8:30 a.m. to 4:30 p.m. and Tuesday, April 26, 1996, from 8:30 a.m. to 3:30 p.m.
- The training topics, which include:
  Communication Skills
  Group Development
  Team Building
  Conflict Resolution

Save the letter and name it u01act02. Print and then close u01act02.

## RESEARCH ACTIVITY

*Note: For the research activity for this unit and future units, you will need access to the Word for Windows User's Guide. Check with your instructor to determine if this guide is available.*

## Activity 1

Answer the following questions about information in the Word for Windows User's Guide.

1. What chapter covers typing and revising? _____
2. What is the first part of each chapter called that gives a brief overview of all sections in the User's Guide? _____
3. On what page(s) do you find information on starting a new paragraph? _____
4. In chapter 1, you learned that pressing the Enter key begins a new line. What command, mentioned in the User's Guide, will also begin a new line? _____
5. On what page(s) do you find information on moving the insertion point and scrolling? _____
6. In the section on moving the insertion point and scrolling, a command is mentioned that, when pressed, returns the insertion point to a previous editing location. What is this command? _____
7. What chapter in the User's Guide covers formatting text characters? _____
8. On what page are the shortcut commands listed for applying character formatting? _____
9. On what page(s) do you find information about points vs. pitch? _____

# Basic Page Formatting

UNIT

2

*In this unit, you will learn to create and proof full-page and multi-page business documents, such as business letters and reports.*

# Using Writing Tools 6

Upon successful completion of chapter 6, you will be able to check the spelling of words in documents, improve the writing in documents by finding appropriate synonyms, and improve the grammar and style of written business documents.

Word for Windows includes writing tools to help create a thoughtful and well-written document. One of these writing tools, a spelling checker, finds misspelled words and offers replacement words. It also finds duplicate words and irregular capitalizations. Another tool, the thesaurus, provides a list of synonyms for a particular word. A grammar checker finds grammar and style errors in documents and provides possible corrections.

## ■ Spell Checking a Document

When you use the spelling checker program in a document, the spelling checker matches the words in your document with the words in its dictionary (or a user's dictionary or your own custom dictionary). If a match is found, the word is passed over. If there is no match for the word, the spelling checker will stop and select the word for correction if it fits one of the following situations:

- a misspelled word if the misspelling does not match another word that exists in the dictionary
- typographical errors such as transposed letters
- double word occurrences (such as *and and*)
- irregular capitalization
- some proper names
- jargon and some technical terms

A small number of words in the spelling checker dictionary are proper names. You will find that many proper names will not appear in this dictionary. The spelling checker will not find a match for these proper names and will select the names for correction. The spelling checker may not, however, stop at all proper names. For example, the spelling checker would assume the first name *June* is spelled correctly and pass over it because June would appear in its dictionary as a month.

The spelling checker will not identify words that are spelled correctly but used incorrectly. For example, if you want the word *from* in a document but you key it as *form*, it will be passed over. The spelling checker matches *form* with a word in its dictionary and assumes it is spelled correctly.

Figure 6.1
Spelling: English
(US) Dialog Box

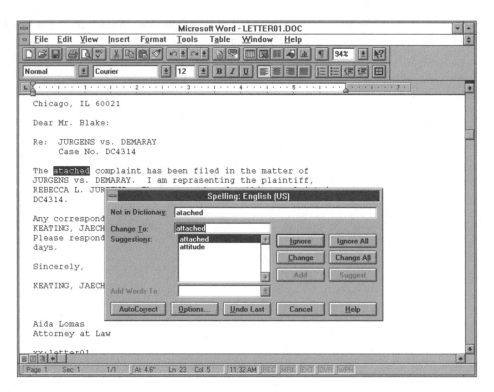

The spelling checker cannot check grammar usage. For example, if the wrong verb tense is used in a document but the verb is spelled correctly, it is passed over.

The spelling checker does not eliminate the need for proofreading, but it does provide assistance in editing a document.

## Checking the Spelling of a Document

Before using the spelling checker, save the document currently displayed in the document screen or open a document. You would complete the following steps to check a document for spelling:

1. Choose Tools, Spelling; press F7; or click on the Spelling button on the Standard toolbar (the sixth button from the left).
2. The spelling checker checks the document for a word that does not match words in its dictionary, selects the word, then displays the Spelling: English (US) dialog box shown in figure 6.1.
3. With the word selected, replace it with the correct spelling, or tell Word to ignore it and move to the next word.
4. When the spelling check is completed, Word inserts an information box with the message *The spelling check is complete.* At this information box, choose OK or press Enter.

## Using Command Buttons

When completing a spelling check, you need to determine if the word should be corrected or if it should be ignored. Word provides command buttons at the right side and the bottom of the Spelling: English (US) dialog box to make decisions.

**Ignore and Ignore All:** In some situations, the spelling checker will select a word for correction that you want to leave alone. This may happen with words such as proper names or abbreviations. To leave the word as written, choose the Ignore command button or the Ignore All command button.

If you choose Ignore, the spelling checker will skip that occurrence of the word but will select occurrences in other locations in the document.

If the word appears in other locations in the document and you want it skipped in those locations also, choose Ignore All. This tells the spelling checker to skip all occurrences of that particular word.

**Change and Change All:** When the spelling checker encounters a word that is not in its dictionary, suggestions for correct spelling are inserted in the Suggestions list box and the most likely choice (as determined by the spelling checker) is inserted in the Change To text box. To replace the selected word in the document with the word in the Change To text box, choose Change.

If you want to replace the selected word in the document with one of the words displayed in the Suggestions list box, double-click on the desired replacement word in the list box. If you are using the keyboard, press Alt + N, press the down arrow key until the desired replacement word is selected, then press Alt + C.

If you want to correct the same word in other locations in the document, choose the Change All command button rather than the Change command button.

**Add:** Besides the spelling checker dictionary, a custom dictionary is available in which you can add words. For example, you may want to add your name, a company name, or any other word that you use in documents that is not currently found in the main spelling checker dictionary. The name of the custom dictionary, CUSTOM.DIC, is displayed in the Add Words To text box. To add a selected word to the custom dictionary, choose the Add command button.

**Suggest:** By default, the spelling checker displays suggestions for correcting the word and the Suggest command button is dimmed. If you change spelling options so that no suggestions display by default, choose the Suggest command button if you want to see possible replacements. Later in this chapter you will learn how to change spelling checker options.

**AutoCorrect:** In chapter 1, you learned that Word for Windows includes an AutoCorrect feature that automatically changes certain words in a document. For example, if you key *teh* AutoCorrect changes this to *the*. You can add misspelled words with the correct spelling in the AutoCorrect. To do this during a spelling check, you would complete the following steps:

1. When the spelling checker selects the misspelled word, make sure the proper spelling is inserted in the Change To text box. If not, choose Change To, then key the correct spelling.
2. Choose AutoCorrect.

The misspelling of the word and the correct spelling of the word are inserted in the AutoCorrect dialog box. The next time you key the incorrect word in a document, then press the space bar, AutoCorrect will automatically correct it with the proper spelling.

**Options:** If you choose the Options command button from the Spelling: English (US) dialog box, the Options dialog box with the Spelling tab selected as shown in figure 6.2 displays in the document screen.

*Figure 6.2*
*Options Dialog Box*
*with Spelling Tab*
*Selected*

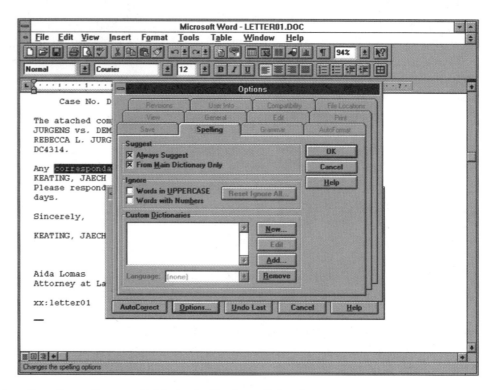

Figure 6.3 describes the options available in the Options dialog box.

*Figure 6.3*
*Options Dialog Box*
*Options*

| Choose this option | and Word will... |
|---|---|
| A**l**ways Suggest | always suggest corrections. Make this option inactive if you do not want suggestions (spelling checker will work faster). |
| From **M**ain Dictionary Only | provide suggestions only from the main dictionary, not from any custom dictionaries. |
| Words in UPPERCASE | ignore words in all uppercase letters. |
| Words with Num**b**ers | ignore words that include numbers. |
| Reset Ignore All | remove all words that have been added during the current session to the Ignore All list. (The next time you complete a spelling check, Word will not ignore these words.) |

At the Options dialog box, you can also create or edit a custom dictionary. Custom dictionaries can be created for specialized terms or a specific profession. Using and creating custom dictionaries is explained in the next section of this chapter.

You can also display the Options dialog box by choosing Tools, then Options. At the Options dialog box, make sure the Spelling tab is selected.

**Undo Last:** The Undo Last command button from the Spelling: English (US) dialog box will undo the last spelling replacement made. This option is dimmed until a replacement is made. When you choose Undo Last, Word goes back to the last spelling correction made, returns the word to its original spelling, and leaves the word selected. You can then either ignore the word or change to a different spelling.

**Cancel:** Use the Cancel command button to stop the spelling checker and remove the Spelling: English (US) dialog box from the screen.

**Help:** You can use Word's Help feature by choosing the Help command button from the Spelling: English (US) dialog box.

## Editing While Spell Checking

When spell checking a document, you can temporarily leave the Spelling: English (US) dialog box, make corrections in the document, then resume spell checking. For example, suppose while spell checking you notice a sentence that you want to change. You would complete the following steps to correct the sentence:

1. With the Spelling: English (US) dialog box displayed, move the arrow pointer to the location in the sentence where the change is to occur, then click the left mouse button.
2. Click the left mouse button again to deselect the word.
3. Make changes to the sentence.
4. Move the arrow pointer to the Start command button (previously the Ignore command button), then click the left mouse button. This resumes the spelling check.

To edit while spell checking using the keyboard, you would complete the following steps:

1. With the Spelling: English (US) dialog box displayed, press Ctrl + tab. (This makes the document screen active rather than the dialog box.)
2. Make changes to the sentence as needed.
3. Press Ctrl + tab to make the Spelling: English (US) dialog box active.
4. Press Alt + S to begin spell check.

## Using and Creating Custom Dictionaries

When Word for Windows is installed, a custom dictionary named CUSTOM.DIC is provided along with the main dictionary. If you use words or terms that do not appear in the main dictionary, you can add them to the custom dictionary during a spelling check. Word uses the custom dictionary when completing a spelling check. If words in your document match words in either the main or custom dictionary, the words are passed over during a spelling check.

## Creating a Custom Dictionary

You can create your own custom dictionary. For example, you may want to create a custom dictionary for legal terms or medical terms. As an example of how to create a custom dictionary, you would complete the following steps to create a custom dictionary named COMPANY.DIC:

1. Choose Tools, Options.
2. At the Options dialog box, select the Spelling tab.
3. Choose New.
4. At the Create Custom Dictionary dialog box, key **COMPANY.DIC**.
5. Choose OK or press Enter.
6. At the Options dialog box, choose OK.

## Adding Words to a Custom Dictionary

During a spelling check, you can add words to a custom dictionary other than the default. For example, to add the word *Mariah* to the custom dictionary named COMPANY.DIC during a spelling check, you would complete the following steps:

1. Open a document containing the word *Mariah*.
2. Choose Tools, Spelling; press F7; or click on the Spelling button on the Standard toolbar.
3. When the spelling checker selects *Mariah*, change the custom dictionary to COMPANY.DIC and add *Mariah* to the dictionary by completing the following steps:
   a. Choose Add Words To, then COMPANY.DIC. To do this with the mouse, click on the down-pointing arrow to the right of the Add Words To text box, then click on COMPANY.DIC. If you are using the keyboard, press Alt + W, then press the down arrow key until COMPANY.DIC is selected.
   b. Choose Add.
4. Complete spell checking the remaining words in the document.
5. When checking is completed, choose OK or press Enter.

## Editing a Custom Dictionary

A custom dictionary can be edited. For example, you may want to remove words from the custom dictionary. As an example of how to edit a custom dictionary, you would complete the following steps to delete the word *Mariah* from the COMPANY.DIC custom dictionary:

1. Choose Tools, Options.
2. At the Options dialog box, select COMPANY.DIC in the Custom Dictionaries list box. To do this with the mouse, click on COMPANY.DIC. If you are using the keyboard, press Alt + D, then press the down arrow key until COMPANY.DIC is selected.
3. Choose Edit.
4. Word displays the message *This operation will allow you to edit the custom dictionary as a Word document. Do you want to continue?* At this message, choose Yes.
5. Choose Cancel to remove the Options dialog box from the document screen. (The COMPANY.DIC document displays in the document screen.)
6. Delete *Mariah* from the COMPANY.DIC document.
7. Choose File, Save.
8. Choose File, Close.

## Removing a Custom Dictionary

You can remove a custom dictionary at the Options dialog box. For example, to remove the custom dictionary named COMPANY.DIC, you would complete the following steps:

1. Choose Tools, Options.
2. At the Options dialog box, select the Spelling tab.
3. Click on the check box before COMPANY.DIC to remove the X.
4. With COMPANY.DIC selected, choose Remove.
5. Choose OK.

## ■ Customizing AutoCorrect

Earlier in this chapter, you learned how to add a selected word to AutoCorrect during a spelling check. You can add, delete, or change words at the AutoCorrect dialog box. To display the AutoCorrect dialog box shown in figure 6.4 choose Tools, then AutoCorrect.

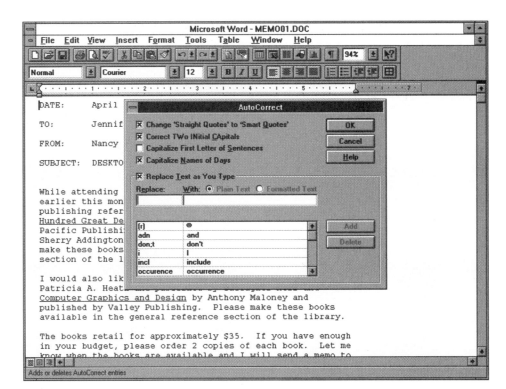

**Figure 6.4**
*AutoCorrect Dialog Box*

Several options display at the beginning of the AutoCorrect dialog box. If a check appears in the check box before the option, the option is active. Figure 6.5 describes what will occur if the option is active.

**Figure 6.5**
*AutoCorrect Options*

| If this option is active | Word will... |
|---|---|
| Change 'Straight Quotes' to 'Smart Quotes' | change straight quotes to "curly" quotes. |
| Correct TWo INitial CApitals | change the second capital to a lowercase letter. |
| Capitalize First Letter of Sentences | capitalize the first letter of a word beginning a sentence. |
| Capitalize Names of Days | capitalize the first letter of days of the week. |
| Replace Text as You Type | replace misspelled word with correct spelling as displayed in the list box at the bottom of the AutoCorrect dialog box. |

## Adding a Word to AutoCorrect

Commonly misspelled words or typographical errors can be added to AutoCorrect. For example, if you consistently key *oopen* instead of *open*, you can add *oopen* to AutoCorrect and tell it to correct it as *open*. To do this, you would complete the following steps:

1. Choose Tools, AutoCorrect.
2. At the AutoCorrect dialog box, choose Replace.
3. Key **oopen.**
4. Choose With.
5. Key **open.**
6. Choose Add.
7. Choose OK or press Enter.

The next time you type *oopen,* then press the space bar, AutoCorrect corrects it as *open.*

## Deleting a Word from AutoCorrect

A word that is contained in AutoCorrect can be deleted. For example, to delete the word *oopen* and its correction, *open*, you would complete the following steps:

1. Choose Tools, AutoCorrect.
2. At the AutoCorrect dialog box, click on the *oopen* option in the list box. (If *oopen* is not visible, click on the down-pointing arrow in the list box scroll bar until it is visible.)
3. Choose Delete.
4. Choose OK or press Enter.

Go To
Exercise
5

## ■ *Using the Thesaurus*

Word offers a thesaurus program that can be used to find synonyms for words. Synonyms are words that have the same or nearly the same meaning. When using the thesaurus, Word may display antonyms for some words. Antonyms are words with opposite meanings. With the thesaurus, you can improve the clarity of business documents.

As an example of how to use the thesaurus, you would complete the following steps to look up synonyms for the word *subtle* and replace it with the word *faint:*

1. Open the document containing the word *subtle* or key the word *subtle.*
2. Position the insertion point next to any character in the word *subtle.*
3. Choose Tools, Thesaurus; or press Shift + F7.
4. At the Thesaurus: English (US) dialog box shown in figure 6.6, select *faint* in the Meanings list box. To do this with the mouse, click on *faint.* If you are using the keyboard, press the down arrow key until *faint* is selected.
5. Choose Replace.

At the Thesaurus: English (US) dialog box, a list of words displays in the Meanings list box. Depending on the word you are looking up, the words in the Meanings list box may display followed by *(noun)* or *(adj).* You might also see the words *Antonym* and *Related Words.* The first word in the Meanings list box is selected by default and synonyms for that word are displayed in the Replace with Synonym list box.

*Figure 6.6*
*Thesaurus: English*
*(US) Dialog Box*

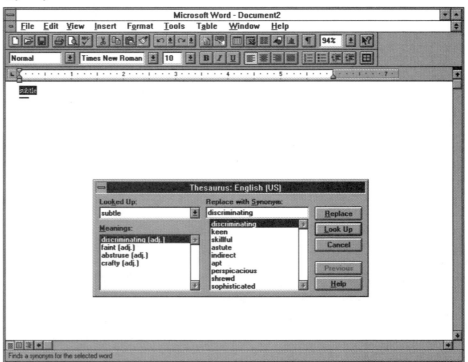

You can view synonyms in the Replace with <u>S</u>ynonyms list box for the words shown in the <u>M</u>eanings list box by clicking on the desired word or pressing the down arrow key until the desired word is selected.

## Using Command Buttons

Use the command buttons at the right side of the Thesaurus: English (US) dialog box to replace a word, look up a different word, or display the previous word.

**<u>R</u>eplace:** Use the <u>R</u>eplace command button to replace the word in the document with the word displayed in the Replace with <u>S</u>ynonym text box.

**<u>L</u>ook Up:** You can look up synonyms for words displayed in either the <u>M</u>eanings list box or the Replace with <u>S</u>ynonyms list box. To do this, select the word for which you want to look up synonyms, then choose <u>L</u>ook Up. If you are using the mouse, you can also double-click on the word for which you want synonyms displayed.

**Cancel:** Choose the Cancel command button to remove the Thesaurus: English (US) dialog box from the document screen without making a change.

**<u>P</u>revious:** Choose the <u>P</u>revious command button to display the previous word you looked up.

**<u>H</u>elp:** Use the <u>H</u>elp command button to access Word's Help feature.

# ◼ *Displaying Word Count*

With the <u>W</u>ord Count option from the <u>T</u>ools menu, the number of pages, words, characters, paragraphs, and lines in a document can be displayed. As an example of how to use the <u>W</u>ord Count option, you would complete the following steps to display a word count for the document named *report01*:

1. Open report01.
2. Choose <u>T</u>ools, <u>W</u>ord Count.
3. At the Word Count dialog box shown in figure 6.7, read the information, then choose Close.

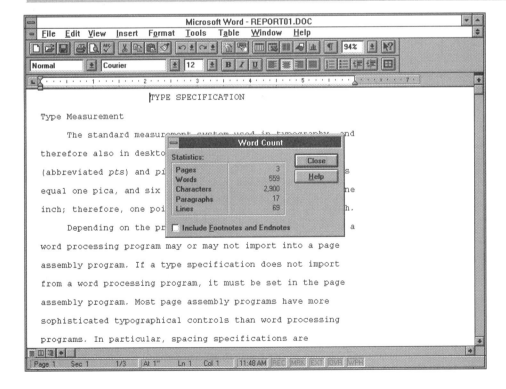

*Figure 6.7*
*Word Count Dialog Box*

# ■ Checking the Grammar and Style of a Document

Word for Windows includes a grammar checking feature that you can use to search a document for correct grammar, style, punctuation, and word usage. Like the spelling checker, the grammar checker does not find every error in a document and may stop at correct phrases. The grammar checker can help you create a well-written document but does not replace the need for proofreading.

To complete a grammar check on a document, you would complete the following steps:

1. Open the document to be checked.
2. Choose Tools, then Grammar.
3. The grammar checker selects the first sentence with an error and displays the sentence in the Sentence section of the Grammar: English (US) dialog box.
4. Choose to ignore or change errors found by the grammar checker.
5. When the grammar checking is completed, Word displays the Readability Statistics dialog box with information about the current document. At this dialog box, choose OK or press Enter.

When the grammar checker is done, the open document is displayed on the screen. The changes made during the check are inserted in the document. You can save the document with the same name, overwriting the original; or you can save the document with a different name, retaining the original.

By default, a spelling check is completed on a document during a grammar check. If a word is found in the document that does not match a word in the spelling dictionary, the word is selected and the Spelling: English (US) dialog box is displayed. Make selections at this dialog box as described earlier in this chapter in the section titled *Spell Checking a Document*.

When you choose Tools, then Grammar, the Grammar: English (US) dialog box shown in figure 6.8 displays in the document screen.

In figure 6.8, the grammar checker selects the sentence *Please send your reference book requests to Tom or I.* and offers the suggestion *Consider me instead of I.*

**Figure 6.8**
*Grammar: English (US) Dialog Box*

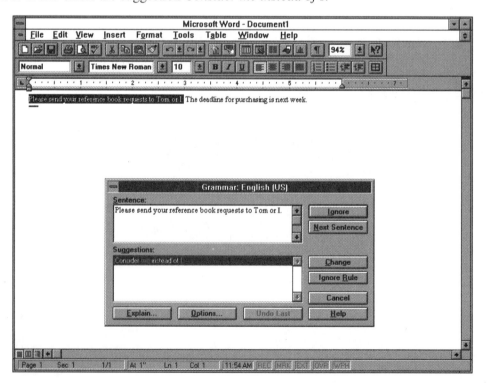

## Making Changes

When an error is detected during a grammar check, replacement word(s) may be listed in the Suggestions box. If you agree with the suggested change, choose the Change command button.

If the grammar checker does not offer a replacement word or words, you can temporarily leave the grammar checker and edit the text. To do this, you would complete the following steps:

1. Position the I-beam pointer in the document screen (outside the Grammar: English (US) dialog box), then click the left mouse button. If you are using the keyboard, press Ctrl + Tab.
2. Edit the text in the document.
3. To resume grammar checking with the mouse, click on the Start button. If you are using the keyboard, press Ctrl + Tab, then press Alt + S.

When you choose the Start command button, the grammar checking is resumed at the location of the insertion point after you edited the document.

## Ignoring Text

At times, the grammar checker will select text that you want left as written. Choose the Ignore command button to tell the grammar checker to ignore the selected text and move to the next error.

The grammar checker checks a document for a variety of grammar and style errors. In some situations, you may want the grammar checker to ignore a particular grammar or style rule. To do this, choose the Ignore Rule command button the first time the grammar checker displays text breaking the particular grammar or style rule you want ignored.

If the grammar checker selects a sentence in a document containing a grammar or style error and you want that sentence left as written, choose the Next Sentence command button. This tells the grammar checker to leave the current sentence unchanged and move to the next sentence.

## Explaining Grammar and Style Rules

When an error is detected you can display information about the specific error by choosing the Explain command button. When you choose Explain, a window displays describing the grammar or style rule. After reading the information in the window, press the Esc key to close the window and return to the Grammar: English (US) dialog box. You can also close the window by clicking on the document control box in the upper left corner of the window (the box containing the hyphen), then clicking on Close.

Figure 6.9 displays the Grammar: English (US) dialog box with a window displayed containing information on passive voice.

Figure 6.9
Passive Voice
Explanation

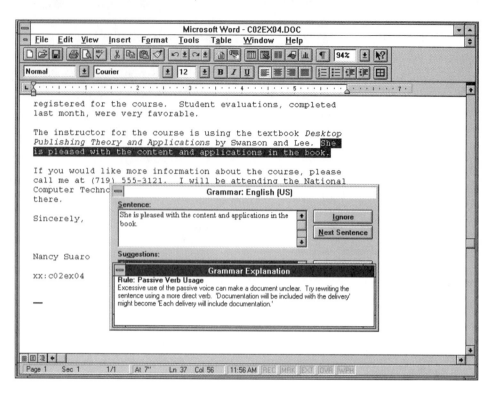

## Changing Options

The grammar checker uses rules of style and grammar when checking a document. The number of rules used is determined by options set at the Options dialog box. To display the Options dialog box shown in figure 6.10, choose the Options command button from the Grammar: English (US) dialog box. You can also display the Options dialog box by choosing Tools, Options, then selecting the Grammar tab.

Figure 6.10
Options Dialog Box
with Grammar Tab
Selected

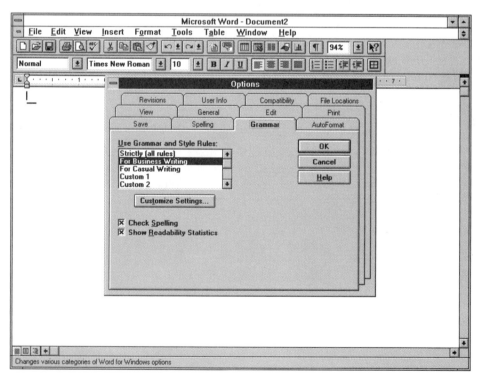

At the Options dialog box, with the Grammar tab selected, the Use Grammar and Style Rules option is set at For Business Writing. This can be changed to Strictly (all rules), For Casual Writing, Custom 1, Custom 2, or Custom 3. Figure 6.11 describes the options.

| This Option | Applies This |
|---|---|
| Strictly (all rules) | All grammar and style rules. |
| For Business Writing | Fewer rules—those appropriate for written business communications. |
| For Casual Writing | The least number of rules—those appropriate for informal written communications. |
| Custom 1, 2, or 3 | Rules applied by you. |

*Figure 6.11*
*Grammar Check*
*Rules Options*

As an example of how to change rule options, you would complete the following steps to change rule options to Strictly (all rules):

1. Choose Tools, Options.
2. At the Options dialog box, click on the Grammar tab to select it.
3. Select Strictly (all rules). To do this with the mouse, click on Strictly (all rules). If you are using the keyboard, press the up arrow key until Strictly (all rules) is selected.
4. Choose OK or press Enter.

**Customizing Settings:** You can specify which rules of grammar and/or style are used by Word when checking a document at the Customize Grammar Settings dialog box. At this dialog box, you can customize the rules used for the three types of grammar and style rules—Strictly (all rules), For Business Writing, and For Casual Writing—as well as create custom grammar and style rules.

To display the Customize Grammar Settings dialog box shown in figure 6.12, choose the Customize Settings option from the Options dialog box.

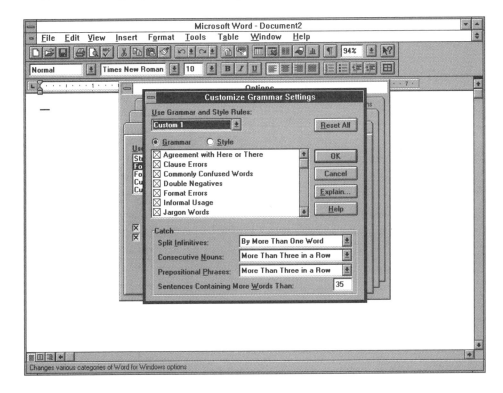

*Figure 6.12*
*Customize*
*Grammar Settings*
*Dialog Box*

At the Customize Grammar Settings dialog box, you can specify which grammar and style rules are used when checking a document. You can also determine whether you want the grammar checker to catch errors such as split infinitives, prepositional phrases, and/or sentences containing more words than 35.

**Checking Spelling:** By default, spelling in a document is checked when you complete a grammar check. If you do not want spelling checked during a grammar check, remove the X from the Check Spelling check box at the Options dialog box.

**Showing Readability Statistics:** When a grammar check is completed, Word displays readability statistics for the document. If you do not want these statistics displayed, remove the X from the Show Readability Statistics check box at the Options dialog box.

### Understanding Readability Statistics

When a grammar check is completed, Word analyzes the document, then provides readability statistics for the document. Most of the options are self-explanatory. Figure 6.13 describes the last four statistics.

*Figure 6.13*
*Readability*
*Statistics*

| | |
|---|---|
| **Flesch Reading Ease** | The Flesch reading ease is based on the average number of syllables per word and the average number of words per sentence. The higher the number, the greater the number of people who will be able to understand the text in the document. Standard writing generally scores in the 60-70 range. |
| **Flesch-Kincaid Grade Level** | The Flesch-Kincaid grade level index is based on the average number of syllables per word and the average number of words per sentence. The score indicates a grade level. Standard writing is generally written at the seventh- or eighth-grade level. |
| **Coleman-Liau Grade Level** | The Coleman-Liau grade level index uses word length in characters and sentences to determine a grade level. |
| **Bormuth Grade Level** | The Bormuth grade level index uses word length characters and sentences to determine a grade level. |

## CHAPTER SUMMARY

- Word for Windows includes these writing tools: a spell checker, a thesaurus, and a grammar checker.
- The spelling checker matches the words in your document with the words in its dictionary. It will not identify words that are spelled correctly but used incorrectly, nor does it identify misspellings that match other words in its dictionaries. The spelling checker cannot check grammar usage.
- While the spelling checker is at work, these command button options are available: Ignore and Ignore All, Change and Change All, Add, Suggest, or AutoCorrect. Several others are available at the Options dialog box.
- When spell checking a document, you can temporarily leave the Spelling: English (US) dialog box, make corrections in the document, then resume spell checking.

- Words that do not appear in the main dictionary can be added to the custom dictionary during a spelling check.
- Words can be added to AutoCorrect during a spelling check, as well as at the AutoCorrect dialog box.
- Use the thesaurus to find synonyms and antonyms for words in your document.
- While the thesaurus is at work, these command button options are available: Replace, Look Up, Cancel, Previous, and Help.
- With the Word Count option from the Tools menu, the number of pages, words, characters, paragraphs, and lines in a document can be displayed.
- Word for Windows includes a grammar checker that you can use to search a document for correct grammar, style, punctuation, and word usage.
- While the grammar checker is at work, these command button options are available: Change, Ignore, Ignore Rule, Explain, and Add.
- When a grammar error is detected by the grammar checker, you can display information about the specific error by choosing the Explain command button.
- The grammar checker uses rules of style and grammar when checking a document. The number of rules used is determined by options set at the Options dialog box.
- By default, spelling in a document is checked when you complete a grammar check. If you do not want the spelling checked, make a change at the Options dialog box.
- When a grammar check is completed, Word analyzes the document, then provides readability statistics for the document.

## COMMANDS REVIEW

| | Mouse | Keyboard |
|---|---|---|
| Activate the spelling checker | Tools, Spelling; or click on the Spelling button on the Standard toolbar (sixth from left) | F7 |
| Spelling Options dialog box | Tools, Options, then select the Spelling tab or choose the Options command button from the Spelling: English (US) dialog box | Tools, Options, then select the Spelling tab |
| AutoCorrect dialog box | Tools, AutoCorrect | Tools, AutoCorrect |
| Thesaurus dialog box | Tools, Thesaurus | SHIFT + F7 |
| Word Count dialog box | Tools, Word Count | Tools, Word Count |
| Activate the grammar checker | Tools, Grammar | Tools, Grammar |
| Grammar Options dialog box | Tools, Options, then select the Grammar tab; or choose the Options command button from the Grammar: English (US) dialog box | Tools, Options, then select Grammar tab |

**True/False:** Circle the letter T if the statement is true; circle the letter F if the statement is false.

T F 1. The spelling checker will stop at a correctly spelled word that is used improperly.

T F 2. Words not in the main dictionary that are used frequently should be added to AutoCorrect.

T F 3. There are no proper names in the spelling checker's main dictionary.

T F 4. Double word occurrences (such as *the the*) will be passed over by the spelling checker if both words are spelled correctly.

T F 5. The thesaurus is used to find synonyms and antonyms for words in a document.

T F 6. Antonyms are words with similar meanings.

T F 7. A document's word count will automatically appear on the screen after using the spelling checker.

T F 8. Unlike the spelling checker, Word's grammar checker will find every grammar error in a document.

T F 9. When an error is detected by the grammar checker, you can display information about the error by choosing the Explain command button.

T F 10. When a grammar check is completed, Word displays readability statistics for the document.

<u>Underline</u> the words in the paragraph below that the spelling checker *would* highlight for correction.

```
The cost for a larje nubmer of listings is assessed monthly. It is
recommend that the number of companys in your business category be
determined, if posssible. Then try to learn what percentge of there
business each month comes form people who have located them thru
the yellow pages. This percentage cna range from 6 to 50 percent.
```

Using the same paragraph above, <u>underline twice</u> the incorrect words that the spelling checker *would not* highlight.

## Exercise 1

1. Open memo03. This document is located on your student data disk.
2. Save the memo with Save As and name it c06ex01.
3. Complete a spelling check by completing the following steps:
   a. Choose <u>T</u>ools, <u>S</u>pelling; press F7; or click on the Spelling button on the Standard toolbar (the sixth button from the left).
   b. The spelling checker selects the word *Struebing*. This word is spelled properly (it is a proper name) so choose Ignore All. To do this with the mouse, click on the I<u>g</u>nore All command button. If you are using the keyboard, press Alt + G.
   c. The spelling checker selects the word *Rivera*. This name is spelled properly so choose Ignore All.
   d. The spelling checker selects the word *infermation*. The proper spelling is displayed in the Change <u>T</u>o box so choose <u>C</u>hange (or Change A<u>l</u>l).
   e. The spelling checker selects the word *PIeces*. The proper case of the word is displayed in the Change <u>T</u>o box so choose <u>C</u>hange (or Change A<u>l</u>l).
   f. The spelling checker selects *colected*. The proper spelling is displayed in the Change <u>T</u>o box so choose <u>C</u>hange (or Change A<u>l</u>l).

g. The spelling checker selects the word *fom*. Select the correct spelling, *from*, then choose Change. To do this with the mouse, click on the down scroll arrow in the Suggestions list box until *from* is visible, click on *from*, then click on Change. If you are using the keyboard, press Alt + S, press the down arrow key until *from* is selected, then press Alt + C.

h. The spelling checker selects the word *Lakeview*. This proper name is spelled correctly, so choose Ignore (or Ignore All).

i. The spelling checker selects the word *the*. Choose Delete to delete *the*. (The word *the* is repeated twice.)

j. The spelling checker selects the word *Cora*. This proper name is spelled correctly, so choose Ignore (or Ignore All).

k. The spelling checker selects *xx:memo03*. Choose Ignore.

l. At *The spelling check complete* message, choose OK or press Enter.

4. Save the memo again with the same name (c06ex01).

5. Print c06ex01.

6. Close c06ex01.

## Exercise 2

1. Open letter01. This document is located on your student data disk.

2. Save the letter with Save As and name it c06ex02.

3. Change spell checking options by completing the following steps:

   a. Choose Tools, Options.

   b. At the Options dialog box, choose the Spelling tab.

   c. Choose Words in UPPERCASE. (This inserts an X in the check box and tells the spelling checker to ignore words in uppercase letters.)

   d. Choose Words with Numbers. (This inserts an X in the check box and tells the spelling checker to ignore words containing numbers.)

   e. Choose OK or press Enter.

4. Complete a spelling check by completing the following steps:

   a. Choose Tools, Spelling; press F7; or click on the Spelling button on the Standard toolbar.

   b. The spelling checker selects the word *atached*. The proper spelling is displayed in the Change To box so choose Change (or Change All).

   c. The spelling checker selects the word *reprasenting*. The proper spelling of the word is displayed in the Change To box so choose Change (or Change All).

   d. The spelling checker selects *corresondances*. The proper spelling is displayed in the Change To box so choose Change (or Change All).

   e. The spelling checker selects the word *suld* and does not offer the correct spelling (which is *should*). To correct the word with the mouse, click the arrow pointer in the document window, then click on *suld*. Add the *h* and the *o* to *suld*, then click on the Start button in the Spelling: English (US) dialog box. If you are using the keyboard, press Ctrl + Tab, add the *h* and the *o* to *suld*, press Ctrl + Tab, then press Alt + S (to start the spelling checker).

   f. The spelling checker selects the word *Streat*. The proper spelling is displayed in the Change To box  so choose Change (or Change All).

   g. The spelling checker selects *Aida*. Change this to *Aid*.

   h. When the spelling checker selects *Lomas*, you realize that *Aida* was a proper name and should have remained as written. To undo the correction, choose Undo Last at the bottom of the Spelling: English (US) dialog box.

   i. When the spelling checker selects *Aida* again, choose Ignore.

   j. The spelling checker selects *Lomas*. This proper name is spelled correctly so choose Ignore.

k. When the spell check is completed, choose OK or press Enter.
5. Save the letter again with the same name (c06ex02).
6. Print c06ex02.
7. Change the spell checking options back to the default by completing the following steps:
   a. Choose Tools, Options.
   b. At the Options dialog box, make sure the Spelling tab is selected.
   c. Choose Words in UPPERCASE. (This removes the X from the check box.)
   d. Choose Words with Numbers. (This removes the X from the check box.)
   e. Choose OK or press Enter.
8. Close c06ex02.

## Exercise 3

1. At a clear document screen, create a custom dictionary named HOSPITAL.DIC by completing the following steps:
   a. Choose Tools, Options.
   b. At the Options dialog box, select the Spelling tab.
   c. Choose New.
   d. At the Create Custom Dictionary dialog box, key **hospital.dic**.
   e. Choose OK or press Enter.
   f. At the Options dialog box, choose OK.
2. Open memo04. This document is located on your student data disk.
3. Save the memo with Save As and name it c06ex03.
4. Complete a spelling check on the document and add words to the HOSPITAL.DIC custom dictionary by completing the following steps:
   a. Choose Tools, Spelling; press F7; or click on the Spelling button on the Standard toolbar.
   b. The spelling checker selects *Alison*. Add this to the HOSPITAL.DIC custom dictionary by completing the following steps:
      (1) Make sure HOSPITAL.DIC displays in the Add Word To text box. If it does not, click on the down-pointing arrow to the right of the text box, then click on HOSPITAL.DIC. If you are using the keyboard, press Alt + W, then press the down arrow key until HOSPITAL.DIC is selected.
      (2) Choose Add.
   c. The spelling checker selects *Germaine*. Choose Add to add this name to the HOSPITAL.DIC custom dictionary.
   d. The spelling checker selects *Averson*. Choose Add to add this name to the HOSPITAL.DIC custom dictionary.
   e. The spelling checker selects *Roland*. Choose Add to add this name to the HOSPITAL.DIC custom dictionary.
   f. The spelling checker selects *Lavel*. Choose Add to add this name to the HOSPITAL.DIC custom dictionary.
   g. The spelling checker selects *Greerson*. Choose Add to add this name to the HOSPITAL.DIC custom dictionary.
   h. The spelling checker selects *xx:memo04*. Choose Ignore.
   i. When the spell check is completed, choose OK or press Enter.
5. Close c06ex03.

## Exercise 4

1. Open memo05. This document is located on your student data disk.
2. Save the memo with Save As and name it c06ex04.
3. Edit the HOSPITAL.DIC custom dictionary by completing the following steps:
   a. Choose Tools, Options.

b. At the Options dialog box, select HOSPITAL.DIC in the Custom Dictionaries list box. To do this with the mouse, click on HOSPITAL.DIC. If you are using the keyboard, press Alt + D, then press the down arrow key until HOSPITAL.DIC is selected.

c. Choose Edit.

d. Word displays the message *This operation will allow you to edit the custom dictionary as a Word document. Do you want to continue?* At this message, choose Yes.

e. Choose Cancel to remove the Options dialog box from the document screen. (The HOSPITAL.DIC document displays in the document screen.)

f. Edit *Alison* so it is spelled *Allison*.

g. Edit *Averson* so it is spelled *Aversen*.

h. Edit *Lavel* so it is spelled *Lavell*.

i. Choose File, Save.

j. Choose File, Close.

4. Complete a spelling check on the memorandum. Make corrections as needed. (Proper names are spelled correctly.)

5. Save the memo again with the same name (c06ex04).

6. Print c06ex04.

7. Remove the HOSPITAL.DIC dictionary by completing the following steps:

a. Choose Tools, Options.

b. At the Options dialog box, make sure the Spelling tab is selected.

c. Click on the check box before HOSPITAL.DIC to remove the X.

d. With HOSPITAL.DIC selected, choose Remove.

e. Choose OK.

8. Close c06ex04.

## Exercise 5

1. At a clear document screen, add words to AutoCorrect by completing the following steps:

a. Choose Tools, AutoCorrect.

b. At the AutoCorrect dialog box, make sure the insertion point is positioned in the Replace text box. If not, choose Replace.

c. Key **prefered.**

d. Choose With.

e. Key **preferred**.

f. Choose Add.

g. Choose Replace.

h. Key **thumnails**.

i. Choose With.

j. Key **thumbnails**.

k. Choose Add.

l. Choose Replace.

m. Key **dtp**.

n. Choose With.

o. Key **desktop publishing**.

p. Choose Add.

q. Choose OK or press Enter.

2. Key the text shown in figure 6.14. (Key the text exactly as shown. AutoCorrect will correct words as you key.)

3. Save the document and name it c06ex05.

4. Print c06ex05.

5. Delete the words you added to AutoCorrect by completing the following steps:

a. Choose Tools, AutoCorrect.

    b. At the AutoCorrect dialog box, click on the *dtp* option in the list box.

    c. Choose <u>D</u>elete.

    d. Click on the *prefered* option in the list box. (If *prefered* is not visible, click on the down-pointing arrow in the list box scroll bar until it is visible.)

    e. Choose <u>D</u>elete.

    f. Click on the *thumnail* option in the list box. (If *thumnail* is not visible, click on the down-pointing arrow in the list box scroll bar until it is visible.)

    g. Choose <u>D</u>elete.

    h. Choose OK or press Enter.

6. Close c06ex05.

**Figure 6.14**

The preliminary design tasks are common to both traditional and dtp. The first stage involves sketching of ideas in thumnails, or miniature drafts. Sketching thumnails is like thinking on paper (or on teh screen). The second stage is to create roughs from teh best sketches. These are refined thumnails, showing more detail and usually drawn at actual size. Roughs are often used for the first client review.

The prefered rough is then precisely specified with actual type adn graphic effects. The resulting comprehensive layout (also known as a comp) is a blueprint of the publication, showing exactly how teh type will be set adn positioned, and teh treatment, sizing, adn placement of illustrations on the page. In traditional publishing, the designer may either draw a carefully detailed comp, or actually paste up sample pages with typeset text and graphics in place.

A good designer knows in advance what the type and artwork specifications will produce. In traditional publishing, the designer spends a substantial amount of time calculating, copyfitting, and sizing illustrations. When using traditional methods, resetting type and rephotographing art means substantial delays adn added costs. In WYSIWYG dtp the computer does much of the calculating, adn type adn art specifications can be previewed and adjusted on teh screen.

## Exercise 6

1. At a clear document screen, look up synonyms for the word *rhetoric* by completing the following steps:

    a. Key **rhetoric**.

    b. With the insertion point positioned in the word or immediately right of the word, choose <u>T</u>ools, <u>T</u>hesaurus; or press Shift + F7.

    c. After viewing the synonyms for *rhetoric*, close the Thesaurus: English (US) dialog box by choosing Cancel.

2. Look up synonyms for the word *subtle* by completing steps similar to those in 1a through 1c.

3. Look up synonyms for the word *insipid* by completing steps similar to those in 1a through 1c.

4. Close the document without saving it.

# Exercise 7

1. Open memo01. This document is located on your student data disk.
2. Save the memo with Save As and name it c06ex07.
3. Change the word *discovered* in the first paragraph to *located* using the thesaurus by completing the following steps:
   a. Position the insertion point in the word *discovered*.
   b. Display the Thesaurus: English (US) dialog box.
   c. At the Thesaurus: English (US) dialog box, select *located*, then choose Replace.
4. Follow similar steps to make the following changes using the thesaurus:
   a. Change *excellent* in the first paragraph to *superior*.
   b. Change *retail* in the third paragraph to *sell*.
5. Save the memo again with the same name (c06ex07).
6. Print c06ex07.
7. Close c06ex07.

# Exercise 8

1. Open letter01. This document is located on your student data disk.
2. Display a word count for the document by completing the following steps:
   a. Choose Tools, Word Count.
   b. After reading the statistics in the Word Count dialog box, choose Close.
3. Close letter01 without saving changes.
4. Open report02.
5. Display the word count for the document by completing steps 2a and 2b.
6. Close report02 without saving changes.

# Exercise 9

1. Open memo06. This document is located on your student data disk.
2. Save the memo with Save As and name it c06ex09.
3. Complete a grammar check by completing the following steps:
   a. Choose Tools, Grammar.
   b. The word *Aversen* is selected and the Spelling: English (US) dialog box is displayed. This proper name is correct so choose Ignore.
   c. The word *Greerson* is selected and the Spelling: English (US) dialog box is displayed. This proper name is correct so choose Ignore.
   d. The word *Roland* is selected and the Spelling: English (US) dialog box is displayed. This proper name is correct so choose Ignore.
   e. The grammar checker selects the sentence *I would likes information from Roland and you on requirements for administering the survey.* and offers the suggestion *Consider **like** instead of **likes***. This suggestion is correct, so choose Change.
   f. The grammar checker selects the sentence *Please contact me any day next week accept Thursday.* and offers the suggestion *Consider **except** instead of **accept***. This suggestion is correct, so choose Change.
   g. The grammar checker selects the sentence *I feel confident that it will illicit the information needed to determines employee requirements.* and offers the suggestion *Consider **elicit** instead of **illicit***. This suggestion is correct, so choose Change.
   h. The grammar checker selects the sentence *I feel confident that it will elicit the information needed to determines employee requirements.* and offers the suggestion *Consider **determine** instead of **determines***. This suggestion is correct, so choose Change.
   i. The text *xx:memo06* is selected and the Spelling: English (US) dialog box is displayed. This text is correct so choose Ignore.
   j. The grammar checker displays the Readability Statistics for the document. Read these statistics, then choose OK or press Enter.
4. Save the memo again with the same name (c06ex09).
5. Print c06ex09.
6. Close c06ex09.

## Exercise 10

1. Open para06. This document is located on your student data disk.
2. Save the document with Save As and name it c06ex10.
3. Change grammar check options by completing the following steps:
   a. Choose Tools, Options.
   b. At the Options dialog box, click on the Grammar tab to select it.
   c. Choose Strictly (all rules) in the Use Grammar and Style Rules list box.
   d. Choose Check Spelling. (This removes the X from the check box.)
   e. Choose OK or press Enter.
4. Complete a grammar check by completing the following steps:
   a. Choose Tools, Grammar.
   b. The grammar checker selects the sentence *You recall that just a short time ago, only selected workers had terminals, and they were used primarily for text and data-manipulation activities.* and offers the suggestion *"This main clause may contain a verb in the passive voice."* View information about passive voice, by choosing Explain.
   c. After reading the information about passive voice, close the Explain window. To do this with the mouse, click on the document control box in the upper left corner of the Explain window (the box containing the hyphen), then click on Close. If you are using the keyboard, press the Esc key.
   d. Delete *and they were* from the sentence so it reads *You recall that just a short time ago, only selected workers had terminals, used primarily for text and data-manipulation activities.* To do this with the mouse, position the arrow pointer in the selected text, then click the left mouse button. Click the left mouse button again to deselect the text, delete the words, then click on the Grammar: English (US) dialog box title bar (this selects it). If you are using the keyboard, press Ctrl + Tab, move the insertion point to the location where text is to be deleted, delete the words, then press Ctrl + Tab.
   e. Choose Start to begin the grammar checker.
   f. The grammar checker selects the sentence *Incoming correspondence that is not transmitted electronically to your work station is converted to a digitized format via laser scanners and input into the electronic filing system.* with *is not transmitted* displayed in red and offers the suggestion *This verb group may be in the passive voice.* Choose Ignore to leave this as written.
   g. The grammar checker selects the same sentence only this time *is converted* is displayed in red. Choose Ignore to leave this as written.
   h. The grammar checker selects the same sentence only this time *via* is displayed in red and offers the suggestion *Try a simpler term like **through**, **by way of**, or **by**.* Choose Change to change the word *via* to *through*.
   i. The grammar checker selects the same sentence only this time *input* is displayed in red. Choose Ignore to leave this as written.
   j. The grammar checker selects the sentence *An added bonus is that you don't have a pile of papers cluttering your desk.* and offers the suggestion *Consider replacing with do not in a formal document.* Choose Change to change *don't* to *do not*.
   k. The grammar checker displays the Readability Statistics for the document. Read these statistics, then choose OK or press Enter.
5. Change the grammar check options back to the default by completing the following steps:
   a. Choose Tools, Options.
   b. At the Options dialog box, make sure the Grammar tab is selected.
   c. Choose For Business Writing in the Use Grammar and Style Rules list box.
   d. Choose Check Spelling. (This inserts the X in the check box.)
   e. Choose OK or press Enter.
6. Save the document again with the same name (c06ex10).
7. Print c06ex10.
8. Close c06ex10.

## Assessment 1

1. Open para05. This document is located on your student data disk.
2. Save the document with Save As and name it c06sa01.
3. Complete a spell check on the document.
4. Save the document again with the same name (c06sa01).
5. Print c06sa01.
6. Close c06sa01.

## Assessment 2

1. Open letter02. This document is located on your student data disk.
2. Save the letter with Save As and name it c06sa02.
3. Change spell checking so that words in uppercase are ignored as well as words containing numbers. You determine whether to ignore words or make corrections. (Proper names are spelled correctly.)
4. After the spell check is completed, proofread the letter and make necessary changes. (There are mistakes that the spelling checker will not select.)
5. Change the spell checking options so that words in uppercase or words containing numbers are not ignored.
6. Save the letter again with the same name (c06sa02).
7. Print c06sa02.
8. Close c06sa02.

## Assessment 3

1. Open para02. This document is located on your student data disk.
2. Save the document with Save As and name it c06sa03.
3. Use the thesaurus to make the following changes:
   a. Change *vital* in the first paragraph to *critical*.
   b. Change *versatile* in the first paragraph to *flexible*.
   c. Change all occurrences of *via* in the first paragraph to *by way of*.
   d. Change *astounding* in the second paragraph to *amazing*.
4. Save the document again with the same name (c06sa03).
5. Print c06sa03.
6. Close c06sa03.

## Assessment 4

1. Open letter03. This document is located on your student data disk.
2. Save the letter with Save As and name it c06sa04.
3. This letter overuses the words *manage* (in various forms), and *efficient* and *efficiently*. Use the thesaurus to make changes to some of the occurrences of *manage*, *manages*, and/or *managed* to make the letter read better. Also, use the thesaurus to make changes to one of the occurrences of *efficient* or *efficiently*.
4. Save the letter again with the same name (c06sa04).
5. Print c06sa04.
6. Close c06sa04.

## Assessment 5

1. Open letter04. This document is located on your student data disk.
2. Save the letter with Save As and name it c06sa05.
3. Change the grammar check option to *Strictly (all rules),* then complete a grammar check. (Proper names are spelled correctly; leave passive sentences as written.)
4. After completing the grammar check, proofread the letter and make necessary changes. (There are mistakes in the letter that the grammar checker will not select.)
5. Change the grammar check option back to *For Business Writing*.
6. Save the letter again with the same name (c06sa05).
7. Print c06sa05.
8. Close c06sa05.

# Formatting Pages 7

Upon successful completion of chapter 7, you will be able to enhance business memoranda, letters, and reports by changing margins, adjusting page breaks, changing the widow/orphan control, and centering text vertically on pages in documents.

Word assumes that you are using standard-sized paper, which is 8.5 inches wide and 11 inches long. By default, a Word document contains 1-inch top and bottom margins and 1.25-inch left and right margins. At the default top and bottom margins, a total of 9 inches of text will print on a page. As you create long documents, you will notice that when the insertion point nears line 9.8 inches (or line 54) a page break is inserted in the document. The page break is inserted at the next line (line 10"). The line below the page break is the beginning of the next page.

The display of the page break will change depending on the viewing mode. Word provides more than one viewing mode. By default, the Normal viewing mode is selected. At this viewing mode, a page break displays as a row of dots. If you change to the Page Layout viewing mode, a page break displays as an actual break in the page. To change to the Page Layout viewing mode, choose View, then Page Mode or click on the Page Layout View button at the left side of the horizontal scroll bar. (The Page Layout View button is the second button from the left.) To change back to the Normal viewing mode, choose View, then Normal or click on the Normal View button at the left side of the horizontal scroll bar. (The Normal View button is the first button on the left.)

While Word's default settings break each page near line 10" (after line 54), there are several features that can affect the location of page breaks within text in a document.

## ■ Changing Margins

The default top, bottom, left, and right margin settings are displayed in the Page Setup dialog box shown in figure 7.1. To display the Page Setup dialog box, choose File, then Page Setup. Make sure the Margins tab is selected. If not, choose Margins at the Page Setup dialog box.

Figure 7.1
Page Setup Dialog
Box with Margins
Tab Selected

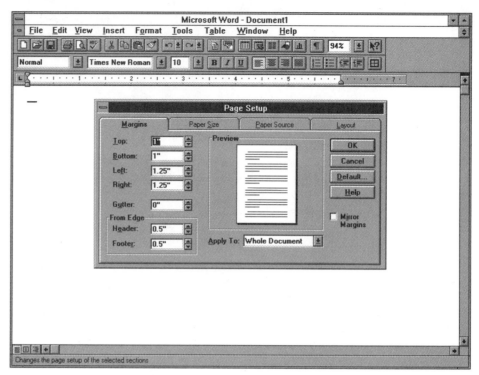

To change margins in a document, you would complete the following steps:

1. Choose File, Page Setup. (Make sure the Margins tab is selected.)
2. At the Page Setup dialog box, choose Top, Bottom, Left, or Right.
3. Key the new measurement for the margin.
4. Choose OK or press Enter.

As you make changes to the margin measurements at the Page Setup dialog box, the sample page in the Preview box illustrates the effects of the margins. If you are using the mouse, you can click on the up- and down-pointing triangles after each margin option to increase or decrease the margin measurement.

If you want the new margins to affect the entire document, position the insertion point anywhere within the document, then make margin changes at the Page Setup dialog box. If you want the new margins to affect only a portion of the text in a document, select the text in the document first, then change the margins. You can also make changes to margins within sections. You will learn more about sections later in this chapter.

You can also specify that margin changes affect the text in a document from the position of the insertion point to the end of the document. To do this, you would complete the following steps:

1. Choose File, Page Setup. (Make sure the Margins tab is selected.)
2. At the Page Setup dialog box, choose Top, Bottom, Left, or Right.
3. Key the new measurement for the margin.
4. Choose Apply To, then choose This Point Forward. To do this with the mouse, click on the down-pointing arrow to the right of the Apply To text box, then click on This Point Forward. If you are using the keyboard, press Alt + A, then press the down arrow key until This Point Forward is selected.
5. Choose OK or press Enter.

Go To
Exercises
1 & 2

## Changing Margins with the Ruler

You can change margins at the Page Setup dialog box or with the Ruler. At the Page Setup dialog box, you can enter specific margin measurements; at the Ruler, you can visually set margins. Before changing margins on the Ruler, the Ruler must be displayed. To turn on or off the display of the Ruler, choose View, then Ruler.

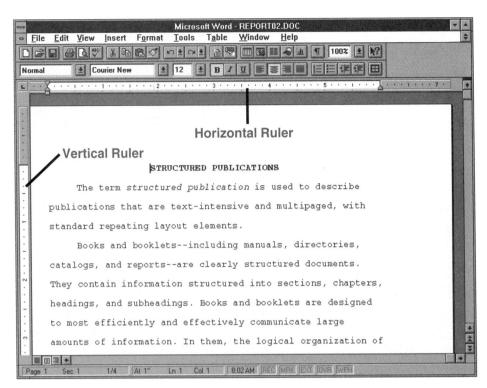

Figure 7.2
Page Layout
Viewing Mode

Word provides more than one viewing mode. By default, the Normal viewing mode is selected. At this viewing mode, a horizontal ruler displays below the Formatting toolbar. You can change paragraph indents with this ruler in the Normal viewing mode but you cannot make changes to the left and right margins. If you want to make changes to the left, right, top, or bottom margins using rulers, the viewing mode must be changed to Page Layout. At this viewing mode, the horizontal ruler displays below the Formatting toolbar and a vertical ruler displays along the left side of the screen. Figure 7.2 shows a document in the Page Layout viewing mode and identifies the horizontal and vertical rulers.

The horizontal and vertical rulers each contain a gray area and a white area. The gray area indicates the margin while the white area indicates the space between margins. The edge between the gray and white areas is called the margin boundary.

To change margins using the ruler, position the arrow pointer on the margin boundary. This causes the arrow pointer to turn into a double-headed arrow. Drag the margin boundary to change the margin. For example, to increase the left and right margins in a document about 0.5 inches (decrease the amount of space available for text), you would complete the following steps:

1. Open a document containing text for which you want to change the left and right margins.
2. Change the viewing mode to Page Layout by choosing <u>V</u>iew, then <u>P</u>age Layout or clicking on the Page Layout View button at the left side of the horizontal scroll bar.
3. Position the arrow pointer on the margin boundary at the left side of the horizontal ruler until the pointer turns into a double-headed arrow pointing left and right.
4. Hold down the left mouse button, drag the margin boundary to the right approximately 0.5 inches, then release the mouse button. (As you drag the mouse, a dashed vertical line appears in the document screen. Use this to help you position the left margin. When you drag the mouse, the entire ruler moves.)
5. Position the arrow pointer on the margin boundary at the right side of the horizontal ruler until it turns into a double-headed arrow pointing left and right.
6. Hold down the left mouse button, drag the margin boundary to the left about 0.5 inches, then release the mouse button. (When you drag the right margin boundary, the ruler is stationary and the margin boundary moves along the ruler.)

You can make changes to the top and bottom margins in a document using the vertical ruler by completing similar steps. For example, to increase the top and bottom margins approximately 0.5 inches in a document (decrease the amount of space available for text) using the vertical ruler, you would complete the following steps:

1. Open a document containing text for which you want to change the top and bottom margins.
2. Change the viewing mode to Page Layout by choosing <u>V</u>iew, then <u>P</u>age Layout or clicking on the Page Layout View button at the left side of the horizontal scroll bar.
3. Position the arrow pointer on the margin boundary toward the top of the vertical ruler until it turns into a double-headed arrow pointing up and down.
4. Hold down the left mouse button, drag the margin boundary down approximately 0.5 inches, then release the mouse button. (As you drag the mouse, a dashed horizontal line appears in the document screen. Use this to help you position the top margin. When you drag the mouse, the entire ruler moves.)
5. Display the bottom margin boundary. To do this, click on the down arrow in the vertical scroll bar until the bottom margin boundary is visible.
6. Position the arrow pointer on the bottom margin boundary until it turns into a double-headed arrow pointing up and down.
7. Hold down the left mouse button, drag the margin boundary up approximately 0.5 inches, then release the mouse button. (When you drag the bottom margin boundary, the ruler is stationary and the margin boundary moves along the ruler.)

When you move the left margin boundary on the horizontal ruler or the top margin boundary on the vertical ruler, the entire ruler moves. If you want to try and move margin boundaries to a precise measurement, you can use the Alt key when dragging a margin boundary. For example, to change the left and right margins in a document to 1.75 inches using the horizontal ruler, you would complete the following steps:

1. Open a document containing text for which you want to change the left and right margins.
2. Change the viewing mode to Page Layout by choosing <u>V</u>iew, then <u>P</u>age Layout or clicking on the Page Layout View button at the left side of the horizontal scroll bar.
3. Position the arrow pointer on the margin boundary at the left side of the horizontal ruler until the pointer turns into a double-headed arrow pointing left and right.
4. Hold down the Alt key, hold down the left mouse button, drag the margin boundary to the right until the measurement in the horizontal ruler displays as *5.5"*, then release the mouse button and the Alt key.
5. Position the arrow pointer on the margin boundary at the right side of the horizontal ruler until it turns into a double-headed arrow pointing left and right.
6. Hold down the Alt key, hold down the left mouse button, drag the margin boundary to the left until the measurement in the horizontal ruler displays as *5"*, then release the mouse button.

You can also display the top and bottom margin measurements when dragging the margin boundary on the vertical ruler by holding down the Alt key.

## Adding a Gutter Margin

The G<u>u</u>tter option at the Page Setup dialog box can be used to create gutter margins for bound material. The default setting for gutter margins is 0 inches. When creating a document that is to be bound and printed on both sides, such as a report or manual, change the gutter margin measurement to properly position text on the page.

For left-bound material to properly display on the page, change the gutter margins to approximately 0.5 inches. When you make this change, Word adds the 0.5 inches of extra margin to the right margin on even pages and to the left margin on odd pages. When the material is bound, even-numbered pages are generally located at the left and odd-numbered pages are generally located at the right. The 0.5-inch gutter margin allows room for the binding.

To change gutter margins in a document, you would complete the following steps:

1. Choose File, Page Setup. (Make sure the Margins tab is selected.)
2. At the Page Setup dialog box, choose Gutter.
3. Key the new measurement for the margin. (If you are using the mouse, you can also click on the up-pointing triangle after the Gutter option until *0.5"* displays in the Gutter text box.)
4. Choose OK or press Enter.

As you change the measurements in the Gutter text box, the display page in the Preview box shows the changes.

## Creating Mirror Margins

The Page Setup dialog box contains the option, Mirror Margins. If this option is active (an X appears in the check box), the measurements for left and right margins are applied to odd-numbered pages and reversed for even-numbered pages.

For example, if you change the left margin to 2.5 inches and the right margin to 1 inch, odd-numbered pages will have these margins but even-numbered pages will have a left margin of 1 inch and a right margin of 2.5 inches. If you apply a gutter margin to a document with mirrored margins, the gutter margin is added to the inside of the page.

To create mirrored margins, display the Page Setup dialog box, make sure the Margins tab is selected, then choose Mirror Margins. This inserts an X in the Mirror Margins option.

# Inserting a Section Break

By default, changes made to margins in a document are applied to all text in the document. If you want margin changes to apply to specific text in a document, select the text first. Text in a document can also be divided into sections.

When a document is divided into sections, each section can be formatted separately. For example, different margin settings can be applied to each section in a document. In chapter 9 you will learn about headers and footers. Sections in a document can contain different headers and/or footers.

A section can insert a page break in a document or a continuous section can be created that does not insert a page break. To insert a continuous section break in a document, you would complete the following steps:

1. Position the insertion point at the location in the document where you want the new section to begin.
2. Choose Insert, Break.
3. At the Break dialog box, choose Continuous.
4. Choose OK or press Enter.

A section break displays in the Normal viewing mode as a line of dots across the screen with the words *End of Section* inserted in the middle.

To create a section break and begin a new page, you would complete the following steps:

1. Position the insertion point at the location in the document where you want the new section to begin.
2. Choose Insert, Break.
3. At the Break dialog box, choose Next Page.
4. Choose OK or press Enter.

A section break that begins a new page displays in the same manner as a continuous section break. At the Break dialog box, choose Even Page if you want to insert a section break and begin the next page with an even number. Choose Odd page if you want to insert a section break and begin the next page with an odd number. For example, if you position the insertion point somewhere in the middle of page 4, then insert a section break with the Even Page option, a section break is inserted and the page below the section break is page 6.

If you change margins to a section of text, the Apply To option at the Page Setup dialog box will have the default setting of This Section.

## ■ Affecting Text Flow

There are several options from the Paragraph dialog box with the Text Flow tab selected that will affect the position of the page break within a document. To display the Paragragh dialog box with the Text Flow tab selected as shown in figure 7.3, choose Format, Paragraph, then choose Text Flow.

### Turning Widow/Orphan Control On/Off

In a long document, you will want to avoid creating widows or orphans. A widow is the last line of a paragraph that appears at the top of a page. An orphan is the first line of a paragraph that appears at the bottom of a page.

In Word, widows and orphans are automatically prevented from appearing in text. Word accomplishes this by adjusting the page breaks in a document. Because of this, the last line of text on various pages will not always occur at the same line measurement or count.

*Figure 7.3*
*Paragraph Dialog*
*Box with Text Flow*
*Tab Selected*

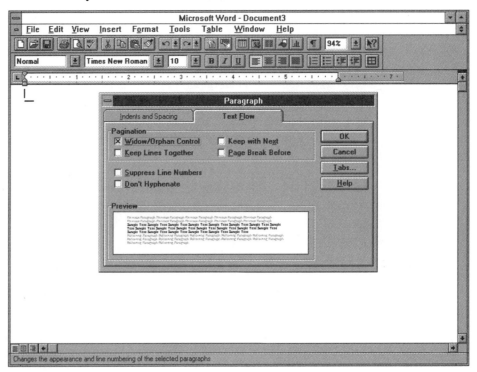

If you wish to turn off the widow and orphan control, you would complete the following steps:

1. Choose Format, Paragraph.
2. At the Paragraph dialog box, select the Text Flow tab.
3. Choose Widow/Orphan Control.
4. Choose OK or press Enter.

When you choose Widow/Orphan Control, the X is removed from the check box and the feature is turned off. If you want to turn on Widow/Orphan Control, repeat the steps above. This inserts the X in the check box.

## Keeping a Paragraph of Text Together

Even with widow/orphan control on, Word may insert a page break in a document between text in a paragraph or several paragraphs that should stay together as a unit. The Paragraph dialog box with the Text Flow tab selected contains options to keep a paragraph, a group of paragraphs, or a group of lines together.

To keep a paragraph together, you can instruct Word to not insert a page break within a paragraph. This format instruction is stored in the paragraph mark, so as the paragraph is moved within the document, the format instruction moves with it.

To tell Word not to insert a page break within a paragraph, you would complete the following steps:

1. Position the insertion point in the paragraph you want to keep together.
2. Choose Format, Paragraph.
3. At the Paragraph dialog box, make sure the Text Flow tab is selected.
4. Choose Keep Lines Together.
5. Choose OK or press Enter.

The same steps can be used to keep a group of consecutive paragraphs together. To do this, select the paragraphs first, then complete the steps above.

With the Keep with Next option from the Paragraph dialog box, you can tell Word to keep the paragraph where the insertion point is located together with the next paragraph. If there is not enough room for the paragraph and the next paragraph, Word moves both paragraphs to the next page.

Use the Page Break Before option if you want a particular paragraph to print at the top of a page. Position the insertion point in the paragraph that you want to begin a new page, display the Paragraph dialog box with the Text Flow tab selected, then choose Page Break Before.

# Inserting Hard Page Breaks

Word's default settings break each page after line 9.8" (line 54). Word automatically inserts page breaks in a document as you edit it. Since Word does this automatically, sometimes you may find that the page breaks occur in undesirable locations. To remedy this, you can insert your own page break.

In the Normal viewing mode, the Word page break called a *soft* page break displays as a row of dots across the screen. In the Page Layout viewing mode the page break displays as a gray bar between two pages. If you do not like where the soft page break is inserted in a document, you can insert your own page break. A page break that you insert in a document is called a *hard* page break. To insert a hard page break in a document, you would complete the following steps:

1. Position the insertion point in the location in the document where you want the break to occur.
2. Choose Insert, Break.
3. At the Break dialog box, make sure Page Break is selected, then choose OK or press Enter.

You can also insert a hard page break by positioning the insertion point at the location in the document where you want the break to occur, then pressing Ctrl + Enter.

A hard page break displays in the Normal viewing mode as a line of dots with the words *Page Break* in the middle of the line. A hard page break displays in the same manner as a soft page break in the Page Layout viewing mode.

Soft page breaks automatically adjust if text is added to or deleted from a document. A hard page break does not adjust and is therefore less flexible than a soft page break. If you add or delete text from a document with a hard page break, check the break to determine whether it is still in a desirable location.

A hard page break can be deleted from a document. To delete a hard page break, position the insertion point on the page break, then press the Delete key.

## Changing Paper Size

Word assumes that you are printing on standard stationery—8.5 inches wide by 11 inches long. If you need to print text on different size stationery, change the paper size at the Page Setup dialog box with the Paper Size tab selected as shown in figure 7.4.

To display the Page Setup dialog box with the Paper Size tab selected choose File, Page Setup, then Paper Size tab.

Word provides several predefined paper sizes including Letter (the default), Letter Small, Legal, and Custom Size. The number and type of paper sizes will vary depending on the printer you are using. Use the predefined paper sizes if they are the needed sizes. If the predefined sizes do not include what you need, create your own paper size with the Custom Size option. If you choose the Custom Size option at the Page Setup dialog box, you can enter the desired measurement for the width and height of the paper size.

*Figure 7.4*
*Page Setup Dialog*
*Box with Paper Size*
*Tab Selected*

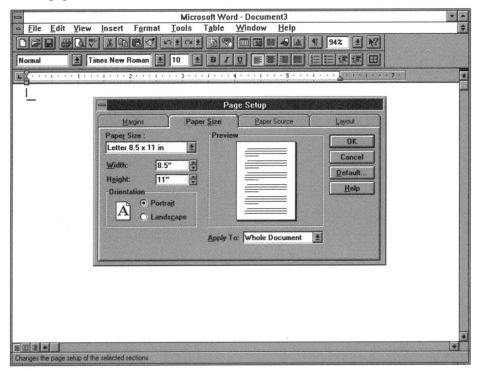

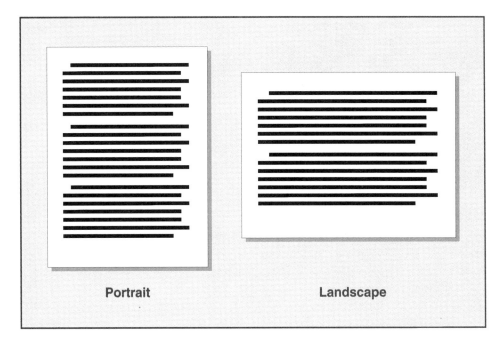

**Figure 7.5**
*Portrait and
Landscape
Orientations*

**Portrait**          **Landscape**

Word provides two orientations for paper sizes—Portrait and Landscape. Figure 7.5 illustrates how text appears on the page in portrait and landscape orientations.

As an example of how to change the paper size, you would complete the following steps to change the paper size to Legal (8.5 x 14 inches):

1. Choose File, Page Setup.
2. At the Page Setup dialog box, select the Paper Size tab. (Skip this step if the Paper Size tab is already selected.)
3. Choose Paper Size, then *Legal 8.5 x 14 in.* To do this with the mouse, click on the down-pointing arrow at the right side of the Paper Size text box, then click on *Legal 8.5 x 14 in.* If you are using the keyboard, press the space bar to display the list of paper sizes, then press the down arrow key until *Legal 8.5 x 14 in* is selected.
4. Choose OK or press Enter.

By default, the change in paper size will affect the entire document. At the Page Setup dialog box, the Apply To option has a default setting of Whole Document. This can be changed to This Point Forward. At this setting, the paper size change will affect text from the current position of the insertion point to the end of the document.

## Centering Text on the Page

Text in a Word document is aligned at the top of the page by default. You can change this alignment with the Vertical Alignment option at the Page Setup dialog box with the Layout tab selected as shown in figure 7.6.

*Figure 7.6*
*Page Setup Dialog*
*Box with Layout*
*Tab Selected*

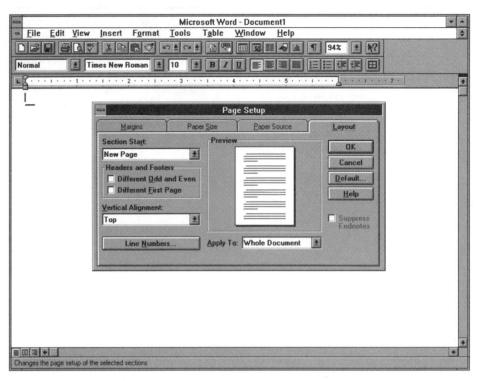

The Vertical Alignment option from the Page Setup dialog box contains three choices—Top, Center, and Justified. The default setting is Top which aligns text at the top of the page. Choose Center if you want text centered vertically on the page. The Justified option will align text between the top and the bottom margins. The Center option positions text in the middle of the page vertically, while the Justified option adds space between paragraphs of text (not within) to fill the page from the top to bottom margins.

As an example of how to use the Vertical Alignment option, you would complete the following steps to vertically center text on the page:

1.  Open the document containing the text to be centered.
2.  Choose File, Page Setup.
3.  At the Page Setup dialog box, select the Layout tab. (Skip this step if the Layout tab is already selected.)
4.  Choose Vertical Alignment, then Center. To do this with the mouse, click on the down-pointing arrow to the right of the Vertical Alignment text box, then click on Center. If you are using the keyboard, press Alt + V, press the space bar, then press the down arrow key until Center is selected.
5.  Choose OK or press Enter.

If you center or justify text, the text does not display centered or justified on the screen (in either viewing mode). Text will print properly, however, on the page. In the next section of this chapter you will learn about the Print Preview feature. This feature can be used to view the document to see how the text will appear on the page when printed.

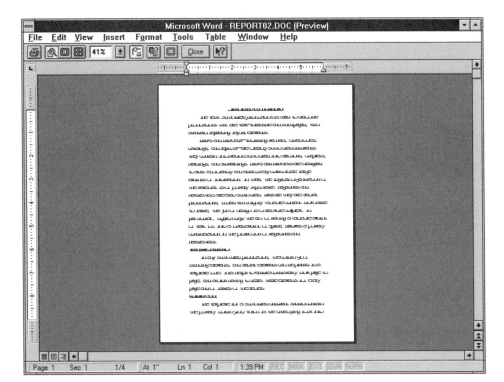

Figure 7.7
Document in Print
Preview

## ▉ *P*reviewing a *D*ocument

Before printing a document, you may find it useful to view the document before printing. Word's Print Preview feature displays the document on the screen as it will appear when printed. With this feature, you can view a partial page, single page, multiple pages, or zoom in on a particular area of a page.

To view a document, choose File, Print Preview or click on the Print Preview button on the Standard toolbar. (The Print Preview button is the fifth button from the left on the Standard toolbar and contains an icon of a page with a magnifying glass.)

When Print Preview is displayed, the page where the insertion point is located is displayed on the screen. Figure 7.7 shows a document in Print Preview.

The toolbar along the top of the screen in Print Preview is called the Preview Bar. With buttons from this bar, you can change the display of the document, send a document to the printer, and turn on or off the display of the ruler. Figure 7.8 shows each button from the Preview Bar and describes what the button will perform.

*Figure 7.8*
*Preview Bar*
*Buttons*

| Click on this button | Named | To do this: |
|---|---|---|
| ⬛ | Print | Send the current document to the printer. |
| ⬛ | Magnifier | Toggle the mouse pointer between a magnifying glass which is used to view the document and the normal mouse pointer which is used to edit the document. |
| ⬛ | One Page | Display individual pages in the document. |
| ⬛ | Multiple Pages | Display multiple pages in the document (up to 18 pages). |
| 41% ⬛ | Zoom Control | Change viewing by percentage option or to Page Width, Whole Page, or Two Pages. |
| ⬛ | View Ruler | Turn on or off the display of the ruler. |
| ⬛ | Shrink to Fit | Try to "shrink" contents of last page in document on to the previous page if there is only a small amount of text on the last page. |
| ⬛ | Full Screen | Toggle the screen display between the normal display and full screen display, which removes everything from the Print Preview screen except the document and the Preview Bar. |
| Close | Close | Close Print Preview and return to document screen. |
| ⬛ | Help | Display context-sensitive help. |

Earlier in this chapter, you learned that you can change the viewing mode by clicking on the Normal View button on the horizontal scroll bar or the Page Layout View button. These buttons are also available in Print Preview. Clicking on either of these buttons causes the document to display in the viewing mode you choose and also closes Print Preview.

While in Print Preview, you can move through a document using the insertion point movement keys, the horizontal and vertical scroll bars, and/or the Page Up and Page Down keys.

## Editing in Print Preview

Print Preview is used to view a document before printing but it can also be used to edit a document. To edit a document in Print Preview, you would complete the following steps:

1. Open the document containing text to be edited.
2. Display Print Preview by choosing File, Print Preview or clicking on the Print Preview button on the Standard toolbar.
3. Make sure the Magnifier button on the Preview Bar is active. (If the Magnifier button is active, it displays with a lighter gray background than the other buttons. By default, the Magnifier button is active when you first display Print Preview.)
4. Position the mouse pointer (displays as a magnifying glass) in the part of the document you want to edit, then click the left button. This changes the display to 100% magnification.
5. Click on the Magnifier glass to turn it off. This returns the mouse pointer to normal.
6. Edit the document in the normal manner.
7. Click on the Magnifier button, then click on the document. This returns the display of the document to the previous magnification.

In Print Preview you can change the top, bottom, left, and right margins using the rulers. In Print Preview, a horizontal ruler displays above the document and a vertical ruler displays at the left side of the document. If these rulers are not visible, clicking on the View Ruler button on the Preview Bar will display them.

Use the horizontal and vertical ruler to change margins in the same manner as the horizontal and vertical rulers in the normal document screen. The horizontal ruler contains a left and right margin boundary and the vertical ruler contains a top and bottom margin boundary. To change a margin, position the mouse pointer on the margin boundary until it turns into a double-headed arrow, then drag the margin boundary to the desired position.

## ■ Changing the Document Zoom

In the previous section of this chapter you learned about the Zoom Control button on the Preview Bar. With this button, you can change the percentage of display in Print Preview or change the display to Page Width, Whole Page, or Two Pages. The Zoom Control button changes the display of the document in Print Preview. You can also change the display of text at the document screen (not Print Preview) with the Zoom Control button on the Standard toolbar or with the Zoom option from View.

If you click on the Zoom Control button on the Standard toolbar, the drop-down menu shown in figure 7.9 displays. Choose one of the percentage options to change the display to that percentage. Choose the Page Width and the screen display will change so that you can view text from the left to the right margins.

When you make a change at the Zoom Control drop-down menu, that change stays in effect for all future documents or until you change to another option.

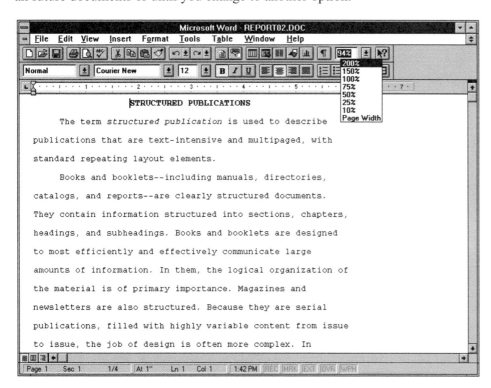

*Figure 7.9*
*Zoom Control Drop-Down Menu*

Figure 7.10
Zoom Dialog Box

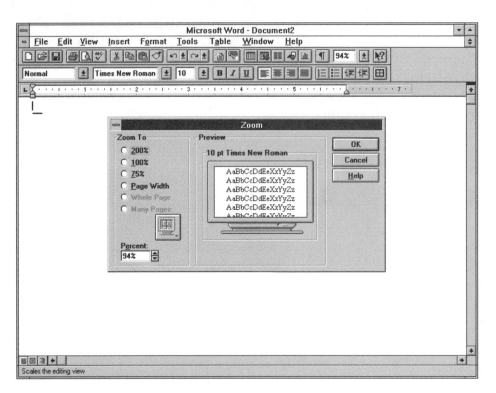

You can change the display of text at the document screen with options from the Zoom Control drop-down menu and also at the Zoom dialog box shown in figure 7.10. To display the Zoom dialog box, choose View, then Zoom.

At the Zoom dialog box you can change the display to 200%, 100%, or 75%. You can also change the display to Page Width. The Whole Page and Many Pages options are dimmed if the viewing mode is Normal. If the viewing mode is changed to Page Layout, these two options are available. To specify a percentage measurement, use the Percent option.

Changes made at the Zoom dialog box stay in effect for future documents or until another change is made.

## Change Screen Display

You can change the display of the screen so only the screen and not the Title bar, Menu bar, toolbars, or Ruler displays. To do this, choose View, then Full Screen. This causes the screen to display with just the insertion point, end of document marker, and Full Screen button in the bottom right corner of the screen. To return the screen back to the previous viewing mode, click on the Full Screen button or press the Esc key.

## CHAPTER SUMMARY

- By default, a Word document contains 1.25-inch left and right margins and 1-inch top and bottom margins.
- Word inserts a page break at approximately 10 inches from the top of each page. With the default 1-inch top and bottom margins, this allows a total of 9 inches to be printed on a standard page. The page break displays as a row of dots in Normal viewing mode and as an actual break in the page in Page Layout.
- If you want new margins to affect the entire document, position the insertion point anywhere within the document, then display the Page Setup dialog box. If you want new margins to affect only a portion of the text in a document, select the text in the document before displaying the Page Setup dialog box.
- Margin settings can be changed visually with the Ruler. The Page Layout viewing mode must be displayed to do this.

- For left-bound material to properly display on the page, change the gutter margins at the Page Setup dialog box from the default 0 inches to approximately 0.5 inches.
- Mirror margins can be created at the Page Setup dialog box. With this option, the measurements for left and right margins are applied to odd-numbered pages and reversed for even-numbered pages.
- Formatting is generally applied to an entire document or to selected text. A document can also be divided into sections to which separate formatting can be applied.
- In Word, widows and orphans are automatically prevented from appearing in text. Turn off this feature at the Paragraph dialog box.
- The Paragraph dialog box with the Text Flow tab selected contains options to keep a paragraph, a group of paragraphs, or a group of lines together.
- The page break that Word inserts automatically is a soft page break. A page break that you insert is a hard page break.
- To print text on a paper size that is different from the default 8.5 by 11, display the Page Setup dialog box with the Paper Size tab selected.
- The Vertical Alignment option from the Page Setup dialog box contains three choices—Top, Center, and Justified.
- With Word's Print Preview feature, you can view a partial page, single page, multiple pages, or zoom in on a particular area of a page. With buttons from the Preview Bar at the top of the Print Preview screen, you can change the display of the document, send a document to the printer, and turn on or off the display of the rulers.
- In addition to viewing how a document will look when printed, you can edit a document while in Print Preview. You can also change the margins while in Print Preview by using the rulers.
- The Zoom Control changes the display of the document in Print Preview. You can also change the display of text at the document screen with the Zoom Control button on the Standard toolbar or with the Zoom option from View.

## COMMANDS REVIEW

| | Mouse | Keyboard |
|---|---|---|
| Page viewing mode | View, Page Mode; or click on Page Layout View button (left side of horizontal scroll bar) | View, Page Mode |
| Normal viewing mode (default) | View, Normal; or click on Normal View button (left side of horizontal scroll bar) | View, Normal |
| Page Setup dialog box | File, Page Setup | File, Page Setup |
| Display Ruler (or turn off display) | View, Ruler | View, Ruler |
| Insert continuous section break | Insert, Break, Continuous | Insert, Break, Continuous |
| Insert section break and begin new page | Insert, Break, Next Page | Insert, Break, Next Page |
| Paragraph dialog box | Format, Paragraph | Format, Paragraph |
| Insert a hard page break | Insert, Break, Page Break | CTRL + ENTER |
| Print Preview | File, Print Preview; or click on Print Preview button on the Standard toolbar. | File, Print Preview |
| Full Screen display | View, Full Screen | View, Full Screen |

**True/False:** Circle the letter T if the statement is true; circle the letter F if the statement is false.

**T   F**   1.   When margin changes are made at the Page Setup dialog box, the sample page in the Preview box illustrates the effects of the margins.

**T   F**   2.   When making margin changes using rulers, the viewing mode must be changed to Page Layout.

**T   F**   3.   A widow or an orphan is one line of a paragraph that appears alone on a page.

**T   F**   4.   The keyboard command to insert a hard page break is Shift + Enter.

**T   F**   5.   With mirrored margins, the left and right margins are applied to odd-numbered pages and reversed for even-numbered pages.

**T   F**   6.   A document can be divided into sections only when the outline function is active.

**T   F**   7.   Instructions can be given at the Paragraph dialog box to keep a group of lines together in a document.

**T   F**   8.   The paper size can only be changed to Word's predefined paper sizes such as Letter, Letter Small, and Legal.

**T   F**   9.   A document cannot be edited while Print Preview is displayed.

**T   F**   10.  The Zoom Control button only affects the Print Preview display.

**Matching:** In the space provided, indicate the correct letter that matches each description. Some choices may be used more than once.

| | | | |
|---|---|---|---|
| A. | 1 inch | G. | 1.25 inches |
| B. | 8.5 inches | H. | 10 inches |
| C. | 9 inches | I. | 11 inches |
| D. | 11.5 inches | J. | 9.5 inches |
| E. | Line 54 | K. | 0 inches |
| F. | Line 60 | L. | 1.5 inches |

1.   Length of a standard piece of paper.                                                    _____
2.   Default top margin.                                                                              _____
3.   Approximate number of vertical inches of text on a page.                      _____
4.   Approximate line number at which an automatic page break occurs on a page.                                                                                                          _____
5.   Width of a standard piece of paper.                                                       _____
6.   Default left margin.                                                                             _____
7.   Default right margin.                                                                           _____
8.   Default bottom margin.                                                                        _____
9.   Default gutter margin.                                                                          _____
10.  Approximate number of inches from the top of the page at which an automatic page break occurs on a page.                                                    _____

### Exercise 1

1.   Open para06. This document is located on your student data disk.
2.   Save the document with Save As and name it c07ex01.
3.   Change the left and right margins to 1.75 inches by completing the following steps:
     a.   Choose File, Page Setup.
     b.   At the Page Setup dialog box make sure the Margins tab is selected.
     c.   Choose Left, then key **1.75**.

d. Choose Right, then key **1.75**.

e. Choose OK or press Enter.

4. Save the document again with the same name (c07ex01).

5. Print c07ex01.

6. Close c07ex01.

## Exercise 2

1. Open report01. This document is located on your student data disk.

2. Save the document with Save As and name it c07ex02.

3. Change the top margin to 1.5 inches and the left and right margins to 1 inch by completing the following steps:

   a. Choose File, Page Setup.

   b. At the Page Setup dialog box, make sure the Margins tab is selected.

   c. Click on the up-pointing triangle after the Top option until *1.5″* displays in the Top text box.

   d. Click on the down-pointing triangle after the Left option until *1″* displays in the Left text box.

   e. Click on the down-pointing triangle after the Right option until *1″* displays in the Right text box.

   f. Choose OK or press Enter.

4. Make the following changes to the document:

   a. Select the entire document, then change the font to 12-point Times New Roman.

   b. Select the title, *TYPE SPECIFICATION*, then change the font to 18-point Times New Roman Bold.

   c. Select the heading *Type Measurement,* then change the font to 14-point Times New Roman Bold.

   d. Use Format Painter to change the formatting to 14-point Times New Roman Bold for the headings *Type Size* and *Type Style*.

   e. Select the last four paragraphs (lines) of text in the document, then click on the Bullets button on the Formatting toolbar to add bullets before each selected paragraph.

5. Save the document again with the same name (c07ex02).

6. Print c07ex02.

7. Close c07ex02.

## Exercise 3

1. Open para02. This document is located on your student data disk.

2. Save the document with Save As and name it c07ex03.

3. Increase the left and right margins in the document approximately 0.5 inches using the Ruler by completing the following steps:

   a. Make sure the Ruler is displayed. If it is not, choose View, Ruler.

   b. Change the viewing mode to Page Layout by choosing View, then Page Layout or clicking on the Page Layout View button at the left side of the horizontal scroll bar.

   c. Position the arrow pointer on the margin boundary at the left side of the horizontal ruler until the pointer turns into a double-headed arrow pointing left and right.

   d. Hold down the left mouse button, drag the margin boundary to the right approximately 0.5 inches, then release the mouse button. (As you drag the mouse, a dashed vertical line appears in the document screen. Use this to help you position the left margin. When you drag the mouse, the entire ruler moves.)

   e. Position the arrow pointer on the margin boundary at the right side of the horizontal ruler until it turns into a double-headed arrow pointing left and right.

   f. Hold down the left mouse button, drag the margin boundary to the left about 0.5 inches, then release the mouse button. (When you drag the right margin boundary, the ruler is stationary and the margin boundary moves along the Ruler.)

4. Change the viewing mode back to <u>N</u>ormal by choosing <u>V</u>iew, then <u>N</u>ormal or clicking on the Normal View button at the left side of the horizontal scroll bar.
5. Save the document again with the same name (c07ex03).
6. Print c07ex03.
7. Close c07ex03.

## Exercise 4

1. Open legal01. This document is located on your student data disk.
2. Save the document with Save As and name it c07ex04.
3. Change the top margin to 2 inches and the left and right margins to 1 inch using the Ruler by completing the following steps:
   a. Make sure the Ruler is displayed. If it is not, choose <u>V</u>iew, <u>R</u>uler.
   b. Choose <u>V</u>iew, <u>P</u>age Layout or click on the Page Layout View button at the left side of the horizontal scroll bar.
   c. Position the arrow pointer on the left margin boundary on the horizontal ruler until the pointer turns into a double-headed arrow pointing left and right.
   d. Hold down the left mouse button, drag the margin boundary to the left until the left edge of the page displays, drag the mouse to the right until the gray 1-inch mark is positioned at the left edge of the horizontal ruler, then release the mouse button.
   e. Display the right margin boundary. To do this, position the arrow pointer on the scroll box in the horizontal scroll bar, hold down the left mouse button, drag the scroll box to the right edge of the horizontal scroll bar, then release the mouse button.
   f. Position the arrow pointer on the right margin boundary until it turns into a double-headed arrow pointing left and right.
   g. Hold down the left mouse button, drag the right margin boundary to the 6.5-inch mark on the horizontal ruler, then release the mouse button.
   h. Position the arrow pointer on the top margin boundary on the vertical ruler until it turns into a double-headed arrow pointing up and down.
   i. Drag the top margin boundary down until the 2-inch gray mark displays at the top of the vertical ruler.
4. Change the viewing mode back to Normal.
5. Save the document again with the same name (c07ex04).
6. Print c07ex04.
7. Close c07ex04.

## Exercise 5

1. Open legal02. This document is located on your student data disk.
2. Save the document with Save As and name it c07ex05.
3. Change the top margin to 2 inches and the left and right margins to 1 inch by completing the following steps:
   a. Make sure the Ruler is displayed. If it is not, choose <u>V</u>iew, <u>R</u>uler.
   b. Choose <u>V</u>iew, <u>P</u>age Layout or click on the Page Layout View button at the left side of the horizontal scroll bar.
   c. Position the arrow pointer on the left margin boundary, hold down the Alt key and the left mouse button, drag the margin boundary to the left until the left edge of the page is displayed. Move the left margin boundary to the left or right until *1"* appears in the gray area and *6.25"* appears in the white area on the horizontal ruler, then release the mouse button and the Alt key.
   d. Display the right margin boundary. To do this, position the arrow pointer on the scroll box in the horizontal scroll bar, hold down the left mouse button, drag the scroll box to the right edge of the horizontal scroll bar, then release the mouse button.
   e. Position the arrow pointer on the right margin boundary until it turns into a double-headed arrow pointing left and right.

f. Hold down the Alt key and the left mouse button, drag the right margin boundary to the right until *6.5"* displays in the white area and *1"* displays in the gray area on the horizontal ruler, then release the mouse button and the Alt key.

g. Position the arrow pointer on the top margin boundary on the vertical ruler until it turns into a double-headed arrow pointing up and down.

h. Hold down the Alt key and the left mouse button, drag the top margin boundary down until *2"* displays in the gray area on the vertical ruler, then release the mouse button and the Alt key.

4. Change the viewing mode back to Normal.
5. Save the document again with the same name (c07ex05).
6. Print c07ex05.
7. Close c07ex05.

## Exercise 6

1. Open c07ex02.
2. Save the document with Save As and name it c07ex06.
3. Change the gutter margin to 0.75 inches by completing the following steps:
   a. Choose File, Page Setup.
   b. At the Page Setup dialog box, make sure the Margins tab is selected.
   c. Choose Gutter.
   d. Key **0.75**.
   e. Choose OK or press Enter.
4. Save the document again with the same name (c07ex06).
5. Print c07ex06.
6. Close c07ex06.

## Exercise 7

1. Open c07ex02.
2. Save the document with Save As and name it c07ex07.
3. Change the left margin to 2 inches and the right margin to 1 inch.
4. Create mirror margins by completing the following steps:
   a. Choose File, Page Setup.
   b. At the Page Setup dialog box, make sure the Margins tab is selected.
   c. Choose Mirror Margins.
   d. Choose OK or press Enter.
5. Save the document again with the same name (c07ex07).
6. Print c07ex07.
7. Close c07ex07.

## Exercise 8

1. Open quote. This document is located on your student data disk.
2. Save the document with Save As and name it c07ex08.
3. Make the following changes to the document:
   a. Insert a section break between the first two paragraphs by completing the following steps:
      (1) Position the insertion point on the blank line between the first and second paragraphs.
      (2) Choose Insert, Break.
      (3) At the Break dialog box, choose Continuous.
      (4) Choose OK or press Enter.
   b. Insert a section break between the second and third paragraphs by completing steps similar to those in 3a(1) through 3a(4).
   c. Insert a section break between the third and fourth paragraphs by completing steps similar to those in 3a(1) through 3a(4).

    d. Position the insertion point anywhere in the second paragraph, then change the left and right margins to 1.75 inches. (At the Page Setup dialog box, make sure the default setting at the Apply To option is This Section.)

    e. Position the insertion point anywhere in the fourth paragraph, then change the left and right margins to 1.75 inches. (At the Page Setup dialog box, make sure the default setting at the Apply To option is This Section.)

4. Save the document again with the same name (c07ex08).
5. Print c07ex08.
6. Close c07ex08.

## Exercise 9

1. Open report03. This document is located on your student data disk.
2. Save the document with Save As and name it c07ex09.
3. Make the following changes to the document:
    a. Insert a section break that begins a new even page by completing the following steps:
      (1) Position the insertion point at the beginning of the line of text containing the title *CHAPTER 2: DEVELOPMENT OF TECHNOLOGY, 1950 - 1960.*
      (2) Choose Insert, Break.
      (3) At the Break dialog box, choose Even Page.
      (4) Choose OK or press Enter.
    b. Position the insertion point anywhere in the first page, then change the left and right margins to 1 inch.
    c. Position the insertion point anywhere in the fourth page, then change the left and right margins to 1.5 inches.
4. Save the document again with the same name (c07ex09).
5. Print c07ex09.
6. Close c07ex09.

## Exercise 10

1. Open c07ex02.
2. Save the document with Save As and name it c07ex10.
3. Change the top margin to 1.3 inches.
4. Tell Word to not insert a page break within the last paragraph of text on the first page (that continues on the top of the second page) by completing the following steps:
    a. Position the insertion point on any character in the last paragraph of text on the first page.
    b. Choose Format, Paragraph.
    c. At the Paragraph dialog box, select the Text Flow tab.
    d. Choose Keep Lines Together.
    e. Choose OK or press Enter.
5. Tell Word to keep the paragraph above the bulleted items at the end of the document with the bulleted paragraphs by completing the following steps:
    a. Position the insertion point anywhere within the paragraph above the bulleted paragraphs. (This paragraph is located toward the end of the document.)
    b. Choose Format, Paragraph.
    c. At the Paragraph dialog box (with the Text Flow tab selected), choose Keep with Next.
    d. Choose OK or press Enter.
6. Save the document again with the same name (c07ex10).
7. Print c07ex10.
8. Close c07ex10.

# Exercise 11

1. Open c07ex02.
2. Save the document with Save As and name it c07ex11.
3. Change the top margin to 1.3 inches.
4. Insert a page break before the last paragraph on the first page by completing the following steps:
   a. Position the insertion point at the beginning of the last paragraph at the end of the first page (the paragraph that begins *For display type, common sizes...*).
   b. Choose Insert, Break.
   c. At the Break dialog box, make sure Page Break is selected, then choose OK or press Enter.
5. Insert a hard page break before the paragraph above the bulleted paragraphs by completing the following steps:
   a. Position the insertion point at the beginning of the paragraph above the bulleted paragraphs (the paragraph that begins *In addition to these styles...*).
   b. Press Ctrl + Enter.
6. Save the document again with the same name (c07ex11).
7. Print c07ex11. (Check with your instructor before printing this document. The document will print the same as c07ex10.)
8. Close c07ex11.

# Exercise 12

1. Open para03. This document is located on your student data disk.
2. Save the document with Save As and name it c07ex12.
3. Change the paper size to 5.5 inches by 8.5 inches by completing the following steps:
   a. Choose File, Page Setup.
   b. At the Page Setup dialog box, choose the Paper Size tab. (Skip this step if the Paper Size tab is already selected.)
   c. Click on the down-pointing triangle to the right of the Width text box until *5.5"* displays in the Width text box.
   d. Click on the down-pointing triangle to the right of the Height text box until *8.5"* displays in the Height text box.
   e. Choose OK or press Enter.
4. Select the entire document, then change the font to 10-point Arial.
5. Save the document again with the same name (c07ex12).
6. Print c07ex12. (If you are printing on 8.5 x 11-inch paper, the text prints on only a portion of the page. If you are printing on paper that is 5.5 x 8.5 inches, check with your instructor on how to feed the paper into the printer.)
7. Close c07ex12.

# Exercise 13

*Note: Check with your instructor before completing this exercise. You may not be able to change the paper size to Legal.*

1. Open c07ex02.
2. Save the document with Save As and name it c07ex13.
3. Change the paper size to Legal by completing the following steps:
   a. Choose File, Page Setup.
   b. At the Page Setup dialog box choose the Paper Size tab. (Skip this step if the Paper Size tab is already selected.)
   c. Choose Paper Size, then *Legal 8.5 x 14 in.* To do this with the mouse, click on the down-pointing arrow at the right side of the Paper Size text box, then click on *Legal 8.5 x 14 in.* If you are using the keyboard, press the space bar to display the list of paper sizes, then press the down arrow key until *Legal 8.5 x 14 in* is selected.

d. Choose OK or press Enter.
4. Save the document again with the same name (c07ex13).
5. Print c07ex13. (Check with your instructor before printing to see if your printer is capable of printing legal-sized documents.)
6. Close c07ex13.

## Exercise 14

1. Open notice02. This document is located on your student data disk.
2. Save the document with Save As and name it c07ex14.
3. Select the text in the document, then change the font to 24-point Algerian (or a decorative serif typeface, if your printer does not support Algerian).
4. Center the text between the top and bottom margins by completing the following steps:
   a. Choose File, Page Setup.
   b. At the Page Setup dialog box, choose the Layout tab. (Skip this step if the Layout tab is already selected.)
   c. Choose Vertical Alignment, then Center. To do this with the mouse, click on the down-pointing arrow to the right of the Vertical Alignment text box, then click on Center. If you are using the keyboard, press Alt + V, then press the down arrow key until Center is selected.
   d. Choose OK or press Enter.
5. Save the document again with the same name (c07ex14).
6. Print c07ex14.
7. Close c07ex14.

## Exercise 15

1. Open c07ex12.
2. Save the document with Save As and name it c07ex15.
3. Justify the text between the top and bottom margins by completing the following steps:
   a. Choose File, Page Setup.
   b. At the Page Setup dialog box make sure the Layout tab is selected.
   c. Choose Vertical Alignment, then Justified.
   d. Choose OK or press Enter.
4. Save the document again with the same name (c07ex15).
5. Print c07ex15.
6. Close c07ex15.

## Exercise 16

1. Open report02.
2. View the document by completing the following steps:
   a. Choose File, Print Preview or click on the Print Preview button on the Standard toolbar.
   b. Click on the Multiple Pages button on the Preview Bar. (This causes a grid to appear immediately below the button.)
   c. Position the arrow pointer in the upper left portion of the grid, hold down the left mouse button, drag the mouse down and to the right until the message at the bottom of the grid displays as *2 x 2 Pages,* then release the mouse button.
   d. Click on the Full Screen button on the Preview Bar. This displays only the pages in the document and the Preview Bar.
   e. Click on the Full Screen button again to restore the full screen display.
   f. Click on the One Page button on the Preview Bar.
   g. Click on the down-pointing arrow at the right of the Zoom Control button. From the drop-down list that displays, click on 50%.
   h. Click on the down-pointing arrow at the right of the Zoom Control button. From the drop-down list that displays, click on 75%.

    i. Click on the One Page button on the Preview Bar.
    j. Click on the Close button on the Preview Bar.
  3. Close report02.

## Exercise 17

  1. Open notice01. This document is located on your student data disk.
  2. Save the document with Save As and name it c07ex17.
  3. Display Print Preview and make changes to the document by completing the following steps:
    a. Choose File, Print Preview or click on the Print Preview button on the Standard toolbar.
    b. Position the mouse pointer (displays as a magnifying glass) in the middle of the first paragraph of text in the document, then click the left button. This changes the display to 100% magnification.
    c. Click on the Magnifier button on the toolbar to turn magnification off. This returns the mouse pointer to normal.
    d. Make the following edits to text in the first paragraph of the document:
       (1) Change *6:00* to *6:30*.
       (2) Change *9:30* to *10:00*.
       (3) Change *John McNary* to *Sylvia Joiner*.
    e. Make the following edits to the text in the third paragraph of the document:
       (1) Add *hamburgers,* after the word *Hotdogs,*.
       (2) Change *8:30* to *9:00*.
    f. Click on the Magnifier button on the toolbar, then click on the document. This returns the display of the document to the previous magnification.
    g. Make sure the rulers are displayed. (If they are not displayed, click on the View Ruler button on the Preview Bar.)
    h. Make the following changes to the left, right, and top margins:
       (1) Drag the left margin boundary to the right on the horizontal ruler until the 2-inch mark displays in the gray area.
       (2) Drag the right margin boundary to the left on the horizontal ruler to the 4.5-inch mark in the white area.
       (3) Drag the top margin boundary down on the vertical ruler until the 3-inch mark displays in the gray area.
    i. Click on Close to close Print Preview.
  4. Save the document again with the same name (c07ex17).
  5. Print c07ex17.
  6. Close c07ex17.

## Exercise 18

  1. Open report02. This document is located on your student data disk.
  2. Change the display by completing the following steps:
    a. Click on the Zoom Control button on the Standard toolbar, then click on 50%.
    b. Click on the Zoom Control button on the Standard toolbar, then click on Page Width.
    c. Choose View, Zoom.
    d. At the Zoom dialog box, choose 200%.
    e. Choose OK or press Enter.
    f. Choose View, Page Layout.
    g. Choose View, Zoom.
    h. At the Zoom dialog box, choose Whole Page.
    i. Choose OK or press Enter.
    j. Click on the Zoom Control button on the Standard toolbar, then click on 100%.
  3. Close report02.

## Assessment 1

1. Open report02. This document is located on your student data disk.
2. Save the document with Save As and name it c07sa01.
3. Make the following changes to the document:
    a. Change the left and right margins to 1 inch.
    b. Position the insertion point in the subheading *Column Grid,* then tell Word to keep the subheading together with the next paragraph.
4. Save the document again with the same name (c07sa01).
5. Print c07sa01.
6. Close c07sa01.

## Assessment 2

1. Open report02.
2. Save the document with Save As and name it c07sa02.
3. Make the following changes to the document:
    a. Change the left margin to 2 inches and the right margin to 1 inch.
    b. Select the Mirror Margins option at the Page Setup dialog box.
    c. Select the entire document, then change the font to 12-point Times New Roman.
    d. Select the title, *STRUCTURED PUBLICATIONS*, then change the font to 14-point Century Gothic Bold.
    e. Select each of the following headings and subheadings individually, then change the font to 12-point Century Gothic Bold (hint: use the Format Painter):
        TEMPLATE ELEMENTS
        Column Grid
        STANDING ELEMENTS
        Running Heads/Feet
        Page Numbers (Folios)
        SERIAL ELEMENTS
    f. Check the page breaks in the document and make changes, if needed.
4. Save the document again with the same name (c07sa02).
5. Print c07sa02.
6. Close c07sa02.

## Assessment 3

1. Open para04. This document is located on your student data disk.
2. Save the document with Save As and name it c07sa03.
3. Make the following changes to the document:
    a. Change the paper size to 5.5 inches by 8.5 inches.
    b. Change the top and bottom margins to 1.5 inches.
    c. Change the left and right margins to 1 inch.
    d. Select the entire document, then change the font to 10-point Arial.
    e. Change the vertical alignment of the text in the document to Justified.
4. Preview the document before printing.
5. Save the document again with the same name (c07sa03).
6. Print c07sa03.
7. Close c07sa03.

## Assessment 4

1. At a clear document screen, key the text shown in figure 7.11. Center and bold the text as indicated. Press the Enter key the number of times indicated in the brackets. (Do not key the information in brackets.)
2. Center the text vertically on the page.
3. Preview the document before printing.
4. Save the document and name it c07sa04.
5. Print c07sa04.
6. Close c07sa04.

**Figure 7.11**

**DESKTOP PUBLISHING TECHNIQUES**
[press Enter 15 times]


**by Gina Swanson**
[press Enter 15 times]


**OA 230**
**March 12, 1996**

# *Manipulating* **8** *Tabs*

Upon successful completion of chapter 8, you will be able to enhance business memoranda and letters and generate two- and three-column tables with tab stops including left, right, center, and decimal.

When you work with a document, Word offers a variety of default settings such as margins and line spacing. One Word default setting is tab stops every 0.5 inches. In some situations, these default tab stops are appropriate; in others, you may want to create your own tab stops.

There are two methods for setting tabs. Tabs can be set on the Ruler or at the Tabs dialog box.

## ■ *Manipulating* *Tabs on the* *Ruler*

The Ruler can be used, together with the mouse, to set, move, and/or delete tabs. To display the Ruler shown in figure 8.1, choose <u>V</u>iew, then <u>R</u>uler.

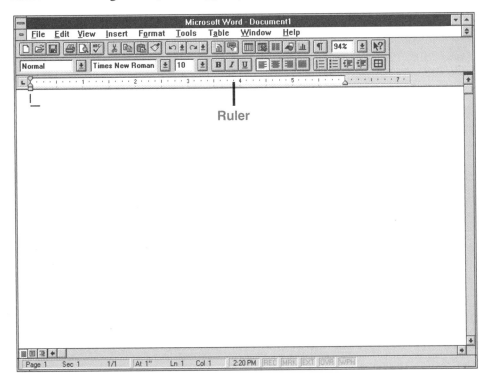

*Figure 8.1*
*Ruler*

Ruler

The Ruler, by default, contains left tabs every 0.5 inches. These default tabs are indicated by tiny vertical lines along the bottom of the ruler. At a left tab, text aligns at the left edge of the tab. The other types of tabs that can be set on the Ruler are Center, Right, and Decimal.

The small button at the left side of the Ruler is called the Tab Alignment button. Click on this button to display the various tab alignment options. Each time you click on the Tab Alignment button a different tab alignment symbol displays. Figure 8.2 shows each symbol and what kind of tab it will set.

| Figure 8.2 Tab Alignment Symbols | **L** = left alignment tab <br> **⊥** = center alignment tab <br> **⅃** = right alignment tab <br> **工.** = decimal alignment tab |
| --- | --- |

The columns displayed in figure 8.3 show text aligned at different tabs. The text in the first column was keyed at a left tab. The second column of text was keyed at a center tab, the third column at a right tab, and the fourth column at a decimal tab.

| Figure 8.3 Types of Tabs | Emery | British Columbia | Victoria | 34.56 |
| --- | --- | --- | --- | --- |
| | Wilson | Saskatchewan | Regina | 2,314.08 |
| | Drew | Alberta | Edmonton | 368.92 |

## Setting Tabs

To set a left tab on the Ruler, make sure the left alignment symbol ( **L** ) displays in the Tab Alignment button. Position the arrow pointer just below the tick mark (the marks on the Ruler) on the Ruler where you want the tab symbol to appear, then click the left mouse button. When you set a tab on the Ruler, any tabs to the left are automatically deleted by Word.

Set a center, right, or decimal tab on the Ruler in a similar manner. Before setting the tab on the Ruler, click on the Tab Alignment button at the left side of the Ruler until the appropriate tab symbol is displayed, then set the tab.

As an example of how to set tabs on the Ruler, you would complete the following steps to set a left tab at the 1-inch mark on the Ruler, a center tab at the 2.5-inch mark on the Ruler, and a right tab at the 5-inch mark on the Ruler:

1. Choose View, Ruler to display the Ruler. (Skip this step if the Ruler is already displayed.)
2. Make sure the left tab symbol displays in the Tab Alignment button at the left side of the Ruler.
3. Position the arrow pointer below the 1-inch tick mark on the Ruler, then click the left mouse button.
4. Position the arrow pointer on the Tab Alignment button at the left side of the Ruler, then click the left mouse button until the center tab symbol ( **⊥** ) displays.
5. Position the arrow pointer below the 2.5-inch tick mark on the Ruler, then click the left mouse button.
6. Position the arrow pointer on the Tab Alignment button at the left side of the Ruler, then click the left mouse button until the right tab symbol ( **⅃** ) displays.
7. Position the arrow pointer below the 5-inch tick mark on the Ruler, then click the left mouse button.

If you change the tab symbol in the Tab Alignment button, the symbol remains until you change it again or you exit Word. If you exit then reenter Word, the tab symbol returns to the default of left.

You can set the tabs first and then key the text or key the text at the default tab stops, then set tabs. If you set tabs and then key text, the tab formatting is inserted in the paragraph mark. As you press the Enter key, the paragraph mark is copied down to the next line and the tab formatting is carried with the paragraph mark.

When you press the Enter key, the insertion point is moved down to the next line and a paragraph mark is inserted in the document. Paragraph formatting is stored in this paragraph mark. For example, if you make changes to tab stops, these changes are inserted in the paragraph mark. In some situations, you may want to start a new line but not a new paragraph. To do this, press Shift + Enter. Word inserts a line break symbol (visible when nonprinting characters have been turned on) and moves the insertion point to the next line.

If you change tab stops, then create columns of text using the New Line command, Shift + Enter, the tab formatting is stored in the paragraph mark at the end of the columns. If you want to make changes to the tab stops for the columns, position the insertion point anywhere within the columns (the columns do not have to be selected), then make the changes.

If you set tabs for existing text, you must press the Tab key before keying each column entry. After the text is keyed, select the lines of text you want to be formatted with the new tab stops, then set the tabs on the Ruler.

Turning on the display of nonprinting characters is useful when creating tabbed text. With nonprinting characters turned on, the paragraph mark containing the tab formatting displays. Also, when the Tab key is pressed, a right-pointing arrow displays in the document screen. To turn on the display of nonprinting characters, click on the Show/Hide button on the Standard toolbar or press Shift + Ctrl + *.

## Moving Tabs

After a tab has been set on the Ruler, it can be moved to a new location. To move a single tab, you would complete the following steps:

1. Position the arrow pointer on the tab symbol on the Ruler to be moved.
2. Hold down the left mouse button.
3. Drag the symbol to the new location on the Ruler, then release the mouse button.

## Deleting Tabs

A tab can be removed from the Ruler. To delete a tab from the Ruler, you would complete the following steps:

1. Position the arrow pointer on the tab symbol you want deleted from the Ruler.
2. Hold down the left mouse button, drag the symbol down into the document screen, then release the mouse button.

# ■ Manipulating Tabs at the Tabs Dialog Box

Use the Tabs dialog box shown in figure 8.4 to set tabs at a specific measurement. You can also use the Tabs dialog box to set tabs with preceding leaders and clear one tab or all tabs. To display the Tabs dialog box, choose Format, Tabs. You can also display the Tabs dialog box by double-clicking on a tab symbol on the Ruler.

## Clearing Tabs

At the Tabs dialog box, you can clear an individual tab or all tabs. To clear all tabs, choose Clear All. To do this with the mouse, click on the Clear All button in the dialog box. If you are using the keyboard, press Alt + A.

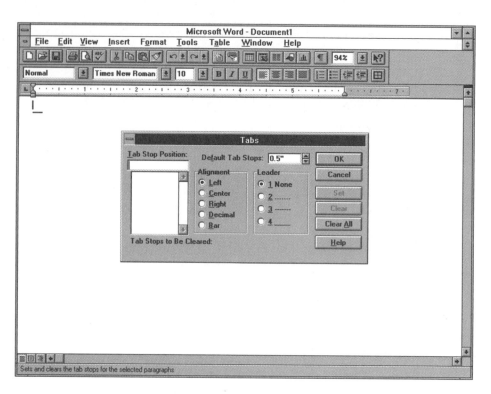

**Figure 8.4**
*Tabs Dialog Box*

To clear an individual tab, identify the tab position, then choose Clear. For example, to clear a tab at the 2-inch mark on the Ruler, you would complete the following steps:

1.  Choose Format, Tabs.
2.  At the Tabs dialog box, select 2″ in the Tab Stop Position list box. To do this with the mouse, click on 2″ in the list box. If you are using the keyboard, press Alt + T, then press the down arrow key until 2″ is selected.
3.  Choose Clear.
4.  Choose OK or press Enter.

## Setting Tabs

At the Tabs dialog box, you can set a left, right, center, or decimal tab as well as a vertical bar. You can also set a left, right, center, or decimal tab with preceding leaders. To change the type of tab at the Tabs dialog box, display the dialog box, then choose the desired tab in the Alignment section. If you set a vertical bar tab stop, Word will insert a vertical bar at the tab stop when you press the Tab key. You do not enter text at a vertical bar tab stop.

The Tab Stop Position option at the Tabs dialog box is used to identify the specific measurement where the tab is to be set. To set a tab, choose the desired tab alignment, choose Tab Stop Position, then key the desired measurement.

As an example of how to clear and set tabs at the Tabs dialog box, you would complete the following steps to set a left tab at the 2-inch mark and a decimal tab at the 4-inch mark on the Ruler:

1.  Choose Format, Tabs.
2.  At the Tabs dialog box choose Clear All.
3.  Key **2**. (The insertion point should automatically be positioned in the Tab Stop Position text box.)
4.  Choose Set.
5.  Choose Decimal. To do this with the mouse, click on the circle before the Decimal option in the Alignment section of the dialog box. If you are using the keyboard, press Alt + D.

6. Select the *2″* in the <u>T</u>ab Stop Position text box.
7. Key **4**.
8. Choose <u>S</u>et.
9. Choose OK or press Enter.

## Setting Leader Tabs

The four types of tabs can also be set with leaders. Leaders are useful in a table of contents or other material where you want to direct the reader's eyes across the page. Figure 8.5 shows an example of leaders. The text in the first column was keyed at a left tab. The text in the second column was keyed at a right tab with leaders.

| | |
|---|---|
| British Columbia ............................................................................ Victoria |
| Alberta ...............................................................................Edmonton |
| Saskatchewan ................................................................... Regina |
| Manitoba ..............................................................................Winnipeg |
| Ontario .......................................................................... Toronto |
| Quebec ........................................................................Montreal |

*Figure 8.5*
*Leader Tabs*

Leaders can be periods (.), hyphens (-), or underlines (_). To add leaders to a tab, choose the type of leader desired in the Leader section of the Tabs dialog box.

As an example of how to create tabs with leaders, you would complete the following steps to set a left tab at the 1-inch mark and a right tab with period leaders at the 6-inch mark on the Ruler:

1. Choose F<u>o</u>rmat, <u>T</u>abs.
2. At the Tabs dialog box choose Clear <u>A</u>ll.
3. Make sure <u>L</u>eft is selected in the Alignment section of the dialog box. (If not, choose <u>L</u>eft.)
4. Make sure the insertion point is positioned in the <u>T</u>ab Stop Position text box, then key **1**.
5. Choose <u>S</u>et.
6. Choose <u>R</u>ight. To do this with the mouse, click on the circle before the <u>R</u>ight option in the Alignment section of the dialog box. If you are using the keyboard, press Alt + R.
7. Choose <u>2</u> ..... To do this with the mouse, click on the circle before the <u>2</u> .... option in the Leader section of the dialog box. If you are using the keyboard, press Alt + 2.
8. Select the *1″* in the <u>T</u>ab Stop Position text box.
9. Key **6**.
10. Choose <u>S</u>et.
11. Choose OK or press Enter.

## Resetting Default Tab Stops

Word sets left tabs every 0.5 inches by default. If you set a tab on the Ruler or at the Tabs dialog box, any tabs to the left are automatically deleted.

The interval between default tabs can be changed with the De<u>f</u>ault Tab Stops option at the Tabs dialog box. For example, if you want to set tabs every inch, you would enter a *1* in the De<u>f</u>ault Tab Stops text box.

# Determining Tabs Using the Key Line Method

Columns of text or data in a document are usually centered between the left and right margins to provide a balanced look. A variety of methods can be used to determine the position of columns on the page. In a Word document, one of the easiest methods for determining column positions is the *key line* method.

To use the key line method for determining column positions, you would complete the following steps:

1. Display the Ruler.
2. Turn on the display of nonprinting characters.
3. Identify the longest entry in each column.
4. Determine the number of spaces between columns.
5. Change to Center alignment.
6. Key the longest entry in the first column, then press the space bar the number of desired spaces between columns. Continue this procedure until all of the longest entries in each column and the spaces between columns have been entered.
7. Set a tab at the position on the Ruler immediately above the first letter, above the character (such as a decimal point), above the character that represents the center of the column, or immediately to the right of the character. (The location depends on whether you are setting a left tab, decimal tab, center tab, or right tab.)
8. Delete the key line (but not the paragraph mark containing the tab formatting).
9. Press Ctrl + L or click on the Left button on the Standard toolbar to return paragraph alignment to left.

As an example of how to use the key line method to set tabs for columns, you would complete the following steps to set tabs for the following columns of text.

| Leah Aversen | Director | $561.50 |
| Mariah Jackson | Vice President | 98.45 |
| Roland Lavell | Nurse | 854.23 |

1. At a clear document screen, display the Ruler. (Skip this step if the Ruler is already displayed.)
2. Click on the Show/Hide button on the Standard toolbar to turn on the display of nonprinting characters.
3. Identify the longest entry in each column. (In this example, the longest entries are *Mariah Jackson*, *Vice President*, and *$561.50.*)
4. Determine the number of spaces between columns. Generally, six to ten spaces between columns are appropriate. (In this example, use eight spaces to separate the columns.)
5. Press Ctrl + E or click on the Center button on the Standard toolbar.
6. Key **Mariah Jackson**, then press the space bar eight times.
7. Key **Vice President**, then press the space bar eight times.
8. Key **$561.50**.
9. Position the arrow pointer on the Ruler immediately above the *M* in *Mariah*, then click the left mouse button. (This inserts a left tab on the Ruler. Before setting the tab, make sure the left tab symbol displays in the Tab Alignment button.)
10. Click on the Tab Alignment button on the left side of the Ruler until the center tab symbol ( ⊥ ) displays.

11. Position the arrow pointer on the Ruler immediately above the first *e* in *President*, then click the left mouse button. (This is a center tab so the insertion point must be positioned at the center of the longest entry.)
12. Click on the Tab Alignment button on the left side of the Ruler until the decimal tab symbol ( ⊥ ) displays.
13. Position the arrow pointer on the Ruler Bar immediately above the decimal point in $561.50, then click the left mouse button.
14. Click on the Tab Alignment button until the left tab symbol ( L ) displays. (This step is optional.)
15. Delete the key line text but *not* the paragraph mark.
16. Press Ctrl + L or click on the Left button on the Standard toolbar. (This changes the paragraph alignment to left.)

## Keying Column Headings

If the column heading is the longest line in the column, use it when creating the key line. Column headings that are shorter than the column entries can be visually centered above the entries. To do this, key the column entries first, leaving blank lines above the columns for the headings. After the column entries have been keyed, move the cursor above the columns, visually determine the center of the columns, then key the headings.

Some businesses are accepting column headings aligned at the tab stops rather than centered. Keying column headings at the tab stops takes less time than centering headings.

## CHAPTER SUMMARY

- One Word default setting is tab stops every 0.5 inches. These settings can be changed on the Ruler or at the Tabs dialog box.
- Use the Tab Alignment button at the left side of the Ruler to select a left, right, center, or decimal tab. When you set a tab on the Ruler, any tabs to the left are automatically deleted.
- You can set tab stops before or after keying text. If before, the tab formatting is inserted in the paragraph mark. As you press the Enter key, the tab formatting is copied to the next paragraph mark. If you set tab stops after keying text, select the lines of text you want to be formatted with the new tab stops, then set the tabs on the Ruler or at the Tabs dialog box.
- Turning on the display of nonprinting characters, such as those for paragraphs and tabs, is useful when creating tabbed text.
- After a tab has been set on the Ruler, it can be moved or deleted using the arrow pointer.
- At the Tabs dialog box, you can set any of the four types of tabs as well as a vertical bar at a specific measurement. You can also set tabs with preceding leaders and clear one tab or all tabs.
- Preceding leaders can be periods, hyphens, or underlines.
- The 0.5-inch interval between default tabs can be changed with the Default Tab Stops option at the Tabs dialog box.
- The key line method is an easy way to determine column positions when centering columns of text or data between the left and right margins. Begin by identifying the longest entry in each column and determining the number of spaces between columns.

|  | **Mouse** | **Keyboard** |
|---|---|---|
| Display the Ruler | View, Ruler | View, Ruler |
| Display nonprinting characters | Click on the Show/Hide button on the Standard toolbar | SHIFT + CTRL + ✳ |
| Tabs dialog box | Format, Tabs | Format, Tabs |

## CHECK YOUR UNDERSTANDING

**Completion:** In the space provided, indicate the correct command, term, or number.

1. By default, each tab is set apart from the other by this measurement. _____
2. The four types of tabs that can be set at the Ruler are Left, Right, Center, and this. _____
3. This is the default tab type. _____
4. Tabs can be set on the Ruler or here. _____
5. When setting tabs on the Ruler, choose the tab type with this button. _____
6. This is the name for the line of periods that can run between columns. _____
7. The tab formatting is inserted in this symbol if you set tabs before keying text. _____
8. This is the first step in the key line method of setting tabs for columns. _____
9. Column headings that are shorter than the column entries can be centered this way. _____
10. In many situations it is acceptable to align column headings here rather than center each one. _____

**Use the computer to determine answers for the situations below.**

Determine the left tab stops needed to center the two columns below between the left and right margins. Use the key line method. Allow for eight spaces between the columns.

| | |
|---|---|
| Valerie Smith | Director |
| Kim Sung | Assistant Director |
| Torvald Henderson | Office Manager |

1. Left tab stop for first column: _____
2. Left tab stop for second column: _____

Determine the tab stops needed to center the three columns below between the left and right margins. Use the key line method. Allow for ten spaces between the columns.

| | | |
|---|---|---|
| 5 reams stationery | @ 4.95 | 24.75 |
| 6 boxes pencils | @ 1.95 | 11.70 |
| 1 ergonomic chair | @ 345.62 | 345.62 |

3. Left tab stop for first column: _____
4. Decimal tab stop for second column: _____
5. Decimal tab stop for third column: _____

## Exercise 1

1. At a clear document screen, key the document shown in figure 8.6 by completing the following steps:
   a. Key the heading, **TRAINING & EDUCATION DEPARTMENT**, centered and bolded.
   b. Press Enter three times. (Be sure to return the paragraph alignment back to left.)
   c. Set left tabs at the 0.5-inch mark and the 3-inch mark on the Ruler by completing the following steps:
      (1) Click on the Show/Hide button on the Standard toolbar or press Shift + Ctrl + * to turn on the display of nonprinting characters.
      (2) Choose <u>V</u>iew, <u>R</u>uler to display the Ruler. (Skip this step if the Ruler is already displayed.)
      (3) Make sure the left tab symbol displays in the Tab Alignment button at the left side of the Ruler.
      (4) Position the arrow pointer below the 0.5-inch tick mark on the Ruler, then click the left mouse button.
      (5) Position the arrow pointer below the 3-inch tick mark on the Ruler, then click the left mouse button.
   d. Key the text in columns as shown in figure 8.6. Press the Tab key before keying each column entry. (Make sure you press Tab before keying the text in the first and second columns.)
2. Save the document and name it c08ex01.
3. Print c08ex01.
4. Close c08ex01.

**Figure 8.6**

```
           TRAINING & EDUCATION DEPARTMENT


      Brenda Hogue          Director
      Pauline Coffey        Trainer Supervisor
      James Zekes           Trainer Specialist
      Daniel Lagasa         Trainer Specialist
      Scott Sideres         Administrative Assistant
      My Trinh              Administrative Assistant
```

## Exercise 2

1. At a clear document screen, key the document shown in figure 8.7 by completing the following steps:
   a. Key the heading, **TRAINING SCHEDULE AND COSTS**, centered and bolded.
   b. Press Enter three times. (Be sure to return the paragraph alignment back to left.)
   c. Set a left tab at the 0.5-inch mark, a center tab at the 3.6-inch mark, and a right tab at the 5.5-inch mark by completing the following steps:
      (1) Choose <u>V</u>iew, <u>R</u>uler to display the Ruler. (Skip this step if the Ruler is already displayed.)
      (2) Make sure the left tab symbol displays in the Tab Alignment button at the left side of the Ruler.
      (3) Position the arrow pointer below the 0.5-inch tick mark on the Ruler, then click the left mouse button.

(4) Position the arrow pointer on the Tab Alignment button at the left side of the Ruler, then click the left mouse button until the center tab symbol displays.

(5) Position the arrow pointer below the 3.6-inch tick mark on the Ruler then click the left mouse button.

(6) Position the arrow pointer on the Tab Alignment button at the left side of the Ruler, then click the left mouse button until the right tab symbol displays.

(7) Position the arrow pointer below the 5.5-inch tick mark on the Ruler, then click the left mouse button.

d. Key the text in columns as shown in figure 8.7. Press the Tab key before keying each column entry. (Make sure you press Tab before keying the text in the first, second, and third columns. Press Shift + Enter twice after each line of text in the columns. This begins a new line without beginning a new paragraph.)

2. Save the document and name it c08ex02.
3. Print c08ex02.
4. Close c08ex02.

**Figure 8.7**

TRAINING SCHEDULE AND COSTS

| | | |
|---|---|---|
| Spreadsheet | February 28 | $195 |
| Word processing | March 5 | 170 |
| Desktop publishing | March 20 | 240 |
| Electronic mail | April 3 | 95 |

## Exercise 3

1. Open tab01. This document is located on your student data disk.
2. Save the document with Save As and name it c08ex03.
3. Move the tab stops so the columns are more balanced by completing the following steps:
   a. Position the insertion point on any character in the columns (the lines end with Shift + Enter).
   b. Position the arrow pointer on the left tab symbol at the 0.5-inch mark.
   c. Hold down the left mouse button, drag the left tab symbol to the 1.2-inch mark on the Ruler, then release the mouse button.
   d. Position the arrow pointer on the decimal tab symbol at the 3.5-inch mark.
   e. Hold down the left mouse button, drag the decimal tab symbol into the document screen, then release the mouse button. (This deletes the tab and merges the second column of text with the first column.)
   f. Click on the Tab Alignment button at the left side of the Ruler until the decimal tab symbol displays.
   g. Position the arrow pointer on the 4.5-inch mark on the Ruler, then click the left mouse button.
   h. Deselect the text.
4. Center the document vertically on the page.
5. Save the document again with the same name (c08ex03).
6. Print c08ex03.
7. Close c08ex03.

# Exercise 4

1. At a clear document screen, key the document shown in figure 8.8 by completing the following steps:
   a. Key the headings in the memorandum, the first paragraph, then center and bold the title, *MAY ACTIVITIES*. (Be sure to return the paragraph alignment back to left.)
   b. With the cursor a double space below the title, use the Tabs dialog box to set a left tab at the 1-inch mark and the 2.2-inch mark by completing the following steps:
      (1) Choose Format, Tabs.
      (2) At the Tabs dialog box choose Clear All.
      (3) Make sure Left is selected in the Alignment section, of the dialog box. (If not, position the arrow pointer in the circle before the Left option, then click the left mouse button.)
      (4) Key **1**. (The insertion point should automatically be positioned in the Tab Stop Position text box. If not, choose Tab Stop Position.)
      (5) Choose Set.
      (6) Key **2.2**.
      (7) Choose Set.
      (8) Choose OK or press Enter.
   c. Key the text in columns as shown in figure 8.8. Press the Tab key before keying each column entry. (Make sure you press Tab before keying the text in the first and second columns.)
2. Key the remaining text in the memorandum.
3. Save the memorandum and name it c08ex04.
4. Print c08ex04.
5. Close c08ex04.

**Figure 8.8**

```
DATE:      April 6, 1996

TO:        Jon Struebing, Editor

FROM:      Martha Carl-Rivera

SUBJECT: MAY NEWSLETTER


A variety of exciting activities are planned for May.  Please
include the following information in the May newsletter.

                      MAY ACTIVITIES

          May 6        Teacher Appreciation Week
          May 10       Senior Prom
          May 13       Bicycle Safety Week
          May 18       High School Special Olympics
          May 20       Student Leadership Week

The Activities Committee is busy planning end-of-the-school-year
activities.  If the final schedule is ready before the publication
date of the May newsletter, I will fax it to you.

xx:c08ex04
```

## Exercise 5

1. At a clear document screen, key the document shown in figure 8.9 by completing the following steps:
   a. Key the title, **PETERSBURG CLINIC**, bolded and centered, then press the Enter key twice.
   b. Key the subtitle, **Immunization Dates**, bolded and centered, then press the Enter key three times. (Be sure to return the paragraph alignment to left.)
   c. Display the Tabs dialog box, then set left tabs at the 1-inch mark, the 2.7-inch mark, and the 4.2-inch mark; set vertical bar tabs at the 2.2-inch mark and the 3.8-inch mark by completing the following steps:
      (1) Choose Format, Tabs.
      (2) At the Tabs dialog box choose Clear All.
      (3) Make sure Left is selected in the Alignment section of the dialog box. (If not, position the arrow pointer in the circle before the Left option, then click the left mouse button.)
      (4) Key **1**. (The insertion point should automatically be positioned in the Tab Stop Position text box. If not, choose Tab Stop Position.)
      (5) Choose Set.
      (6) Key **2.7**.
      (7) Choose Set.
      (8) Key **4.2**.
      (9) Choose Set.
      (10) Key **2.2**.
      (11) Choose Bar.
      (12) Choose Set.
      (13) Key **3.8**.
      (14) Choose Bar.
      (15) Choose Set.
      (16) Choose OK or press Enter.
   d. Key the text in columns as shown in figure 8.9. Press the Tab key before keying each column entry. (Word will automatically insert the vertical bar.)
2. Save the document and name it c08ex05.
3. Print c08ex05.
4. Close c08ex05.

**Figure 8.9**

PETERSBURG CLINIC

Immunization Dates

| April 2 | May 8 | June 6 |
| April 9 | May 15 | June 13 |
| April 16 | May 22 | June 20 |
| April 23 | May 29 | June 27 |

## Exercise 6

1. At a clear document screen, create the document shown in figure 8.10 by completing the following steps:
   a. Change the font to 12-point Colonna MT.
   b. Change the line spacing to double (2).
   c. Center and bold the title, *TABLE OF CONTENTS*.

d. Press Enter once. (Be sure to return the alignment of the paragraph back to left.)
e. Set a left tab at the 0.5-inch mark and a right tab with dot leaders at the 5.5-inch mark by completing the following steps:
    (1) Choose Format, Tabs.
    (2) At the Tabs dialog box choose Clear All.
    (3) Make sure Left is selected in the Alignment section of the dialog box. (If not, choose Left.)
    (4) Make sure the insertion point is positioned in the Tab Stop Position text box, then key **0.5**.
    (5) Choose Set.
    (6) Key **5.5**.
    (7) Choose Right. To do this with the mouse, click on the circle before the Right option in the Alignment section of the dialog box. If you are using the keyboard, press Alt + R.
    (8) Choose 2 ..... To do this with the mouse, click on the circle before the 2 .... option in the Leader section of the dialog box. If you are using the keyboard, press Alt + 2.
    (9) Choose Set.
    (10) Choose OK or press Enter.
f. Key the text in columns as shown in figure 8.10. Press the Tab key before keying each column entry. (Make sure you press Tab before keying the text in the first and second columns.)
2. Save the document and name it c08ex06.
3. Print c08ex06.
4. Close c08ex06.

**Figure 8.10**

TABLE OF CONTENTS

What is Desktop Publishing?........................................................................2

Basic Hardware ..........................................................................................5

Basic Software ...........................................................................................8

Design and Gestalt ......................................................................................11

Basic Principles of Design .............................................................................15

Graphics Modes...........................................................................................21

Graphics Production .....................................................................................24

Graphics Applications ...................................................................................28

Design of Graphics .......................................................................................32

## Exercise 7

1. At a clear document screen, key the document shown in figure 8.11 by completing the following steps:
    a. Key the letter through the first paragraph.
    b. With the insertion point a double space below the first paragraph, set a left tab at the 1-inch mark and a right tab with hyphen leaders at the 5-inch mark by completing the following steps:
        (1) Choose Format, Tabs.
        (2) At the Tabs dialog box choose Clear All.
        (3) Make sure Left is selected in the Alignment section of the dialog box. (If not, choose Left.)

(4) Make sure the insertion point is positioned in the <u>T</u>ab Stop Position text box, then key **1**.

(5) Choose <u>S</u>et.

(6) Key **5**.

(7) Choose <u>R</u>ight. To do this with the mouse, click on the circle before the <u>R</u>ight option in the Alignment section of the dialog box. If you are using the keyboard, press Alt + R.

(8) Choose <u>3</u> -----. To do this with the mouse, click on the circle before the <u>3</u> ----- option in the Leader section of the dialog box. If you are using the keyboard, press Alt + 3.

(9) Choose <u>S</u>et.

(10) Choose OK or press Enter.

c. Key the text in columns as shown in figure 8.11. Press the Tab key before keying each column entry. (Make sure you press Tab before keying the text in the first and second columns.)

d. After keying the column text, press the Enter key twice, then key the remaining text of the letter.

2. Save the document and name it c08ex07.

3. Print c08ex07.

4. Close c08ex07.

---

**Figure 8.11**

May 7, 1996


Mr. and Mrs. Larry Caldwell
12032 South 42nd Street
San Francisco, CA 97043

Dear Mr. and Mrs. Caldwell:

Hotel reservations for your trip to the Hawaiian Islands have been finalized. As you requested, all hotel reservations have been made at Grand Palace hotels. Reservations have been confirmed for the following dates:

          Maui Grand Palace --------------- July 2-6
          Grand Palace Resort ------------ July 7-9
          Grand Palace Seaside --------- July 10-15
          Honolulu Grand Palace -------- July 16-20

Your airline reservations have not been confirmed. I am still waiting for a reduction in price. I have heard that airlines will be lowering their rates during the next two weeks. As soon as the airfare is reduced below $500, I will make your flight reservations.

Will you need a car while you are vacationing in Hawaii? Please let me know if you would like me to reserve a car for you at each island.

Sincerely,


Jennifer Price

xx:c08ex07

# Exercise 8

1. At a clear document screen, key the document shown in figure 8.12 by completing the following steps:
   a. Key the title, **PETERSBURG SCHOOL DISTRICT**, centered and bolded.
   b. Press the Enter key three times.
   c. Determine the tab stops using the key line method by completing the following steps:
      (1) Display the Ruler. (Skip this step if the Ruler is already displayed.)
      (2) Click on the Show/Hide button on the Standard toolbar to turn on the display of nonprinting characters. (Skip this step if nonprinting characters are already displayed.)
      (3) Press Ctrl + E or click on the Center button on the Standard toolbar.
      (4) Key **Assistant Superintendent**, then press the space bar eight times.
      (5) Key **Dorothy Warner**.
      (6) Position the arrow pointer on the Ruler immediately above the *A* in *Assistant*, then click the left mouse button. (This inserts a left tab on the Ruler. Before setting the tab, make sure the left tab symbol displays in the Tab Alignment button.)
      (7) Position the arrow pointer on the Ruler immediately above the *D* in *Dorothy* then click the left mouse button.
      (8) Delete the key line text but *not* the paragraph mark.
      (9) Press Ctrl + L or click on the Left button on the Standard toolbar. (This changes the paragraph alignment to left.)
   d. Key the text in columns as shown in figure 8.12. Press the Tab key before keying each column entry. (Make sure you press Tab before keying the text in the first and second columns. Press the Enter key twice after each line of text.)
2. Save the document and name it c08ex08.
3. Print c08ex08.
4. Close c08ex08.

**Figure 8.12**

| PETERSBURG SCHOOL DISTRICT | |
|---|---|
| Superintendent | Dorothy Warner |
| Assistant Superintendent | David O'Shea |
| Curriculum/Instruction | Damion Japhet |
| Support Services | Donna Schmitt |
| Information Services | Alex Perozzo |

# Exercise 9

1. At a clear document screen, key the document shown in figure 8.13 by completing the following steps:
   a. Key the title, **KEYBOARDING CLASS**, centered and bolded.
   b. Press the Enter key three times.
   c. Determine the tab stops using the key line method by completing the following steps:
      (1) Display the Ruler. (Skip this step if the Ruler is already displayed.)
      (2) Press Ctrl + E or click on the Center button on the Standard toolbar.
      (3) Key **Wendy Thomas-Hart**, then press the space bar six times.
      (4) Key **100**, then press the space bar six times.
      (5) Key **100**, then press the space bar six times.

(6) Key **100**.

(7) Position the arrow pointer on the Ruler immediately above the *W* in *Wendy*, then click the left mouse button. (This inserts a left tab on the Ruler. Before setting the tab, make sure the left tab symbol displays in the Tab Alignment button.)

(8) Click on the Tab Alignment button at the left side of the Ruler until the right tab symbol displays.

(9) Position the arrow pointer on the Ruler immediately above the space just after the *100* in the second column, then click the left mouse button.

(10) Position the arrow pointer on the Ruler immediately above the space just after the *100* in the third column, then click the left mouse button.

(11) Position the arrow pointer on the Ruler immediately above the space just after the *100* in the fourth column, then click the left mouse button.

(12) Delete the key line text but *not* the paragraph mark.

(13) Press Ctrl + L or click on the Left button on the Standard toolbar. (This changes the paragraph alignment to left.)

(14) Click on the Tab Alignment button until the left tab symbol displays.

   d. Key the text in columns as shown in figure 8.13. Bold the column headings. Press the Tab key before keying each column entry.

2. Save the document and name it c08ex09.
3. Print c08ex09.
4. Close c08ex09.

**Figure 8.13**

**KEYBOARDING CLASS**

| Name | #1 | #2 | #3 |
|------|----|----|----|
| Charles Silvers | 78 | 80 | 84 |
| Wendy Thomas-Hart | 75 | 80 | 78 |
| Jane Harmsen | 96 | 94 | 98 |
| Alma Frazier | 74 | 68 | 73 |
| Jeff Wayman | 100 | 94 | 97 |
| Monica Churchill | 64 | 74 | 82 |
| Pat DeRosier | 97 | 89 | 100 |
| Diane Garneau | 74 | 85 | 78 |
| Richard Itami | 98 | 100 | 94 |

## SKILL ASSESSMENTS

### Assessment 1

1. At a clear document screen, change the font to 12-point Arial, then key the document shown in figure 8.14. (Be sure to bold the title.) Before keying the text in columns, set a left tab at the 0.8-inch mark, the 3.1-inch mark, and the 4.3-inch mark on the Ruler.
2. After keying the text in the columns, center the document vertically on the page.
3. Save the document and name it c08sa01.
4. Print c08sa01.
5. Close c08sa01.

Figure 8.14

**FINANCIAL PLANNING WORKSHOPS**

| | | |
|---|---|---|
| Estate Planning | 04/09/96 | 6:30 - 8:30 |
| Saving for College | 04/16/96 | 7:00 - 8:30 |
| Preparing for Retirement | 05/08/96 | 6:00 - 8:00 |
| High-Yield Investments | 05/15/96 | 7:00 - 9:00 |

## Assessment 2

1. At a clear document screen, key the document shown in figure 8.15. Before keying the text in columns, display the Tabs dialog box, clear all tabs, then set a left tab at the 0.8-inch mark, and right tabs at the 2.9-inch mark, the 4-inch mark, and the 5.1-inch mark.
2. After keying the memorandum, save the document and name it c08sa02.
3. Print c08sa02.
4. Close c08sa02.

Figure 8.15

```
DATE:     October 15, 1996

TO:       Jon Struebing, Editor

FROM:     Dorothy Warner, Superintendent

SUBJECT:  SCHOOL LEVY


With the recent passing of the school levy, I would like the  following
information presented in the next newsletter to help community members
understand how levy dollars are utilized.

The operations levy will raise $6.3 million in 1997 and $6.9 million in
1998.  The computer levy will raise $4 million over three years.  The bus
levy will raise $1 million over two years.  The bond was approved by
voters in 1993.

The following information shows the projected tax rates per $1,000 of
assessed property value for 1997, 1998, and 1999.

                   1997      1998      1999

         Operations    $3.98     $3.95     $0.00
         Computers      1.04      0.98      0.77
         Bus            0.31      0.28      0.00
         Bond           3.12      3.12      3.12

Money from the school bus levy will help purchase new school buses.  These
new buses will save taxpayers thousands of dollars through lower
maintenance and fuel costs.  The computer levy will purchase computers,
printers, and related hardware and software for student use.  Computers
and communications technology are an essential part of ensuring that every
student who graduates has the skills to compete in the job market.  Every
school in the district will receive equipment funded by the computer levy.

xx:c08sa02
```

## Assessment 3

1. At a clear document window, key the document shown in figure 8.16 with the following specifications:
   a. Change the font to 12-point Times New Roman.
   b. Bold and center the title as shown.
   c. Press the Enter key three times, then change the line spacing to 2.
   d. Before keying the text in columns, display the Tabs dialog box, then set a left tab at the 1-inch mark and the 1.5-inch mark, and a right tab with dot leaders at the 5-inch mark. Press Shift + Enter to end each line in the columns.
2. Save the document and name it c08sa03.
3. Print c08sa03.
4. Close c08sa03.

---

**Figure 8.16**

**TABLE OF CONTENTS**

Introduction ............................................................. 1

Page Assembly Basics ............................................. 2

    Source Files ..................................................... 7

    Text Functions ................................................. 9

    Graphics Functions ........................................ 11

    Conclusion ...................................................... 14

Word Processing and Page Assembly .................. 15

    Tagging and Coding ...................................... 17

    Data Processing and ASCII ......................... 19

    Conclusion ...................................................... 21

---

## Assessment 4

1. Open c08sa03.
2. Save the document with Save As and name it c08sa04.
3. Position the insertion point anywhere in the columns of text, then move the tab symbols on the Ruler as follows:
   a. Move the left tab symbol at the 1-inch mark to the 0.5-inch mark.
   b. Move the left tab symbol at the 1.5-inch mark to the 1-inch mark.
   c. Move the right tab symbol at the 5-inch mark to the 5.5-inch mark.
4. Center the document vertically on the page.
5. Save the document again with the same name (c08sa04).
6. Print c08sa04.
7. Close c08sa04.

## Assessment 5

1. At a clear document screen, key the document shown in figure 8.17. Use the key line method to determine the tab settings.
2. Save the document and name it c08sa05.
3. Print c08sa05.
4. Close c08sa05.

Figure 8.17

**NURSING DEPARTMENT**

| | |
|---|---|
| Intensive Care Unit | Benjamin Moon |
| Emergency Room | Rosemary Stratten |
| Labor and Delivery | Rafael Ohala |
| Coronary Care Unit | Lisa Murray |
| Surgical Unit | Joan Harris-Lee |
| Medical Services | Sandra Ellerbe |
| Pediatrics | Alyce Arevalo |

## Assessment 6

1. At a clear document screen, change the left and right margins to 1 inch, then key the text shown in figure 8.18 in an appropriate business letter format. Use the key-line method to determine the tab stops for the text shown in columns.
2. After keying the letter, save it and name it c08sa06.
3. Print c08sa06.
4. Close c08sa06.

Figure 8.18

March 20, 1996


Mr. and Mrs. James Henning
3220 South Soundview Drive
Tacoma, WA 98044

Dear Mr. and Mrs. Henning:

The travel experts at Travel Advantage have specially chosen the most exciting and inviting vacation destinations for you and your family.  This month, we are offering a package travel plan to St. Thomas, a dazzling Caribbean island.  At St. Thomas, you will be able to enjoy boating, swimming, sailing, windsurfing, scuba diving, golfing, and tennis.

The St. Thomas package includes round-trip airfare, seven nights' hotel accommodations, and round-trip airport transfers.  The prices for this exciting vacation vary depending on the city of departure. Sample prices are shown below.

|  | Regular | TA Price |
|---|---|---|
| Los Angeles | $1,320 | $1,088 |
| Dallas | 1,220 | 930 |
| Chicago | 1,250 | 980 |
| New York | 1,040 | 880 |

This package offer includes a bonus of 2-for-1 pricing on sightseeing tours, a diving course at Bolongo Bay, and a full-day or half-day catamaran cruise.

Call us now to make your reservations for beautiful St. Thomas. All prices are firm through the end of April.  After that, prices may vary depending on hotel availability.

Sincerely,

TRAVEL ADVANTAGE



Edward McMillan
Travel Consultant

xx:c08sa06

# Inserting Headers and Footers

Upon successful completion of chapter 9, you will be able to finish multiple-page reports with specific page characteristics including headers, footers, and page numbering.

In a Word document, text can be created that prints at the top of every page and/or that prints at the bottom of every page. In addition, page numbering can be added to a Word document.

## Working with Headers and Footers

Text that appears at the top of every page is called a *header* and text that appears at the bottom of every page is referred to as a *footer*. Headers and footers are common in manuscripts, textbooks, reports, and other publications.

### Creating a Header or Footer

With the Header and Footer option from View, you can create a header or a footer. When you choose View, then Header and Footer, Word automatically changes the viewing mode to Page Layout, dims the text in the document, inserts a pane where the header or footer is entered, and inserts the Header and Footer toolbar. Figure 9.1 shows a document with a header pane and the Header and Footer toolbar displayed.

By default, the insertion point is inserted in the header pane. Key the header text in the header pane. Header text can be formatted in the same manner as text in the document. For example, the font of header text can be changed, character formatting such as bolding, italicizing, and underlining can be added, margins can be changed, and much more.

*Figure 9.1*
*Header Pane and*
*Header and Footer*
*Toolbar*

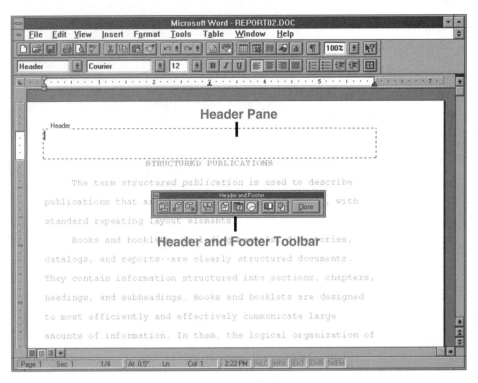

As an example of how to create a header, you would complete the following steps to create the header *Desktop Publishing in the 90s*:

1. Open the document where you want the header created.
2. Choose View, Header and Footer.
3. Key **Desktop Publishing in the 90s** in the header pane.
4. Choose Close. (To do this with the mouse, click on the Close button. If you are using the keyboard, press Alt + Shift + C.)

Choosing Close returns you to the previous view and displays the document text in black and the header text dimmed. If the Normal viewing mode was selected before a header was created, you are returned to the Normal viewing mode. If the Page Layout view was selected before a header was created, you are returned to that viewing mode.

In the Normal viewing mode a header or footer does not display on the screen. A header or footer will display dimmed in the Page Layout viewing mode. If you want to view how a header and/or footer will print, display Print Preview.

By default, a header and/or footer prints on every page in the document. Later in this chapter you will learn how to create headers/footers for specific sections of a document.

Creating a footer is similar to creating a header. To create a footer you must switch to the footer pane. To do this, click on the Switch Between Header and Footer button on the Header and Footer toolbar. Figure 9.2 displays the buttons on the Header and Footer toolbar, the name of the button, and what each button will perform.

| Click on this button | Named | To do this: |
|---|---|---|
| | Switch Between Header and Footer | Switch between the header pane and the footer pane. |
| | Show Previous | Show previous section's header/footer. |
| | Show Next | Show next section's header/footer. |
| | Same As Previous | Link/Unlink header/footer to or from previous section. |
| | Page Numbers | Insert page number in header/footer. |
| | Date | Insert date in header/footer. |
| | Time | Insert time in header/footer. |
| | Page Setup | Display Page Setup dialog box. |
| | Show/Hide Document Text | Turn on/off the display of document text. |
| Close | Close | Close header/footer pane. |

Figure 9.2
Header and Footer
Toolbar Buttons

As an example of how to create a footer, you would complete the following steps to create the footer *Trends in Desktop Publishing*:

1. Open the document where you want the footer created.
2. Choose View, Header and Footer.
3. Click on the Switch Between Header and Footer button on the Header and Footer toolbar (the first button). (Clicking on this button switches from a header pane to a footer pane.)
4. Key **Trends in Desktop Publishing**.
5. Choose Close.

When creating a header or footer, the main document text is displayed but dimmed. This dimmed text can be hidden while creating a header or footer by clicking on the Show/Hide Document Text button on the Header and Footer toolbar. To redisplay the dimmed document text, click on the button again.

## Formatting a Header or Footer

Header or footer text does not take on the character formatting of the document. For example, if you change the font for the document text, header or footer text remains at the default font. Margin changes made to the document text, however, do affect header or footer text.

If you want header or footer text character formatting to be the same as the document text, you must format the header or footer text. Format header or footer text in the header or footer pane in the normal manner.

A header or footer contains three alignment settings. If you want text aligned at the left margin, make sure the insertion point is positioned at the left side of the header or footer pane, then key the text. To center text in the header or footer pane, press the Tab key. This moves the insertion point to a preset tab stop. Pressing the Tab key twice will move the insertion point to the right margin of the header or footer pane. Text keyed at this tab stop will be right aligned.

With buttons on the Header and Footer toolbar, you can insert page numbering and the date and/or time in a header or footer. To insert page numbering in a header or footer, display the header or footer pane, then click on the Page Numbers button on the Header and Footer toolbar. This inserts the page number of the page where the insertion point is currently located. The correct page number will also appear on all other pages in the document. Click on the Date button on the Header and Footer toolbar to insert the current date in a header or footer and click on the Time button to insert the current time in a header or footer.

### Editing a Header or Footer

Changes can be made to a header or footer in a document. There are two methods you can use to display a header or footer for editing.

You can display a header or footer for editing in the Page Layout viewing mode. To do this, you would complete the following steps:

1. Open the document containing the header or footer to be edited.
2. Choose View, Page Layout or click on the Page Layout View button to the left of the horizontal scroll bar.
3. Double-click on the dimmed header or footer you want to edit.
4. Edit the header or footer as needed.
5. Double-click on the dimmed document text to make it active.

You can also display a header or footer for editing by completing the following steps:

1. Open the document containing the header or footer to be edited.
2. Choose View, Header and Footer.
3. Click on the Switch Between Header and Footer button (if you want to edit a footer), click on the Show Next button or the Show Previous, if necessary, to display the header or footer you want to edit.
4. When the proper header or footer pane is displayed, edit the header or footer as needed.
5. Click on the Close button on the Header and Footer toolbar.

### Deleting a Header or Footer

A header or footer can be deleted from a document by deleting it from the header or footer pane. To delete a header or footer, you would complete the following steps:

1. Open the document containing the header or footer to be deleted.
2. Change to the Page Layout viewing mode.
3. Double-click on the header or footer to be deleted.
4. With the header or footer displayed in the header or footer pane, select the header or footer text, then press the Delete key.
5. Click on the Close button on the Header and Footer toolbar to close the header or footer pane. (You can also close the header or footer pane by double-clicking on the dimmed document text.)

A header or footer pane can also be displayed by choosing View, Header and Footer, then clicking on the Switch Between Header and Footer, the Show Next, or the Show Previous buttons until the desired header or footer is displayed.

## Positioning a Header or Footer

Word inserts a header or footer 0.5 inches from the edge of the page. You can change this default position at the Page Setup dialog box. As an example of how to reposition a header, you would complete the following steps to change the distance from the edge of the paper for a header to 0.3 inches:

1. Open the document containing the header you want to reposition.
2. Choose View, Header and Footer.
3. Make sure the header you want to reposition is displayed. If not, click on the Show Next button or Show Previous button until it is visible.
4. Click on the Page Setup button on the Header and Footer toolbar.
5. At the Page Setup dialog box, click on the Margins tab to select it.
6. Click on the down-pointing triangle after Header until *0.3"* displays in the text box.
7. Choose OK or press Enter.
8. Click on the Close button on the Header and Footer toolbar to close the header pane.

A header or footer can be positioned closer to the edge of the page by decreasing the number in the Header or Footer text box at the Page Setup dialog box. A header or footer can be positioned further from the edge of the page by increasing the number in the Header or Footer text box. If you increase the number, make sure the document top or bottom margin can accommodate the header or footer.

# ■ Creating Different Headers/Footers in a Document

By default, Word will insert a header or footer on every page in the document. You can create different headers or footers in a document. For example, you can do the following:

- create a unique header or footer on the first page;
- omit a header or footer on the first page;
- create different headers or footers for odd and even pages; or
- create different headers or footers for sections in a document.

## Creating a First Page Header/Footer

A different header or footer can be created on the first page of a document. As an example of how to create a different first page footer, you would complete the following steps to create the footer *Procedures Manual* at the bottom of the first page and the footer *Preparing Documents* on all other pages in the document:

1. Open the document where you want the footers created.
2. Position the insertion point anywhere in the first page.
3. Choose View, Header and Footer.
4. Click on the Switch Between Header and Footer button. (This displays a footer pane.)
5. Click on the Page Setup button on the Header and Footer toolbar.
6. At the Page Setup dialog box, make sure the Layout tab is selected, then choose Different First Page.
7. Choose OK or press Enter.
8. Key the footer **Procedures Manual**.
9. Click on the Show Next button on the Header and Footer toolbar. (This opens another footer pane.)
10. Key **Preparing Documents**.
11. Click on the Close button on the Header and Footer toolbar.

After creating the footers, preview the document to see how the footers will display when printed.

You can follow similar steps to omit a header or footer on the first page. For example, to omit a footer on the first page, complete the same steps as listed above except do not key the text in step 8.

## Creating a Header/Footer for Odd/Even Pages

You may find it useful to print one header or footer on even pages and another header or footer on odd pages. You may want to do this in a document that will be bound after printing.

As an example of how to create footers on odd and even pages, you would complete the following steps to create the footer *Creative Designs* that prints on odd pages and the footer *Chapter 1* that prints on even pages:

1. Open the document where you want the footers created.
2. Position the insertion point anywhere in the first paragraph.
3. Choose View, Header and Footer.
4. Click on the Switch Between Header and Footer button. (This displays a footer pane.)
5. Click on the Page Setup button.
6. At the Page Setup dialog box, make sure the Layout tab is selected, then choose Different Odd and Even. (Make sure there is no X in the Different First Page option.)
7. Choose OK or press Enter.
8. At the odd footer pane, key **Creative Designs**.
9. Click on the Show Next button on the Header and Footer toolbar.
10. At the even footer pane, key **Chapter 1**.
11. Click on the Close button on the Header and Footer toolbar.

## Creating a Header/Footer for Different Sections

In chapter 7, you learned how to create different sections in a document. A section can be created that begins a new page or a continuous section can be created. If you want different headers and/or footers for pages in a document, divide the document into sections.

For example, if a document contains several chapters, you can create a section for each chapter, then create a different header or footer for each section. When dividing a document into sections by chapter, insert a section break that also begins a new page.

When a header or footer is created for a specific section in a document, the header or footer can be created for all previous and next sections or just for next sections. If you want a header or footer to print on only those pages in a section and not the previous or next sections, you must deactivate the Same As Previous button. This tells Word to not print the header or footer on previous sections. Word will, however, print the header or footer on following sections. If you do not want the header or footer to print on following sections, create a blank header or footer at the next section.

As an example of how to create a footer for a section of a document, you would complete the following steps to create the footer *Chapter 2: Contemporary Designs* for the second section of a document (not the first section or sections following the second section):

1. Open the document where you want the footer.
2. Position the insertion point in the second section.
3. Choose View, Header and Footer.
4. Click on the Switch Between Header and Footer button.
5. Click on the Same As Previous button to deactivate it.
6. At the footer pane, key **Chapter 2: Contemporary Designs**.
7. Click on the Show Next button.

Go To
Exercise
8

8. Click on the Same As Previous button to deactivate it.
9. At the footer pane, select the text (*Chapter 2: Contemporary Designs*), then delete it.
10. Click on the Close button on the Header and Footer toolbar.

When creating a header or footer for a specific section in a document, preview the document to determine if the header or footer appears on the correct pages.

## Inserting Page Numbering in a Document

Word, by default, does not print page numbers on a page. For documents such as memos and letters, this is appropriate. For longer documents, however, page numbers may be needed. Page numbers can be added to documents with options from the Page Numbers dialog box or in a header or footer.

Earlier in this chapter, you learned about the Page Numbers button on the Header and Footer toolbar. Clicking on this button inserts page numbering in a header or footer.

In addition to a header or footer, page numbering can be added to a document with options from the Page Numbers dialog box shown in figure 9.3. To display this dialog box, choose Insert, then Page Numbers.

The Position option at the Page Numbers dialog box contains two choices—Top of Page (Header) and Bottom of Page (Footer). With choices from the Alignment option, you can choose to insert page numbering at the left margin, center of the page, right margin, at the inside margin (the margin closest to the binding in bound material), and at the outside margin (the margin furthest from the binding in bound material).

If you turn on page numbering in a document, the page number will appear on all pages in the document including the first page. If you do not want page numbering to appear on the first page, remove the X from the Show Number on First Page option at the Page Numbers dialog box.

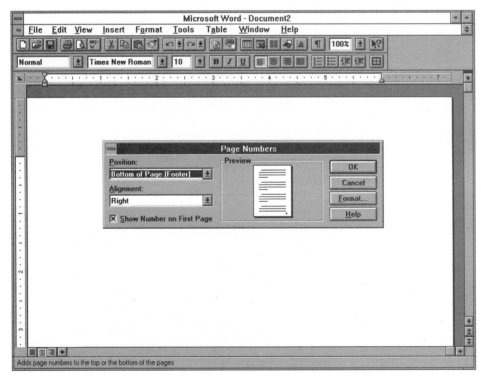

*Figure 9.3*
*Page Numbers*
*Dialog Box*

As an example of how to number pages in a document, you would complete the following steps to number all pages except the first page at the left margin at the bottom of the page:

1. Open the document where you want page numbering inserted.
2. Choose Insert, Page Numbers.
3. At the Page Numbers dialog box, make sure the Position option is Bottom of Page (Footer). If not, click on the down-pointing arrow after the option, then click on Bottom of Page (Footer).
4. Choose Alignment, then Left. To do this with the mouse, click on the down-pointing arrow to the right of the Alignment text box, then click on Left. If you are using the keyboard, press Alt + A, then press the down arrow key until Left is selected.
5. Choose Show Number on First Page (this removes the X from the option).
6. Choose OK or press Enter.

Page numbers, like headers and footers, do not display in the Normal viewing mode. To see page numbers in a document, change to the Page Layout viewing mode or display Print Preview.

### Deleting Page Numbering

Page numbering in a document can be deleted in the same manner as deleting a header or footer. To delete page numbering in a document, you would complete the following steps:

1. Open the document containing page numbering you want to delete.
2. Choose View, Header and Footer.
3. Display the header or footer pane containing the page numbering.
4. Select the page numbering, then press the Delete key.
5. Choose Close from the Header and Footer toolbar.

### Changing Page Numbering Format

At the Page Number Format dialog box shown in figure 9.4, you can change the numbering format, add chapter numbering, and specify where you want page numbering to begin and in what sections you want page numbering to appear. To display the Page Number Format dialog box, choose Insert, then Page Numbers. At the Page Numbers dialog box, choose Format.

*Figure 9.4*
*Page Number*
*Format Dialog Box*

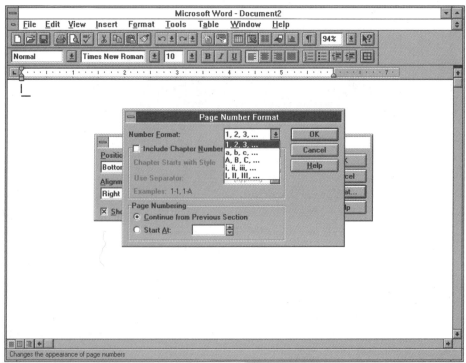

Choose the Number Format option from the Page Number Format dialog box to change the numbering from Arabic numbers (1, 2, 3, etc.), to lowercase letters (a, b, c, etc.), uppercase letters (A, B, C, etc.), lowercase Roman numerals (i, ii, iii, etc.), or uppercase Roman numerals (I, II, III, etc.).

Chapter numbering can be included in a document. Word will number chapters in a document if the chapter heading is formatted with a heading style. You will learn about heading styles in a later chapter.

By default, page numbering begins with 1 and continues sequentially from 1 through all pages and sections in a document. You can change the beginning page number with the Start At option at the Page Number Format dialog box. You can change the beginning page number at the beginning of the document or change the page number at the beginning of a section. As an example of how to change the beginning page number, you would complete the following steps to change the beginning page number to 1 for the third section of a document:

1. Open the document.
2. Position the insertion point in the third section of the document.
3. Choose Insert, Page Numbers.
4. At the Page Numbers dialog box, choose Format.
5. At the Page Number Format dialog box, choose Start At. (This inserts a 1 in the Start At text box.)
6. Choose OK or press Enter.
7. Choose OK or press Enter to close the Page Numbers dialog box.

## CHAPTER SUMMARY

- Text that appears at the top of every page is called a header; text that appears at the bottom of every page is called a footer.
- When you choose View then Header and Footer, Word automatically changes the viewing mode to Page Layout, dims the text in the document, inserts a pane where the header is entered, and also inserts the Header and Footer toolbar.
- To create a footer, switch to the footer pane by clicking on the Switch Between Header and Footer button on the Header and Footer toolbar.
- A header or footer does not display in the Normal viewing mode but will display dimmed in the Page Layout viewing mode. To see how the header or footer will print, display Print Preview.
- Header or footer text does not take on any character formatting applied to the document. If you want header or footer text character formatting to be the same as the document text, format that text in the header or footer pane in the normal manner.
- A header or footer contains three alignment settings: left, center, and right. Press the Tab key to move the insertion point to the center alignment setting, then press the Tab key again to move the insertion point to the right alignment setting.
- With buttons on the Header and Footer toolbar, you can insert page numbering and the date and/or time in a header or footer.
- You can edit a header or footer in the Page Layout viewing mode or in the header or footer pane.
- A header or footer can be deleted at the header or footer pane. In the Page Layout viewing mode, double-click on the header or footer. With the header or footer pane displayed, select the text, then press the Delete key.
- Word inserts a header or footer 0.5 inches from the edge of the page. A header or footer can be repositioned at the Page Setup dialog box.
- You can create more than one header or footer in a document.
- Insert page numbering in a document with options from the Page Numbers dialog box or in a header or footer.

| | **Mouse** | **Keyboard** |
|---|---|---|
| Create a Header/Footer | View, Header and Footer | View, Header and Footer |
| Print Preview | File, Print Preview; or click on Print Preview button on the Standard Toolbar | File, Print Preview |
| Page Setup dialog box | Click on Page Setup button on Header and Footer toolbar | |
| Page Numbers dialog box | Insert, Page Numbers | Insert, Page Numbers |

## CHECK YOUR UNDERSTANDING

**True/False:** Circle the letter T if the statement is true; circle the letter F if the statement is false.

T   F   1.   Text that appears at the top of every page is called a header.

T   F   2.   When creating a footer, Word automatically changes the viewing mode to Normal.

T   F   3.   Header or footer text is positioned 0.5" from the edge of the paper by default.

T   F   4.   The Header and Footer toolbar contains 12 buttons that can assist you in creating headers and footers.

T   F   5.   No more than two footers can be created in the same document.

T   F   6.   Any formatting that is applied to a document will automatically be applied to all headers and footers in the document.

T   F   7.   The only way to begin editing a header/footer is by choosing View, then Header and Footer.

T   F   8.   A unique header/footer is created on the first page of a document by choosing Different First Page at the Header and Footer toolbar.

T   F   9.   Delete a header/footer by deleting the first letter of the header/footer in the document.

T   F   10.   If you do not want the header or footer to print on following sections, create a blank header or footer at the next section.

**Completion:**   In the space provided, indicate the correct term, command, or number needed to complete the sentence.

1.   After choosing View, Header and Footer, the insertion point is automatically inserted in the _____ pane.

2.   To create a footer, click on the _____ button on the Header and Footer toolbar.

3.   A _____ appears at the bottom of every page.

4.   In addition to creating headers/footers for different pages in a document, they can also be created for different _____.

5.   If the header you wish to edit is not visible in the header/footer pane, choose _____ or _____ from the Header and Footer toolbar.

6.   Choose _____ to see how headers/footers will look on the page when printed.

7.   Create footers on odd and even pages at the _____ dialog box.

8.   Page numbers do not display in the _____ viewing mode.

9.   Delete page numbers in a document by first displaying the _____.

10.   Display the Page Number Format dialog box by choosing _____, then Page Numbers.

11.   Change the beginning page number with the _____ option at the Page Number Format dialog box.

## Exercise 1

1. Open report01.
2. Save the document with Save As and name it c09ex01.
3. Bold the title, *TYPE SPECIFICATION*, and the three headings: *Type Measurement*, *Type Size*, and *Type Style*.
4. Select the last four paragraphs of the document, then insert bullets. (Use the Bullets button on the Formatting toolbar.)
5. Create the header *Chapter 1: Basic Typography* that is bolded and prints at the left margin on every page by completing the following steps:
   a. Choose View, Header and Footer.
   b. Key **Chapter 1: Basic Typography** in the header pane.
   c. Click on the Close button on the Header and Footer toolbar.
6. Display Print Preview to see how the header will appear on each page when printed. (Press the Page Down key to view the second, then third page of the report.)
7. Check page breaks in the document and, if necessary, make corrections to the page breaks.
8. Save the document again with the same name (c09ex01).
9. Print c09ex01.
10. Close c09ex01.

## Exercise 2

1. Open report01.
2. Save the document with Save As and name it c09ex02.
3. Select the entire document, then change the font to 12-point Times New Roman.
4. Bold the title, *TYPE SPECIFICATION*, and the three headings: *Type Measurement*, *Type Size*, and *Type Style*.
5. Select the last four paragraphs (lines) of the document, then insert bullets. (Use the Bullets button on the Standard toolbar.)
6. Create the footer *Type Specification* in 12-point Times New Roman Bold that prints at the left margin of every page and *Page #* (where # represents the page number) in 12-point Times New Roman Bold that prints at the right margin of every page by completing the following steps:
   a. Choose View, Header and Footer.
   b. Click on the Switch Between Header and Footer button on the Header and Footer toolbar. (This displays the footer pane.)
   c. Change the font to 12-point Times New Roman Bold.
   d. Key **Type Specification**.
   e. Press the Tab key twice.
   f. Key **Page**, then press the space bar once.
   g. Click on the Page Numbers button on the Header and Footer toolbar. (The page number will display in the default font. After inserting the page number, select the number, then change the font to 12-point Times New Roman Bold.)
   h. Click on the Close button on the Header and Footer toolbar.
7. View the document in Print Preview.
8. Check page breaks in the document and, if necessary, make corrections to the page breaks.
9. Save the document again with the same name (c09ex02).
10. Print c09ex02.
11. Close c09ex02.

## Exercise 3

1. Open c09ex02.
2. Save the document with Save As and name it c09ex03.
3. Change the top margin for the report to 1.5 inches and the left and right margins to 1 inch.
4. Edit the footer by completing the following steps:
   a. Choose View, Header and Footer.
   b. Click on the Switch Between Header and Footer button on the Header and Footer toolbar. (This will display the footer pane containing the footer created in exercise 2.)
   c. Delete *Type Specification* from the footer pane. (Leave *Page #* at the right margin.)
   d. Key **Chapter 1: Basic Typography** at the left margin in the footer pane.
   e. Click on the Close button on the Header and Footer toolbar.
5. View the document in Print Preview.
6. Check page breaks in the document and, if necessary, make corrections to the page breaks.
7. Save the document again with the same name (c09ex03).
8. Print c09ex03.
9. Close c09ex03.

## Exercise 4

1. Open c09ex01.
2. Save the document with Save As and name it c09ex04.
3. Select the entire document, then change the font to 12-point Palatino (or Times New Roman, if your printer does not support Palatino).
4. Delete the header *Chapter 1: Basic Typography* by completing the following steps:
   a. Change to the Page Layout view.
   b. Double-click on the dimmed header.
   c. With the header displayed in the header pane, select the header text, then press the Delete key.
   d. Close the header pane by double-clicking on the dimmed document text.
5. Create the footer *Page - #* that prints centered and is set in 12-point Palatino (or Times New Roman). (Press the Tab key once to move the insertion point to the preset tab stop at the center of the footer. Click on the Page Numbers button on the Header and Footer toolbar to insert page numbering. The page number will display in the default font. Select the number, then change the font to 12-point Paltino or Times New Roman.)
6. Change the viewing mode back to Normal.
7. Check page breaks in the document and, if necessary, make corrections to the page breaks.
8. Save the document again with the same name (c09ex04).
9. Print c09ex04. (You may want to preview the document before printing.)
10. Close c09ex04.

## Exercise 5

1. Open c09ex04.
2. Save the document with Save As and name it c09ex05.
3. Change the top and bottom margins to 1.5 inches.
4. Change the position of the footer to 1 inch by completing the following steps:
   a. Choose View, Header and Footer.
   b. Click on the Switch Between Header and Footer button to display the footer pane containing the footer *Page - #*.
   c. Click on the Page Setup button on the Header and Footer toolbar.
   d. At the Page Setup dialog box, click on the Margins tab to select it.
   e. Click on the up-pointing triangle after Footer until *1"* displays in the text box.
   f. Choose OK or press Enter.
   g. Click on the Close button on the Header and Footer toolbar.

5. Check page breaks in the document and, if necessary, make corrections to the page breaks.
6. Save the document again with the same name (c09ex05).
7. Print c09ex05. (You may want to preview the document before printing.)
8. Close c09ex05.

## Exercise 6

1. Open c09ex01.
2. Save the document with Save As and name it c09ex06.
3. Delete the header containing the text *Chapter 1: Basic Typography*.
4. Create the header *Type Specification* that is bolded and prints at the right margin on all pages except the first page by completing the following steps:
   a. Position the insertion point anywhere in the first page.
   b. Choose View, Header and Footer.
   c. Click on the Page Setup button on the Header and Footer toolbar.
   d. At the Page Setup dialog box, make sure the Layout tab is selected, then choose Different First Page. (This inserts an X in the check box.)
   e. Choose OK or press Enter.
   f. With the header pane displayed, click on the Show Next button on the Header and Footer toolbar. (This opens another header pane.)
   g. Press the Tab key twice, turn on bold, then key **Type Specification**.
   h. Choose Close at the Header and Footer toolbar.
5. Save the document again with the same name (c09ex06).
6. Print c09ex06. (You may want to preview the document before printing.)
7. Close c09ex06.

## Exercise 7

1. Open c09ex04.
2. Save the document with Save As and name it c09ex07.
3. Delete the footer *Page - #*.
4. Create the footer *CHAPTER 1* that is set in 12-point Palatino Bold (or Times New Roman Bold) and prints at the left margin on all even pages and the footer *TYPE SPECIFICATION* that is set in 12-point Palatino Bold (or Times New Roman Bold) and prints at the right margin on all odd pages by completing the following steps:
   a. Choose View, Header and Footer.
   b. Click on the Switch Between Header and Footer button. (This displays the footer pane.)
   c. Click on the Page Setup button.
   d. At the Page Setup dialog box, make sure the Layout tab is selected, then choose Different Odd and Even. (Make sure there is no X in the Different First Page option.)
   e. Choose OK or press Enter.
   f. At the odd footer pane press the Tab key twice, then key **TYPE SPECIFICATION**.
   g. Select the footer text, *TYPE SPECIFICATION*, then change the font to 12-point Palatino Bold (or Times New Roman Bold).
   h. Click on the Show Next button on the Header and Footer toolbar.
   i. At the even footer pane key **CHAPTER 1**.
   j. Select the footer text, *CHAPTER 1*, then change the font to 12-point Palatino Bold (or Times New Roman Bold).
   k. Click on the Close button on the Header and Footer toolbar.
5. Save the document again with the same name (c09ex07).
6. Print c09ex07. (You may want to preview the document before printing.)
7. Close c09ex07.

## Exercise 8

1. Open report03. This document is located on your student data disk.
2. Save the document with Save As and name it c09ex08.
3. Change the top margin to 1.5 inches.
4. Insert a section break that begins a new page at the line containing the chapter title *CHAPTER 2: DEVELOPMENT OF TECHNOLOGY, 1950 - 1960.*
5. Create chapter and page numbering footers for each chapter by completing the following steps:
   a. Position the insertion point anywhere in the first page.
   b. Choose View, Header and Footer.
   c. Click on the Switch Between Header and Footer button.
   d. At the footer pane, turn on bold, key **Chapter 1**, then press the Tab key twice. This moves the insertion point to the right margin. Key **Page -** (select the page number, then bold it) then click on the Page Numbers button on the Header and Footer toolbar.
   e. Click on the Show Next button.
   f. Click on the Same As Previous button to deactivate it.
   g. Change *Chapter 1* to *Chapter 2* in the footer.
   h. Click on the Close button on the Header and Footer toolbar.
6. Check page breaks in the document and, if necessary, make corrections to the page breaks.
7. Save the document again with the same name (c09ex08).
8. Print c09ex08. (You may want to preview the document before printing.)
9. Close c09ex08.

## Exercise 9

1. Open report02. This document is located on your student data disk.
2. Save the document with Save As and name it c09ex09.
3. Change the top margin to 1.5 inches and the left and right margins to 1 inch.
4. Number pages at the bottom of the page at the right margin by completing the following steps:
   a. Choose Insert, Page Numbers.
   b. At the Page Numbers dialog box, make sure the Position option is Bottom of Page (Footer). If not, click on the down-pointing arrow after the option, then click on Bottom of Page (Footer).
   c. Choose Alignment, then Right. To do this with the mouse, click on the down-pointing arrow to the right of the Alignment text box, then click on Right. If you are using the keyboard, press Alt + A, then press the down arrow key until Right is selected.
   d. Choose OK or press Enter.
5. Check page breaks in the document and, if necessary, make corrections to the page breaks.
6. Save the document again with the same name (c09ex09).
7. Print c09ex09. (You may want to preview the document before printing.)
8. Close c09ex09.

## Exercise 10

1. Open c09ex09.
2. Save the document with Save As and name it c09ex10.
3. Change the page numbering to outside margins, use lowercase Roman numerals, and change the beginning number to 3 by completing the following steps:
   a. Choose Insert, Page Numbers.
   b. At the Page Numbers dialog box, change the Alignment to Outside.
   c. Choose Format.

    d. At the Page Number Format dialog box, change the Number Format to lowercase Roman numerals. To do this with the keyboard, click on the down-pointing arrow to the right of the Number Format option, then click on *i, ii, iii, ....* If you are using the keyboard, press Alt + F, then press the down arrow key until *i, ii, iii, ...* is selected.

    e. At the Page Number Format dialog box, choose Start At, then key **3**.

    f. Choose OK or press Enter.

    g. Choose OK or press Enter to close the Page Numbers dialog box.

4. Save the document again with the same name (c09ex10).
5. Print c09ex10. (You may want to preview the document before printing.)
6. Close c09ex10.

## SKILL ASSESSMENTS

### Assessment 1

1. Open report02. This document is located on your student data disk.
2. Save the document with Save As and name it c09sa01.
3. Make the following changes to the document:
   a. Select the entire document, then change the font to 12-point Times New Roman.
   b. Select the title, *STRUCTURED PUBLICATIONS*, then change the font to 14-point Arial Bold.
   c. Select the heading *TEMPLATE ELEMENTS*, then change the font to 12-point Arial Bold.
   d. Use the Format Painter to change the font to 12-point Arial Bold for the following headings and subheadings:

   > Column Grid
   > STANDING ELEMENTS
   > Running Heads/Feet
   > Page Numbers (Folios)
   > SERIAL ELEMENTS

   e. Create the footer *STRUCTURED PUBLICATIONS* that is set in 12-point Arial Bold and prints at the center of the footer pane.
4. Check page breaks in the document and, if necessary, make corrections to the page breaks.
5. Save the document again with the same name (c09sa01).
6. Print c09sa01. (You may want to preview the document before printing.)
7. Close c09sa01.

### Assessment 2

1. Open c09sa01.
2. Save the document with Save As and name it c09sa02.
3. Make the following changes to the document:
   a. Delete the footer in the document.
   b. Create the footer *Page #* (where the correct page number is inserted at the #) that is set in 12-point Arial Bold and prints at the right margin on all odd pages.
   c. Create the footer *STRUCTURED PUBLICATIONS* that is set in 12-point Arial Bold and prints at the left margin on all even pages.
4. Save the document again with the same name (c09sa02).
5. Print c09sa02. (You may want to preview the document before printing.)
6. Close c09sa02.

## Assessment 3

1. Open report04. This document is located on your student data disk.
2. Save the document with Save As and name it c09sa03.
3. Make the following changes to the document:
   a. Select the entire document, then change the font to 12-point New Century Schoolbook (or Times New Roman, if your printer does not support New Century Schoolbook).
   b. Select the title, *CHAPTER 1: FINISHED PUBLICATIONS,* then change the font to 12-point Century Gothic Bold.
   c. Use the Format Painter to change the font to 12-point Century Gothic Bold for the following titles, headings, and subheadings:
      LASER PRINTOUTS
      Time and Cost Considerations
      REPRODUCTION QUALITY
      Color
      CHAPTER 2: OFFSET PRINTING
      IMAGESETTING
      WYSIWYG
      Output Options
      METAL-PLATE OFFSET PRINTING
      Preparing Mechanicals
      Pasteup
   d. Insert a section break that begins a new page at the beginning of the line containing the title *CHAPTER 2: OFFSET PRINTING.*
   e. Create the footer *CHAPTER 1: FINISHED PUBLICATIONS* that is set in 12-point Century Gothic Bold, is centered, and prints in the first section (the chapter 1 section).
   f. Create the footer *CHAPTER 2: OFFSET PRINTING* that is set in 12-point Century Gothic Bold, is centered, and prints in the second section (the chapter 2 section).
4. Check page breaks in the document and, if necessary, make corrections to the page breaks.
5. Save the document again with the same name (c09sa03).
6. Print c09sa03. (You may want to preview the document before printing.)
7. Close c09sa03.

# Creating Footnotes & Endnotes  10

Upon successful completion of chapter 10, you will be able to amend a researched business report with properly formatted footnotes or endnotes.

A research paper or report contains information from a variety of sources. To give credit to those sources, a footnote can be inserted in the document. A *footnote* is an explanatory note or reference that is printed at the bottom of the page. An *endnote* is also an explanatory note or reference that is printed at the end of the document.

Two steps are involved when creating a footnote or endnote. First, the note reference number is inserted in the document at the location where the note is referred to. The second step when creating a footnote or endnote is to key the note entry text.

## Creating Footnotes and Endnotes

Footnotes and endnotes are created in a similar manner. To create a footnote in a document, you would complete the following steps:

1. Position the insertion point at the location in the document where the reference number is to appear.
2. Choose Insert, Footnote.
3. At the Footnote and Endnote dialog box shown in figure 10.1, make sure Footnote is selected, then choose OK or press Enter.
4. At the footnote pane shown in figure 10.2, key the footnote entry text.
5. Choose Close or press Alt + Shift + C to close the footnote pane.

You can also create a footnote by positioning the insertion point at the location in the document where the reference number is to appear, then pressing Alt + Ctrl + F. This displays the footnote pane. Key the footnote text, then choose Close or press Alt + Shift + C to close the footnote pane.

Figure 10.1
Footnote and
Endnote Dialog Box

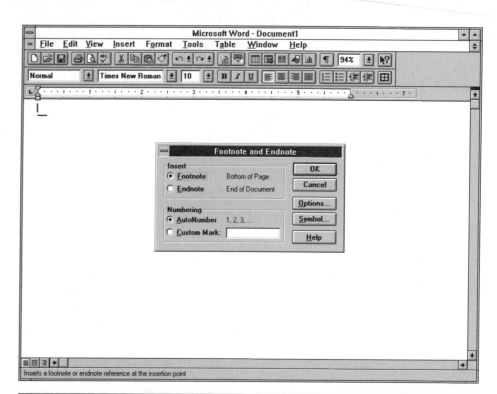

Figure 10.2
Footnote Pane

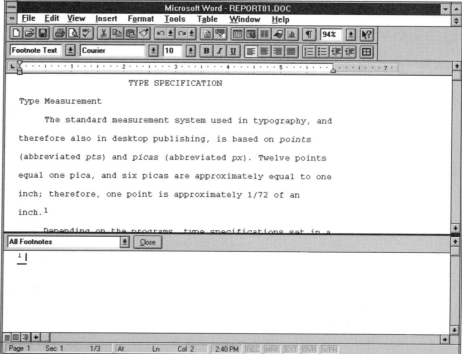

When creating footnotes, Word numbers footnotes with Arabic numbers (1, 2, 3, etc.).

If you press the Enter key after keying the footnote entry text, footnotes will be separated by a blank line (double space). If you do not want footnote text separated by a blank line, do not press the Enter key after keying the footnote entry text.

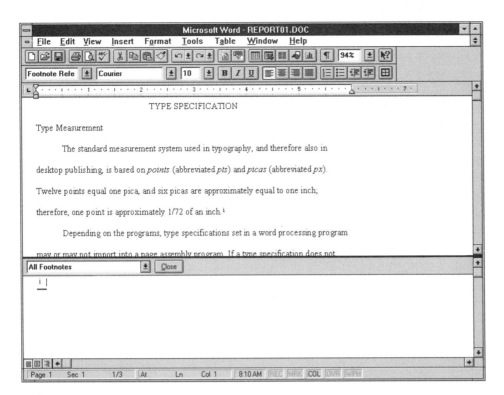

Figure 10.3
Endnote Pane

To create an endnote, you would complete the following steps:

1. Position the insertion point at the location in the document where the endnote reference number is to appear.
2. Choose Insert, Footnote.
3. At the Footnote and Endnote dialog box shown in figure 10.1, choose Endnote, then choose OK or press Enter.
4. At the endnote pane shown in figure 10.3, key the endnote entry text.
5. Choose Close or press Alt + Shift + C to close the endnote pane.

You can also create an endnote by positioning the insertion point at the location in the document where the endnote reference number is to appear, then pressing Alt + Ctrl + E. This displays the endnote pane. Key the endnote text, then choose Close or press Alt + Shift + C to close the endnote pane.

When creating endnotes, Word numbers endnotes with lowercase Roman numerals (i, ii, iii, etc.).

Press the Enter key after keying the endnote entry text if you want the endnote separated from the next endnote by a blank line (double space).

Footnotes and endnotes can be formatted in the normal manner. The note reference number and the note entry number print in the default font at 8-point. The note entry text prints in the default font at 10-point. The note reference and the note entry text can be formatted, if desired, to match the formatting of the document text.

## Printing Footnotes and Endnotes

When a document containing footnotes is printed, Word automatically reduces the number of text lines on a page by the number of lines in the footnote plus two lines for spacing between the text and the footnote. If there is not enough room on the page, the footnote number and footnote entry text are taken to the next page. Word separates the footnotes from the text with a 2-inch separator line that begins at the left margin. The footnote reference number in the document and the footnote number before the entry text print as a superscript number above the text line.

When endnotes are created in a document, Word prints all endnote references at the end of the document separated from the text by a 2-inch separator line.

## Viewing and Editing Footnotes and Endnotes

To edit existing footnote or endnote entry text, display the footnote or endnote text or the pane. There are several methods you can use for displaying the footnote or endnote text or pane.

In the Normal viewing mode, the footnote or endnote text does not display. To display footnotes or endnotes, change the viewing mode to Page Layout. Footnotes will display at the bottom of the page where they are referenced and endnotes will display at the end of the document. Footnotes or endnotes can be edited in the normal manner in the Page Layout viewing mode.

Display a footnote or endnote pane by choosing View, then Footnotes. (The Footnotes option is dimmed unless a document is open that contains footnotes or endnotes.) If the document contains footnotes, the footnote pane is opened. If the document contains endnotes, the endnote pane is opened. If the document contains both footnotes and endnotes, you can switch between the panes by choosing All Footnotes or All Endnotes from the view text box at the top of the footnote or endnote pane. To do this, click on the down-pointing arrow at the right side of the view text box at the top of the pane, then click on All Footnotes or All Endnotes.

You can display a footnote or endnote pane in the Normal viewing mode with the split bar. The split bar is the small black bar located above the up-pointing arrow at the top of the vertical scroll bar as shown in figure 10.4. To view a footnote or endnote pane, you would complete the following steps:

1. Position the arrow pointer on the split bar until it turns into a double line with an up- and down-pointing arrow.
2. Hold down the Shift key and the left mouse button.
3. Drag the split bar down to somewhere in the middle of the document screen, then release the mouse button and the Shift key.

To close a footnote or endnote pane, you can click on the Close button, drag the split bar back up to the top of the screen, or double-click on the split bar.

Another method for opening a footnote or endnote pane is to double-click on the footnote or endnote reference number in the document text. You can close a footnote or endnote pane by double-clicking on the number before the footnote or endnote entry text in the pane.

*Figure 10.4*
*Split Bar*

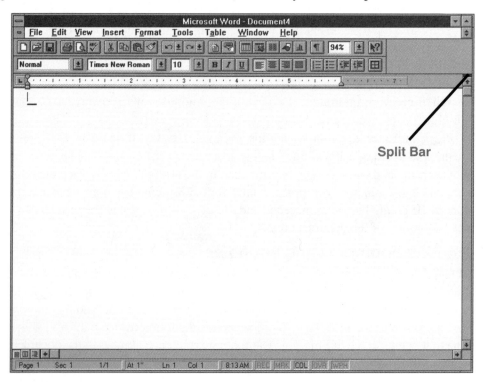

Split Bar

With the footnote or endnote pane visible, you can move the insertion point between the pane and the document. To do this with the mouse, position the arrow pointer in the document text, then click the left mouse button or position the arrow pointer in the pane, then click the left mouse button. If you are using the keyboard, press F6 to move the insertion point to the next pane. You can also press Shift + F6 which moves the insertion point to the previous pane.

## Finding Footnotes or Endnotes

In a document containing footnotes or endnotes, you can use the Go To option to move the insertion point to a particular footnote or endnote. For example, to move the insertion point to the footnote reference number 4, you would complete the following steps:

1. Open the document containing footnotes.
2. Choose Edit, Go To; press F5; or press Ctrl + G.
3. At the Go To dialog box, choose Go To What, then Footnote.
4. Choose Enter Footnote Number, then key **4**.
5. Choose Go To.
6. When the insertion point is positioned on footnote reference number 4, click on the Close button to close the Go To dialog box.

In the Page Layout view, you can move the insertion point to a particular footnote or endnote reference number in the document text or to an entry number in a footnote or endnote pane. To move the insertion point to a specific entry number in a footnote pane, position the insertion point on the reference number in the document text, then double-click the left mouse button. To move the insertion point to a specific reference number in the text document, double-click on the entry text number in the footnote or endnote pane.

## Moving, Copying, or Deleting Footnotes or Endnotes

Footnote or endnote reference numbers can be moved, copied, or deleted in a document. If a footnote or endnote reference number is moved, copied, or deleted, all footnotes or endnotes remaining in the document are automatically renumbered.

To move a footnote or endnote in a document, you would complete the following steps:

1. Select the reference mark of the footnote or endnote that you want moved.
2. Choose Edit, Cut.
3. Position the insertion point at the location where you want the footnote or endnote reference inserted.
4. Choose Edit, Paste.

You can also move a reference number to a different location in the document by selecting the reference number, then dragging it to the desired location.

To copy a reference number, complete steps similar to those listed above except you would choose Edit, Copy at step 2.

You can also copy a reference number to a different location in the document by selecting the reference number, holding down the Ctrl key, then dragging the reference number to the desired location.

To delete a footnote or endnote from a document, select the reference number, then press the Delete key or the Backspace key. When the reference number is deleted, the entry text is also deleted.

Figure 10.5
Footnote Pane Text
Box Drop-Down
Menu

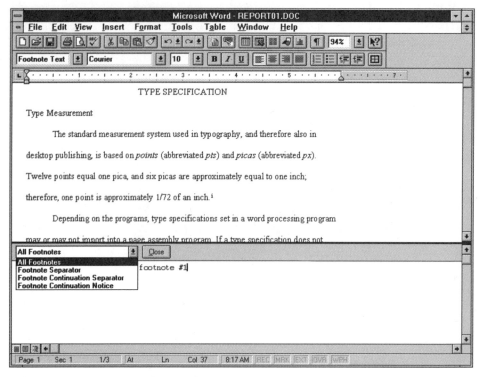

## Customizing Footnote or Endnote Settings

Footnotes or endnotes contain default settings. These default settings can be changed with options from the footnote or endnote pane or with options from the Note Options dialog box.

When a footnote or endnote pane is visible, a view text box displays at the upper left corner of the pane. If you click on the down-pointing arrow at the right side of this text box, a drop-down menu will display as shown in figure 10.5. (The options will change depending on whether a footnote or endnote pane is open.)

By default, Word inserts a 2-inch separator line that begins at the left margin and separates footnotes or endnotes from document text. Choose the *Footnote Separator* option to customize this line. When you choose *Footnote Separator*, the pane display changes and shows the default separator line. Edit this line as desired. For example, you can delete it or change the position of the line. After customizing the line, choose Close. Choose Reset if you want to reset the separator line back to the default. Complete similar steps to customize the Endnote separator line.

If a footnote or endnote continues across more than one page, Word inserts a continuation separator line between the note and the document text. This continuation separator line prints from the left to the right margin. Choose the *Footnote Continuation Separator* option if you want to customize the footnote continuation separator line. After customizing the line, choose Close to close the pane. Complete similar steps to customize a continuation separator line for endnotes.

If a footnote or endnote is continued on the next page you can add text indicating that the note is continued on the next page. To do this, choose the *Footnote Continuation Notice* option from the drop-down menu, key the text you want to indicate that the note is continued, then choose Close. Complete similar steps to add continuation text to endnotes.

With options from the Note Options dialog box with the All Footnotes tab selected shown in figure 10.6, you can further customize footnotes. The Note Options dialog box will display in a similar manner if the All Endnotes tab is selected. To display the Note Options dialog box, choose Insert, then Footnote. At the Footnote and Endnote dialog box, choose Options.

With the Place At option you can specify whether footnotes are printed at the bottom of the page or beneath text. By default, Word prints footnotes at the bottom of the page even if the text does not fill the entire page. Choose the Beneath Text option from Place At if you want the footnote to print below the last line of text on the page.

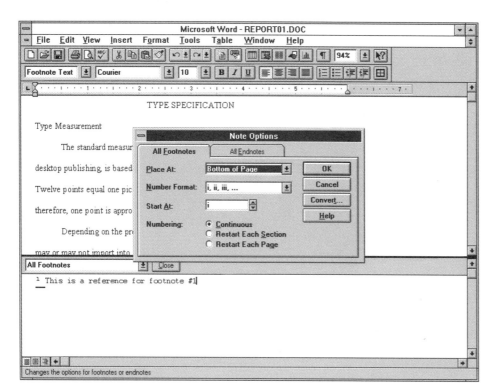

Figure 10.6
Note Options Dialog
Box with All
Footnotes Tab
Selected

The <u>P</u>lace At option at the Note Options dialog box with the All <u>E</u>ndnotes tab selected contains the choices End of Document or End of Section. At the default setting of End of Document, endnotes print at the end of the document. Change this to End of Section if you want endnotes to print at the end of the section in the document.

Word numbers footnotes with Arabic numbers and endnotes with lowercase Roman numerals. Change this default numbering with the <u>N</u>umber Format option at the Note Options dialog box. You can choose Arabic numbers, lowercase letters, uppercase letters, lowercase Roman numerals, uppercase Roman numerals, or special symbols.

Footnotes or endnotes are numbered sequentially beginning with 1. Use the Start <u>A</u>t option from the Note Options dialog box if you want to change the beginning footnote or endnote number.

Word numbers footnotes or endnotes sequentially from the beginning to the end of a document. With options from the Numbering section of the Note Options dialog box you can change this to Restart Each <u>S</u>ection which restarts numbering at the beginning of each section or Restart Each Page which restarts numbering at the beginning of each page. (The Restart Each Page option is not available if the All <u>E</u>ndnotes tab is selected.)

Footnotes are numbered with Arabic numbers and endnotes are numbered with lowercase Roman numerals. This can be changed to a symbol, if necessary. If you want to number footnotes or endnotes with a symbol, choose the <u>C</u>ustom Mark option at the Footnote and Endnote dialog box. (To display the Header and Footer dialog box, choose <u>I</u>nsert, <u>F</u>ootnote.) To specify a symbol, choose <u>S</u>ymbol. This displays the Symbol dialog box. At the Symbol dialog box, choose the desired symbol, then choose OK or press Enter. This inserts the selected symbol in the <u>C</u>ustom Mark text box. Continue creating the footnote or endnote in the normal manner.

**Figure 10.7**
**Convert Notes**
**Dialog Box**

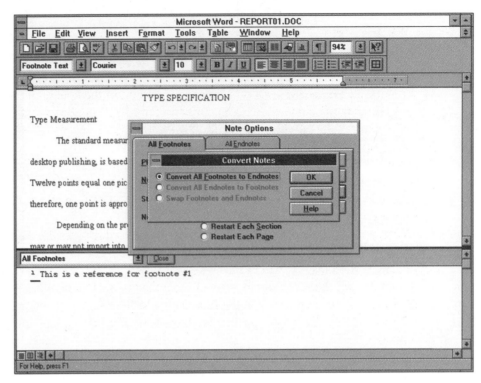

**Figure 10.7**
**Convert Notes**
**Dialog Box**

# **C**onverting **F**ootnotes and **E**ndnotes

Word provides an option that lets you convert footnotes to endnotes or endnotes to footnotes. As an example of how to use this option, you would complete the following steps to convert footnotes in a document to endnotes:

1. Open the document containing the footnotes you want to convert to endnotes.
2. Choose Insert, Footnote.
3. At the Footnote and Endnote dialog box, choose Options.
4. At the Note Options dialog box, choose Convert.
5. At the Convert Notes dialog box shown in figure 10.7, the Convert All Footnotes to Endnotes option is already selected.
6. Choose OK or press Enter to close the Convert Notes dialog box.
7. Choose OK or press Enter to close the Note Options dialog box.
8. Choose Close to close the Footnote and Endnote dialog box.

The steps described above convert all footnotes to endnotes in the document. You can also convert an individual footnote to an endnote or an endnote to a footnote. For example, to convert an endnote to a footnote, you would complete the following steps:

1. Open the document containing the endnote you want converted to a footnote.
2. Make sure the viewing mode is Normal.
3. Choose View, Footnotes.
4. Make sure *All Endnotes* displays in the view text box in the endnote pane.
5. Select the endnote you want converted to a footnote.
6. With the insertion point positioned in the endnote pane, click the right mouse button.
7. At the shortcut menu that displays, choose Convert to Footnote.
8. Choose Close or press Alt + Shift + C to close the footnote pane.

# CHAPTER SUMMARY

- Footnotes and endnotes are explanatory notes or references. Footnotes are printed at the bottom of the page; endnotes, at the end of the document.
- The first step in creating a footnote/endnote is to insert the note reference number at the location in the document where the note is referred to. The second step is to key the note entry text.
- The footnote/endnote text is keyed at the footnote or endnote pane.
- By default, footnotes are numbered with Arabic numbers; endnotes are numbered with lowercase Roman numerals.
- The note reference number and the note entry text can be formatted to match the formatting of the document text.
- When printing a document containing footnotes, Word reduces the number of text lines on a page by the number of lines in the footnote plus two lines. Word separates footnotes and endnotes from the text with a 2-inch separator line.
- Footnotes and endnotes can be viewed and edited in the Page Layout viewing mode. Several methods can be used to edit at the footnote/endnote pane.
- You can use the Go To option to move the insertion point to a particular footnote or endnote.
- Several methods can be used to move or copy a reference number within a document. If a footnote or endnote reference number is moved, copied, or deleted, all other footnotes/endnotes are automatically renumbered.
- To delete a footnote or endnote, select the reference number, then press the Delete key or the Backspace key.
- The footnote or endnote default settings can be changed with options from the footnote or endnote pane or from the Note Options dialog box. Customizing changes can be made to the separator line, the footnote location, and the reference numbers.
- Footnotes can be converted to endnotes, or vice versa, at the Convert Notes dialog box. You can also convert an individual footnote to an endnote, or vice versa.

## COMMANDS REVIEW

| | Mouse | Keyboard |
|---|---|---|
| Footnote and Endnote dialog box | Insert, Footnote | Insert, Footnote |
| Create a footnote at the Footnote pane | Insert, Footnote, Footnote | ALT + CTRL + F |
| Create an endnote at the Endnote pane | Insert, Footnote, Endnote | ALT + CTRL + E |
| Close footnote or endnote pane | Close | ALT + SHIFT + C |
| Edit the footnote | View, Footnote; or with arrow pointer on split bar, hold shift key and left mouse button, drag to middle of screen, release; or double-click on reference number | ALT + CTRL + F |
| Edit the endnote | View, Footnote; or with arrow pointer on split bar, hold Shift key and left mouse button, drag to middle of screen, release; or double-click on reference number | ALT + CTRL + E |

|  | **Mouse** | **Keyboard** |
|---|---|---|
| Locate specific footnote or endnote | Edit, Go To | F5 ; or CTRL + G |
| Note Options dialog box | At the Footnote and Endnote dialog box, choose Options | At the Footnote and Endnote dialog box, choose Options |
| Convert Notes dialog box | At the Footnote and Endnote dialog box, choose Options, then choose Convert | At the Footnote and Endnote dialog box, choose Options, then choose Convert |

## CHECK YOUR UNDERSTANDING

**True/False:** Circle the letter T if the statement is true; circle the letter F if the statement is false.

**T  F**  1. When creating a footnote or endnote, the insertion point must be at the location where the reference number is to appear.

**T  F**  2. All footnotes in a document are printed on the last page.

**T  F**  3. When the endnote reference information has been keyed, press Enter if you want to insert a blank line between endnotes.

**T  F**  4. You can use the Backspace key to delete a reference number after selecting it.

**T  F**  5. When an endnote is deleted, Word automatically renumbers the remaining endnotes.

**T  F**  6. By default, Word separates footnotes from the text by a 1-inch separator line.

**T  F**  7. Footnotes and endnotes will print in the default font unless the note entry text formatting is changed.

**T  F**  8. The footnote reference number in the document and before the entry text prints as a superscript number.

**T  F**  9. Neither footnotes nor endnotes can be edited in the Page Layout viewing mode.

**T  F**  10. Footnotes can be converted to endnotes.

**Completion:** In the space provided, indicate the correct term, command, or number.

1. To display the Footnote and Endnote dialog box, first choose this from the menu bar.  _____

2. The footnote entry text is keyed here.  _____

3. By default, each footnote is separated by this number of blank lines.  _____

4. This is the keyboard command to display the endnote pane.  _____

5. Word numbers footnotes with Arabic numbers and endnotes with these numerals.  _____

6. You can display a footnote or endnote pane in the Normal viewing mode with this bar.  _____

7. Use this command to locate a specific footnote or endnote.  _____

8. One way to begin moving a reference number to another location is by selecting the reference mark, then choosing this at the Menu bar.  _____

9. One way to copy a reference number to a different location is to select the number, hold down this key, then drag the number to the desired location.  _____

10. If you want footnotes to begin with a number other than 1, display this dialog box.  _____

## Exercise 1

1. Open report02.
2. Save the report with Save As and name it c10ex01.
3. Create the first footnote shown in figure 10.8 at the end of the second paragraph (directly above *TEMPLATE ELEMENTS*) by completing the following steps:
   a. Position the insertion point at the end of the second paragraph.
   b. Choose Insert, Footnote.
   c. At the Footnote and Endnote dialog box, make sure Footnote is selected, then choose OK or press Enter.
   d. At the footnote pane, key the first footnote shown in figure 10.8. Press the Enter key once after keying the footnote text (this will separate the first footnote from the second footnote by a blank line).
   e. Choose Close or press Alt + Shift + C to close the footnote pane.
4. Move the insertion point to the end of the last paragraph in the *Column Grid* section, then create the second footnote shown in figure 10.8 by completing the following steps:
   a. Position the insertion point at the end of the last paragraph in the *Column Grid* section.
   b. Press Alt + Ctrl + F.
   c. At the footnote pane, key the second footnote shown in figure 10.8. Press the Enter key once after keying the second footnote.
   d. Choose Close or press Alt + Shift + C to close the footnote pane.
5. Move the insertion point to the end of the only paragraph in the *Running Heads/Feet* section, then create the third footnote shown in figure 10.8 by completing steps similar to those in 3 or 4.
6. Move the insertion point to the end of the last paragraph in the *Page Numbers (Folios)* section, then create the fourth footnote shown in figure 10.8.
7. Move the insertion point to the end of the last paragraph in the *SERIAL ELEMENTS* section (the last paragraph in the document), then create the fifth footnote shown in figure 10.8.
8. Check page breaks in the document and, if necessary, make corrections to the page breaks.
9. Save the report again with the same name (c10ex01).
10. Print c10ex01. (You may want to preview the document before printing.)
11. Close c10ex01.

**Figure 10.8**

Yasui, Holly. *Desktop Publishing Technology and Design.* Paradigm Publishing, 1989, pages 163-166.

Libby, Margot, and Edward Ostgard. "Designing Your Brochure," *Computer Technologies.* July/August 1995, pages 4-7.

Haisch, Timothy. "Binding Documents," *Design and Style.* September 1996, pages 5-9.

Elstrom, Lisa. *Design Concepts.* Greenleaf Publishing House, 1995, pages 103-110.

Addington, Terry. "Maintaining Consistency in Publications," *Computing Plus.* October 1996, pages 31-35.

## Exercise 2

1. Open report01.
2. Save the report with Save As and name it c10ex02.
3. Make the following changes to the document:
   a. Select the entire document, then change the font to 12-point Times New Roman.
   b. Select the title, *TYPE SPECIFICATION*, then change the font to 14-point Times New Roman Bold. Select each of the headings, *Type Measurement*, *Type Size*, and *Type Style,* then change the font to 14-point Times New Roman Bold. (Hint: Use the Format Painter button on the Formatting toolbar.)
   c. Select the last four paragraphs (lines) of the document, then insert bullets. (Use the Bullets button on the Formatting toolbar.)
4. Create the first endnote shown in figure 10.9 at the end of the last paragraph in the *Type Measurement* section by completing the following steps:
   a. Position the insertion point at the end of the last paragraph in the *Type Measurement* section.
   b. Choose Insert, Footnote.
   c. At the Footnote and Endnote dialog box, choose Endnote.
   d. Choose OK or press Enter.
   e. At the endnote pane, key the first endnote shown in figure 10.9. Press the Enter key once after keying the endnote text.
   f. Choose Close or press Alt + Shift + C to close the endnote pane.
5. Move the insertion point to the end of the first paragraph in the *Type Size* section, then create the second endnote shown in figure 10.9 by completing the following steps:
   a. Position the insertion point at the end of the first paragraph in the *Type Size* section.
   b. Press Alt + Ctrl + E.
   c. At the endnote pane, key the second endnote shown in figure 10.9. Press the Enter key once after keying the second endnote.
   d. Choose Close or press Alt + Shift + C to close the endnote pane.
6. Move the insertion point to the end of the third paragraph in the *Type Style* section, then create the third endnote shown in figure 10.9 by completing steps similar to those in 4 or 5.
7. Check page breaks in the document and, if necessary, make corrections to the page breaks.
8. Save the report with the same name (c10ex02).
9. Print c10ex02. (You may want to preview the document before printing.)
10. Close c10ex02.

### Figure 10.9

Yasui, Holly. *Desktop Publishing Technology and Design.* Paradigm Publishing, 1989, pages 96-98.

Dernovich, Arthur, and Sandy McRae. "Choosing the Appropriate Font," *Design Technologies.* May 1996, pages 53-57.

Nunoz, Juanita. "Form and Function," *Computer Technologies.* January/February 1996, pages 45-53.

## Exercise 3

1. Open c10ex01.
2. Save the document with Save As and name it c10ex03.
3. Edit the footnotes by completing the following steps:
   a. Change the viewing mode to Page Layout.
   b. Move the insertion point to the bottom of the second page until the second footnote is visible.
   c. Make the following changes to the second footnote:
      (1) Change *July/August* to *September/October*.
      (2) Change *4-7* to *6-9*.
   d. Move the insertion point to the bottom of the fourth page until the fourth footnote is visible, then make the following changes to the fourth footnote:
      (1) Change *Greenleaf Publishing House* to *Old Town Publishing*.
      (2) Change *1995* to *1996*.
   e. Change the viewing mode back to Normal.
4. Save the document again with the same name (c10ex03).
5. Print c10ex03.
6. Close c10ex03.

## Exercise 4

1. Open c10ex02.
2. Save the document with Save As and name it c10ex04.
3. Display the endnote pane, then change the font of the endnotes by completing the following steps:
   a. Choose View, Footnotes.
   b. At the endnote pane, select all endnote entry text and endnote numbers, then change the font to 12-point Times New Roman.
   c. Choose Close or press Alt + Shift + C to close the endnote pane.
4. Save the document again with the same name (c10ex04).
5. Print c10ex04. (You may want to preview the document before printing.)
6. Close c10ex04.

## Exercise 5

1. Open c10ex01.
2. Save the document with Save As and name it c10ex05.
3. Go to footnote number 3, then edit the footnote by completing the following steps:
   a. Choose Edit, Go To; press F5; or press Ctrl + G.
   b. At the Go To dialog box, choose Footnote in the Go To What list box.
   c. Choose Enter Footnote Number, then key **3**.
   d. Choose Go To.
   e. When the insertion point is positioned on footnote reference number 3, click on the Close button to close the Go To dialog box.
   f. With the insertion point still positioned on the footnote reference number, double-click the mouse button. (This displays the footnote pane.)
   g. Make the following changes to the third footnote:
      (1) Change the name from *Haisch, Timothy* to *Keppler, Susan*.
      (2) Change the page numbers from *5-9* to *10-14*.
   h. Choose Close to close the footnote pane.
4. Save the document again with the same name (c10ex05).
5. Print c10ex05. (You may want to preview the document before printing.)
6. Close c10ex05.

## Exercise 6

1. Open c10ex01.
2. Save the document with Save As and name it c10ex06.
3. Select the entire document, then change the font to 12-point Palatino (or Times New Roman, if your printer does not support Palatino).
4. Display the footnote pane, then change the font to 12-point Palatino (or Times New Roman) by completing the following steps:
   a. Choose View, Footnotes.
   b. At the footnote pane, select all footnote entry text and footnote numbers, then change the font to 12-point Palatino (or Times New Roman).
   c. Choose Close or press Alt + Shift + C to close the footnote pane.
5. Delete the fourth footnote by completing the following steps:
   a. Move the insertion point to the fourth footnote reference number in the document text.
   b. Select the fourth footnote reference number, then press the Delete key or the Backspace key.
6. Move the third footnote reference number from the end of the only paragraph in the *Running Heads/Feet* section to the end of the first paragraph in the *Page Numbers (Folios)* section by completing the following steps:
   a. Move the insertion point to the third footnote reference number.
   b. Select the third footnote reference number.
   c. Choose Edit, Cut.
   d. Position the insertion point at the end of the first paragraph in the *Page Numbers (Folios)* section.
   e. Choose Edit, Paste.
7. Check page breaks in the document and, if necessary, make corrections to the page breaks.
8. Save the document again with the same name (c10ex06).
9. Print c10ex06. (You may want to preview the document before printing.)
10. Close c10ex06.

## Exercise 7

1. Open c10ex06.
2. Save the document with Save As and name it c10ex07.
3. Customize the footnotes by completing the following steps:
   a. Choose View, Footnotes.
   b. At the footnote pane, click on the down-pointing arrow to the right of the view text box containing the words All Footnotes, then click on *Footnote Separator*.
   c. At the footnote separator pane, press Ctrl + E or click on the Center button on the Standard toolbar. (This centers the separator line between the left and right margins.)
   d. Click on Close to close the separator pane.
   e. Choose Insert, Footnote, then Options.
   f. At the Note Options dialog box, make sure the All Footnotes tab is selected.
   g. Choose Place At, then Beneath Text.
   h. Click on the up-pointing triangle after the Start At option until *5* displays in the text box.
   i. Choose OK or press Enter to close the Note Options dialog box.
   j. Choose OK to close the Footnote and Endnote dialog box.
   k. Choose Close to close the footnote pane.
4. Check page breaks in the document and, if necessary, make corrections to the page breaks.
5. Save the document again with the same name (c10ex07).
6. Print c10ex07. (You may want to preview the document before printing.)
7. Close c10ex07.

## Exercise 8

1. Open c10ex06.
2. Save the document with Save As and name it c10ex08.
3. Convert the footnotes to endnotes by completing the following steps:
   a. Choose Insert, Footnote.
   b. At the Footnote and Endnote dialog box, choose Options.
   c. At the Note Options dialog box, choose Convert.
   d. At the Convert Notes dialog box, the Convert All Footnotes to Endnotes option is already selected so choose OK or press Enter to close the Convert Notes dialog box.
   e. At the Note Options dialog box, choose the All Endnotes tab.
   f. Choose Number Format, then 1, 2, 3,....
   g. Choose OK or press Enter to close the Note Options dialog box.
   h. Choose Close to close the Footnote and Endnote dialog box.
4. Check page breaks in the document and, if necessary, make corrections to the page breaks.
5. Save the document again with the same name (c10ex08).
6. Print c10ex08. (You may want to preview the document before printing.)
7. Close c10ex08.

## SKILL ASSESSMENTS

## Assessment 1

1. Open report04.
2. Save the document with Save As and name it c10sa01.
3. Make the following changes to the report:
   a. Insert a section break that begins a new page at the line containing the title *CHAPTER 2: OFFSET PRINTING*.
   b. Number each page of the entire document except the first page at the upper right corner of the page.
   c. Create the first footnote shown in figure 10.10 at the end of the last paragraph in the *Time and Cost Considerations* section of the report.
   d. Create the second footnote shown in figure 10.10 at the end of the last paragraph in the *Color* section of the report.
   e. Create the third footnote shown in figure 10.10 at the end of the last paragraph in the *IMAGESETTING* section of the report.
   f. Create the fourth footnote shown in figure 10.10 at the end of the only paragraph in the *Output Options* section of the report.
   g. Create the fifth footnote shown in figure 10.10 at the end of the last paragraph of the report.
4. Check page breaks in the document and, if necessary, make corrections to the page breaks.
5. Save the document again with the same name (c10sa01).
6. Print c10sa01. (You may want to preview the document before printing.)
7. Close c10sa01.

Figure 10.10

```
Worley, Beverly.  "Should You Buy a Laser Printer?" Microcomputing.
March/April 1996, pages 61-65.

Lapinski, Frank.  "Choosing a Color Printer," Computer Technology.
August 1995, pages 15-19.

Casada, Sara.  "Typesetting Equipment," Power Computing.  February
12, 1996, pages 23-28.

Sihto, Richard.  "Imagesetting Options," Design Technologies.
April 1996, pages 17-22.

Wittenberg, Robin.  "Creating a Pasteup," Design Technologies.
April 1996, pages 41-48.
```

## Assessment 2

1. Open c10sa01.
2. Save the document with Save As and name it c10sa02.
3. Make the following changes to the report:
   a. Select the entire document, then change the font to 12-point Times New Roman.
   b. Display the footnote pane, select all the footnotes, then change the font to 12-point Times New Roman.
   c. Move the third footnote (the one after the last paragraph in the *IMAGE SETTING* section) to the end of the last paragraph in the *WYSIWYG* section.
   d. Delete the first footnote.
   e. Change the beginning footnote number to 6.
   f. Center the footnote separator line between the left and right margins.
4. Check page breaks in the document and, if necessary, make corrections to the page breaks.
5. Save the document again with the same name (c10sa02).
6. Print c10sa02.
7. Close c10sa02.

## Assessment 3

1. Open c10sa01.
2. Save the document with Save As and name it c10sa03.
3. Make the following changes to the report:
   a. Change the font to 12-point New Century Schoolbook (or Times New Roman, if your printer does not support New Century Schoolbook) for the document text and the footnotes.
   b. Convert the footnotes to endnotes.
   c. Change the numbering format for the endnotes to Arabic numbers.
4. Check page breaks in the document and, if necessary, make corrections to the page breaks.
5. Save the document again with the same name (c10sa03).
6. Print c10sa03.
7. Close c10sa03.

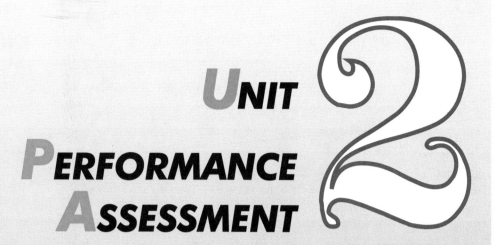

# UNIT 2

## PERFORMANCE ASSESSMENT

In this unit, you have learned to create and proof full-page and multi-page business documents, such as business letters and reports.

## Assessment 1

1. At a clear document screen, key the text shown in figure U2.1 in an appropriate business letter format with the following specifications:
   a. Change the left and right margins to 1 inch.
   b. After keying the letter, change the alignment of the paragraphs within the body of the letter to Justified.
   c. After keying the letter, complete a spelling check. (Proper names are spelled correctly.)
   d. Use the thesaurus to find appropriate synonyms for the following words:
      (1) *growth* in the first paragraph
      (2) *best* in the first paragraph
      (3) *many* in the last paragraph
      (4) *choosing* in the last paragraph
2. Save the letter and name it u02pa01.
3. Print u02pa01.
4. Close u02pa01.

April 15, 1996

Ms. Regina Delmarr
1232 Cascade Drive
Tacoma, WA 98032

Dear Ms. Delmarr:

As the next stage in the growth of Seaview Airlines' Frequent
Traveler program, I am plaesed to anounce a new program, AIR MILES,
affective May 1, 1996.  In designing this new program, Seaview
relied on thorough reserch to make key business decesions and
provide you with a program which you will discover to be the best
in the industry.  Here are some of the highlights you have to look
forward to in 1996:

• a free ticket for traval within the continental United States
  has been reduced from 30,000 to 25,000 miles;

• unlike some other carriers, miles earned in Seaview's new
  program will never expire, just take one qualifing Seaview
  flight every 2 years;

• an enhanced elite level program with new qualafication levels, a
  streamlined upgrade program, and richer rewards.

Our thanks to the many Frequent Traveler program members we invited
to help us design the new program.  Seaview Airlines is committed
to providing you with the best programs and becoming your airline
of choice.  Thank you for choosing Seaview.  We look forward to
serving your futere travel needs.

Sincerely,



Candace Sandberg
Senior Vice President

xx:u02pa01

# Assessment 2

1. At a clear document screen, key the text shown in figure U2.2 in an appropriate memorandum format with the following specifications:
   a. Change the font to 12-point Times New Roman.
   b. Use the key line method to set tabs for the text columns. (You determine the number of spaces between columns.)
2. Complete a grammar check on the document. (Proper names are spelled correctly. When the grammar checker highlights a sentence in passive voice, tell it to ignore the sentence.) You determine what to change and what to ignore. After completing the grammar check, proofread the document and correct any errors not found by the grammar checker.
3. Save the memorandum and name it u02pa02.
4. Print u02pa02.
5. Close u02pa02.

**Figure U2.2**

DATE: April 16, 1996

TO: College Faculty and Staff

FROM: Leah Adamson

SUBJECT: COLLEGE TRANSFER DAY

Its that time of year when our students begin thinking about transferring to a four-year college. Mountain Community College are hosting college transfer day on May 7. Representatives from local four-year colleges and universities will answer specific question about admission and transfer requirement. Please encourages students to attend if they are planning to transfer to a four-year college.

The college and university representatives will provide information and answer questions in the atrium area on Tuesday, May 7, 1996, from 9:30 a.m. to 2:00 p.m. The following schools will be participating:

Mountain University　　　　University of Colorado
Colorado State College　　　Whitman College
Riger Women's College　　　East Colorado University
Chapman University　　　　West Colorado University

You is invited to meet with the representatives during an informal coffee time from 9:00 a.m. to 9:30 a.m. in the conference room. Please stop by if you're schedule permits.

xx:u02pa02

## Assessment 3

1. At a clear document screen, make the following changes:
   a. Change the paper size to 5.5 inches by 8.5 inches.
   b. Change the left and right margins to 1 inch.
   c. Change the font to 12-point Times New Roman.
2. Key the memorandum shown in figure U2.3. Use the key line method to determine the tab stops for the text in columns. (You determine the number of spaces between columns.)
3. Save the memorandum and name it u02pa03.
4. Print u02pa03.
5. Close u02pa03.

**Figure U2.3**

```
DATE:     March 5, 1996

TO:       Brenda Hogue

FROM:     James Zekes

SUBJECT: TRAINING


Listed below are the dates that I have attended cultural diversity
training sessions.  I have completed over 70 hours of training
which qualifies me as a cultural diversity specialist.  Not listed
are the hours I attended prior to my tenure as Trainer.


              Date          Hrs

              01/02/96        8
              01/04/96        8
              01/15/96        6
              01/17/96        6
              01/23/96        8
              01/25/96        8
              02/13/96        6
              02/15/96        6
              02/19/96        8
              02/21/96        8

If you need further documentation, I can provide you with my
training material.

xx:u02pa03
```

## Assessment 4

1.  At a clear document screen, create the document shown in figure U2.4 with the following specifications:
    a.  Bold and center text as indicated.
    b.  Use the key line method to determine the tab settings. (You determine the number of spaces between columns.)
    c.  Center the document vertically on the page.
2.  Save the document and name it u02pa04.
3.  Print u02pa04.
4.  Close u02pa04.

**Figure U2.4**

**PETERSBURG SCHOOL DISTRICT**

**Enrollment Comparisons**

| School | 1995 | 1996 |
|--------|------|------|
| Meeker Senior High | 1,160 | 1,033 |
| Rollings Senior High | 890 | 993 |
| Lakeview Middle School | 690 | 587 |
| Oakridge Middle School | 681 | 801 |
| Cedar Middle School | 702 | 745 |
| Stewart Elementary | 521 | 498 |
| Overman Elementary | 386 | 404 |
| Grant Elementary | 478 | 512 |
| Curtiss Elementary | 403 | 455 |

## Assessment 5

1.  Open report01.
2.  Save the document with Save As and name it u02pa05.
3.  Make the following changes to the report:
    a.  Select the entire document, then change the font to 12-point Times New Roman.
    b.  Set the title and headings in 14-point Arial Bold.
    c.  Insert bullets before the last four paragraphs (lines) in the report.
    d.  Number pages, except the first page, at the upper right margin.
    e.  Create the footer *DESIGN TECHNIQUES* that prints centered at the bottom of every page and is set in 12-point Arial Bold.
4.  Save the document again with the same name (u02pa05).
5.  Print u02pa05.
6.  Close u02pa05.

## Assessment 6

1.  Open report05.
2.  Save the report with Save As and name it u02pa06.
3.  Make the following changes to the document:
    a.  Select the entire document, then change the font to 12-point Palatino (or Times New Roman, if your printer does not support Palatino).
    b.  Change the left and right margins to 1 inch.
    c.  Insert a section break that begins a new page at the line containing the title *CHAPTER 4: CHOOSING INK*.

d. Create the footer *Chapter 3: Choosing Paper* that prints at the left margin and *Page #* that prints at the right margin on each page in the first section and is set in 12-point Palatino Bold (or Times New Roman Bold).

e. Create the footer *Chapter 4: Choosing Ink* that prints at the left margin and *Page #* that prints at the right margin on each page in the second section and is set in 12-point Palatino Bold (or Times New Roman Bold).

4. Save the report again with the same name (u02pa06).
5. Print u02pa06.
6. Close u02pa06.

## Assessment 7

1. Open u02pa06.
2. Save the document with Save As and name it u02pa07.
3. Make the following changes to the document:
   a. Delete the footer in the first section.
   b. Delete the footer in the second section.
   c. Create the header, *Page #* that prints at the top right margin on every page except the first page. Select the header, then change the font to 12-point Palatino (or Times New Roman).
   d. Create the first footnote shown in figure U2.5 at the end of the last paragraph in the *General Characteristics* section of the report.
   e. Create the second footnote shown in figure U2.5 at the end of the last paragraph in the *Grades of Paper* section of the report.
   f. Create the third footnote shown in figure U2.5 at the end of the last paragraph in the *Specialty Inks* section of the report.
   g. Create the fourth footnote shown in figure U2.5 at the end of the last paragraph in the *Special Effects* section of the report.
   h. Display the footnote pane, select all the footnotes, then change the font to 12-point Palatino (or Times New Roman).
4. Save the document again with the same name (u02pa07).
5. Print u02pa07. (You may want to preview the document before printing.)
6. Close u02pa07.

**Figure U2.5**

```
Yasui, Holly.  Desktop Publishing Technology and Design.  Paradigm
Publishing, 1989, pages 190-194.


Myton, Gail.  "Choosing the Right Paper," Desktop Publishing.  June
1996, pages 14-19.


Heath, Anthony.  Desktop Publishing in Style.  Monroe-Ackerman
Publishing, 1996, pages 102-109.


Sears, Laurie.  Desktop Publishing Tips and Tricks.  Aurora
Publishing House, 1995, pages 56-66.
```

## Assessment 8

1. Open u02pa07.
2. Save the document with Save As and name it u02pa08.
3. Make the following changes to the report:
   a. Convert the footnotes to endnotes.
   b. Change the numbering format for endnotes to Arabic numbers.
   c. Change the separator line to a 2-inch line that prints centered between the left and right margins.
   d. Edit endnote number 3 and change the publication year from *1996* to *1995* and change the pages from *102-109* to *96-104*.
   e. Move the first endnote reference number from the last paragraph in the *General Characteristics* section of the report to the end of the second paragraph in the document.
4. Save the report again with the same name (u02pa08).
5. Print u02pa08.
6. Close u02pa08.


## COMPOSING ACTIVITIES

The following activities give you the opportunity to practice your writing skills along with demonstrating an understanding of some of the important Word features you have mastered in this unit. In planning the documents, remember to shape the information according to the writing purpose and the audience. Use correct grammar, appropriate word choices, and clear sentence constructions.

### Activity 1

**Situation:** You are responsible for formatting the report in the document named *report06* on your student data disk. This report will be left bound and should include page numbers and headers and/or footers. Change to a serif font for the body of the report and a sans serif font for the title and headings. Correct the spelling in the document.

After formatting the report, create an appropriate title page for the report. Include your name as the author of the report. Save the document and name it u02act01. Print then close u02act01.

### Activity 2

**Situation:** You are Brenda Hogue, director of the Training and Education Department at St. Francis Medical Center. Compose a memo to the employees of the Training and Education Department informing them that it is time for their semi-annual employee review. You want to schedule meetings with them on the following days and times:

| | | |
|---|---|---|
| Pauline Coffey | July 25 | 1:00 p.m. |
| James Zekes | July 30 | 10:30 a.m. |
| Daniel Lagasa | August 1 | 9:00 a.m. |
| Scott Sideres | August 3 | 10:00 a.m. |
| My Trinh | August 8 | 2:30 p.m. |

Use the key line method to set the names, days, and times in columns. Save the letter and name it u02act02. Print then close u02act02.

*Note: For the research activity for this unit and future units, you will need access to the Word for Windows User's Guide. Check with your instructor to determine if this guide is available.*

### Activity 1

Answer the following questions about information in the Word for Windows User's Guide.

1. What chapter covers checking spelling and grammar? _____

2. If the Grammar command does not appear in the Tools menu, what do you need to do to make it appear?

   _____

3. What chapter covers headers and footers? _____

4. Answer the following questions about *background pagination*?
   a. What is background pagination? _____
   b. In what viewing modes is it always on? _____
   c. Why might you want to turn off background pagination? _____
   d. What steps would you complete to turn off background pagination? _____

# Basic Document Formatting

UNIT

3

*In this unit, you will learn to create, revise, copy, delete, print, and maintain standard business memoranda , letters, and reports.*

# Cutting and Pasting Text 11

Upon successful completion of chapter 11, you will be able to manipulate blocks and columns of text between areas of different business documents.

Some documents may need to be heavily revised, and these revisions may include deleting, moving, or copying blocks of text. This kind of editing is generally referred to as *cut and paste*.

## Working with Blocks of Text

When cutting and pasting, you work with blocks of text. A block of text is a portion of text that you have selected. (Chapter 2 explained the various methods for selecting text.) A block of text can be as small as one character or as large as an entire page or document. Once a block of text has been selected, it can be:

- deleted,
- moved to a new location, or
- copied and placed in a certain location within a document.

The last two operations involve using Word's Cut, Copy, and Paste features.

### Deleting a Block of Text

Word offers different methods for deleting text from a document. To delete a single character, you can use either the Delete key or the Backspace key. To delete more than a single character, select the portion of text to be deleted, then choose one of the following options:

- Press Delete.
- Choose Edit, Cut.
- Click on the Cut button on the Standard toolbar.
- Press Shift + Delete.
- Press Ctrl + X.

If you press Delete, the text is deleted permanently. (You can restore deleted text with the Undo option from the Edit menu or with the Undo or Redo buttons on the Standard toolbar.) Cut from the Edit menu, the Cut button on the Standard toolbar, Shift + Delete, and Ctrl + X will delete the selected text and insert it in the *Clipboard*. Word's Clipboard is a temporary area of memory. The

Clipboard holds text while it is being moved or copied to a new location in the document or to a different document. Text inserted in the Clipboard stays there until other text is inserted or until Word is exited.

Delete selected text with the Delete key if you do not need it again. Use the other methods if you might want to insert deleted text in the current document or a different document.

## Moving a Block of Text

Word offers a variety of methods for moving text. After you have selected a block of text, move text with options from the Edit menu, shortcut commands, buttons on the Standard toolbar, the mouse, or the mouse and a shortcut menu.

To move a block of selected text from one location to another using the Edit menu, you would complete the following steps:

1. Select the text.
2. Choose Edit, Cut.
3. Position the insertion point at the location where the selected text is to be inserted.
4. Choose Edit, Paste.

To move a block of selected text from one location to another using shortcut commands, you would complete the following steps:

1. Select the text.
2. Press Ctrl + X; or Shift + Delete.
3. Position the insertion point at the location where the selected text is to be inserted.
4. Press Ctrl + V; or Shift + Insert.

To move a block of selected text from one location to another using buttons on the Standard toolbar, you would complete the following steps:

1. Select the text.
2. Click on the Cut button on the Standard toolbar.
3. Position the insertion point at the location where the selected text is to be inserted.
4. Click on the Paste button on the Standard toolbar.

In addition to the methods just described, a block of selected text can also be moved with the mouse. There are two methods for moving text with the mouse. You can move selected text by completing the following steps:

1. Select the text to be moved with the mouse.
2. Move the I-beam pointer inside the selected text until it becomes an arrow pointer.
3. Hold down the left mouse button, drag the insertion point (displays as a grayed vertical bar) to the location where you want the selected text inserted, then release the button.
4. Deselect the text.

As you hold down the left mouse button and drag the mouse, the arrow pointer displays with a small gray box attached. In addition, the insertion point displays as a grayed vertical bar. When the insertion point (grayed vertical bar) is located in the desired position, release the mouse button. The selected text is removed from its original position and inserted in the new location.

A shortcut menu can also be used to move selected text with the mouse. To do this, you would complete the following steps:

1. Select the text to be moved with the mouse.
2. Move the I-beam pointer inside the selected text until it becomes an arrow pointer.
3. Click the *right* mouse button.
4. At the shortcut menu that displays, click on Cut.
5. Position the insertion point where the text is to be inserted.
6. Click the *right* mouse button to display the shortcut menu, then click on Paste.

When selected text is cut from a document and inserted in the Clipboard, it stays in the Clipboard until other text is inserted in the Clipboard or until Word is exited. For this reason, you can paste text from the Clipboard more than just once. For example, if you cut text to the Clipboard, you can paste this text in different locations within the document or other documents as many times as desired.

In addition to the methods mentioned above, you can also move a selected paragraph above the preceding one or below the following one. To move a selected paragraph above the preceding paragraph, select the paragraph, then press Alt + Shift + up arrow. To move a selected paragraph below the following paragraph, select the paragraph, then press Alt + Shift + down arrow.

## Copying a Block of Text

Copying selected text can be useful in documents that contain repetitive portions of text. You can use this function to insert duplicate portions of text in a document instead of rekeying the text. After you have selected a block of text, copy the text with options from the Edit menu, shortcut commands, buttons on the Standard toolbar, the mouse, or the mouse and a shortcut menu.

To copy text with the Edit menu, you would complete the following steps:

1. Select the text to be copied.
2. Choose Edit, Copy.
3. Move the insertion point to the location where the copied text is to be inserted.
4. Choose Edit, Paste.

To copy text with shortcut commands, you would complete the following steps:

1. Select the text to be copied.
2. Press Ctrl + Insert.
3. Move the insertion point to the location where the copied text is to be inserted.
4. Press Shift + Insert.

For another way to copy text with shortcut commands, you would complete the following steps:

1. Select the text to be copied.
2. Press Ctrl + C.
3. Move the insertion point to the location where the copied text is to be inserted.
4. Press Ctrl + V.

To copy text with the buttons on the Standard toolbar, you would complete the following steps:

1. Select the text to be copied.
2. Click on the Copy button on the Standard toolbar (the eighth button from the left).
3. Move the insertion point to the location where the copied text is to be inserted.
4. Click on the Paste button on the Standard toolbar.

The mouse can also be used to copy a block of text in a document and insert the copy in a new location. To do this, you would complete the following steps:

1. Select the text with the mouse.
2. Move the I-beam pointer inside the selected text until it becomes an arrow pointer.
3. Hold down the left mouse button and hold down the Ctrl key. Drag the insertion point (displays as a grayed vertical bar) to the location where you want the copied text inserted, then release the mouse button and the Ctrl key.
4. Deselect the text.

With the Ctrl key down, a plus symbol (+) displays above the small gray box by the arrow pointer.

When text is copied, the text remains in the document screen and a copy is inserted in the Clipboard. Once text has been cut or copied to the Clipboard, it can be inserted in a document any number of times without copying it again. The text will remain in the Clipboard until other text is cut or copied to the Clipboard or until you exit Word.

If you select a block of text and then decide you selected the wrong text or you do not want to do anything with the block, you can deselect it. If you are using the mouse, click the left mouse button outside the selected text. If you are using the keyboard, press Esc to turn off the Extend mode, then move the insertion point.

## ■ Working with Columns of Text

Text keyed in columns and separated by tabs can be selected and then deleted, moved, or copied within the document. (Refer to chapter 8 for a review of setting tabs and entering text into columns.) A column of text can be selected using the mouse or the keyboard.

To select a column of text using the mouse, you would complete the following steps:

1. Move the I-beam pointer immediately left of the first character in the upper left corner of the column.
2. Hold down the Alt key and the left mouse button, drag the I-beam pointer down and to the right to the lower right corner of the column of text. When dragging the I-beam pointer, be sure to include the longest entry in the column and the nonprinting tab character, if necessary.
3. Release the mouse button and the Alt key.

Figure 11.1 shows a document with nonprinting characters displayed and a column of text selected.

To select a column of text using the keyboard, you would complete the following steps:

1. Position the insertion point on the first character in the upper left corner of the column.
2. Press Ctrl + Shift + F8. (This turns on the Column Extend feature.)
3. Press the down arrow key and the right arrow key until the insertion point is positioned in the lower right corner of the column. (Be sure to move the insertion point to the right to include the longest entry in the column along with the nonprinting tab character, if necessary.)

When selecting columns to be moved you need to consider where the columns will be moved. For example, in the columns shown in figure 11.1, to reverse the order of the two columns the tab characters before the first column and the first column of text would be selected. You would not be able to select the second column effectively because of the paragraph marks at the end of each line. Other times you will want to select the column of text and the tab characters after the text. This depends on where you will be moving the column. Once a column of text has been selected, it can be moved, copied, or deleted.

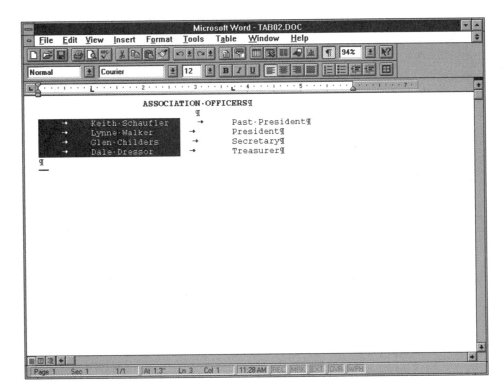

Figure 11.1
Selected Column

## Moving a Column

To understand how to move a column, look at the columns shown in figure 11.2.

The three columns were keyed with left tab stops set at the 0.5-inch, 2.5-inch, and 4.5-inch marks on the Ruler. The Tab key was pressed to move from one column to the next when keying the text. To reverse the order of the first two columns, you would complete the following steps:

1. Move the I-beam pointer immediately left of the *V* in *Vice President*.
2. Hold down the Alt key and the left mouse button.
3. Drag the I-beam pointer down and to the right until it is positioned in the bottom right corner of the column past the longest entry and the nonprinting tab character (as shown in figure 11.3).
4. Release the left mouse button and the Alt key.
5. Click on the Cut button on the Standard toolbar.
6. Position the insertion point immediately left of the *M* in *Mariah*.
7. Click on the Paste button on the Standard toolbar.

To reverse the order of the first two columns using the keyboard, you would complete the following steps:

1. Move the insertion point immediately left of the *V* in *Vice President*.
2. Press Ctrl + Shift + F8.
3. Press the down arrow key and the right arrow key until the insertion point is positioned at the bottom right corner of the column past the longest entry and the nonprinting tab character.
4. Choose Edit, Cut.
5. Position the insertion point immediately left of the *M* in *Mariah*.
6. Choose Edit, Paste.

Go To
Exercise
5

Figure 11.2
Columns

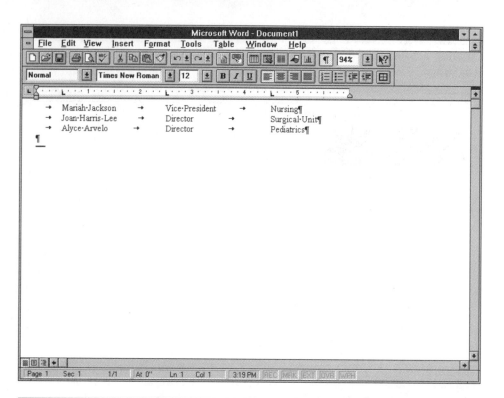

Figure 11.3
Selected Column

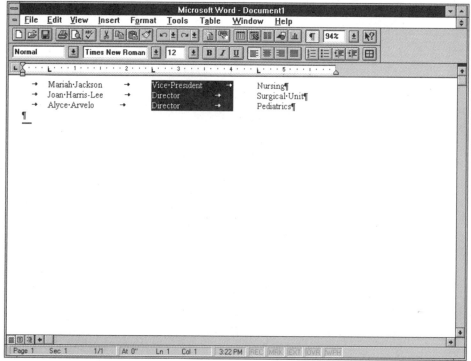

## Copying a Column

Copying a column of text is very similar to moving a column. For example, to copy the second column in figure 11.2 a double space below the three columns, you would complete the following steps:

> 1. Move the insertion point to the end of the columns, then press Enter twice (to make sure you will be able to move the insertion point below the columns).
> 2. Select the second column using either the Alt key together with the mouse or the Column Select command, Ctrl + Shift + F8, together with the keyboard. (Be sure to include the longest entry and the nonprinting tab character in the block.)
> 3. Choose Edit, Copy; press Ctrl + C; press Ctrl + Insert; or click on the Copy button on the Standard toolbar.
> 4. Position the insertion point at the left margin a double space below the columns, then choose Edit, Paste; press Ctrl + V; press Shift + Insert; or click on the Paste button on the Standard toolbar.
> 5. Deselect the text.

To copy the second column in figure 11.2 a double space below the three columns using the mouse, you would complete the following steps:

> 1. Move the insertion point immediately left of the *V* in *Vice President*.
> 2. Hold down the Alt key and the left mouse button.
> 3. Drag the I-beam pointer down and to the right until it is positioned in the bottom right corner of the column past the longest entry and the nonprinting tab character.
> 4. Release the mouse button and the Alt key.
> 5. Move the I-beam pointer inside the selected text until it becomes an arrow pointer.
> 6. Hold down the Ctrl key and the left mouse button, drag the insertion point (displays as a grayed vertical bar) to the left margin a double space below the columns, then release the left mouse button and the Ctrl key.
> 7. Deselect the text.

## Deleting a Column

To delete a column of text, select the column, then press the Delete key. You can also delete a column of text by selecting the column, then choosing Edit, Cut; pressing Ctrl + X; pressing Shift + Delete; or clicking on the Cut button on the Standard toolbar. These methods, except the Delete key, remove the column from the document and insert it in the Clipboard.

## ■ Working with Documents

Some documents may contain standard information—information that remains the same. For example, a legal document, such as a will, may contain text that is standard and appears in all wills. Repetitive text can be saved as a separate document and then retrieved into an existing document whenever needed.

There are two methods that can be used for saving text into a separate document. The first is to save a document just as you have been doing. The other method is to select standard text within a document and save it as a separate document.

## Saving Standard Text

If you know in advance what information or text is standard and will be used again, you can save it as a separate document. You should determine how to break down the information based on how it will be used. After deciding how to break down the information, key the text at a clear document screen, then save it with the Save option or Save As option from the File menu.

## Saving Selected Text

When you create a document and then realize that a portion of the text in the document will be needed for future documents, you can save it as a separate document. To do this, you would copy the text, paste it into a new document screen, then save it in the normal manner. For example, to save a paragraph as a separate document, you would complete the following steps:

1. Open the document containing the paragraph you want to save.
2. Select the paragraph.
3. Choose Edit, Copy; press Ctrl + C; press Ctrl + Insert; or click on the Copy button on the Standard toolbar.
4. Click on the New button on the Standard toolbar.
5. At the clear document screen, paste the paragraph by choosing Edit, Paste; pressing Ctrl + V; pressing Shift + Insert; or clicking on the Paste button on the Standard toolbar.
6. Save the new document in the normal manner.
7. Close the document, then close the first document.

## Inserting a Document

A document containing standard text can be inserted into an existing document with the File option from the Insert menu. For example, suppose you are keying a will and want to retrieve a standard document into the current will document. To do this, you would complete the following steps:

1. Position the insertion point in the will document at the location where you want the standard text.
2. Choose Insert, then File.
3. At the File dialog box shown in figure 11.4, double-click on the document name to be inserted, or key the document name, then choose OK or press Enter.

Word brings the entire document to the screen including any formatting. If you want standard text to conform to the formatting of the current document, do not insert any formatting in the standard document.

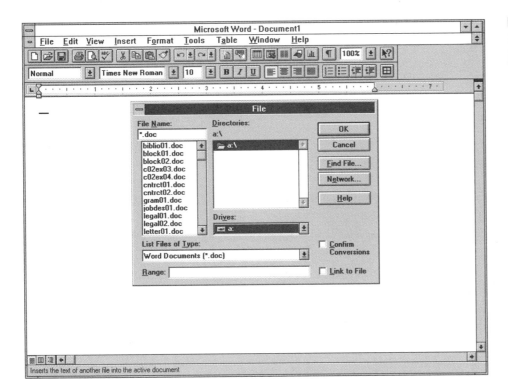

Figure 11.4
File Dialog Box

## CHAPTER SUMMARY

- Deleting, moving, or copying blocks of text within a document is generally referred to as *cutting and pasting*. A block of text can be as small as one character or as large as an entire page or document.

- When deleting a block of text, use the Delete key if you do not need that text again; use other methods if you might want to insert the deleted text in the current or a different document.

- Several methods described below in Commands Review can be used to move or copy a block of text. In addition, the mouse can be used to drag the selected block of text to a new location.

- When text keyed in columns and separated by tabs has been selected, the columns can be deleted, moved, or copied within the document with the same commands as other blocks of text.

- Text that will be repeatedly used in one or more documents can be saved as a separate document. This text can be keyed and the document saved as usual, or the text can be selected within a document and saved as a separate document. This separate document can then be inserted into an existing document with the File option from the Insert menu.

|  | **Mouse** | **Keyboard** |
|---|---|---|
| Delete one character | | DEL or BACK SPACE |
| Delete selected text permanently | | DEL |
| Delete selected text and insert it in the Clipboard | Edit, Cut; or click on Cut button on Standard toolbar; or with I-beam pointer inside text block, click right mouse button, click on Cut | SHIFT + DEL ; or CTRL + X |
| Insert text from Clipboard to new location | Edit, Paste; or click on Paste button on Standard toolbar; or click right mouse button, click on Paste | SHIFT + INS ; or CTRL + V |
| Move selected paragraph above preceding paragraph | | ALT + SHIFT + ↑ |
| Move selected paragraph below following paragraph | | ALT + SHIFT + ↓ |
| Copy selected text | Edit, Copy; move insertion point to new location, then Edit, Paste; or click on Copy button on Standard toolbar, then click on Paste | CTRL + INS , then SHIFT + INS ; or CTRL + C , then CTRL + V |
| Deselect text block | Click left mouse button outside selected text | ESC |
| Select column of text | With I-beam pointer on first character in upper left corner of column, hold down Alt key and left mouse button, drag I-beam pointer to lower right corner of column | With insertion point on first character in upper left corner of column, press CTRL + SHIFT + F8, then press ↓ and → keys until insertion point is positioned in the lower right corner of column |
| Save selected paragraph as separate document | Edit, Copy; or click on Copy button on Standard toolbar; click on the New button on the Standard toolbar; then choose Edit, Paste; or click on Paste on Standard toolbar; then save in the normal manner | CTRL + C ; or CTRL + INS ; then choose File, New, Enter; then press CTRL + V ; then save in the normal manner |
| Insert document into another document | With insertion point at the desired location for the standard text, choose Insert, then File, double-click on document name desired, click on OK | With insertion point at the desired location for the standard text, choose Insert, File, key document name, then press ENTER |

**True/False:** Circle the letter T if the statement is true; circle the letter F if the statement is false.

T   F   1.   One word could be considered a block of text.

T   F   2.   When text is copied, it remains in its original position, and a copy is inserted in a new location.

T   F   3.   Cutting and pasting are other terms for deleting and moving.

T   F   4.   Once text has been selected, it cannot be deselected.

T   F   5.   After text has been inserted in the Clipboard, it can be reinserted into a document only once.

T   F   6.   A block of text can be moved by dragging it with the mouse, but this method cannot be used to copy text.

T   F   7.   A document containing standard text can be retrieved into an existing document by choosing File, Open.

T   F   8.   Selected text that has been deleted with the Delete key cannot be restored.

T   F   9.   To move a selected paragraph below the following paragraph, press Alt + Shift + down arrow.

T   F   10.   Selected text can be saved as a separate document by choosing File, then Save As.

**Completion:** In the space provided, indicate the correct word or words relating to the table below.

| Director | Rose Palermo | Room 130 |
| Executive Assistant | Steven Kingston | Room 130A |
| Assistant Director | Carol Kwan | Room 130B |

Assume you wish to move the second column to the left of the first column.

1.   Where should the insertion point be placed before selecting the text?   _____

2.   What keyboard command will then turn on the Column Extend feature?   _____

3.   When selecting the column, the longest column entry must be included in the block as well as this.   _____

4.   After selecting the column, what button on the Standard toolbar would you then choose if using the mouse?   _____

5.   Where should the insertion point be placed in order to insert the second column to the left of the first column?   _____

## AT THE COMPUTER

### Exercise 1

1.   Open report01. This document is located on your student data disk.

2.   Save the document with Save As and name it c11ex01.

3.   Make the following changes to the document:

   a.   Select and bold the title, *TYPE SPECIFICATION*, and the headings *Type Measurement*, *Type Size*, and *Type Style*.

   b.   Insert bullets before the last four paragraphs of text in the document.

4.   Delete the following text in the report:

   a.   Delete the sentence *In particular, spacing specifications are generally set in a page assembly program.* which is the last sentence in the second paragraph, by completing the following steps:

   (1)   Select the sentence.

   (2)   Press Delete.

b. Delete the second bulleted item at the end of the document by completing the following steps:
   (1) Select the second bulleted paragraph at the end of the document. (The bullet will not be selected.)
   (2) Choose Edit, then Cut.
c. Delete the third paragraph in the *Type Size* section of the report.
5. Check page breaks in the document and, if necessary, make adjustments to the page breaks.
6. Save the document again with the same name (c11ex01).
7. Print c11ex01.
8. Close c11ex01.

## Exercise 2

1. Open para04. This document is located on your student data disk.
2. Save the document with Save As and name it c11ex02.
3. Move the following text in the document:
  a. Move the second paragraph (beginning with *Having studied...*) above the first paragraph by completing the following steps:
    (1) Select the second paragraph, including the blank line below the paragraph.
    (2) Choose Edit, Cut.
    (3) Position the insertion point at the beginning of the first paragraph.
    (4) Choose Edit, Paste.
  b. Move the third paragraph (begins with *When you deliver...*) above the second paragraph by completing the following steps:
    (1) Select the third paragraph including the blank line below the paragraph.
    (2) Click on the Cut button on the Standard toolbar.
    (3) Position the insertion point at the beginning of the second paragraph (begins with *Every time a...*) .
    (4) Click on the Paste button on the Standard toolbar.
  c. Move the first paragraph (beginning with *Having studied...*) to the end of the document using the mouse by completing the following steps:
    (1) Using the mouse, select the first paragraph including the blank line below the paragraph. (You must use the mouse to select the paragraph.)
    (2) Move the I-beam pointer inside the selected text until it becomes an arrow pointer.
    (3) Hold down the left mouse button, drag the insertion point (displays as a grayed vertical bar) a double space below the last paragraph, then release the mouse button.
    (4) Deselect the text.
4. Save the document again with the same name (c11ex02).
5. Print c11ex02.
6. Close c11ex02.

## Exercise 3

1. Open block01. This document is located on your student data disk.
2. Save the document with Save As and name it c11ex03.
3. Select the entire document, then change the font to 14-point Braggadocio.
4. Copy all the text to the end of the document by completing the following steps:
  a. Select the entire document (five lines of text plus two blank lines below the text).
  b. Choose Edit, Copy.
  c. Move the insertion point to the end of the document.
  d. Choose Edit, Paste.
5. Copy the text again at the end of the document. To do this, position the insertion point at the end of the document, then click on the Paste button on the Standard toolbar. (This inserts a copy of the text from the Clipboard.)

6. Save the document again with the same name (c11ex03).
7. Print c11ex03.
8. Close c11ex03.

## Exercise 4

1. Open block02. This document is located on your student data disk.
2. Save the document with Save As and name it c11ex04.
3. Copy the text in the document using the mouse by completing the following steps:
   a. Select the text with the mouse. Include the two blank lines below the text.
   b. Move the I-beam pointer inside the selected text until it becomes an arrow pointer.
   c. Hold down the Ctrl key and then the left mouse button. Drag the insertion point (displays as a grayed vertical bar) to the end of the document (immediately above the end-of-document marker), then release the mouse button and then the Ctrl key. (The Ctrl key must be released last.)
   d. Deselect the text.
4. Select the entire document, then copy it to the end of the document.
5. Select one form, then copy it at the end of the document. (You should have a total of five forms.)
6. Save the document again with the same name (c11ex04).
7. Print c11ex04.
8. Close c11ex04.

## Exercise 5

1. Open tab02. This document is located on your student data disk.
2. Save the document with Save As and name it c11ex05.
3. Reverse the order of the columns by completing the following steps:
   a. Click on the Show/Hide button on the Standard toolbar to turn on the display of nonprinting characters.
   b. Move the I-beam pointer immediately left of the tab character in front of *Keith Schaufler*.
   c. Hold down the Alt key first and then the left mouse button.
   d. Drag the I-beam pointer down and to the right until it is positioned in the bottom right corner of the column past the longest entry (the *r* in *Schaufler*), then release the mouse button and the Alt key.
   e. Click on the Cut button on the Standard toolbar.
   f. Position the I-beam pointer immediately right of the last *t* in *Past President* (between the *t* and the paragraph mark at the end of the line).
   g. Click on the Paste button on the Standard toolbar.
4. Turn off the display of nonprinting characters.
5. Save the document again with the same name (c11ex05).
6. Print c11ex05.
7. Close c11ex05.

## Exercise 6

1. Open tab03. This document is located on your student data disk.
2. Save the document with Save As and name it c11ex06.
3. Make a copy of the first column of text below *Surgical Unit* and insert it below *Coronary Care Unit* by completing the following steps:
   a. Turn on the display of nonprinting characters.
   b. Move the I-beam pointer immediately left of the tab character in front of *Insurance Forms*.
   c. Hold down the Alt key and the left mouse button.
   d. Drag the I-beam pointer down and to the right until it is positioned in the bottom right corner of the column past the longest entry (the last *s* in *Consultant's Reports*).
   e. Release the mouse button and the Alt key.

f. Move the I-beam pointer inside the selected text until it becomes an arrow pointer.

g. Hold down the Ctrl key first and then the left mouse button, drag the insertion point (displays as a grayed vertical bar) a double space below *Coronary Care Unit*, at the left margin, then release the mouse button, then the Ctrl key.

4. Key the following colors after the entries below *Coronary Care Unit* as indicated below:

| | |
|---|---|
| Insurance Forms | White |
| Patient Records | Brown |
| Doctor's Reports | Green |
| Consultant's Reports | Gray |
| Pharmacology | Blue |
| Medical Supplies | Red |

To key the colors after the column entries, position the insertion point after the first entry, *Insurance Forms*. Press the Tab key, then key *White*. Press the down arrow key to move the insertion point down to the next line (do not press the Enter key). Press the Tab key, then key the next color, *Brown*. Continue in this manner until all colors have been keyed.

5. Turn off the display of nonprinting characters.

6. Save the document again with the same name (c11ex06).

7. Print c11ex06.

8. Close c11ex06.

## Exercise 7

1. Open tab04. This document is located on your student data disk.

2. Save the document with Save As and name it c11ex07.

3. Delete the second column by completing the following steps:

   a. Turn on the display of nonprinting characters.

   b. Position the insertion point immediately left of the *A* in *April*.

   c. Press Ctrl + Shift + F8. (This turns on the Column Extend feature.)

   d. Press the down arrow key and the right arrow key until the insertion point is positioned immediately *left* of the *8* in *89%* (the last entry in the third column). (This selects the second column and the space after the second column up to the third column.)

   e. Click on the Cut button on the Standard toolbar.

4. Delete the tab symbol at the 4-inch mark on the Ruler by completing the following steps:

   a. Select all the text in the document except the title.

   b. Position the arrow pointer on the tab symbol at the 4-inch mark on the Ruler, hold down the left mouse button, drag the insertion point into the document screen, then release the mouse button.

   c. Deselect the text.

5. Turn off the display of nonprinting characters.

6. Save the document again with the same name (c11ex07).

7. Print c11ex07.

8. Close c11ex07.

## Exercise 8

1. Open memo02. This document is located on your student data disk.

2. Select the paragraphs containing book titles (the second paragraph through the fifth paragraph), then save them as a separate document named *books* by completing the following steps:

   a. Select the second paragraph through the fifth paragraph (the paragraphs containing book titles).

   b. Click on the Copy button on the Standard toolbar.

   c. Click on the New button on the Standard toolbar.

   d. At the clear document screen, click on the Paste button on the Standard toolbar.

   e. Save the document and name it *books*.

    f. Close the books document.
3. Close memo02.
4. At a clear document screen, key the memorandum headings and the first paragraph of the text shown in figure 11.5. Use an appropriate memorandum format. After keying the first paragraph, press Enter twice, then insert the books document by completing the following steps:
    a. Choose Insert, then File.
    b. At the File dialog box, key **books**, then choose OK or press Enter.
5. Move the insertion point a double space below the last paragraph, then key the last paragraph shown in figure 11.5. Include your initials and the document name a double space below the last line of the paragraph.
6. Select the second through the fifth paragraphs (the paragraphs containing book titles), then insert bullets before the paragraphs. (Use the Bullets button on the Formatting toolbar.)
7. Save the memorandum and name it c11ex08.
8. Print c11ex08.
9. Close c11ex08.

**Figure 11.5**

```
DATE: May 16, 1996; TO: All OT Staff; FROM: Nancy Suaro; SUBJECT:
REFERENCE BOOKS

The library has recently purchased several reference books on
graphics and graphics design.  These books are now available at the
library.  The books that are available include:

[Insert books document here.]

You may want to use these reference books for your desktop
publishing and graphics design classes.  Students may also want to
use them for preparing documents or writing reports.

xx:c11ex08
```

## SKILL ASSESSMENTS

### Assessment 1

1. Open report02. This document is located on your student data disk.
2. Save the document with Save As and name it c11sa01.
3. Make the following changes to the report:
    a. Select then delete the last sentence in the second paragraph of the report (begins with *In particular...*).
    b. Select then delete the third paragraph (begins with *Page-assembly programs...*) in the *Page Numbers (Folios)* section of the report.
    c. Move the section on *SERIAL ELEMENTS* above the section on *TEMPLATE ELEMENTS*.
    d. Select the entire document, then change to a serif font (you determine the font).
    e. Number pages at the bottom center of each page.
    f. Check page breaks in the document and, if necessary, make adjustments to the page breaks.
4. Save the document again with the same name (c11sa01).
5. Print c11sa01.
6. Close c11sa01.

## Assessment 2

1. At a clear document screen, create the document shown in figure 11.6. Triple space after the last line in the document.
2. Select the entire document, then change the font to 14-point Algerian.
3. Select and copy the text a triple space below the original text.
4. Copy the text two more times. (There should be a total of four forms when you are done and they should fit on one page.)
5. Save the document and name it c11sa02.
6. Print c11sa02.
7. Close c11sa02.

---

**Figure 11.6**

```
                    NEWS FLASH!!


              CURTISS ELEMENTARY SCHOOL


         No school, Monday, June 10, 1996


           Elementary Teacher Work Day!
```

---

## Assessment 3

1. At a clear document screen, create the document shown in figure 11.7. You determine the tab stops for the columns. (Set a left tab for the first column and right tabs for the second and third columns.)
2. Save the document and name it c11sa03.
3. With c11sa03 open, reverse the second and third columns. (*Hint: Select the third column including the tab characters before the column but* not *the paragraph marks. After cutting the column, position the insertion point immediately right of the* n *in* Region, *then paste the column.*)
4. Center the text vertically on the page.
5. Save the document again with the same name (c11sa03).
6. Print c11sa03.
7. Delete the second column. (*Hint: Select the second column and the tab characters before the column.*)
8. Change the tab stops so the remaining columns are more balanced on the page.
9. Save the document again with the same name (c11sa03).
10. Print c11sa03.
11. Close c11sa03.

Figure 11.7

**REGIONAL SALES**

| Region | September | August |
|--------|-----------|---------|
| North | $120,459 | $143,200 |
| South | 213,209 | 235,309 |
| East | 255,304 | 274,302 |
| West | 132,095 | 129,433 |

## Assessment 4

1. Open cntrct01. This document is located on your student data disk.
2. Complete the following steps:
   a. Select the first paragraph, copy it to a new document, save it and name it *cont01*, then close cont01.
   b. Select the second paragraph, copy it to a new document, save it and name it *cont02*, then close cont02.
   c. Select the third paragraph, copy it to a new document, save it and name it *cont03*, then close cont03.
   d. Select the fourth paragraph, copy it to a new document, save it and name it *cont04*, then close cont04.
   e. Select the fifth paragraph, copy it to a new document, save it and name it *cont05*, then close cont05.
   f. Select the sixth paragraph, copy it to a new document, save it and name it *cont06*, then close cont06.
   g. Select the seventh paragraph, copy it to a new document, save it and name it *cont07*, then close cont07.
3. Close cntrct01.
4. At a clear document screen, key the information shown in figure 11.8. Insert the documents as identified in the bracketed text.
5. Make the following changes to the document:
   a. Change the top margin to 1.5 inches.
   b. Select the paragraphs within the body of the document (excluding the signature lines), then change line spacing to 2 and the First Line indent to 0.5 inches. (Make sure there is only a double space between paragraphs. If there is more, delete the extra space.)
   c. Create a footer that prints *AGREEMENT* at the left margin and the page number at the right margin.
6. Save the document and name it c11sa04.
7. Print c11sa04.
8. Close c11sa04.

**Figure 11.8**

**AGREEMENT BETWEEN SEAVIEW AIRLINES**

**AND**

**AIRLINE WORKERS UNION**

**PURPOSE AND SCOPE**

**[Insert cont04 here.]**

**[Insert cont03 here.]**

**[Insert cont02 here.]**

**[Insert cont05 here.]**

**[Insert cont07 here.]**

_____
KELLY EDWARDS, President
Seaview Airlines


_____
JULIETTE CHANNING, President
Airline Workers Union

# Working with Multiple Windows 12

Upon successful completion of chapter 12, you will be able to open multiple windows to move or copy text between business documents.

Word for Windows operates within the Windows environment created by the Windows program. However, when working in Word, a *window* refers to the document screen.

The Windows program creates an environment in which various software programs are used with menu bars, scroll bars, and icons to represent programs and files. With the Windows program, you can load several different software programs and move between them quickly. Similarly, using windows in Word, you can open several different documents and move between them quickly.

## ■ Opening Windows

With multiple documents open, you can move the insertion point between them. You can move or copy information between documents or compare the contents of several documents.

The maximum number of windows that you can have open at one time is nine. (Depending on your computer's memory, this number may be lower.) When you open a new window, it is placed on top of the original window. Once multiple windows are opened, you can resize the windows to see all or a portion of them on the screen.

A new window can be opened with the New option from the File menu. This will open an empty document. You can also open a new document window with the shortcut command, Ctrl + N, or by clicking on the New button on the Standard toolbar. (The New button is the first button from the left on the Standard toolbar.)

When you are working in a document, the document fills the entire document screen. If you open another document without closing the first, the newly opened document will fill the document screen. The first document is still open, but it is covered by the new one. To see what documents are currently open, choose Window from the Menu Bar. When you choose Window, the Window drop-down menu shown in figure 12.1 displays. (The number of documents and document names displayed at the bottom of the menu will vary.)

Figure 12.1
Window Menu

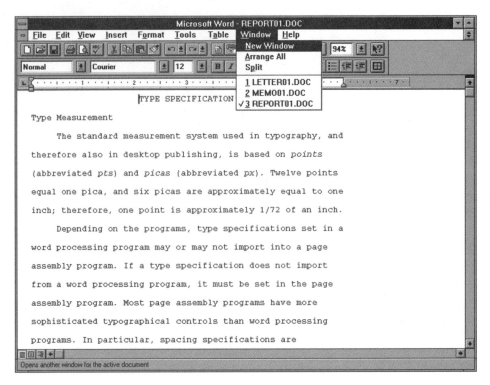

The open document names are displayed at the bottom of the drop-down menu. The document name with the check mark in front of it is the *active* document. The active document is the document containing the insertion point.

To make one of the other documents active, move the arrow pointer to the desired document name, then click the left mouse button. If you are using the keyboard, key the number shown in front of the desired document. When you change the active document, the Window drop-down menu is removed and the new active document is displayed. You can also use the Next Document Window command, Ctrl + F6, to display the next window; or the Previous Document Window command, Ctrl + Shift + F6, to display the previous window.

## ■ *S*plitting a *W*indow

With the Split command from the Window menu you can divide a window into two *panes*. This is helpful if you want to view different parts of the same document at one time. You may wish to display an outline for a report in one pane, for example, and the portion of the report that you are editing in the other. The split occurs vertically; the original window is split into two panes that extend horizontally across the screen.

A window can be split with the Split option from the Window menu or with the Split icon. To split the current document window using the Split option, you would complete the following steps:

1. Open the document.
2. Choose Window, Split.
3. Press the Enter key or click the left mouse button.

When you choose Split from the Window menu, a double line displays in the middle of the screen. Move this line up or down if desired by dragging the mouse or by pressing the up and/or down arrow keys on the keyboard. When the double line is positioned at the desired location in the document, click the left mouse button or press the Enter key.

You can also split the window with the Split icon. The Split icon is the solid black horizontal bar above the up scroll arrow on the vertical scroll bar as identified in figure 12.2.

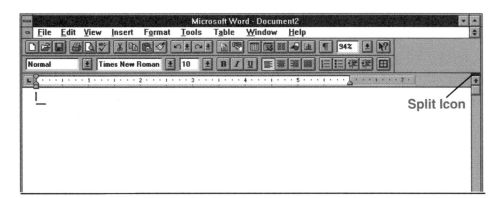

*Figure 12.2*
*Split Icon*

Split Icon

To split the window with the Split icon, you would complete the following steps:

1. Position the arrow pointer on the Split icon until it turns into a short double line with an up- and down-pointing arrow.
2. Hold down the left mouse button, drag the Split icon down into the document screen to the location where you want the window split, then release the mouse button.

When a window is split, the insertion point is positioned in the bottom pane. To move the insertion point to the other pane with the mouse, position the I-beam pointer in the other pane, then click the left mouse button. If you are using the keyboard, press F6 to move to the next pane. (You can also press Shift + F6 which is the Previous Pane command.) Figure 12.3 displays a document split into two windows. If the Ruler is displayed when you split the window, the Ruler will display above the split line.

To remove the split line from the document, choose Window, then Remove Split. You can also remove the split with the mouse by completing the following steps:

1. Position the arrow pointer on the Split line until it turns into a short double line with an up- and down-pointing arrow.
2. Hold down the left mouse button, drag the split line up to the top of the screen or down to the bottom of the screen, then release the mouse button.

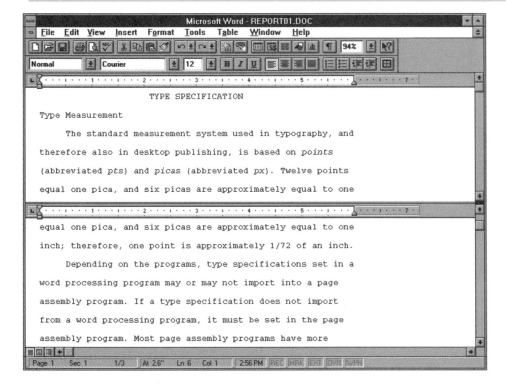

*Figure 12.3*
*Split Window*

# ■ *Arranging Windows*

If you have more than one document open, you can use the <u>A</u>rrange All option from the <u>W</u>indow menu to view a portion of all open documents. To do this, choose <u>W</u>indow, <u>A</u>rrange All. Figure 12.4 shows a document screen with three documents open that have been arranged.

When open documents are arranged, a portion of each window is displayed on the screen. The Title bar for each document is displayed along with the vertical and horizontal scroll bars.

# ■ *Sizing Windows*

You can use the maximize, minimize, and restore buttons in the upper right corner of the active document. The maximize button is the button in the upper right corner of the active document containing the up-pointing triangle. The minimize button is the button in the upper right corner containing the down-pointing triangle. The restore button is the button in the upper right corner containing the up- and down-pointing triangles.

If you arrange all open documents, then click on the maximize button in the active document, the active document expands to fill the document screen. To return the active document back to its size before it was maximized, click on the restore button. If you click on the minimize button in the active document, the document is reduced to an icon that displays at the bottom of the screen. To restore a document that has been reduced to an icon, move the arrow pointer to the icon, then double-click the left mouse button. Figure 12.5 shows an example of the document named *memo01* that has been minimized to an icon.

The top gray box in the upper left corner of the screen is called the Application control button. It is used to change the size of the Windows application window. The second gray box in the upper left corner of the screen is called the Document control button. The Document control button is used to change the size of the Word for Windows application window.

*Figure 12.4*
*Arranged*
*Documents*

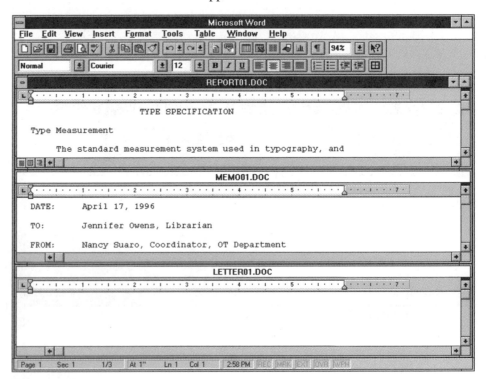

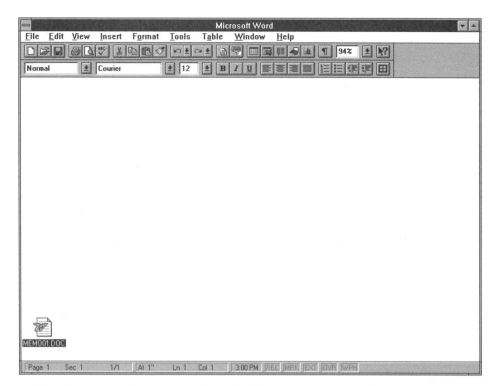

Figure 12.5
Minimized
Document

To minimize a document using the Document control button with the mouse, you would complete the following steps:

1. Open the document you want to minimize.
2. Click on the Document control button (the second one in the upper left corner of the screen).
3. At the Document control drop-down menu, click on Minimize.

To minimize a document using the Document control button with the keyboard, you would complete the following steps:

1. Open the document you want to minimize.
2. Press Alt + hyphen (-).
3. At the Document control drop-down menu, key **N** for Minimize.

When a document has been minimized, it can be restored or maximized with the mouse or keyboard and the Document control button. To maximize a minimized document using the mouse, position the mouse cursor on the icon, then double-click the left mouse button.

To maximize a document using the Document control button with the keyboard, you would complete the following steps:

1. Make the icon the active document by pressing Ctrl + F6 until the document name below the icon displays with white letters on a blue background.
2. Press Alt + hyphen (-).
3. At the Document control drop-down menu, key **X** for Maximize or key **R** for Restore.

The difference between the Maximize and Restore options is that Maximize increases the size of the document to fill the entire document screen while Restore returns the icon to its previous size.

Go To
Exercise
4

The size of documents that have been arranged can be increased or decreased using the mouse. To increase or decrease the size of the active document window vertically, move the arrow pointer to the double line border at the right or left side of the window until the arrow pointer becomes a left- and right-pointing arrow. Hold down the left mouse button, then drag the border to the right or left. When the window is the desired size, release the mouse button.

To increase or decrease the size of the active window horizontally, move the mouse cursor to the double line border at the top or bottom of the window until the mouse cursor becomes an up- and down-pointing arrow. Hold down the left mouse button, then drag the mouse up or down to increase or decrease the size. When the window is the desired size, release the mouse button.

## ■ Cutting and Pasting Text Between Windows

With several documents open, you can easily move, copy, and/or paste text from one document to another. To move, copy, and/or paste text between documents, use the cutting and pasting options you learned in chapter 11 together with the information about windows in this chapter.

For example, suppose you want to cut a paragraph from a document named *contract* and paste it in a document named *myerscon*. To do this using windows and cutting and pasting, you would complete the following steps:

1. Open the *myerscon* document.
2. Open the *contract* document.
3. Arrange the windows by choosing <u>W</u>indow, then <u>A</u>rrange All.
4. With the window containing the *contract* document as the active window, complete the following steps:
   a. Select the paragraph to be cut.
   b. Click on the Cut button on the Standard toolbar.
5. Click on the Title bar for *myerscon* to make it active.
6. Move the insertion point to the location where the paragraph is to be inserted, then click on the Paste button on the Standard toolbar.
7. Save the *myerscon* document, then close it. (This will close the window.)
8. With the window containing the *contract* document the active window, save and then close the document.

You would complete similar steps to copy and then paste text from one open document to another.

### CHAPTER SUMMARY

- When working in Word for Windows, a window refers to the document screen.
- You can open up to nine documents at one time, depending on your computer's memory. With multiple documents open, you can copy or move text between documents or compare the contents of several documents.
- A new (empty) window can be opened in several ways.
- Each document that is opened will fill the entire editing window. Move among the open documents by choosing <u>W</u>indow, then clicking the left mouse button on the desired document name or keying the number in front of that document name. The active document is the document containing the insertion point.
- With the Split command from the Window menu, you can divide a window into two panes. This enables you to view different parts of the same document at one time.
- You can use the <u>A</u>rrange All option from the <u>W</u>indow menu to view a portion of all open documents.

- Use the maximize, minimize, and restore buttons in the upper right corner of the window to reduce or increase the size of the active window.
- The Application control button, the top gray box in the upper left corner of the screen, is used to change the size of the Windows application window.
- The Document control button, the second gray box in the upper left corner of the screen, is used to change the size of the Word for Windows application window.
- With several documents open, you can easily move, copy, and/or paste text from one document to another.

## COMMANDS REVIEW

| | Mouse | Keyboard |
|---|---|---|
| Open a new (empty) document | File, then New; or click on New button on Standard toolbar | CTRL + N |
| Next Document Window | | CTRL + F6 |
| Previous Document Window | | CTRL + SHIFT + F6 |
| Split a window | Window, Split; or position arrow pointer on Split icon until it becomes an up- and down-pointing arrow, then hold down left mouse button, drag the Split icon down into document screen to desired location, release mouse button | Window, Split |
| Remove split window | Window, Remove Split | Window, Remove Split |
| Move insertion point to other window | Position I-beam pointer in pane, click left mouse button | F6 |
| Arrange all open documents | Window, Arrange All | Window, Arrange All |
| Minimize a document | Click on button with down-pointing triangle in upper right corner of active window; or click on Document control button | ALT + − , then key N for Minimize |
| Maximize a document | Click on button with up-pointing triangle in upper right corner of active window; or click on Document control button | ALT + − , then key X for Maximize or R for Restore |
| Size a document using the mouse | With arrow pointer on double line border at right/left or top/bottom, hold left mouse button, drag the border to increase or decrease window size | |

**True/False:** Circle the letter T if the statement is true; circle the letter F if the statement is false.

T    F    1.    You must tell Word to either Arrange All or Split the documents before you open more than one.

T    F    2.    With other documents open, you cannot open an empty document window.

T    F    3.    Documents displayed in windows can be increased or decreased vertically and/or horizontally using the mouse.

T    F    4.    When a document is minimized, it becomes half the size of a normal document.

T    F    5.    The Restore button is in the upper left corner of an open document and contains the up- and down-pointing triangles.

T    F    6.    Click on the Restore button to return an active document back to its size before it was maximized.

T    F    7.    You can move, copy, and/or paste text from one open document to another.

T    F    8.    The second gray box in the upper left corner of the screen is called the Document control button.

T    F    9.    To minimize a document using the Document control button with the keyboard, first press Alt + hyphen (-).

T    F    10.    When several documents are open, Word will automatically arrange each window so the document name is visible.

**Completion:** In the space provided, indicate the correct term, command, or number.

1.    This is the maximum number of documents that can be open at one time.    _____

2.    This choice causes each open document to appear in a separate window with no windows overlapping.    _____

3.    A document is reduced to this when it is minimized.    _____

4.    The word that describes the document where the insertion point is located.    _____

5.    Do this if you want a document to fill the editing window.    _____

6.    The top gray box in the upper left corner of the screen is called this.    _____

7.    This is the button in the upper right corner of the screen with the down-pointing triangle.    _____

8.    Choose this from the Menu bar to see what documents are open.    _____

9.    The Split command divides a window into these.    _____

10.    With several documents open, use this keyboard command to display the next window.    _____

## AT THE COMPUTER

### Exercise 1

1.    Open block01.
2.    Open memo01.
3.    Open letter01.
4.    Make memo01 the active document by choosing <u>W</u>indow, then <u>3</u>.
5.    Make block01 the active document by choosing <u>W</u>indow, then <u>1</u>.
6.    Close block01.
7.    Close memo01.
8.    Close letter01.

## Exercise 2

1. Open report04.
2. Save the document with Save As and name it c12ex02.
3. Split the window by completing the following steps:
   a. Choose Window, Split.
   b. With the split line displayed in the middle of the document screen, click the left mouse button.
   c. With the insertion point located in the bottom pane, move the *REPRODUCTION QUALITY* section above the *LASER PRINTOUTS* section by completing the following steps:
      (1) Press the down arrow key until *REPRODUCTION QUALITY* is visible.
      (2) Select the *REPRODUCTION QUALITY* section from the heading, *REPRODUCTION QUALITY*, to right above *CHAPTER 2: OFFSET PRINTING*.
      (3) Click on the Cut button on the Standard toolbar.
      (4) Position the arrow pointer immediately left of *LASER PRINTOUTS* in the top window pane, then click the left mouse button. (This inserts the insertion point immediately left of the *L* in *LASER PRINTOUTS*.)
      (5) Click on the Paste button on the Standard toolbar.
4. Insert a section break that begins a new page above *CHAPTER 2: OFFSET PRINTING* by completing the following steps:
   a. Position the arrow pointer immediately left of the *C* in *CHAPTER 2: OFFSET PRINTING* in the bottom window pane, then click the left mouse button.
   b. Choose Insert, Break.
   c. At the Break dialog box, choose Next Page.
   d. Choose OK or press Enter.
5. Remove the split from the window by choosing Window, Remove Split.
6. Number all pages in the document at the bottom right margin of the page.
7. Check page breaks in the document and, if necessary, make adjustments to the page breaks.
8. Save the document again with the same name (c12ex02).
9. Print c12ex02.
10. Close c12ex02.

## Exercise 3

1. Open para02.
2. Open memo02.
3. Open letter02.
4. Open report02.
5. Arrange the windows by choosing Window, then Arrange All.
6. Make letter02 the active document by positioning the arrow pointer on the title bar for letter02, then clicking the left mouse button.
7. Close letter02.
8. Make para02 active, then close it.
9. Make memo02 active, then close it.
10. Close report02.

## Exercise 4

1. Open tab03.
2. Maximize tab03 by clicking on the Maximize button at the right side of the Title bar. (The Maximize button is the button at the right side of the Title bar containing an up-pointing triangle.)
3. Open memo03.
4. Open report03.
5. Arrange the windows.
6. Make memo03 the active window.
7. Minimize memo03 to an icon using the mouse by clicking on the Minimize button in the upper right corner of the active window. (The Minimize button is the button with the down-pointing triangle.)
8. Make tab03 the active document, then minimize tab03 using the Document control button by completing the following steps:
   a. Click on the Document control button (the gray button in the upper left corner of the active document window).
   b. At the Document control drop-down menu, click on Mi<u>n</u>imize.
9. Restore the size of tab03 using the mouse by double-clicking on the tab03 icon.
10. Restore the size of memo03 using the mouse by double-clicking on the memo03 icon.
11. Make report03 the active document, then close it.
12. Close memo03.
13. Maximize tab03 by clicking on the Maximize button at the right side of the Title bar.
14. Close tab03.

## Exercise 5

1. Open memo05.
2. Open report01.
3. Arrange the windows.
4. Change the size of the report01 document window by completing the following steps:
   a. Position the arrow pointer on the double line border at the right side of the window until it turns into a left- and right-pointing arrow.
   b. Hold down the left mouse button, drag the border to the left approximately 1 inch, then release the mouse button.
   c. Position the arrow pointer on the double line border at the left side of the window until it turns into a left- and right-pointing arrow.
   d. Hold down the left mouse button, drag the border to the right approximately 1 inch, then release the mouse button.
5. Make the same changes to memo05.
6. Close memo05.
7. Maximize report01 by clicking on the Maximize button at the upper right side of the report01 window.
8. Close report01.

## Exercise 6

1. At a clear document screen, key the entire memorandum shown in figure 12.6 in an appropriate memorandum format. (Press the Enter key three times after keying the first paragraph and before you key the second paragraph.)
2. Save the memorandum and name it c12ex06.
3. With c12ex06 still open on the screen, open memo02, then arrange the windows.
4. With memo02 the active document, copy the first three books listed in the memorandum and place them after the first paragraph in c12ex06 by completing the following steps:

a. Select the three paragraphs containing the first three book titles.
b. Click on the Copy button on the Standard toolbar.
c. Deselect the text.
d. Make c12ex06 the active document.
e. Position the insertion point a double space below the first paragraph, then click on the Paste button on the Standard toolbar.
5. Save the memorandum again with the same name (c12ex06).
6. Print c12ex06.
7. Close c12ex06.
8. Close memo02.

**Figure 12.6**

```
DATE: April 23, 1996; TO: Jennifer Owens, Librarian; FROM: Alan
VanDruff, Assistant Librarian; SUBJECT: REFERENCE BOOKS

I found $75.50 in the library reference fund and $24.00 in the
emergency fund.  With these combined amounts, I was able to
purchase the following books:

[Insert book titles here.]

With funds that will become available May 1, we should be able to
purchase the remaining two books.

xx:c12ex06
```

## SKILL ASSESSMENTS

### Assessment 1

1. Open biblio01, letter01, notice01, and quiz01.
2. Make notice01 the active document.
3. Make biblio01 the active document.
4. Arrange all the windows.
5. Make quiz01 the active document, then minimize it.
6. Minimize the remaining documents.
7. Make biblio01 active, then restore it.
8. Restore letter01.
9. Restore notice01.
10. Restore quiz01.
11. Close quiz01.
12. Close notice01.
13. Close letter01.
14. Maximize biblio01.
15. Close biblio01.

## Assessment 2

1. At a clear document screen, key the letter shown in figure 12.7 in an appropriate letter format through the first paragraph (to the location where the bolded message is displayed).
2. Save the letter and name it c12sa02.
3. With c12sa02 still open, open cntrct01.
4. Arrange the windows.
5. With cntrct01 the active document, copy the first paragraph a double space below the first paragraph in the letter in c12sa02.
6. Key the third paragraph in the letter (begin with *Additionally, I...*) as shown in figure 12.7.
7. Make cntrct01 the active document, then copy the sixth paragraph a double space below the third paragraph in the letter in c12sa02.
8. Make cntrct01 the active document, then close it.
9. Maximize c12sa02.
10. Key the remaining text in the letter.
11. Save the letter again with the same name (c12sa02).
12. Print c12sa02.
13. Close c12sa02.

---

**Figure 12.7**

```
May 14, 1996

Ms. Juliette Channing, President
Airline Workers Union
230 Greentree Boulevard
Seattle, WA 98012

Dear Ms. Channing:

I received the draft of the purpose and scope for the agreement
between Seaview Airlines and the Airline Workers Union.  In this
first section of the agreement, I recommend adding the following
paragraph between the third and fourth paragraphs:

[Insert the first paragraph from cntrct01 here.]

Additionally, I recommend adding the following paragraph between
the fifth and sixth paragraphs:

[Insert the sixth paragraph from cntrct01 here.]

The preliminary agreement looks good.  I feel confident that we can
complete these contract negotiations by the end of the month.

Sincerely,

SUNDE & MAZINSKY



Elena Watts
Attorney at Law

xx:c12sa02
```

# Conducting a Find and Replace 13

Upon successful completion of chapter 13, you will be able to revise text and formatting in standard business letters and reports by using Word's find and replace features.

With Word's Find feature, you can look for a specific word or words or formatting within a document. This is helpful in locating the specific name of a person or company, a particular phrase, or a format. Once Word finds the text or formatting, you can delete it or edit the text as needed.

If you compose many documents at the keyboard, the Find feature can be helpful in locating words or phrases that are overused within a document. For example, if you overuse the phrase *I feel that...* in a document, you can find every occurrence of the phrase, then decide to leave it in the document or edit it.

The Find feature can also be used to move quickly to a specific location in a document. This is particularly useful in long documents if you want to position the insertion point at a specific location within a page.

## ▪ *Finding Text*

With the Find feature, you can search for text and formatting. You can enter up to 256 characters in the Find What text box at the Find dialog box. A search begins at the position of the insertion point. You search from the insertion point to the beginning of the document or from the location of the insertion point to the end of the document. If you want to search the entire document, position the insertion point at the beginning or end of the document before beginning the search. To conduct a search, you would complete the following steps:

1.  Choose Edit, Find; or press Ctrl + F.
2.  At the Find dialog box shown in figure 13.1, enter the characters you are searching for in the Find What text box.
3.  Choose Find Next.
4.  Word searches for and selects the first occurrence of the text in the document. Position the insertion point in the document if you want to make changes.
5.  Search for the next occurrence by choosing Find Next, or choose Cancel to close the Find dialog box.

Figure 13.1
Find Dialog Box

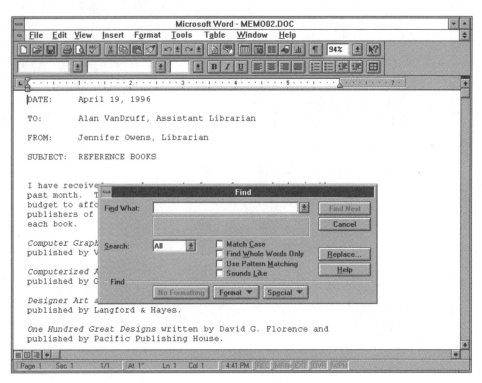

As an example of how to use the Find feature, you would complete the following steps to find all occurrences of the words *desktop publishing* in a document.

1. Position the insertion point at the beginning of the document.
2. Choose Edit, Find; or press Ctrl + F.
3. At the Find dialog box, key *desktop publishing* in the Find What text box.
4. Choose Find Next.
5. Continue choosing Find Next until Word displays the message *Word has finished searching the document.* At this message, choose OK or press Enter.
6. Choose Cancel to close the Find dialog box.

The second time you open the Find dialog box, you can display a list of text you have searched for by clicking on the down-pointing arrow after the Find What text box. For example, if you searched for *type size* and then performed another search for *type style*, the third time you open the Find dialog box, clicking on the down-pointing arrow after the Find What text box will display a drop-down menu with *type style* and *type size* listed. Click on text from this drop-down menu if you want to perform a search on that text.

## Replacing Text

If you are searching for characters and then decide to replace each occurrence with the same replacement text, choose Replace from the Find dialog box. This displays the Replace dialog box. Information on the Replace dialog box is presented later in this chapter.

## Choosing Find Check Box Options

The Find dialog box contains a variety of check boxes with options you can choose for completing a search. Figure 13.2 describes each option and what will occur if it is selected.

| Choose this option | To |
|---|---|
| Match Case | Exactly match the case of the search text. For example, if you search for *Book* and select the Match Case option, Word will stop at *Book* but not *book* or *BOOK*. |
| Find Whole Words Only | Find a whole word, not a part of a word. For example, if you search for *her* and *did not* select Find Whole Word Only, Word will stop at *there, here, hers*, etc. |
| Use Pattern Matching | Search for special operators and expressions. |
| Sound Like | Match words that sound alike but are spelled differently such as *know* and *no*. |

Figure 13.2
*Find Check Box
Options*

## Choosing a Find Direction

The Search option at the Find dialog box has a default setting of All. At this setting, Word will search the entire document. This can be changed to Up or Down. Choose Up and Word will search the document from the insertion point to the beginning of the document. Choose Down and Word will search the document from the insertion point to the end of the document.

## Finding Formatting

You can search a document for some character and paragraph formatting. For example, you can search for bold characters, characters set in a specific font, as well as some paragraph formatting such as indents and spacing.

As an example of how to search for formatting, you would complete the following steps to find the words *Type Size* that are set in 14-point Times New Roman:

1. Open the document containing the text you are searching for.
2. Make sure the insertion point is positioned at the beginning of the document, then choose Edit, Find; or press Ctrl + F.
3. Key **Type Size** in the Find What text box.
4. Choose Format.
5. Choose Font.
6. At the Find Font dialog box, choose Times New Roman in the Font list box.
7. Choose 14 in the Size list box.
8. Choose OK or press Enter.
9. At the Find dialog box, choose Find Next.
10. Continue choosing Find Next until Word displays the message *Word has finished searching the document.* At this message, choose OK or press Enter.
11. Choose Cancel to close the Find dialog box.

When you search for formatting, the formatting displays below the Find What text box in the Find dialog box.

The text and/or formatting that you searched for previously remains in the Find What text box. The next time you perform a search, the text you key in the Find What text box will replace the existing text. This does not, however, remove formatting. To remove previous formatting, choose No Formatting at the bottom of the Find dialog box.

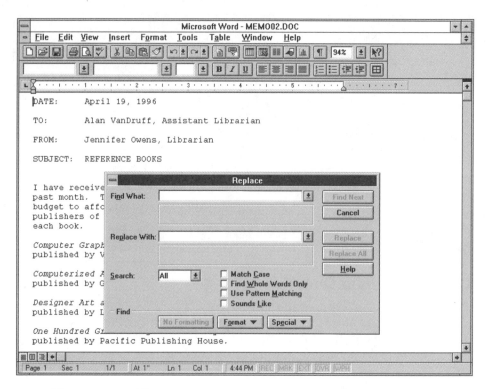

**Figure 13.3**
Replace Dialog Box

# Finding and Replacing Text

With Word's Find and Replace feature, you can look for specific characters or formatting and replace them with other characters or formatting. With the Find and Replace feature, you can:

- Correct a misspelled word by searching for it and replacing it throughout a document with the correct spelling.
- Use abbreviations for common phrases when entering text, then replace the abbreviations with the actual text later.
- Set up standard documents with generic names and replace them with other names to make personalized documents.
- Find and replace formatting.

This is just a short list of how the Find and Replace feature can make your keyboarding job easier. As you use this feature, you may find more ways that it can benefit you.

When you choose Edit, then Replace or press Ctrl + H, the Replace dialog box shown in figure 13.3 displays.

Enter the characters and/or formatting you are searching for in the Find What text box. Choose Replace With, then enter the characters or formatting you want to replace the characters or formatting in the Find What text box.

The Replace dialog box contains five command buttons at the right side. Choose the Find Next button to tell Word to find the next occurrence of the characters and/or formatting. Choose the Replace button to replace the characters or formatting and find the next occurrence. If you know that you want all occurrences of the characters or formatting in the Find What text box replaced with the characters or formatting in the Replace With text box, choose Replace All. This replaces every occurrence from the location of the insertion point to the beginning or end of the document (depending on the search direction). Choose Cancel to close the Replace dialog box.

If you choose Help, Word will display information about the Find and Replace feature.

As an example of how to complete a find and replace, you would complete the following steps to find the abbreviation *MCC* and replace it with *Mountain Community College*:

1. Open the document containing the abbreviation.
2. Position the insertion point at the beginning of the document.
3. Choose Edit, Replace; or press Ctrl + H.
4. At the Replace dialog box, key **MCC** in the Find What text box.
5. Choose Replace With.
6. Key **Mountain Community College**.
7. Choose Replace All.
8. At the message *Word has finished searching the document. X replacements were made.*, choose OK or press Enter. (Word will insert the number of replacements made in place of the *X*.)
9. Choose Close to close the Replace dialog box.

After replacements are made, the Cancel button in the Replace dialog box becomes the Close button.

In the above example, Word makes all replacements without getting confirmation from you. If you want to confirm each replacement before it is made, you would complete the following steps:

1. Open the document containing the abbreviation.
2. Position the insertion point at the beginning of the document.
3. Choose Edit, Replace; or press Ctrl + H.
4. At the Replace dialog box, key **MCC** in the Find What text box.
5. Choose Replace With.
6. Key **Mountain Community College**.
7. Choose Find Next.
8. Word stops at the first occurrence of *MCC*. If you want to replace the abbreviation, choose Replace. This replaces the text and finds the next occurrence of the abbreviation.
9. At the next occurrence, choose Replace if you want to replace the abbreviation with the name.
10. Continue in this manner until Word displays the message *Word has finished searching the document.* At this message, choose OK or press Enter.
11. Choose Close to close the Replace dialog box.

If you did not want to replace an occurrence with the replace text, choose Find Next. This tells Word to find the next occurrence without replacing the current occurrence.

The second time you open the Replace dialog box, you can display a list of text you have entered in the Replace With text box. To do this, click on the down-pointing arrow after the Replace With text box. To choose text from the Replace With list box, click on the desired text.

## Choosing Find Check Box Options

The Replace dialog box contains the same check box options as the Find dialog box. Refer to figure 13.2 to determine what will occur if a check box option is selected.

## Finding and Replacing Formatting

With Word's Find and Replace feature, you can find specific formatting or characters containing specific formatting and replace it with other characters or formatting. For example, you can find the text *Type Style* set in 14-point Courier and replace it with the text *Type Style* set in 18-point Times New Roman. You can also find specific formatting and delete it. For example, you can find bold formatting and replace it with nothing. This will remove bold formatting from the document leaving the text.

As an example of how to find and replace formatting, you would complete the following steps to find justified paragraph alignment and replace it with left paragraph alignment:

1. Open the document containing the formatting you want to change.
2. Position the insertion point at the beginning of the document.
3. Choose Edit, Replace; or press Ctrl + H.
4. Delete any characters in the Find What text box. If there is any formatting displayed below the Find What text box, choose No Formatting at the bottom of the dialog box.
5. Make sure the insertion point is positioned in the Find What text box, then choose Format, then Paragraph.
6. At the Find Paragraph dialog box, make sure the Indents and Spacing tab is selected, then choose Alignment, then Justified.
7. Choose OK or press Enter to close the Find Paragraph dialog box.
8. At the Replace dialog box, choose Replace With. Delete any characters in the Replace With text box. If there is any formatting displayed below the Replace With text box, choose No Formatting at the bottom of the dialog box.
9. Make sure the insertion point is positioned in the Replace With text box, then choose Format, then Paragraph.
10. At the Replace Paragraph dialog box, choose Alignment, then Left.
11. Choose OK or press Enter to close the Replace Paragraph dialog box.
12. At the Replace dialog box, choose Replace All.
13. When Word displays the message *Word has finished searching the document. X replacements were made.*, choose OK or press Enter.
14. Choose Close to close the Replace dialog box.

## Finding and Replacing Special Characters

In this chapter you have learned how to find text and/or formatting in a document. You have also learned how to find and replace text and/or formatting. You can also find and replace special characters such as paragraph marks, tab characters, blank spaces, and much more.

When you choose the Special button at the bottom of the Find dialog box or the Replace dialog box, a list of special symbols displays. The number of options at this list will vary depending on whether you are entering the character in the Find What text box or the Replace With text box. Figure 13.4 shows the special character and identifies if it is available only for find or replace.

*Figure 13.4*
*Special Characters*

| Choosing this | Inserts this |
| --- | --- |
| Paragraph Mark | ^p |
| Tab Character | ^t |
| Annotation Mark (Find only) | ^a |
| Any Character (Find only) | ^? |
| Any Digit (Find only) | ^# |
| Any Letter (Find only) | ^$ |
| Caret Character | ^^ |
| Column Break | ^n |
| Em Dash | ^+ |
| En Dash | ^= |
| Endnote Mark (Find only) | ^e |
| Field (Find only) | ^d |
| Footnote Mark (Find only) | ^f |

| Choosing this | Inserts this |
|---|---|
| Graphic (Find only) | ^g |
| Manual Line Break | ^l |
| Manual Page Break | ^m |
| Nonbreaking Hyphen | ^~ |
| Nonbreaking Space | ^s |
| Optional Hyphen | ^- |
| Section Break (Find only) | ^b |
| White Space (any space—one space, multiple spaces, tab spaces—bordered by characters (Find only) | ^w |
| Clipboard Contents (Replace only) | ^c |
| Find What Text (Replace only) | ^& |

If you want to find or replace special characters, turning on the display of nonprinting characters is helpful. As an example of how to use special characters, you would complete the following steps to find all section breaks in a document and replace them with manual page breaks:

1. Open the document containing the section breaks you want changed to manual page breaks.
2. Position the insertion point at the beginning of the document.
3. Choose Edit, Replace; or press Ctrl + H.
4. Delete any characters in the Find What text box. If there is any formatting displayed below the Find What text box, choose No Formatting at the bottom of the dialog box.
5. Make sure the insertion point is positioned in the Find What text box, then choose Special. (This command button is located at the bottom of the dialog box.)
6. At the list of special characters, choose Section Break. To do this with the mouse, click on Section Break. If you are using the keyboard, press the letter B.
7. At the Replace dialog box, choose Replace With. Delete any characters in the Replace With text box. If there is any formatting displayed below the Replace With text box, choose No Formatting at the bottom of the dialog box.
8. Make sure the insertion point is positioned in the Replace With text box, then choose Special.
9. At the list of special characters, choose Manual Page Break. To do this with the mouse, click on Manual Page Break. If you are using the keyboard, press the letter K.
10. At the Replace dialog box, choose Replace All.
11. When Word displays the message *Word has finished searching the document. X replacements were made.*, choose OK or press Enter.
12. Choose Close to close the Replace dialog box.

Go To
Exercise
7

- With the Find feature you can quickly locate specific words, phrases, or formatting. Once located, these items can then be edited or deleted.
- A find begins at the location of the insertion point and searches from there to the beginning of the document (Up) or to the end (Down).
- The second time you open the Find dialog box, you can display a list of text you have searched for by clicking on the down-pointing arrow after the Find What text box.
- If you are searching for characters and then decide to replace each occurrence with the same replacement text, choose Replace from the Find dialog box to display the Replace dialog box.
- The Find dialog box contains a variety of check boxes with options for completing a search, such as Match Case, Find Whole Words Only, Use Pattern Matching, and Sounds Like.
- You can search a document for some character and paragraph formatting such as bold characters, specific fonts, indents, and spacing.
- With Word's Find and Replace feature, you can look for specific characters or formatting and replace with other characters or formatting.
- The Replace dialog box contains these five options: Find Next, Cancel, Replace, Replace All, and Help. With these options, you can choose to skip an occurrence of the search item, replace it, or replace all occurrences at once.
- The second time you open the Replace dialog box, you can display a list of text you have entered in the Replace With text box.
- When you choose the Special button at the bottom of the Find dialog box or the Replace dialog box, a list of special symbols displays that you can find or replace such as a paragraph mark, tab character, or graphic.

## COMMANDS REVIEW

|  | Mouse | Keyboard |
|---|---|---|
| Find dialog box | Edit, Find | CTRL + F |
| Replace dialog box | Edit, Replace | CTRL + H |

## CHECK YOUR UNDERSTANDING

**True/False:** Circle the letter T if the statement is true; circle the letter F if the statement is false.

T  F  1.  You can enter no more than 80 characters in the Find What text box.

T  F  2.  Word will automatically search through the entire document, no matter where the insertion point is located.

T  F  3.  You can use Word's Find and Replace feature to remove all bold formatting from a document.

T  F  4.  You can change the type style of specific text using Word's Find and Replace feature.

T  F  5.  You can use Word's Find feature to search for spaces in a document.

**Completion:** In the space provided, indicate the correct term, command, or number.

1.  If you want to search from the insertion point to the end of the document, choose this at the Find dialog box.    _____

2.  Use these for common phrases when entering text, then replace them with the actual text using find and replace.    _____

3.  The second time you open the Find dialog box, you can display this list.    _____

4. Use this keyboard command to display the Replace dialog box.  _____
5. If you want to replace every occurrence of what you are searching for in a document, choose this at the Replace dialog box.  _____
6. Choose this command button at the Replace dialog box if you do not want to replace an occurrence with the replace text.  _____
7. When you choose the Special button at the bottom of the Find dialog box, this displays.  _____
8. Use this keyboard command to display the Find dialog box.  _____
9. Display a list of text you have entered previously in the Replace With text box by clicking here.  _____

## AT THE COMPUTER

### Exercise 1

1. Open report01.
2. Find every occurrence of *program* in the document by completing the following steps:
   a. With the insertion point positioned at the beginning of the document, choose Edit, Find; or press Ctrl + F.
   b. At the Find dialog box, key **program** in the Find What text box.
   c. Choose Find Next.
   d. Word searches for and selects the first occurrence of *program*.
   e. Search for the next occurrence of *program* by choosing Find Next.
   f. Continue choosing Find Next until Word displays the message *Word has finished searching the document.* At this message, choose OK or press Enter.
   g. Choose Cancel to close the Find dialog box.
3. Close report01.

### Exercise 2

1. Open report02.
2. Find every occurrence of the word *publication* that exactly matches the case by completing the following steps:
   a. Move the insertion point to the end of the document.
   b. Choose Edit, Find; or press Ctrl + F.
   c. At the Find dialog box, key **publication** in the Find What text box.
   d. Choose Match Case.
   e. Choose Find Whole Words Only.
   f. Choose Search, then Up.
   g. Choose Find Next.
   h. Word searches for and selects the first occurrence (from the end of the document) of *publication*.
   i. Search for the next occurrence of *publication* by choosing Find Next.
   j. Continue choosing Find Next until Word displays the message *Word has finished searching the document.* At this message, choose OK or press Enter.
   k. Choose Cancel to close the Find dialog box.
3. Close report02.

### Exercise 3

1. Open report02.
2. Find all text set in italics by completing the following steps:
   a. Make sure the insertion point is positioned at the beginning of the document, then choose Edit, Find; or press Ctrl + F.
   b. With the insertion point positioned in the Find What text box, press the Delete key. (This deletes any text that displays in the text box.)

c. Choose F<u>o</u>rmat.

d. Choose <u>F</u>ont.

e. At the Find Font dialog box, choose Italic in the F<u>o</u>nt Style list box.

f. Choose OK or press Enter.

g. At the Find dialog box, choose Match <u>C</u>ase to remove the X from the check box. (Skip this step if the X does not appear in the check box.)

h. Choose Find <u>W</u>hole Word Only to remove the X from the check box. (Skip this step if the X does not appear in the check box.)

i. Choose <u>S</u>earch, then All.

j. Choose <u>F</u>ind Next.

k. Continue choosing <u>F</u>ind Next until Word displays the message *Word has finished searching the document.* At this message, choose OK or press Enter.

l. Choose Cancel to close the Find dialog box.

3. Close report02.

## Exercise 4

1. Open legal01. This document is located on your student data disk.

2. Save the document with Save As and name it c13ex04.

3. Find all occurrences of *NAME1* and replace with *PAUL G. AVEY* by completing the following steps:

   a. With the insertion point positioned at the beginning of the document, choose <u>E</u>dit, <u>R</u>eplace; or press Ctrl + H.

   b. At the Replace dialog box, choose No Forma<u>t</u>ting. (This removes the Italic formatting from the previous exercise.)

   c. Key **NAME1** in the Fi<u>n</u>d What text box.

   d. Choose Re<u>p</u>lace With.(If any text displays in the Re<u>p</u>lace With dialog box, delete it.)

   e. Key **PAUL G. AVEY**.

   f. Choose Replace <u>A</u>ll.

   g. At the message *Word has finished searching the document. 5 replacements were made.*, choose OK or press Enter.

   h. Choose Close to close the Replace dialog box.

4. Complete steps similar to those in 3a through 3h to find all occurrences of *NAME2* and replace with *TRACY A. ROSS.*

5. Complete steps similar to those in 3a through 3h to find the one occurrence of *NUMBER* and replace with *C-5403.*

6. Adjust the right parenthesis in the heading. (A couple of right parentheses became misaligned when the names were inserted.)

7. Save the document again with the same name (c13ex04).

8. Print c13ex04.

9. Close c13ex04.

## Exercise 5

1. Open report05.

2. Select all the text in chapter 3, copy then paste the text to a new document screen, then save the document as c13ex05.

3. Make report05 the active window, then close it.

4. With c13ex05 open, find all occurrences of *paper* and replace with *stationery* by completing the following steps:

   a. With the insertion point positioned at the beginning of the document, choose <u>E</u>dit, <u>R</u>eplace; or press Ctrl + H.

   b. At the Replace dialog box, choose Find <u>W</u>hole Words Only.

   c. Choose Fi<u>n</u>d What.

    d. Key **paper.**

    e. Choose Replace With.

    f. Key **stationery**.

    g. Choose Find Next. When Word stops at the first occurrence of *paper* (in the title), choose Find Next. (This tells Word to leave the first occurrence alone and search for the next occurrence.)

    h. Continue choosing Replace when Word stops at an occurrence of *paper*, except in the heading *Grades of Paper*. At this occurrence, choose Find Next.

    i. At the message *Word has finished searching the document. X replacements were made.*, choose OK or press Enter. (Word will insert the number of replacements made in place of the *X*.)

    j. Choose Find Whole Words Only to remove the X from the check box.

    k. Choose Close to close the Replace dialog box.

5. Save the document again with the same name (c13ex05).

6. Print c13ex05.

7. Close c13ex05.

## Exercise 6

1. Open report01.

2. Save the document with Save As and name it c13ex06.

3. Find all italics and *add* bold formatting by completing the following steps:

    a. With the insertion point positioned at the beginning of the document, choose Edit, Replace; or press Ctrl + H.

    b. Delete any characters in the Find What text box. If there is any formatting displayed below the Find What text box, choose No Formatting at the bottom of the dialog box.

    c. Make sure the insertion point is positioned in the Find What text box, then choose Format, then Font.

    d. At the Find Font dialog box, choose Font Style, then Italic.

    e. Choose OK or press Enter to close the Find Font dialog box.

    f. At the Replace dialog box, choose Replace With. Delete any characters in the Replace With text box. If there is any formatting displayed below the Replace With text box, choose No Formatting at the bottom of the dialog box.

    g. Make sure the insertion point is positioned in the Replace With text box, then choose Format, then Font.

    h. At the Replace Font dialog box, choose Font Style, then Bold.

    i. Choose OK or press Enter to close the Replace Font dialog box.

    j. At the Replace dialog box, choose Replace All.

    k. When Word displays the message *Word has finished searching the document. 7 replacements were made.*, choose OK or press Enter.

    l. Choose Close to close the Replace dialog box.

4. Make the following changes to the document:

    a. Change the left and right margins to 1 inch.

    b. Select the entire document, then change the font to 12-point Times New Roman.

    c. Select the title, then change the font to 14-point Times New Roman Bold.

    d. Set the headings (*Type Measurement*, *Type Size*, and *Type Style*) in 14-point Times New Roman Bold.

    e. Insert bullets before the last four paragraphs of the document.

    f. Create a footer that prints *TYPE SPECIFICATION* at the left margin and the page number at the right margin, is set in 12-point Times New Roman Bold, and prints on every page.

5. Save the document again with the same name (c13ex06).

6. Print c13ex06. (The italics text will print in bold.)

7. Close c13ex06.

## Exercise 7

1. Open para03.
2. Save the document with Save As and name it c13ex07.
3. Find all occurrences of paragraph marks and replace them with nothing (this removes all paragraph marks from the document) by completing the following steps:
    a. With the insertion point positioned at the beginning of the document, choose Edit, Replace; or press Ctrl + H.
    b. Delete any characters in the Find What text box. If there is any formatting displayed below the Find What text box, choose No Formatting at the bottom of the dialog box.
    c. Make sure the insertion point is positioned in the Find What text box, then choose Special. (This command button is located at the bottom of the dialog box.)
    d. At the list of special characters, choose Paragraph Mark. To do this with the mouse, click on Paragraph Mark. If you are using the keyboard, press the letter P.
    e. At the Replace dialog box, choose Replace With. Delete any characters in the Replace With text box. If there is any formatting displayed below the Replace With text box, choose No Formatting at the bottom of the dialog box.
    f. Choose Replace All.
    g. When Word displays the message *Word has finished searching the document. 7 replacements were made.*, choose OK or press Enter.
    h. Choose Close to close the Replace dialog box.
4. Save the document again with the same name (c13ex07).
5. Print c13ex07.
6. Close c13ex07.

## SKILL ASSESSMENTS

### Assessment 1

1. Open cntrct02. This document is located on your student data disk.
2. Save the document with Save As and name it c13sa01.
3. Make the following changes to the document:
    a. Find all occurrences of *HAYES CORPORATION* and replace with *CASCADE MANUFACTURING*.
    b. Find all occurrences of *HC* and replace with *CM*.
    c. Find all occurrences of *OFFICE WORKERS UNION* and replace with *SUPPORT SERVICES UNION*.
    d. Find all occurrences of *OWU* and replace with *SSU*.
4. Save the document again with the same name (c13sa01).
5. Print c13sa01.
6. Close c13sa01.

## Assessment 2

1. Open legal02.
2. Save the document with Save As and name it c13sa02.
3. Make the following changes to the document:
   a. Find all occurrences of *NAME1* and replace with *SEAN A. WINSLOW*.
   b. Find the one occurrence of *NUMBER* and replace with *C-8532*.
   c. Find all bold formatting and add italic formatting to text, except the following:
      > *IN DISTRICT COURT NO. 4, COOK COUNTY*
      > *STATE OF ILLINOIS*
      > *EUGENE BLAKE*
4. Save the document again with the same name (c13sa02).
5. Print c13sa02.
6. Close c13sa02.

## Assessment 3

1. Open c13sa01.
2. Save the document with Save As and name it c13sa03.
3. Make the following changes to the document:
   a. Find bold formatting and add italic formatting to text in the document *except* the title and headings.
   b. Find all occurrences of justified paragraph alignment and replace with left paragraph alignment.
4. Save the document again with the same name (c13sa03).
5. Print c13sa03.
6. Close c13sa03.

# Printing 14

Upon successful completion of chapter 14, you will be able to control printing features for simple business documents and print envelopes and mailing labels.

In chapter 2, you learned to print the document displayed in the document screen at the Print dialog box. By default, one copy of all pages is printed of the currently open document. In this chapter, you will learn to customize a print job with selections from the Print dialog box.

## ■ Using the Print Dialog Box

To display the Print dialog box shown in figure 14.1, choose one of the following methods:

- Choose File, Print.
- Press Ctrl + P.
- Press Ctrl + Shift + F12.

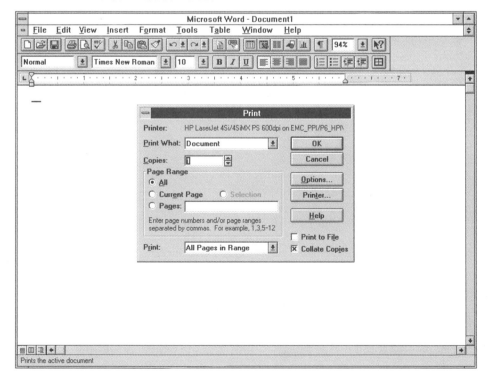

*Figure 14.1*
*Print Dialog Box*

The name of the selected printer is displayed after the Printer option at the top of the Print dialog box. When Word for Windows was installed on the hard drive or network, a printer was selected. The printer displayed after *Printer* should be the printer you are using.

By default, Word prints the document currently displayed in the document screen. With Print What options you can print various parts of a document. If you click on the down-pointing arrow after the Print What text box, a drop-down list displays with the options, Document Summary Info, Annotations, Styles, AutoText Entries, and Key Assignments. As you learn about these options, you can print these sections by choosing the desired option.

To cancel a print job, press the Esc key or choose Cancel from the Print dialog box.

## Printing Multiple Copies

If you want to print more than one copy of a document, use the Copies option from the Print dialog box. To print more copies of the document, increase the number in the Copies text box. As an example of how to use this feature, you would complete the following steps to print three copies of the document currently displayed in the document screen:

1. Display the Print dialog box.
2. Key **3** (or click on the up-pointing triangle after the Copies text box until *3* displays in the box). (When the Print dialog box is first displayed, the insertion point is automatically positioned in the Copies text box.)
3. Choose OK or press Enter.

If you print several copies of a document containing multiple pages, Word prints the pages in the document collated. For example, if you print two copies of a three-page document, pages 1, 2, and 3 are printed; then the pages are printed a second time. Printing pages collated is helpful but takes more printing time. To speed up the printing time, you can tell Word to print the pages *not* collated. To do this, remove the X from the Collate Copies option at the bottom of the Print dialog box. With the X removed, Word will print all copies of the first page, then all copies of the second page, and so on.

## Printing Specific Text or Pages

The Page Range section of the Print dialog box contains settings you can use to specify the amount of text you want printed. At the default setting of All, all pages of the current document are printed. Choose the Current Page option to print the page where the insertion point is located. If you want to select then print a portion of the document, choose the Selection option at the Print dialog box. This prints only the text that has been selected in the current document. (This option is dimmed unless text is selected in the document.)

With the Pages option, you can identify a specific page for printing, multiple pages, and/or a range of pages. If you want specific multiple pages printed, use a comma (,) to indicate *and* and use a hyphen (-) to indicate *through*. For example, to print pages 2 and 5, you would key 2,5 in the Pages text box. To print pages 6 through 11, you would key 6-11. Figure 14.2 illustrates options for printing pages (X, Y, and Z denote page numbers):

*Figure 14.2*
*Page Printing Options*

| Entry | Action |
|---|---|
| X | Page X printed |
| X,Y | Pages X and Y printed |
| X- | Pages X to end of document printed |
| X-Y | Pages X through Y printed |
| -X | Beginning of document through page X printed |
| X-Y,Z | Pages X through Y and page Z printed |

As illustrated in the last entry in figure 14.2, the hyphen and comma can be used in the same print job. As an example of how to print multiple pages in a document, you would complete the following steps to print pages 3 through 6 and pages 9 and 12 of the current document:

1. Open the document containing pages to be printed.
2. Display the Print dialog box.
3. At the Print dialog box, choose Pages.
4. Key **3-6,9,12**.
5. Choose OK or press Enter.

In addition to specifying pages in the document, you can print pages in a specific section. For example, if you want to print the pages in the third section of a document, you would key **s3** in the Pages text box.

### Printing Odd and/or Even Pages

If you are printing on both sides of the paper, the Odd Pages and Even Pages selections from the Print option are useful. For example, you can print all odd pages in the document, turn the pages over, then print all even pages on the back side.

To print odd or even pages, you would complete the following steps:

1. Open the document containing pages to be printed.
2. Display the Print dialog box.
3. Choose Print, then Odd Pages or Even Pages. To do this with the mouse, click on the down-pointing arrow after the Print text box, then click on Odd Pages or Even Pages. If you are using the keyboard, press Alt + R, then press the down arrow key until Odd Pages or Even Pages is selected.
4. Choose OK or press Enter.

### Printing to a File

Use the Print to File option at the Print dialog box to print a document to a file. This is useful if you want to print a document from a computer that does not have Word for Windows installed. Switching printers can change page breaks and font spacing in a document.

### Changing Print Options

Choosing Options from the Print dialog box causes the Options dialog box with the Print tab selected to display as shown in figure 14.3.

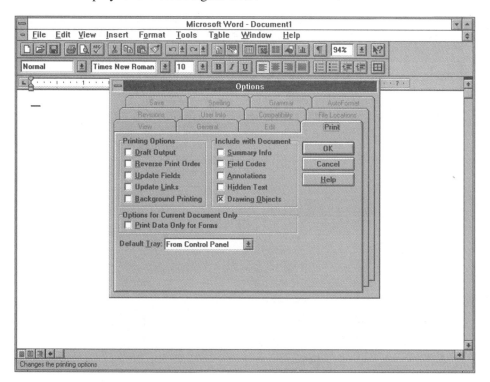

*Figure 14.3*
*Options Dialog Box with Print Tab Selected*

With the selections from the Printing Options section, you can print the document in draft, reverse the print order (last pages first, etc.), and update fields and links. With the Include with Document options, you can identify what additional information or text you want printed with the document such as the summary information, annotations, or hidden text.

### Selecting Printers

If more than one printer was selected when Word for Windows was installed, you can select another printer at the Print Setup dialog box. To display the Print Setup dialog box, choose Printer from the Print dialog box. To select another printer, double-click on the desired printer in the Printers section of the dialog box, then click on Close.

If you want to change the default printer, choose the Set as Default Printer button at the bottom of the Print Setup dialog box. This will change the default printer for Word and all Windows-based applications.

## ■ *Printing Envelopes*

With Word's envelope feature, you can create and print an envelope. You can use the delivery address in the current document or enter the delivery address and return address at the Envelopes and Labels dialog box.

### Creating an Envelope at a Clear Document Screen

To create an envelope document at a clear document screen using the envelope feature, you would complete the following steps:

1. Choose Tools, Envelopes and Labels.
2. At the Envelopes and Labels dialog box with the Envelopes tab selected shown in figure 14.4, key the delivery address. (When the Envelopes and Labels dialog box is displayed, the insertion point is automatically displayed in the Delivery Address text box.) Press the Enter key to end each line in the address.
3. Choose Return Address.
4. Key the return address. Press the Enter key to end each line in the address.
5. Choose Print to print the envelope or choose Add to Document to insert the envelope delivery address and return address in the current document screen.

*Figure 14.4
Envelopes and
Labels Dialog Box
with Envelopes Tab
Selected*

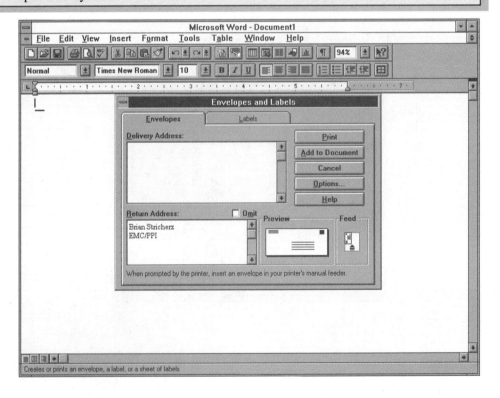

If you entered a return address before printing the envelope, Word will display the question *Do you want to save the new return address as the default return address?* At this question, choose Yes if you want the current return address available for future envelopes. Choose No if you do not want the current return address used as the default.

When you send the envelope text to the printer, you may be prompted to insert the envelope in the printer. This is dependent upon the printer you are using.

If a default return address displays in the Return Address section of the dialog box, you can tell Word to omit the return address when printing the envelope by choosing Omit. This inserts an X in the Omit check box.

The Envelopes and Labels dialog box contains a Preview sample box and a Feed sample box. The Preview sample box shows how the envelope will appear when printed and the Feed sample box shows how the envelope will be fed into the printer.

## Creating an Envelope with an Existing Document

If you open the Envelopes and Labels dialog box in a document containing a name and address, the name and address are automatically inserted in the Delivery Address section of the dialog box.

To create an envelope document in an existing document and add it to the document, you would complete the following steps:

1. Open a document containing a name and address.
2. Choose Tools, Envelopes and Labels.
3. At the Envelopes and Labels dialog box (with the Envelopes tab selected), make sure the delivery address displays properly in the Delivery Address section.
4. Choose Add to Document.

When you choose Add to Document, the envelope is inserted at the beginning of the document followed by a section break.

If you want to send the envelope directly to the printer without inserting it in the document, choose Print instead of Add to Document. When you choose Print, the envelope is sent directly to the printer (but not the text in the document).

## Changing Envelope Options

If you choose Options from the Envelopes and Labels dialog box, the Envelope Options dialog box with the Envelope Options tab selected displays as shown in figure 14.5.

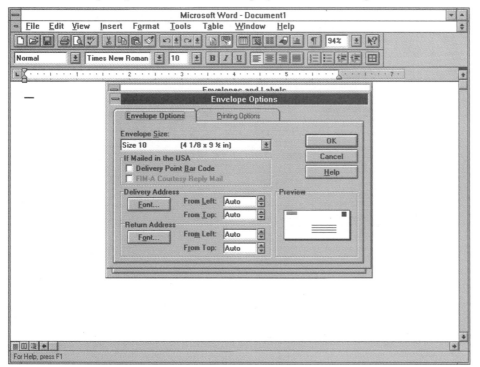

*Figure 14.5*
*Envelope Options Dialog Box with Envelope Options Tab Selected*

Word provides a variety of envelope sizes from which you can choose. To view the list of envelope sizes, click on the down-pointing arrow after the Envelope Size text box. If you are using the keyboard, press Alt + S. From this list, select the desired envelope size.

You can include a POSTNET (POSTal Numeric Encoding Technique) bar code for the delivery address at the Envelope Options dialog box. The bar code is a machine-readable representation of the ZIP Code and speeds mail sorting, increases the accuracy of delivery, and reduces postage costs.

To create a POSTNET bar code for the delivery address, choose Delivery Point Bar Code at the Envelope Options dialog box. Word automatically converts the ZIP Code displayed in the Delivery Address section of the Envelopes and Labels dialog box into short and tall lines that create the bar code.

The Envelope Options dialog box also contains a FIM-A Courtesy Reply Mail option. This option is dimmed unless the Delivery Point Bar Code option is selected. A FIM (Facing Identification Mark) identifies the front (face) of the envelope during presorting. A courtesy reply envelope is provided as a service to the recipient and is preprinted with the sender's name and address. To add a FIM to an envelope, choose the FIM-A Courtesy Reply Mail option at the Envelope Options dialog box.

The delivery address and the return address will print with the default font. If you want to change the delivery address font, choose Font from the Envelope Options dialog box. This displays the Envelope Address dialog box with the Font tab selected as shown in figure 14.6.

The options at the Envelope Address dialog box with the Font tab selected are the same as the options available at the Font dialog box. At this dialog box, choose the desired font, then choose OK or press Enter. This returns you to the Envelope Options dialog box.

To change the font for the return address, choose Font from the Envelope Options dialog box. This displays the Envelope Address dialog box with the Font tab selected as shown in figure 14.6. Choose the desired font at this dialog box, then choose OK or press Enter.

Word automatically determines the location of the delivery and return addresses from the top and left edges of the envelope. If you want to control where the delivery address is printed on the envelope, choose From Left from the Envelope Options dialog box, then enter the desired measurement from the left edge of the envelope. Choose From Top, then enter the desired measurement from the top edge of the envelope. Choose From Left and From Top to enter the measurement for the return address.

*Figure 14.6*
*Envelope Address*
*Dialog Box with*
*Font Tab Selected*

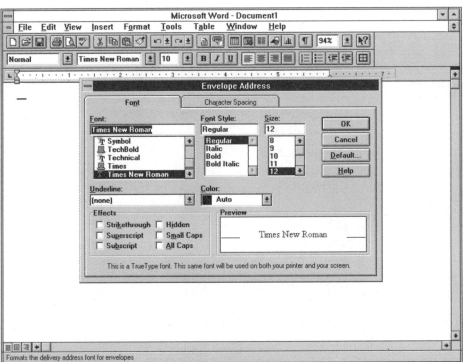

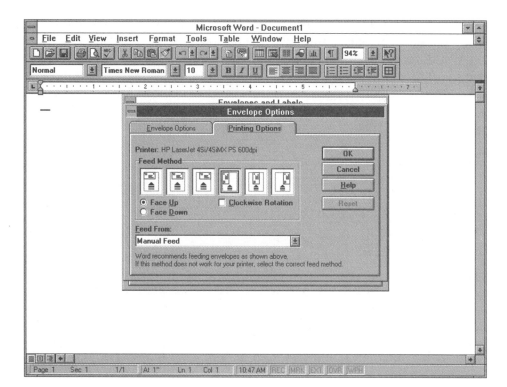

Figure 14.7
Envelope Options
Dialog Box with
Printing Options
Tab Selected

The Preview box at the Envelope Options dialog box displays how the envelope will appear when printed. The Preview box changes as changes are made to the dialog box.

If you choose the Printing Options tab from the Envelope Options dialog box, the dialog box displays as shown in figure 14.7.

Word determines the feed method for envelopes and the feed form. If this method does not work for your printer, choose the correct feed method and feed form at the Envelope Options dialog box with the Printing Options tab selected. Feed methods are visually displayed at the dialog box. You can also determine if the envelope is fed into the printer face up or face down.

# ■ *Printing Labels*

Use Word's labels feature to print text on mailing labels, file labels, disk labels, or other types of labels. Word includes a variety of predefined labels that can be purchased at an office supply store. To create a sheet of mailing labels with the same name and address using the default options, you would complete the following steps:

1. At a clear document screen, choose Tools, Envelopes and Labels.
2. At the Envelopes and Labels dialog box, choose the Labels tab.
3. Key the address you want to appear on the labels in the Address text box.
4. Choose New Document to insert the mailing label in a new document or choose Print to send the mailing label directly to the printer.

If you open the Envelopes and Labels dialog box (with the Labels tab selected) in a document containing a name and address, the name and address are automatically inserted in the Delivery Address section of the dialog box.

To enter different names in each of the mailing labels, you would complete the following steps:

1. At a clear document screen, choose Tools, Envelopes and Labels.
2. At the Envelopes and Labels dialog box, choose Labels.
3. Choose New Document.

Figure 14.8
Label Options
Dialog Box

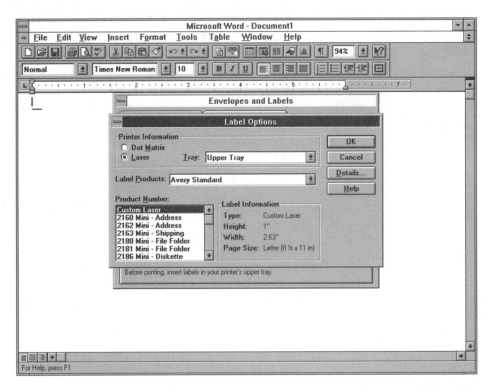

When you choose New Document, the Envelopes and Labels dialog box is removed from the screen, and the document screen displays with label forms. The insertion point is positioned in the first label form. Key the name and address in this label. Press the Tab key to move the insertion point to the next label. Pressing Shift + Tab will move the insertion point to the preceding label. Because labels are designed primarily for merging with the data source (covered in chapter 25) or for one name and address, the first label has a different format than the other labels.

## Changing Label Options

If you choose Options from the Envelopes and Labels dialog box (with the Labels tab selected), the Label Options dialog box shown in figure 14.8 displays.

In the Printer Information section of the dialog box, the type of printer you are using is selected. If you are using a laser printer, you can specify where labels are located. The default setting depends on the selected printer.

The Label Products option lets you choose Avery Standard, Avery Pan European, or Other. The list of labels in the Product Number list box will change depending on what label product you select.

To select a different label product number, choose Product Number, then select the desired label. When you select a label, information about that label is displayed in the Label Information section of the Label Options dialog box including the type, height, width, and paper size.

When you select a label, Word automatically determines label margins. If, however, you want to customize these default settings, choose Details from the Label Options dialog box. This causes the Custom Laser Information dialog box as shown in figure 14.9 to display. If a dot matrix printer is the selected printer, the Custom Dot Matrix dialog box displays.

The Preview box displays a label with the margins and pitch measurements described. At this dialog box, you can customize the top and side margins, vertical and horizontal pitch, the label height and width, and the number of labels across and down the label page. After making changes to this dialog box, choose OK or press Enter. This returns the insertion point to the Label Options dialog box.

As an example of how to use the labels feature, you would complete the following steps to print a name and address on an Avery 5161 address label at a new document screen:

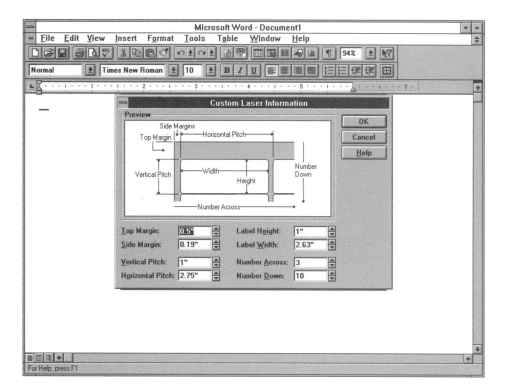

*Figure 14.9*
*Custom Laser*
*Information Dialog*
*Box*

1. At a clear document screen, choose Tools, Envelopes and Labels.
2. At the Envelopes and Labels dialog box, choose the Labels tab.
3. Key the name and address you want to appear on the labels in the Address text box.
4. Choose Options.
5. At the Label Options dialog box, choose Product Number, then choose *5161 - Address*. To do this with the mouse, click on the down-pointing arrow in the Product Number scroll bar until *5161 - Address* is displayed, then click on it. If you are using the keyboard, press Alt + N, then press the down arrow key until *5161 - Address* is selected.
6. Choose OK or press Enter.
7. At the Envelopes and Labels dialog box, choose New Document.

These steps will cause the same name and address to print on each label on the sheet. To print different names and addresses on each label, you would complete the following steps:

1. At a clear document screen, choose Tools, Envelopes and Labels.
2. At the Envelopes and Labels dialog box, choose the Labels tab.
3. Make sure there is not an address displayed in the Address section of the dialog box.
4. Choose Options.
5. At the Label Options dialog box, choose Product Number, then choose *5161 - Address*. To do this with the mouse, click on the down-pointing arrow in the Product Number scroll bar until *5161 - Address* is displayed, then click on it. If you are using the keyboard, press Alt + N, then press the down arrow key until *5161 - Address* is selected.
6. Choose OK or press Enter.
7. At the Envelopes and Labels dialog box, choose New Document.
8. At the document screen, key the name and address in the first label.
9. Press Tab to move the insertion point to the next label. Continue in this manner until all names and addresses have been entered.

Go To
Exercise
10

# CHAPTER SUMMARY

- The options available at the Print dialog box can help to customize a print job.
- The printer displayed after the Printer option should be the printer you are using.
- With Print What options you can print various parts of a document. If you click on the down-pointing arrow after the Print What text box, a drop-down list displays with these options: Document, Summary Info, Annotations, Style, AutoText Entries, and Key Assignments.
- To cancel a print job, press Esc or choose Cancel from the Print dialog box.
- If you want to print more than one copy of a document, use the Copies option from the Print dialog box.
- The Page Range section of the Print dialog box contains settings you can use to specify the amount of text you want printed. With the Pages option, you can identify a specific page for printing, multiple pages, and/or a range of pages. You can also specify a section to be printed or pages within a section for printing.
- The Odd Pages and Even Pages selections from the Print option are useful if you are printing on both sides of the paper.
- If you want to print a document from a computer that does not have Word for Windows installed, use the Print to File option at the Print dialog box.
- You can select another printer at the Print Setup dialog box if more than one printer was selected when Word for Windows was installed.
- With Word's envelope feature you can create and print an envelope at the Envelopes and Labels dialog box. This dialog box contains a Preview sample box, which shows how the envelope will appear when printed, and a Feed sample box, which shows how the envelope will be fed into the printer.
- If you open the Envelopes and Labels dialog box in a document containing a name and address, that information is automatically inserted in the Delivery Address section of the dialog box.
- You can include a POSTNET (POSTal Numeric Encoding Technique) bar code for the delivery address at the Envelope Options dialog box.
- These additional options are available at the Envelope Options dialog box: Envelope Size, FIM-A Courtesy Reply Mail, Delivery and Return Address Fonts, From Left and From Top (to change location of addresses).
- Use Word's labels feature to print text on mailing labels, file labels, disk labels, or other types of labels.
- These additional options are available at the Label Options dialog box: Printer Information, Label Products (to choose the type of label), and Details (to change label margins).
- Choosing Details at the Label Options dialog box displays a label with the margins and pitch measurements described. You can customize the label at this dialog box.

## COMMANDS REVIEW

|  | Mouse | Keyboard |
| --- | --- | --- |
| Print dialog box | File, Print | CTRL + P ; or |
|  |  | CTRL + SHIFT + F12 |
| Envelopes and Labels dialog box | Tools, Envelopes and Labels | Tools, Envelopes and Labels |

**True/False:** Circle the letter T if the statement is true; circle the letter F if the statement is false.

**T    F    1.**   If you print several copies of a document containing multiple pages, by default Word prints the pages in the document collated.

**T    F    2.**   When specifying a range of pages to be printed, a hyphen specifies *and,* a comma means *through.*

**T    F    3.**   Even-numbered pages can be identified for printing at the Print dialog box.

**T    F    4.**   You cannot create an envelope in Word for Windows without first creating the letter that will be mailed in the envelope.

**T    F    5.**   When the Envelopes and Labels dialog box is opened in a document containing a name and address, that data is automatically inserted on the envelope.

**T    F    6.**   A POSTNET bar code converts the street name into short and tall lines that are printed on the envelope.

**T    F    7.**   When a label type is selected at the Label Options dialog box, information about that label is displayed in the Label Information section.

**T    F    8.**   You can customize the margins, pitch, height, and width of a label at the Preview box.

**Completion:** In the space provided, indicate what should be keyed in the Pages text box of the Print menu to most efficiently print the following pages.

1.   Page 4 only.                                                      _____
2.   Beginning of the document through page 5.      _____
3.   Pages 3, 4, 5, and 8.                                        _____
4.   Page 7 to the end of the document.               _____
5.   Pages 7 and 9.                                                 _____

### Exercise 1

1.   Open memo01.
2.   Print three copies of the memo by completing the following steps:
     a.   Display the Print dialog box. To do this, choose *one* of the following methods:
          (1)   Choose File, Print.
          (2)   Press Ctrl + P.
          (3)   Press Ctrl + Shift + F12.
     b.   Key **3**.
     c.   Choose OK or press Enter.
3.   Close memo01.

### Exercise 2

1.   Open report02.
2.   Print pages 1 and 4 by completing the following steps:
     a.   Display the Print dialog box.
     b.   At the Print dialog box, choose Pages.
     c.   Key **1,4**.
     d.   Choose OK or press Enter.
3.   Close report02.

## Exercise 3

1. Open report04.
2. Insert a section break that begins a new page at the line containing the title, *CHAPTER 2: OFFSET PRINTING*.
3. Print the pages in section 2 by completing the following steps:
   a. Display the Print dialog box.
   b. At the Print dialog box, choose Pages.
   c. Key **s2**.
   d. Choose OK or press Enter.
4. Close report04 without saving the changes.

## Exercise 4

1. Open report05.
2. Print only odd-numbered pages by completing the following steps:
   a. Display the Print dialog box.
   b. At the Print dialog box, choose Print, then Odd Pages. To do this with the mouse, click on the down-pointing arrow after the Print text box, then click on Odd Pages. If you are using the keyboard, press Alt + R, then press the down arrow key until Odd Pages is selected.
   c. Choose OK or press Enter.
3. Close report05.

## Exercise 5

1. Open report03.
2. Print this document in reverse order by completing the following steps:
   a. Display the Print dialog box.
   b. Choose Options.
   c. At the Options dialog box with the Print tab selected, choose Reverse Print Order. (This inserts an X in the check box.)
   d. Choose OK or press Enter.
   e. At the Print dialog box, choose OK or press Enter.
3. After the document is printed, remove the X from the Reverse Print Order check box by completing the following steps:
   a. Display the Print dialog box.
   b. Choose Options.
   c. At the Options dialog box with the Print tab selected, choose Reverse Print Order. (This removes the X from the check box.)
   d. Choose OK or press Enter.
   e. At the Print dialog box, choose Close.
4. Close report03.

## Exercise 6

1. At a clear document screen, create an envelope that prints the delivery address and return address shown in figure 14.10 by completing the following steps:
   a. Choose Tools, Envelopes and Labels.
   b. At the Envelopes and Labels dialog box with the Envelopes tab selected, key the delivery address shown in figure 14.10 (the one containing the name *Mr. Jared Holstad*). (Press the Enter key to end each line in the name and address.)
   c. Choose Return Address.
   d. Key the return address shown in figure 14.10 (the one containing the name *Mrs. Faith Reid*). (Press the Enter key to end each line in the name and address.)
   e. Choose Add to Document.

f. At the message *Do you want to save the new return address as the default return address?*, choose <u>N</u>o.
2. Save the document and name it c14ex06.
3. Print c14ex06.
4. Close c14ex06.

Figure 14.10

```
Mrs. Faith Reid
712 North Columbia
Portland, OR 97032




                        Mr. Jared Holstad
                        8208 Ruby Drive
                        Portland, OR 97034
```

## Exercise 7

1. Open letter01.
2. Create and print an envelope for the document by completing the following steps:
   a. Choose <u>T</u>ools, <u>E</u>nvelopes and Labels.
   b. At the Envelopes and Labels dialog box (with the <u>E</u>nvelopes tab selected), make sure the delivery address displays properly in the <u>D</u>elivery Address section.
   c. Make sure there is no text in the <u>R</u>eturn Address text box. If there is, choose <u>R</u>eturn Address, then delete the text.
   d. Choose <u>P</u>rint.
3. Close letter01 without saving the changes.

## Exercise 8

1. Open c14ex06.
2. Save the document with Save As and name it c14ex08.
3. Add a POSTNET Bar Code and a FIM to the envelope and change the font of the delivery address by completing the following steps:
   a. Choose <u>T</u>ools, <u>E</u>nvelopes and Labels.
   b. At the Envelopes and Labels dialog box (with the <u>E</u>nvelopes tab selected), choose <u>O</u>ptions.
   c. At the Envelope Options dialog box, choose Delivery Point <u>B</u>ar Code.
   d. Choose FIM-<u>A</u> Courtesy Reply Mail.
   e. Choose <u>F</u>ont. (This option is located in the Delivery Address section of the dialog box.)
   f. At the Envelope Address dialog box with the Fo<u>n</u>t tab selected, choose Times New Roman in the <u>F</u>ont list box.
   g. Choose 12 in the <u>S</u>ize list box.
   h. Choose OK or press Enter.
   i. At the Envelope Options dialog box, choose O<u>m</u>it. This inserts an X in the check box and omits the return address from the envelope.
   j. Choose OK or press Enter.
   k. At the Envelopes and Labels dialog box, choose Ch<u>a</u>nge Document.
   l. At the message *Do you want to save the new return address as the default return address?*, choose <u>N</u>o.
4. Save the document again with the same name (c14ex08).
5. Print c14ex08.
6. Close c14ex08.

## Exercise 9

1.  Open letter01.
2.  Create mailing labels with the delivery address by completing the following steps:
    a.  Choose Tools, Envelopes and Labels.
    b.  At the Envelopes and Labels dialog box, choose the Labels tab.
    c.  Make sure the delivery address displays properly in the Address section.
    d.  If there is an X in the Delivery Point Bar Code check box, choose Delivery Point Bar Code to remove the X.
    e.  Choose New Document.
3.  Save the mailing label document and name it c14ex09.
4.  Print c14ex09. (The name and address in letter01 will print on every label.)
5.  Close c14ex09.
6.  Close letter01 without saving the changes.

## Exercise 10

1.  At a clear document screen, create mailing labels for the names and addresses shown in figure 14.11 by completing the following steps:
    a.  Choose Tools, Envelopes and Labels.
    b.  Make sure the Labels tab is selected. If not, choose Labels.
    c.  Make sure there is no name and address in the Address section of the dialog box. (If there is, choose Address, then delete the name and address.)
    d.  Choose Options.
    e.  At the Label Options dialog box, choose Product Number, then choose *5662 - Address* (or a numer provided by your instructor). To do this with the mouse, click on the down-pointing arrow in the Product Number scroll bar until *5662 - Address* is displayed, then click on it. If you are using the keyboard, press Alt + N, then press the down arrow key until *5662 - Address* is selected.
    f.  Choose OK or press Enter.
    g.  At the Envelopes and Labels dialog box, choose New Document.
    h.  At the document screen, key the first name and address in the first label. (This label will contain different formatting than the other labels.)
    i.  Press Tab to move the insertion point to the next label, then key the second name and address shown in figure 14.11. Continue in this manner until all names and addresses have been keyed.
2.  Save the document and name it c14ex10.
3.  Print c14ex10.
4.  Close c14ex10.
5.  At the clear document screen, close the document screen without saving changes.

---

**Figure 14.11**

```
Mr. Donald G. Thompson      Mrs. Wanda Holmes
Bonney Lake Services        Career Management Consultants
1604 Old Pioneer Way        24138 Harman Avenue
Bonney Lake, WA 98033       Federal Way, WA 98133

Dr. Barbara Sharpe          Mr. Craig Simmons
Puget Sound Center          Lakeside Business Management
4005 East Mall Boulevard    935 North Pearl Street
Tacoma, WA 98412            Tacoma, WA 98409
```

## Assessment 1

1. Open report01.
2. Print two copies of page 2.
3. Close report01.

## Assessment 2

1. Open report04.
2. Print pages 4 through 6 of the report.
3. Close report04.

## Assessment 3

1. Open letter02.
2. Create an envelope for the document that is sent directly to the printer. Include the POSTNET bar code and the FIM.
3. Close letter02.

## Assessment 4

1. At a clear document screen, create mailing labels for the name and address shown in figure 14.12. Use the custom label (this will be Custom Laser or Custom Dot Matrix, depending on your printer). Key the name and address shown in figure 14.12 in the Address section of the Envelopes and Labels dialog box.
2. Save the mailing label in a new document and name it c14sa04.
3. Print c14sa04. (The name and address in figure 14.12 will print on every label.)
4. Close c14sa04.
5. Close the clear document screen without saving changes.

**Figure 14.12**

```
Ms. Ann Sloan
1202 South Third
Jennings, LA 73021
```

# Maintaining Documents 15

Upon successful completion of chapter 15, you will be able to copy, move, and print documents; create document summaries; and search for documents that match specific criteria.

Almost every company that conducts business maintains a filing system. The system may consist of documents, folders, and cabinets; or it may be a computerized filing system where information is stored on tapes and disks. Whatever kind of filing system a business uses, daily maintenance of files is important to a company's operation. Maintaining files in Word for Windows can include such activities as printing, copying, and deleting documents as well as searching for specific documents.

## Changing Options at the Open and Save As Dialog Boxes

In chapter 1 you learned how to open and save documents as well as how to choose a different directory or drive. The Open dialog box shown in figure 15.1 contains options you can use to change to a different directory or subdirectory as well as display document names with different extensions. The same options are available at the Save As dialog box.

### Changing to a Different Directory and Subdirectory

By default, Word saves documents in the *winword* subdirectory on the hard drive or network (unless customized during installation). A directory or subdirectory is a specific portion of the disk space reserved for files that have something in common. The *winword* subdirectory is reserved for files that provide information about the Word for Windows program. In chapter 1, you learned how to change the default from the *winword* subdirectory to the drive where your student data disk is located.

A directory is a logical location where documents are saved. There might also be directories within directories called *subdirectories*. The main directory on a disk or drive is called the *root* directory (like the roots of a tree), and subdirectories branch off from this root directory. A hard drive or a floppy disk can contain a root directory and one or more subdirectories.

*Figure 15.1*
*Open Dialog Box*

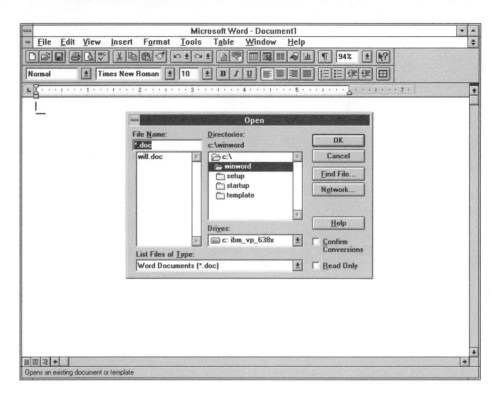

The hard drive on many computers is referred to as drive C. The steps you take to move from a directory to a subdirectory is called the *path* or *path name*. A directory and subdirectories are separated in the path name by a backslash (\). The path name for the root directory for the hard drive is c:\. (This may vary depending on how the hard drive is partitioned.)

At the Open dialog box shown in figure 15.1, directories and subdirectories are displayed in the Directories list box preceded by a file folder icon. Subdirectories are listed below directories and are slightly indented. This provides a visual display of the directories and subdirectories on the drive or disk. The directory or subdirectory preceded by an open file folder (rather than a closed file folder) is the current directory.

To choose a different directory or subdirectory you would select the desired directory or subdirectory in the Directories list box at the Open or Save As dialog box. To do this with the mouse, position the arrow pointer on the desired directory or subdirectory, then double-click the left mouse button. If you are using the keyboard, press Alt + D, press the up or down arrow key until the desired directory or subdirectory is selected, then press Enter.

## Opening Documents with Different Extensions

Documents are displayed in the Open or Save As dialog box that end with the extension *.doc*. At the Open dialog box, *\*.doc* displays in the File Name text box as shown in figure 15.1. With choices from the List Files of Type option, you can choose to display documents with different extensions. When you choose List of Files of Type, a drop-down menu displays as shown in figure 15.2. At this menu, choose *All Files (\*.\*)* to display all documents (with any extension) that are saved in the directory or subdirectory. Choose the other options to display documents with the *.dot*, *.rtf*, or the *.txt* extension.

Go To
Exercise
1

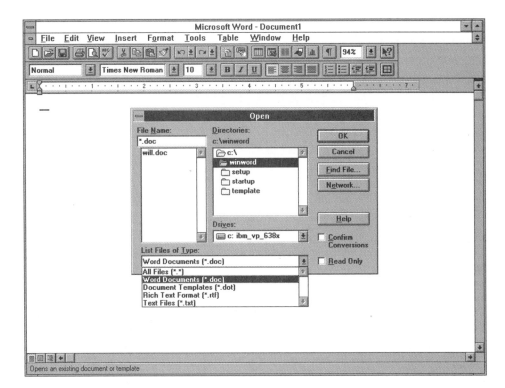

*Figure 15.2*
*List of Files of Type*
*Options*

# ◼ *Changing **S**ave **O**ptions*

When working in Word, a document is automatically saved every 10 minutes. This default setting can be changed at the Options dialog box with the Save tab selected as shown in figure 15.3. To display the Options dialog box, choose Tools, then Options. At the Options dialog box, select the Save tab.

If you would like Word to create a backup of documents, choose Always Create Backup at the Options dialog box. With this option selected, Word will create a backup copy of a document every time you save the document.

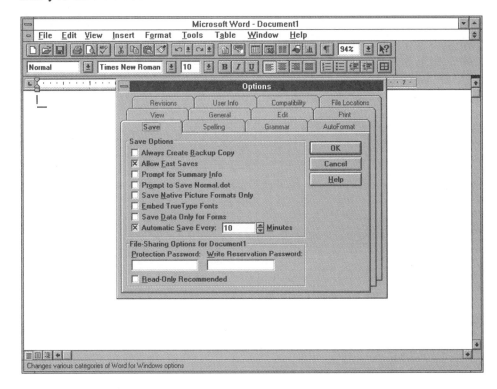

*Figure 15.3*
*Options Dialog Box*
*with Save Tab*
*Selected*

You can create a summary that includes information about the document such as title, subject, author, keywords, and comments. If you would like Word to display the Summary Info dialog box each time you save a document, choose Prompt for Summary Info at the Options dialog box. Creating a summary is covered later in this chapter.

The other options at the Options dialog box with the Save tab selected let you specify what happens when a Word document is saved.

## Managing Documents

Maintaining files such as copying, printing, and deleting can be accomplished at the Find File dialog box. At the Find File dialog box, you can perform the following functions:

- view the contents of a document or related information
- open one or more documents
- print, delete, or copy one or more documents
- create a subdirectory
- search for certain documents
- change the summary information for a document

*Note: The File Manager program within the Windows program can also be used to perform many of the same functions. Refer to your Windows documentation or ask your instructor for assistance in using the File Manager program.*

There are two methods for displaying the Find File dialog box. One method is to choose File, then Find File. The Find File dialog box displays as shown in figure 15.4 and displays documents in the current drive and/or directory.

*Figure 15.4*
*Find File Dialog Box*

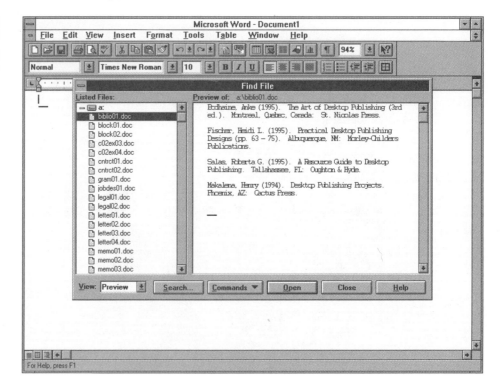

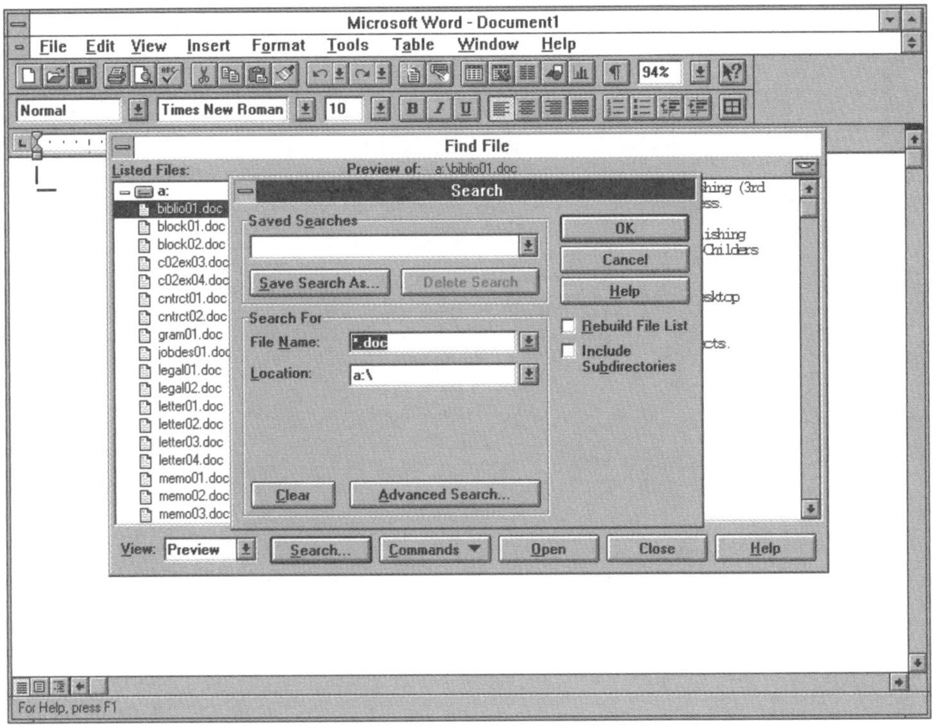

**Figure 15.5**
*Search Dialog Box*

You can also display the Find File dialog box with the Find File option at the Open dialog box. To display the Find File dialog box from the Open dialog box, you need to identify the location of documents to be displayed at the Search dialog box. For example, to display a list of documents in the Find File dialog box for the disk in drive A, you would complete the following steps:

1. Choose File, Open; or press Ctrl + O.
2. At the Open dialog box, choose Find File.
3. At the Search dialog box, shown in figure 15.5, choose Location.
4. Key **a:\**.
5. Choose OK or press Enter.

When you choose OK or press Enter, the Find File dialog box displays with a list of documents located on the disk in the drive as shown in figure 15.4.

The first time you choose File, then Find File, the Search dialog box displays. At this dialog box, specify in the Location text box the drive or directory you want displayed at the Find File dialog box.

Later in this chapter, you will learn how to specify search criteria to display specific documents.

## Viewing Documents

When the Find File dialog box is displayed, the first document in the Listed Files list box is selected. The contents of this document are displayed in the Preview of preview box. You can view the contents of a document by selecting the document name in the Listed Files list box.

If you choose View at the Find File dialog box, a drop-down menu displays with three choices—Preview, File Info, and Summary. The Preview option is the default and displays the document contents in the Preview of preview box as shown in figure 15.6.

Figure 15.6
Find File Dialog Box
with Document
Previewed

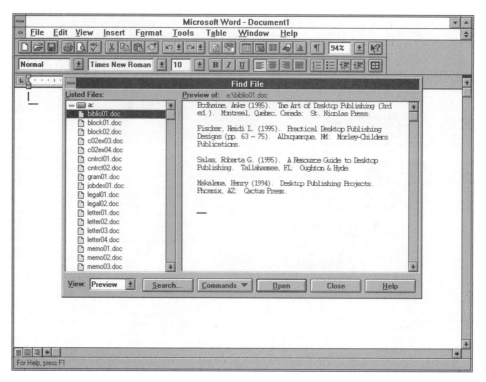

Use the arrow pointer with the up and down scroll arrows on the vertical scroll bar to view different parts of the document in the Preview of preview box. If you are using the keyboard, press Alt + P to make the Preview of preview box active, then press the up or down arrow key on the keyboard to view different parts of the document. You can also press the Page Up and Page Down keys to scroll through the document.

If you choose File Info from the View drop-down menu, the following information is displayed about the document: File Name, Title, Size, Author, and Last Saved. Figure 15.7 displays the Find File dialog box with File Info selected at the View option.

Figure 15.7
Find File with File
Info Displayed

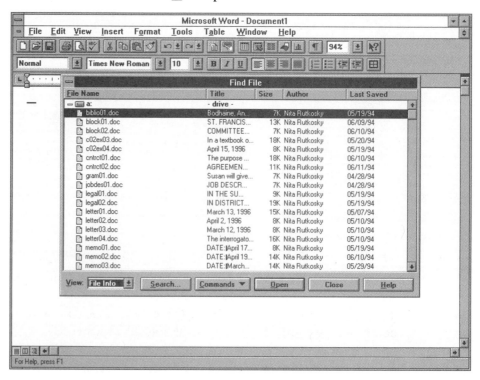

If a summary was created for a document, that summary can be displayed in the Preview of preview box. To do this, choose View, then Summary.

## Selecting Documents in Find File

At the Find File dialog box you can copy, move, delete, or print individual documents or selected documents. To copy, move, delete, or print more than one document, the documents must first be selected.

To select a group of adjacent documents in the Listed Files list box at the Find File dialog box, you would complete the following steps:

1. Position the arrow pointer on the first document in the group.
2. Hold down the left mouse button.
3. Drag the arrow pointer to the last document in the group.
4. Release the mouse button.

To select a group of adjacent documents in the Listed Files list box using the keyboard, you would complete the following steps:

1. Position the insertion point on the first document in the group.
2. Hold down the Shift key, then press the down arrow key until the insertion point is positioned on the last document in the group.
3. Release the Shift key.

You can also select documents that are not adjacent in the Listed Files list box. To do this with the mouse, you would complete the following steps:

1. Position the arrow pointer on the first document to be selected.
2. Hold down the Ctrl key.
3. Click on the desired document names. (Keep the Ctrl key down the entire time.)
4. When all desired documents are selected, release the Ctrl key.

To deselect a document name with the mouse, hold the Ctrl key down, then click on the document name.

To select documents that are not adjacent in the Listed Files list box using the keyboard, you would complete the following steps:

1. Press Shift + F8.
2. Use the arrow keys to move the insertion point to the desired document.
3. Press the space bar to select the document.
4. Move to the next document name, then press the space bar. Continue in this manner until all desired documents are selected.

To deselect a document name with the keyboard, move to the document name, then press the space bar.

## Opening Documents

A document or selected documents can be opened at the Find File dialog box. To open one document, select the document in the Listed Files list box, then choose Open. To open more than one document, select the documents, then choose Open. Up to nine documents can be open at one time. (This number may be lower, depending on the computer's memory.)

A document can be opened that is read only. At a read only document, you can make changes to a document but you cannot save those changes with the same name. Word protects the original document and does not allow you to save the changes to the document with the same name. You can, however, open a document, make changes to it, then save the document with a different name. To open a read only document, you would complete the following steps:

1. Choose File, Find File.
2. At the Find File dialog box, select the document you want to open.
3. Choose Commands.
4. From the menu that displays, choose Open Read Only.

## Printing Documents

Up to this point, you have opened a document and then printed it. With Print from the Commands option from the Find File dialog box, you can print a document or several documents without opening them. Printing a document without opening it is referred to as *background printing*. In background printing the printing occurs in the background, allowing you to work on other documents.

To print a document from the Find File dialog box, you would complete the following steps:

1. Choose File, Find File.
2. At the Find File dialog box, make sure the list of documents on your data disk is displayed in the Listed Files section of the screen, then select the document you want printed. To do this with the mouse, click on the desired document. If you are using the keyboard, press the down arrow key until the desired document is selected.
3. Choose Commands.
4. From the menu that displays, choose Print.
5. At the Print dialog box, make any necessary changes, then choose OK or press Enter.

If you want to print more than one document, select the documents first, then choose Commands, Print.

## Deleting Documents

At some point, you may want to delete certain documents from your student data disk or any other disk you may be working with. If you work with Word for Windows on a regular basis, you should establish a system for deleting documents. The system you choose depends on the work you are doing.

To delete a document, you would complete the following steps:

1. Choose File, Find File.
2. At the Find File dialog box, select the document in the Listed Files section that you want deleted.
3. Choose Commands, Delete.
4. At the question *Do you want to delete X?* (where X is the document name), choose Yes.

To delete more than one document, select the documents to be deleted, then choose Commands, Delete. Word displays the question *Do you want to delete X?* and inserts all the selected document names (or as many as can fit in the dialog box) in place of the X. If you want to delete all the selected documents, choose Yes.

## Copying Documents

At the Find File dialog box, you can make an exact copy of a document and save it on the same disk, another disk, or into a directory or subdirectory. If you copy a document to the same directory, you must give it a different name than the original. If you copy a document to another drive, directory, or subdirectory, it can retain its original name.

As an example of how to copy a document, you would complete the following steps to copy the *memo01.doc* document and name it *owens.doc*:

1. Choose File, Find File.
2. At the Find File dialog box, select the *memo01.doc* document.
3. Choose Commands, Copy.
4. At the Copy dialog box, key **owens.doc** in the Path text box.
5. Choose OK or press Enter.

You can also copy a document to another drive or directory. For example, to copy the document named *memo01.doc* from the disk in drive a to a disk in drive b, you would complete the following steps:

1. Choose File, Find File.
2. At the Find File dialog box, select the *memo01.doc* document.
3. Choose Commands, Copy.
4. At the Copy dialog box, key **b:** in the Path text box.
5. Choose OK or press Enter.

When a document is copied, the original document is retained and an exact copy is made.

Selected documents can be copied at the Find File dialog box. When more then one document is selected for copying, enter a drive letter, directory, or subdirectory in the Path text box. You cannot key a specific name for the document since more than one document is selected. What you can do is specify where you want the copied documents to be saved. Word saves the copied documents in the new location with the same names.

## Creating a Directory

At the Copy dialog box, you can create a new directory. Use the New command button at the Copy dialog box to create a new directory or subdirectory. For example, to create a subdirectory named *letters* from the *a:\* root directory, you would complete the following steps:

1. Choose File, Find File.
2. At the Find File dialog box, choose Commands, Copy.
3. At the Copy dialog box, choose New.
4. At the Create Directory dialog box, key **letters** in the Name text box.
5. Choose OK or press Enter.
6. At the Copy dialog box, choose OK or press Enter.
7. Choose Close to close the Find File dialog box.

Directories can be created at the Find File dialog box but cannot be deleted. Directories must be deleted at the File Manager in Windows.

## Creating a Summary

A summary can be created for a document that identifies important information about the document such as the title, subject, author, keywords, and comments. You can create a summary for a document with the Summary Info option from the File menu or at the Find File dialog box. To create a summary for a document with the File menu, you would complete the following steps:

Figure 15.8
Summary Info
Dialog Box

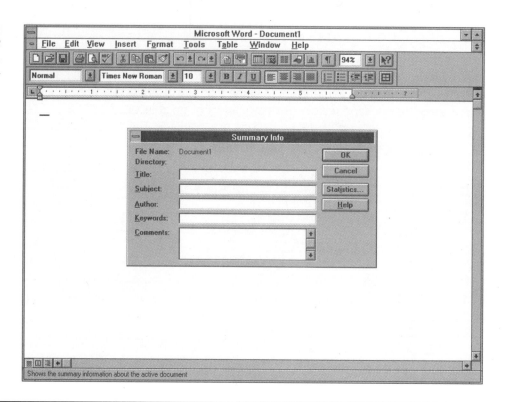

1. Open the document for which you want to create a summary.
2. Choose File, Summary Info.
3. At the Summary Info dialog box shown in figure 15.8, enter information in the text boxes.
4. Choose OK or press Enter.

To create a summary for a document at the Find File dialog box, you would complete the following steps:

1. Choose File, Find File.
2. At the Find File dialog box, select the document for which you are creating a summary.
3. Choose Commands.
4. From the menu that displays, choose Summary.
5. At the Summary Info dialog box, enter information in the text boxes.
6. Choose OK or press Enter.
7. Choose Close to close the Find File dialog box.

The document name and the directory where the document is located display at the top of the Summary Info dialog box.

Choose the other options to insert information about the document. Key a title for the document in the Title text box. At the Subject text box, enter information about the main point of the document. Identify the author of the document at the Author text box. Enter important words or phrases included in the document at the Keywords option. Use the last option, Comments, to add additional comments about the document.

Choosing the Statistics button at the right side of the Summary Info dialog box causes statistics about the document to display. For example, if you open the document named *report04.doc*, display the Summary Info dialog box, then choose Statistics, the Document Statistics dialog box shown in figure 15.9 displays.

Go To
Exercises
7, 8, & 9

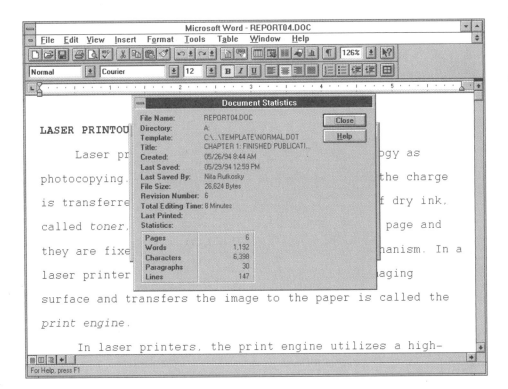

Figure 15.9
Document Statistics
Dialog Box

## ■ *Searching for* *Documents*

With the Search option at the Find File dialog box, you can search for a specific document or documents, or display documents in another drive or directory. When you choose Search, the Search dialog box shown in figure 15.10 displays.

To search for specific documents on a disk, in a directory or subdirectory, or on a drive, enter the search criteria at the Search dialog box. You can search for a document with a specific name, search for all documents with a specific extension, or limit the search to a particular drive, directory, or subdirectory.

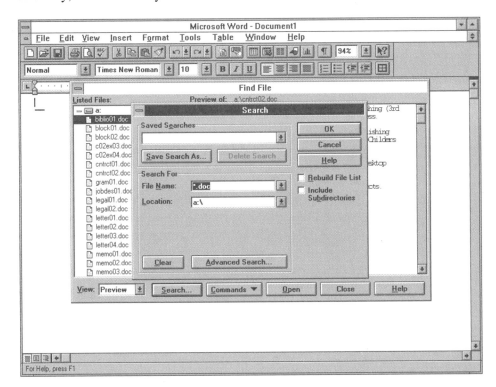

Figure 15.10
Search Dialog Box

## Searching for a Specific Document

At the Search dialog box, you can enter a document name in the File Name text box, and Word will display only that document at the Find File dialog box. For example, to search for *report03.doc*, you would complete the following steps:

1. Choose File, Find File.
2. At the Find File dialog box, choose Search.
3. At the Search dialog box, key **report03.doc** in the File Name text box. (When the Search dialog box is displayed, the insertion point is automatically positioned in the File Name text box.)
4. Make sure the correct drive and/or directory is displayed in the Location text box. For example, if you are searching the disk in drive a for the document, make sure *a:\* displays in the Location text box. (If not, choose Location, then key **a:\**.)
5. Choose OK or press Enter.

When you choose OK or press Enter, Word searches for the *report03.doc* on the disk in drive a, then displays the document in the Find File dialog box.

## Searching for Documents

At the File Name option, you can limit the number of documents Word searches for by using a wildcard character. Use the asterisk (*) to indicate a range of characters or use the question mark (?) to indicate one character. For example, if you want to search for only those documents that begin *c03* you would enter *c03*.doc* in the File Name list box. Word searches for and finds documents such as *c03ex01.doc, c03ex02.doc, c03ex03.doc* and so on. As an example of how to use the question mark (?), entering *c0?ex01.doc* in the File Name text box tells Word to search for exercise one documents from chapters one through nine (such as *c01ex01.doc, c02ex01.doc, c03ex01.doc*, etc.). In this example, the question mark indicates one character (the 1 through 9).

## Saving and Deleting Searches

At the Search dialog box, you can save search criteria. For example, if you search for all letter documents on the disk in drive a, you can enter the search criteria, then save the criteria. To do this and name the search *letters*, you would complete the following steps:

1. Choose File, Find File.
2. At the Find File dialog box, choose Search.
3. At the Search dialog box, key **letter*.doc** in the File Name text box.
4. Choose Location, then key **a:\**.
5. Choose Save Search As.
6. At the Save Search As dialog box, key **letters** in the Search Name text box.
7. Choose OK or press Enter.

When you choose OK or press Enter, the Search dialog box displays. To display the *letters* search, choose Saved Searches. To do this with the mouse, click on the down-pointing arrow after the Saved Searches text box. If you are using the keyboard, press Alt + E. This causes a drop-down list to display with *letters* included and any other searches that have been saved. If you choose *letters* from this list, Word will display the search criteria for letters in the File Name and Location text boxes. Choose OK or press Enter and the Find File dialog box displays with letters that match the criteria.

Searches that have been added at the Search dialog box can be deleted. For example, to delete the *letters* search, you would complete the following steps:

Go To
Exercise
12

1. Choose File, Find File.
2. At the Find File dialog box, choose Search.
3. At the Search dialog box, choose Saved Searches.
4. From the drop-down list that displays, select *letters*.
5. Choose Delete Search.
6. At the question *Do you want to delete "letters"?*, choose Yes.

## Changing the Search

At the Search dialog box choose the Clear button at the bottom of the dialog box to clear the search criteria from the File Name and Location text boxes. Choose Include Subdirectories to insert an X in the check box if you want Word to display any subdirectories in the directory you are searching. Choosing Rebuild File List causes Word to replace all files previously found with a new list that meets the new set of criteria.

## Performing an Advanced Search

Word provides an Advanced Search dialog box where you can further specify search criteria. For example, you can search for documents created on a certain date, by a certain author, with a certain summary, or for specific words or phrases.

If you choose Advanced Search from the Search dialog box, the Advanced Search dialog box with the Location tab selected shown in figure 15.11 displays.

At the right side of the Advanced Search dialog box, a list of directories displays in the Directories list box. If the current directory is drive a, there may not be any subdirectories displayed when you display the Advanced Search dialog box.

If you want to search in a different drive, choose Drives at the Advanced Search dialog box. From the drop-down list that displays, select the desired drive. When the drive is changed, the display of directories and/or subdirectories in the Directories list box changes.

To search for a particular document, enter the document name including the .doc extension in the File Name text box at the Advanced Search dialog box. You can tell Word to search in a specific directory or a number of directories and subdirectories. To tell Word to search in a

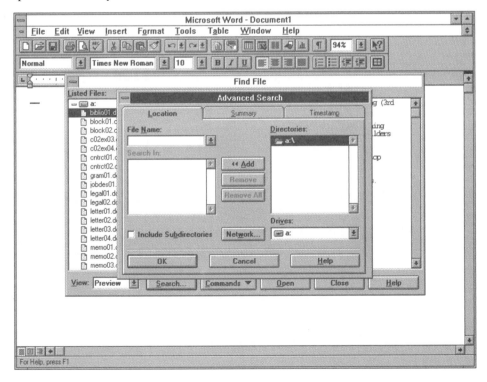

*Figure 15.11*
*Advanced Search*
*Dialog Box with*
*Location Tab*
*Selected*

directory or subdirectory, add the directory in the Search In list box. To do this, select the desired directory in the <u>D</u>irectories list box, then choose <u>A</u>dd. This adds the directory to the Search In list box. Add any desired directories or subdirectories to the Search In list box, then complete the search.

To remove a directory or subdirectory from the Search In list box, select the directory or subdirectory in the Search In list box, then choose <u>R</u>emove. If you want to remove all directories or subdirectories from the list box, choose Re<u>m</u>ove All.

If you want to include subdirectories in the search, insert an X in the Include Su<u>b</u>directories check box.

## Searching Summaries

If summaries are created for documents, you can search for documents containing specific information in the summary or specific information within the document. To specify summary information for the search, choose the <u>S</u>ummary tab at the Advanced Search dialog box. This causes the Advanced Search dialog box with the <u>S</u>ummary tab selected to display as shown in figure 15.12.

To search for documents with a particular title, author, keywords, or subject, enter the search text in these options. For example, to search for all documents pertaining to the subject desktop publishing, enter *desktop publishing* in the Su<u>b</u>ject text box.

If you want Word to match exactly the case of the search criteria, insert an X in the <u>M</u>atch Case option.

Choose <u>O</u>ptions and a drop-down list displays with three options. Choose the Create New List option to replace the existing list at the Find File dialog box. Choose Add Matches to List to add the new list to the existing list. Choose Search Only in List to tell Word to search for criteria only in the existing list.

Search for documents containing special text with the <u>C</u>ontaining Text option. To specify the text, choose <u>C</u>ontaining Text, then key the text in the text box.

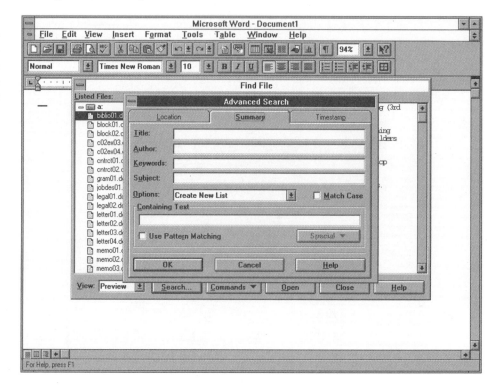

*Figure 15.12*
*Advanced Search*
*Dialog Box with*
*Summary Tab*
*Selected*

When specifying text, you can use wildcard characters. Figure 15.13 shows wildcard characters and what the search results will be.

| Wildcard entered | Will find documents |
|---|---|
| educa* | containing words that begin **educa** and end with any combination of letters |
| probabl? | containing words that begin with **probabl** and end with any one character (such as **probable** and **probably**) |
| "desktop publishing" | containing the words desktop publishing |
| Lawson&Sideres | containing Lawson and Sideres |
| Lawson,Sideres | containing Lawson or Sideres |
| ~Sideres | that do not contain Sideres |

*Figure 15.13*
*Wildcard Examples*

## Searching by Date Saved or Created

You can search for documents that were saved or created on or between specific dates. To do this, display the Advanced Search dialog box with the Timestamp tab selected as shown in figure 15.14.

At the Advanced Search dialog box with the Timestamp tab selected, search for documents saved or created during a particular period of time. For example, to search for documents saved between March 1, 1996, and April 1, 1996, enter *3/1/96* in the From text box and *4/1/96* in the To text box. If you are searching for documents created by a specific author, enter the author's name at the By text box. Complete similar steps to search for documents created during a specific period of time.

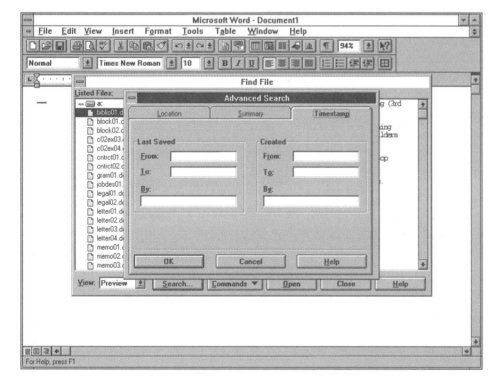

*Figure 15.14*
*Advanced Search Dialog Box with Timestamp Tab Selected*

- The Open dialog box contains options for changing to a different directory as well as displaying document names with different extensions. The same options are available at the Save As dialog box.
- By default, Word saves documents in the *winword* subdirectory on the hard drive or network. Generally, you will change the default from the *winword* subdirectory to the drive where your student data disk is located.
- The main directory on a disk or drive is called the *root* directory. Subdirectories can be created that branch off from this root directory.
- The hard drive on many computers is referred to as drive c. The steps you take to move from a directory to a subdirectory is called the *path* or *path name*. A directory and subdirectories are separated in the path name by a backslash (\).
- The Open dialog box provides a visual display of the directories and subdirectories on the drive or disk.
- To choose a different directory, select the desired directory or subdirectory in the Directories list box at the Open or Save As dialog box.
- With choices from the List Files of Type option at the File Name text box in the Open dialog box, you can choose to display documents with extensions other than the default *.doc*.
- Several choices are available at the Options dialog box that affect how and when a document is saved. These choices include automatic save, automatic backup, and document summary creation.
- At the Find File dialog box, you can perform the following functions: view the contents of a document; open one or more documents; print; delete or copy one or more documents; create a subdirectory; search for certain documents; and create a summary for a document.
- With the Search option at the Find File dialog box, you can search for a specific document or documents, display documents in another drive or directory, and add to or save search criteria.

## COMMANDS REVIEW

|  | Mouse | Keyboard |
|---|---|---|
| Open dialog box | File, Open | `CTRL` + `O` |
| Save As dialog box | File, Save As | File, Save As |
| Options dialog box | Tools, Options (with Save tab selected) | Tools, Options (with Save tab selected) |
| Find File dialog box | File, Find File | File, Find File |
| Search dialog box | Choose Search at the Find File dialog box | Choose Search at the Find File dialog box |

**True/False:** Circle the letter T if the statement is true; circle the letter F if the statement is false.

T  F  1.  By default, Word saves documents in the *wordwin* subdirectory.
T  F  2.  Several documents in the Listed Files list box at the Find File dialog box can be selected at the same time only if they are adjacent to each other.
T  F  3.  To create a new directory, begin at the Find File dialog box.
T  F  4.  A summary is automatically created for every document.
T  F  5.  As you select a document name in the Listed Files list box at the Find File dialog box, the document contents are displayed in the Preview of text box.
T  F  6.  When using wildcard characters, use the question mark (?) to indicate a range of characters.
T  F  7.  To save a complex search criteria, you need to write it down by hand.
T  F  8.  A document is automatically saved every 15 minutes.
T  F  9.  Tell Word to create an automatic backup of documents at the Backup dialog box.
T  F  10.  The File Manager program within the Windows program can also be used to perform many of the same document maintenance functions as described in this chapter.

**Completion:** In the space provided, indicate the correct term, command, or number.

1.  Many of the same document maintenance functions can be performed at the Open dialog box and this dialog box.                                    _____
2.  This is a directory within a directory.                                    _____
3.  The main directory on a disk or drive is called this.                                    _____
4.  This is the set of steps you take to move from a directory to a subdirectory.                                    _____
5.  At the Open dialog box, this icon indicates the current directory.                                    _____
6.  Choose the Statistics button at this dialog box to display statistics about a document.                                    _____
7.  At this dialog box, you can search a directory for documents with specific words or phrases.                                    _____
8.  Key this in the appropriate location to search for all documents containing either the name Smith or Smyth.                                    _____
9.  When a document is opened as this, you can make changes to it, but you cannot save those changes with the same name.                                    _____
10.  Printing a document without opening it is referred to as this.                                    _____

### Exercise 1

*Note: Check with your instructor before completing this exercise. Depending on your computer system setup, you may need specialized directions from your instructor.*

1.  Change the drive to c: by completing the following steps:
    a.  Display the Open dialog box.
    b.  At the Open dialog box, choose Drives, then *c:*. To do this with the mouse, click on the down-pointing arrow after the Drives text box, then click on *c:*. If you are using the keyboard, press Alt + V, press the down arrow key until *c:* is selected, then press Enter.
    c.  Choose Cancel to close the Open dialog box.
2.  Change directories by completing the following steps:
    a.  Display the Open dialog box.
    b.  Double-click on *c:\* in the Directories list box.

c. Double-click on *winword* in the Directories list box. (You may need to click on the down-pointing arrow to display the *winword* directory.)

d. Choose Cancel to close the Open dialog box.

3. Display all documents in the *c:\winword* subdirectory by completing the following steps:

a. Display the Open dialog box.

b. At the Open dialog box, choose List Files of Type, then All Files (*.*). To do this with the mouse, click on the down-pointing arrow after the List Files of Type text box, then click on *All Files (*.*)*. If you are using the keyboard, press Alt + T, press the down arrow key until *All Files (*.*)* is selected, then press Enter.

c. Choose Cancel to close the Open dialog box.

4. Display the Open dialog box, then make the following changes:

a. Change the directory to the drive where your student data disk is located.

b. Change the List Files of Type option to *Word Documents (*.doc)*.

c. Choose Cancel to close the Open dialog box.

## Exercise 2

1. Display the Find File dialog box and view documents by completing the following steps:

a. Choose File, Find File.

b. At the Find File dialog box, click on the *letter01.doc* in the Listed Files list box. (This displays the document in the Preview of preview box.)

c. Click on *memo01.doc* to display the document in the Preview of preview box. (If the *memo01.doc* is not displayed in the Listed Files list box, click on the down-pointing arrow on the vertical scroll bar until the document is visible.)

d. Click on *report01.doc* to display the document in the Preview of preview box.

2. Close the Find File dialog box by clicking on the Close button.

## Exercise 3

1. Select then open several documents at the Find File dialog box by completing the following steps:

a. Choose File, Find File.

b. At the Find File dialog box, select all the letter documents using the mouse, then open them by completing the following steps:

(1) Position the arrow pointer on *letter01.doc* in the Listed Files list box, hold down the left mouse button, drag the arrow pointer to the last letter document, then release the mouse button.

(2) Choose Open.

2. Close each document.

## Exercise 4

1. Select then print several documents at the Find File dialog box by completing the following steps:

a. Choose File, Find File.

b. At the Find File dialog box select *notice01.doc, notice02.doc,* and *notice03.doc*.

c. Choose Commands, Print.

d. At the Print dialog box, choose OK or press Enter.

## Exercise 5

1. Select then delete all documents created in chapters 6 and 7 by completing the following steps:

a. Choose File, Find File.

b. At the Find File dialog box select all documents that *begin* with *c06* and *c07*.

c. Choose Commands, Delete.

d. When Word asks if you want to delete all the documents, choose Yes.

2. Close the Find File dialog box.

## Exercise 6

1. Copy the document named *memo06.doc* and name it *aversen.doc* by completing the following steps:
   a. Choose <u>F</u>ile, <u>F</u>ind File.
   b. At the Find File dialog box select *memo06.doc*.
   c. Choose <u>C</u>ommands, <u>C</u>opy.
   d. At the Copy dialog box, key **aversen.doc** in the <u>P</u>ath text box.
   e. Choose OK or press Enter.
2. Close the Find File dialog box.
3. Copy the document named *letter01.doc* and name it *blake.doc* by completing steps similar to those in 1a through 1e.

## Exercise 7

1. Create a summary for *report01.doc* by completing the following steps:
   a. Open *report01.doc*.
   b. Save the document with Save As and name it c15ex07.
   c. Choose <u>F</u>ile, Summary <u>I</u>nfo.
   d. At the Summary Info dialog box, choose <u>S</u>ubject, then key **desktop publishing**.
   e. Choose <u>A</u>uthor, then key your name in the text box.
   f. Choose <u>K</u>eywords, then key **type measurement size style**.
   g. Choose OK or press Enter.
2. Save the document again with the same name (c15ex07).
3. Print the document summary by completing the following steps:
   a. Display the Print dialog box.
   b. At the Print dialog box, choose <u>P</u>rint What, Summary Info.
   c. Choose OK or press Enter.
4. Close c15ex07.

## Exercise 8

1. Open report02.
2. Save the document with Save As and name it c15ex08.
3. Create a document summary by completing steps similar to those in exercise 7. At the Summary Info dialog box, key **desktop publishing** in the <u>S</u>ubject text box; your name in the <u>A</u>uthor text box; and **multipage documents** in the <u>K</u>eywords text box.
4. Save the document again with the same name (c15ex08).
5. Print the document summary.
6. Close c15ex08.

## Exercise 9

1. Open report03.
2. Save the document with Save As and name it c15ex09.
3. Create a document summary by completing steps similar to those in exercise 7. At the Summary Info dialog box, key **telecommunications** in the <u>S</u>ubject text box; your name in the <u>A</u>uthor text box; and **history technology** in the <u>K</u>eywords text box.
4. Save the document again with the same name (c15ex09).
5. Print the document summary.
6. Close c15ex09.

## Exercise 10

1. Search for *quiz01.doc* by completing the following steps:
   a. Choose <u>F</u>ile, <u>F</u>ind File.
   b. At the Find File dialog box, choose <u>S</u>earch.

     c.  At the Search dialog box, key **quiz01.doc** in the File <u>N</u>ame text box. (When the Search dialog box is displayed, the insertion point is automatically positioned in the File <u>N</u>ame text box.)

     d.  Make sure the correct drive and/or directory is displayed in the <u>L</u>ocation text box. For example, if you are searching the disk in drive a for the document, make sure *a:\* displays in the <u>L</u>ocation text box. (If not, choose <u>L</u>ocation, then key **a:\**.)

     e.  Choose OK or press Enter.

  2.  Close the Find File dialog box.

## Exercise 11

  1.  Search for all documents created in chapter 8 by completing the following steps:

     a.  Choose <u>F</u>ile, <u>F</u>ind File.

     b.  At the Find File dialog box, choose <u>S</u>earch.

     c.  At the Search dialog box, key **c08\*.doc** in the File <u>N</u>ame text box.

     d.  Make sure the correct drive and/or directory is displayed in the <u>L</u>ocation text box.

     e.  Choose OK or press Enter.

  2.  Close the Find File dialog box.

## Exercise 12

  1.  Create then save a search criteria for all report documents and name the search criteria *reports* by completing the following steps:

     a.  Choose <u>F</u>ile, <u>F</u>ind File.

     b.  At the Find File dialog box, choose <u>S</u>earch.

     c.  At the Search dialog box, key **report\*.doc** in the File <u>N</u>ame text box.

     d.  Choose <u>L</u>ocation, then key **a:\** (or the drive letter where your student data disk is located).

     e.  Choose <u>S</u>ave Search As.

     f.  At the Save Search As dialog box, key **reports** in the <u>S</u>earch Name text box.

     g.  Choose OK or press Enter.

     h.  At the Search dialog box, choose OK or press Enter.

     i.  Close the Find File dialog box.

  2.  Delete the *reports* search criteria by completing the following steps:

     a.  Choose <u>F</u>ile, <u>F</u>ind File.

     b.  At the Find File dialog box, choose <u>S</u>earch.

     c.  At the Search dialog box, make sure *reports* displays in the Saved S<u>e</u>arches text box. If not, choose Saved S<u>e</u>arches, then select *reports* from the drop-down menu.

     d.  Choose <u>D</u>elete Search.

     e.  At the question *Do you want to delete "reports"?*, choose <u>Y</u>es.

     f.  Choose Close to close the Search dialog box.

     g.  At the Find File dialog box, choose <u>S</u>earch.

     h.  At the Search dialog box, key **\*.doc** in the File <u>N</u>ame list box.

     i.  Choose <u>L</u>ocation, then key **a:\** (or the drive where your student data disk is located).

     j.  Choose OK or press Enter.

     k.  Close the Find File dialog box.

## Exercise 13

  1.  Search for all documents containing *desktop publishing* in the summary by completing the following steps:

     a.  Choose <u>F</u>ile, <u>F</u>ind File.

     b.  At the Find File dialog box, choose <u>S</u>earch.

     c.  At the Search dialog box, choose <u>A</u>dvanced Search.

     d.  At the Advanced Search dialog box, choose the <u>S</u>ummary tab.

    e.  Choose S<u>u</u>bject, then key **desktop publishing**.

    f.  Choose OK or press Enter.

    g.  At the Search dialog box, choose OK or press Enter.

    h.  Close the Find File dialog box.

2.  Display the list of documents in drive a (or the drive where your student data disk is located) by completing the following steps:

    a.  Choose <u>F</u>ile, <u>F</u>ind File.

    b.  At the Find File dialog box, choose <u>S</u>earch.

    c.  At the Search dialog box, make sure *.*doc* displays in the File <u>N</u>ame list box and *a:\* displays in the <u>L</u>ocation text box (or the drive where your student data disk is located).

    d.  Choose <u>A</u>dvanced Search.

    e.  At the Advanced Search dialog box, delete the text in the S<u>u</u>bject text box.

    f.  Choose OK or press Enter.

    g.  At the Search dialog box, choose OK or press Enter.

    h.  Close the Find File dialog box.

## Exercise 14

1.  Search for all documents last saved in the current month by completing the following steps:

    a.  Choose <u>F</u>ile, <u>F</u>ind File.

    b.  At the Find File dialog box, choose <u>S</u>earch.

    c.  At the Search dialog box, choose <u>A</u>dvanced Search.

    d.  At the Advanced Search dialog box, choose the Timestam<u>p</u> tab.

    e.  Choose <u>F</u>rom, then key the month, day, and year for the beginning of the current month. (For example, if the current month is April in the year 1996, you would key **04-01-96**.)

    f.  Choose <u>T</u>o, then key the month, day, and year for the end of the current month.

    g.  Choose OK or press Enter.

    h.  At the Search dialog box, choose OK or press Enter.

    i.  Close the Find File dialog box.

2.  Display the list of documents in drive a (or the drive where your student data disk is located) by completing the following steps:

    a.  Choose <u>F</u>ile, <u>F</u>ind File.

    b.  At the Find File dialog box, choose <u>S</u>earch.

    c.  At the Search dialog box, make sure *.*doc* displays in the File <u>N</u>ame list box and *a:\* displays in the <u>L</u>ocation text box (or the drive where your student data disk is located).

    d.  Choose <u>A</u>dvanced Search.

    e.  At the Advanced Search dialog box with the Timestam<u>p</u> tab selected, delete the text in the <u>F</u>rom and the <u>T</u>o text boxes.

    f.  Choose OK or press Enter.

    g.  At the Search dialog box, choose OK or press Enter.

    h.  Close the Find File dialog box.

## SKILL ASSESSMENTS

## Assessment 1

1.  Display the Find File dialog box, then open all documents created in chapter 15.

2.  Make c15ex08 the active document, then print the summary.

3.  Close all documents.

## Assessment 2

1. Display the Find File dialog box, then delete the following documents: *aversen.doc* and *blake.doc*.
2. At the Find File dialog box, select then delete all documents created in chapters 8, 9, and 10.
3. At the Find File dialog box, select then delete all documents created in chapters 1 through 5. (Skip this step if the documents have already been deleted.)
4. At the Find File dialog box, select then delete all documents created for the unit 1 Performance Assessment. (These documents begin with *u01*. Skip this step if the documents have already been deleted.)
5. At the Find File dialog box, select then delete all documents created for the unit 2 Performance Assessment. (These documents begin with *u02*.
6. Close the Find File dialog box.

## Assessment 3

1. Open report05.
2. Save the document with Save As and name it c15sa03.
3. Create a summary for the document with the following information: *desktop publishing* in the Subject text box; your name in the Author text box; and *stationery* in the Keywords text box. (Make sure the title, *CHAPTER 3: CHOOSING PAPER*, displays in the Title text box.)
4. Save the document again with the same name (c15sa03).
5. Print the summary.
6. Close c15sa03.

# UNIT 3

## PERFORMANCE ASSESSMENT

In this unit, you have learned to create, revise, copy, delete, print, and maintain standard business memoranda, letters, and reports.

## Assessment 1

1. Open mortgage. This document is located on your student data disk.
2. Complete the following steps:
   a. Select the first paragraph, copy it to a new document, save it and name it *mort01*, then close mort01.
   b. Select the second paragraph, copy it to a new document, save it and name it *mort02*, then close mort02.
   c. Select the third paragraph, copy it to a new document, save it and name it *mort03*, then close mort03.
   d. Select the fourth paragraph, copy it to a new document, save it and name it *mort04*, then close mort04.
   e. Select the fifth paragraph, copy it to a new document, save it and name it *mort05*, then close mort05.
   f. Select the sixth paragraph, copy it to a new document, save it and name it *mort06*, then close mort06.
   g. Select the seventh paragraph, copy it to a new document, save it and name it *mort07*, then close mort07.
3. Close mortgage.
4. At a clear document screen, create the document shown in figure U3.1. Insert the documents as indicated by the bracketed items.
5. Make the following changes to the document:
   a. Select the entire document, then change to a serif font in 12-point size.
   b. Change the top margin to 1.5 inches and the left and right margins to 1 inch.
6. Save the document and name it u03pa01.
7. Print u03pa01.
8. Close u03pa01.

## CONTRACT AND SECURITY AGREEMENT

### BETWEEN

### TAHOMA MORTGAGE AND

### SAMUEL H. MONROE AND NORA G. MONROE

This contract is made this _____ day of _____, 1996 between TAHOMA MORTGAGE, Seller, and SAMUEL H. MONROE and NORA G. MONROE, Buyers. Having been quoted a cash price and a credit price and having chosen to pay the credit price, the Buyers agree to buy and Seller agrees to sell, subject to all the terms of this contract, the land parcel located at 1232 Southeast 144th Street, Olympia, WA 98430.

[Insert mort03 here.]

[Insert mort01 here.]

[Insert mort02 here.]

[Insert mort05 here.]

[Insert mort07 here.]

[Insert mort04 here.]

```
_____
AMANDA J. BAKER, President
TAHOMA MORTGAGE



_____
SAMUEL H. MONROE, Buyer



_____
NORA G. MONROE, Buyer
```

## Assessment 2

1. Open u03pa01.
2. Save the document with Save As and name it u03pa02.
3. Make the following changes to the document:
   a. Double space the paragraphs within the body of the contract.
   b. Indent the first line of each paragraph.
   c. Delete the blank lines between paragraphs. (There should only be a double space between all text in the body of the contract.)

    d.  Create a footer that prints on every page, is set in the same font as the document text, is bolded, and contains *CONTRACT* at the left margin and *Page* followed by the page number at the right margin.

    e.  Complete the following find and replaces:

       (1)  Find SAMUEL H. MONROE and replace with ERIC L. RIVERS.

       (2)  Find NORA G. MONROE and replace with MONICA A. RIVERS.

4.  Create a summary for this document. (You determine the information to enter after the options.)

5.  Save the document again with the same name (u03pa02).

6.  Print the summary.

7.  Print u03pa02.

8.  Close u03pa02.

## Assessment 3

1.  At a clear document screen, create the document shown in figure U3.2 by completing the following steps:

    a.  Change the left and right margins to 2 inches.

    b.  Key the document shown in figure U3.2.

    c.  Save the document and name it u03out.

2.  With u03out still open, open mortgage, then complete the following steps:

    a.  Save the mortgage document with Save As and name it u03pa03.

    b.  Arrange the windows.

    c.  With u03pa03 the active window, select and move paragraphs so they are in the order shown in the outline. (Make sure the spacing between paragraphs is correct.)

    d.  Save the u03pa03 document again with the same name.

    e.  Print u03pa03.

    f.  Close u03pa03.

    g.  With u03out the active document, print u03out.

    h.  Close u03out.

**Figure U3.2**

```
              CONTRACT AND SECURITY OUTLINE


    1.  Prepayment
    2.  Delinquency
    3.  Taxes
    4.  Insurance
    5.  Use of the Collateral
    6.  Ownership of the Collateral
    7.  Demand for Full Payment
```

## Assessment 4

1.  At a clear document screen, create an envelope with the delivery address and return address shown in figure U3.3. Include the following:

    a.  POSTNET Bar Code

    b.  FIM

2.  Save the envelope and name it u03pa04.

3.  Print u03pa04.

4.  Close u03pa04.

```
Dr. Lyle Cornish
Northwest Clinic
1324 Kirkland Avenue
Seattle, WA 98012



                    Mrs. Diana King
                    304 North 144th
                    Seattle, WA 98044
```

## Assessment 5

1. Create mailing labels for the return address shown in figure U3.3 (containing the name *Dr. Lyle Cornish*). Use the Custom Laser or Custom Dot Matrix label form.
2. Save the label document and name it u03pa05.
3. Print u03pa05.
4. Close u03pa05.

## COMPOSING ACTIVITIES

The following activities give you the opportunity to practice your writing skills along with demonstrating an understanding of some of the important Word features you have mastered in this unit. In planning the documents, remember to shape the information according to the writing purpose and the audience. Use correct grammar, appropriate word choices, and clear sentence constructions.

### Activity 1

**Situation:** You are responsible for creating a report with the *report04.doc* and the *report05.doc* documents. (*Hint: Use Insert, File to do this.*) This report should include page numbers and headers and/or footers. Change to a serif font for the body of the report and a sans serif font for the title and headings.

After formatting the report, create a table of contents for the report and an appropriate title page for the report. Include your name as the author of the report. Save the document and name it u03act01. Print then close u03act01.

### Activity 2

**Situation:** You are Karen Delano, assistant editor for the Petersburg School District newsletter. You have been asked by Jon Struebing, editor of the newsletter, to present information on the types of paper available for printing the newsletter. Prepare a memo to Jon Struebing discussing information on how to choose paper. Use the information in chapter 3 in the report you prepared for activity 1 and create a synopsis of this information for the memo.

Save the memo and name it u03act02. Print then close u03act02.

*Note: For this research activity you will need access to the Microsoft Word User's Guide.*
Answer the following questions about information in the Word for Windows User's Guide.

1. Find information in the user's guide on restoring lost work. (*Hint: This information is located in chapter 21.*) What two options does Word provide that can help you recover work if there is a power failure or other problem?

   _____

   _____

2. If you tell Word to create backup documents, what extension does Word add to backup documents? _____

3. If the Backup option is turned on, what steps would you follow to display backup documents in the Open dialog box?

   _____

   _____

4. On what page do you find information on printing a document in the draft mode?

   _____

5. What steps would you take to change to the draft mode?

   _____

   _____

   _____

6. Word contains a feature called *Spike* that is a special type of AutoText entry that enables you to move selected text from different places in a document, collect them, and then insert them into a document as a group. The word *Spike* comes from the office spikes that were used in offices to impale bills and invoices until they could be dealt with. Text stored in the Spike can be inserted in a document just as a regular AutoText entry. Answer the following questions about the Spike:

   What is the keyboard command to move selected text to the Spike? _____

   What is the keyboard command to paste Spike contents into a document? _____

# *A*dvanced *C*haracter and *L*ine *F*ormatting

U N I T

*In this unit you will learn to automate the preparation of business documents and enhance the visual display of documents with borders, frames, pictures, shapes, and WordArt text.*

# Advanced Line Formatting 16

Upon successful completion of chapter 16, you will be able to manipulate the length of lines in business documents, create a document more quickly with the date and AutoText features, and improve the visual appeal of a document with drop caps and nonbreaking spaces.

Word's hyphenation feature can be used to hyphenate words at the end of lines. Use the AutoText feature to simplify inserting commonly used words, names, or phrases in a document. The visual appeal of a document can be improved with drop caps and/or nonbreaking spaces. Bookmarks can be inserted in specific locations in a document to help you find those locations later.

## Hyphenating Words

In some Word documents, especially documents with left and right margins wider than 1 inch, the right margin may appear quite ragged. If the paragraph alignment is changed to justified, the right margin will appear even, but there will be extra space added throughout the line. In these situations, hyphenating long words that fall at the end of the text line provides the document with a more balanced look.

### Automatically Hyphenating Words

When using the hyphenation feature, you can tell Word to automatically hyphenate words in a document or you can manually insert hyphens.

To automatically hyphenate words in a document, you would complete the following steps:

1. Open the document in which you want to insert hyphens.
2. Choose Tools, Hyphenation.
3. At the Hyphenation dialog box shown in figure 16.1, choose Automatically Hyphenate Document.
4. Choose OK or press Enter.

*Figure 16.1
Hyphenation Dialog
Box*

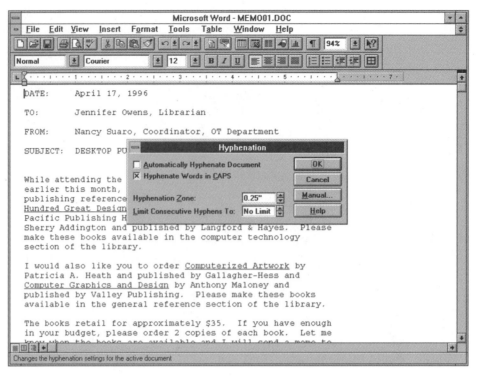

After hyphens are inserted automatically in the document, scroll through the document and check to see if hyphens display in the appropriate location within the word.

If, after hyphenating words in a document, you want to remove all hyphens, immediately click on the Undo button on the Standard toolbar; choose Edit, then Undo Hyphenation; or press Ctrl + Z. This must be done immediately after hyphenating since the Undo feature undoes the last function.

By default, Word hyphenates words in all capital letters. If you do not want words in all capital letters hyphenated, choose Hyphenate Words in CAPS. This removes the X from the check box.

With the Limit Consecutive Hyphens To option at the Hyphenation dialog box, you can limit the number of lines that can end in hyphens. Generally, no more than two lines of text should display with a hyphen. To limit the hyphenation to two lines, display the Hyphenation dialog box, choose Limit Consecutive Hyphens To, then key 2. You can also increase the number of lines by clicking on the up-pointing triangle after the option. Click on the down-pointing arrow to decrease the number of consecutive lines.

You can tell Word to ignore text in a paragraph or selected paragraphs when hyphenating. To do this, you would complete the following steps:

1. Position the insertion point in the paragraph where you do not want words hyphenated or select paragraphs.
2. Choose Format, Paragraph.
3. At the Paragraph dialog box, choose the Text Flow tab.
4. At the Paragraph dialog box with the Text Flow tab selected, choose Don't Hyphenate.
5. Choose OK or press Enter.

Word will ignore the text in the paragraph or text in the selected paragraphs when hyphenating words in the document.

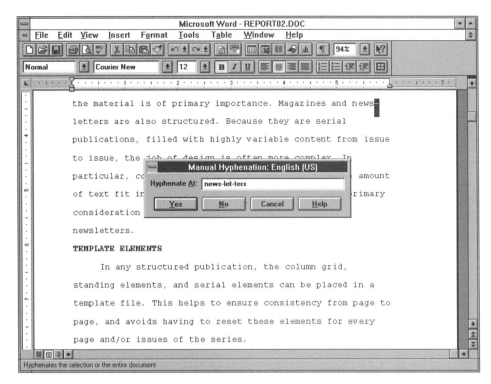

Figure 16.2
Manual
Hyphenation:
English (US) Dialog
Box

## Manually Hyphenating Words

If you want to control where a hyphen appears in a word during hyphenation, choose manual hyphenation. To do this, you would complete the following steps:

1. Open the document in which you want to insert hyphens.
2. Choose Tools, Hyphenation.
3. At the Hyphenation dialog box, choose Manual.
4. Word displays the Manual Hyphenation: English (US) dialog box as shown in figure 16.2. (The word in the Hyphenate At text box will vary.) At this dialog box, choose Yes to hyphenate the word as indicated in the Hyphenate At text box. Choose No if you do not want the word hyphenated, or choose Cancel to cancel hyphenation.
5. Continue choosing Yes or No at the Manual Hyphenation: English (US) dialog box.
6. When Word displays the message *Hyphenation is complete.*, choose OK or press Enter.

At the Manual Hyphenation: English (US) dialog box, you can reposition the hyphen in the Hyphenate At text box. Word displays the word with syllable breaks indicated by a hyphen. The position where Word will hyphenate the word displays as a blinking black bar. If you want to hyphenate at a different location in the word, position the I-beam pointer at the desired location, then click the left mouse button. If you are using the keyboard, press the left or right arrow key until the hyphen is positioned in the desired location. After positioning the hyphen, choose Yes.

If you want to remove all manual hyphenations in a document, immediately click on the Undo button on the Standard toolbar; choose Edit, then Undo Hyphenation; or press Ctrl + Z.

To delete a few hyphens, but not all, in a document, use the Replace dialog box. To do this, you would complete the following steps:

1. Open the document containing hyphens to be removed.
2. Choose Edit, Replace; or press Ctrl + H.
3. At the Replace dialog box, make sure there is no text in the Find What text box. If there is, press the Delete key. Make sure there is no formatting displayed below the Find What text box. If there is, choose No Formatting.
4. With the insertion point positioned in the Find What text box, choose Special.
5. At the list of special characters, choose Optional Hyphen.
6. Make sure there is no text in the Replace With text box and no formatting below the box. (This tells Word to replace the optional hyphen with nothing.)
7. Choose Find Next.
8. When Word stops at the first occurrence of an optional hyphen (a hyphen inserted during hyphenation), choose Replace to remove the hyphen or choose Find Next to leave the hyphen in the document and move to the next hyphen.
9. Continue choosing Find Next or Replace until all hyphens have been found.
10. When Word displays the message *Word has finished searching the document.*, choose OK or press Enter.
11. Choose Close to close the Replace dialog box.

## Changing the Hyphenation Zone

Word uses a hyphenation zone of 0.25 inches from the right margin. If a word begins after the beginning of the hyphenation zone and extends beyond the end of the hyphenation zone, the word is wrapped to the next line. If a word begins at or before the beginning of the hyphenation zone and extends beyond the end of the hyphenation zone, it will be hyphenated during automatic hyphenation or presented for hyphenation during manual hyphenation.

If the hyphenation zone measurement is decreased, more words will be hyphenated. If the hyphenation zone measurement is increased, fewer words will be hyphenated.

To change the hyphenation zone measurement, you would complete the following steps:

1. Choose Tools, Hyphenation.
2. At the Hyphenation dialog box, choose Hyphenation Zone, then key the desired measurement. You can also click on the up-pointing triangle after the Hyphenation Zone dialog box to increase the hyphenation zone, or click on the down-pointing triangle to decrease the hyphenation zone. If you are using the keyboard, press Alt + Z, then press the up arrow key to increase the zone or press the down arrow key to decrease the zone.

After changing the hyphenation zone measurement, continue hyphenation by completing steps similar to those presented earlier.

## Inserting Hyphens

There are several ways that a hyphen is inserted in a document. The type of hyphen in a word like *co-worker* is called a *regular* hyphen. This hyphen is inserted by keying the minus sign on the keyboard. During hyphenation, Word will break hyphenated words, if necessary, at the hyphen.

A hyphen that you or Word inserts during hyphenation is considered an *optional* hyphen. An optional hyphen appears in the document screen and prints only if the word falls at the end of the text line. If text is adjusted and the word no longer falls at the end of the line, the optional hyphen is removed from the document screen and will not print. To view optional hyphens, turn on the display of nonprinting characters. An optional hyphen displays as (-).

An optional hyphen can be inserted in a word by pressing Ctrl + -. If a word containing an optional hyphen falls at the end of the line, Word automatically breaks the word at the optional hyphen.

In some text, such as telephone numbers and Social Security numbers, you may want to insert a *nonbreaking* hyphen rather than a regular hyphen. A nonbreaking hyphen tells Word that the text is to be considered a unit and not to break it between lines. A nonbreaking hyphen is inserted in text by pressing Ctrl + Shift + -.

## ▪ Spacing Between Paragraphs

Space before and after a paragraph can be added by pressing the Enter key. If you want more control over the spacing above or below paragraphs, use the Before and/or After options at the Paragraph dialog box with the Indents and Spacing tab selected.

If spacing before or after a paragraph is added at the Paragraph dialog box, the spacing is part of the paragraph and will be moved, copied, or deleted with the paragraph. If a paragraph, such as a heading, contains spacing above it, and the paragraph falls at the top of a page, the spacing is ignored.

Spacing above or below paragraphs is added in points. As an example of how to add spacing to a paragraph, you would complete the following steps to add 6 points of space below selected paragraphs:

1. Select the paragraphs.
2. Choose Format, Paragraph.
3. At the Paragraph dialog box, make sure the Indents and Spacing tab is selected. If not, choose Indents and Spacing.
4. Choose After, then key **6**. (If you are using the mouse, you can click on the up-pointing arrow after the After text box until *6 pt* displays.)
5. Choose OK or press Enter.

With the shortcut command, Ctrl + 0 (the zero), you can add 12 points of space before a paragraph.

## ▪ Turning on Line Numbering

Lines in a document can be numbered with options from the Line Numbering dialog box. This has practical applications for certain legal papers or for reference purposes. To number lines in a document, you would complete the following steps:

1. Open the document in which you want to add line numbers.
2. Choose File, Page Setup.
3. At the Page Setup dialog box, choose the Layout tab.
4. Choose Line Numbers.
5. At the Line Numbers dialog box shown in figure 16.3, choose Add Line Numbering.
6. Choose OK or press Enter.
7. At the Page Setup dialog box, choose OK or press Enter.

When you choose Add Line Numbering at the Line Numbers dialog box, a variety of options becomes available. By default, Word begins line numbering with number 1. With the Start At option, you can change to a different beginning number. To change the beginning number, choose Start At, then key the new beginning number; or click on the up-pointing or down-pointing triangles after the option.

The From Text option at the Line Numbers dialog box has a default setting of *Auto*. At this setting, line numbers are printed 0.25 inches from the text in the document. This measurement can be increased or decreased with the From Text option.

Figure 16.3
Line Numbers
Dialog Box

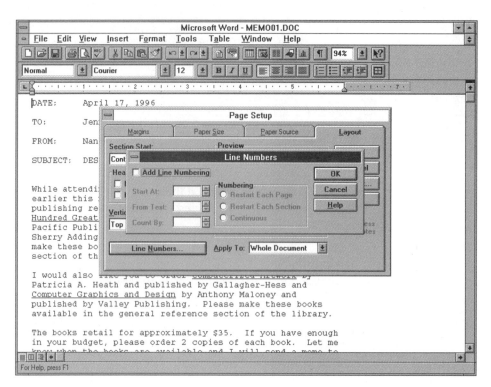

With the Count <u>B</u>y option at the Line Numbers dialog box, you can specify the interval between printed line numbers. For example, if you want every second line numbered, you would enter 2 in the Count <u>B</u>y text box.

Word starts numbering over at the beginning of each page. This is because the Restart Each <u>P</u>age option is selected. If you want line numbering to start over at the beginning of each section, choose Restart Each <u>S</u>ection. If you want lines numbered in a document consecutively, choose <u>C</u>ontinuous.

When line numbering is turned on, line numbers will display in the Page viewing mode or in Print Preview. At the Page viewing mode, you may need to scroll the text in the document screen to the right to see the line numbers.

# ■ <u>U</u>sing <u>A</u>uto<u>T</u>ext

Word's AutoText feature is similar to the AutoCorrect feature you learned about in a previous chapter. With AutoCorrect, the text is automatically inserted in a document when the space bar is pressed. For example, if you assigned the letters *MCC* to *Mountain Community College*, when you key MCC, then press the space bar, *Mountain Community College* is automatically inserted in the document.

If you use text on a less frequent basis and do not want it automatically inserted in the document, use Word's AutoText feature. An AutoText entry is inserted in the document if you click on the Insert AutoText button on the Standard toolbar or at the AutoText dialog box.

## Saving an AutoText Entry

The AutoText feature is useful for items such as addresses, a company logo, lists, standard text, or a closing to a letter. As an example of how to create an AutoText entry, you would complete the following steps to save *KNOXVILLE COMMUNITY COLLEGE* set in 18-point Arial Bold with the name *KCC*:

1. Key **KNOXVILLE COMMUNITY COLLEGE**.
2. Select *KNOXVILLE COMMUNITY COLLEGE,* then change the font to 18-point Arial Bold.

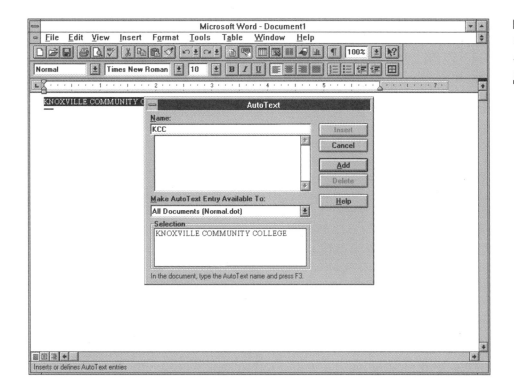

Figure 16.4
AutoText Dialog
Box

3. With the text still selected, click on the Edit AutoText button on the Standard toolbar (the ninth button from the right).
4. At the AutoText dialog box shown in figure 16.4, key **KCC**.
5. Choose <u>A</u>dd.
6. Deselect the text.

When you save selected text as an AutoText entry, the formatting applied to the text is also saved. In the example above, the 18-point Arial Bold formatting was saved with the text. If you are saving a paragraph or paragraphs of text that have paragraph formatting applied, make sure you include the paragraph mark with the selected text. To make sure the paragraph mark is included, turn on the display of nonprinting characters before selecting the text.

An AutoText entry name can contain a maximum of 32 characters and can include spaces. Try to name the AutoText something that is short but also gives you an idea of the contents of the entry.

## Inserting an AutoText Entry

An AutoText entry can be inserted in a document with a button on the Standard toolbar, with a shortcut command, or through the AutoText dialog box. Use the button on the Standard toolbar or the shortcut command if you want the AutoText entry and all formatting to be inserted in the document. Use the AutoText dialog box if you want to insert the text but not the formatting of an AutoText entry.

As an example of how to insert an AutoText entry, you would complete the following steps to insert the AutoText entry *KNOXVILLE COMMUNITY COLLEGE* into a document:

1. Key **KCC**.
2. Click on the Insert AutoText button on the Standard toolbar; press F3; or press Alt + Ctrl + V.

The Insert AutoText button and the Edit AutoText button are the same button on the Standard toolbar. It is the Edit AutoText button when text is selected in a document and the Insert AutoText button when text is not selected.

When an AutoText entry is saved, the formatting applied to the text is also saved. An AutoText entry can be inserted in a document without the formatting. For example, the AutoText entry KCC can insert the words *KNOXVILLE COMMUNITY COLLEGE* in a document without being set in 18-point Arial Bold. To do this, you would complete the following steps:

1. Choose Edit, AutoText.
2. At the AutoText dialog box, select *KCC* in the Name list box. To do this with the mouse, click on *KCC*. If you are using the keyboard, press the down arrow key until *KCC* is selected.
3. Choose Plain Text.
4. Choose Insert.

The text *KNOXVILLE COMMUNITY COLLEGE* is inserted in the document at the location of the insertion point and takes on the formatting of surrounding text.

At the AutoText dialog box, the Preview box displays the contents of the entry. This is useful if you cannot remember the name of the desired entry. Click on each entry in the Name list box and view the contents in the Preview box.

## Editing an AutoText Entry

An AutoText entry can be edited by inserting the entry in a document, making any necessary changes, then saving it again with the same AutoText entry name. When Word asks if you want to redefine the AutoText entry, choose Yes.

As an example of how to edit an AutoText entry, you would complete the following steps to edit the KCC AutoText entry so it is formatted with 14-point Times New Roman Bold (rather than 18-point Arial Bold):

1. At a document screen, key **KCC**.
2. Click on the Insert AutoText button on the Standard toolbar. (This inserts *KNOXVILLE COMMUNITY COLLEGE* in the document screen.)
3. Select *KNOXVILLE COMMUNITY COLLEGE*, display the Font dialog box, then change the font to 14-point Times New Roman Bold.
4. Choose OK or press Enter to close the Font dialog box and return to the document screen.
5. With *KNOXVILLE COMMUNITY COLLEGE* still selected, click on the Edit AutoText button on the Standard toolbar.
6. At the AutoText dialog box, key **KCC**.
7. Choose Add.
8. At the message *Do you want to redefine the AutoText entry?*, choose Yes.
9. Deselect the text.

## Deleting an AutoText Entry

An AutoText entry can be removed from the AutoText dialog box. To do this, display the AutoText dialog box, select the entry to be deleted, then choose Delete. As an example of how to delete an AutoText entry, you would complete the following steps to delete the KCC AutoText entry:

1. Choose Edit, AutoText.
2. At the AutoText dialog box, key **KCC** in the Name text box, or select *KCC* in the list box below the Name text box.
3. Choose Delete.
4. Choose Close to close the AutoText dialog box.

# Inserting a Nonbreaking Space

As you key text in a document, Word makes line-end decisions and automatically wraps text to the next line. Word wrap is a time-saving feature that can increase your keyboarding speed.

Even though word wrap is helpful, there may be times when word wrap breaks up words or phrases that should remain together. For example, a name such as *Daniel C. Lagasa* can be broken after, but should not be broken before, the initial *C*. The phrase *World War II* can be broken between *World* and *War*, but should not be broken between *War* and *II*.

To control what text is wrapped to the next line, a nonbreaking space can be inserted between words. When a nonbreaking space is inserted, Word considers the words as one unit and will not divide them.

A nonbreaking space can be inserted at the Symbol dialog box or with a shortcut command. To insert a nonbreaking space between words, key the first word, press Ctrl + Shift + space bar, then key the second word.

To insert a nonbreaking space between two words using the Symbol dialog box, you would complete the following steps:

1. Key the first word.
2. Choose Insert, Symbol.
3. At the Symbol dialog box, select the Special Characters tab.
4. Select Nonbreaking Space in the Character list box.
5. Choose Insert.
6. Choose Close.

If nonprinting characters are displayed, a normal space displays as a dot. A nonbreaking space displays as a degree symbol. When creating nonbreaking spaces, turn on the display of nonprinting characters to see the difference between a normal space and a nonbreaking space.

# Inserting the Date and Time

The current date and/or time can be inserted in a document with options from the Date and Time dialog box shown in figure 16.5. To display the Date and Time dialog box, choose Insert, then Date and Time. The current date and time will display in various formats in the Available Formats list box.

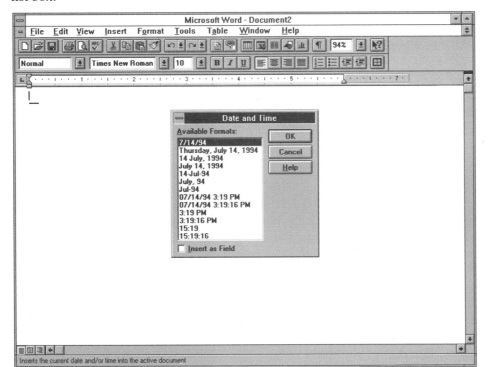

*Figure 16.5*
*Date and Time*
*Dialog Box*

The Date and Time dialog box contains a list of date and time options in the Available Formats list box. Select the desired date or time format, then choose OK or press Enter.

The date can be inserted in a document with the shortcut command Alt + Shift + D. When you press Alt + Shift + D, the date is inserted in the format that you last chose at the Date and Time dialog box. Press Alt + Shift + T to insert the current time in the document. The time is inserted in the format that you last chose at the Date and Time dialog box.

The date and/or time is inserted in the document as regular text. The date and/or time can also be inserted in a document as a field. If a date is inserted in a document as a field, the date is automatically updated if the document is opened on a different day. If the time is inserted as a field, the time is automatically updated when the document is opened again. To insert the date and/or time as a field, choose Insert as Field at the Date and Time dialog box. This inserts an X in the check box.

## Using Bookmarks

In long documents, you may find it useful to mark a location in the document so you can quickly move the insertion point to the location. Create bookmarks for locations in a document at the Bookmark dialog box. When you create bookmarks, you can insert as many as needed in a document. To create a bookmark, you would complete the following steps:

1. Position the insertion point at the location in the document where the bookmark is to appear.
2. Choose Edit, then Bookmark.
3. At the Bookmark dialog box, key a name for the bookmark in the Bookmark Name text box.
4. Choose Add.

Repeat these steps as many times as needed in a document to insert bookmarks. Make sure you give each bookmark a unique name. A bookmark name can contain a maximum of 40 characters and can include letters, numbers, and the underscore character (_). You cannot use spaces in a bookmark name.

When you insert a bookmark in a document, by default the bookmark is not visible. To make a bookmark visible, you would complete the following steps:

1. Choose Tools, Options.
2. At the Options dialog box, select the View tab.
3. Choose Bookmark in the Show section of the dialog box. (This inserts an X in the Bookmark check box.)
4. Choose OK or press Enter.

Complete the same steps to turn off the display of bookmarks. A bookmark displays as an I-beam marker.

You can also create a bookmark for selected text. To do this, select the text first then complete the steps listed above. When you create a bookmark for selected text, a left bracket ([) indicates the beginning of the selected text and a right bracket (]) indicates the end of the selected text.

After bookmarks have been inserted in a document, you can move the insertion point to a specific bookmark by completing the following steps:

1. Choose Edit, Bookmark.
2. At the Bookmark dialog box, key the bookmark name in the Bookmark Name text box. You can also select the bookmark name in the Bookmark Name list box with the mouse by clicking on the desired bookmark. If you are using the keyboard, press the up or down arrow key until the bookmark name is selected.

3. Choose <u>G</u>o To.
4. When Word stops at the location of the bookmark, choose Close to close the Bookmark dialog box.

If you move the insertion point to a bookmark created with selected text, Word moves the insertion point to the bookmark and selects the text.

Bookmarks in a document are deleted at the Bookmark dialog box (not the document). To delete a bookmark, you would complete the following steps:

1. Choose <u>E</u>dit, <u>B</u>ookmark.
2. At the Bookmark dialog box, key the bookmark name in the <u>B</u>ookmark Name text box or select the name in the list box.
3. Choose <u>D</u>elete.
4. Choose Close to close the Bookmark dialog box.

## ■ Creating a Dropped Capital Letter

In publications such as magazines, newsletters, or brochures, a graphic feature called "dropped caps" can be used to enhance the appearance of the text. A drop cap is the first letter of the first word of a paragraph that is set into a paragraph and set in a larger font size. Drop caps identify the beginning of major sections or parts of a document.

Drop caps look best when set in a paragraph containing text set in a proportional font. The drop cap can be set in the same font as the paragraph text or it can be set in a complementary font. For example, a drop cap can be set in a sans serif font while the paragraph text is set in a serif font.

Figure 16.6 illustrates three paragraphs with different types of drop caps. The paragraph text and the drop cap in the first paragraph are set in Times New Roman. The drop caps in the second paragraph are set in Colonna MT and the paragraph text is set in Times New Roman. The drop cap in the third paragraph is set in Algerian and the paragraph text is set in Times New Roman. The first paragraph shows the first letter of the paragraph as the drop cap. The first word of the paragraph is used as drop caps in the second paragraph. The first letter of the third paragraph is a drop cap that displays in the left margin of the paragraph.

O n the most apparent level, graphics and the content of the text communicate characteristics such as humor, elegance, and warmth. Red and yellow are warm, while blue and purple are cool. Illustrations and color should be chosen for their appropriateness in terms of the content of the publication.

On the most apparent level, graphics and the content of the text communicate characteristics such as humor, elegance, and warmth. Red and yellow are warm, while blue and purple are cool. Illustrations and color should be chosen for their appropriateness in terms of the content of the publication.

O n the most apparent level, graphics and the content of the text communicate characteristics such as humor, elegance, and warmth. Red and yellow are warm, while blue and purple are cool. Illustrations and color should be chosen for their appropriateness in terms of the content of the publication.

*Figure 16.6*
*Paragraphs with Drop Caps*

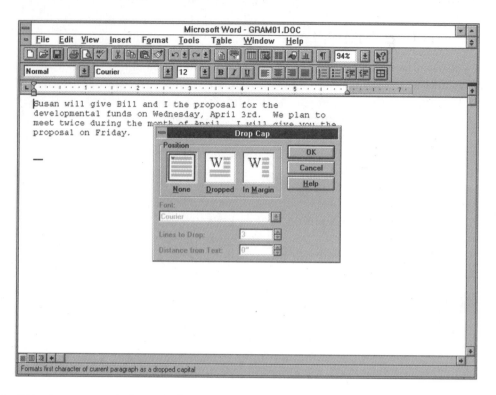

*Figure 16.7*
*Drop Cap Dialog*
*Box*

Drop caps in Word are created through the Drop Cap dialog box shown in figure 16.7. To display this dialog box, choose Format, then Drop Cap. At the Drop Cap dialog box, choose the desired drop cap option, then choose OK or press Enter.

As an example of how to create a drop cap, you would complete the following steps to create a drop cap for the first letter of the first paragraph shown in figure 16.6:

1. Change to the Page Layout viewing mode.
2. Position the insertion point in the paragraph.
3. Choose Format, Drop Cap.
4. At the Drop Cap dialog box, choose Dropped in the Position section of the dialog box.
5. Choose OK or press Enter.

If you want more than the first letter of a paragraph to be set in drop caps, you must select the word before displaying the Drop Cap dialog box. For example, to set the first word in drop caps for the second paragraph shown in figure 16.6, you would complete the following steps:

1. Change to the Page Layout viewing mode.
2. Select the word *On*.
3. Choose Format, Drop Cap.
4. At the Drop Cap dialog box, choose Dropped in the Position section of the dialog box.
5. Choose Font, then Colonna MT.
6. Choose OK or press Enter.

To remove drop caps from a paragraph, you would complete the following steps:

1. Position the insertion point in the paragraph.
2. Choose Format, Drop Cap.
3. At the Drop Cap dialog box, choose None in the Position section of the dialog box.
4. Choose OK or press Enter.

# ■ Creating Annotations

If you want to make comments in a document you are creating, or if a reviewer wants to make comments in a document written by someone else, use *annotations*. An annotation includes the initials of the person whose name was entered as the user information and a number. (In a school setting, this may not be your name.) For example, if *Linda Chambers* was the user's name, the first annotation in a document would be named *LC1*. To determine what name is entered as the user, choose Tools, Options, then click on the User Info tab. The name and initials of the user are displayed at this dialog box.

## Creating an Annotation

An annotation is similar to a footnote or endnote in that a reference mark is inserted in a document and annotation text is keyed at an annotation pane. The annotation mark will not display in the document screen by default. To show annotation marks, turn on the display of nonprinting characters. You can also display annotation marks by completing the following steps:

1. Choose Tools, Options.
2. At the Options dialog box, click on the View tab.
3. At the Options dialog box with the View tab selected, choose Hidden Text.
4. Choose OK or press Enter.

As an example of how to create an annotation with the comment *Add more information here.*, you would complete the following steps:

1. Open the document in which you want to insert the annotation.
2. Position the insertion point at the location in the document where you want the annotation mark to appear.
3. Choose Insert, Annotation; or press Alt + Ctrl + A.
4. At the Annotation pane, key **Add more information here**.
5. Choose Close.

When inserting an annotation mark in a document, position the insertion point where you want the mark to appear, or select text then create the annotation.

## Viewing Annotation Text

If you turn on the display of nonprinting characters or hidden text, the annotation mark is visible but not the annotation text. To view the annotation text, choose View, then Annotation, or double-click on an annotation mark. This displays the annotation pane with the annotation text. After viewing the annotation text, choose Close to close the annotation pane.

## Deleting an Annotation

Delete an annotation in the same manner as a footnote or endnote is deleted. To delete an annotation, select the annotation mark, then press the Delete key. When the mark is deleted, the corresponding annotation text is also deleted.

## Printing an Annotation

A document containing annotations can be printed with the annotations, or you can choose to print just the annotations and not the document.

To print a document and annotations, you would complete the following steps:

1. Choose File, Print; or press Ctrl + P.
2. At the Print dialog box, choose Options.
3. At the Options dialog box, choose Annotations. (This inserts an X in the check box.)
4. Choose OK or press Enter.
5. At the Print dialog box, choose OK or press Enter.

To print only annotations in a document, you would complete the following steps:

1. Choose File, Print; or press Ctrl + P.
2. At the Print dialog box, choose Print What, then Annotations.
3. Choose OK or press Enter.

Annotations are printed on a separate page from the document. The page number where the annotation occurs in the document is printed along with the annotation mark and the annotation text.

## CHAPTER SUMMARY

- Word's hyphenation feature can help achieve a more balanced look when the right margin of a left-justified document is particularly ragged, or when the lines in justified paragraphs include large spaces.
- In addition to automatic or manual hyphenation, these options are also available at the Hyphenation dialog box: choose to hyphenate words that are in all capital letters, limit the number of consecutive lines that can end in hyphens, or tell Word to ignore text in selected text when hyphenating.
- To remove all manual or automatic hyphenations immediately after hyphenating, use the Undo feature. Delete specific hyphens at the Replace dialog box.
- The default hyphenation zone is 0.25 inches from the right margin. If the hyphenation zone is decreased at the Hyphenation dialog box, more words will be hyphenated. If the zone is increased, fewer words will be hyphenated.
- Keying a minus sign in a document inserts a *regular* hyphen. A hyphen inserted during the hyphenation process is called an *optional* hyphen. Insert a *nonbreaking* hyphen in words or groups of numbers that should be kept together on one line.
- Additional spacing, measured in points, above or below selected paragraphs can be added at the Paragraph dialog box with the Indents and Spacing tab showing.
- Lines in a document can be numbered with options from the Line Numbering dialog box.
- Text that is used frequently can be saved as an AutoText entry at the AutoText dialog box, then inserted in a document. An AutoText entry is inserted in the document if you click on the Insert AutoText button on the Standard toolbar or at the AutoText dialog box.
- When a nonbreaking space is inserted between words, Word considers these words as one unit and will not divide them. Insert a nonbreaking space at the Symbol dialog box or with a shortcut command.
- The current date and/or time can be inserted in a document with options from the Date and Time dialog box or with shortcut commands.
- Create bookmarks to mark a location in the document so you can later move the insertion point quickly to that location. Create or delete bookmarks at the Bookmark dialog box.
- A dropped cap can be used to identify the beginning of major sections of a document. Create a dropped cap at the Drop Cap dialog box.
- Use annotations to make comments in a document. The annotation marks and/or the annotation text can be hidden or displayed.

| | Mouse | Keyboard |
|---|---|---|
| Hyphenation dialog box | Tools, Hyphenation | Tools, Hyphenation |
| Remove all manual or automatic hyphenations | Click on Undo button on the Standard toolbar; or choose Edit, then Undo Hyphenation | `CTRL` + `Z` |
| Replace dialog box | Edit, Replace | `CTRL` + `H` |
| Insert an optional hyphen | | `CTRL` + `—` |
| Insert a nonbreaking hyphen | | `CTRL` + `SHIFT` + `—` |
| Paragraph dialog box | Format, Paragraph | Format, Paragraph |
| Line Numbers dialog box | File, Page Setup, choose the Layout tab, then Line Numbers | File, Page Setup, choose Layout tab, then Line Numbers |
| AutoText dialog box | Click on the Edit AutoText button on the Standard toolbar | Edit, AutoText |
| Insert AutoText in document | Click on Insert AutoText button on Standard toolbar | `ALT` + `CTRL` + `V` ; or `F3` |
| Insert nonbreaking space | Insert, Symbol (with Special Characters tab selected), click on Nonbreaking Space | `CTRL` + `SHIFT` + space bar |
| Insert date/time | Insert, Date and Time, click on your choice, choose OK or press Enter | `ALT` + `SHIFT` + T(ime) or D(ate) |
| Create a bookmark | Edit, Bookmark, key unique name for the bookmark, choose Add | Edit, Bookmark, key unique name for the bookmark, choose Add |
| Move insertion point to a bookmark | Edit, Bookmark, key or select name, choose Go To, choose Close | Edit, Bookmark, key or select name, choose Go To, choose Close |
| Drop Cap dialog box | Format, Drop Cap | Format, Drop Cap |
| Insert annotation | Insert, Annotation, key remarks, choose Close | `ALT` + `CTRL` + `A` , key remarks, choose Close |

## CHECK YOUR UNDERSTANDING

**True/False:** Circle the letter T if the statement is true; circle the letter F if the statement is false.

**T F** 1. A hyphen inserted during hyphenation will not print if the word no longer falls at the end of the line.

**T F** 2. If the hyphenation zone is decreased, fewer words will be hyphenated.

**T F** 3. By default, Word starts line numbering over at the beginning of each page.

**T F** 4. Only one bookmark can be located in a document at one time.

**T F** 5. If you cannot remember the name of an AutoText entry, display the Preview box at the Open dialog box.

**T F** 6. If the time is inserted automatically in a document as a field, the time will be updated whenever the document is opened.

| T | F | 7. | With AutoText, the desired text is automatically inserted in the document when the space bar is pressed. |
|---|---|---|---|
| T | F | 8. | Display the Drop Cap dialog box by first choosing Format from the Menu bar. |
| T | F | 9. | By default, the annotation mark will not display in the document screen. |
| T | F | 10. | You can choose to print just the annotations in a document and not the document. |

**Completion:** In the space provided at the right, indicate the correct term, command, or number.

1. The command to insert an optional hyphen from the keyboard when hyphenation is off. _____

2. The default hyphenation zone. _____

3. When increasing the space before or after paragraphs, be sure this tab is selected at the Paragraph dialog box. _____

4. The shortcut command from the keyboard to insert a nonbreaking space. _____

5. Press this key to insert a regular hyphen. _____

6. The feature that will delete all hyphens immediately after hyphenation. _____

7. The shortcut command that will add 12 points of space before a paragraph. _____

8. The feature that can simplify insertion of frequently used text. _____

9. The distance from the text that line numbers are printed. _____

10. The shortcut command to insert the current date. _____

## AT THE COMPUTER

### Exercise 1

1. Open report01.
2. Save the document with Save As and name it c16ex01.
3. Hyphenate words automatically in the report and limit hyphenations to two lines by completing the following steps:
   a. Choose Tools, Hyphenation.
   b. At the Hyphenation dialog box, click on the up-pointing triangle at the right of the Limit Consecutive Hyphens To text box until 2 displays in the text box.
   c. Choose Automatically Hyphenate Document.
   d. Choose OK or press Enter.
4. Save the document again with the same name (c16ex01).
5. Print c16ex01.
6. Close c16ex01.

### Exercise 2

1. Open report03.
2. Save the document with Save As and name it c16ex02.
3. Manually hyphenate documents by completing the following steps:
   a. Choose Tools, Hyphenation.
   b. At the Hyphenation dialog box, choose Limit Consecutive Hyphens To, then key **2**.
   c. Choose Manual.
   d. At the Manual Hyphenation: English (US) dialog box, choose Yes to hyphenate the word as indicated in the Hyphenate At text box; move the hyphen in the word to a more desirable location, then choose Yes; choose No if you do not want the word hyphenated; or choose Cancel to cancel hyphenation. You make each hyphenation decision.
   e. Continue choosing Yes or No at the Manual Hyphenation: English (US) dialog box.
   f. When Word displays the message *Hyphenation is complete,* choose OK or press Enter.
4. Save the document again with the same name (c16ex02).
5. Print c16ex02.
6. Close c16ex02.

## Exercise 3

1. Open c16ex02.
2. Save the document with Save As and name it c16ex03.
3. Delete the second, fourth, and sixth hyphen in the document by completing the following steps:
   a. Choose Edit, Replace; or press Ctrl + H.
   b. At the Replace dialog box, make sure there is no text in the Find What text box. If there is, press the Delete key. Make sure there is no formatting displayed below the Find What text box. If there is, choose No Formatting.
   c. With the insertion point positioned in the Find What text box, choose Special.
   d. At the list of special characters, choose Optional Hyphen.
   e. Make sure there is no text in the Replace With text box and no formatting below the box.
   f. Choose Find Next.
   g. When Word stops at the first occurrence of an optional hyphen (a hyphen inserted during hyphenation), choose Find Next to leave the hyphen in the document and move to the next hyphen.
   h. When Word stops at the second occurrence of an optional hyphen, choose Replace.
   i. Continue choosing Find Next or Replace until all hyphens have been found. (Replace the fourth and sixth optional hyphens. Leave the other hyphens in the document.)
   j. When Word displays the message *Word has finished searching the document.*, choose OK or press Enter.
   k. Choose Close to close the Replace dialog box.
4. Save the document again with the same name (c16ex03).
5. Print c16ex03.
6. Close c16ex03.

## Exercise 4

1. Open para03.
2. Save the document with Save As and name it c16ex04.
3. Change the hyphenation zone, then hyphenate the text in the document automatically by completing the following steps:
   a. Choose Tools, Hyphenation.
   b. At the Hyphenation dialog box, click on the up-pointing triangle at the right of the Hyphenation Zone text box until *0.7"* displays in the text box.
   c. Choose Automatically Hyphenate Document.
   d. Choose OK or press Enter.
4. Save the document again with the same name (c16ex04).
5. Print c16ex04.
6. Close c16ex04.

## Exercise 5

1. At a clear document screen, key the memo shown in figure 16.8. Insert a nonbreaking hyphen between the numbers in the Social Security numbers and the telephone numbers. (Insert a nonbreaking hyphen by pressing Ctrl + Shift + -.)
2. Save the document and name it c16ex05.
3. Print c16ex05.
4. Close c16ex05.

Figure 16.8

```
DATE:      May 16, 1996

TO:        Tina Marzano

FROM:      Dirk Gaines

SUBJECT:   NEW EMPLOYEE VERIFICATION


A New Employee Verification form has been received for Troy
Hoffman, Carol Ishikawa, William Kreis, and Nicole Diorio.  Please
confirm the following numbers:  Troy Hoffman, 536-40-5422; Carol
Ishikawa, 340-45-0049; William Kreis, 403-76-4832; and Nicole
Diorio, 231-29-3942.

Many employees have asked for a toll-free number they can call from
home to check on benefits.  As a response to these requests, a new
toll-free number has been added which is 1-800-555-3033.  Please
provide the new employees with this number.

xx:c16ex05
```

## Exercise 6

1. Open report02.
2. Save the document with Save As and name it c16ex06.
3. Select all the text in the document (except the title), then change the line spacing to single.
4. With the text still selected, change the spacing before and after paragraphs to 6 points by completing the following steps:
   a. Choose Format, Paragraph.
   b. At the Paragraph dialog box, make sure the Indents and Spacing tab is selected. If not, choose Indents and Spacing.
   c. Choose Before, then key **6**. (If you are using the mouse, you can click on the up-pointing arrow after the Before text box until *6 pt* displays.)
   d. Choose After, then key **6**. (If you are using the mouse, you can click on the up-pointing arrow after the After text box until *6 pt* displays.)
   e. Choose OK or press Enter.
5. Check the page breaks in the document and, if necessary, adjust the page breaks.
6. Save the document again with the same name (c16ex06).
7. Print c16ex06.
8. Close c16ex06.

## Exercise 7

1. Open legal01.
2. Save the document with Save As and name it c16ex07.
3. Complete the following instances of find and replace:
   a. Find NAME1 and replace with BRIAN G. COOK.
   b. Find NAME2 and replace with LEAH R. JOHANSON.
   c. Find NUMBER and replace with C-4432.
4. Adjust the right parentheses after the names.

5. Turn on line numbering by completing the following steps:
   a. Choose File, Page Setup.
   b. At the Page Setup dialog box, choose the Layout tab.
   c. Choose Line Numbers.
   d. At the Line Numbers dialog box, choose Add Line Numbering.
   e. Choose OK or press Enter.
   f. At the Page Setup dialog box, choose OK or press Enter.
6. Save the document again with the same name (c16ex07).
7. Print c16ex07.
8. Close c16ex07.

## Exercise 8

1. At a clear document screen, create an AutoText entry for the name OAKRIDGE MIDDLE SCHOOL that is centered and set in 18-point Algerian Bold by completing the following steps:
   a. Turn on the display of nonprinting characters.
   b. Press Ctrl + E, or click on the Center button on the Formatting toolbar.
   c. Key **OAKRIDGE MIDDLE SCHOOL**.
   d. Select *OAKRIDGE MIDDLE SCHOOL*, including the paragraph mark.
   e. Change the font to 18-point Algerian Bold.
   f. With the text still selected, click on the Edit AutoText button on the Standard toolbar (the ninth button from the right).
   g. At the AutoText dialog box, key **OMS**.
   h. Choose Add.
   i. Deselect the text.
   j. Turn off the display of nonprinting characters.
   k. Close the document without saving it.
2. At a clear document screen, create an AutoText entry for the letter complimentary closing shown in figure 16.9 by completing the following steps:
   a. Key the text as shown in figure 16.9. (Insert your initials where you see the *xx*.)
   b. Select the text.
   c. Click on the Edit AutoText button on the Standard toolbar.
   d. At the AutoText dialog box, key **cc**.
   e. Choose Add.
   f. Deselect the text.
3. Close the document without saving it.
4. At a clear document screen, create the letter shown in figure 16.10 by completing the following steps:
   a. Insert the OMS AutoText entry by completing the following steps:
      (1) Key **OMS**.
      (2) Click on the Insert AutoText button on the Standard toolbar; press F3; or press Alt + Ctrl + V.
      (3) Press Enter twice.
   b. Key the body of the letter. To insert the OMS AutoText entry in the body of the letter without the formatting, complete the following steps:
      (1) Choose Edit, AutoText.
      (2) At the AutoText dialog box, select *OMS* in the Name List Box.
      (3) Choose Plain Text.
      (4) Choose Insert.
   c. Insert the *cc* AutoText entry at the end of the letter (where *cc* is located) by completing the following steps:
      (1) Key **cc**.
      (2) Click on the Insert AutoText button on the Standard toolbar; press F3; or press Alt + Ctrl + V.
5. When the letter is completed, save it and name it c16ex08.
6. Print c16ex08.
7. Close c16ex08.

**Figure 16.9**

Very truly yours,


Douglas McKenzie
Principal

xx:c16ex08

**Figure 16.10**

OMS

September 9, 1996



Dear Parents:

The 1996 OMS Open House will be held on Thursday, September 26.  A
short program explaining OMS opportunities and activities will be
presented in the school gym.  After the program, you can visit your
child's classroom and speak with teachers.  The program begins at
6:30 p.m. and the classroom visitations begin at 7:00 p.m.

During the school year, you can help make your child's school year
a success by considering the following suggestions:

• Schedule a teacher conference within the first month of school
  and during each major grading period.

• Ask the teacher for expectations.

• Be sure you oversee your child's work and review any graded
  tests.

• Help your child set a time and place for homework.  Be sure to
  provide support, materials, and encouragement.

During the classroom visitation, find out each teacher's planning
hour so you can schedule a private visitation when needed.  Each of
us at OMS looks forward to a great year!

cc

# Exercise 9

1. At a clear document screen, edit the *cc* AutoText entry by completing the following steps:
   a. Key **cc**.
   b. Click on the Insert AutoText button on the Standard toolbar. (This inserts the complimentary close text.)
   c. Delete the name *Douglas McKenzie*, then key **Dorothy Warner**.
   d. Delete the title *Principal*, then key **Superintendent**.
   e. Select the complimentary close text.
   f. Click on the Edit AutoText button on the Standard toolbar.
   g. At the AutoText dialog box, key **cc**.
   h. Choose <u>A</u>dd.
   i. At the message *Do you want to redefine the AutoText entry?*, choose <u>Y</u>es.
   j. Deselect the text.
2. Close the document without saving it.
3. At a clear document screen, create an AutoText entry named *PSD* that includes the text shown in figure 16.11 by completing the following steps:
   a. Click on the Center button on the Formatting toolbar.
   b. Key **PETERSBURG SCHOOL DISTRICT**.
   c. Press Enter.
   d. Key **7900 North Briar Road**.
   e. Press Enter.
   f. Key **Petersburg, ND 76231**.
   g. Press Enter.
   h. Click on the Align Left button on the Formatting toolbar.
   i. Press Enter.
   j. Select the text and the hard return below the text.
   k. Change the font to 18-point Colonna MT Bold.
   l. With the text still selected, click on the Edit AutoText button on the Standard toolbar.
   m. At the AutoText dialog box, key **PSD**.
   n. Choose <u>A</u>dd.
4. Close the document without saving it.
5. At a clear document screen, create an AutoText entry named *CMS* for CEDAR MIDDLE SCHOOL that is set in 18-point Algerian Bold.
6. Close the document without saving it.
7. At a clear document screen, create the letter shown in figure 16.12. Insert the AutoText entry where you see the AutoText entry name. (When inserting the AutoText entries OMS and CMS in the body of the letter, insert the entry as plain text.)
8. After creating the letter, save it and name it c16ex09.
9. Print c16ex09.
10. Close c16ex09.
11. At a clear document screen, delete the CMS AutoText entry by completing the following steps:
    a. Choose <u>E</u>dit, AutoTe<u>x</u>t.
    b. At the AutoText dialog box, select CMS in the list box below the <u>N</u>ame text box.
    c. Choose <u>D</u>elete.
    d. Choose Close to close the AutoText dialog box.
12. Complete steps similiar to those in 11a through 11d to delete the following AutoText entries: OMS, cc, and PSD.
13. Close the document.

**Figure 16.11**

# PETERSBURG SCHOOL DISTRICT
## 7900 North Briar Road
## Petersburg, ND 76231

**Figure 16.12**

PSD

October 9, 1996

Dear Parents:

Child Psychologist Dr. Marie Sadler, from the University of North Dakota, will be speaking at OMS and CMS. Her topic is "Preparing all students for success in the 21st century." Dr. Sadler will speak at CMS on Tuesday, October 21, from 7:30 to 8:30 p.m. in the multipurpose room. She will speak on Thursday, October 23, from 7:30 to 8:30 p.m. in the gym at OMS.

After speaking, Dr. Sadler will accept questions from the audience. She will address the following issues:

- The knowledge, skills, attitudes, and maturity that will be required of our students in the future world of work.

- The areas of education that need to be reconsidered to better prepare students for a future of fluctuating economy and global competition.

- The need for a comprehensive, integrated approach to education.

We are excited to have Dr. Sadler as our guest speaker. The information she provides will help us and you make sound educational decisions.

cc

## Exercise 10

1. At a clear document screen, turn on the display of nonprinting characters, then key the memo shown in figure 16.13. Insert nonbreaking spaces between the commands in the memorandum (for example, between *Ctrl + B* and *Ctrl + I*). Insert a nonbreaking space by pressing Ctrl + Shift + space bar. Insert a nonbreaking space before and after the plus symbol in all the shortcut commands.
2. After keying the document, change the left and right margins to 1.5 inches.
3. Save the memorandum and name it c16ex10.

4. Turn off the display of nonprinting characters.
5. Print c16ex10.
6. Close c16ex10.

**Figure 16.13**

```
DATE:      April 11, 1996

TO:        All Medical Transcribers

FROM:      Monica Nevins

SUBJECT:  SHORTCUT COMMANDS


Word for Windows version 6 provides a variety of shortcut commands
that lets you quickly access features and functions.  For example,
to bold text press Ctrl + B and to italicize text use the command
Ctrl + I.  To underline text, use the command Ctrl + U.

In addition to the shortcut commands for applying character
formatting, you can use shortcut commands to display certain dialog
boxes.  For example, press Ctrl + F to display the Find dialog box
and press Ctrl + H to display the Replace dialog box.  Press Ctrl +
G to display the Go To dialog box.

xx:c16ex10
```

## Exercise 11

1. Open memo01.
2. Save the document with Save As and name it c16ex11.
3. Delete the date *April 17, 1996*, then insert the current date by pressing Alt + Shift + D.
4. Print c16ex11.
5. Delete the current date you just inserted, then insert the current date in a different format by completing the following steps:
   a. Select the current date with the mouse, then press the Delete key.
   b. Choose Insert, Date and Time.
   c. At the Date and Time dialog box, select the third option in the Available Formats list box.
   d. Choose OK or press Enter.
6. Save the document again with the same name (c16ex11).
7. Print c16ex11.
8. Change the date format back to the original format by completing the following steps:
   a. Choose Insert, Date and Time.
   b. At the Date and Time dialog box, select the fourth option in the Available Formats list box (or the option that displays with the month spelled out and the day and year in figures).
   c. Choose OK or press Enter.
9. Close c16ex11.

## Exercise 12

1. Open report03.
2. Turn on the display of bookmarks by completing the following steps:
   a. Choose Tools, Options.
   b. At the Options dialog box, select the View tab.

    c. Choose Bookmarks in the Show section. (This inserts an X in the Bookmarks check box.)

    d. Choose OK or press Enter.

3. Insert a bookmark at the beginning of the heading *World War I* by completing the following steps:

    a. Position the insertion point at the beginning of the line containing the heading *World War I*.

    b. Choose Edit, Bookmark.

    c. At the Bookmark dialog box, key **WWI**.

    d. Choose Add.

4. Insert a bookmark at the beginning of the following headings with the names listed by following steps similar to those in 3a through 3d.

| | | |
|---|---|---|
| *World War II* | = | WWII |
| *Korean War* | = | KW |
| *Cold War and Vietnam* | = | CWV |

5. Position the insertion point at the KW bookmark by completing the following steps:

    a. Choose Edit, Bookmark.

    b. At the Bookmark dialog box, select *KW* in the Bookmark Name list box.

    c. Choose Go To.

    d. When Word stops at the heading *Korean War*, choose Close to close the Bookmark dialog box.

6. Complete steps similar to those in 5a through 5d to move the insertion point to the WWII, CWV, and WWI bookmarks.

7. Turn off the display of bookmarks by completing steps similar to those in 2a through 2d.

8. Close the report without saving the changes.

## Exercise 13

1. Open para04.

2. Save the document with Save As and name it c16ex13.

3. Select the entire document, then change the font to 12-point Times New Roman.

4. Create a drop cap for the first paragraph by completing the following steps:

    a. Change to the Page Layout viewing mode.

    b. Position the insertion point anywhere in the first paragraph.

    c. Choose Format, Drop Cap.

    d. At the Drop Cap dialog box, choose Dropped in the Position section.

    e. Choose OK or press Enter.

5. Complete steps similar to those in 4b through 4e to create a drop cap for the second paragraph and the third paragraph.

6. Save the document again with the same name (c16ex13).

7. Print c16ex13.

8. Close c16ex13.

## Exercise 14

1. Open para03.

2. Save the document with Save As and name it c16ex14.

3. Select the entire document, then change the font to 12-point Times New Roman.

4. Create a drop cap for the first word of the first paragraph and change the font of the word by completing the following steps:

    a. Change to the Page Layout viewing mode.

    b. Select the first word (*You*) of the first paragraph.

    c. Choose Format, Drop Cap.

    d. At the Drop Cap dialog box, choose Dropped in the Position section.

    e. Choose Font, then select *Desdemona* from the drop-down menu.

  f. Choose OK or press Enter.
5. Save the document again with the same name (c16ex14).
6. Print c16ex14.
7. Close c16ex14.

## Exercise 15

1. Open c16ex13.
2. Save the document with Save As and name it c16ex15.
3. Remove the drop cap from the second paragraph by completing the following steps:
  a. Position the insertion point anywhere in the second paragraph.
  b. Choose Format, Drop Cap.
  c. At the Drop Cap dialog box, choose None in the Position section of the dialog box.
  d. Choose OK or press Enter.
4. Complete steps similar to those in 3a through 3d to remove the dropped cap from the third paragraph.
5. Save the document again with the same name (c16ex15).
6. Print c16ex15.
7. Close c16ex15.

## Exercise 16

1. Open report02.
2. Save the document with Save As and name it c16ex16.
3. Turn on the display of annotation marks by completing the following steps:
  a. Choose Tools, Options.
  b. At the Options dialog box, click on the View tab.
  c. At the Options dialog box with the View tab selected, choose Hidden text in the Nonprinting Characters section.
  d. Choose OK or press Enter.
4. Create an annotation at the end of the first paragraph in the report by completing the following steps:
  a. Position the insertion point at the end of the first paragraph in the report.
  b. Choose Insert, Annotation; or press Alt + Ctrl + A.
  c. At the Annotation pane, key **Add the source.**
  d. Choose Close.
5. Create an annotation at the end of the second paragraph in the report that contains the text *Include more information on copyfitting.* by completing steps similar to those in 4a through 4d.
6. Create an annotation at the end of the first paragraph below *Column Grid* that contains the text *Add an illustration of a grid.* by completing steps similar to those in 4a through 4d.
7. Create an annotation at the end of the first paragraph below *SERIAL ELEMENTS* that contains the text *Add an illustration of a banner.* by completing steps similar to those in 4a through 4d.
8. Save the document again with the same name (c16ex16).
9. Print the document and the annotations by completing the following steps:
  a. Choose File, Print; or press Ctrl + P.
  b. At the Print dialog box, choose Options.
  c. At the Options dialog box, choose Annotations. (This inserts an X in the Annotation text box and the Hidden Text box.)
  d. Choose OK or press Enter.
  e. At the Print dialog box, choose OK or press Enter.
10. Turn off the display of annotation marks by completing steps similar to those in 3a through 3d.
11. Turn off the printing of annotations by completing the following steps:

    a. Choose File, Print; or press Ctrl + P.

    b. At the Print dialog box, choose Options.

    c. At the Options dialog box, choose Annotations. (This removes the X.)

    d. Choose Hidden Text. (This removes the X.)

    e. Choose OK or press Enter.

    f. Choose Close to close the Print dialog box.

12. Close c16ex16.

## SKILL ASSESSMENTS

### Assessment 1

1. Open para04.
2. Save the document with Save As and name it c16sa01.
3. Make the following changes to the document:
   a. Select the entire document, then change the font to 12-point Arial.
   b. Change the left and right margins for the document to 2 inches.
   c. Change the hyphenation zone to 0.5 inches, then hyphenate the text in the document automatically.
4. Save the document again with the same name (c16sa01).
5. Print c16sa01.
6. Close c16sa01.

### Assessment 2

1. Open report01.
2. Save the document with Save As and name it c16sa02.
3. Make the following changes to the report:
   a. Select the entire document, then change the font to 12-point Times New Roman.
   b. Set the title and the headings in 14-point Times New Roman Bold.
   c. Select the text in the body of the report (everything except the title), then make the following changes:
      (1) Change the line spacing to single.
      (2) Change the spacing before and after paragraphs to 6 points.
      (3) Change the paragraph alignment to justified.
   d. Select the last four paragraphs (lines) of text in the report, then insert bullets.
   e. Hyphenate the document manually.
   f. Create an annotation at the end of the second paragraph in the *Type Measurement* section of the report that contains the text *Include more information on type specification.*
   g. Create an annotation at the end of the third paragraph in the *Type Style* section of the report that contains the text *Add an illustration of the three type styles.*
4. Save the document again with the same name (c16sa02).
5. Print the document and the annotations. (After printing the document and the annotations, be sure to remove the X's in the Annotation and Hidden Text check boxes at the Options dialog box.)
6. Close c16sa02.

### Assessment 3

1. Open legal02.
2. Save the document with Save As and name it c16sa03.
3. Make the following changes to the document:
   a. Select the entire document, then change the font to 12-point Arial.
   b. Complete the following instances of find and replace:

      (1)  Find NAME1 and replace with JOYCE CHAN.

      (2)  Find NUMBER and replace with C-9903.

  c.  Adjust the right parentheses in the heading.

  d.  Automatically hyphenate the text in the document.

  e.  Begin line numbering with 1.

4.  Save the document again with the same name (c16sa03).

5.  Print c16sa03.

6.  Close c16sa03.

## Assessment 4

1.  At a clear document screen, create the memorandum shown in figure 16.14. Insert the current date with the Date and Time dialog box or with a shortcut command. Insert nonbreaking spaces between the shortcut commands.

2.  After keying the memorandum, change the left and right margins to 1.5 inches.

3.  Save the document and name it c16sa04.

4.  Print c16sa04.

5.  Close c16sa04.

**Figure 16.14**

```
DATE:      (current date)

TO:        Medical Transcribers

FROM:      Monica Nevins

SUBJECT: SHORTCUT COMMANDS


Shortcut commands can be used to format text, display dialog boxes,
and insert special characters.  For example, you can insert a
nonbreaking space with Ctrl + Shift + space bar.  You can press
Ctrl + Shift + - to insert a nonbreaking hyphen in a document.
Other shortcut commands include Alt + Ctrl + C which inserts a
copyright symbol and Alt + Ctrl + R which inserts a registered
trademark symbol.

A Word for Windows training session has been scheduled for next
month.  At this training, additional shortcut commands will be
introduced.

xx:c16sa04
```

# Formatting with Templates & Macros 17

Upon successful completion of chapter 17, you will be able to create business documents such as letters, memoranda, and calendars using templates and Wizards. You will also be able to record keystrokes for commands, then play those keystrokes in many different business documents.

In this chapter, you will learn about two time-saving features—templates and macros. Word has included a number of *template* documents containing formatting for producing a variety of documents such as memos, letters, reports, invoices, and resumes. Word also includes Wizards that guide you through the creation of documents.

In chapter 16, you learned about the AutoText feature that simplifies inserting commonly used words, names, or phrases in a document. Word includes another time-saving feature called *macros*. With macros, you can automate the formatting of a document. The word *macro* was coined by computer programmers for a collection of commands used to make a large programming job easier and save time. A Word macro is a document containing recorded commands that can accomplish a task automatically and save time.

In Word, creating a macro is referred to as *recording*. As a macro is being recorded, all the keys pressed and the menus and dialog boxes accessed are recorded and become part of the macro. For example, you can record a macro to change the left or right margins or insert page numbering in a document.

In this chapter, you will learn to record and play macros. Word's macro feature can also be used to write macros. For more information on writing macros, refer to the *Microsoft Word Developer's Kit*.

## ■ Using Templates

Word has included a number of *template* documents that are formatted for specific uses. Each Word document is based on a template document with the *Normal* template the default. With Word templates, you can easily create a variety of documents such as letters, memos, and awards, with specialized formatting. Along with templates, Word also includes *Wizards*. Wizards are templates that do most of the work for you.

To display the templates and Wizards provided by Word, display the New dialog box shown in figure 17.1. To do this, choose File, then New.

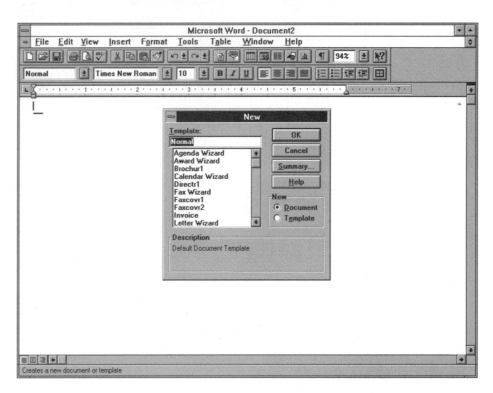

*Figure 17.1*
*New Dialog Box*

At the New dialog box, document templates are displayed in the Template list box. Each template document contains the extension *.dot* but this extension does not display in the list box. To create a document based on a different template, select the desired template in the Template list box, then choose OK or press Enter.

As an example of how to use templates, you would complete the following steps to use the *Memo1* template to create a memo:

1. Choose File, New.
2. At the New dialog box, select the *Memo1* template in the Template list box. To do this with the mouse, click on the down-pointing arrow to the right of the list box until *Memo1* is visible, then click on *Memo1*. If you are using the keyboard, press the up arrow key until *Memo1* is selected.
3. Choose OK or press Enter.
4. Word inserts the memo as shown in figure 17.2. At this screen, complete the following steps:
   a. Select *[Names]* after *TO:*.
   b. Press the Delete key.
   c. Key the name (or names) of the person to receive the memo.
   d. Select *[Names]* after *FROM:*.
   e. Press the Delete key.
   f. Key the name (or names) of the person sending the memo.
   g. Continue selecting the text in brackets, deleting it, then keying the information for the memo.
5. When the memo is completed, save it in the normal manner.

Use the other template documents in a similar manner. The formatting and text will vary for each template document. Figure 17.3 shows the template documents available in Word and what the template will create.

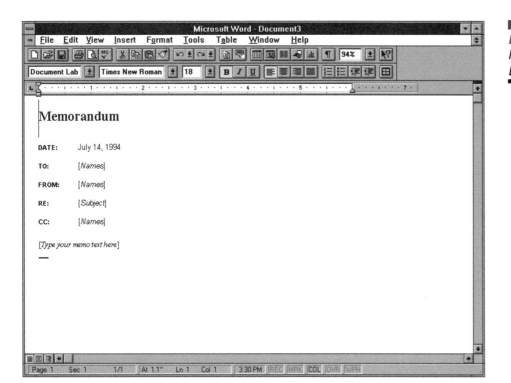

Figure 17.2
Memo Template
Document

Figure 17.3
Template
Documents

| Use this Template | to create a |
|---|---|
| Brochur1 | classic brochure |
| Dirctr1 | classic directory |
| Faxcovr1 | classic FAX cover sheet |
| Faxcovr2 | contemporary FAX cover sheet |
| Invoice | standard invoice |
| Letter1 | classic letter |
| Letter2 | contemporary letter |
| Letter3 | typewriter letter |
| Manual1 | classic manual |
| Manuscr1 | classic manuscript |
| Manuscr3 | typewriter manuscript |
| Memo1 | classic memo |
| Memo2 | contemporary memo |
| Memo3 | typewriter memo |
| Present1 | classic presentation |
| Presrel1 | classic press release |
| Presrel2 | contemporary press release |
| Presrel3 | typewriter press release |
| Purchord | standard purchase order |
| Report1 | classic report |
| Report2 | contemporary report |
| Report3 | typewriter report |
| Resume1 | classic resume |
| Resume2 | contemporary resume |
| Resume4 | elegant resume |
| Thesis1 | classic thesis |
| Weektime | weekly time sheets |

## Using Wizards

Wizards are template documents that do most of the work for you. When you select a Wizard template document, Word asks you questions and gives you choices about what type of document you want to create. Follow the steps provided by the Wizard to complete the document. For example, to create a calendar for January through December in the year 1996, you would complete the following steps:

1. Choose File, New.
2. At the New dialog box, select *Calendar Wizard* in the Template list box.
3. Choose OK or press Enter.
4. When Word asks if you want to print the calendar in landscape or portrait, choose Portrait, then Next.
5. When Word asks what kind of calendar you want to create, choose Jazzy, then Next.
6. When Word asks if you want to leave room for a picture, choose Next.
7. At the next screen, make sure the starting month is January and the ending month is December. Choose Year, then key **1996**. Choose Year, then key **1996**. Choose Next.
8. When Word asks if you want to display Help after the calendar is created, choose No, then choose Finish.
9. Word generates each month of the year (a generating message displays at the left side of the Status bar). When all months have been generated, a portion of the first page of the calendar is displayed in the document screen. Save the calendar document in the normal manner.

When the calendar document is created, each month appears on a different page. This makes the document twelve pages long. Since this document is heavily formatted, it takes some time to generate and print.

Use the other Wizard template documents in a similar manner. The questions, formatting, and text will vary for each Wizard. Figure 17.4 shows the Wizard template documents available in Word and what the Wizard will create.

*Figure 17.4*
*Wizard Template*
*Documents*

| Use this Wizard | to create a |
|---|---|
| Agenda Wizard | meeting agenda |
| Award Wizard | customized award certificate |
| Calendar Wizard | a calendar for week, month, or year |
| Fax Wizard | customized FAX cover sheet |
| Letter Wizard | prewritten or customized letter |
| Memo Wizard | customized memo |
| Newsltr Wizard | newsletter |
| Pleading Wizard | legal pleading paper |
| Resume Wizard | customized resume |
| Table Wizard | table |

## Creating a Document Template

Word provides a large number of document templates for specialized needs. If, however, none of the predesigned templates contain the desired formatting, you can create your own document template. One of the easiest ways to create a new document template is to base it on an existing template. (If you are using a network system, you will need to check with your instructor to determine the location of the *template* subdirectory.) For example, to create a template named *report.dot* that contains a top margin of 1.5 inches and double spacing and is based on the *normal.dot* template, you would complete the following steps:

1. Choose <u>F</u>ile, <u>O</u>pen; or click on the Open button on the Standard toolbar.
2. At the Open dialog box, key **c:\winword\template\\*.dot** in the File <u>N</u>ame text box. (This tells Word to display all documents in the *template* subdirectory from the *winword* directory, that contain the extension *.dot*.)
3. Select the *normal.dot* document in the File <u>N</u>ame list box, then choose OK or press Enter. (If you are using the mouse, you can double-click on *normal.dot*.)
4. At the document screen, save the document with Save As and name it *c:\winword\template\report.dot*.
5. Close the document.
6. Open *c:\winword\template\report.dot* following the same basic steps as those in steps 1 through 3.
7. At the document screen, change the top margin to 1.5 inches and line spacing to double.
8. Save the document again with the same name (*c:\winword\template\report.dot*).
9. Close the document.

To create a document based on the new template document, *report.dot,* rather than the default of *normal.dot*, select the *report.dot* template (displays as *Report*) at the New dialog box, then create a document in the normal manner.

# Creating Macros

Word's Macro feature is similar to the AutoText feature. The difference is that AutoText is primarily used for text while macros are primarily used for executing certain commands. For example, you can create a macro that changes the left and right margins in a document or a macro that selects then applies character formatting to the selected text.

When macros are created, they are stored in the document template. By default, this is the *normal.dot* template. Macros that are stored in the *normal.dot* template are available for use in any document. Macros stored in a different document template are available for use only in documents that are based on that template.

There are two steps involved in working with macros: recording a macro and running a macro.

## Recording a Macro

Recording a macro involves turning on the macro recorder, performing the steps to be recorded, then turning off the recorder. To create a macro, you would complete the following steps:

1. To begin recording the macro, complete one of the following steps:
   - Double-click on the *REC* mode button on the Status bar.
   - Choose <u>T</u>ools, <u>M</u>acro, then Rec<u>o</u>rd.
2. At the Record Macro dialog box shown in figure 17.5, key a name for the macro or use the name proposed by Word. (A macro name can contain a maximum of 80 characters and may not contain spaces, commas, or periods.)
3. Choose <u>D</u>escription, then key a description for the macro. (A macro description can contain a maximum of 255 characters and may include spaces.)
4. Choose OK or press Enter.
5. At the document screen with the Macro Record toolbar displayed as shown in figure 17.6, perform the actions to be recorded.
6. To stop the recording of the macro, complete one of the following steps:
   - Click on the Stop button (first button) on the Macro Record toolbar.
   - Double-click on the *REC* mode button on the Status bar.
   - Choose <u>T</u>ools, <u>M</u>acro, then Stop Rec<u>o</u>rding.

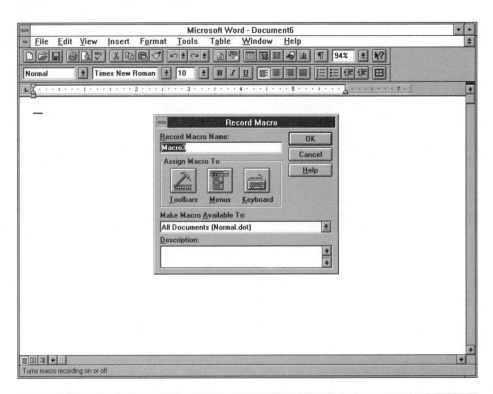

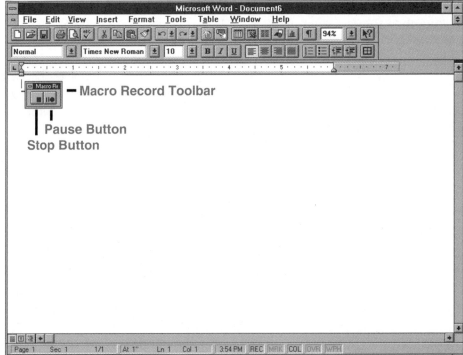

*Figure 17.5*
*Record Macro*
*Dialog Box*

*Figure 17.6*
*Macro Record*
*Toolbar*

## Copying Macros to a Different Template

When a macro is recorded, it is stored in the *normal.dot* template document by default. This makes the macro available for all documents based on the *normal.dot* template document. In a school setting, you may want to store macros you create in your own template. In this manner, you can use your own macros for formatting documents.

Copy macros from the *normal.dot* document template to another document template at the Organizer dialog box shown in figure 17.7. The Organizer dialog box displays macros that have been recorded in the In NORMAL.DOT list box. To copy these macros to another template, choose the desired template document, then use the Copy button to copy the macros.

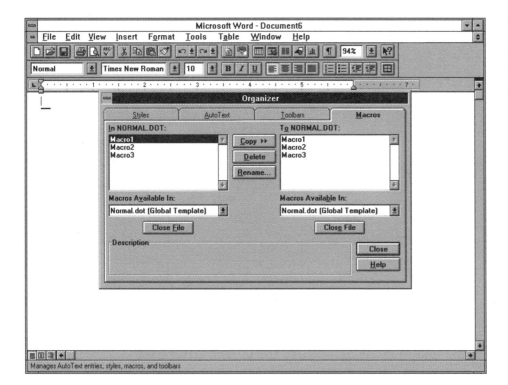

*Figure 17.7*
*Organizer Dialog*
*Box with Macros*
*Tab Selected*

As an example of how to copy macros to a different template document, you would complete the following steps to copy macros to the *report.dot* template document:

1. Record macros as described earlier.
2. At a clear document screen, choose Tools, Macro.
3. At the Macro dialog box, choose Organizer.
4. At the Organizer dialog box with the Macros tab selected as shown in figure 17.7, choose Close File. (This button is located at the right side of the dialog box, toward the bottom. When you choose the Close File button it becomes the Open File button.)
5. Choose Open File.
6. At the Open dialog box, select the *report.dot* template document in the File Name list box.
7. Choose OK or press Enter.
8. At the Organizer dialog box, make sure the first macro to be copied is displayed in the In NORMAL.DOT list box, then choose Copy. (This copies the macro to the To REPORT.DOT list box.)
9. Continue selecting then copying macros to the *report.dot* template.
10. If you do not want the macros to remain in the *normal.dot* template document, select each macro in the In NORMAL.DOT list box, then choose Delete. When Word asks if you want to delete the macro, choose Yes.
11. After macros have been copied (and deleted, if necessary), choose Close.
12. When Word asks if you want to save the changes to REPORT.DOT, choose Yes.

Go To
Exercise
5

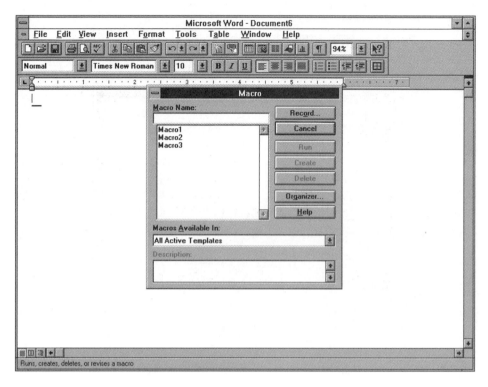

**Figure 17.8**
*Macro Dialog Box*

## Running a Macro

After a macro has been recorded, it can be run in a document. To run a macro, you would complete the following steps:

1. Choose Tools, Macro.
2. At the Macro dialog box shown in figure 17.8, select the macro to be run in the Macro Name list box.
3. Choose Run.

## Pausing then Resuming a Macro

When recording a macro, you can temporarily suspend the recording, perform actions that are not recorded, then resume recording the macro. To pause the recording of a macro, click on the Pause button on the Macro Record toolbar. To resume recording the macro, click on the Pause button again.

## Deleting a Macro

If you no longer need a macro that has been recorded, it can be deleted. To delete a macro, you would complete the following steps:

1. Choose Tools, Macro.
2. At the Macro dialog box, select the macro in the Macro Name list box that is to be deleted.
3. Choose Delete.
4. At the message asking if you want to delete the macro, choose Yes.
5. Choose Close to close the Macro dialog box.

Macros can also be deleted at the Organizer dialog box, as described earlier.

## Renaming Macros

Macros can be renamed at the Organizer dialog box. This might be useful in a situation where you want to rename macros to follow a particular system or pattern. To rename a macro, you would complete the following steps:

1. Choose Tools, Macro.
2. At the Macro dialog box, choose Organizer.
3. At the Organizer dialog box, select the macro to be renamed in the In NORMAL.DOT list box, then choose Rename.
4. At the Rename dialog box, key the new name for the macro.
5. Choose OK or press Enter.
6. Choose Close to close the Organizer dialog box.

## Assigning a Macro a Shortcut Command

If you use a macro on a regular basis, you may want to assign it a shortcut command. To run a macro that has been assigned a shortcut command, all you do is press the keys assigned to the macro. A macro can be assigned a shortcut command with a letter plus Alt + Ctrl, Ctrl + Shift, or Alt + Shift. Word has already used many combinations for Word functions. For example, pressing Ctrl + Shift + M decreases the paragraph indent.

With the Alt + Ctrl combination, the following letters are available for assigning to a macro: B, D, G, H, J, K, L, M, Q, W, and X. With the Ctrl + Shift combination, the following letters are available for assigning to a macro: E, G, J, O, R, X, and Y. The following letters are available with the Alt + Shift combination: B, G, H, J, Q, S, V, W, Y, and Z. (This may vary depending on the configuration of your computer system.)

Assign a shortcut command to a macro at the Record Macro dialog box. For example, to create a macro named *formpara* that increases the spacing before and after a paragraph to 6 points, and is assigned the shortcut command, Alt + Shift + S, you would complete the following steps:

1. Double-click on the *REC* mode button on the Status bar.
2. At the Record Macro dialog box, key **formpara**.
3. Choose Description, then key **Add spacing before and after paragraphs**.
4. Choose Keyboard.
5. At the Customize dialog box, with the insertion point positioned in the Press New Shortcut Keys text box, press Alt + Shift + S.
6. Choose Assign.
7. Choose Close.
8. At the document screen with the Macro Record toolbar displayed, complete the necessary steps to increase spacing before and after paragraphs to 6 points.
9. Click on the Stop button (first button) on the Macro Record toolbar.
10. Close the document without saving changes.

After assigning a shortcut key to a macro, it can be copied to a different template document if necessary. To do this, you would follow the steps listed earlier in the "Copying Macros to a Different Template" section of the chapter.

If you delete the macro, the shortcut command is also deleted. This allows you to use the shortcut key combination again.

## Assigning a Macro to a Menu

A macro that you use on a frequent basis can be assigned to a menu. If a macro is assigned to a menu, it appears when the drop-down menu is displayed. By default, Word assigns a macro to the

Tools drop-down menu at the bottom of the menu. For example to create a macro named *Formtabs* that sets left tabs at the 2-inch mark and the 4-inch mark and is assigned to the Tools menu, you would complete the following steps:

1. Choose Tools, Macro, then Record.
2. At the Record Macro dialog box, key **Formtabs**.
3. Choose Description, then key **Set left tabs at 2 and 4.**
4. Choose Menus.
5. At the Customize dialog box, make sure the *Formtabs* macro is selected in the Commands list box, then choose Add.
6. Choose Close to close the Customize dialog box.
7. At the document screen with the Macro Record toolbar displayed, complete the necessary steps to set left tabs at the 2-inch and the 4-inch mark. (Use the Tabs dialog box.)
8. Double-click on the *REC* mode button on the Status bar to stop the recording of the macro.

At the Customize dialog box, the Change What Menu option has a default setting of *&Tools*. (This may vary depending on your system setup.) At this setting, the macro is added to the Tools drop-down menu. If you want to add a macro to a different drop-down menu, choose Change What Menu then select the desired menu from the drop-down list.

The Position on Menu option at the Customize dialog box has a default setting of *(Auto)*. At this setting, the macro is automatically added to the end of the menu. To add the macro to a different location on the menu, choose Position on Menu, then select the desired location.

Word will add the macro on the menu with the name you gave the macro. This name is displayed in the Name on Menu text box. If you want the macro to display on the menu with a different name, choose Name on Menu, then key the desired name.

If, after adding a macro to a menu, you want to remove it, delete the macro at the Macro dialog box. When the macro is deleted from the dialog box, it is also removed from the menu.

## Assigning a Macro to the Toolbar

A macro that you use on a very regular basis can be added to a toolbar. To run a macro from a toolbar, just click on the button. As an example of how to add a macro to a toolbar, you would complete the following steps to record a macro named *Tab* that sets a left tab at the 0.5-inch mark and a right tab at the 5.5-inch mark, is assigned to the Standard toolbar, and displays with the word *Tab* on the button:

1. Double-click on the *REC* mode button on the Status bar.
2. At the Record Macro dialog box, key **Tab**.
3. Choose Description, then key **Set left tab at 0.5 and right at 5.5.**
4. Choose Toolbars.
5. At the Customize dialog box, position the arrow pointer on the *Tab* macro name in the second list box, hold down the left mouse button, drag the outline of the button to the location on the Standard toolbar where you want the button to appear, then release the mouse button. (This inserts the button on the Standard toolbar with no text or image and also inserts the Custom Button dialog box.)
6. At the Custom Button dialog box, choose Assign. (This assigns the name of the macro inside the button on the toolbar. If you want to assign an icon, click on the desired icon, then choose Assign.)
7. Choose Close to close the Customize dialog box.
8. At the document screen with the Macro Record toolbar displayed, complete the necessary steps to set a left tab at the 0.5-inch mark and a right tab at the 5.5-inch mark. (Use the Tabs dialog box.)
9. Double-click on the *REC* mode button on the Status bar.

A macro can be assigned to any toolbar that is displayed. For example, a macro can be assigned to the Formatting toolbar if that toolbar is displayed in the document screen.

An existing macro can also be assigned to a toolbar. To assign an existing macro to the Standard toolbar, you would complete the following steps:

1.  At a clear document screen, choose <u>T</u>ools, <u>C</u>ustomize.
2.  At the Customize dialog box, choose *Macros* in the <u>C</u>ategories list box. To do this with the mouse, click on the down-pointing arrow in the <u>C</u>ategories list box until *Macros* is visible, then click on *Macros*. If you are using the keyboard, press the down arrow key until *Macros* is selected.
3.  Position the arrow pointer on the desired macro in the Macr<u>o</u>s list box, hold down the left mouse button, drag the outline of the button to the desired location on the Standard toolbar, then release the mouse button.
4.  At the Custom button dialog box, choose <u>A</u>ssign.
5.  Choose Close to close the Customize dialog box.

A macro button can be removed from a toolbar at the Customize dialog box. For example, to remove the *Tab* button from the Standard toolbar, you would complete the following steps:

1.  Choose <u>T</u>ools, <u>C</u>ustomize.
2.  At the Customize dialog box, select the <u>T</u>oolbars tab.
3.  Position the arrow pointer on the *Tab* button on the Standard toolbar, hold down the left mouse button, drag the outline of the button off the toolbar, then release the mouse button.
4.  Choose Close to close the Customize dialog box.

When a macro button is removed from a toolbar, the macro is not deleted. Delete the macro at the Macro dialog box.

## CHAPTER SUMMARY

- With Word templates, you can easily create a variety of documents, such as letters, memos, and awards, with specialized formatting.
- Wizards are templates that do most of the work for you.
- To see the templates and Wizards provided by Word, display the New dialog box. You can also create your own document template.
- Word's Macro feature is primarily used for executing certain commands.
- Recording a macro involves turning on the macro recorder, performing the steps to be recorded, then turning off the recorder.
- By default, macros are stored in the *normal.dot* template and so are available for all documents and for everyone using that computer. To copy macros from the *normal.dot* template to your own template, display the Organizer dialog box.
- You can temporarily suspend the recording of a macro by clicking on the Pause button on the Macro Record toolbar.
- Run, delete, or rename a macro from the Macro dialog box.
- Assign a shortcut command to a macro at the Record Macro dialog box.
- A macro that you use on a frequent basis can be assigned to a menu and will appear when the drop-down menu is displayed. A macro that you use quite often can be added to a toolbar.

|  | **Mouse** | **Keyboard** |
|---|---|---|
| New dialog box | File, New | File, New |
| Macro dialog box | Tools, Macro | Tools, Macro |
| Record Macro dialog box | Double-click on the *REC* mode button on the Status bar; or choose Tools, Macro, then Record | Tools, Macro, Record |
| Organizer dialog box | Tools, Macro, Organizer | Tools, Macro, Organizer |

## CHECK YOUR UNDERSTANDING

**True/False:** Circle the letter T if the statement is true; circle the letter F if the statement is false.

**T  F**  1. The variety of templates provided by Word includes invoices and resumes.

**T  F**  2. At the Open dialog box, document templates are displayed in the Template list box.

**T  F**  3. One of the easiest ways to create your own document template is to base it on an existing template.

**T  F**  4. A macro document can contain letters, words, or commands.

**T  F**  5. A macro name can contain a maximum of 10 characters.

**T  F**  6. When a macro is recorded, it is stored in the *general.dot* template document by default.

**T  F**  7. Once you begin recording a macro, you cannot pause before you are finished.

**T  F**  8. A macro can be assigned a shortcut command such as the Alt key + a letter of the alphabet.

**T  F**  9. A macro can be assigned to a drop-down menu at the Customize dialog box.

**T  F**  10. When assigning a macro to a toolbar, you must be sure you will use it often because it cannot be deleted.

**List the steps needed to record a macro that changes the font to 18-point Arial Bold. Name the macro Font18.**

_____

_____

_____

_____

**List the steps needed to run the Font18 macro recorded above.**

_____

_____

_____

_____

## Exercise 1

1. Use the Faxcovr1 template to create a fax cover sheet by completing the following steps:
   a. Choose File, New.
   b. At the New dialog box, select the *Faxcovr1* template in the Template list box. To do this with the mouse, click on the down-pointing arrow to the right of the list box until *Faxcovr1* is visible, then click on *Faxcovr1*. If you are using the keyboard, press the up arrow key until *Faxcovr1* is selected.
   c. Choose OK or press Enter.
   d. At the fax cover document, turn on the display of nonprinting characters, then complete the following steps to insert *St. Francis Medical Center* where *[Company Name]* displays:
      (1) Select *[Company Name]* at the top of the document. (Do not select the paragraph mark after *[Company Name]*.)
      (2) Press the Delete key.
      (3) Key **St. Francis Medical Center**.
   e. Follow steps similar to those in 1d(1) through 1d(3) to select the text in brackets, delete it, then key the information as shown below each bracketed item:

   *[Street Address]*
   **300 Blue Ridge Boulevard**
   *[City, State/Province Zip/Postal Code]*
   **Kansas City, MO 63009**
   *[Names]* (after *TO:*)
   **Jerry Rhodes**
   *[Company Name]* (after *TO:*)
   **RD Pharmaceuticals**
   *[Their phone number]*
   **(816) 555-9055**
   *[Their fax number]*
   **(816) 555-3448**
   *[Names]* (after *FROM:*)
   **Melissa Aurand**
   *[Company Name]* (after *FROM:*)
   **St. Francis Medical Center**
   *[Your phone number]*
   **(816) 555-2145**
   *[Your fax number]*
   **(816) 555-2300**
   *[Subject]*
   **Rush Order**
   *[Names]* (after *CC:*)
   **Peter Hagan, Director**
   *[Type number of pages here]*
   **2**
   *[Type your message here]*
   **The purchase order form is attached. Please send these supplies by overnight carrier.**

2. After keying all the text, save the document and name it c17ex01.
3. Turn off the display of nonprinting characters.
4. Print c17ex01.
5. Close c17ex01.

## Exercise 2

1. Use the Award Wizard to create an award by completing the following steps:
   a. Choose File, New.
   b. At the New dialog box, double-click on *Award Wizard* in the Template list box.
   c. When Word asks what kind of award you want to create, choose Jazzy, then Next.
   d. At the next screen, choose Portrait, then Next.
   e. At the next screen, choose *Type the name of the person who will receive award*, then key **Lisa Murray**.
   f. Choose *Type the title of the award*, then key **Distinguished Employee Award**.
   g. Choose Next.
   h. At the next screen, choose *Type the name of the people who will sign the award*, key **Allison St. Germaine**, then choose Next.
   i. At the next screen, choose Next. (There are no presenters' names.)
   j. At the next screen, choose *Type the date for the award*, then key **Wednesday, June 5, 1996**.
   k. Choose *Type any additional text that you want on the award*, key **QUALITY PATIENT CARE**, then choose Next.
   l. At the next screen, make sure *No just display the award* is selected, then choose Finish.
2. Save the award and name it c17ex02.
3. Print c17ex02.
4. Close c17ex02.

## Exercise 3

*Note: Before completing this assignment, check with your instructor to determine if you can complete the exercises as written or if customized instructions are needed.*

1. Create a document template named *xxxtemp.dot* (where *xxx* are your initials; if you do not have a middle initial, use *x*) that contains left and right margins of 1 inch and is based on the *normal.dot* template, by completing the following steps:
   a. Choose File, Open; or click on the Open button on the Standard toolbar.
   b. At the Open dialog box, key **c:\winword\template\*.dot** in the File Name text box. (This tells Word to display all documents in the *template* subdirectory from the *winword* directory that contain the extension *.dot*.)
   c. Choose OK or press Enter.
   d. Select the *normal.dot* document in the File Name list box, then choose OK or press Enter. (If you are using the mouse, you can double-click on *normal.dot*.)
   e. At the document screen, save the document with Save As and name it *c:\winword\template\xxxtemp.dot* (where your initials are inserted instead of the *xxx*).
   f. Close the document.
   g. Open *c:\winword\template\xxxtemp.dot* following the same basic steps as those in steps 1a through 1c.
   h. At the document screen, change the left and right margins to 1 inch.
   i. Save the document again with the same name (*c:\winword\template\xxxtemp.dot*).
   j. Close the document.
2. Open a clear document screen based on the *xxxtemp.dot* by completing the following steps:
   a. Choose File, New.
   b. At the New dialog box, select *Xxxtemp*, then choose OK or press Enter.
3. At the clear document screen based on the *xxxtemp.dot* document template, insert the document named *report01* by completing the following steps:
   a. Choose Insert, File.
   b. At the File dialog box, key **a:\*.doc** (or **b:\*.doc** depending on where your student data disk is located), then press Enter.
   c. Select *report01.doc* in the File Name list box, then choose OK or press Enter.

4. Save the document and name it c17ex03.
5. Print page 1 of c17ex03.
6. Close c17ex03.

## Exercise 4

1. Create a macro named *Ind01* that indents text in a paragraph 0.5 inches and hang indents second and subsequent lines of the paragraph by completing the following steps:
   a. At a clear document screen, double-click on the *REC* mode button on the Status bar.
   b. At the Record Macro dialog box, key **Ind01**.
   c. Choose Description, then key **Indent and hang text in paragraph**.
   d. Choose OK or press Enter.
   e. At the document screen with the Macro Record toolbar displayed, complete the following steps:
      (1) Choose Format, Paragraph.
      (2) Choose Left, then key **0.5**.
      (3) Choose Special, then Hanging.
      (4) Choose OK or press Enter.
   f. Double-click on the REC mode button on the Status bar.
2. Complete steps similar to those in 1a through 1f to create a macro named *Ind02* that indents text in a paragraph 1 inch and hang indents second and subsequent lines of the paragraph.
3. Close the document without saving it.

## Exercise 5

1. Copy the *Ind01* and the *Ind02* macros from the *normal.dot* to the *xxxtemp.dot* document template by completing the following steps:
   a. At a clear document screen, choose Tools, Macro.
   b. At the Macro dialog box, choose Organizer.
   c. At the Organizer dialog box with the Macros tab selected, choose Close File. (This button is located at the right side of the dialog box, toward the bottom. When you choose the Close File button, it becomes the Open File button.)
   d. Choose Open File.
   e. At the Open dialog box, select the *xxxtemp.dot* template document in the File Name list box.
   f. Choose OK or press Enter.
   g. At the Organizer dialog box, make sure *Ind01* is selected in the In NORMAL.DOT list box, then choose Copy. (This copies the macro to the To XXXTEMP.DOT list box.)
   h. Select *Ind02* in the In NORMAL.DOT list box, then choose Copy.
   i. Choose Close. (This button is located at the bottom right side of the dialog box.)
   j. When Word asks if you want to save the changes to XXXTEMP.DOT, choose Yes.
2. Close the document.

## Exercise 6

1. Open a new document based on the *xxxtemp.dot* template document (displays as *Xxxtemp* in the New dialog box).
2. Insert the document named *survey01* into the document screen. (Use the File option from the Insert menu to do this. The document *survey01* is located on your student data disk.)
3. Run the *Ind01* macro for the first numbered paragraph by completing the following steps:
   a. Position the insertion point anywhere in the paragraph that begins with 1.
   b. Choose Tools, Macro.
   c. At the Macro dialog box, choose *Ind01* in the Macro Name list box, then choose Run.
4. Complete steps similar to those in 3a through 3c to run the macro for each of the numbered paragraphs (just the numbered paragraphs, not the lettered paragraphs).
5. Run the *Ind02* macro for the lettered paragraphs (a through d) after the first numbered paragraph by completing the following steps:

a. Select paragraphs a through d below the first numbered paragraph.

b. Choose Tools, Macro.

c. At the Macro dialog box, choose *Ind02* in the Macro Name list box, then choose Run.

6. Complete steps similar to those in 5a through 5c to run the macro for the lettered paragraphs below each of the numbered paragraphs.

7. Check to see if the document fits on one page. If not, change margins or font size so it does.

8. Save the document and name it c17ex06.

9. Print c17ex06.

10. Close c17ex06.

## Exercise 7

1. Click on the New button on the Standard toolbar. (This opens a document based on the *normal.dot* template document.)

2. Delete the *Ind01* and the *Ind02* macros from the *normal.dot* template document by completing the following steps:

   a. Choose Tools, Macro.

   b. At the Macro dialog box, select *Ind01* in the Macro Name list box.

   c. Choose Delete.

   d. At the message asking if you want to delete *Ind01*, choose Yes.

   e. Make sure *Ind02* is selected in the Macro Name list box.

   f. Choose Delete.

   g. At the message asking if you want to delete *Ind02*, choose Yes.

   h. Choose Close to close the Macro dialog box.

3. Close the document.

## Exercise 8

1. Open a new document based on the *xxxtemp.dot* template document (displays as *Xxxtemp* in the New dialog box).

2. Rename the *Ind01* and *Ind02* macros by completing the following steps:

   a. Choose Tools, Macro.

   b. At the Macro dialog box, choose Organizer.

   c. At the Organizer dialog box, select *Ind01* in the In XXXTEMP.DOT list box, then choose Rename.

   d. At the Rename dialog box, key **I01**.

   e. Choose OK or press Enter.

   f. Select *Ind02* in the In XXXTEMP.DOT list box, then choose Rename.

   g. At the Rename dialog box, key **I02**.

   h. Choose OK or press Enter.

   i. Choose Close to close the Organizer dialog box.

   j. When Word asks if you want to save changes to the XXXTEMP.DOT document, choose Yes.

3. Close the document without saving it.

## Exercise 9

1. Create a macro named *ltrhd01* that contains the letterhead text shown in figure 17.9 and assign it the shortcut command, Alt + Ctrl + L by completing the following steps:

   a. At a clear document screen, double-click on the *REC* mode button on the Status bar.

   b. At the Record Macro dialog box, key **ltrhd01**.

   c. Choose Description, then key **St. Francis Letterhead**.

   d. Choose Keyboard.

   e. At the Customize dialog box, with the insertion point positioned in the Press New Shortcut Key text box, press Alt + Ctrl + L.

   f. Choose Assign.

g. Choose Close.

h. At the document screen with the Macro Record toolbar displayed, create the letterhead shown in figure 17.9 by completing the following steps:

(1) Press Ctrl + E.

(2) Key **ST. FRANCIS MEDICAL CENTER**.

(3) Press Enter, then key **300 Blue Ridge Boulevard**.

(4) Press Enter, then key **Kansas City, MO 63009**.

(5) Press Enter, then key **(816) 555-2000**.

(6) Press Enter.

(7) Press Ctrl + L to return the paragraph alignment to left.

(8) Press Enter.

(9) Select the hospital name, address, and telephone number, then change the font to 18-point Colonna MT Bold. (You must use the keyboard to select the text.)

(10) Deselect the text.

i. Click on the Stop button on the Macro Record toolbar.

j. Close the document without saving changes.

2. At a clear document screen, copy the *ltrhd01* macro to the *xxxtemp.dot* template document, then delete the *ltrhd01* macro from the *normal.dot* template document. (*Hint: Exercise 5 contains steps for copying macros from one template document to another.*)

3. Close the document.

4. Change the default directory to the drive where your student data disk is located. (When you changed to the XXXTEMP.DOT template document at the Organizer dialog box, this changed the default drive.)

5. Open a new document based on the *xxxtemp.dot* template document (displays as *Xxxtemp* in the New dialog box).

6. With the insertion point positioned at the beginning of the document, run the *ltrhd01* macro by pressing Alt + Ctrl + L.

7. With the insertion point a double space below the letterhead, key the letter shown in figure 17.10. After keying the letter, run the *l01* macro for the numbered paragraphs and the *l02* macro for the lettered paragraphs.

8. Save the letter and name it c17ex09.

9. Print c17ex09.

10. Close c17ex09.

**Figure 17.9**

ST. FRANCIS MEDICAL CENTER

300 Blue Ridge Boulevard

Kansas City, MO 63009

(816) 555-2000

Figure 17.10

May 14, 1996


Mr. Victor Durham
Good Samaritan Hospital
1201 James Street
St. Louis, MO 62033

Dear Victor:

Congratulations on obtaining eight new nursing positions at your
hospital. The attached registered nurse job description is
generic. Depending on the specialty, additional responsibilities
are added such as:

1. Uses the nursing process to prescribe, coordinate, and delegate
patient care from admission through discharge.
a. Analyzes the patient's condition and reports changes to the
appropriate health care provider.
b. Observes patient for signs and symptoms; collects data on
patient; reports and documents results.
2. Teaches patient, family, staff, and students.
a. Assumes responsibility for patient and family teaching and
discharge planning.
b. Participates in orientation of new staff and/or acts as
preceptor.

I am interested in hearing about your recruitment plan. Additional
medical personnel will be hired in the fall at St. Francis so I
need to begin formulating a recruitment plan.

Sincerely,


Mariah Jackson

xx:c17ex09

Attachment

## Exercise 10

1. At a clear document screen (based on the *normal.dot* template document), create a macro named *Tab01* that sets left tabs at the 0.5-inch mark and the 1-inch mark and a right tab with preceding period leaders at the 5.5-inch mark and is assigned to the <u>T</u>ools menu by completing the following steps:

   a. Choose <u>T</u>ools, <u>M</u>acro, then Rec<u>o</u>rd.

b. At the Record Macro dialog box, key **Tab01**.

c. Choose <u>D</u>escription, then key **Set left tabs at 0.5 and 1 and right tab with leaders at 5.5.**

d. Choose <u>M</u>enus.

e. At the Customize dialog box, make sure the *Tab01* macro is selected in the C<u>o</u>mmands list box, then choose <u>A</u>dd.

f. Choose Close to close the Customize dialog box.

g. At the document screen with the Macro Record toolbar displayed, complete the necessary steps to set left tabs at the 0.5-inch mark and the 1-inch mark and a right tab with preceding leaders at the 5.5-inch mark. (You must display the Tabs dialog box to do this.)

h. After setting tabs, double-click on the *REC* mode button on the Status bar.

2. Close the document without saving it.

3. At a clear document screen (based on the *normal.dot* template document), create the table of contents shown in figure 17.11 by completing the following steps:

a. Run the *Tab01* macro by clicking on <u>T</u>ools on the Menu bar, then clicking on <u>T</u>ab01 in the drop-down menu.

b. Key the table of contents as shown in figure 17.11.

4. Save the document and name it c17ex10.

5. Print c17ex10.

6. Close c17ex10.

**Figure 17.11**

**TABLE OF CONTENTS**

Traditional Desktop Publishing . . . . . . . . . . . . . 2

    Traditional Process . . . . . . . . . . . . . . . . 3

    Computerized Process . . . . . . . . . . . . . . . 5

Design and Gestalt . . . . . . . . . . . . . . . . . . 7

    Figure and Ground . . . . . . . . . . . . . . . . . 9

    Special Graphics Effects . . . . . . . . . . . . . 12

Basic Principles of Design . . . . . . . . . . . . . . 14

    Focus . . . . . . . . . . . . . . . . . . . . . . . 15

    Balance . . . . . . . . . . . . . . . . . . . . . . 17

    Visual Weight . . . . . . . . . . . . . . . . . . . 20

    Directional Flow . . . . . . . . . . . . . . . . . 23

    Unity . . . . . . . . . . . . . . . . . . . . . . . 25

    Visual Identity . . . . . . . . . . . . . . . . . . 28

## Exercise 11

1. At a clear document screen (based on the *normal.dot* document template), assign the *Tab01* macro to the Standard toolbar by completing the following steps:
   a. Choose Tools, Customize.
   b. At the Customize dialog box, choose *Macros* in the Categories list box. To do this with the mouse, click on the down-pointing arrow in the Categories list box until *Macros* is visible, then click on *Macros*. If you are using the keyboard, press the down arrow key until *Macros* is selected.
   c. Position the arrow pointer on *Tab01* in the Macros list box, hold down the left mouse button, drag the outline of the button between the Print Preview button and the Spelling button on the Standard toolbar, then release the mouse button.
   d. At the Custom button dialog box, choose Assign.
   e. Choose Close to close the Customize dialog box.
2. Create the document shown in figure 17.12 by completing the following steps:
   a. Click on the *Tab01* button on the Standard toolbar.
   b. Key the directory listing as shown in figure 17.12.
3. Save the document and name it c17ex11.
4. Print c17ex11.
5. Close c17ex11.
6. Remove the *Tab01* button from the Standard toolbar by completing the following steps:
   a. At a clear document screen, choose Tools, Customize.
   b. At the Customize dialog box, select the Toolbars tab.
   c. Position the arrow pointer on the *Tab01* button on the Standard toolbar, hold down the left mouse button, drag the outline of the button off the toolbar, then release the mouse button.
   d. Choose Close to close the Customize dialog box.

**Figure 17.12**

```
                    ST. FRANCIS MEDICAL CENTER

                      Medical Unit Directors


        Benjamin Moon  . . . . . . . .      Intensive Care

        Rosemary Stratten  . . . . . . .    Emergency Room

        Rafael Ohala . . . . . . . .    Labor and Delivery

        Lisa Murray  . . . . . . . .    Coronary Care Unit

        Joan Harris-Lee  . . . . . . . . .    Surgical Unit

        Sandra Ellerbe . . . . . . . .    Medical Services

        Alyce Arevalo  . . . . . . . . . .      Pediatrics
```

## Assessment 1

1. Use the Letter2 template document to create a business letter. Select the text in brackets, delete it, then key the information as shown below each bracketed item:

    [COMPANY NAME]
    > **GOOD SAMARITAN HOSPITAL**

    [Street Address]
    > **1201 James Street**

    [City, State/Province Zip/Postal Code]
    > **St. Louis, MO 62033**

    [Recipient Name]
    > **Mariah Jackson**

    [Address]
    > **300 Blue Ridge Boulevard**

    [City, State/Province Zip/Postal Code]
    > **Kansas City, MO 63009**

    [Recipient]
    > **Mariah**

    [Type the body of your letter here]
    > **Thank you for the registered nurse job description. I will be including the additional job requirements listed in your letter.**
    >
    > **A committee spent several months designing a recruitment plan. A copy of that plan is attached. The plan is very thorough and will help us recruit highly qualified nurses.**
    >
    > **I will contact you after the eight registered nursing positions have been filled.**

    [Your name]
    > **Victor Durham**

    [Your position]
    > **Director of Nursing**

    [Typist's initials]
    > (insert your initials)

    [Number]
    > **1**

    [Name]
    > **Carrie Ehnat**

2. After creating the letter, save it and name it c17sa01.
3. Print c17sa01.
4. Close c17sa01.

## Assessment 2

1. Use the Calendar Wizard to create a calendar for the month of March 1996. (At the screen where you are asked for the starting and ending months, key **March** in both text boxes. Make sure *1996* displays in the year text boxes.) You determine the style and orientation for the calendar.
2. Save the calendar document and name it c17sa02.
3. Print c17sa02.
4. Close c17sa02.

## Assessment 3

1. Create a macro named *ltrhd02* that contains the letterhead text shown in figure 17.13 and assign it the shortcut command, Alt + Ctrl + G. (Set the text in 18-point Colonna MT Bold.)
2. Copy the *ltrhd02* macro to the *xxxtemp.dot* template document.
3. Delete the *ltrhd02* macro from the *normal.dot* template document.
4. Change the default directory to the drive where your student data disk is located.
5. Open a new document based on the *xxxtemp.dot* template document.
6. With the insertion point positioned at the beginning of the document, run the *ltrhd02* macro.
7. With the insertion point a double space below the letterhead, key the letter shown in figure 17.14. After keying the letter, run the *l01* macro for the numbered paragraphs and the *l02* macro for the lettered paragraphs.
8. Save the letter and name it c17sa03.
9. Print c17sa03.
10. Close c17sa03.

**Figure 17.13**

GOOD SAMARITAN HOSPITAL

1201 James Street

St. Louis, MO 62033

(816) 555-1201

**Figure 17.14**

May 20, 1996

Ms. Mariah Jackson
St. Francis Medical Center
300 Blue Ridge Boulevard
Kansas City, MO 63009

Dear Mariah:

The registered nurse job description was very timely. I was able
to use the basic outline to create a job description for the
hospital. For one of the positions, the following information was
included:

1. Functions with the awareness of safety needs and implements
appropriate safety measures.
a. Demonstrates adherence to all unit hospital safety standards.
b. Follows established standards in emergency situations.
c. Recognizes, communicates, delegates, and coordinates management
of emergency situations.

2. Demonstrates awareness of legal issues on all aspects of
patient care and unit function and takes action to limit or reduce
risks.
a. Completes unusual occurrence form for all patient incidents.
b. Adheres to organizational standards in the area of patient
confidentiality.

The information was provided by our legal department. Safety and
legal issues are an integral part of medical services.

Very truly yours,


Victor Durham

xx:c17sa03

## Assessment 4

1. At a clear document screen (based on the *normal.dot* template document), run the *Tab01* macro, then create the document shown in figure 17.15.
2. After creating the document, save it and name it c17sa04.
3. Print c17sa04.
4. Close c17sa04.

---

**Figure 17.15**

**ST. FRANCIS MEDICAL CENTER**

**Extension Numbers**

```
Allison St. Germaine . . . . . . . . . . . . . . . . . .    2200

Kenneth Levine . . . . . . . . . . . . . . . . . . .       2230

Mariah Jackson . . . . . . . . . . . . . . . . . . .       2244

Leslie Greerson  . . . . . . . . . . . . . . . . . .       2211

Brenda Hogue . . . . . . . . . . . . . . . . .            2237

Leah Aversen . . . . . . . . . . . . . . . . . . . .       2209
```

---

## Assessment 5

1. Delete all the macros displayed in the Macro dialog box.
2. Delete the *xxxtemp.dot* document by completing the following steps:
   a. Choose File, Open.
   b. At the Open dialog box, choose Find File.
   c. At the Search dialog box, choose File Name, then key **xxxtemp.dot** in the File Name list box. (Be sure to key your initials instead of the *xxx*.)
   d. Choose Location, then key **c:\winword\template**. (Check with your instructor to determine if this is the correct directory and subdirectory.)
   e. Choose OK or press Enter.
   f. At the Find File dialog box, make sure *xxxtemp.dot* displays in the Listed Files list box and it is selected.
   g. Choose Commands, then Delete.
   h. When Word asks if you want to delete the document, choose Yes.
   i. Choose Close to close the Find File dialog box.

# Adding Borders, Frames, & Pictures 18

Upon successful completion of chapter 18, you will be able to enhance the visual appeal of documents by adding borders to paragraphs, framing text and pictures, and customizing frames and pictures.

Word for Windows contains a variety of features you can use to make a document more visually appealing. For example, you can add a border to a paragraph or selected paragraphs in a document. You can also insert a picture in a document and add a frame to text or a picture.

## Adding Borders

Every paragraph you create in Word contains an invisible frame. A border can be added to a paragraph that appears around this frame. A border can be added to specific sides of the paragraph or to all sides. The type of border line and thickness of the line can be customized. In addition, you can add shading and fill to the border.

When a border is added to a paragraph of text, the border expands and contracts as text is inserted or deleted from the paragraph. You can create a border around a single paragraph or a border around selected paragraphs.

### Creating a Border

To create a border, display the Borders toolbar shown in figure 18.1 by clicking on the Borders button (▦) on the Formatting toolbar or by completing the following steps:

1. Choose View, Toolbars.
2. At the Toolbars dialog box, insert an X in the Borders check box in the Toolbars list box.
3. Choose OK or press Enter.

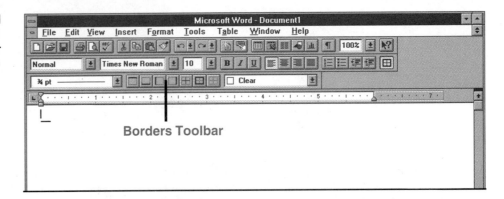

*Figure 18.1*
*Borders Toolbar*

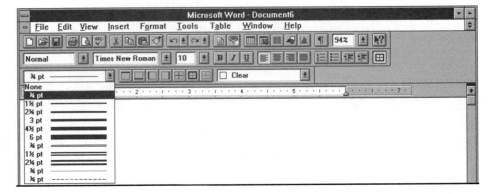

*Figure 18.2*
*Border Line Style*
*Options*

The first option at the left side of the Borders toolbar, the Line Style option, contains a variety of choices for changing the thickness or style of the border. When you click on the down-pointing arrow to the right of the Line Style option, a drop-down menu displays as shown in figure 18.2.

With the options from the Line Style drop-down menu, you can make the border line thicker or choose a double, dotted, or dashed line.

The seven buttons on the Borders toolbar will perform the functions shown in figure 18.3.

*Figure 18.3*
*Borders Toolbar*
*Buttons*

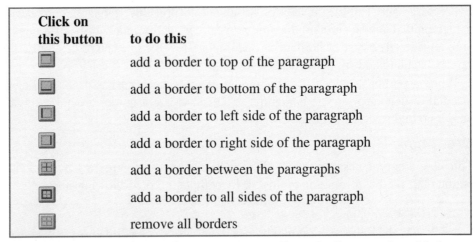

With choices from the Shading option on the Borders toolbar, shading can be added to a paragraph or selected paragraphs. If you click on the down-pointing arrow to the right of the Shading option, a drop-down list displays as shown in figure 18.4.

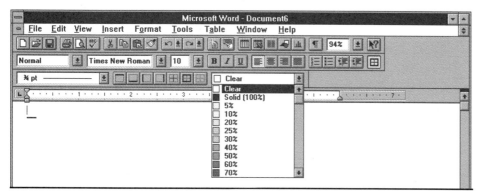

Figure 18.4
Border Shading
Options

Not all the shading options are visible at one time in the Shading drop-down menu. With shading choices, you can specify the amount of shading by percentage or add a pattern shading such as horizontal lines, vertical lines, diagonal lines, trellis lines, or a grid.

As an example of how to add a border, you would complete the following steps to add an outside border to selected paragraphs that is 3 points thick and contains 20% shading:

1. Select the paragraphs you want surrounded by a border.
2. Click on the Borders button on the Formatting toolbar to display the Borders toolbar.
3. Click on the down-pointing arrow to the right of the Line Style option on the Borders toolbar. From the drop-down list that displays, click on *3 pt*.
4. Click on the Outside Border button on the Borders toolbar.
5. Click on the down-pointing arrow to the right of the Shading option. From the drop-down menu that displays, click on *20%*.

If you want to remove a border from a paragraph, position the insertion point anywhere within the paragraph, then click on the No Border button on the Borders toolbar. To remove shading, click on the down-pointing arrow after Shading option, then click on Clear.

Word's border feature can be used to add lines in headers and/or footers. For example, you can add a line below text in a header or add a line above text in a footer. This line acts as a graphic element that adds visual appeal to a document. As an example of how to add a line to a header, you would complete the following steps to add a 3-point line below a header in a document:

1. Open the document in which you want to add a header.
2. Choose View, Header and Footer.
3. At the Header pane, key the header text.
4. Click on the down-pointing arrow to the right of the Line Style option. From the drop-down menu that displays, click on *3 pt*.
5. Click on the Bottom Border button on the Borders toolbar.
6. Click on the Close button to close the header pane.

You would complete similar steps to add a border line to a footer.

## Customizing Borders

The options on the Borders toolbar let you create a variety of borders. If you want to further customize a border, use options from the Paragraph Borders and Shading dialog box shown in figure 18.5. To display this dialog box, choose Format, then Borders and Shading.

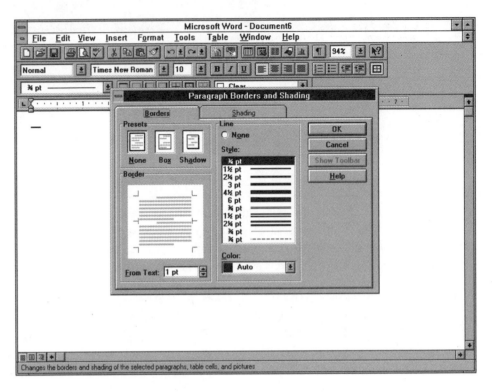

At the Paragraph Borders and Shading dialog box with the Borders tab selected, choose Box or Shadow in the Presets section to add a border. If a paragraph contains a border and you want to remove it, choose None at the Paragraph Borders and Shading dialog box.

At the preview page in the Border section of the dialog box, you can add or remove a border line. To do this, position the arrow pointer on the side of the preview page where you want to add or remove a border, then click the left mouse button. To add a border between paragraphs, position the arrow pointer between the two paragraphs shown in the preview page, then click the left mouse button.

By default, Word separates text from the border by one point of space. To increase or decrease the space between the text and the border, choose From Text at the Paragraph Borders and Shading dialog box, then key the desired distance in points. You can also click on the up- or down-pointing triangle to the right of the From Text text box to increase or decrease the amount of space between text and the border.

Change the line style with the Style options displayed in the middle of the dialog box. To choose an option, position the arrow pointer on the desired style, then click the left mouse button.

You can change the color of the border line with the Color option at the Paragraph Borders and Shading dialog box. To change the border line color, choose Color, then click on an option from the drop-down menu. The border line color will print only if you have access to a color printer.

Shading can be added to text within a border with options on the Borders toolbar or at the Paragraph Borders and Shading dialog box with the Shading tab selected as shown in figure 18.6.

Choose an option in the Shading list box to add shading inside a border. With the Foreground option, you can select the color of the dots and lines that create the shading pattern. Choose Background, then select a color option for the background color of the shading pattern. In the Shading list box, choose Clear to apply the selected background color. Choose Solid to apply the

selected foreground color. To print reverse text (white text on black background) choose White for the foreground color and black for the background color.

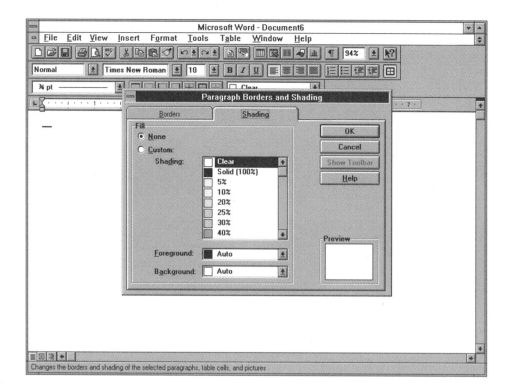

# ◼ *I*nserting a *F*rame

Text in a document or an object such as a picture can be positioned precisely in a document when it is placed in a frame. When an item is enclosed in a frame, you can drag the frame to a different position in the document using the mouse or you can specify a measurement at the Frame dialog box.

## Framing Text

A frame can be inserted around existing text or a picture. The frame is sized automatically to the text or picture. An empty frame can also be inserted in a document. This might be useful in a document where you want to hold a spot open for a photograph or other graphic element to be inserted later.

The viewing mode should be changed to Page Layout before inserting a frame. If the viewing mode is Normal and you try to insert a frame, Word will ask if you want to switch to the Page Layout mode. At the Page Layout mode, you can view, size, or reposition the frame.

To insert a frame around existing text, you would complete the following steps:

1. Change the viewing mode to Page Layout by choosing View, Page Layout or clicking on the Page Layout View button to the left of the horizontal scroll bar.
2. Select the text to be framed.
3. Choose Insert, Frame.
4. Deselect the frame. To do this with the mouse, click anywhere outside the frame in the document screen. If you are using the keyboard, press one of the arrow keys.

When you insert a frame, the frame is automatically selected as shown in figure 18.7. The black squares around the frame are called *sizing handles* and are used to change the size of the frame. Sizing frames is discussed in a later section of this chapter.

*Figure 18.7*
*Framed Text*

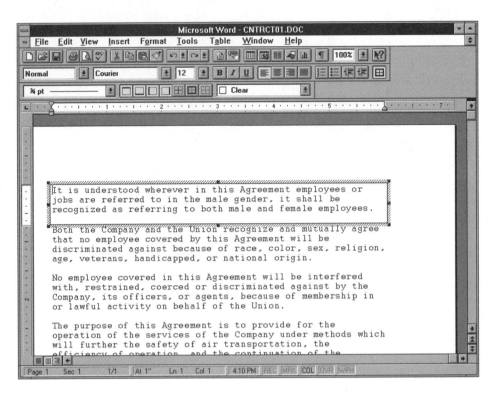

A frame inserted around selected text assumes the size of the text. If text is inserted or deleted, the frame changes to accommodate the text size. The frame inserted by Word contains a single line border around all sides.

## Framing a Picture

A graphic image such as a picture can be inserted in a Word document. This graphic image can be created in a separate draw or paint program and then inserted in a Word document. Or, you can use one of the 94 predesigned pictures provided by Word. These predesigned pictures are displayed in appendix G at the end of this textbook and include the document names. These pictures were created in a program called ClipArt and are easily inserted in a Word document.

A ClipArt picture can be inserted in a document without a frame. The advantage to framing the picture is that you can move the frame and the image is automatically moved with it. You can also customize the frame by precisely positioning it in the document allowing you to size the picture to the frame.

To insert a picture in a document, you would complete the following steps:

1. Change to the Page Layout viewing mode.
2. Choose Insert, Picture.
3. At the Insert Picture dialog box shown in figure 18.8, select a document displayed in the File Name list box.
4. Choose OK or press Enter.

The picture is inserted in the document at the location of the insertion point. The width and height of the picture will vary depending on the picture.

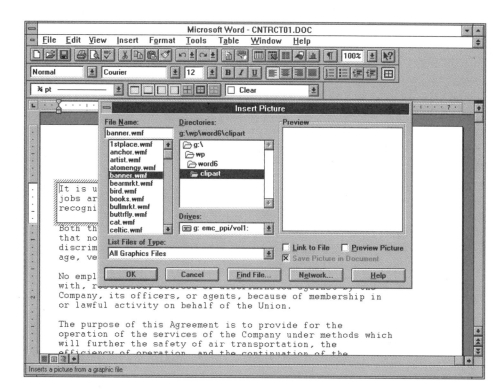

**Figure 18.8**
*Insert Picture Dialog Box*

If you select a picture, black boxes appear around the picture. These black boxes are called *sizing handles*. You can change the width and height of the picture using these sizing handles.

Use the middle sizing handles at the left or right side of the picture to make it wider or thinner. Use the middle sizing handles at the top or bottom of the picture to make it taller or shorter. Use the sizing handles at the corners of the picture to change both the width and height at the same time.

To change the size of a picture, you would complete the following steps:

1. Select the picture. To do this, position the I-beam pointer inside the picture, then click the left mouse button. This causes the sizing handles to display.
2. Position the arrow pointer on a sizing handle until it turns into a double-headed arrow.
3. Hold down the left mouse button, drag the sizing handle in or out to increase or decrease the size of the picture, then release the mouse button.

The size of a picture can be changed with the sizing handles. If, however, you want to move the picture in the document, insert a frame around the picture. To frame a picture, you would complete the following steps:

1. Change to the Page Layout viewing mode.
2. Insert the desired picture in the document.
3. Select the picture. To do this, position the I-beam pointer on the picture, then click the left mouse button.
4. With the picture selected, choose Insert, Frame.

The picture displays in the document with a frame and sizing handles. These sizing handles can be used to change the size of the picture. To deselect the picture frame, click anywhere in the document screen outside the frame. If you are using the keyboard, press one of the arrow keys. Text that has been framed contains a single line border on all sides of the text. A framed picture, however, does not contain any border lines.

Go To Exercise 8

## Drawing a Frame

When framing text or a picture, the frame is positioned around the object you are framing. In addition to framing an object, you can draw a frame in a document. You can draw a frame in a document to hold a spot for something to be inserted such as a photograph, or you can draw a frame in a specific location in a document, then insert text or a picture.

To draw a frame in a document, you would complete the following steps:

1. Open the document in which you want to draw the frame.
2. Change to the Page Layout viewing mode.
3. Choose Insert, Frame.
4. Position the arrow pointer, which displays as cross hairs, where you want the top left corner of the frame to appear.
5. Hold down the left mouse button, drag the outline of the frame to the location where you want the lower right corner of the frame to appear, then release the mouse button.

After a frame is drawn, you can key text inside the frame, cut or copy text into the frame, or insert a picture.

## Sizing a Frame

In a previous section, you learned how to size a picture that was not framed using sizing handles. A picture that has been framed can also be sized. Change the size of a frame in the same manner as you learned to change the size of a picture.

To size text that is framed you must first select the frame. To do this, position the I-beam pointer on any line of the frame until it becomes an arrow pointer with a four-headed arrow attached, then click the left mouse button. This selects the frame and adds sizing handles to the frame.

After a frame is selected, it can be sized with the sizing handles. For example, to make the frame wider or thinner, position the arrow pointer on the middle sizing handle at the left or right side of the frame until it turns into a double-headed arrow pointing left or right. Hold down the left mouse button, drag the double-headed arrow to the left or right until the frame is the desired size, then release the mouse button. You would complete similar steps using the middle sizing handles at the top or bottom of the frame to make the frame taller or shorter. Change both the width and the height of the frame at the same time with the corner sizing handles.

If you change the size of a frame around a picture using the sizing handles, the size of the picture is also changed. However, when a frame around text is changed, the size of the text does not change.

## Positioning a Frame

One of the biggest advantages to framing text or a picture is the ability to reposition the frame in the document. To reposition framed text, you would complete the following steps:

1. Position the I-beam pointer on any side of the text frame until it turns into an arrow pointer with a four-headed arrow attached.
2. Hold down the left mouse button, drag the outline of the frame to the desired location, then release the mouse button.

To reposition a framed picture, you would complete the following steps:

1. Position the I-beam pointer inside the picture until it turns into an arrow pointer with a four-headed arrow attached.
2. Hold down the left mouse button, drag the outline of the frame to the desired location, then release the mouse button.

When repositioning text or a picture in a frame, changing the page display can be helpful. For example, to reposition a framed picture on the page, changing the page display to Whole Page lets you see the entire page on the screen. Select the frame, reposition it, then return the display back to 100%.

To change the page display to Whole Page, make sure the viewing mode is Page Layout, click on the Zoom Control button on the Standard toolbar, then click on Whole Page. You can also change the page display by completing the following steps:

1. Change to the Page Layout viewing mode.
2. Choose View, Zoom.
3. At the Zoom dialog box, choose Whole Page.
4. Choose OK or press Enter.

## Customizing at the Frame Dialog Box

You can size and position a frame using sizing handles and the mouse. If you want to precisely size and/or position a frame, use options from the Frame dialog box shown in figure 18.9. To display this dialog box, select a frame, then choose Format, then Frame.

### Changing a Frame Size

With options in the Size section of the Frame dialog box, you can enter specific measurements for the width and height of the frame. If you have not sized the frame at the document screen, the Width and Height options have a default setting of *Auto*.

If you want to specify an exact width measurement for a frame, choose Width. From the drop-down menu that displays, choose *Exactly*. Choose At, then key the desired measurement. If you are using the mouse, you can click on the up-pointing triangle after the At text box to specify the width measurement. Make changes to the Height option in a similar manner. By default, the height is determined automatically either by the amount of text in the frame or the size of the picture.

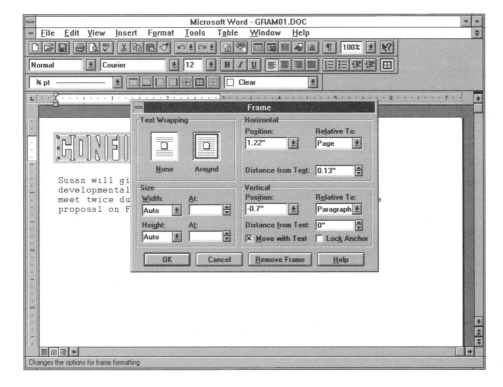

*Figure 18.9*
*Frame Dialog Box*

## Positioning the Frame Horizontally

In the Horizontal section of the Frame dialog box, you can specify the horizontal position of the frame. When a frame is inserted around text or a picture, the frame is automatically positioned horizontally at the left side of the document. This horizontal position can be changed with the Position option. When you choose Position, a drop-down menu displays with *Left, Right, Center, Inside,* and *Outside* options. Where the frame is positioned when choosing one of these options is determined by the setting at the Relative To option.

If Relative To is set at *Margin,* choosing Left in the Position option aligns the frame horizontally at the left margin; Right aligns the frame at the right margin; Center aligns the frame between the left and right margins; Inside aligns the frame inside the margin; and Outside aligns the frame outside the margin.

If Relative To is set at *Page,* choosing Left in the Position option aligns the frame horizontally at the left edge of the page; Right aligns the frame at the right edge of the page; Center aligns the frame between the left and right edges of the page; Inside aligns the frame at the left side of odd-numbered pages and the right side of even-numbered pages; and Outside aligns the frame at the right side of odd-numbered pages and the left side of even-numbered pages.

If Relative To is set at *Column,* the Position options will align the frame relative to the columns. You will learn more about columns in a later chapter.

Use the Distance from Text option to specify the amount of space you want to appear between the frame and the text on the left and right sides.

## Positioning the Frame Vertically

The frame can be positioned vertically relative to the top or bottom edge of the page, margin, or paragraph. Specify if you want the frame positioned relative to the page, margin, or paragraph at the Relative To option in the Vertical section of the Frame dialog box.

Choose Top, Bottom, or Center at the Position option in the Vertical section. You can also enter an exact measurement in the Position text box. This measurement specifies the distance between the top edge of the page, margin, or paragraph and the top of the frame.

Choose Distance from Text in the Vertical section of the dialog box, then enter the measurement for the amount of space you want to appear between the frame and the text above and below the frame.

## Anchoring a Frame

By default, a frame is anchored to the nearest paragraph. As a frame is moved, the anchor moves to the nearest paragraph to the anchor. A frame always appears on the same page as the paragraph to which it is anchored.

When a frame is inserted in a document, an anchor symbol displays to the left of the paragraph to which the frame is anchored. To view this anchor, click on the Show/Hide button on the Standard toolbar to turn on the display of nonprinting characters. You can also display anchor icons by completing the following steps:

1. Choose Tools, Options.
2. At the Options dialog box, select the View tab.
3. Choose Object Anchors in the Show section of the Options dialog box. (This inserts an X in the check box.)
4. Choose OK or press Enter.

The Object Anchors option at the Options dialog box with the View tab selected displays only if the current document contains a frame. Turn off the display of anchor icons by completing the same steps. (This removes the X from the Object Anchors dialog box.)

A frame's anchor can be moved to another paragraph without moving the frame itself. Then, if the anchor is locked, the frame remains in the same position on the page but always prints on the same page as the paragraph. For example, if you center a frame horizontally and vertically on a page and then the paragraph to which the frame is anchored moves to the next page, the frame also moves and displays in the center of the next page. Also, if a frame is too big to fit on a page with the paragraph to which it is anchored, the frame and the paragraph are moved to the next page. To move an anchor, you would complete the following steps:

1. Open the document containing the anchor to be moved.
2. Change the viewing mode to Page Layout.
3. Click on the Show/Hide button on the Standard toolbar to turn on the display of nonprinting characters.
4. Select the frame.
5. Position the I-beam pointer on the anchor icon until the pointer turns into an arrow with a four-headed arrow attached.
6. Hold down the left mouse button, drag the anchor icon to the desired paragraph, then release the mouse button.

When you move an anchor icon, the frame does not move. If, however, the paragraph containing the anchor is moved to another page, the frame will move also.

If you want a frame to stay on a specific page and not move with the paragraph to which it is anchored, you would choose Format, Frame to display the Frame dialog box, then remove the X from the Move with Text option and the Lock Anchor option.

## Wrapping Text Around a Frame

By default, text in a document will wrap around a frame. If you do not want text to wrap around a frame in a document, choose Format, Frame to display the Frame dialog box, then choose None in the Text Wrapping section. If you turn off wrapping and then decide to turn it back on, choose Around.

## Removing a Frame

Choose Remove Frame at the Frame dialog box to remove the frame from the selected object in the document. The frame is removed leaving the text or the picture. If you want to delete a frame and its contents, select the frame, then press the Delete key.

# Customizing a Picture

As you learned earlier in this chapter, a picture can be inserted in a document, a frame can be inserted around the picture, and the picture frame can be customized. The picture itself can also be customized. For example, the size and scale of a picture can be changed and a picture can be cropped.

A picture can be customized using the mouse or options from the Picture dialog box shown in figure 18.10. To display this dialog box, select a picture in the document, then choose Format, then Picture.

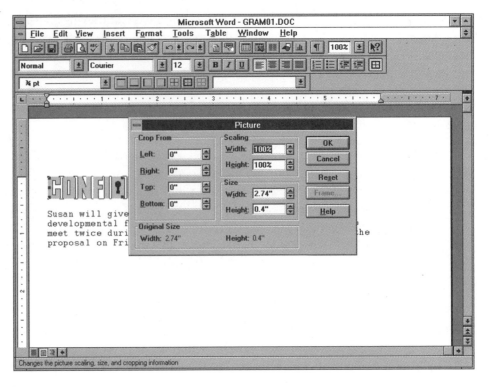

*Figure 18.10*
*Picture Dialog Box*

## Sizing and Scaling a Picture

The width and height of a picture in a document can be changed with sizing handles in a selected picture or at the Picture dialog box shown in figure 18.10. At the Picture dialog box, you can change the width and the height of a picture or you can scale the picture by a percentage. To size a picture, you would complete the following steps:

1. Select the picture in the document.
2. Choose Format, Picture.
3. At the Picture dialog box, choose Width in the Size section, then key the desired measurement. (You can also click on the up- or down-pointing triangles to the right of the Width text box to change the measurement.)
4. Choose Height in the Size section, then key the desired measurement (or click on the up- or down-pointing triangles to the right of the Height text box.)
5. Choose OK or press Enter.

To scale a picture you would complete similar steps except key a percentage measurement in the Width text box and a percentage in the Height text box. You can also increase or decrease the percentage measurement by clicking on the up- or down-pointing triangles after the Width and Height text boxes in the Scaling section.

## Cropping a Picture

At the Picture dialog box you can crop a picture, cutting off areas you do not want to display. You can also add white space around a picture. A picture can be cropped using the mouse or with options at the Picture dialog box.

To crop a picture using the mouse, you would complete the following steps:

1. Select the picture in the document.
2. Hold down the Shift key, position the arrow pointer on one of the sizing handles until it turns into a square with overlapping corners, then hold down the left mouse button.
3. Drag the outline of the frame into the image. When the outline is in the desired location, release the mouse button and the Shift key.

When you drag the frame outline into the image, the image is cropped where the outline is positioned. If you want to increase white space around a picture, drag the outline of the frame away from the picture.

To crop a picture using the Picture dialog box, you would complete the following steps:

1. Select the picture.
2. Choose Format, Picture.
3. At the Picture dialog box, enter a positive number in the Left, Right, Top, or Bottom text box to crop off a portion of the picture. Enter a negative number to add white space around the picture.
4. Choose OK or press Enter.

If you enter a positive number in a text box in the Crop From section of the Picture dialog box, a portion of the picture will be cropped. If you enter a negative number in a text box in the Crop From section, white space will be added to the picture. You can click on the up-pointing triangle after a text box to insert a positive number or click on the down-pointing arrow to insert a negative number.

## Resetting the Picture Size

At the Picture dialog box, the original width and height of a picture is displayed at the bottom of the Picture dialog box. You can return the picture to its original size by keying the measurements in the Width text box and the Height text box. Or, you can return the picture to its original size by choosing the Reset button.

## CHAPTER SUMMARY

- You can create a border around a single paragraph or selected paragraphs with buttons on the Borders toolbar.
- With options from the Line Style drop-down menu at the Borders toolbar, you can make the border line thicker or choose a double, dotted, or dashed line. Add shading to a paragraph with choices from the Shading options on the Borders toolbar.
- To remove a border from a paragraph, position the insertion point anywhere within the paragraph, then click on the No Border button on the Borders toolbar.
- Word's border feature can be used to add lines in headers and/or footers.
- To further customize a border, use options from the Paragraph Borders and Shading dialog box. At the preview page in the Border section of this dialog box, you can add or remove a border line.
- When text or an object is enclosed in a frame, you can drag the frame to a different position in the document, or you can specify a measurement at the Frame dialog box. An empty frame can also be inserted in a document.
- A frame assumes the size of the text, even if the text is later inserted or deleted.
- Word provides 94 predesigned pictures in a program called ClipArt. A ClipArt picture can be inserted in a document without a frame. The advantage to framing the picture is that you can move the frame and the picture is automatically moved with it.
- Insert a picture in a document at the Insert Picture dialog box. To frame the selected picture in the Page Layout viewing mode, choose Insert, then Frame.
- To draw a frame in a document, choose Insert, then Frame. At the desired location, drag the mouse from the top left corner to the lower right corner, then release the mouse button.
- An existing frame can be selected; sizing handles appear when the frame is selected.
- You can size and position a frame using sizing handles and the mouse. If you want to precisely size and/or position a frame, use options from the Frame dialog box.
- By default, a frame is anchored to the closest paragraph. You can lock an anchor to a specific paragraph so that the frame stays with the paragraph, even if the paragraph is moved.
- Whether or not a picture is inside a frame, the selected picture itself can be customized using the sizing handles or options at the Picture dialog box.
- You can crop a picture, cutting off areas you do not want to display. Do this using the mouse or with options at the Picture dialog box.

| | Mouse | Keyboard |
|---|---|---|
| Borders toolbar | Click on the Borders button on Formatting toolbar | View, Toolbars; select Borders; press Enter |
| Paragraph Borders and Shading dialog box | Format, Borders and Shading | Format, Borders and Shading |
| Insert frame around selected text | Insert, Frame | Insert, Frame |
| Insert Picture dialog box | Insert, Picture | Insert, Picture |
| Frame dialog box | Format, Frame | Format, Frame |
| Picture dialog box | Format, Picture | Format, Picture |

## CHECK YOUR UNDERSTANDING

**True/False:** Circle the letter T if the statement is true; circle the letter F if the statement is false.

T   F   1.   Every paragraph you create in Word contains an invisible frame.

T   F   2.   You can add a pattern of diagonal lines to a paragraph at the Shading drop-down menu.

T   F   3.   Borders cannot be added to only one side of a paragraph.

T   F   4.   A border and a frame are used for the same purpose.

T   F   5.   An empty frame can be inserted in a document.

T   F   6.   The major advantage to framing a picture is that it looks more professional.

T   F   7.   A framed picture does not contain any border lines.

T   F   8.   When a frame is inserted around text, the frame is automatically positioned at the right side of the document.

T   F   9.   A picture can be customized using options from the Picture dialog box.

T   F   10.   You can make a picture larger or smaller, but you cannot cut off part of the picture.

**Completion:** In the space provided at the right, indicate the correct term, command, or number.

1.   Create a border at this toolbar.   _____

2.   By default, Word separates text from the border by this amount of space.   _____

3.   Change the color of the border line at this dialog box.   _____

4.   Change to this viewing mode before inserting a frame in a document.   _____

5.   The black squares around a frame are called this.   _____

6.   The pictures provided by Word are created in this program.   _____

7.   Click here to deselect a picture frame.   _____

8.   To draw a frame in a document, complete the necessary steps until the arrow pointer looks like this.   _____

9.   At the Frame dialog box, this is the default setting for Width and Height.   _____

10.   If you want a frame to follow a paragraph wherever it is moved, you must do this.   _____

## AT THE COMPUTER

### Exercise 1

1.   Open para04.

2.   Save the document with Save As and name it c18ex01.

3.   Create a border around the first paragraph by completing the following steps:

   a.   Position the insertion point anywhere in the first paragraph.

   b.   Click on the Borders button on the Formatting toolbar to display the Borders toolbar. (Skip this step if the Borders toolbar is already displayed.)

    c.  Click on the Outside Border button on the Borders toolbar.

4. Complete steps similar to those in 3a through 3c to add a border to the second paragraph.
5. Complete steps similar to those in 3a through 3c to add a border to the third paragraph.
6. Save the document again with the same name (c18ex01).
7. Print c18ex01.
8. Close c18ex01.

## Exercise 2

1. Open para04.
2. Save the document with Save As and name it c18ex02.
3. Create a border around all the paragraphs in the document that is 3 points thick and contains 25% shading by completing the following steps:
   a. Select all paragraphs in the document.
   b. Make sure the Borders toolbar is displayed, then click on the down-pointing arrow to the right of the Line Style option. From the drop-down menu that displays, click on *3 pt*.
   c. Click on the Outside Border button on the Borders toolbar.
   d. Click on the down-pointing arrow to the right of the Shading option. From the drop-down menu that displays, click on *25%*.
4. Save the document again with the same name (c18ex02).
5. Print c18ex02.
6. Close c18ex02.

## Exercise 3

1. Open report02.
2. Save the document with Save As and name it c18ex03.
3. Create a footer that prints on every page of the document and contains a border line by completing the following steps:
   a. Display the Borders toolbar. (Skip this step if the Borders toolbar is already displayed.)
   b. Choose <u>V</u>iew, <u>H</u>eader and Footer.
   c. At the header pane, click on the Switch Between Header and Footer button on the Header and Footer toolbar.
   d. At the footer pane, click on the down-pointing arrow to the right of the Line Style option, then click on *3 pt* in the drop-down menu.
   e. Click on the Top Border button on the Borders toolbar.
   f. Key **Structured Publications** at the left margin.
   g. Press the Tab key twice.
   h. Key **Page,** then press the space bar.
   i. Click on the Page Numbers button on the Header and Footer toolbar.
   j. Click on the <u>C</u>lose button on the Header and Footer toolbar to close the footer pane.
4. Check the page breaks in the report and, if necessary, adjust the page breaks.
5. Save the document again with the same name (c18ex03).
6. Print c18ex03.
7. Close c18ex03.

## Exercise 4

1. Open notice02.
2. Save the document with Save As and name it c18ex04.
3. Make the following changes to the document:
   a. With the insertion point at the beginning of the document, press the Enter key once.
   b. Select the entire document, then change the font to 14-point Brush Script MT.
   c. With the entire document selected, add a shadow border by completing the following steps:

        (1)  Choose Format, Borders and Shading.

        (2)  At the Paragraph Borders and Shading dialog box with the Borders tab selected, choose Shadow.

        (3)  Click on the *4 1/2 pt* option in the Style list box.

        (4)  Choose OK or press Enter.

4.   Save the document again with the same name (c18ex04).

5.   Print c18ex04.

6.   Close c18ex04.

## Exercise 5

1.   Open notice03.

2.   Save the document with Save As and name it c18ex05.

3.   Make the following changes to the document:

    a.  With the insertion point positioned at the beginning of the document, press the Enter key. (This adds a hard return at the beginning of the document.)

    b.  Select the entire document, then change the paragraph alignment to centered.

    c.  With the entire document still selected, add a border and shading by completing the following steps:

        (1)  Choose Format, Border and Shading.

        (2)  At the Paragraph Borders and Shading dialog box with the Borders tab selected, choose Box.

        (3)  Click on the *2 1/4 pt* option in the Style list box.

        (4)  Click on the bottom line of the preview page. (This removes the line.)

        (5)  Click on the top line of the preview page. (This removes the line.)

        (6)  Click on the Shading tab.

        (7)  At the Paragraph Borders and Shading dialog box with the Shading tab selected, choose Background. At the drop-down menu that displays, click on *Cyan*.

        (8)  Click on *25%* in the Shading list box.

        (9)  Choose OK or press Enter.

4.   Save the document again with the same name (c18ex05).

5.   Print c18ex05.

6.   Close c18ex05.

## Exercise 6

1.   Open block01.

2.   Save the document with Save As and name it c18ex06.

3.   Insert a frame around the text in the document by completing the following steps:

    a.  Choose View, Page Layout to change the viewing mode.

    b.  Press Ctrl + A to select all the text in the document.

    c.  Choose Insert, Frame.

    d.  Deselect the frame.

4.   Press Ctrl + Home to move the insertion point to the beginning of the document (immediately left of the *H*) then press the Enter key.

5.   Select the text in the document, then change the font to 16-point Brush Script MT.

6.   Save the document again with the same name (c18ex06).

7.   Print c18ex06.

8.   Close c18ex06.

## Exercise 7

1.   Open para02.

2.   Save the document with Save As and name it c18ex07.

3.   Insert a picture at the beginning of the document by completing the following steps:

a. Make sure the insertion point is positioned at the beginning of the document.

b. Change the viewing mode to Page Layout.

c. Choose Insert, Picture.

d. At the Insert Picture dialog box, click on the down-pointing arrow in the File Name list box until *computer.wmf* is visible.

e. Double-click on *computer.wmf*.

4. Insert a frame around the picture by completing the following steps:

a. Position the I-beam pointer inside the picture, then click the left mouse button. (This selects the picture.)

b. Choose Insert, Frame.

c. Click in the document screen outside the picture to deselect the picture and the frame.

5. Save the document again with the same name (c18ex07).

6. Print c18ex07.

7. Close c18ex07.

## Exercise 8

1. Open notice01.

2. Save the document with Save As and name it c18ex08.

3. Make the following changes to the document:

a. Select the entire document, then change the font to 12-point Colonna MT.

b. Select the title, *RIDGWAY ELEMENTARY SCHOOL CARNIVAL,* then change the font to 14-point Colonna MT Bold.

4. Insert the ClipArt picture named *spring.wmf* by completing the following steps:

a. Position the insertion point at the beginning of the document (immediately left of the *R* in *RIDGWAY*).

b. Choose Insert, Picture.

c. At the Insert Picture dialog box, click on the down-pointing arrow in the File Name list box until *spring.wmf* is visible.

d. Double-click on *spring.wmf*.

5. Save the document again with the same name (c18ex08).

6. Print c18ex08.

7. Insert a frame around the picture by completing the following steps:

a. Change to the Page Layout viewing mode.

b. Click on the picture to select it.

c. Choose Insert, Frame.

8. Deselect the frame.

9. Save the document again with the same name (c18ex08).

10. Print c18ex08.

11. Close c18ex08.

## Exercise 9

1. Open para02.

2. Save the document with Save As and name it c18ex09.

3. Draw a frame spanning the two paragraphs and insert a picture in the frame by completing the following steps:

a. Change to the Page Layout viewing mode.

b. Choose Insert, Frame.

c. Position the arrow pointer, which displays as cross hairs, at the beginning of the word *compact* in the seventh line of the first paraghaph.

d. Hold down the left mouse button, then move the outline of the frame until the cross hairs are positioned on the word *astounding* in the fifth line of the second paragraph, then release the mouse button.

e. Choose Insert, Picture.

f. At the Insert Picture dialog box, double-click on the *computer.wmf* document name. (You will need to scroll down the list to see this document name.)

g. With the computer image inserted in the frame and the frame still selected, add a border by completing the following steps:

    (1) Display the Borders toolbar.

    (2) Click on the down-pointing arrow to the right of the Line Style option, then click on *2 1/4 pt*.

    (3) Click on the Outside Border button on the Borders toolbar.

h. Deselect the frame.

4. Save the document again with the same name (c18ex09).

5. Print c18ex09.

6. Close c18ex09.

## Exercise 10

1. At a clear document screen, insert a frame around text then size the frame by completing the following steps:

    a. Change to the Page Layout viewing mode.

    b. Press Ctrl + E.

    c. Key **MEEKER HIGH SCHOOL**.

    d. Select *MEEKER HIGH SCHOOL*.

    e. Change the font to 18-point Algerian.

    f. With *MEEKER HIGH SCHOOL* still selected, choose Insert, Frame.

    g. Widen the frame by completing the following steps:

        (1) Position the arrow pointer on the middle sizing handle at the right side of the frame until it turns into a double-headed arrow pointing left and right.

        (2) Hold down the left mouse button, drag the frame to the right to about the 6-inch mark on the horizontal ruler, then release the mouse button.

    h. Deselect the frame.

2. Save the document and name it c18ex10.

3. Print c18ex10.

4. Close c18ex10.

## Exercise 11

1. Open c18ex10.

2. Save the document with Save As and name it c18ex11.

3. Move the frame to the middle of the page by completing the following steps:

    a. Change the zoom display to whole page by completing the following steps:

        (1) Choose View, Zoom.

        (2) At the Zoom dialog box, choose Whole Page.

        (3) Choose OK or press Enter.

    b. Position the arrow pointer at the bottom of the frame until the arrow pointer displays with a four-headed arrow attached.

    c. Hold down the left mouse button, drag the frame outline to the middle of the page, then release the mouse button.

    d. Deselect the frame.

    e. Change the viewing mode back to 100% by completing the following steps:

        (1) Choose View, Zoom.

        (2) At the Zoom dialog box, choose 100%.

        (3) Choose OK or press Enter.

4. Save the document again with the same name (c18ex11).

5. Print c18ex11.

6. Close c18ex11.

# Exercise 12

1. Open notice01.
2. Save the document with Save As and name it c18ex12.
3. Insert a picture above and below the text in the document and change the location of the picture by completing the following steps:
   a. With the insertion point at the beginning of the document, press the Enter key four times.
   b. Select the entire document, then change the font to 12-point Colonna MT.
   c. Deselect the text, then change the left and right margins to 2 inches.
   d. Move the insertion point to the beginning of the document, then insert a picture, frame the picture, then change the location of the frame by completing the following steps:
      (1) Change to the Page Layout viewing mode.
      (2) Choose Insert, Picture.
      (3) At the Insert Picture dialog box, double-click on the *divider1.wmf* document name. (You will need to scroll down the list to see this document name.)
      (4) Select the picture.
      (5) Choose Insert, Frame.
      (6) With the picture and frame still selected, choose Format, Frame.
      (7) At the Frame dialog box, choose Position in the Horizontal section of the dialog box, then choose *Center* from the drop-down menu.
      (8) Choose Relative To in the Horizontal section of the dialog box, then choose *Margin* from the drop-down menu.
      (9) Choose OK or press Enter.
   e. Move the insertion point to the end of the document, then complete steps 3d(2) through 3d(9) above.
4. Save the document again with the same name (c18ex12).
5. Print c18ex12.
6. Close c18ex12.

# Exercise 13

1. Open report01.
2. Save the document with Save As and name it c18ex13.
3. Make the following changes to the report:
   a. Select the entire document, then change the font to 12-point Times New Roman.
   b. Select the title and each of the three headings (individually), then change the font to 14-point Times New Roman Bold.
   c. Select the text of the report from the first heading, *Type Measurement,* to the end, then change the line spacing to single.
   d. With the text still selected change the spacing before and after paragraphs to 3 points.
   e. Insert bullets before the last four paragraphs (lines).
   f. Insert the computer picture that is anchored on the page by completing the following steps:
      (1) Move the insertion point to the beginning of the document.
      (2) Choose Insert, Picture.
      (3) At the Insert Picture dialog box, double-click on *computer.wmf.*
      (4) At the document screen, click inside the picture to select it.
      (5) Choose Insert, Frame.
      (6) Choose Format, Frame.
      (7) At the Frame dialog box, change the Position option to *Center* and the Relative To option to *Page* in the Horizontal section of the dialog box.
      (8) Change the Position option to *Center* and the Relative To option to *Page* in the Vertical section of the dialog box.

(9) Make sure there is no X in the Move with Text check box and the Lock Anchor check box. (If there is, select the option to remove the X.)

(10) Choose OK or press Enter.

    g. Move the *Type Size* section of the report (including the heading) below the *Type Style* section.

    h. Check the page break in the report and, if necessary, adjust page breaks.

4. Save the document again with the same name (c18ex13).

5. Print c18ex13.

6. Close c18ex13.

## Exercise 14

1. Open c18ex06.

2. Save the document with Save As and name it c18ex14.

3. Remove the frame around the text by completing the following steps:

    a. Choose Format, Frame.

    b. At the Frame dialog box, choose Remove Frame.

4. Save the document again with the same name (c18ex14).

5. Print c18ex14.

6. Close c18ex14.

## Exercise 15

1. At a clear document screen, create the invitation shown in figure 18.11 by completing the following steps:

    a. Change to the Page Layout viewing mode.

    b. Insert the picture by completing the following steps:

        (1) Choose Insert, Picture.

        (2) At the Insert Picture dialog box, double-click on *party.wmf*. (You will need to scroll down the list to see this document name.)

        (3) Select the picture, then choose Format, Picture.

        (4) At the Picture dialog box, choose Width in the Size section of the dialog box, then key **2**. (If you are using the mouse, you can click on the up-pointing triangle until *2"* displays in the Width text box.)

        (5) Choose Height in the Size section of the dialog box, then key **2.5**. (If you are using the mouse, you can click on the up-pointing triangle until *2.5"* displays in the Height text box.)

        (6) Choose OK or press Enter.

        (7) With the picture selected, choose Insert, Frame.

        (8) Position the arrow pointer outside the picture, then click the left mouse button.

    c. Press the Enter key twice.

    d. Change the paragraph alignment to center.

    e. Key the text shown in figure 18.11.

    f. Select the text, then change the font to 14-point Brush Script MT.

2. Save the document and name it c18ex15.

3. Print c18ex15.

4. Close c18ex15.

Figure 18.11

HAPPY BIRTHDAY PAULA!

Come celebrate Paula's birthday

Wednesday, August 7, 1996

3:00 - 4:30 p.m.

Room 320

## Exercise 16

1. At a clear document screen, create the letterhead shown in figure 18.12 by completing the following steps:

   a. Change to the Page Layout viewing mode.

   b. Choose Insert, Picture.

   c. At the Insert Picture dialog box, double-click on the *continen.wmf* document name. (You will need to scroll down the list to display this document name.)

   d. At the document screen, change the zoom display to whole page by completing the following steps:

      (1) Click on the down-pointing arrow after the Zoom Control button on the Standard toolbar.

      (2) At the drop-down list that displays, click on *Whole Page*.

   e. With the full page of the document displayed, crop the continents so only Australia is displayed. To do this, complete the following steps:

      (1) Select the picture by positioning the arrow pointer inside the picture, then clicking the left mouse.

      (2) Crop the picture so only Australia displays by holding down the Shift key, positioning the arrow pointer on one of the sizing handles until it turns into a square with overlapping corners, holding down the left mouse button, then dragging the outline into the picture.

      (3) Continue using different sizing handles together with the Shift key to crop the image until only Australia is visible.

   f. Change the zoom display back to 100%. To do this, click on the down-pointing arrow after the Zoom Control button, then click on *100%*.

   g. At the document screen, crop the picture some more, if necessary, to make it look similar to the picture shown in figure 18.12.

   h. Insert a frame around the picture. (To do this, select the picture, then choose Insert, Frame.)

   i. With the picture still selected, change the width and height of the picture by completing the following steps:

      (1) Choose Format, Picture.

      (2) At the Picture dialog box, choose Width in the Size section of the dialog box, then key **1.8**.

      (3) Choose Height in the Size section of the dialog box, then key **1.5**.

      (4) Choose OK or press Enter.

    j.  Deselect the picture.

    k.  Press the Enter key once, change the paragraph alignment to right, then key the company name, address, and telephone number as shown in figure 18.12. (This will appear in the default font and without the line border.)

    l.  Select the company name, *AUSTRALIAN IMPORTS*, then change the font to 18-point Bookman Old Style Bold.

    m.  Select the address and the telephone number, then change the font to 14-point Bookman Old Style Bold.

    n.  Insert a border at the bottom of the paragraph containing the company name by completing the following steps:

        (1)  Position the insertion point on any letter of the company name.

        (2)  Make sure the Borders toolbar is visible. (If not, click on the Borders button on the Formatting toolbar.)

        (3)  Change the Line Style option to *3 pt*.

        (4)  Click on the Bottom Border button.

    o.  Insert a 3-point line border around the picture.

2.  Save the document and name it c18ex16.

3.  Print c18ex16.

4.  Close c18ex16.

**Figure 18.12**

# AUSTRALIAN IMPORTS

**430 Fifth Avenue**
**Los Angeles, CA 97443**
**1-800-555-3033**

## SKILL ASSESSMENTS

### Assessment 1

1.  Open survey01.

2.  Save the document with Save As and name it c18sa01.

3.  Make the following changes to the document:

    a.  Select the entire document, then change the font to 12-point Times New Roman.

    b.  Select the title and the subtitle, then change the font to 14-point Times New Roman Bold.

    c.  Hang indent each numbered paragraph.

    d.  Indent 0.5 inches each of the lettered paragraphs.

    e.  Select the first numbered paragraph and the four lettered paragraphs below it, then add a 3/4 point border with 10% shading. (A border will display around the paragraphs and between the numbered paragraph and the lettered paragraphs.)

    f.  Select the second numbered paragraph and the four lettered paragraphs below it, then add a 3/4 point border with 10% shading.

    g.  Select the third numbered paragraph and the four lettered paragraphs below it, then add a 3/4 point border with 10% shading.

    h. Select the fourth numbered paragraph and the four lettered paragraphs below it, then add a 3/4 point border with 10% shading.

    i. Select the fifth numbered paragraph and the four lettered paragraphs below it, then add a 3/4 point border with 10% shading.

4. Save the document again with the same name (c18sa01).
5. Print c18sa01.
6. Close c18sa01.

## Assessment 2

1. Open c18ex08.
2. Save the document with Save As and name it c18sa02.
3. Move the picture below all the text in the document and center it visually between the left and right edges of the page.
4. Save the document again with the same name (c18sa02).
5. Print c18sa02.
6. Close c18sa02.

## Assessment 3

1. Open para02.
2. Save the document with Save As and name it c18sa03.
3. Insert a picture in the first paragraph by completing the following steps:
    a. Change to the Page Layout viewing mode.
    b. With the insertion point positioned at the beginning of the first paragraph, display the Insert Picture dialog box, then double-click on *disk.wmf*.
    c. At the document screen, select the picture then insert a frame.
    d. With the picture still selected, choose Format, Frame to display the Frame dialog box.
    e. At the Frame dialog box, change the Position option in the Horizontal section of the dialog box to *Right*. (Leave the Relative To option at the default setting of *Column*.)
    f. Choose OK or press Enter to close the Frame dialog box.
4. Complete steps similar to those in 3b through 3f to insert the picture named *computer.wmf* at the beginning of the second paragraph except leave the horizontal position of the picture at the left.
5. Save the document again with the same name (c18sa03).
6. Print c18sa03.
7. Close c18sa03.

## Assessment 4

1. At a clear document screen, create the letterhead shown in figure 18.13 by completing the following steps:
    a. Insert the picture named *pharmacy.wmf*.
    b. Frame the picture.
    c. Deselect the frame.
    d. Press the Enter key twice, change the paragraph alignment to right, then key the company name and address as shown in figure 18.13.
    e. Select *MYERS PHARMACEUTICALS*, then change the font to 18-point Desdemona Bold.
    f. Select the address and the telephone number, then change the font to 14-point Desdemona Bold.
    g. Position the insertion point on any character in the company name *MYERS PHARMACEUTICALS*, then insert a 3-point border line at the bottom of the paragraph.
2. Save the document and name it c18sa04.
3. Print c18sa04.
4. Close c18sa04.

**Figure 18.13**

MYERS PHARMACEUTICALS

3500 RIGGS BOULEVARD
MIAMI, FL 33190
(813) 555-7990

# Using Microsoft Draw 19

Upon completion of chapter 19, you will be able to enhance documents by creating shapes, images, or text in the Microsoft Draw program.

Word for Windows, Version 6, provides many predesigned ClipArt pictures. You used some of these pictures in exercises in chapter 18. If you would like to create your own images and pictures, you can do so with Word's Draw program. This program was included with Word for Windows and provides many of the features of a standalone draw program. With Draw, you can draw shapes, draw freehand, and create and customize text.

In this chapter, you will learn the basic functions of Draw. For more sophisticated and varying ideas on how to use Draw, please refer to the Word for Windows User's Guide.

## Drawing Shapes

You can use the Draw program to draw a variety of shapes such as circles, squares, rectangles, ellipses, ovals, and much more.

To use the Draw program, the Drawing toolbar must be displayed. To turn on the display of the toolbar, choose one of the following methods:

- Click on the Drawing button on the Standard toolbar.
- Choose View, Toolbars, click on Drawing, then choose OK or press Enter.
- Position the arrow pointer in the gray area of any displayed toolbar, click the right mouse button, then click on Drawing at the drop-down menu.

Change the viewing mode to Page Layout when using buttons on the Drawing toolbar. If you do not, Word will prompt you to change to Page Layout when you click on a button on the Drawing toolbar.

When you turn on the display of the Drawing toolbar, the toolbar displays at the bottom of the screen above the Status bar. Figure 19.1 identifies the buttons on the Drawing toolbar.

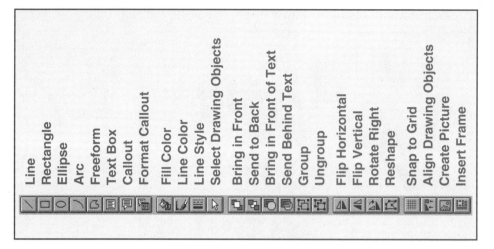

*Figure 19.1*
*Buttons on the*
*Drawing Toolbar*

The buttons on the Drawing toolbar are used for a variety of functions such as selecting, drawing, and changing the fill and attributes of shapes and images. There are five buttons on the toolbar that you can use to draw shapes. These five buttons are shown in figure 19.2.

*Figure 19.2*
*Buttons for Drawing*
*Shapes*

| Use this button | To |
|---|---|
| | draw straight vertical or horizontal lines or at a 30-, 45-, or 60-degree angle if the Shift key is down. |
| | draw rectangles or hold down the Shift key to draw squares. |
| | draw ellipses or hold down the Shift key to draw circles. |
| | draw an elliptical arc or hold down the Shift key to draw a circular arc. |
| | draw a straight or curving line, or vertical, horizontal, or at 30-, 45-, and 60-degree angles if the Shift key is down. |

To draw a shape with a drawing button, you would complete the following steps:

1. At a clear screen, change to the Page Layout viewing mode.
2. Position the arrow pointer on the desired drawing button on the Drawing toolbar, then click the left mouse button.
3. Position the arrow pointer in the document screen (the arrow pointer displays as cross hairs).
4. Hold down the left mouse button, drag the mouse in the desired direction, then release the mouse button.

If you use the Line button to draw a shape, the shape you draw is considered a line drawing. If you draw a shape with the Rectangle, Ellipse, Arc, or Freeform button, the shape you draw is considered an enclosed object. Later in this chapter you will learn how to add fill color to an enclosed object.

If you want to draw the same shape more than once, double-click on the shape button on the Drawing toolbar. After drawing the shapes, click on the button again to deactivate it.

As an example of how to draw a shape, you would complete the following steps to draw a circle:

1. At a clear document screen, change to the Page Layout viewing mode.
2. Turn on the display of the Drawing toolbar by clicking on the Drawing button on the Standard toolbar.
3. Position the arrow pointer on the Ellipse tool, then click the left mouse button.
4. Position the cross hairs in the middle of the document screen.
5. Hold down the Shift key and the left mouse button, drag the mouse down until the circle is the desired size, then release the mouse button.
6. If desired, click on the Drawing button on the Standard toolbar to turn off the display of the Drawing toolbar.

With the Line button, you can draw a line in the document screen. To do this, you would complete the following steps:

1. Click on the Line button on the Drawing toolbar.
2. Position the cross hairs where you want to begin the line.
3. Hold down the left mouse button, drag the line to the location where you want the line to end, then release the mouse button.

You can add as many lines as desired in the document screen by repeating the steps above. For example, you can draw a triangle by drawing three lines. If you want to draw more than one line, double-click on the Line button. This makes the button active. After drawing all the necessary lines, click on the Line button again to deactivate it.

In addition to dragging the mouse to create a shape, you can use the Freeform button to click at specific locations in the document screen to mark a point. When you connect points, Draw will select the shape. For example, to draw a triangle using the Freeform button, you would complete the following steps:

1. At a clear document screen, change to the Page Layout viewing mode.
2. Display the Drawing toolbar.
3. Click on the Freeform button.
4. Position the cross hairs approximately in the middle of the document screen.
5. Click the left mouse button once. This marks a point.
6. Move the cross hairs down and to the right approximately 1 inch, then click the left mouse button. This marks another point.
7. Move the cross hairs across and to the left approximately 1 inch, then click the left mouse button.
8. Move the cross hairs to the beginning of the triangle, then click the left mouse button. (This selects the shape.)

## Creating Text in Draw

In Draw, you can create a box and then insert text inside the box. Text inside a box can be formatted in the normal manner. For example, you can change the font, the alignment, or indent of the text.

Figure 19.3
Text Box

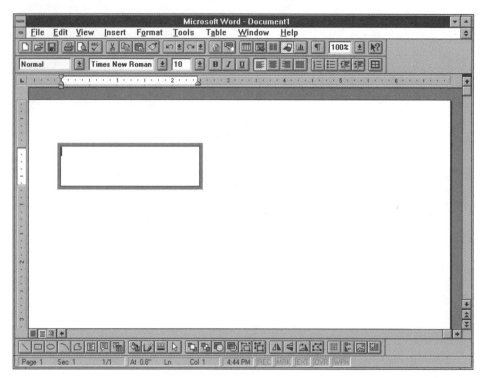

To create a box in Draw and then insert text inside the box, you would complete the following steps:

1. At a clear document screen, change to the Page Layout viewing mode.
2. Turn on the display of the Drawing toolbar.
3. Click on the Text Box button on the Drawing toolbar (the sixth button from the left).
4. Position the cross hairs in the document screen where you want the text to appear. Hold down the left mouse button, drag the outline down and to the right to draw a box, then click the left mouse button. This causes a box to appear in the drawing area as shown in figure 19.3.
5. Key the text in the box. If the text you key fills more than the first line in the box, the text wraps to the next line. (The box, however, will not increase in size. If you need more room in the text box, select the box, then use the sizing handles to make it bigger.)
6. After keying the text, click outside the text box to deselect it.

As an example of how to create a text box, you would complete the following steps to create a text box with the words *ST. FRANCIS MEDICAL CENTER* inside:

1. At a clear document screen, change to the Page Layout viewing mode.
2. Display the Drawing toolbar.
3. Click on the Text Box button on the Drawing toolbar (the sixth button from the left).
4. Position the cross hairs in the document screen then draw a box that is approximately 1 inch high and 3 inches wide. When the box is the desired size, release the mouse button.
5. Change the paragraph alignment to center.
6. Press the Enter key until the insertion point is located approximately in the middle of the box.
7. Key **ST. FRANCIS MEDICAL CENTER**.
8. Click outside the box to deselect it.

Go To
Exercise
3

Text keyed in the drawing area can be edited and formatted in the same manner as normal text.

# Changing Objects

Shapes and text boxes created in Draw, called objects, can be customized. For example, an object can be selected then moved, copied, or deleted. You can also change the size of an object.

## Selecting an Object

After an object has been created in a document, you may decide to make changes or delete the object. To do this, the object must be selected. To select one object, position the I-beam pointer on one of the lines of the object until the I-beam pointer turns into an arrow with a four-headed arrow attached, then click the left mouse button. When an object is selected, it displays with sizing handles. Once an object is selected, it can be edited such as changing the fill and the line, it can be moved, or it can be deleted.

If a document screen contains more than one object, you can select several objects at once using the Select Drawing Objects button on the Drawing toolbar. This is the twelfth button from the left containing the arrow. To do this, you would complete the following steps:

1. Click on the Select Drawing Objects button on the Drawing toolbar.
2. Position the cross hairs in the upper left corner of the area containing the objects.
3. Hold down the left mouse button, drag the outline to the lower right corner of the area containing the objects, then release the mouse button.

Each object in the selected area displays with sizing handles. Objects in the selected area are connected. For example, if you move one of the objects in the selected area, the other objects move relatively. You can also select more than one object by holding down the Shift key as you select each object.

## Deleting an Object

An object you have drawn can be deleted from the document screen. To do this, select the object, then press the Delete key.

## Moving an Object

An object can be moved to a different location in this document. To do this, you would complete the following steps:

1. Position the I-beam pointer on a line of the object until it turns into an arrow with a four-headed arrow attached.
2. Hold down the left mouse button, drag the outline of the object to the new location, then release the mouse button.

If you select more than one object, moving one of the objects will also move the other objects.

You can move a selected object with the keyboard by pressing one of the arrow keys. For example, to move an object down the screen, select the object, then press the down arrow key.

## Copying an Object

Moving an object removes the object from its original position and inserts it into a new location. If you want the object to stay in its original location and an exact copy to be inserted in a new location, you would complete the following steps:

1. Position the I-beam pointer on a line of the object until it turns into an arrow with a four-headed arrow attached.
2. Hold down the Ctrl key, then the left mouse button, drag the outline to the new location, then release the left mouse button, and then the Ctrl key.

Go To
Exercise
4

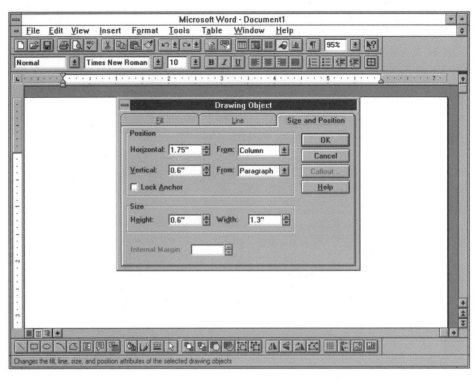

## Sizing an Object

With the sizing handles that appear around an object when it is selected, the size of the object can be changed. For example, to make an object wider, you would complete the following steps:

1.  Select the object.
2.  Position the I-beam pointer or the arrow pointer on the middle sizing handle at the left or right side of the object until it turns into a double-headed arrow.
3.  Hold down the left mouse button, drag the outline of the shape away from the center of the object until it is the desired size, then release the mouse button.

You would complete similar steps as those above to make an object thinner, taller, or shorter. If you want to change the width and height of the object at the same time, use one of the corner sizing handles.

A selected object can also be sized at the Drawing Object dialog box with the Size and Position tab selected as shown in figure 19.4. To display this dialog box, select an object, then choose Format, then Drawing Object. At the Drawing Object dialog box, select the Size and Position tab. You can also display the Drawing Object dialog box by positioning the I-beam pointer on any line of an object until it turns into an arrow pointer with a four-headed arrow attached, then double-clicking the left mouse button. At the Drawing Object dialog box, select the Size and Position tab.

At the Drawing Object dialog box with the Size and Position tab selected, you can specify the distance you want the object positioned horizontally from the margin, page, or column. You can also specify the vertical distance for the object relative to the margin, page, or paragraph. The height and width of the selected object can be specified at this dialog box. These options are similar to the options you learned about in chapter 18 for sizing frames.

## ■ *Customizing Objects*

With buttons on the Drawing toolbar, you can add fill color or pattern to an enclosed object, change the thickness and color of the line that draws the object, and change the position of the object. Although fill and line color will display on the screen, they will print in color only if you are using a color printer.

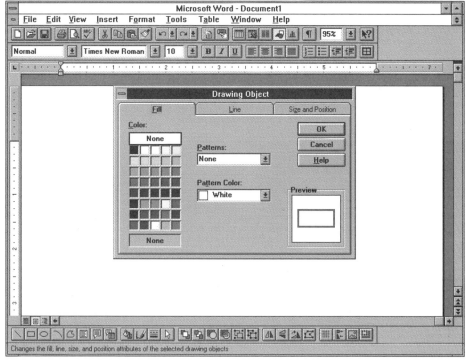

Figure 19.5
*Fill Color Options*

## Adding Fill Shading or Color

With the Fill Color button on the Drawing toolbar, shading or color can be added to an enclosed object such as a shape or a text box. To add shading or color to an enclosed object, you would complete the following steps:

1. Select the object to which you want shading or color added.
2. Click on the Fill Color button on the Drawing toolbar (the ninth button from the left).
3. At the pop-up menu that displays as shown in figure 19.5, click on the desired shade or color.
4. Click in the document screen outside the object to deselect it.

You can also add fill color and pattern to an object at the Drawing Object dialog box with the Fill tab selected as shown in figure 19.6.

Figure 19.6
*Drawing Object
Dialog Box with Fill
Tab Selected*

To display the Drawing Object dialog box, position the I-beam pointer on any line of an object until it turns into an arrow with a four-headed arrow attached, then double-click the left mouse button. You can also display the Drawing Object dialog box by selecting the drawing object, then choosing Format, Drawing Object.

At the Drawing Object dialog box with the Fill tab selected, change the fill color with options in the Color section; add a pattern to the selected object with options from the Patterns drop-down menu; and add a color to the pattern with the Pattern Color option. The preview box in the lower right corner of the dialog box displays how the object will appear in the document screen.

## Changing Line Color

Draw uses a black line when drawing shapes or creating a text box. The color of this line can be changed with the Line Color button on the Drawing toolbar. Clicking on the Line Color button (tenth button from the left) causes a pop-up menu to display with the same shading and color options as the Fill Color button. Change line color in the same manner as adding color or shading to an enclosed object.

In some situations, you may want to remove the line around an object. For example, you may want to remove the lines of a text box after text has been added to it. To remove lines, select the object, click on the Line Color button, then click on *None*.

## Changing Line Style

By default, Word draws shapes and text boxes with a thin black line. This line can be changed to a thicker line, a broken line, or a line with an arrow pointer. To change the line style, choose an option from the Line Style button. For example, to change the line style to a thick line, you would complete the following steps:

1. Select the object containing lines you want thicker.
2. Click on the Line Style button on the Drawing toolbar.
3. From the pop-up menu that displays as shown in figure 19.7, click on the fourth line from the top.
4. Deselect the object.

*Figure 19.7*
*Line Style Options*

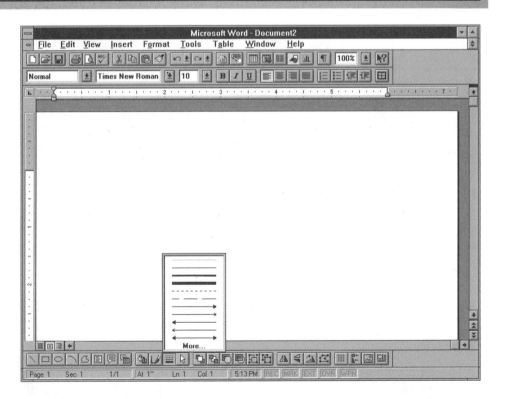

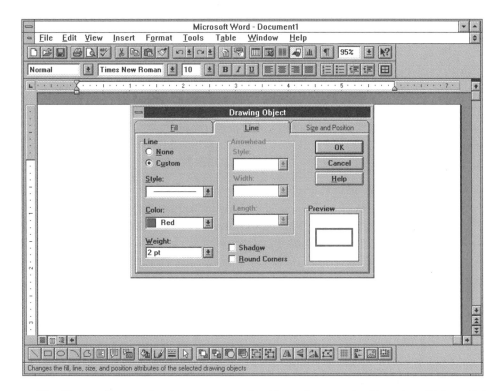

Figure 19.8
Drawing Object
Dialog Box with
Line Tab Selected

The line style can also be customized with options at the Drawing Object dialog box with the Line tab selected as shown in figure 19.8.

At the Drawing Object dialog box with the Line tab selected, you can choose a line color and style. You can also add a shadow to the selected object by choosing the Shadow option. Choose the Round Corners option to round the corners of the selected object. This option is dimmed if the selected object does not contain corners (such as a circle or oval).

If you change the line style to an arrowhead, you can change the style, width, and length of the arrowhead line.

## Moving an Object Front/Back

Objects created in Draw can overlap. With the Bring to Front and Send to Back buttons on the Drawing toolbar, you can bring an object to the front or move it to the back.

If an object overlaps and is in front of another, it can be moved behind by selecting the front object, then clicking on the Send to Back button (the fourteenth button from the left). To bring the back object to the front, select the object, then click on the Bring to Front button (the thirteenth button from the left).

## Moving an Object in Front or Behind Text

A Word document contains three levels, the text layer, a layer in front of the text, and a layer behind. The text layer is the one in which you generally work in a document. An object created by the Draw program can be drawn in a document containing text. By default, the object will display in front of the text layer, covering the text. If you want the object and the text in the document to display, move the object behind the text.

Use the Send Behind Text button (the sixteenth button from the left) on the Drawing toolbar to send the selected object behind the text layer. If an object displays behind the text layer, it can be moved in front of the text layer with the Bring in Front of Text button (the eighteenth button from the left).

As an example of how to send a selected object behind text in a document, you would complete the following steps:

1. Open a document containing text.
2. Draw an object with the Draw program.
3. Select the object.
4. Click on the Send Behind Text button on the Drawing toolbar.
5. Deselect the object.

## Flipping and Rotating an Object

Use the Flip Horizontal and Flip Vertical buttons on the Drawing toolbar to flip the display of a selected object. If you click on the Flip Horizontal button, the selected object reverses left and right. If you click on the Flip Vertical, the selected object reverses top and bottom.

Click on the Rotate Right button on the Drawing toolbar to rotate the shape or object 90 degrees to the right. If you rotate a text box, the box rotates but the text does not.

## Reshaping an Object

If an object is drawn with the Freeform tool, that object can be reshaped using the Reshape button on the Drawing toolbar. When you select an object, then click on the Reshape button, the selected object displays with a large number of sizing handles. To reshape an object drawn with Freeform, you would complete the following steps:

1. Select the object.
2. Click on the Reshape button on the Drawing toolbar.
3. Position the I-beam pointer on one of the sizing handles until it turns into cross hairs, hold the left mouse button down, drag the mouse to reshape that portion of the object, then release the mouse button.

## ■ Creating Callouts

Callouts are a useful tool for identifying parts of an illustration or picture. Many figures in this textbook include callouts identifying Word features. For example, figure 19.1 includes a callout identifying the Drawing toolbar.

Callouts can be created with the Callout button on the Drawing toolbar. To create a callout, you would complete the following steps:

1. Click on the Callout button (the seventh button from the left).
2. Position the cross hairs at the location where you want the callout to point.
3. Hold down the left mouse button, drag to the location where callout text is to display, then release the mouse button. (This inserts a text box in the document screen.)
4. Key the callout text in the text box.
5. Deselect the callout text box.

## Formatting a Callout

Earlier in this chapter, you learned that color can be added to a selected object and the line color and style can be customized. These same options are available for a callout. To customize a callout, select the callout, then make the desired changes.

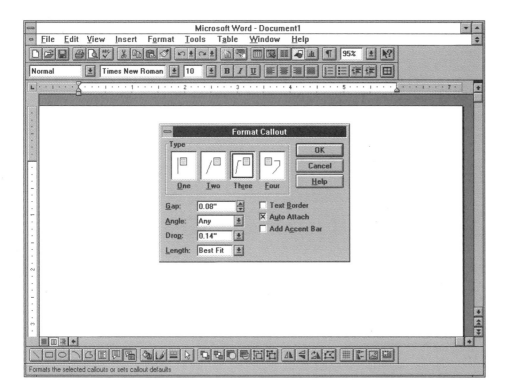

*Figure 19.9*
*Format Callout*
*Dialog Box*

In addition to changing the line and fill color and style, a callout can be customized at the Format Callout dialog box. To display the Format Callout dialog box shown in figure 19.9, select a callout, then click on the Format Callout button on the Drawing toolbar.

With the choices in the Type section of the dialog box, you can specify whether a callout uses a straight line (choices One and Two), a two-part line (choice Three), or a three-part line (choice Four).

Use the Gap option to specify the distance between the callout line and the callout text. Choose Angle if you want to change the angle by degrees. Use the Drop option to select the position where the callout line attaches to the callout text. This can be an exact distance from the top or attached to the top, center, or bottom. The Length option at the Format Callout dialog box has a default setting of *Best Fit*. At this setting, Word determines the best length for the callout line. If you want the callout line to be a specific length, choose Length, then key the measurement.

If you want a border around the callout text, choose Text Border in the Format Callout dialog box. This inserts an X in the check box. Choose the Auto Attach option if you want the callout line at the bottom of the callout text when text is to the left of the callout line. If you choose the Add Accent Bar option, a vertical line will be inserted next to the callout line.

Changes made to the Format Callout dialog box stay in effect for the current and future callouts.

# Framing an Object

If an object is drawn using a button on the Drawing toolbar in a document containing text, the object is positioned in front of the text or it can be positioned behind. If you want the text in the document to wrap around the object, it must be framed.

To frame an object, select the object, then click on the Insert Frame button on the Drawing toolbar (the last button at the right side of the toolbar.)

# Using the Grid

A drawing grid can be used when drawing a shape or box with the Draw program. The grid contains invisible intersecting lines that constrain the cross hairs within the lines. With the grid turned on, an object is pulled into alignment with the nearest intersection of grid lines. This is referred to as the *snap-to-grid* effect.

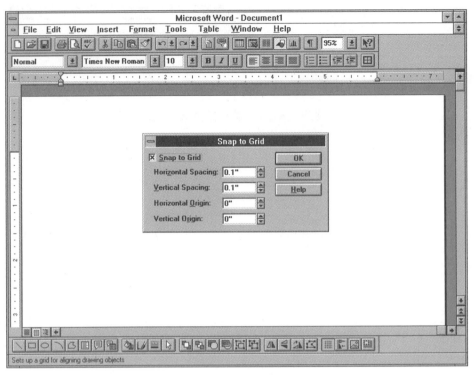

*Figure 19.10*
*Snap to Grid Dialog*
*Box*

You can turn on the grid, specify the vertical and horizontal spacing, and specify the horizontal and vertical origin of the lines at the Snap to Grid dialog box shown in figure 19.10. To display the Snap to Grid dialog box, click on the Snap to Grid button (fourth button from the right) on the Drawing toolbar.

To turn on the grid, choose the Snap to Grid option at the Snap to Grid dialog box. This inserts an X in the check box. The default spacing for the grid lines is 0.1 inches. This can be changed with the Horizontal Spacing and Vertical Spacing options. For example, to increase the horizontal and vertical space between grid lines, increase the number in each of these options.

The grid, by default, begins in the upper left corner of the page. You can change this with the Horizontal Origin and Vertical Origin options. The change made to these options changes the point from which Word starts to measure the horizontal and vertical grid lines.

To turn off the snap-to-grid effect, click on the Snap to Grid button on the Drawing toolbar, then choose Snap to Grid at the Snap to Grid dialog box.

The snap-to-grid effect can also be turned on by holding down the Alt key while you draw an object. If the snap-to-grid effect is turned on, holding down the Alt key while you draw an object will turn it off.

## ■ *Aligning Objects*

Selected objects can be aligned with options at the Align dialog box. To display the Align dialog box shown in figure 19.11, select the objects you want aligned, then click on the Align Drawing Objects button (the third button from the right) on the Drawing toolbar.

At the Align dialog box, you can specify the horizontal and vertical alignment of the selected objects. For example, you can align the objects horizontally at the left side of the objects, the center of the objects, or the right side of the objects. Selected objects can be aligned vertically at the top of the objects, the center, or the bottom. The alignment of the objects can be relative to each other or the page.

Go To
Exercise
11

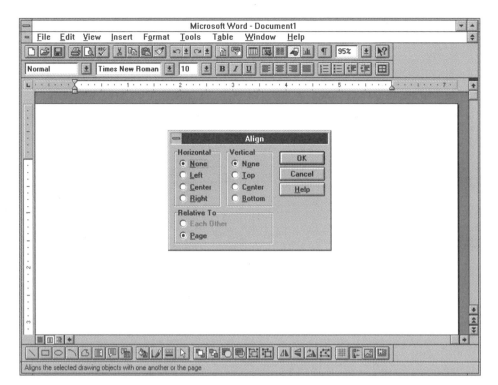

Figure 19.11
*Align Dialog Box*

# ■ *G*rouping and *U*ngrouping *O*bjects

You learned in an earlier section of this chapter how to select one object or how to select several objects. All objects can be included in one group with the Group button (the tenth button from the right) on the Drawing toolbar. With the Group button, you can group two or more objects together as a single unit. Grouped objects are faster and easier for Word to manipulate.

To group objects, you would complete the following steps:

1. Click on the Select Drawing Objects button on the Drawing toolbar.
2. Position the cross hairs in the upper left corner of the area containing the objects.
3. Hold down the left mouse button, drag the outline to the lower right corner of the area containing the objects, then release the mouse button.
4. Click on the Group button on the Drawing toolbar.

To ungroup objects, select the objects using the Select Drawing Objects button, then click on the Ungroup button (the eleventh button from the right) on the Drawing toolbar.

## CHAPTER SUMMARY

- Create your own shapes and images with Word's Draw program. With Draw, you can draw shapes, draw freehand, and create and customize text.
- To use the Draw program, display the Drawing toolbar and change the viewing mode to Page Layout. Click the left mouse button on the desired drawing button on the Drawing toolbar.
- In Draw, you can create a box and then insert text inside the box.
- Shapes and text boxes created in Draw, called objects, can be customized. For example, an object can be selected then moved, copied, or deleted. You can also change the size of an object.
- When an object is selected, it displays with sizing handles.
- With buttons on the Drawing toolbar, you can add fill color or pattern to an enclosed object, change thickness and color of the line that draws the object, and change the position of the object.

- Objects created in Draw can overlap. With the Bring to Front and Send to Back buttons on the Drawing toolbar, you can bring an object to the front or move it to the back. You can also move an object in front or behind text.
- Callouts can be created with the Callout button on the Drawing toolbar. A callout can be customized at the Format Callout dialog box.
- If you want the text in the document to wrap around an object, the object must be framed.
- A drawing grid can be used when drawing a shape or box with the Draw program. With the grid turned on, an object is pulled into alignment with the nearest intersection of grid lines.
- Selected objects can be aligned with options at the Align dialog box.
- With the Group button on the Drawing toolbar, you can group two or more objects together as a single unit. Grouped objects are faster and easier for Word to manipulate.

## COMMANDS REVIEW

|  | Mouse | Keyboard |
|---|---|---|
| Display Drawing toolbar | Click on Drawing button on Standard toolbar; or position arrow pointer in gray area of any displayed toolbar, click right mouse button, click on Drawing | View, Toolbars, select Drawing, then press Enter |
| Format Callout dialog box | Click on Format Callout button on Drawing toolbar | |
| Turn on grid | Click on Snap to Grid button on Drawing toolbar, then choose Snap to Grid | |

## CHECK YOUR UNDERSTANDING

**True/False:** Circle the letter T if the statement is true; circle the letter F if the statement is false.

T    F    1.    The Drawing toolbar displays at the bottom of the screen.

T    F    2.    Be sure the viewing mode is Normal when using buttons on the Drawing toolbar.

T    F    3.    If more than one object is selected, dragging one will also drag the other objects.

T    F    4.    By default, Word draws shapes and text boxes with a thin black line.

T    F    5.    A Word document contains three levels: the text layer, a layer in front of the text, and a layer behind the text.

T    F    6.    To reverse a selected object from top to bottom, click on the Flip Horizontal button on the Drawing toolbar.

T    F    7.    An object drawn with the Freeform button can be reshaped using the Reshape button on the Drawing toolbar.

T    F    8.    The snap-to-grid effect can be turned on by holding down the Alt key while you draw an object.

T    F    9.    Once objects have been grouped, this grouping cannot be changed.

T    F    10.    If you rotate a text box, the box rotates but the text does not.

**Completion:** In the space provided at the right, indicate the correct term, command, or number.

1. This program is included with Word for Windows and provides many of the features of a standalone draw program. _____

2. If you draw a shape with any button except the Line button, the shape is considered to be this. _____

3. To create a box in Draw and then insert text inside the box, click on this button on the Drawing toolbar. _____

4. To select one object, position the I-beam pointer on the object until the pointer turns into this. _____

5. To change the width and height of an object at the same time, use one of these sizing handles. _____

6. The line style of an object can be customized with options at this dialog box. _____

7. This is a useful tool for identifying parts of an illustration or picture. _____

8. At this dialog box you can specify the horizontal and vertical alignment of selected objects. _____

9. The five buttons on the Drawing toolbar you can use to draw shapes are Line, Rectangle, Freeform, Ellipse, and this. _____

10. If you want to draw the same shape more than once, do this on the shape button on the Drawing toolbar. _____

## AT THE COMPUTER

### Exercise 1

1. At a clear document screen, draw a circle and a square using Draw by completing the following steps:
   a. Change to the Page Layout viewing mode.
   b. Click on the Draw button on the Standard toolbar to turn on the display of the Drawing toolbar. (Skip this step if the Drawing toolbar is already displayed.)
   c. Position the arrow pointer on the Ellipse tool, then click the left mouse button.
   d. Position the cross hairs in the document screen towards the left side.
   e. Hold down the Shift key and the left mouse button, drag the mouse down and to the right until the outline image displays as approximately a 2-inch circle, then release the mouse button, then the Shift key.
   f. Click on the Rectangle button on the Drawing toolbar.
   g. Position the cross hairs in the document screen toward the right side.
   h. Hold down the Shift key and the left mouse button, drag the mouse down and to the right until the outline image displays as approximately a 2-inch square, then release the mouse button, then the Shift key.
2. Save the document and name it c19ex01.
3. Print c19ex01.
4. Close c19ex01.

### Exercise 2

1. At a clear document screen, write your first name using Draw by completing the following steps:
   a. Change to the Page Layout viewing mode.
   b. Make sure the Drawing toolbar is displayed. (If not, click on the Drawing button on the Standard toolbar.)
   c. Click on the Freeform button.

    d. Position the cross hairs in the document screen, hold down the left mouse button, then move the mouse in the necessary directions to draw your first name. When finished, double-click the left mouse button. (If you are not satisfied with the results, close the document without saving it, then start again.)

2. Save the document and name it c19ex02.
3. Print c19ex02.
4. Close c19ex02.

## Exercise 3

1. At a clear document screen, create an oval shape, then create a text box inside the oval with the words *Mariah Jackson* and *Vice President* by completing the following steps:
    a. Change to the Page Layout viewing mode.
    b. Make sure the Drawing toolbar is displayed.
    c. Click on the Ellipse button.
    d. Position the cross hairs in the document screen (approximately below the 1.5-inch mark on the horizontal ruler), hold down the left mouse button, drag the mouse down and to the right until you have drawn an oval that is approximately 3 inches wide and 2 inches tall, then release the mouse button.
    e. Click on the Text Box button.
    f. Draw a text box inside the oval shape from the left side to the right side that is approximately an inch tall.
    g. Click on the Center button on the Formatting toolbar, then press the Enter key once.
    h. Key **Mariah Jackson** in the text box, then press Enter.
    i. Key **Vice President.** (The name and title should be centered vertically in the oval. If not, insert or delete hard returns until the text appears centered.)

2. Save the document and name it c19ex03.
3. Print c19ex03.
4. Close c19ex03.

## Exercise 4

1. At a clear document screen, create the organizational chart shown in figure 19.12 by completing the following steps:
    a. Change to the Page Layout viewing mode.
    b. Make sure the Drawing toolbar is displayed.
    c. Click on the Text Box button on the Drawing toolbar.
    d. Draw a text box from approximately the 2-inch mark on the horizontal ruler to the 4-inch mark on the ruler.
    e. Change the font to 12-point Times New Roman Bold.
    f. Press Enter to move the insertion point down one line inside the text box.
    g. Click on the Center button on the Formatting toolbar.
    h. Key **Allison St. Germaine**.
    i. Press Enter, then key **President**.
    j. Position the I-beam pointer at the bottom of the text box until it turns into an arrow with a four-headed arrow attached.
    k. Hold down the Ctrl key and the left mouse button, drag the outline of the text box down and to the left as shown in figure 19.12, then release the left mouse button. (Do not release the Ctrl key.)
    l. With the Ctrl key still down, hold down the left mouse button, drag the outline of the text box to the right as shown in figure 19.12, then release the mouse button, then the Ctrl key.
    m. After copying the text box, key the names and titles shown in figure 19.12 in the second and third text boxes over the name *Allison St. Germaine* and *President*.

2. Save the document and name it c19ex04.
3. Print c19ex04.
4. Close c19ex04.

Figure 19.12

**Allison St. Germaine**
**President**

**Mariah Jackson**
**Vice President**

**Kenneth Levine**
**Vice President**

## Exercise 5

1. At a clear document screen, create a text box, key text in the box, then size the box by completing the following steps:
   a. Change to the Page Layout viewing mode.
   b. Make sure the Drawing toolbar is displayed.
   c. Click on the Text Box button, then draw a text box in the document screen that is approximately 2 inches wide and 2.5 inches tall.
   d. With the insertion point inside the text box, change the font to 14-point Arial Bold.
   e. Click on the Center align button on the Formatting toolbar.
   f. Key **ST. FRANCIS MEDICAL CENTER** (this will wrap).
   g. Press the Enter key.
   h. Key **300 Blue Ridge Boulevard** (this will also wrap).
   i. Press Enter.
   j. Key **Kansas City, MO 63009**.
   k. Press Enter.
   l. Key **(816) 555-2000**.
   m. Select the text box, then use the sizing handles around the text box to make the box wider until the company name displays on one line and you can see all the text.
   n. Move the text box to the middle of the document screen.
2. Save the document and name it c19ex05.
3. Print c19ex05.
4. Close c19ex05.

## Exercise 6

1. Open c19ex03.
2. Save the document with Save As and name it c19ex06.
3. Change the fill color of the oval shape by completing the following steps:
   a. Select the oval shape by positioning the I-beam pointer on the line that forms the oval until it turns into an arrow with a four-headed arrow attached, then clicking the left mouse button.
   b. Click on the Fill Color button on the Drawing toolbar.
   c. At the palette that displays, click on the blue button (the first button from the left in the third row from the bottom).
   d. Select the text box.
   e. Click on the Fill Color button on the Drawing toolbar.
   f. At the palette that displays, click on the cyan button (the second button from the left in the third row from the bottom).

4. Save the document again with the same name (c19ex06).
5. Print c19ex06.
6. Change the fill color back to None. To do this, click on the Fill Color button on the Drawing toolbar, then click on *None* (at the top of the palette).
7. Close c19ex06.

## Exercise 7

1. Open c19ex04.
2. Save the document with Save As and name it c19ex07.
3. Change the line style and color of the top box by completing the following steps:
   a. Position the I-beam pointer on one of the lines of the text box containing the name *Allison St. Germaine* until it turns into an arrow with a four-headed arrow attached, then double-click the left mouse button. (This displays the Drawing Object dialog box.)
   b. At the Drawing Object dialog box, make sure the Line tab is selected.
   c. Click on the down-pointing arrow to the right of the Color option in the Drawing Object dialog box, then click on *Red*.
   d. Click on the down-pointing arrow to the right of the Weight option, then click on *4 pt*.
   e. Choose Round Corners.
   f. Choose OK or press Enter to close the Drawing Object dialog box.
4. Complete steps similar to those in 3a through 3f to change the line style and color for the text box at the left (containing the name *Mariah Jackson*).
5. Complete steps similar to those in 3a through 3f to change the line style and color for the text box at the right (containing the name *Kenneth Levine*).
6. Save the document again with the same name (c19ex07).
7. Print c19ex07.
8. Return the line color and weight back to the default and remove rounded corners by completing the following steps:
   a. Choose Format, Drawing Object.
   b. At the Drawing Defaults dialog box (called the Drawing Object dialog box if an object is selected) with the Line tab selected, make the following changes:
      (1) Click on the down-pointing arrow to the right of the Color option, then click on *Black*.
      (2) Click on the down-pointing arrow to the right of the Weight option, then click on *3/4 pt*.
      (3) Choose Round Corners. (This removes the X from the check box.)
   c. Choose OK or press Enter to close the Drawing Defaults dialog box.
9. Close c19ex07.

## Exercise 8

1. Open notice01.
2. Save the document with Save As and name it c19ex08.
3. Create a text box in the document, then insert a picture inside the box by completing the following steps:
   a. Change to the Page Layout viewing mode.
   b. Make sure the Drawing toolbar is displayed.
   c. Click on the Text Box button.
   d. Draw a box from the second line of the first paragraph beginning at approximately the 2-inch mark on the horizontal ruler to the first line of the last paragraph ending at approximately the 4-inch mark on the horizontal ruler.
   e. Choose Insert, then Picture.
   f. At the Insert Picture dialog box, double-click on *party.wmf* in the File Name list box. (You will need to click on the down-pointing arrow to the right of the list box to make *party.wmf* visible.)

g. Select the text box, click on the Line Color button, then click on *None* at the color palette.
h. With the text box still selected, click on the Send Behind Text button.
i. Deselect the text box.
4. Save the document again with the same name (c19ex08).
5. Print c19ex08.
6. Click on the Line Color button, then click on the black button (first button on the left in the second row).
7. Close c19ex08.

## Exercise 9

1. Open c19ex04.
2. Save the document with Save As and name it c19ex09.
3. Rotate the top text box by completing the following steps:
   a. Select the top text box (containing the name *Allison St. Germaine*).
   b. Click once on the Rotate Right button on the Drawing toolbar.
4. Complete steps similar to those in 3a and 3b to rotate the text box at the left (containing the name *Mariah Jackson*).
5. Complete steps similar to those in 3a and 3b to rotate the text box at the right (containing the name *Kenneth Levine*).
6. Resize the boxes to fit more closely to the text inside the boxes.
7. Save the document again with the same name (c19ex09).
8. Print c19ex09.
9. Close c19ex09.

## Exercise 10

1. At a clear document screen, insert the butterfly picture shown in figure 19.13 and add the callouts as shown by completing the following steps:
   a. Change to the Page Layout viewing mode.
   b. Make sure the Drawing toolbar is displayed.
   c. Click on the Center button on the Formatting toolbar.
   d. Change the alignment of the document to center. (Do this with the Vertical Alignment option at the Page Setup dialog box with the Layout tab selected.)
   e. Insert the butterfly picture by completing the following steps:
      (1) Choose Insert, then Picture.
      (2) At the Insert Picture dialog box, double-click on *buttrfly.wmf*.
   f. Create the callout for the antennae by completing the following steps:
      (1) Click on the Format Callout button on the Drawing toolbar.
      (2) At the Format dialog box choose Two in the Type section.
      (3) Choose Drop, then Bottom.
      (4) Choose OK or press Enter.
      (5) Click on the Callout button on the Drawing toolbar.
      (6) Position the cross hairs on the antennae, hold down the left mouse button, drag the line to the left (make sure the line is straight and not jagged), then release the mouse button.
      (7) With the insertion point inside the callout box, press the Enter key until the insertion point is positioned in the bottom of the box by the callout line.
      (8) Click on the Align Right button on the Formatting toolbar. (This moves the insertion point closer to the callout line.)
      (9) Key **Antennae**.

g. Complete steps similar to those in 1f(5) through 1f(9) to create a callout for *Front Wing* and another for *Back Wing* as shown in figure 19.13. (Make sure the text in the callout box fits on one line. If not, size the box and make it wider.)

2. Save the document and name it c19ex10.
3. Print c19ex10.
4. Close c19ex10.

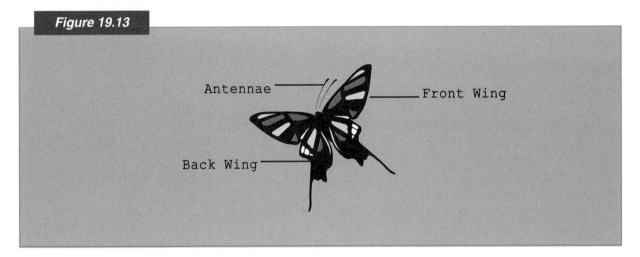

**Figure 19.13**

## Exercise 11

1. At a clear document screen, create the text boxes (in the unarranged form) as shown in figure 19.14 by completing the following steps:
   a. Change to the Page Layout viewing mode.
   b. Make sure the Drawing toolbar is displayed.
   c. Change the alignment of the document to center. (Do this with the Vertical Alignment option at the Page Setup dialog box with the Layout tab selected.)
   d. Turn on the snap-to-grid effect by completing the following steps:
      (1) Click on the Snap to Grid button on the Drawing toolbar.
      (2) At the Snap to Grid dialog box, choose Snap to Grid to insert an X in the check box. (Skip this step if the box already contains an X.)
      (3) Choose OK or press Enter.
   e. Click on the Text Box button, then draw a text box that is approximately 1.5 inches wide and 1 inch tall.
   f. Key the name, *Brenda Hogue,* and the title, *Director*, in the text box by completing the following steps:
      (1) With the insertion point inside the text box, change the font to 12-point Times New Roman Bold.
      (2) Press the Enter key at least once to better center the insertion point vertically in the text box.
      (3) Press Ctrl + E or click on the Center button on the Formatting toolbar to horizontally center the insertion point.
      (4) Key **Brenda Hogue**.
      (5) Press Enter.
      (6) Key **Director**.
   g. If the text does not look centered in the text box, size the box.
   h. Copy the text box three times below the first box as shown in figure 19.14.
   i. After copying the text box, key the names and titles shown in figure 19.14 in the second, third, and fourth text boxes over the name *Brenda Hogue* and the title *Director*.
   j. Align the boxes horizontally at the left by completing the following steps:
      (1) Click on the down-pointing arrow to the right of the Zoom Control button on the Standard toolbar, then click on *Whole Page*.

(2) Click on the Select Drawing Objects button on the Drawing toolbar.

(3) Draw a box around all four boxes.

(4) Click on the Align Drawing Objects button on the Drawing toolbar.

(5) At the Align dialog box, choose Left in the Horizontal section of the dialog box.

(6) Choose OK or press Enter.

(7) Change the view back to 100%.

2. Save the document and name it c19ex11.

3. Print c19ex11.

4. Turn off the snap-to-grid effect by completing steps 1d(1) through 1d(3).

5. Close c19ex11.

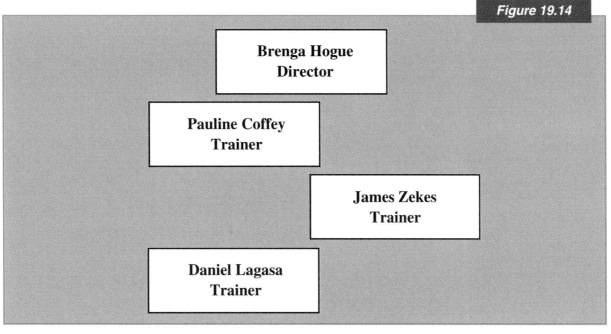

**Figure 19.14**

## Exercise 12

1. At a clear document screen, create the shapes shown in figure 19.15 by completing the following steps:

a. Change to the Page Layout viewing mode.

b. Make sure the Drawing toolbar is displayed.

c. Click on the Line Style button on the Drawing toolbar, then click on the third option from the top of the palette.

d. Use the Line button on the Drawing toolbar to draw a triangle about the size shown in figure 19.15. (You will need to click on the Line button before drawing each side of the triangle.)

e. After drawing the triangle, select it, then group it by completing the following steps:

(1) Click on the Select Drawing Objects button on the Drawing toolbar.

(2) Draw a box around the triangle.

(3) Click on the Group button on the Drawing toolbar.

f. With the triangle selected, copy it two times to the right.

g. Select the second triangle, then click on the Flip Vertical button on the Drawing toolbar.

h. Select then move the second and the third triangles until they are closer together as shown in figure 19.15.

2. Save the document and name it c19ex12.

3. Print c19ex12.

4. Click on the Line Style button on the Drawing toolbar, then click on the second option from the top of the palette. (This returns the line back to the default thickness.)

5. Close c19ex12.

*Figure 19.15*

## SKILL ASSESSMENTS

### Assessment 1

1. At a clear document screen, draw the square, circle, and rectangle shown in figure 19.16. After drawing the shapes, make the following changes:
   a. Select each shape, click on the Line Style button on the Drawing toolbar, then click on the third option from the top. (This makes the line thicker.)
   b. Add red fill to the circle, yellow fill to the square, and blue fill to the rectangle.
2. Save the document and name it c19sa01.
3. Print c19sa01.
4. Click on the Line Style button on the Drawing toolbar, then click on the second option from the top of the palette. (This returns the line thickness back to the default.)
5. Click on the Fill Color button on the Drawing toolbar, then click on *None*.
6. Close c19sa01.

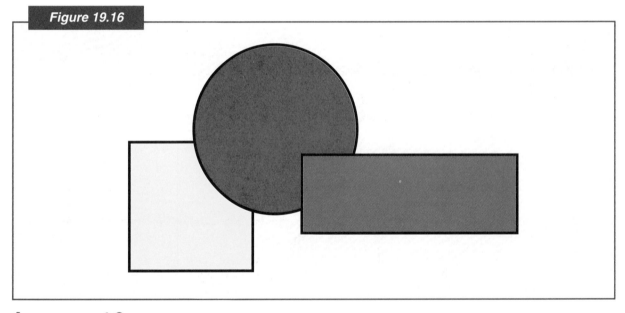

*Figure 19.16*

### Assessment 2

1. At a clear document screen, create the organizational chart shown in figure 19.17 with the following specifications:
   a. Create the first text box with rounded corners and cyan (light blue) fill. Change the font to 12-point Times New Roman Bold for the text.
   b. After creating the first text box, copy the text box the number of times needed for the document. Change the title inside the boxes as shown in figure 19.17.
   c. Use the Line button on the Drawing toolbar to create the lines connecting the rectangles.
2. Save the document with Save As and name it c19sa02.

3. Print c19sa02.
4. Display the Drawing Defaults dialog box, select the Line tab, then choose Round Corners (this removes the X from the check box). Select the Fill tab, then change the Color to *None*.
5. Close c19sa02.

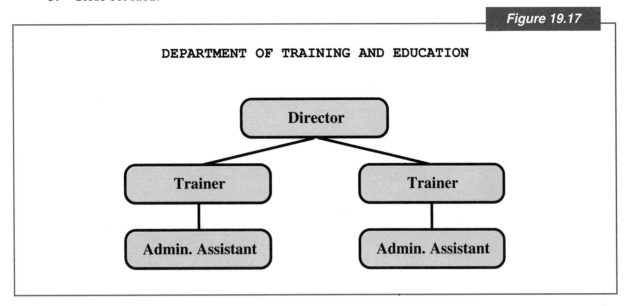

**Figure 19.17**

DEPARTMENT OF TRAINING AND EDUCATION

## Assessment 3

1. Open c19ex11.
2. Save the document with Save As and name it c19sa03.
3. Make the following changes to each text box:
    a. Display the Drawing Objects dialog box with the Line tab selected, then change the weight of the line to 2 points, the color of the line to blue, and round the corners.
    b. Change the fill color to cyan (light blue).
    c. Draw a line between each box (to connect the boxes).
4. Save the document again with the same name (c19sa03).
5. Print c19sa03.
6. Display the Drawing Defaults dialog box, select the Line tab, then change the Weight to *3/4 pt*. Select the Fill tab, then change the Color to *None*.
7. Close c19sa03.

## Assessment 4

1. At a clear document screen, create the document shown in figure 19.18 using the Draw program.
2. Save the document and name it c19sa04.
3. Print c19sa04.
4. Return line style and color back to the default settings.
5. Close c19sa04.

**Figure 19.18**

# Using WordArt & Equation Editor 20

Upon completion of chapter 20, you will be able to enhance the visual appeal of documents with text created with WordArt. You will also be able to create equations in a document using the equation editor.

Word provides supplementary applications including an application called WordArt that you can use to modify and conform text to a variety of shapes and an equation editor named Microsoft Equation 2.0. These applications use object linking and embedding (OLE) to create and add objects to a Word document. Use the WordArt application to create text in a variety of shapes and alignments and add 3-D effects. Use the Equation Editor to apply formatting to mathematical elements such as integers, fractions, and exponents.

To complete this chapter, the WordArt and Equation Editor applications must be installed. Check with your instructor before proceeding with this chapter.

## ■ Using WordArt

With the WordArt application, you can distort or modify text to conform to a variety of shapes. This is useful for creating company logos and headings. With WordArt, you can change the font, style, and alignment of text. You can also add a shadow to the text, use different fills and outlines, and resize the text.

To enter WordArt, choose Insert, then Object. At the Object dialog box with the Create New tab selected as shown in figure 20.1, double-click on *Microsoft WordArt 2.0* in the Object Type list box.

When you double-click on *Microsoft WordArt 2.0*, a text entry box displays in the document screen as well as a WordArt text box as shown in figure 20.2. A WordArt menu bar and toolbar replace the normal Menu bar and the Standard and Formatting toolbars.

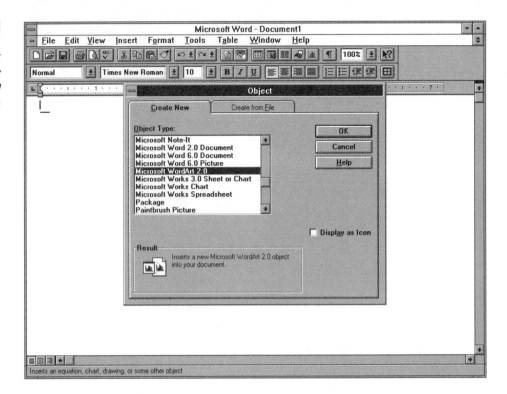

Figure 20.1
Object Dialog Box
with Create New
Tab Selected

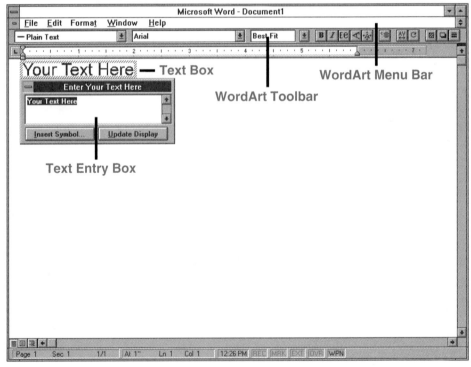

Figure 20.2
WordArt Screen

## Entering Text

When you first enter the WordArt application, the insertion point is positioned in the Enter Your Text Here text entry box. The words *Enter Your Text Here* display in the text entry box and are selected. Key the text in the text entry box and the original words are removed. Press the Enter key if you want to move the insertion point to the next line.

To view how the text you enter will display in the text box, choose the Update Display button at the right side of the text entry box. By default, WordArt uses *Best Fit* when displaying text in the text box. For example, a short word in the text box will display larger than several words will display in the text box.

If you want to insert a symbol in the text entry box, choose Insert Symbol. This option displays at the left side of the text entry box. When you choose Insert Symbol, the Symbol dialog box displays. This is the same dialog box you learned about in chapter 5.

After keying text in the text entry box, remove the box. To do this with the mouse, click outside the text entry box. You can also remove the text entry box by clicking on the document control button (the button with the hyphen) in the upper left corner of the text entry box, then clicking on Close. If you are using the keyboard, press Alt + F4.

## Sizing a WordArt Text Box

Text in a WordArt text box can be sized. To do this, select the text in the WordArt text box by positioning the I-beam pointer in the text box, then clicking the left mouse button. Use the sizing handles that display around the WordArt text box to increase or decrease the size of the text.

## Changing Shapes

The WordArt toolbar contains buttons for customizing the WordArt text. Figure 20.3 displays the WordArt toolbar with the buttons identified.

When you click on the down-pointing arrow to the right of the Line and Shape button, a palette of line and shape options displays as shown in figure 20.4.

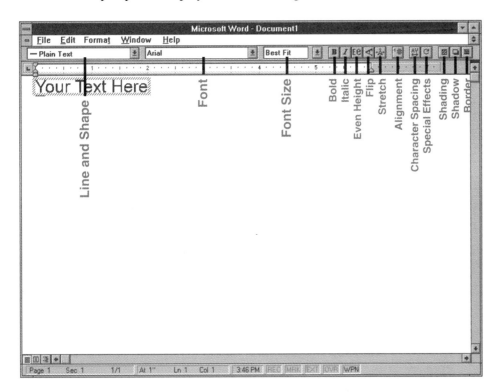

*Figure 20.3
WordArt Toolbar
Buttons*

Figure 20.4
Line and Shape
Palette

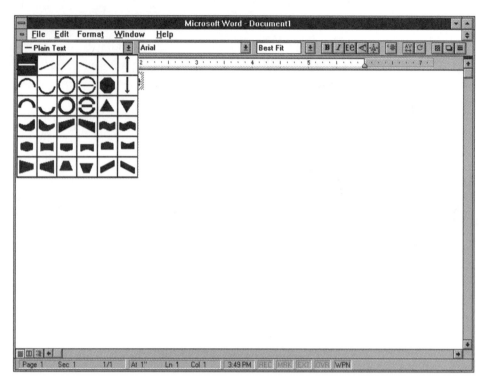

With the choices from the Line and Shape palette shown in figure 20.4, you can conform text to a variety of shapes. To select a shape, click on the desired shape. The text in the text box will conform to the selected shape. If you want to return text to the default shape, click on the first shape in the first row.

As an example of how to use WordArt, you would complete the following steps to create the text *Rollins High School* and shape it in a semi-circle:

1. At a clear document screen, choose Insert, Object.
2. At the Object dialog box make sure the Create New tab is selected, then select *Microsoft WordArt 2.0* in the Object Type list box.
3. Choose OK or press Enter. (You can also just double-click on *Microsoft WordArt 2.0*.)
4. Key **Rollins High School** in the text entry box.
5. Choose Update Display. (This displays *Rollins High School* in the text box in the document screen.)
6. Click on the down-pointing arrow to the right of the Line and Shape button on the WordArt toolbar.
7. Click on the first shape in the second row (the semi-circle shape).
8. Click in the document screen outside the text entry box to remove the text entry box.
9. Click in the document screen outside the text box to deselect the box.

## Changing Fonts

More than likely, WordArt applies the Arial font to text. (This may vary, depending on your printer.) You can change to a different font with options at the Font drop-down menu. To display this menu, click on the Font button on the WordArt toolbar. Click on the desired font at the drop-down menu. When you change to a different font, the text in the text box reflects the new font.

With options from the Font Size button, you can change the size of the WordArt text. WordArt uses the Best Fit option by default. At this option, WordArt sizes the text to best fit in the text box. If you want to control the size of the text, click on the Font Size button on the WordArt toolbar.

This causes a drop-down menu to display with a variety of font sizes. To change the font size, click on the desired size.

The WordArt toolbar contains a Bold button and an Italic button. Click on the Bold and/or Italic button to apply that style to the text.

Clicking on the Even Height button on the WordArt toolbar makes each letter in the text box the same height. Click on the Flip button on the WordArt toolbar to flip each letter in the text box on its side (90 degrees counterclockwise).

## Changing Spacing

Use the Stretch button on the WordArt toolbar or the Character Spacing button to change the spacing of text in the text box. If you want text to fit in the text box both vertically and horizontally, click on the Stretch button on the toolbar. Click on the Character Spacing button and the Spacing Between Characters dialog box displays as shown in figure 20.5.

The Tracking section of the Spacing Between Characters dialog box contains options to determine character spacing. By default, Normal is selected. Choose one of the other options to either tighten up or loosen the spacing between characters. Kerning is a term that refers to the decreasing of space between specific letter pairs. By default the Automatically Kern Character Pairs option is selected. If you do not want letter pairs kerned, remove the X from this option.

## Changing Alignment

Text in a WordArt text box is center aligned by default. With options from the Alignment button on the WordArt toolbar, this alignment can be changed. When you click on the Alignment button, a drop-down menu displays with alignment options.

Click on the *Left* option if you want text aligned at the left side of the WordArt text box. Choose *Right* to align text at the right side of the text box. Use the Stretch Justify option to stretch letters to fit in the text box. Choosing the *Letter Justify* option will cause the letters to space out to fit the text box. Use the last option, *Word Justify*, to space the words to fit in the text box.

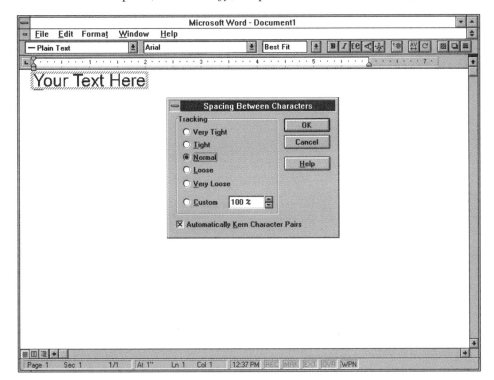

*Figure 20.5*
*Spacing Between Characters Dialog Box*

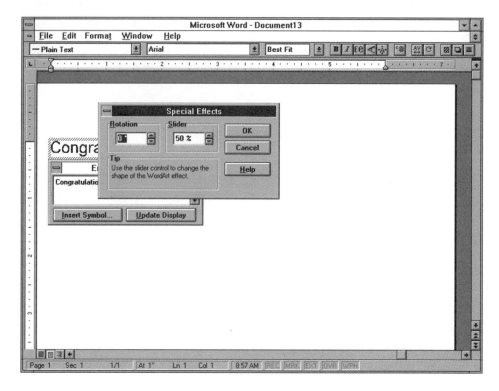

*Figure 20.6*
*Special Effects*
*Dialog Box for*
*Noncircular Text*

## Rotating and Arcing Text

You can rotate, arc, and slant WordArt text at the Special Effects dialog box. To display the Special Effects dialog box, click on the Special Effects button on the WordArt toolbar. The Special Effects dialog box that displays is dependent on the shape you have selected for the WordArt text. Text in a noncircular shape can be rotated and slanted. Text in a circular shape can be rotated and arced.

If you click on the Special Effects button and the text in the text box is noncircular, the Special Effects dialog box shown in figure 20.6 displays.

Enter a degree of rotation in the Rotation text box or click on the up- or down-pointing triangles after the Rotation text box to change the degree.

Use the Slider option to slant the text. The default setting is 50%, which does not slant the text. Increase the percentage to slant the text backwards or decrease the percentage to slant the text forwards.

If you click on the Special Effects button on the WordArt toolbar and the text in the text box is in a circular shape, the Special Effects dialog box shown in figure 20.7 displays.

Choose the Rotation option to rotate the text in the text box by degrees. For example, to rotate the image upside down, change the rotation to 180 degrees.

By default, the arc of circular text is 180 degrees. This number can be decreased to flatten the arc. To do this, choose Arc Angle, then key a number less than 180.

If you want to reduce the height of letters, choose the Reduce Letter Height by option, then key a percentage number less than 100%.

## Adding a Pattern, Shading, and Color

Color, shading, and a pattern can be added to WordArt text. The foreground and background colors of shading or a pattern for text can be changed. To display the color, shading, and pattern options, click on the Shading button on the WordArt toolbar. This causes the Shading dialog box shown in figure 20.8 to display.

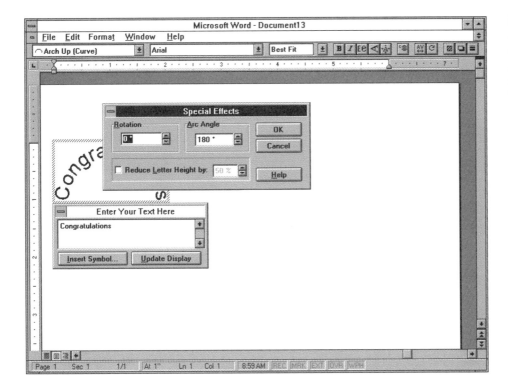

*Figure 20.7*
*Special Effects*
*Dialog Box for*
*Circular Text*

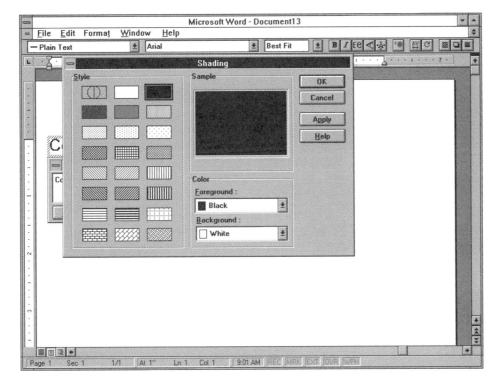

*Figure 20.8*
*Shading Dialog Box*

Pattern options display in the <u>S</u>tyle section of the Shading dialog box. To choose a pattern, click on the desired pattern. To change the foreground color, click on the down-pointing arrow to the right of the <u>F</u>oreground text box, then click on the desired color at the drop-down menu. Complete similar steps to choose a <u>B</u>ackground color. When you change the foreground and/or background color, the pattern options in the <u>S</u>tyle section reflect the color changes.

If you want to see the change to the text in the text box, choose A<u>p</u>ply. (The Shading dialog box may partially obscure the text box.) After making changes to the Shading dialog box, choose OK or press Enter. This removes the Shading dialog box from the screen and applies the changes to the text in the WordArt text box.

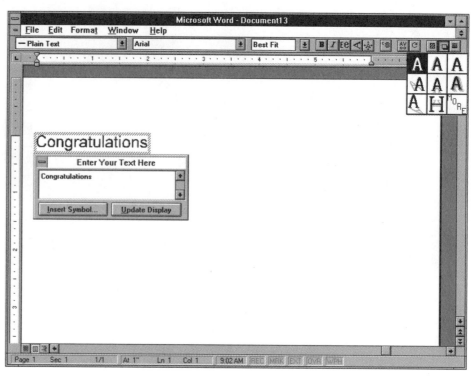

*Figure 20.9*
*Shadow Palette*

## Adding a Shadow

To add a three-dimensional look to WordArt text, click on the Shadow button on the WordArt toolbar. This causes the Shadow palette to display as shown in figure 20.9.

Choose a shadow option by clicking on the desired option on the palette. To see more shadow and color options, click on the More button. This causes the Shadow dialog box to display as shown in figure 20.10.

At the Shadow dialog box, click on the desired shadow effect in the Choose a Shadow section. To change the shadow color, click on the down-pointing arrow to the right of the Shadow Color text box, then click on the desired color from the drop-down menu. The color you choose is applied to the shadow.

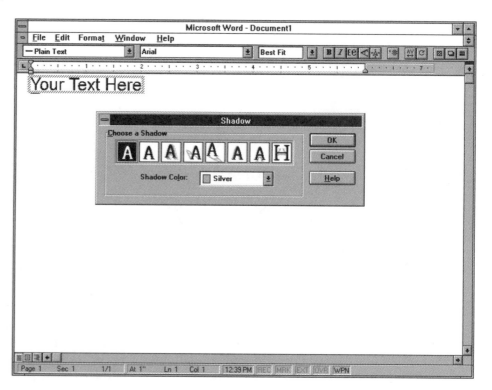

*Figure 20.10*
*Shadow Dialog Box*

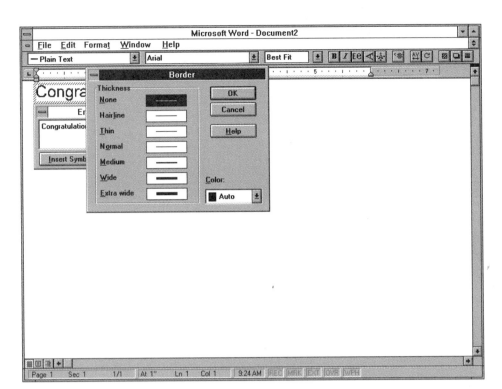

Figure 20.11
Border Dialog Box

## Adding a Border

A border can be added to letters in the WordArt text box. To add a border around letters, click on the Border button on the WordArt toolbar. This causes the Border dialog box to display as shown in figure 20.11.

Choose a border for letters in the Thickness section of the Border dialog box. By default, the border color is Auto (usually black). To change the color, click on the down-pointing arrow to the right of the Color text box, then click on the desired color at the drop-down menu.

## Formatting Using the WordArt Menu Bar

You can use the Format option on the WordArt menu bar to customize WordArt text as described earlier in this chapter. When you choose Format from the WordArt menu bar, a drop-down menu displays with the following options: Spacing Between Characters, Border, Shading, Shadow, Stretch to Frame, and Rotation and Effects.

Choose the Spacing Between Characters option and the Spacing Between Characters dialog box shown in figure 20.5 displays. Choose the other options to display a dialog box to make changes to the WordArt text. For example, choose Shading to display the Shading dialog box shown in figure 20.8 or choose Shadow to display the Shadow dialog box shown in figure 20.10.

## Editing WordArt Text

WordArt text that has been inserted in a document can be edited. To do this, position the arrow pointer on the WordArt text, then double-click the left mouse button. This displays the WordArt text box and the text entry box.

You can also edit WordArt text by positioning the arrow pointer on the WordArt text, clicking the *right* mouse button, then clicking on Edit WordArt.

In addition to editing WordArt text in the text entry box, you can edit text at the WordArt 2.0 dialog box shown in figure 20.12. To display this dialog box, position the arrow pointer on WordArt text, click the *right* mouse button, then click on Open WordArt.

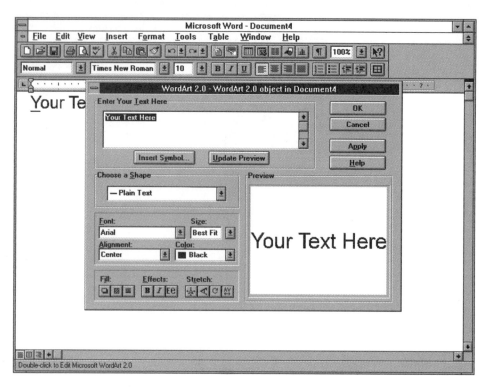

**Figure 20.12**
*WordArt 2.0 Dialog Box*

The WordArt 2.0 dialog box contains all the same features as the WordArt toolbar. Make changes to the text in the WordArt text box at this dialog box, then choose OK or press Enter.

## ■ *Framing WordArt Text*

After text has been created in WordArt, the text can be framed. When WordArt text is framed, the text can be moved or sized as you learned in chapter 18. As an example of how to frame WordArt text, you would complete the following steps to create the text *Oakridge Middle School,* shape it in a circle, then frame it:

1.  At a clear document screen, choose Insert, Object.
2.  At the Object dialog box make sure the Create New tab is selected, then select *Microsoft WordArt 2.0* in the Object Type list box.
3.  Choose OK or press Enter. (You can also just double-click on *Microsoft WordArt 2.0.*)
4.  Key **Oakridge Middle School** in the text entry box.
5.  Choose Update Display.
6.  Click on the down-pointing arrow to the right of the Line and Shape button on the WordArt toolbar.
7.  Click on the third shape in the second row (the circle shape).
8.  Click in the document screen outside the text entry box to remove the text entry box.
9.  With the text box selected, choose Insert, then Frame.
10. At the question asking if you want to change to the Page Layout viewing mode, choose Yes.

After the frame has been inserted around the WordArt text, the size of the frame can be changed with the sizing handles. The frame can be moved and the WordArt text will move with the frame. The frame can also be edited as described in chapter 18.

## ■ *Using the Equation Editor*

With WordArt's equation editor application called Microsoft Equation 2.0, you can create mathematical equations with proper formatting. The equation editor does the formatting for you such as reducing the font size of exponents, applying italics to variables, and adjusting the spacing between equation elements.

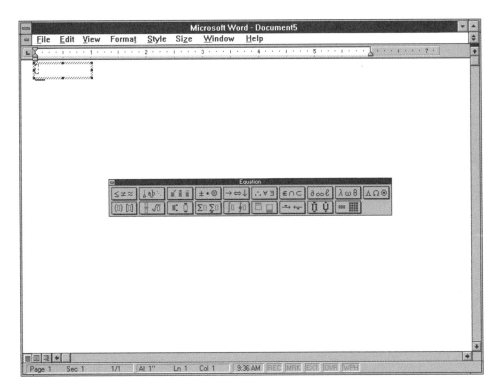

*Figure 20.13*
*Equation Editor*
*Screen*

## Creating an Equation

To create an equation, you must access the equation editor application, Microsoft Equation 2.0. To do this, choose Insert, then Object. At the Object dialog box with the Create New tab selected, select *Microsoft Equation 2.0* in the Object Type list box, then choose OK or press Enter. (You can also just double-click on *Microsoft Equation 2.0.*) When you enter the equation editor, the screen displays as shown in figure 20.13.

A text box displays in the upper left corner of the document screen. Key text for the equation in this box, or insert symbols and templates from the Equation Editor toolbar.

The Equation Editor toolbar contains options for creating an equation. The top row on the toolbar contains symbols such as Greek characters that are used to write an equation. The bottom row of the toolbar contains templates. These templates contain such things as fractions and radicals, integrals, overbars and underbars, and arrows. Figure 20.14 identifies the name of each button on the Equation Editor toolbar.

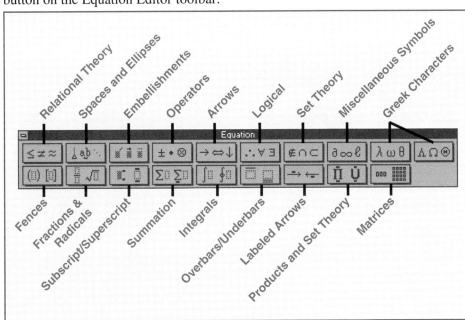

*Figure 20.14*
*Equation Editor*
*Buttons*

When you first open the equation editor, a text box is inserted in the upper left corner of the screen and the insertion point is positioned inside this box in a *slot* (a small box with a dashed border). The Equation Editor toolbar displays below this text box. With the insertion point inside the text box in the slot, key text or add symbols or templates with buttons on the Equation Editor toolbar.

As you enter text or insert symbols in the slot inside the text box, the slot expands. Some options from an Equation Editor toolbar button insert a slot such as the subscript and superscript options. To add an item from the Equation Editor toolbar, position the arrow pointer on the desired button on the toolbar, then click the left mouse button. This causes a palette to display with a variety of options. Click on one of the options on the palette. This causes the symbol or character to be inserted in the text box in the slot where the insertion point is located.

When creating a symbol with the equation editor, you do not add spacing or formatting—the equation editor does that for you.

As an example of how to create an equation, you would complete the following steps to create the equation shown below:

$$P \ = \ \frac{A}{(1 + rt)}$$

1. At a clear document screen, choose Insert, Object.
2. At the Object dialog box with the Create New tab selected, select *Microsoft Equation 2.0.*
3. Choose OK or press Enter. (You can also just double-click on *Microsoft Equation 2.0.*)
4. With the insertion point positioned in the slot inside the text box, key **P**, then **=**. (Do not press the space bar. The equation editor will determine the spacing.)
5. Click on the Fractions and Radicals button on the Equation Editor toolbar (the second button from the left in the bottom row).
6. At the palette that displays, click on the option at the left in the second row.
7. With the insertion point inside the top slot, key **A**.
8. Position the tip of the arrow pointer inside the bottom slot, then click the left mouse button.
9. Click on the Fences button on the Equation Editor toolbar (the first button from the left in the bottom row).
10. At the palette that displays, click on the first option at the left side.
11. Key **1+rt**.
12. Click in the document screen outside the text box and the Equation Editor toolbar. This closes the equation editor.
13. Click in the document screen outside the text box to deselect the box.

The steps to create equations in the exercises at the end of this chapter are provided. For more information on writing extensive equations, please refer to the *Microsoft Word User's Guide*.

## Editing an Equation

An equation created with the equation editor can be edited. To do this, position the arrow pointer on the equation, then double-click the left mouse button. This displays the equation in a text box and inserts the Equation Editor toolbar.

## Framing an Equation

Like other objects you can create in Word, an equation can be framed. When an equation is framed, it can be moved and sized easily. To frame an equation, select the equation, then choose Insert, Frame. When an equation is framed you can move or size the equation. All other editing options are available when the equation is framed as you learned about in chapter 18. For example, you can add a border or shading to the equation.

## CHAPTER SUMMARY

- With the WordArt application, you can distort or modify text to conform to a variety of shapes. With WordArt, you can change the font, style, and alignment of text. You can also add a shadow to the text, use different fills and outlines, and resize the text.
- After accessing *Microsoft WordArt 2.0*, a text entry box displays as well as a WordArt text box. A WordArt menu bar and toolbar replace the normal Menu bar and the Standard and Formatting toolbars.
- To view how the text you enter in the text box will display, choose the Update Display button at the right side of the text entry box.
- After keying text in the text entry box, remove the box.
- To size text in a WordArt text box, select the text. Use the sizing handles that display around the text box to increase or decrease the size of the text.
- The WordArt toolbar contains these buttons for customizing the WordArt text:

| | | |
|---|---|---|
| Line and Shape | Even Height | Special Effects |
| Font | Flip | Shading |
| Font Size | Stretch | Shadow |
| Bold | Alignment | Border |
| Italic | Character Spacing | |

- You can use the Format option on the WordArt menu bar to customize WordArt text.
- Edit WordArt text in the text entry box and at the WordArt 2.0 dialog box.
- After text has been created in WordArt, the text can be framed.
- With WordArt's equation editor application called Microsoft Equation 2.0, you can create mathematical equations with proper formatting.
- To edit an equation created with the equation editor, position the arrow pointer on the equation, then double-click the left mouse button.
- Like other objects you can create in Word, an equation can be framed.

## COMMANDS REVIEW

| | Mouse | Keyboard |
|---|---|---|
| Enter WordArt | Insert, Object, double-click on *Microsoft WordArt 2.0* | Insert, Object, select *Microsoft WordArt 2.0*, press Enter |
| Remove text entry box | Click outside the box; or click on document control button, then choose Close | ALT + F4 |
| WordArt 2.0 dialog box | Position arrow pointer on WordArt text, click *right* mouse button, click on Open WordArt | |
| Access Microsoft Equation 2.0 | Insert, Object, double-click on *Microsoft Equation 2.0* | Insert, Object, select *Microsoft Equation 2.0*, press Enter |

**True/False:** Circle the letter T if the statement is true; circle the letter F if the statement is false.

T   F   1.   WordArt is considered a supplementary application of Word for Windows.

T   F   2.   When entering WordArt, the Create New tab must be selected at the Object dialog box.

T   F   3.   Text in a WordArt text box is left aligned by default.

T   F   4.   Either the foreground color or the background color of shading that is added to WordArt text can be changed, but not both.

T   F   5.   To add a three-dimensional look to WordArt text, choose the 3-D button on the WordArt toolbar.

T   F   6.   A border and/or a frame can be added to WordArt text.

T   F   7.   One way to display WordArt text for editing is to position the arrow pointer on the text, then double-click the left mouse button.

T   F   8.   The equation editor does the formatting of mathematical equations for you.

T   F   9.   By default, WordArt generally applies Arial font to text.

T   F  10.   Choose the Rotate button on the WordArt toolbar to turn each letter in the text box on its side.

**Completion:** In the space provided at the right, indicate the correct term, command, or number.

1.   According to the textbook, the WordArt application is useful when creating these. _____

2.   When using WordArt, the WordArt toolbar and this bar appear in the document screen. _____

3.   To view how the text will display, choose this button near the text entry box. _____

4.   Choose this button on the WordArt toolbar if you want text to fit in the text box both vertically and horizontally. _____

5.   This term refers to the decreasing of space between specific letter pairs. _____

6.   You can rotate and arc WordArt text at this dialog box. _____

7.   Choose this option to slant text. _____

8.   The equation editor application is named this. _____

9.   To create and add objects to a Word document, WordArt text uses object linking and embedding, also called this. _____

10.   Choose from this palette to make text conform to a particular shape. _____

## AT THE COMPUTER

*Note: When closing documents containing WordArt, Word will ask if you want to save changes. At this prompt, choose Yes. This document will display even if you just saved the document.*

### Exercise 1

1.   At a clear document screen, create the letterhead shown in figure 20.15 using WordArt by completing the following steps:

   a.   At a clear document screen, press Enter once, then move the insertion point back up to the first line.

   b.   Choose Insert, Object.

   c.   At the Object dialog box make sure the Create New tab is selected, then select *Microsoft WordArt 2.0* in the Object Type list box.

   d.   Choose OK or press Enter. (You can also just double-click on *Microsoft WordArt 2.0*.)

   e.   Key **Mountain** in the text entry box, then press Enter.

   f.   Key **Community College**.

   g.   Choose Update Display. (This displays *Mountain Community College* in the text box in the document screen.)

h. Click in the document screen outside the text entry box to remove the text entry box.

i. Click in the document screen outside the text box to deselect the box.

j. Position the insertion point at the end of *College*, turn on the display of the Borders toolbar, change the line style to *3 pt,* then insert a border at the bottom of the paragraph.

k. Press the down arrow key to move the insertion point below the border line then click on the Align Right button on the Standard toolbar.

l. Key **A great place to learn!**

m. Select the text *A great place to learn!* then change the font to 12-point Arial Bold.

2. Save the document and name it c20ex01.

3. Print c20ex01. (Depending on your printer's memory, this may take some time to print.)

4. Close c20ex01.

Figure 20.15

# Mountain Community College

## A great place to learn!

## Exercise 2

1. At a clear document screen, create WordArt text, then shape and size the text by completing the following steps:

   a. Choose Insert, Object.

   b. At the Object dialog box make sure the Create New tab is selected, then double-click on *Microsoft WordArt 2.0* in the Object Type list box.

   c. In the text entry box, key **Stewart Elementary School** and press the space bar once.

   d. Choose Update Display. (This displays *Stewart Elementary School* in the text box in the document screen.)

   e. Click on the down-pointing arrow to the right of the Line and Shape button (first button from the left) on the WordArt toolbar.

   f. Click on the third shape from the left in the second row (the circle shape).

   g. Click in the document screen outside the text entry box to remove the text entry box.

   h. With the WordArt text box selected, change the size of the text box by completing the following steps:

      (1) Choose Format, Picture.

      (2) At the Picture dialog box, change the Width to 6 inches and the Height to 3 inches. (These options are located in the Size section of the dialog box.)

      (3) Choose OK or press Enter.

      (4) Deselect the text box.

2. Save the document and name it c20ex02.

3. Print c20ex02. (Depending on your printer's memory, this may take some time to print.)

4. Close c20ex02.

## Exercise 3

1. At a clear document screen, create WordArt text, then change the font, shape, and size of the text by completing the following steps:

   a. Choose Insert, Object.

   b. At the Object dialog box make sure the Create New tab is selected, then double-click on *Microsoft WordArt 2.0* in the Object Type list box.

   c. Key **Now is the time** in the text entry box, then press Enter.

   d. Key **to get out and,** then press Enter.

   e. Key **vote!**

   f. Choose Update Display.

g.  Change the font to Braggadocio by clicking on the down-pointing arrow to the right of
       the Font button (second button from the left) on the WordArt toolbar, then clicking on
       *Braggadocio*.
   h.  Click on the Alignment button (ninth button from the left) on the WordArt toolbar, then
       click on *Letter Justify*.
   i.  Click in the document screen outside the text entry box to remove the text entry box.
   j.  With the WordArt text box selected, change the size of the text box by completing steps
       similar to those in exercise 2, steps 1h(1) through 1h(3).
   k.  Deselect the text box.
2. Save the document and name it c20ex03.
3. Print c20ex03. (Depending on your printer's memory, this may take some time to print.)
4. Close c20ex03.

## Exercise 4

1. At a clear document screen, create the letterhead shown in figure 20.16 using WordArt by
   completing the following steps:
   a.  Choose Insert, Object.
   b.  At the Object dialog box make sure the Create New tab is selected, then double-click on
       *Microsoft WordArt 2.0*.
   c.  Key **The Petersburg Press** in the text entry box.
   d.  Choose Update Display.
   e.  Click on the down-pointing arrow to the right of the Line and Shape button on the
       WordArt toolbar.
   f.  Click on the first shape in the second row (the semi-circle shape).
   g.  Click on the Bold button (fourth button from the left) on the WordArt toolbar. (This
       bolds the text in the text box.)
   h.  Change the arc angle by completing the following steps:
       (1)  Click on the Special Effects button on the WordArt toolbar (the fourth button from the
            right).
       (2)  At the Special Effects dialog box, click on the down-pointing triangle to the right of
            the Arc Angle text box until *100* displays in the text box.
       (3)  Choose OK or press Enter.
   i.  Click in the document screen outside the text entry box to remove the text entry box.
   j.  Widen the text box approximately 1 inch.
   k.  Make the text box taller by approximately 1 inch.
   l.  Click in the document screen outside the text box to deselect the box.
   m. Turn on the display of the Borders toolbar, change the line style to a 2 1/4 point double
      line, then insert a border at the bottom of the paragraph.
2. Save the document and name it c20ex04.
3. Print c20ex04. (Depending on your printer's memory, this may take some time to print.)
4. Close c20ex04.

**Figure 20.16**

# Exercise 5

1. At a clear document screen, create the WordArt text shown in figure 20.17 by completing the following steps:
   a. Open WordArt.
   b. Key **Desktop Publishing Workshop** in the text entry box.
   c. Choose Update Display.
   d. Click on the down-pointing arrow to the right of the Line and Shape button on the WordArt toolbar.
   e. Click on the second shape from the left in the fifth row (the shape called Deflate).
   f. Click on the Stretch button (seventh button from the right) on the WordArt toolbar.
   g. Change the shading color and pattern by completing the following steps:
      (1) Click on the Shading button (third button from the right) on the WordArt toolbar.
      (2) At the Shading dialog box, click on the down-pointing arrow to the right of the Foreground text box, then click on *Fuchsia*.
      (3) Click on the down-pointing arrow to the right of the Background text box, then click on *Aqua*. (You will have to scroll up the list to see *Aqua*.)
      (4) Click on the second option from the left in the seventh row in the Style section of the dialog box.
      (5) Choose OK or press Enter.
   h. Add a thin black border to the letters by completing the following steps:
      (1) Click on the Border button (the last button on the right) on the WordArt toolbar.
      (2) At the Border dialog box, click on the down-pointing arrow after the Color text box, then click on *Black*.
      (3) Click on the Hairline button in the Thickness section of the dialog box.
      (4) Choose OK or press Enter.
   i. Add a shadow to the text by completing the following steps:
      (1) Click on the Shadow button (second button from the right) on the WordArt toolbar.
      (2) At the palette of shadow options, click on the More option.
      (3) At the Shadow dialog box, click on the third button from the left in the Choose a Shadow section of the dialog box.
      (4) Click on the down-pointing arrow to the right of Shadow Color text box, then click on *Gray*.
      (5) Choose OK or press Enter.
   j. Click in the document screen outside the text entry box to remove the text entry box.
   k. With the WordArt text box selected, change the size of the text box by completing steps similar to those in exercise 2, steps 1h(1) through 1h(3).
   l. Deselect the text box.
2. Save the document and name it c20ex05.
3. Print c20ex05. (Depending on your printer's memory, this may take some time to print.)
4. Close c20ex05.

**Figure 20.17**

## Exercise 6

1. Open c20ex04.
2. Save the document with Save As and name it c20ex06.
3. Change the text color and add a border to the letters by completing the following steps:
   a. Position the arrow pointer in the WordArt text (*The Petersburg Press*).
   b. Click the *right* mouse button.
   c. Click on Open WordArt.
   d. At the WordArt 2.0 dialog box, click on the down-pointing arrow to the right of the Color text box, then click on *Yellow*.
   e. Click on the Border button in the Fill section of the dialog box. (The Border button is the third button from the left in the Fill section of the dialog box, which is in the lower left corner.)
   f. At the Border dialog box, click on the Thin button in the Thickness section of the dialog box.
   g. Click on the down-pointing arrow after the Color option, then click on *Black*.
   h. Choose OK or press Enter to close the Border dialog box.
   i. Choose OK or press Enter to close the WordArt 2.0 dialog box.
   j. Deselect the text box.
4. Save the document again with the same name (c20ex06).
5. Print c20ex06. (Depending on your printer's memory, this may take some time to print.)
6. Close c20ex06.

## Exercise 7

1. Open c20ex02.
2. Save the document with Save As and name it c20ex07.
3. Change to the Page Layout viewing mode.
4. Insert a frame around the WordArt text, then format the frame by completing the following steps:
   a. Select the WordArt text (Stewart Elementary School).
   b. With the text selected, choose Insert, then Frame.
   c. Choose Format, then Frame.
   d. At the Frame dialog box, change the Position option in the Horizontal section to *Center* and the Relative To option to *Page*.
   e. Change the Position option in the Vertical section to *Center* and the Relative To option to *Page*.

f.  Change the Width to 6 inches and the Height to 8 inches.

g.  Choose OK or press Enter to close the Frame dialog box.

h.  Click on the down-pointing arrow to the right of the Zoom Control button on the Standard toolbar, then click on *Whole Page*.

i.  Use the sizing handles in the WordArt text box to size the text box to the size of the frame.

j.  Change the zoom back to 100%.

k.  Deselect the text box and the frame.

5.  Save the document again with the same name (c20ex07).

6.  Print c20ex07. (Depending on your printer's memory, this may take some time to print.)

7.  Close c20ex07.

## Exercise 8

1.  At a clear document screen, create the equation shown in figure 20.18 by completing the following steps:

a.  At a clear document screen, choose Insert, Object.

b.  At the Object dialog box with the Create New tab selected, select *Microsoft Equation 2.0*.

c.  Choose OK or press Enter. (You can also just double-click on *Microsoft Equation 2.0*.)

d.  With the insertion point positioned in the slot inside the text box, key **A=P**. (Do not press the space bar. The equation editor will determine the spacing.)

e.  Click on the Fences button on the Equation Editor toolbar (the first button from the left in the bottom row).

f.  At the palette that displays, click on the option at the left in the first row. (This option displays with a black background. The button also displays with a black background. Do not confuse this with the first row of the palette.)

g.  Key **1+**.

h.  Click on the Fractions and Radicals button on the Equation Editor toolbar (the second button from the left in the bottom row).

i.  At the palette that displays, click on the option at the left in the first row. (This option displays with a black background. The button also displays with a black background. Do not confuse this with the first row of the palette.)

j.  With the insertion point inside the top slot, key **1**.

k.  Position the tip of the arrow pointer inside the bottom slot, then click the left mouse button.

l.  Key **m**.

m.  Position the tip of the arrow pointer to the right of the right parenthesis, then click the left mouse button. (This moves the insertion outside of the parentheses.)

n.  Click on the Subscript/Superscript button on the Equation Editor (the third button from the left on the bottom row).

o.  At the palette that displays, click on the option at the left in the first row. (This option displays with a black background. The button also displays with a black background. Do not confuse this with the first row of the palette.)

p.  Key **nm**.

q.  Click in the document screen outside the text box and the Equation Editor toolbar. This closes the equation editor.

r.  Click in the document screen outside the text box to deselect the box.

2.  Save the document and name it c20ex08.

3.  Print c20ex08. (Depending on your printer's memory, this may take some time to print.)

4.  Close c20ex08.

**Figure 20.18**

$$A = P\left(1 + \frac{1}{m}\right)^m$$

## Exercise 9

1.  At a clear document screen, key the title and subtitle of the document shown in figure 20.19, then press Enter three times (leave the paragraph alignment at center). Complete the following steps to create the first formula in the figure:
    a.  Choose Insert, Object.
    b.  At the Object dialog box with the Create New tab selected, double-click on *Microsoft Equation 2.0*.
    c.  With the insertion point positioned in the slot inside the text box, key **P=R**. (Do not press the space bar. The equation editor will determine the spacing.)
    d.  Click on the Fences button on the Equation Editor toolbar (the first button from the left in the bottom row).
    e.  At the palette that displays, click on the second option from the left in the first row.
    f.  Click on the Fractions and Radicals button on the Equation Editor toolbar (the second button from the left in the bottom row).
    g.  At the palette that displays, click on the option at the left in the first row (displays with a black background).
    h.  With the insertion point inside the top slot, key **1-**.
    i.  Click on the Fences button on the Equation Editor toolbar (the first button from the left in the bottom row).
    j.  At the palette that displays, click on the first button from the left in the top row (displays with a black background).
    k.  Key **1+I**.
    l.  Position the tip of the arrow pointer immediately to the right of the right parenthesis but left of the right bracket, then click the left mouse button. (The blinking vertical bar cursor should only be the length of the top row.)
    m.  Click on the Subscript/Superscript button on the Equation Editor toolbar (the third button from the left in the bottom row).
    n.  From the palette that displays, click on the first button from the left in the first row (displays with a black background).
    o.  Key **-n**.
    p.  Position the tip of the arrow pointer in the bottom slot, then click the left mouse button.
    q.  Key **i**.
    r.  Click in the document screen outside the text box and the Equation Editor toolbar. This closes the equation editor.
    s.  Click in the document screen outside the text box to deselect the box.
2.  After creating the first equation, press the Enter key four or five times to separate the first equation from the second equation.
3.  Save the document and name it c20ex09.
4.  Complete the following steps to create the second formula in the figure:
    a.  Choose Insert, Object.
    b.  At the Object dialog box with the Create New tab selected, double-click on *Microsoft Equation 2.0*.
    c.  With the insertion point positioned in the slot inside the text box, key **S=R**. (Do not press the space bar. The equation editor will determine the spacing.)

d. Click on the Fences button on the Equation Editor toolbar (the first button from the left in the bottom row).

e. At the palette that displays, click on the second option from the left in the first row.

f. Click on the Fractions and Radicals button on the Equation Editor toolbar (the second button from the left in the bottom row).

g. At the palette that displays, click on the option at the left in the first row (displays with a black background).

h. Click on the Fences button on the Equation Editor toolbar (the first button from the left in the bottom row).

i. At the palette that displays, click on the first button from the left in the top row.

j. With the insertion point inside the top slot, key **1+i**.

k. Position the tip of the arrow pointer immediately to the right of the right parenthesis but left of the right bracket, then click the left mouse button. (The blinking vertical bar cursor should only be the length of the top row.)

l. Click on the Subscript/Superscript button on the Equation Editor toolbar (the third button from the left in the bottom row).

m. From the palette that displays, click on the first button from the left in the first row (displays with a black background).

n. Key **n**.

o. Position the tip of the arrow pointer immediately to the right of the superscript number but left of the right bracket, then click the left mouse button.

p. Key **-1**.

q. Position the tip of the arrow pointer in the bottom slot, then click the left mouse button.

r. Key **i**.

s. Click in the document screen outside the text box and the Equation Editor toolbar. This closes the equation editor.

t. Click in the document screen outside the text box to deselect the box.

5. Select the first equation, then increase the height and width of the equation text box approximately 0.5 inches.

6. Select the second equation, then increase the height and width of the equation text box approximately 0.5 inches.

7. Save the document again with the same name (c20ex09).

8. Print c20ex09.

9. Close c20ex09.

Figure 20.19

MATH 145

Formulas for Mathematics of Finance

$$P = R\left[\frac{1 - (1 + I)^{-n}}{i}\right]$$

$$S = R\left[\frac{(1 + i)^{n} - 1}{i}\right]$$

## SKILL ASSESSMENTS

### Assessment 1

1. At a clear document screen, create the WordArt text and border line shown in figure 20.20 by completing the following steps:
    a. Open WordArt.
    b. Key **St. Francis**, press Enter, then key **Medical Center**.
    c. Update the display.
    d. Change the shape of the text to a triangle.
    e. Click on the Stretch button on the WordArt toolbar.
    f. Click on the Bold button on the WordArt toolbar.
    g. Close WordArt.
    h. Deselect the WordArt text box.
    i. Insert a 2 1/4 point double line border (use the Borders toolbar to do this) below the center name.
2. Save the document and name it c20sa01.
3. Print c20sa01.
4. Close c20sa01.

Figure 20.20

# Assessment 2

1. At a clear document screen, create the WordArt text shown in figure 20.21 with the following specifications (your text will appear much larger than what you see in figure 20.21):

   a. Open WordArt.

   b. Key the text **Tacoma Water Front** on one line, **Renovation** on the next line, and **and Revitalization** on the third line.

   c. Update the display in the text box.

   d. Change the shape to a circle with a line (the fourth shape from the left in the second row, called the Button [Curve]).

   e. Display the Shading dialog box, then make the following changes:

      (1) Change the shading style to the first shading option in the second row in the <u>S</u>tyle section.

      (2) Change the foreground color to *Aqua*.

      (3) Change the background color to *Blue*.

   f. Display the Border dialog box, then add a medium border line to the letters.

   g. Click in the document screen outside the text entry box and the text box. (This removes the text entry box.)

   h. With the text box still selected, insert a frame around the text box.

   i. Format the frame with the following specifications:

      (1) Change the horizontal position to center, relative to the page.

      (2) Change the vertical position to center, relative to the page.

      (3) Change the width to 5 inches.

      (4) Change the height to 6 inches.

   j. After changing the size of the frame, size the WordArt text box to fill the frame by completing the following steps:

      (1) Change the zoom to whole page.

      (2) Use the sizing handles on the WordArt text box to size the box to fit the frame.

      (3) Change the zoom back to 100%.

   k. Deselect the WordArt text box.

2. Save the document and name it c20sa02.

3. Print c20sa02.

4. Close c20sa02.

**Figure 20.21**

## Assessment 3

1. At a clear document screen, create the text *Curtiss Elementary School* as WordArt text that displays slanted across the entire page by completing the following steps:
   a. Open WordArt.
   b. Key **Curtiss Elementary School.**
   c. Update the display.
   d. Change the shape of the text to a slant (the third button in the first row, called the Slant Up button).
   e. Change the font to Colonna MT.
   f. Display the Shading dialog box, then change the foreground color to white and the background color to red. Choose the second option from the left in the third row in the Style section of the dialog box (this adds a pattern).
   g. Display the Border dialog box, then add a hairline black border to the letters.
   h. Close WordArt.
   i. With the WordArt text box selected, insert a frame.
   j. Format the frame with the following specifications:
      (1) Change the horizontal position to center, relative to the page.
      (2) Change the vertical position to center, relative to the page.
      (3) Change the width to 6 inches.
      (4) Change the height to 9 inches.
   k. After changing the size of the frame, size the WordArt text box to fill the frame by completing the following steps:
      (1) Change the zoom to whole page.
      (2) Use the sizing handles on the WordArt text box to size the box to fit the frame.
      (3) Change the zoom back to 100%.
2. Save the document and name it c20sa03.
3. Print c20sa03.
4. Close c20sa03.

## Assessment 4

1. At a clear document screen, create the document shown in figure 20.22. Create the equation by completing the following steps:
   a. Open Microsoft Equation 2.0.
   b. With the insertion point positioned in the slot inside the text box, key **r=1-.**
   c. Click on the Fractions and Radicals button on the Equation Editor toolbar (the second button from the left in the bottom row).
   d. At the palette that displays, click on the option at the left in the first row (displays with a black background).
   e. With the insertion point inside the top slot, key **6**.
   f. Click on the Greek Character button (the last button in the top row).
   g. From the palette that displays, click on the second option from the left in the fifth row.
   h. Key **d**.
   i. Click on the Subscript/Superscript button on the Equation Editor toolbar (the third button from the left in the bottom row).
   j. From the palette that displays, click on the first option from the left in the first row (displays with a black background).
   k. Key **2**.
   l. Position the tip of the arrow pointer in the bottom slot, then click the left mouse button.
   m. Key **n**.
   n. Click on the Fences button on the Equation Editor toolbar (the first button from the left in the bottom row).

o. At the palette that displays, click on the first option from the left in the top row (displays with a black background).
p. Key **n**.
q. Click on the Subscript/Superscript button on the Equation Editor toolbar (the third button from the left in the bottom row).
r. From the palette that displays, click on the first option from the left in the first row (displays with a black background).
s. Key **2**.
t. Position the tip of the arrow pointer outside the superscript slot but before the right parenthesis, then click the left mouse button.
u. Key **-1**.
v. Click in the document screen outside the text box and the Equation Editor toolbar. This closes the equation editor.
w. With the equation selected, increase the width and height approximately 1 inch.
x. Insert a frame around the equation, then move the equation to the middle of the screen.

2. Save the document and name it c20sa04.
3. Print c20sa04.
4. Close c20sa04.

**Figure 20.22**

**STATISTICS FORMULAS FOR CORRELATION ANALYSIS**

**Rank-Order Correlation**

$$r = 1 - \frac{6\Sigma d^2}{n\left(n^2 - 1\right)}$$

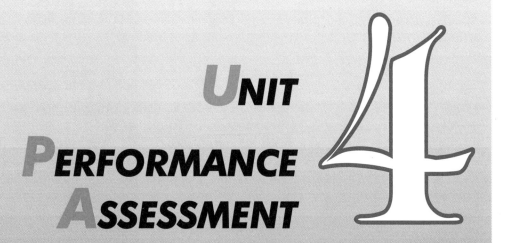

# UNIT 4

## PERFORMANCE ASSESSMENT

In this unit you learned to automate the preparation of business documents and enhance the visual display of documents with borders, frames, pictures, shapes, and WordArt text.

## Assessment 1

1. At a clear document screen, create a macro named *Formhead* that is assigned the shortcut command Ctrl + Alt + H, which selects text and changes the font to 14-point Arial Bold. *(Hint: At the clear document screen key **This is a heading**. This gives you text to select when recording the macro.)*
2. Close the document without saving it.
3. At a clear document screen, open report01.
4. Save the document with Save As and name it u04pa01.
5. Make the following changes to the report:
   a. Select the entire document, then change the font to 12-point Times New Roman.
   b. Select the text in the document except the title, change the line spacing to single, then change the paragraph spacing before and after to 6 points.
   c. Add bullets to the last four paragraphs (lines) of text in the report.
   d. Run the Ctrl + Alt + H macro for the title and the three headings.
   e. Delete the tab before paragraphs to make all paragraphs begin at the left margin.
   f. Add a drop cap to the first paragraph below each heading that is only two lines in length. (Change the <u>L</u>ines to Drop setting to *2* at the Drop Cap dialog box.)
   g. Hyphenate words in the document automatically.
6. Save the document again with the same name (u04pa01).
7. Print u04pa01.
8. Close c04pa01.

## Assessment 2

1. At a clear document screen, create an AutoText entry named **MHS** for the school name *MEEKER HIGH SCHOOL* that is set in 18-point Arial Bold.
2. Close the document without saving it.
3. At a clear document screen, create the memo shown in figure U4.1 with the following specifications:
   a. Insert the MHS AutoText entry where you see *MHS* in the document. Insert the MHS AutoText entry in the body of the memo without formatting.
   b. Use the shortcut command to insert the current date.
   c. Create nonbreaking hyphens where you see hyphens in the document.
4. When the memo is completed, save it and name it u04pa02.
5. Print u04pa02.
6. Close u04pa02.

### Figure U4.1

```
                              MHS

DATE:      (insert current date)

TO:        Martha Wessler

FROM:      Jeremy Chang

SUBJECT: NEW EMPLOYEES


Several new employees have been recently hired at MHS.  The
appropriate forms have been completed and are enclosed.  The new
employees have been assigned school numbers for recordkeeping
purposes.

Scott Jennings has been assigned the school number 645-344-321.
Mr. Jennings is a paraprofessional hired to work in the Special
Services Department.  School number 453-220-333 has been assigned
to Sang Lee who will be working in the school library.  Colleen
Kissel, school number 594-895-904, will be working in the
Counseling Center.

Two additional employees will begin working at MHS the first of
next month.  I will send you the appropriate forms at that time.

xx:u04pa02
```

# Assessment 3

1. Open notice02.
2. Save the document with Save As and name it u04pa03.
3. Insert a divider picture at the top of the document, change the size of the picture, then insert a frame by completing the following steps:
   a. With the insertion point positioned at the beginning of the document, press the Enter key five times.
   b. Select the entire document, then change the font to 16-point Braggadocio.
   c. Position the insertion on the first line in the document (this will be center aligned).
   d. Display the Insert Picture dialog box, then insert the picture named *divider2.wmf*.
   e. Format the picture so it is 4 inches wide and 0.5 inches in height.
   f. Insert a frame around the divider picture.
   g. Format the frame so that the horizontal position is center and relative to the margin.
4. After inserting the divider picture at the beginning of the document, copy the divider picture below the text by completing the following steps:
   a. Change the zoom to whole page.
   b. Position the I-beam pointer on one of the lines that creates the frame around the picture until it turns into an arrow with a four-headed arrow attached.
   c. Hold down the Ctrl key and the left mouse button, drag the outline of the frame until it is centered below the text, then release the mouse button and the Ctrl key.
   d. Change the zoom back to 100%.
5. Save the document again with the same name (u04pa03).
6. Print u04pa03.
7. Close u04pa03.

# Assessment 4

1. At a clear document screen, create the document shown in figure U4.2 by completing the following steps:
   a. Insert the picture named *math.wmf*.
   b. Format the picture so that the width is 2.5 inches and the height is 2 inches.
   c. Insert a frame around the picture.
   d. Deselect the picture.
   e. Change the font to 14-point Arial Bold.
   f. Change the paragraph to center alignment.
   g. Key the text shown in figure U4.2.
2. After creating the document, save it and name it u04pa04.
3. Print u04pa04.
4. Close u04pa04.

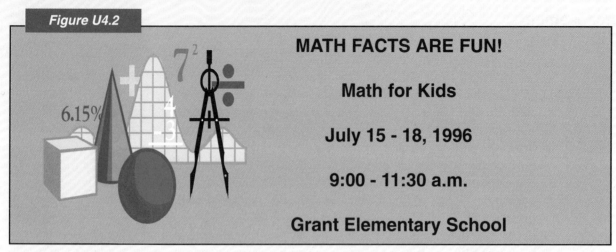

Figure U4.2

**MATH FACTS ARE FUN!**

**Math for Kids**

**July 15 - 18, 1996**

**9:00 - 11:30 a.m.**

**Grant Elementary School**

## Assessment 5

1. At a clear document screen, create the document shown in figure U4.3 by completing the following steps:
   a. Change to the Page Layout viewing mode.
   b. Make sure the Drawing toolbar is displayed.
   c. Select the appropriate buttons to draw the shapes you see in figure U4.3. (*Hint: Draw the first shape with the Rectangle tool, then display the Drawing Object dialog box for the rectangle. Make sure the Line tab is selected, then choose Round Corners. Change the fill color for the rounded rectangle, then copy it below.*)
   d. Draw a text box inside each shape, change the font to 12-point Times New Roman, then key the text shown in each shape center aligned.
   e. Select each text box, then change the line color to none.
   f. Use the Line button on the Drawing toolbar to draw the lines between shapes.
2. Save the document and name it u04pa05.
3. Print u04pa05.
4. Return the fill color back to none and turn off rounded corners.
5. Close u04pa05.

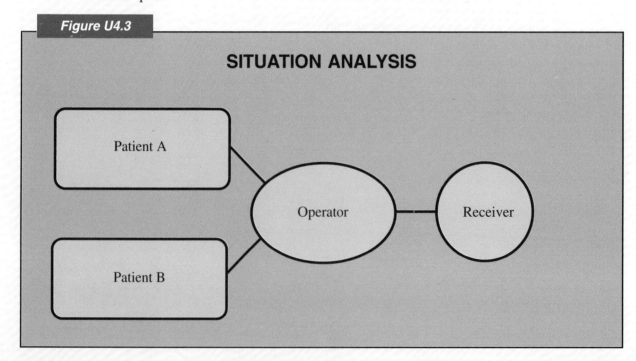

Figure U4.3

**SITUATION ANALYSIS**

Patient A

Operator

Receiver

Patient B

## Assessment 6

1. Open para07.
2. Save the document with Save As and name it u04pa06.
3. Make the following changes to the document:
   a. Select the entire document, then change the font to 12-point Century Gothic.
   b. Run the Ctrl + Alt + H macro for the title of the document.
   c. Draw a text box that spans from the middle of the first paragraph to the middle of the last paragraph and is approximately 4 inches wide.
   d. Insert the picture named *books.wmf* inside the text box.
   e. With the text box selected, move the text box behind the text.
   f. Display the Drawing Object dialog box with the Line tab selected, then change the line to None. (This removes the border around the text box.)
4. Save the document again with the same name (u04pa06).
5. Print u04pa06.
6. Display the Drawing Defaults dialog box with the Line tab selected, then change the line back to Custom.
7. Close u04pa06.

## Assessment 7

1. At a clear document screen, use the WordArt program to create the flyer letterhead shown in figure U4.4. Use buttons on the Borders toolbar to insert the double line.
2. Save the document and name it u04pa07.
3. Print u04pa07.
4. Close u04pa07.

**Figure U4.4**

## Assessment 8

1. Delete the following:
   a. Delete the *Formhead* macro.
   b. Delete the MHS AutoText entry.
   c. Delete all documents created in chapters 11 through 15.
   d. Delete all documents created for unit 3 Performance Assessment.

## COMPOSING ACTIVITIES

The following activities give you the opportunity to practice your writing skills along with demonstrating an understanding of some of the important Word features you have mastered in this unit. In planning the documents, remember to shape the information according to the writing purpose and the audience. Use correct grammar, appropriate word choices, and clear sentence constructions.

## Activity 1

**Situation:** You work for SPORTS WORLD, a sporting goods store. You have been asked to design a letterhead for the store. When designing this letterhead, include the ClipArt picture *sports.wmf* and a border along with this information:

```
SPORTS WORLD
6009 South Meridian
Salt Lake City, UT 84107
(801) 555-7755
```

Save the letterhead document and name it u04act01. Print, then close u04act01.

## Activity 2

**Situation:** You are Richard Granata, assistant manager for SPORTS WORLD. Write a letter to Tennis Suppliers, Inc., 540 Northwest 56th Street, Chicago, IL 66034, using the letterhead you created in Activity 1, stating that the shipment of tennis supplies received today (use the current date) was not complete. SPORTS WORLD ordered 10 each of Pro-Tech Lite, Pro-Tech Ultra Lite, and Pro-Tech Power tennis rackets and received only 5 of each. Additionally, SPORTS WORLD ordered 50 cans of Lovell regular and 30 cans of Lovell heavy-duty tennis balls and only received 25 of each. Ask Tennis Suppliers, Inc., to send the additional supplies by overnight carrier.

Save the letter document and name it u04act02. Print, then close u04act02.

## Activity 3

Use the WordArt application to create a document announcing that all tennis supplies are 40% off on Saturday, April 27, 1996.

Save the document and name it u04act03. Print, then close u04act03.

## Activity 4

Create an announcement regarding graduation for Rollins High School that will be held on Friday, June 7, 1996, beginning at 7:00 p.m. The graduation will be held at the Petersburg Convention Center, 4300 Central Avenue, Petersburg, ND 76321. Include the ClipArt picture *diploma.wmf* in the announcement.

Save the announcement document and name it u04act04. Print, then close u04act04.

## RESEARCH ACTIVITY

*Note: For this research activity you will need access to the Microsoft Word User's Guide.*
Answer the following questions about information in the Word for Windows User's Guide.

1.  What chapter covers the Draw program?  _____
2.  What chapter covers framing?  _____
3.  On what pages do you find troubleshooting tips about frames?  _____
4.  What is a graphics filter?

_____

_____

5.  Word can import graphics drawn in other programs. On what page in the User's Guide are the compatible formats displayed?  _____
6.  What steps would you complete to view more information about compatible file formats in Help?

_____

_____

7.  What steps would you complete to copy a graphic from another application, then paste it into a Word document?

_____

_____

_____

# Advanced Page Formatting

UNIT

5

*In this unit you will learn to enhance the visual display and readability of documents by formatting text into tables, charts, and columns and maintain formatting consistency in documents using styles.*

# Creating & Formatting Tables 21

Upon successful completion of chapter 21, you will be able to create and format business tables according to a variety of format and size considerations and perform mathematical analysis on data in tables.

Word's Tables feature can be used to create columns and rows of information. With Tables, a form can be created that has boxes of information, called *cells.* A cell is the intersection between a row and a column. It can contain text, characters, numbers, data, or formulas. Text within a cell can be formatted to display left, right, or center aligned and can include character formatting such as bold, italics, and underlining. The formatting choices available with Tables are quite extensive and allow flexibility in creating a variety of tables. Calculations can also be performed on numbers in a table.

## Creating a Table

A table can be created with the Insert Table button on the Standard toolbar or the T<u>a</u>ble option from the Menu bar. The Insert Table button is the eighth button from the right on the Standard toolbar. To create a table with the Insert Table button on the Standard toolbar, you would complete the following steps:

1.  Position the arrow pointer on the Insert Table button on the Standard toolbar.
2.  Hold down the left mouse button. This causes a grid to appear as shown in figure 21.1.
3.  Move the arrow pointer down and to the right until the correct number of rows and columns displays below the grid, then release the mouse button.

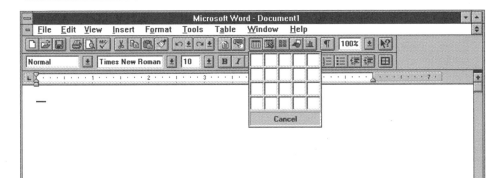

*Figure 21.1*
*Table Grid*

Figure 21.2
Insert Table Dialog
Box

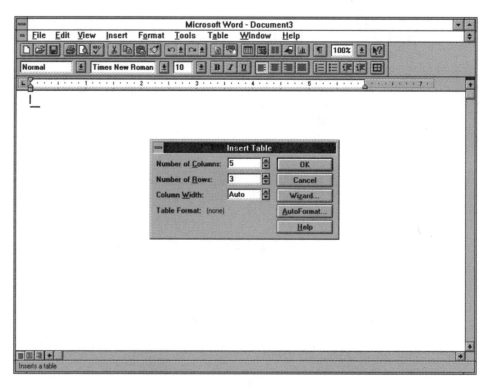

As you move the arrow pointer in step 3, selected columns and rows are displayed in blue, and the number of rows and columns displays below the grid.

A table can also be created with options at the Insert Table dialog box shown in figure 21.2. Display the Insert Table dialog box by choosing Table, then Insert Table. For example, to create a table that contains five columns and three rows, you would complete the following steps:

1. Choose Table, then Insert Table.
2. At the Insert Table dialog box, key **5** in the Number of Columns text box. (The insertion point is automatically positioned in this text box when the dialog box is displayed.)
3. Choose Number of Rows.
4. Key **3**.
5. Choose OK or press Enter.

When you choose OK (or press Enter) at the Insert Table dialog box, a table similar to the one shown in figure 21.3 is inserted in the document at the location of the insertion point.

When a table is created, the insertion point is located in the cell in the upper left corner of the table. Cells in a table contain a cell designation. Columns in a table are lettered from left to right, beginning with A. Rows are numbered from top to bottom beginning with 1. The cell in the upper left corner of the table is cell A1. The cell to the right of A1 is B1, the cell to the right of B1 is C1, and so on. The cells below A1 are A2, A3, A4, and so on. Cell designations are shown in figure 21.4.

The lines that form the cells of the table are called *gridlines* as identified in figure 21.3. Gridlines are visible in the document screen but do not print. If you would like to turn off the display of gridlines, choose Table, then Gridlines. You may find the gridlines useful when creating a table and will want them displayed.

In addition to gridlines, nonprinting characters identify the end of a cell and the end of a row. To view these characters, click on the Show/Hide button on the Standard toolbar or press Shift + Ctrl + *. The end-of-cell marker displays inside each cell and the end-of-row marker displays at the end of a row of cells. These markers are identified in figure 21.3.

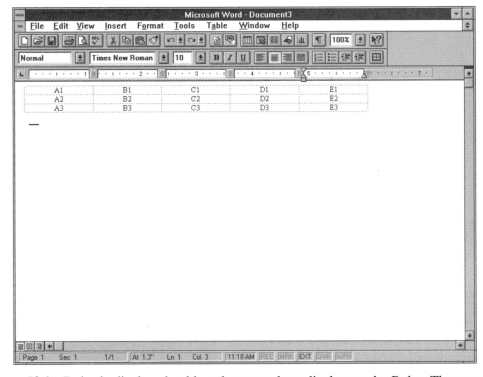

Figure 21.3
Table

Figure 21.4
Cell Designations

If the Ruler is displayed, table column markers display on the Ruler. These markers represent the end of a column and are useful in changing the width of columns. Figure 21.3 identifies a table column marker.

## ■ *Entering Text in Cells*

With the insertion point positioned in a cell, key or edit text as you would normal text. Move the insertion point to other cells with the mouse by positioning the arrow pointer in the desired cell, then clicking the left mouse button. If you are using the keyboard, press Tab to move the insertion point to the next cell or press Shift + Tab to move the insertion point to the previous cell.

If the text you key does not fit on one line, it wraps to the next line within the same cell. Or, if you press Enter within a cell, the insertion point is moved to the next line within the same cell. The cell vertically lengthens to accommodate the text, and all cells in that row also lengthen.

Pressing the Tab key in a table causes the insertion point to move to the next cell in the table. If you want to move the insertion point to a tab stop within a cell, press Ctrl + Tab.

If the insertion point is located in the last cell of the table and you press the Tab key, Word adds another row to the table. To avoid this situation, make sure you do not press the Tab key after entering text in the last cell. You can insert a page break within a table by pressing Ctrl + Enter. The page break is inserted between rows, not within.

When all information has been entered in the cells, move the insertion point below the table and, if necessary, continue keying the document, or save the document in the normal manner.

## Moving the Insertion Point Within a Table

To move the insertion point to different cells within the table using the mouse, position the arrow pointer in the desired cell, then click the left button.

To move the insertion point to different cells within the table using the keyboard, refer to the information shown in figure 21.5.

*Figure 21.5*
*Insertion Point*
*Movement Within a*
*Table*

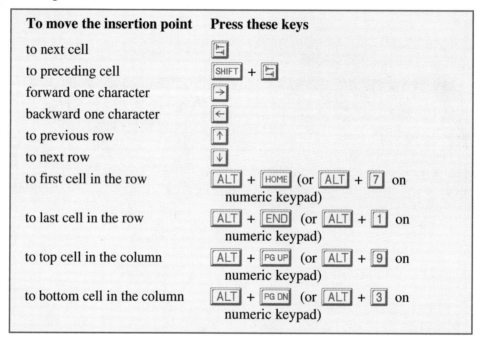

| To move the insertion point | Press these keys |
|---|---|
| to next cell | ⇥ |
| to preceding cell | SHIFT + ⇥ |
| forward one character | → |
| backward one character | ← |
| to previous row | ↑ |
| to next row | ↓ |
| to first cell in the row | ALT + HOME (or ALT + 7 on numeric keypad) |
| to last cell in the row | ALT + END (or ALT + 1 on numeric keypad) |
| to top cell in the column | ALT + PG UP (or ALT + 9 on numeric keypad) |
| to bottom cell in the column | ALT + PG DN (or ALT + 3 on numeric keypad) |

# ■ Selecting Cells

A table can be formatted in special ways. For example, the alignment of text in cells or rows can be changed or character formatting can be added. To identify the cells that are to be affected by the formatting, the specific cells need to be selected.

## Selecting in a Table with the Mouse

The arrow pointer can be used to select a cell, row, column, or an entire table. The left edge of each cell, between the left column border and the end-of-cell marker or first character in the cell, is called the cell selection bar. When the arrow pointer is positioned in the cell selection bar, it turns into an arrow pointing up and to the right (instead of the left).

To select a particular cell, position the arrow pointer in the cell selection bar at the left edge of the cell until it turns into an arrow pointing up and to the right, as shown in figure 21.6, then click the left mouse button.

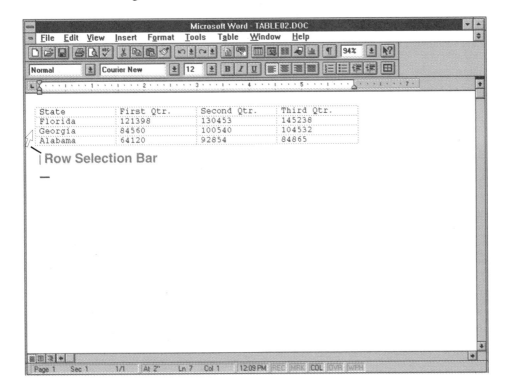

Figure 21.6
Cell Selection Bar

Each row in a table contains a row selection bar, which is the space just to the left of the left edge of the table. Figure 21.7 shows the arrow pointer in the row selection bar. When the arrow pointer is positioned in the row selection bar, the arrow pointer turns into an arrow pointing up and to the right.

To select a row, position the arrow pointer in the row selection bar at the left edge of the table until it turns into an arrow pointing up and to the right, then click the left mouse button. You can also select a row by positioning the arrow pointer in the cell selection bar of any cell in the row, then double-clicking the left mouse button.

Figure 21.7
Row Selection Bar

To select a column, position the arrow pointer on the uppermost horizontal gridline of the table in the appropriate column until it turns into a short, downward-pointing arrow. Click the left mouse button to select the column.

Once you have selected a particular cell, row, or column, you can hold down the Shift key, position the I-beam pointer in another cell, row, or column, then click the left mouse button. This selects cells in the table from the location of the first selected cell, row, or column to the location of the I-beam pointer.

Cells in a table can also be selected by positioning the I-beam pointer in the first cell to be selected, holding down the left mouse button, dragging the I-beam pointer to the last cell to be selected, then releasing the mouse button.

To select all cells within a table using the mouse, position the arrow pointer in the row selection bar at the left edge of the table until it turns into an arrow pointing up and to the right, hold down the left mouse button, drag down to select all rows in the table, then release the left mouse button.

If you want to select a portion of text within a cell (rather than the entire cell), position the I-beam pointer at the beginning of the text, then hold down the left mouse button as you drag the mouse across the text. When a cell is selected, the entire cell is changed to black. When text within a cell is selected, only those lines containing text are selected.

## Selecting in a Table with the Keyboard

The keyboard can be used to select specific cells within a table. Figure 21.8 displays the commands for selecting specific amounts of a table.

*Figure 21.8*
*Selecting in a Table with the Keyboard*

| To select | Press |
|---|---|
| the next cell's contents | ⬚ |
| the preceding cell's contents | SHIFT + ⬚ |
| the entire table | ALT + 5 (on numeric keypad with Num Lock off) |
| adjacent cells | Hold SHIFT, then press an arrow key repeatedly. |
| a column | Position insertion point in top cell of column, hold down SHIFT, then press ↓ until column is selected. |

If you want to select only text within cells, rather than the entire cell, press F8 to turn on the Select mode, then move the insertion point with an arrow key.

When a cell is selected, the entire cell is changed to black. When text within a cell is selected, only those lines containing text are selected.

## Selecting Cells with the Table Drop-Down Menu

A row or column of cells or all cells in a table can be selected with options from the Table drop-down menu. For example, to select a row of cells in a table, you would complete the following steps:

1. Position the insertion point in any cell in the row.
2. Choose Table, then Select Row.

To select cells in a column, position the insertion point in any cell in the column, then choose Table, Select Column. To select all cells in the table, position the insertion point in any cell in the table, then choose Table, Select Table.

# Deleting a Table

All text in cells within a table can be deleted, leaving the table gridlines, or all text and the gridlines can be deleted. To delete the text, leaving the gridlines, you would complete the following steps:

1. Select the table.
2. Press the Delete key.

If just the table is selected, the text in each cell is deleted leaving the gridlines. To delete the text in cells and the gridlines, you would complete the following steps:

1. Select the table and the paragraph mark immediately below the table.
2. Press the Delete key.

If the paragraph mark is also selected, the text in cells as well as the gridlines are deleted from the document. When deleting the text and gridlines, you may want to turn on the display of nonprinting characters so the paragraph mark below the table is visible.

# Formatting a Table

A table that has been created with Word's Tables feature can be formatted in a variety of ways. For example, borders and shading can be added to cells, rows and columns can be inserted or deleted, cells can be split or merged, and the alignment of the table can be changed.

## Adding Borders

The gridlines creating a table do not print. If you want horizontal and vertical lines between cells to print, you must add borders to the table. Borders can be added to one cell, selected cells, or the entire table.

Borders can be added to cells or selected cells with buttons on the Borders toolbar or with options from the Borders and Shading dialog box. You learned about the buttons on the Borders toolbar in chapter 18. To display the Borders toolbar, click on the Borders button on the Formatting toolbar. To add a border to a cell or selected cells, select the cell or cells, then click on the button or buttons on the Borders toolbar that applies the desired format. For example, to add a 3/4-point double-line border to the bottom of all cells in the first row of a table, you would complete the following steps:

1. Select all cells in the first row of the table.
2. Click on the Borders button on the Formatting toolbar to display the Borders toolbar. (Skip this step if the Borders toolbar is already displayed.)
3. Click on the down-pointing arrow to the right of the Line Style button on the Borders toolbar, then click on *3/4 pt* ===== in the drop-down menu (the option that displays with a double line).
4. Click on the Bottom Border button on the Borders toolbar.

You would complete similar steps to add a border to the left, right, or top of a cell or selected cells. For example, if you want to add a 3/4 point single-line border around and between all cells in a table, you would complete the following steps:

1. Select the entire table.
2. Make sure *3/4 pt* (single-line) displays in the Line Style button on the Borders toolbar. (This is the default border line.)
3. Click on the Inside Border button on the Borders toolbar.
4. Click on the Outside Border button on the Borders toolbar.

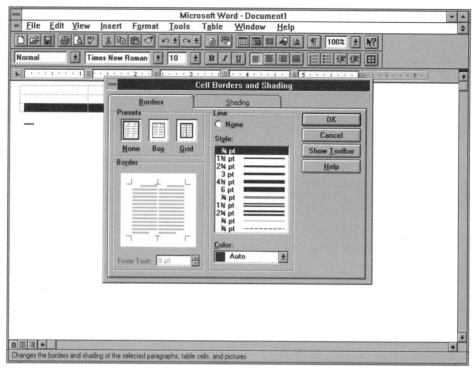

Borders can also be added to selected cells in a table with options from the Cell Borders and Shading dialog box with the Borders tab selected as shown in figure 21.9. To display this dialog box, select a cell or cells, then choose Format, Borders and Shading.

The options available at this dialog box were explained in chapter 18. Make changes to this dialog box as you learned in chapter 18. As an example of how to use this dialog box, you would complete the following steps to add a 2 1/4 point line to the bottom of cells in the second row of the table:

1. Select the second row of cells in the table.
2. Choose Format, Borders and Shading.
3. At the Cell Borders and Shading dialog box with the Borders tab selected, make sure None is selected in the Presets section.
4. Click on *2 1/4 pt* in the Style section of the dialog box.
5. Click on the bottom border of the preview page in the Border section of the dialog box.
6. Choose OK.

Borders can be added around and between all cells in a table. To do this, either select the entire table or have the insertion point positioned in the table with no cells selected. When you choose Format, then Borders and Shading with the entire table selected or the insertion point positioned inside the table, the Table Borders and Shading dialog box displays. This dialog box is similar to the Cell Borders and Shading dialog box shown in figure 21.9. If you want to add borders around and between all cells in the table, you would complete the following steps:

1. Select the entire table or position the insertion point in the table (with no cell selected).
2. Choose Format, Borders and Shading.
3. At the Table Borders and Shading dialog box with the Borders tab selected, choose Grid. (This is located in the Presets section of the dialog box in the upper left corner.)
4. Choose OK.

The Grid option from the Table Borders and Shading dialog box tells Word to add a grid to the table. This inserts lines around and between all cells.

## Adding Shading

To add visual appeal to a table, shading can be added to cells. Shading can be added to cells or selected cells with buttons on the Borders toolbar or with options from the Borders and Shading dialog box.

To display the Borders toolbar, click on the Borders button on the Formatting toolbar. To add shading to a cell or selected cells using the Borders toolbar, you would complete the following steps:

1. Select the cell or cells.
2. Click on the down-pointing arrow to the right of the Shading button.
3. Click on the desired shading option at the drop-down menu.

Shading can also be added to a cell or selected cells with options from the Borders and Shading dialog box. To do this, you would complete the following steps:

1. Select the cell or cells to which you want shading applied.
2. Choose Format, Borders and Shading.
3. At the Cell Borders and Shading dialog box, choose the Shading tab.
4. At the Cell Borders and Shading dialog box with the Shading tab selected, specify the desired shading in the Shading list box. (Click on the down-pointing arrow if necessary to see all options.)
5. After specifying the style of shading desired, choose OK.

To apply the same shading to all cells in a table, either select the entire table or position the insertion point in just one cell of the table (without selecting the cell), then complete steps similar to those listed above. This will display the Table Borders and Shading dialog box rather than the Cell Borders and Shading dialog box.

## Changing Column Width

When a table is created, the columns are the same width. The width of the columns depends on the number of columns as well as the document margins.

In some tables, you may want to change the width of certain columns to accommodate more or less text. You can change the width of columns using the mouse on the Ruler or in a table, or with options from the Cell Height and Width dialog box.

### Changing Column Width with the Ruler

When the insertion point is positioned in a table, the column widths are displayed on the Ruler. These table column markers are identified in figure 21.3. To change the column width with table column markers on the Ruler, you would complete the following steps:

1. Position the arrow pointer on the column width marker to be moved until it turns into a left- and right-pointing arrow.
2. Hold down the left mouse button.
3. Drag the marker to make the column wider or narrower. (As you drag the marker, any table column markers to the right are also moved.)
4. When the column width marker is in the desired position, release the mouse button.

When you move a table column marker, any table column markers to the right are also moved. If you want to see the column measurements as you move a table column marker, hold down the Alt key while you drag the marker. You can also view the column measurements by positioning the arrow pointer on a table column marker, holding down the Alt key, then holding down the left mouse button.

If you want only the table column marker moved where the arrow pointer is positioned, hold down the Shift key, then drag the marker on the Ruler. This does not change the overall size of the table. To change the column width of the column where the insertion point is positioned and all columns to the right and the size of the table, hold down the Ctrl key and the Shift key while you drag the table column marker.

The first-line indent marker, the left indent marker, and the right indent marker display on the Ruler for the column where the insertion point is positioned. These markers can be used to adjust the left or right column margins or indent the first line in a cell. Changes made to the column margins affect only the column where the insertion point is positioned.

### Changing Column Width with the Mouse in the Table

You can use the mouse to change column widths within the table. To change column widths using the mouse, position the arrow pointer on the gridline separating columns until the insertion point turns into a left- and right-pointing arrow with a vertical double line between. Hold down the left mouse button, drag the column line to the desired location, then release the mouse button. This moves the column line where the arrow pointer is positioned and all column lines to the right.

If you hold down the Shift key while you drag a column gridline, only that column line moves and the table width does not change. If you hold down the Ctrl key and the Shift key while you drag a column gridline, the column width changes and all columns to the right move relatively and the size of the table is changed.

### Changing Column Width with the Cell Height and Width Dialog Box

If you know the exact measurement for columns in a table, you can change column widths using the Cell Height and Width dialog box with the Column tab selected as shown in figure 21.10. For example, to change the column width of the second column in a table to 2 inches, you would complete the following steps:

1. Position the insertion point in any cell in the second column.
2. Choose Table, then Cell Height and Width.
3. At the Cell Height and Width dialog box with the Column tab selected, choose Width of Column, then key **2**. (You can also click on the up- or down-pointing triangles to the right of the text box until *2* displays.)
4. Choose OK or press Enter.

Complete similar steps to change the column width for other columns in a table. You can also display the Cell Height and Width dialog box with a shortcut menu. To do this, select the column, click the *right* mouse button, then click on Cell Height and Width at the drop-down menu. At the Cell Height and Width dialog box, make changes as needed, then choose OK or press Enter.

If a table contains text or other features such as pictures, you can tell Word to automatically adjust all column widths in a table to best fit the text or picture. To do this, display the Cell Height and Width dialog box with the Column table selected, then choose Autofit.

In a table containing text or other features, you can adjust the width of one column to accommodate the longest line of text in the column or the picture. To do this, position the I-beam pointer on the right column gridline until it turns into a left- and right-pointing arrow with a vertical double line, then double-click the left mouse button. To automatically size more than one column, select the columns first, then double-click on a gridline.

## Changing Cell Alignment

By default, text in cells aligns at the left side of the cell. Like normal text, this alignment can be changed to center, right, or justified. To change the alignment of cells, select the cells, then click on the desired alignment button on the Standard toolbar. You can also change alignment of selected

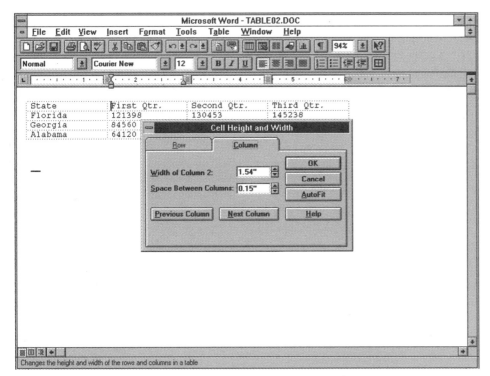

Figure 21.10
*Cell Height and Width Dialog Box with Column Tab Selected*

cells with the Alignment option at the Paragraph dialog box with the Indents and Spacing tab selected or with a shortcut command. For example, to change the alignment of all cells in the second column of a table to centered, you would complete the following steps:

1. Select all cells in the second column.
2. Click on the Center button on the Standard toolbar.

## Aligning the Table

At the Cell Height and Width dialog box with the Row tab selected, the horizontal placement of rows or an entire table can be specified. By default, rows in a table and the table itself are aligned at the left margin. This can be changed to center or right. For example, to center an entire table horizontally between margins in the document, you would complete the following steps:

1. Position the insertion point in any cell in the table.
2. Choose Table, then Cell Height and Width. (Make sure the Row tab is selected.)
3. At the Cell Height and Width dialog box with the Row tab selected, choose Center in the Alignment section of the dialog box.
4. Choose OK or press Enter.

To align a table or selected rows at the right margin, you would choose Right at the Cell Height and Width dialog box.

## Inserting Rows

After a table has been created, rows can be added (inserted) to the table. There are several methods you can use to insert rows.

The Insert Rows option from the Table drop-down menu can be used to insert a row in a table. By default, a row is inserted above the row where the insertion point is positioned. To insert a row in a table, position the insertion point in the row below where the row is to be inserted, then choose Table, Insert Rows.

If you want to insert more than one row, select the number of rows in the table that you want inserted, then choose Table, Insert Rows.

You can also insert rows by selecting a row or several rows, then clicking on the Insert Rows button on the Standard toolbar. The Insert Table button becomes the Insert Rows button on the Standard toolbar when rows in a table are selected.

Another method for inserting a row or several rows is to position the I-beam inside the table, click the *right* mouse button, then click on Insert Rows.

A row can be inserted at the end of the table by positioning the insertion point in the last cell in the table, then pressing the Tab key.

## Inserting Columns

Columns can be inserted in a table in much the same way as rows. To insert a column, select a column or group of columns, then choose T̲able, I̲nsert Columns. You can also insert a column (or columns) by selecting the column, then clicking on the Insert Columns button on the Standard toolbar. The Insert Table button on the Standard toolbar becomes the Insert Columns button when a column or columns are selected.

You can also insert a column or a group of columns by selecting the column(s), clicking the *right* mouse button, then clicking on Insert Columns at the drop-down menu.

Word inserts a column or columns to the left of the selected column or columns. A table can contain a maximum of 31 columns.

If you want to add a column to the right side of the table, select all the end-of-row markers, then click on the Insert Columns button on the Standard toolbar.

## Deleting Cells, Rows, or Columns

Specific cells in a table or rows or columns in a table can be deleted. To delete a specific cell in a table, you would complete the following steps:

1. Select the cell to be deleted.
2. Choose T̲able, then D̲elete Cells.
3. At the Delete Cells dialog box shown in figure 21.11, choose OK or press Enter.

*Figure 21.11*
*Delete Cells Dialog Box*

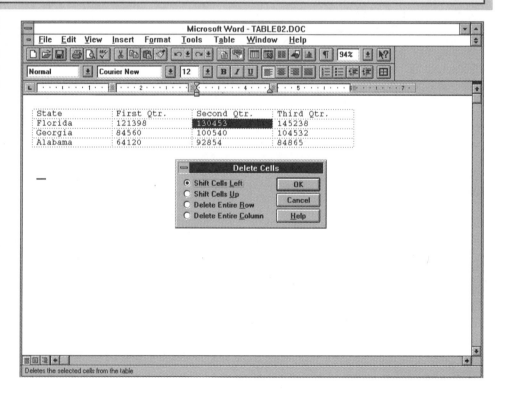

At the Delete Cells dialog box, the Shift Cells Left option is selected by default. At this option, cells will shift left after the selected cell (or cells) is deleted. Choose the Shift Cells Up option if you want cells moved up after the selected cell (or cells) is deleted. Choose Delete Entire Row to delete the row where the insertion point is positioned or choose Delete Entire Column to delete the column where the insertion point is positioned.

The Delete Cells dialog box can also be displayed by positioning the I-beam pointer in the table, clicking the *right* mouse button, then clicking on Delete Cells from the drop-down menu.

A row can be deleted at the Delete Cells dialog box by choosing the Delete Entire Row option. A row or selected rows can also be deleted with the Delete Rows option from the Table drop-down menu. For example, to delete selected rows, you would complete the following steps:

> 1. Select the rows in the table to be deleted.
> 2. Choose Table, then Delete Rows.

A column can be deleted at the Delete Cells dialog box by choosing the Delete Entire Column option. A column or selected columns can also be deleted with the Delete Columns option from the Table drop-down menu. For example, to delete selected columns, you would complete the following steps:

> 1. Select the columns in the table to be deleted.
> 2. Choose Table, then Delete Columns.

## Merging Cells

Cells can be merged with the Merge Cells option from the Table drop-down menu. Before merging cells, the cells to be merged must be selected. As an example of how to merge cells, you would complete the following steps to merge cells A1 through C1:

> 1. Select cells A1 through C1.
> 2. Choose Table, then Merge Cells.

## Splitting Cells

With the Split Cells option from the Table drop-down menu, you can split a cell or a row or column of cells. For example, to split cell D3 into two columns, you would complete the following steps:

> 1. Position the insertion point in cell D3.
> 2. Choose Table, then Split Cells.
> 3. At the Split Cells dialog box shown in figure 21.12, make sure 2 displays in the Number of Columns text box, then choose OK or press Enter.

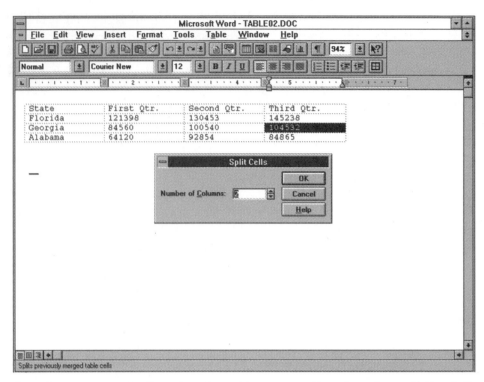

Figure 21.12
Split Cells Dialog
Box

To split an entire column or row of cells, select the column or row first, then choose T<u>a</u>ble, S<u>p</u>lit Cells.

## Changing Row Height

By default, Word determines the amount of vertical space (measured in points) for the height of the row based on how much text is inserted in cells. If you want to control row height, make changes at the Cell Height and Width dialog box with the <u>R</u>ow tab selected as shown in figure 21.13.

The H<u>e</u>ight of Row option at the Cell Height and Width dialog box has a default setting of *Auto*. At this setting, the height of the row is automatically determined based on the amount of text inserted in the cells within the row. The *Auto* option can be changed to *At Least* or *Exactly*.

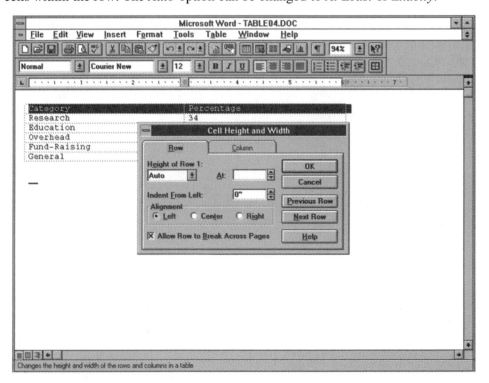

Figure 21.13
Cell Height and
Width Dialog Box
with Row Tab
Selected

If you choose *At Least*, enter a point measurement in the <u>A</u>t text box or click on the up- or down-pointing triangles to the right of the <u>A</u>t text box to increase or decrease the point measurement. If you change the row height to *At Least*, and cell contents exceed the point measurement entered in the <u>A</u>t text box, Word will adjust the height to fit.

You can also choose *Exactly,* then enter a point measurement in the <u>A</u>t text box. If cell contents exceed the point measurement entered in the <u>A</u>t text box, Word cuts off the contents.

By default, Word will allow a row to be divided between pages. If you want pages to be divided above or below a row but not within a row, you would remove the X from the Allow Row to <u>B</u>reak Across Page option at the Cell Height and Width dialog box.

Row height can also be changed with the vertical ruler in the Page Layout viewing mode. In Page Layout, row markers display on the vertical ruler as double lines and identify rows in a table. To increase or decrease the height of a row using the row marker on the vertical ruler, you would complete the following steps:

1.  Change to the Page Layout viewing mode.
2.  Position the arrow pointer on the double-line row marker on the vertical ruler to the left of the row to be changed until the arrow pointer turns into a double-headed arrow pointing up and down.
3.  Hold down the left mouse button, drag the row marker to the desired position, then release the mouse button.

Go To
Exercise
18

## Creating Table Headings

In some tables, columns of text may contain a heading row. This heading row identifies the contents of the columns. If a table contains a heading row and the table is split between pages, the heading row should be repeated on the next page. This provides the reader with information on the column contents. To tell Word to repeat a heading row on the next page, you would complete the following steps:

1.  Select the row containing the heading text.
2.  Choose T<u>a</u>ble, <u>H</u>eadings.

## Cutting and Pasting

In a table, columns and/or rows can be moved or copied to a different location within the table. To copy or move a row or column, select the row or column first, choose <u>E</u>dit from the Menu bar, then choose Cu<u>t</u> or <u>C</u>opy. Move the insertion point to the first cell in the column or row where you want the column or row pasted, choose <u>E</u>dit, then <u>P</u>aste. (The <u>P</u>aste option will display as <u>P</u>aste Columns if you selected a column or it will display as <u>P</u>aste Rows if you selected a row. A column will be inserted to the left of the column where the insertion point is positioned, and a row will be inserted above the row where the insertion point is positioned.)

For example, to reverse the first and second columns in a table, you would complete the following steps:

1.  Select the second column.
2.  Choose <u>E</u>dit, then Cu<u>t</u>; or click on the Cut button on the Standard toolbar.
3.  Position the insertion point in the first cell in the first column.
4.  Chose <u>E</u>dit, then <u>P</u>aste Columns; or click on the Paste button on the Standard toolbar.

To copy a column or row, complete similar steps except choose <u>C</u>opy, rather than Cu<u>t</u> from the <u>E</u>dit drop-down menu; or click on the Copy button on the Standard toolbar.

You can also use a shortcut menu to cut, copy, and paste in a table. For example, to reverse the second and third columns in a table using a shortcut menu, you would complete the following steps:

1. Select the third column.
2. With the arrow pointer positioned within the selected cells in the table, click the *right* mouse button.
3. At the shortcut menu, click on Cut.
4. Select the second column.
5. With the insertion point positioned inside the selected cells in the table, click the *right* mouse button, then click on Paste Columns.

## Splitting a Table

A table can be split into two tables with the Split Table option from the Table drop-down menu. When a table is split, Word inserts a paragraph mark between the two parts of the table. If you want to merge the two tables back into one, delete the paragraph mark.

## Formatting with AutoFormat

Formatting a table such as adding borders or shading, aligning text in cells, changing fonts, etc., can take some time. Word has provided predesigned table formats that can quickly format your table for you.

Table formats are contained in the Table AutoFormat dialog box shown in figure 21.14. To display this dialog box, position the insertion point in any cell in a table, then choose Table, Table AutoFormat.

Predesigned table formats are displayed in the Formats list box. Select a table format in the Formats list box and preview the appearance of the table in the Preview box.

When previewing predesigned table formats, you can make some changes to the predesigned format by removing X's from the options in the Formats to Apply section of the dialog box. For example, suppose you like a predesigned format created by Word except the shading; select the format in the Formats list box in the dialog box, then chose Shading. This removes the X from the Shading check box and also removes the shading from the table shown in the Preview box.

*Figure 21.14*
*Table AutoFormat*
*Dialog Box*

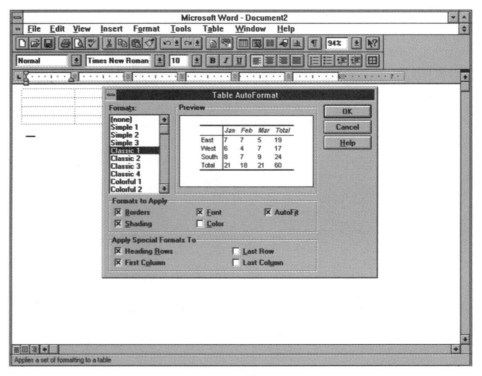

If you want to apply the special formatting only to specific parts of the table, select the parts of the table you want the formatting applied to in the Apply Special Formats To section of the dialog box. For example, if you want the table formatting only applied to the first column in the table, insert an X in the First Column option and remove the X's from the other options.

As an example of how to use one of Word's predesigned table formats, you would complete the following steps to format a table with the *Classic 2* table format:

1. Position the insertion point in any cell in the table.
2. Choose Table, then Table AutoFormat.
3. At the Table AutoFormat dialog box, click on the *Classic 2* option in the Formats section of the dialog box.
4. Choose OK or press Enter.

## Using the Table Wizard

A table can be created with a table Wizard. A Wizard guides you through the process of creating a table, then takes you to the Table AutoFormat dialog box to complete the creation of the table. To use the table Wizard, you would complete the following steps:

1. Position the insertion point at the location where the upper left corner of the table is to display.
2. Choose Table, then Insert Table.
3. At the Insert Table dialog box, choose Wizard.
4. At the Table Wizard dialog box, make decisions based on the choices provided by the Wizard, then choose Next.
5. Continue making decisions, then choosing Next until you have answered all questions, then choose Finish. (This displays the Table AutoFormat dialog box.)
6. At the Table AutoFormat dialog box, choose the predesigned table format, then choose OK or press Enter.

The table created by you and the Wizard is inserted in the document. Enter the text in the cells of the table.

# Converting Text to/from a Table

Text in a document separated by paragraph marks, commas, or tabs can be converted to a table. Text in a table can also be converted to ordinary text.

## Converting Text to a Table

To convert text to a table, the text must be separated by paragraph marks, commas, or tabs. To convert text to a table, you would complete the following steps:

1. Select the text.
2. Click on the Insert Table button on the Standard toolbar.

If you want control over how the text is converted to a table, convert the text with the Convert Text to Table option from the Table drop-down menu. To do this, you would complete the following steps:

1. Select the text to be converted.
2. Choose Table, then Convert Text to Table.
3. At the Convert Text to Table dialog box, shown in figure 21.15, make any necessary changes.
4. Choose OK or press Enter.

Figure 21.15
Convert Text to
Table Dialog Box

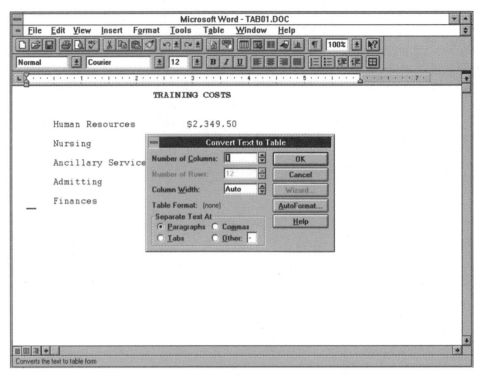

At the Convert Text to Table dialog box, you can specify the number of columns desired in the table. Word will automatically insert a number in the Number of Columns text box based on the text and separators in the document. By default, Word will automatically determine column widths. To specify column widths, choose Column Width, then enter the desired column measurement.

Word will determine what is used to separate text into columns. This is specified in the Separate Text At section of the Convert Text to Table dialog box. Choose a different option in this section if you want to change what Word uses to separate text into columns.

## Converting a Table to Text

Text in a table can be converted to just text. You can specify whether text is separated by paragraph marks, tabs, commas, or other symbols. To convert text in a table to just text, you would complete the following steps:

1. Select the table.
2. Choose Table, then Convert Table to Text.
3. At the Convert Table to Text dialog box shown in figure 21.16, specify whether you want text to be separated by paragraph marks, tabs, commas, or other symbols.
4. Choose OK or press Enter.

# ■ Performing Calculations

Numbers in a table can be calculated. Numbers can be added, subtracted, multiplied, and divided. In addition, you can calculate averages, percentages, minimum, and maximum values. Calculations can be performed in a Word table; for complex calculations, however, use a Microsoft Excel worksheet.

To perform a calculation in a table, position the insertion point in the cell where you want the result of the calculation to display. This cell should be empty. By default, Word assumes that you want to sum cells immediately above or to the left of the cell where the insertion point is positioned. This default calculation can be changed.

As an example of how to calculate sums, you would complete the following steps to calculate the sum of cells in C1 through C5 and insert the result of the calculation in cell C6:

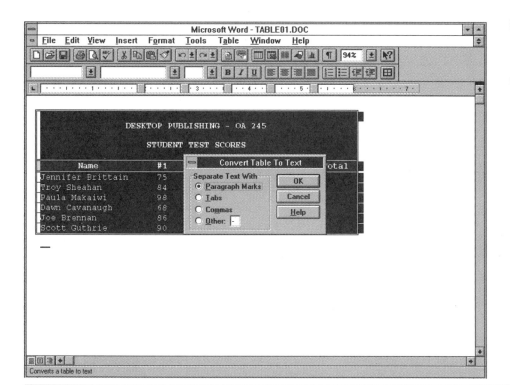

*Figure 21.16*
*Convert Table to*
*Text Dialog Box*

1. Position the insertion point in cell C6.
2. Choose Table, Formula.
3. At the Formula dialog box shown in figure 21.17, the calculation =*SUM(ABOVE)* will display in the Formula text box. This is the desired formula to calculate the sum.
4. Choose OK or press Enter.

Word adds the numbers in cells C1 through C5, then inserts the result of this calculation in cell C6.

To perform other types of calculations such as subtraction, multiplication, and division, the formula displayed in the Formula text box at the Formula dialog box must be changed. You can use an arithmetic sign to write a formula. For example, the formula A2-A3 (A2 minus A3) can be inserted in cell A4, which tells Word to insert the difference of A2 and A3 in cell A4. If changes are made to the numbers in cells A2 and A3, the value in A4 can be recalculated.

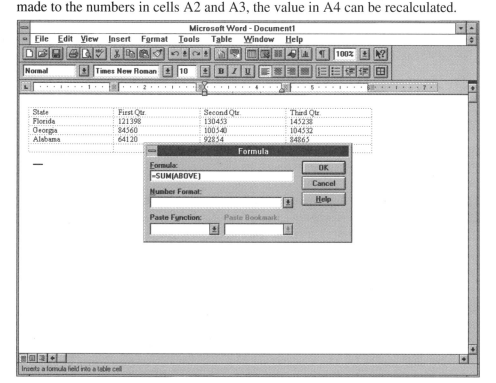

*Figure 21.17*
*Formula Dialog Box*

Four basic operators can be used when writing formulas: the plus sign for addition, the minus sign (hyphen) for subtraction, the asterisk for multiplication, and the forward slash (/) for division.

If there are two or more operators in a calculation, Word calculates from left to right. If you want to change the order of calculation, use parentheses around the part of the calculation to be performed first.

In the default formula, the SUM part of the formula is called a function. Word provides other functions you can use to write a formula. These functions are available with the Paste Function option at the Formula dialog box. For example, you can use the AVERAGE function to average numbers in cells. Examples of how formulas can be written are shown in figure 21.18.

**Figure 21.18**
**Example Formulas**

> **Cell E4 is the total price of items.**
>
> Cell B4 contains the quantity of items, and cell D4 contains the unit price. The formula for cell E4 is =B4*D4. (This formula multiplies the quantity of items in cell B4 by the unit price in cell D4.)
>
> **Cell D3 is the percentage of increase of sales from the previous year.**
>
> Cell B3 contains the amount of sales for the previous year, and cell C3 contains the amount of sales for the current year. The formula for cell D3 is =(C3-B3)/B3*100. (This formula subtracts the amount of sales this year from the amount of sales last year. The remaining amount is divided by the amount of sales last year and then multiplied by 100 to display the product as a percentage.)
>
> **Cell E1 is the average of test scores.**
>
> Cells A1 through D1 contain test scores. The formula for cell E1 to calculate the average score is =(A1+B1+C1+D1)/4. (This formula adds the scores from cells A1 through D1, then divides that sum by 4.) You can also enter the formula as AVERAGE(LEFT). The AVERAGE function tells Word to average all entries left of cell E1.

If changes are made to numbers in cells that are part of a formula, select the result of the calculation, then press the F9 function key. This recalculates the formula and inserts the new result of the calculation in the cell. You can also recalculate by completing the following steps:

1. Select the number in the cell containing the formula.
2. Choose Table, Formula.
3. At the Formula dialog box, choose OK or press Enter.

## CHAPTER SUMMARY

- Word's Tables feature can be used to create columns and rows of information. A cell is the intersection between a row and a column.
- A table can contain text, characters, numbers, data, or formulas. It can be extensively formatted and can include calculations.
- A table can be created with the Insert Table button on the Standard toolbar or by choosing the Table option from the Menu bar.
- Columns in a table are lettered from left to right, beginning with A. Rows are numbered from top to bottom beginning with 1.
- The lines that form the cells of the table are called gridlines. Gridlines are visible in the document screen but do not print.
- With the insertion point positioned in a cell, key or edit text as you would normal text.
- To move the insertion point to different cells within the table using the mouse, position the arrow pointer in the desired cell, then click the left button.

- To move the insertion point to different cells within the table using the keyboard, refer to the information shown in figure 21.5 in this chapter.
- Position the arrow pointer on the cell selection bar, the row selection bar, or the top gridline of a column to select a cell, row, or column. Or, position the I-beam pointer and use the mouse to select a portion of the table.
- To use the keyboard to select specific cells within a table, refer to the information shown in figure 21.8 in this chapter.
- A row or column of cells or all cells in a table can be selected with options from the Table drop-down menu.
- All text in cells within a table can be deleted, leaving the table gridlines, or all text and the gridlines can be deleted.
- Borders and shading can be added to cells, rows and columns can be inserted or deleted, cells can be split or merged, and the alignment of the table can be changed.
- Column width can be changed using the Ruler, the mouse, or at the Cell Height and Width dialog box.
- After a table has been created, various methods can be used to add rows and/or columns.
- Specific cells in a table or rows or columns in a table can be deleted.
- Control the row height at the Cell Height and Width dialog box.
- Some tables may contain a heading row that identifies the contents of the columns. You can tell Word to repeat a heading row on the next page.
- Columns/rows can be moved or copied to a different location within the table.
- Word has provided predesigned table formats in the Table AutoFormat dialog box that can quickly format your table.
- A table Wizard guides you through the process of creating a table, then it takes you to the Table AutoFormat dialog box to complete the creation of the table.
- Text in a document separated by paragraph marks, commas, or tabs can be converted to a table using the Insert Table button on the Standard toolbar or at the Convert Text to Table dialog box. Text in a table can be converted to ordinary text at the Convert Table to Text dialog box.
- Numbers in a table can be calculated by inserting a formula in a cell at the Formula dialog box.

## COMMANDS REVIEW

| | Mouse | Keyboard |
|---|---|---|
| Create table with Standard toolbar | With arrow pointer on Insert Table button on Standard toolbar, hold down left mouse button, move arrow pointer down and right until desired table size displays, release button | |
| Display Insert Table dialog box | Table, Insert Table | Table, Insert Table |
| Turn off display of gridlines | Table, Gridlines | Table, Gridlines |
| Move insertion point to next cell | Position I-beam pointer in next cell, click left mouse button | [TAB] |
| Move insertion point to previous cell | Position I-beam pointer in previous cell, click left mouse button | [SHIFT] + [TAB] |
| Insert tab within a cell | | [CTRL] + [TAB] |
| Insert page break within a table | | [CTRL] + [ENTER] |

| | **Mouse** | **Keyboard** |
|---|---|---|
| Select a row, column, or all cells with Table drop-down menu | Position insertion point, choose Table, then Select Row (or Column or Table) | Position insertion point, choose Table, then Select Row (or Column or Table) |
| Delete text only from table | Select table, press Delete | Select table, press Delete |
| Delete text and gridlines | Select table and the paragraph mark below table, press Delete | Select table and the paragraph mark below table, press Delete |
| Display Cell Height and Width dialog box | Table, Cell Height and Width; or select column, click right mouse button, click on Cell Height and Width | Table, Cell Height and Width |
| Delete cells, rows, or columns | Select cell(s), choose Table, Delete Cells, then Delete Entire Row or Delete Entire Column | Select cell(s), choose Table, Delete Cells, then Delete Entire Row or Delete Entire Column |
| Repeat heading row on next page | Select the heading row, choose Table, Headings | Select the heading row, choose Table, Headings |
| Display Table AutoFormat dialog box | With insertion point in a cell, choose Table, Table AutoFormat | With insertion point in a cell, choose Table, Table AutoFormat |
| Display Table Wizard dialog box | Table, Insert Table, choose Wizard | Table, Insert Table, choose Wizard |
| Display Convert Text to Table dialog box | Table, Convert Text to Table | Table, Convert Text to Table |
| Display Convert Table to Text dialog box | Table, Convert Table to Text | Table, Convert Table to Text |
| Display Formula dialog box | Table, Formula | Table, Formula |

## CHECK YOUR UNDERSTANDING

**Completion:**  In the space provided, indicate the correct term, command, or number.

1. To create a table the quickest way possible, choose this. _____
2. This is another name for the lines that form the cells of the table. _____
3. The end-of-row marker shows only when this is chosen at the Standard toolbar. _____
4. The table column markers display here. _____
5. Use this keyboard command to move the insertion point to the previous cell. _____
6. Use this keyboard command to move the insertion point to a tab stop within a table. _____
7. Use this keyboard command to move the insertion point to the bottom cell in the column. _____
8. This is the name given to the space just to the left of the left edge of a table. _____

9. To select the portion of a table from a selected cell, row, or column to where the I-beam has been repositioned, hold down this key and click the left mouse button.

10. To select all cells within a table, position the arrow pointer in the row selection bar until it becomes an arrow pointing up and right, hold down this button, drag down to select all rows, then release the same button. _____

11. Use this keyboard command to select all cells within a table. _____

12. List the steps needed to delete all text from a table and leave the lines. _____

13. If you want horizontal and vertical lines between cells to print, you must add this to the table. _____

14. To add shading to a cell or selected cells, display this dialog box. _____

15. Change the width of columns using the mouse, the Cell Height and Width dialog box, or this. _____

16. Text in cells aligns at this side of the cell by default. _____

17. One method for inserting rows in a table is to position the I-beam inside the table, click the right mouse button, then click on this. _____

18. A column or group of columns that is added to a table will be inserted on this side of the selected column(s). _____

19. Choose this option at the Delete Cells dialog box if you want cells moved up after selected cells are deleted. _____

20. To merge cells A1 and B1, select A1 and B1, then choose this at the Table drop-down menu. _____

21. To divide one cell into two rows, choose this at the Table drop-down menu. _____

22. The amount of vertical space in each cell can be changed at this dialog box. _____

23. To repeat a table's heading row on the next page, choose this at the Table drop-down menu. _____

24. Choose predesigned table formats at this dialog box. _____

25. This guides you through the process of creating a table. _____

26. Text must be in this format in order to be converted to a table. _____

27. This is the operator for multiplication that is used when writing formulas in a table. _____

28. This is the formula to add cells D2, D3, and D4, then divide the total by 5. _____

29. This is the formula to multiply A1 by B1. _____

30. This calculation will display in the Formula text box in the Formula dialog box by default. _____

## AT THE COMPUTER

### Exercise 1

1. At a clear document screen, create the table shown in figure 21.19 (without the printed gridlines; these are included just as a reference) by completing the following steps:
   a. Change the paragraph alignment to center and turn on bold.
   b. Key **ST. FRANCIS MEDICAL CENTER.**
   c. Press Enter twice.
   d. Key **Training and Education Department**.
   e. Press Enter.
   f. Turn off bold and change the paragraph alignment to left.
   g. Press Enter twice.
   h. Create the table by completing the following steps:
      (1) Position the arrow pointer on the Insert Table button on the Standard toolbar.
      (2) Hold down the left mouse button. This causes a grid to appear.

        (3)  Move the arrow pointer down and to the right until the number below the grid displays as *6x2*, then release the mouse button.

    i.  Key the text in the cells as indicated in figure 21.19. Press the Tab key to move to the next cell or press Shift + Tab to move to the preceding cell. (If you accidentally press the Enter key within a cell, immediately press the Backspace key.)

2.  Save the table and name it c21ex01.

3.  Print c21ex01. (The gridlines will not print.)

4.  Close c21ex01.

**Figure 21.19**

**ST. FRANCIS MEDICAL CENTER**

**Training and Education Department**

| | |
|---|---|
| Brenda Hogue | Director |
| Pauline Coffey | Trainer |
| Daniel Lagasa | Trainer |
| James Zekes | Trainer |
| Scott Sideres | Administrative Assistant |
| My Trinh | Administrative Assistant |

## Exercise 2

1.  At a clear document screen, create the table shown in figure 21.20 (without the printed gridlines; these are included just as a reference) by completing the following steps:

    a.  Change the paragraph alignment to center and turn on bold.

    b.  Key **ST. FRANCIS MEDICAL CENTER.**

    c.  Press Enter twice.

    d.  Key **Executive Officers**.

    e.  Press Enter.

    f.  Turn off bold and change the paragraph alignment to left.

    g.  Press Enter twice.

    h.  Create the table by completing the following steps:

        (1)  Choose Table, then Insert Table.

        (2)  At the Insert Table dialog box, key **3** in the Number of Columns text box. (The insertion point is automatically positioned in this text box.)

        (3)  Choose Number of Rows.

        (4)  Key **5**.

        (5)  Choose OK or press Enter.

    i.  Key the text in the cells as indicated in figure 21.20. Press the Tab key to move to the next cell or press Shift + Tab to move to the preceding cell. To create the text in the third column, press Ctrl + Tab, then key the text. (This moves the insertion point to a tab stop within the cell.)

2.  Save the table and name it c21ex02.

3.  Print c21ex02. (The gridlines will not print.)

4.  Close c21ex02.

## Exercise 3

1.  Open c21ex01.

2.  Save the document with Save As and name it c21ex03.

3.  Select then bold the text in the cells in the first column using the mouse by completing the following steps:

**Figure 21.20**

ST. FRANCIS MEDICAL CENTER

Executive Officers

| President | A. St. Germaine | #2005 |
| Vice President | K. Levine | #2089 |
| Vice President | M. Jackson | #2056 |
| Vice President | N. Lizama | #2143 |
| Vice President | B. Chou-Matheson | #2190 |

    a. Position the arrow pointer on the uppermost horizontal gridline of the first column in the table until it turns into a short, downward-pointing arrow.

    b. Click the left mouse button.

    c. Click on the Bold button on the Standard toolbar.

4. Select then italicize the text in the cells in the second column by completing steps similar to those in 3a through 3c.

5. Save the document again with the same name (c21ex03).

6. Print c21ex03. (The gridlines will not print.)

7. Close c21ex03.

## Exercise 4

1. Open c21ex02.

2. Save the document with Save As and name it c21ex04.

3. Select then bold the text in the cells in the first column using the keyboard by completing the following steps:

    a. Position the insertion point in the first cell of the first column (cell A1).

    b. Hold down the Shift key, then press the down arrow key four times. (This should select all cells in the first column.)

    c. Press Ctrl + B.

4. Select then bold the text in the cells in the second column using the Table drop-down menu by completing the following steps:

    a. Position the insertion point in any cell in the second column.

    b. Choose Table, Select Column.

    c. Click on the Bold button on the Standard toolbar.

5. Select then italicize the text in the cells in the third column by completing steps similar to those in 3a through 3c or 4a through 4c.

6. Save the document again with the same name (c21ex04).

7. Print c21ex04. (The gridlines will not print.)

8. Close c21ex04.

## Exercise 5

1. Open c21ex02.

2. Save the document with Save As and name it c21ex05.

3. Make the following changes to the document:

    a. Select then delete the title, *ST. FRANCIS MEDICAL CENTER*, and the subtitle, *Executive Officers*.

    b. Move the insertion point below the table, then press the Enter key three times.

    c. Select the table by completing the following steps:

      (1) Position the arrow pointer in the row selection bar outside the left edge of the table to the left of the first row until it turns into an arrow pointing up and to the right.

  (2) Hold down the left mouse button, drag down to select all rows in the table, then release the left mouse button.
 d. With the table selected, click on the Copy button on the Standard toolbar.
 e. Move the insertion point to the end of the document, then click on the Paste button on the Standard toolbar. (This inserts a copy of the table at the end of the document.)
 f. Select then delete the first table in the document by completing the following steps:
  (1) Click on the Show/Hide button on the Standard toolbar to turn on the display of nonprinting characters.
  (2) Position the insertion point in the first cell in the first column (cell A1) in the first table.
  (3) Hold down the Shift key, then press the down arrow key until the table *and* the first paragraph mark below the table are selected.
  (4) Release the Shift key.
  (5) Press the Delete key.
  (6) Click on the Show/Hide button on the Standard toolbar to turn off the display of nonprinting characters.
4. Save the document again with the same name (c21ex05).
5. Print c21ex05. (The gridlines will not print.)
6. Close c21ex05.

## Exercise 6

1. At a clear document screen, create the table shown in figure 21.21 by completing the following steps:
 a. Change the paragraph alignment to center and turn on bold.
 b. Key **ST. FRANCIS MEDICAL CENTER.**
 c. Press Enter twice.
 d. Key **Unit Directors**.
 e. Press Enter.
 f. Turn off bold and change the paragraph alignment to left.
 g. Press Enter twice.
 h. Create a table with 2 columns and 8 rows (8x2).
 i. Key the text in the first cell (cell A1) by completing the following steps:
  (1) Click on the Center button on the Formatting toolbar.
  (2) Click on the Bold button on the Formatting toolbar.
  (3) Key **Name**.
 j. Press the Tab key to move the insertion point to the next cell (cell B1). Complete steps similar to those in 1i(1) through 1i(3) to center and bold the column heading *Unit*.
 k. Key the text in the remaining cells as indicated in figure 21.21. Press the Tab key to move to the next cell or press Shift + Tab to move to the preceding cell. Press Ctrl + Tab before keying each entry in the remaining cells.
 l. Add border lines around and between the cells by completing the following steps:
  (1) Select the entire table.
  (2) Click on the Borders button on the Formatting toolbar. (This displays the Borders toolbar.)
  (3) Click on the Inside Border button on the Borders toolbar.
  (4) Click on the Outside Border button on the Borders toolbar.
 m. Add a double-line border to the top and bottom of the cells in the first row by completing the following steps:
  (1) Select the first row in the table (the row containing the cells with *Name* and *Unit*).
  (2) Click on the down-pointing arrow to the right of the Line Style button on the Borders toolbar.
  (3) At the drop-down menu, click on the 3/4-point double-line option.

        (4)  Click on the Top Border button on the Borders toolbar.
        (5)  Click on the Bottom Border button on the Borders toolbar.
  2.  Save the document and name it c21ex06.
  3.  Print c21ex06.
  4.  Close c21ex06.

Figure 21.21

**ST. FRANCIS MEDICAL CENTER**

**Unit Directors**

| Name | Unit |
| --- | --- |
| Alyce Arevalo | Pediatrics |
| Sandra Ellerbe | Medical Services |
| Joan Harris-Lee | Surgical Unit |
| Lisa Murray | Coronary Care Unit |
| Rafael Ohala | Labor & Delivery Unit |
| Rosemary Stratten | Emergency Room |
| Benjamin Moon | Intensive Care Unit |

## Exercise 7

  1.  Open c21ex01.
  2.  Save the document with Save As and name it c21ex07.
  3.  Add a border around and between all cells in the table by completing the following steps:
      a.  Position the insertion point in any cell in the table.
      b.  Choose Format, Borders and Shading.
      c.  At the Table Borders and Shading dialog box with the Borders tab selected, choose Grid.
      d.  Choose OK or press Enter.
  4.  Save the document again with the same name (c21ex07).
  5.  Print c21ex07.
  6.  Close c21ex07.

## Exercise 8

  1.  Open c21ex02.
  2.  Save the document with Save As and name it c21ex08.
  3.  Add a border and shading to the table by completing the following steps:
      a.  Select the entire table.
      b.  Make sure the Borders toolbar is displayed.
      c.  Click on the down-pointing arrow to the right of the Line Style button on the Borders toolbar, then click on the 3/4-point double-line option. (Skip this step if the option is already selected.)
      d.  Click on the Outside Border button on the Borders toolbar.
      e.  Click on the down-pointing arrow to the right of the Shading button on the Borders toolbar.
      f.  Click on the 20% option at the drop-down menu.
  4.  Save the document again with the same name (c21ex08).
  5.  Print c21ex08.
  6.  Close c21ex08.

## Exercise 9

1. Open c21ex06.
2. Save the document with Save As and name it c21ex09.
3. Add a double-line border to the table by completing the following steps:
   a. Select the entire table.
   b. Click on the down-pointing arrow to the right of the Line Style button on the Borders toolbar, then click on the 3/4-point double-line option. (Skip this step if this option is already selected.)
   c. Click on the Outside Border button on the Borders dialog box.
4. Add shading to the first row in the table by completing the following steps:
   a. Select the first row in the table.
   b. Choose Format, Borders and Shading.
   c. At the Cell Borders and Shading dialog box, select the Shading tab.
   d. Click on the 20% option in the Shading list box.
   e. Choose OK or press Enter.
5. Save the document again with the same name (c21ex09).
6. Print c21ex09.
7. Close c21ex09.

## Exercise 10

1. At a clear document screen, create the memo shown in figure 21.22 by completing the following steps:
   a. Key the headings and the first paragraph of the memo.
   b. With the insertion point a double space below the first paragraph, create a table with 3 columns and 7 rows (7x3).
   c. Change the width of the first column using the mouse by completing the following steps:
      (1) Display the Ruler. (Skip this step if the Ruler is already displayed.)
      (2) Position the arrow pointer on the column width marker between the 1-inch mark and the 3-inch mark on the Ruler until it turns into an arrow pointing left and right.
      (3) Hold down the left mouse button, drag the marker to the 3-inch mark on the Ruler, then release the mouse button.
   d. Key the text in the cells. Bold and center the text as shown. Press Ctrl + Tab before keying the text in cells A2 through A7.
   e. Select the table, then add a single border inside the table and a double-line border outside the table. (Use buttons on the Borders toolbar to do this.)
   f. Select the cells in the first row, then add a double-line border to the bottom of the cells and 20% shading.
   g. Move the insertion point below the table, press the Enter key once, then key the last paragraph and the reference line shown in figure 21.22.
2. Save the memo and name it c21ex10.
3. Print c21ex10.
4. Close c21ex10.

Figure 21.22

```
DATE:     April 4, 1996

TO:       Erin Morton

FROM:     Brenda Hogue

SUBJECT: DESKTOP PUBLISHING TRAINING


The deadline for signing up for the desktop publishing training was
March 31.  A total of six employees are registered for the
training.  The list of employees and their departments is displayed
in the table below.
```

| Name | Hospital # | Department |
|------|-----------|------------|
| My Trinh | 234-894-392 | Training |
| Paul Clinton | 843-239-099 | Med. Services |
| Margaret Blackwell | 312-383-743 | Finances |
| Angelina Thompson | 121-896-473 | Med. Services |
| Timothy Benito | 543-354-981 | Pediatrics |
| Cathy Heller-Williams | 187-935-752 | Payroll |

```
Room 200 has been reserved for the training.  Please let me know
what special equipment you will need.  There will be seven
computers available in the room.

xx:c21ex10
```

## Exercise 11

1. Open c21ex02.
2. Save the document with Save As and name it c21ex11.
3. Change the width of the columns and add border lines and shading by completing the following steps:
   a. Position the arrow pointer on the gridline separating the first and second columns until it turns into a left- and right-pointing arrow with a vertical double line between.
   b. Hold down the left mouse button, drag the gridline to the left approximately 0.5 inches, then release the mouse button. (Make sure the text in the first column does not wrap.)
   c. Position the arrow pointer on the gridline separating the second and third columns until it turns into a left- and right-pointing arrow with a vertical double line between.
   d. Hold down the left mouse button, drag the gridline to the left approximately 0.25 inches, then release the mouse button. (Make sure the text in the second column does not wrap.)
   e. Position the insertion point in any cell in the third column.
   f. Choose Table, then Cell Height and Width.
   g. At the Cell Height and Width dialog box, select the Column tab. (Skip this step if the Column tab is already selected.)
   h. Click on the down-pointing triangle to the right of the Width of Column 3 text box until *1.6"* displays in the text box.
   i. Choose OK or press Enter.
   j. Select the entire table, then insert a single-line border between and around the cells in the table.

 k. With the table still selected, add 10% shading to all cells in the table.
4. Save the document again with the same name (c21ex11).
5. Print c21ex11. (The table will not be centered between the margins.)
6. Close c21ex11.

## Exercise 12

1. Open c21ex10.
2. Save the document with Save As and name it c21ex12.
3. Change the alignment of cells B2 through C7 to center by completing the following steps:
 a. Position the insertion point in cell B2 (the cell containing the number *234-894-392*).
 b. Hold down the Shift key, press the down arrow key five times, then the right arrow key once. (This selects cells B2 through C7.)
 c. Click on the Center button on the Formatting toolbar.
 d. Deselect the cells.
4. Save the document again with the same name (c21ex12).
5. Print c21ex12.
6. Close c21ex12.

## Exercise 13

1. Open c21ex11.
2. Save the document with Save As and name it c21ex13.
3. Center the table horizontally by completing the following steps:
 a. Position the insertion point in any cell in the table.
 b. Choose Table, then Cell Height and Width.
 c. At the Cell Height and Width dialog box, select the Row tab. (Skip this step if the Row tab is already selected.)
 d. Choose Center in the Alignment section of the dialog box.
 e. Choose OK or press Enter.
4. Save the document again with the same name (c21ex13).
5. Print c21ex13.
6. Close c21ex13.

## Exercise 14

1. Open c21ex10.
2. Save the document with Save As and name it c21ex14.
3. Add two rows to the table by completing the following steps:
 a. Select the fourth and fifth rows in the table.
 b. Choose Table, then Insert Rows.
 c. Deselect the rows.
 d. Position the insertion point in cell A4 (below *Paul Clinton*), press Ctrl + Tab, then key **Jocelyn Pevan**.
 e. Key the following text in the specified cell:
  B4 = **459-203-294**
  C4 = **Finances**
  A5 = **John Gunderson**
  B5 = **223-983-226**
  C5 = **Admitting**
4. Change the word *six* in the first paragraph to *eight*. Change the word *seven* in the last paragraph to *nine*.
5. Save the document again with the same name (c21ex14).
6. Print c21ex14.
7. Close c21ex14.

# Exercise 15

1. Open c21ex01.
2. Save the document with Save As and name it c21ex15.
3. Make the following changes to the table:
   a. Add a row to the table by completing the following steps:
      (1) Select the first row.
      (2) Choose T_able, then _Insert Rows.
      (3) Deselect the row.
      (4) Position the insertion point in cell A1 (the first cell in the first row), change the alignment to center, turn on bold, then key **Name**.
      (5) Press the Tab key to move the insertion point to the next cell (cell B1), change the alignment to center, turn on bold, then key **Title**.
   b. Add a column to the right side of the table by completing the following steps:
      (1) Click on the Show/Hide button on the Standard toolbar to turn on the display of nonprinting characters.
      (2) Position the I-beam pointer on the first end-of-row marker at the far right side of the table until it turns into a small downward-pointing arrow.
      (3) Click the left mouse button. (This will select all of the end-of-row markers at the right side of the table.)
      (4) Choose T_able, then _Insert Columns.
      (5) Deselect the column.
      (6) Click on the Show/Hide button on the Standard toolbar to turn off the display of nonprinting characters.
   c. Change the width of the first column to 2 inches by completing the following steps:
      (1) Position the insertion point in any cell in the first column.
      (2) Choose T_able, then Cell Height and _Width.
      (3) At the Cell Height and Width dialog box, select the _Column tab. (Skip this step if the _Column tab is already selected.)
      (4) Click on the up- or down-pointing triangle to the right of the _Width of Column 1 text box until *2″* displays in the text box.
      (5) Choose OK or press Enter.
   d. Change the width of the second column to 3 inches and the width of the third column to 1 inch by completing steps similar to those in 3c(1) through 3c(5).
   e. Select the cells in the last column (cells C1 through C7), then change the alignment to center.
   f. Key the following text in the specified cells:

      | C1 | = | **Ext.** |
      |----|---|----------|
      | C2 | = | **2039** |
      | C3 | = | **2435** |
      | C4 | = | **2396** |
      | C5 | = | **2247** |
      | C6 | = | **2834** |
      | C7 | = | **2640** |

   g. Select the entire table, then insert a single-line border for the inside of the table and a double-line border for the outside of the table.
4. Save the document again with the same name (c21ex15).
5. Print c21ex15.
6. Close c21ex15.

# Exercise 16

1. Open c21ex14.
2. Save the document with Save As and name it c21ex16.
3. Make the following changes to the table:
   a. Delete the last row in the table by completing the following steps:
      (1) Select the last row.
      (2) Choose Table, then Delete Rows.
   b. Delete the middle column by completing the following steps:
      (1) Select the middle column.
      (2) Choose Table, then Delete Columns.
   c. Center the table horizontally by completing the following steps:
      (1) Position the insertion point in any cell in the table.
      (2) Choose Table, then Cell Height and Width.
      (3) At the Cell Height and Width dialog box, select the Row tab. (Skip this step if the Row tab is already selected.)
      (4) Choose Center in the Alignment section of the dialog box.
      (5) Choose OK or press Enter.
   d. Change the word *eight* in the first paragraph to *seven*. Change the word *nine* in the last paragraph to *eight*.
4. Save the document again with the same name (c21ex16).
5. Print c21ex16.
6. Close c21ex16.

# Exercise 17

1. At a clear document screen, create the table shown in figure 21.23 by completing the following steps:
   a. Press the Enter key once, then create a table with 3 columns and 10 rows (10x3).
   b. Change the width of the first column to 3 inches, the width of the second column to 2 inches, and the width of the third column to 1 inch.
   c. Merge the cells in the first row by completing the following steps:
      (1) Select the first row.
      (2) Choose Table, then Merge Cells.
   d. Merge the cells in the second row by completing steps similar to those in 1c(1) and 1c(2).
   e. Select the entire table, then change the font to 12-point Arial Bold.
   f. Key the text in the cells as shown. Center and bold the text as indicated.
   g. Add a double-line border around the outside of the table and a single-line border on the inside of the table.
   h. Select the third row, then add 20% shading.
2. Save the document and name it c21ex17.
3. Print c21ex17.
4. Close c21ex17.

Figure 21.23

| TRAINING AND EDUCATION DEPARTMENT | | |
|---|---|---|
| Desktop Publishing Training | | |
| Name | Department | Hosp # |
| | | |
| | | |
| | | |
| | | |
| | | |
| | | |
| | | |

## Exercise 18

1. Open c21ex17.
2. Save the document with Save As and name it c21ex18.
3. Make the following changes to the table:
   a. Change the height of the first row by completing the following steps:
      (1) Select the first row.
      (2) Choose Table, then Cell Height and Width.
      (3) At the Cell Height and Width dialog box, select the Row tab. (Skip this step if the Row tab is already selected.)
      (4) Position the I-beam pointer inside the At text box, then click the left mouse button. (This moves the insertion point into the At text box.)
      (5) Key **48**.
      (6) Choose OK or press Enter.
      (7) Deselect the row.
      (8) Position the insertion point immediately left of the *T* in *TRAINING*, then press the Enter key. (This better centers the title in the cell.)
   b. Change the height of the second row by completing the following steps:
      (1) Change to the Page Layout viewing mode.
      (2) Position the arrow pointer on the second double line at the left side of the screen on the vertical ruler. (This is the double line on the vertical ruler that aligns with the bottom of the second row of cells.)
      (3) Hold down the left mouse button, drag the row marker down until the second row is approximately the same size as the first row (about 2 to 3 marks on the ruler), then release the mouse button.
      (4) Position the insertion point immediately left of the *D* in *Desktop*, then press the Enter key. (This better centers the text in the cell.)
4. Change to the Normal viewing mode.
5. Save the document again with the same name (c21ex18).
6. Print c21ex18.
7. Close c21ex18.

## Exercise 19

1. Open c21ex10.
2. Save the document with Save As and name it c21ex19.
3. Reverse the second and third columns in the table by completing the following steps:
   a. Select the third column.

b. Choose Edit, then Cut; or click on the Cut button on the Standard toolbar.

c. Position the insertion point in the first cell in the second column.

d. Chose Edit, then Paste Columns; or click on the Paste button on the Standard toolbar.

4. Save the document again with the same name (c21ex19).

5. Print c21ex19.

6. Close c21ex19.

## Exercise 20

1. Open c21ex01.

2. Save the document with Save As and name it c21ex20.

3. Make the following changes to the table:

   a. Select the first row, then insert a row.

   b. Key **Name** in the first cell in the first row (cell A1), centered and bolded. Key **Title** in the second cell in the first row (cell A2), centered and bolded.

   c. Automatically format the table by completing the following steps:

   (1) Position the insertion point in any cell in the table.

   (2) Choose Table, then Table AutoFormat.

   (3) At the Table AutoFormat dialog box, click on the down-pointing arrow to the right of the Formats list box, until *Colorful 3* is visible, then click on *Colorful 3*.

   (4) Choose OK or press Enter.

   d. Center the table horizontally.

4. Save the document again with the same name (c21ex20).

5. Print c21ex20.

6. Close c21ex20.

## Exercise 21

1. At a clear document screen, create the table shown in figure 21.24 by completing the following steps:

   a. Key **S & D CORPORATION** centered and bolded.

   b. Press Enter twice, then key **Quarterly Sales - Region 10** centered and bolded.

   c. Press Enter three times.

   d. Change the alignment back to left and turn off bold.

   e. Use the table Wizard to create the table by completing the following steps:

   (1) Choose Table, then Insert Table.

   (2) At the Insert Table dialog box, choose Wizard.

   (3) At the first screen, with Style 1 selected, choose Next.

   (4) At the next screen, choose Quarters (Q1, Q2, Q3, Q4), then choose Next.

   (5) At the next screen, make sure Repeat headings and Center are selected, then choose Next.

   (6) At the next screen, choose Years, then enter **1993** in the first box after Years, then enter **1996** in the second box after Years. Choose Next.

   (7) At the next screen, make sure Left align is selected, then choose Next.

   (8) At the next screen, make sure Numbers: right-aligned is selected, then choose Next.

   (9) At the next screen, make sure Portrait is selected, then choose Next.

   (10) At the next screen, choose Finish.

   (11) At the Table AutoFormat dialog box, choose *Colorful 2*, then choose OK or press Enter.

   (12) At the document screen with the table inserted, key the numbers in the cells as indicated in figure 21.24.

2. Save the document and name it c21ex21.

3. Print c21ex21.

4. Close c21ex21.

Figure 21.24

S & D CORPORATION

Quarterly Sales - Region 10

| | *Q1* | *Q2* | *Q3* | *Q4* |
|------|-----------|-----------|-----------|-----------|
| *1993* | 189,349.50 | 190,309.61 | 187,483.98 | 191,430.34 |
| *1994* | 198,473.98 | 199,082.40 | 189,348.00 | 195,347.05 |
| *1995* | 199,430.80 | 200,430.27 | 203,120.74 | 201,432.79 |
| *1996* | 210,328.34 | 208,573.20 | 207,321.56 | 209,231.89 |

## Exercise 22

1. At a clear document screen, create the document shown in figure 21.25 by completing the following steps:
   a. Key **PETERSBURG SCHOOL DISTRICT** centered and bolded.
   b. Press the Enter key three times.
   c. Change the alignment back to left.
   d. Key the text shown in figure 21.25 exactly as shown.
   e. Convert the text to a table by completing the following steps:
      (1) Select the text (except the title and the blank lines below the title).
      (2) Choose Table, then Convert Text to Table.
      (3) At the Convert Text to Table dialog box, make sure Commas is selected in the Separate Text At section of the dialog box, then choose OK or press Enter.
   f. With the insertion point positioned in any cell within the table, automatically format the table with the *Colorful 1* option at the Table AutoFormat dialog box.
   g. Center the table horizontally.
2. Save the document and name it c21ex22.
3. Print c21ex22.
4. Close c21ex22.

Figure 21.25

**PETERSBURG SCHOOL DISTRICT**


**Title,Name**
Superintendent,Dorothy Warner
Assistant Superintendent,David O'Shea
Curriculum Specialist,Damion Japhet
Support Specialist,Donna Schmitt
Information Specialist,Alex Perozzo

## Exercise 23

1. Open c21ex01.
2. Save the document with Save As and name it c21ex23.
3. Convert the table to text by completing the following steps:
   a. Select the table.
   b. Choose Table, then Convert Table to Text.
   c. At the Convert Table to Text dialog box, make sure Tabs is selected, then choose OK or press Enter.
4. Save the document again with the same name (c21ex23).
5. Print c21ex23.
6. Close c21ex23.

# Exercise 24

1. At a clear document screen, create the table shown in figure 21.26 by completing the following steps:
   a. Press the Enter key once.
   b. Create a table with 4 columns and 6 rows (6x4).
   c. Select the first row, then merge the cells.
   d. Position the insertion point in the first row, press the Enter key once, change the alignment to center, turn on bold, key **S & D CORPORATION**, then press Enter once.
   e. Select the second row in the table, then click on the Center button and the Bold button on the Formatting toolbar.
   f. Select cells A3 through A6, then change the alignment to center.
   g. Select cells B3 through D6, then change the alignment to right.
   h. Key the text in the cells as shown in figure 21.26.
   i. Add border lines and shading to the table as shown in figure 21.26.
   j. Insert a formula in cell D3 by completing the following steps:
      (1) Position the insertion point in cell D3 (the cell below *Net Profit*).
      (2) Choose Table, Formula.
      (3) At the Formula dialog box, delete the formula in the Formula text box.
      (4) Key **=B3-C3** in the Formula text box.
      (5) Choose OK or press Enter.
   k. Insert the formula **=B4-C4** in cell D4 by completing steps similar to those in 1j(1) through 1j(5).
   l. Insert the formula **=B5-C5** in cell D5 by completing steps similar to those in 1j(1) through 1j(5).
   m. Insert the formula **=B6-C6** in cell D6 by completing steps similar to those in 1j(1) through 1j(5).
2. Save the document and name it c21ex24.
3. Print c21ex24.
4. Close c21ex24.

**Figure 21.26**

| S & D CORPORATION | | | |
|---|---|---|---|
| Year | Income | Expenses | Net Profit |
| 1993 | $4,390,130.20 | $3,104,530.45 | |
| 1994 | 4,560,439.86 | 3,239,478.10 | |
| 1995 | 4,687,390.33 | 3,668,092.90 | |
| 1996 | 5,001,058.75 | 3,945,230.68 | |

# Exercise 25

1. Open table01.
2. Save the document with Save As and name it c21ex25.
3. Insert a formula in cell F3 to average test scores by completing the following steps:
   a. Position the insertion point in cell F3 (the cell below *Ave.*).
   b. Choose Table, Formula.
   c. Delete the formula in the Formula text box *except* the equals sign.
   d. With the insertion point positioned immediately after the equals sign, click on the down-pointing arrow to the right of the Paste Function text box.

e. From the drop-down menu that displays, click on *AVERAGE*.

f. With the insertion point positioned between the left and right parentheses, key **left**.

g. Choose OK or press Enter.

4. Position the insertion point in cell F4, then complete steps similar to those in 3a through 3g to insert a formula to average test scores.

5. Position the insertion point in cell F5, then complete steps similar to those in 3a through 3g to insert a formula to average test scores.

6. Position the insertion point in cell F6, then complete steps similar to those in 3a through 3g to insert a formula to average test scores.

7. Position the insertion point in cell F7, then complete steps similar to those in 3a through 3g to insert a formula to average test scores.

8. Position the insertion point in cell F8, then complete steps similar to those in 3a through 3g to insert a formula to average test scores.

9. Save the document again with the same name (c21ex25).

10. Print c21ex25.

11. Close c21ex25.

## Exercise 26

1. Open c21ex25.

2. Save the document with Save As and name it c21ex26.

3. Make the following changes to the table:

   a. Change the number in cell C3 from 81 to 85.

   b. Change the number in cell D5 from 90 to 86.

   c. Change the number in cell D8 from 87 to 92.

   d. Position the I-beam pointer in cell F3, click the left mouse button (this inserts a gray background around the numbers in the cell), then press F9. (Pressing F9 recalculates the average.)

   e. Click on the number in cell F5, then press F9.

   f. Click on the number in cell F8, then press F9.

4. Save the document again with the same name (c21ex26).

5. Print c21ex26.

6. Close c21ex26.

## SKILL ASSESSMENTS

## Assessment 1

1. At a clear document screen, create the table shown in figure 21.27 with the following specifications:

   a. Press the Enter key once, then create a table with 3 columns and 10 rows (10x3).

   b. Change the width of the first column to 2 inches, the width of the second column to 3 inches, and the width of the third column to 1 inch.

   c. Merge the cells in the first row (cells A1, B1, and C1).

   d. Key the text in the cells as indicated. Bold and center text as shown. Before keying the text in the first cell, press the Enter key once. After keying the text in the cell centered and bolded, press the Enter key once.

   e. Add border lines and shading to the table as shown in figure 21.27. (The outside border is a 2 1/4 point line.)

2. Save the document and name it c21sa01.

3. Print c21sa01.

4. Close c21sa01.

Figure 21.27

**PETERSBURG SCHOOL DISTRICT**
**School Principals**

| Name | School | Phone |
|------|--------|-------|
| Rodney Sinclair | Meeker High School | 555-2314 |
| Vanessa Walston | Rollins High School | 555-3049 |
| Marion Nicholson | Cedar Middle School | 555-9088 |
| Douglas McKenzie | Oakridge Middle School | 555-8243 |
| Andy Tanabe | Stewart Elementary School | 555-3834 |
| Kathryn Rosello | Overman Elementary School | 555-1289 |
| Michael Stoddard | Grant Elementary School | 555-3455 |
| Robert Salvus | Curtiss Elementary School | 555-8770 |

## Assessment 2

1. At a clear document screen, create the memo shown in figure 21.28 by completing the following steps:
   a. Key the headings and the first paragraph of the memo.
   b. With the insertion point a double space below the first paragraph of the memo, create a table with 3 columns and 5 rows (5x3).
   c. Change the width of the first column to 2.25 inches, the width of the middle column to 1.5 inches, and the width of the third column to 2.25 inches.
   d. Select the cells in the second column, then change the alignment to center.
   e. Select the cells in the third column, then change the alignment to right.
   f. Add border lines to the table as indicated in figure 21.28.
   g. Select the entire table, then change the font to 12-point Times New Roman.
   h. Key the text in the cells as shown in figure 21.28.
   i. After completing the table, position the insertion point a double space below the table, then key the rest of the memo.
   j. Select the text in the memo, then change the font to 12-point Times New Roman.
2. Save the document and name it c21sa02.
3. Print c21sa02.
4. Close c21sa02.

**Figure 21.28**

DATE:        September 23, 1996

TO:          Karen Delano

FROM:        Jon Struebing

SUBJECT:     OCTOBER NEWSLETTER

The following information needs to be included in the October newsletter under the heading Newsletter Resources.

| | | |
|---|---|---|
| Superintendent | Dorothy Warner | Administrative Offices |
| Assistant Superintendent | David O'Shea | Administrative Offices |
| Curriculum Specialist | Damion Japhet | District Headquarters |
| Newsletter Editor | Jon Struebing | Curtiss Elementary School |
| Newsletter Assistant Editor | Karen Delano | Stewart Elementary School |

Please include how employees can submit articles or items of interest to be published in the newsletter.

xx:c21sa02

## Assessment 3

1. At a clear document screen, create the table shown in figure 21.29 with the following specifications:
   a. Create a table with 4 columns and 11 rows (11x4).
   b. With the insertion point positioned in the table, drag the table column marker on the Ruler between the 1-inch mark and the 2-inch mark to the 4-inch mark on the Ruler.
   c. Merge the cells in the first row.
   d. Merge the cells in the second row.
   e. Select the first two rows in the table, then change the alignment to center.
   f. Select cells B3 through D11, then change the alignment to center.
   g. Select the first two rows in the table, then change the font to 14-point Times New Roman Bold.
   h. Select the cells in the third row, then change the font to 12-point Times New Roman Bold.
   i. Select the remaining cells in the table (rows 4 through 11), then change the font to 10-point Times New Roman and insert a left tab stop at the 0.25-inch mark on the Ruler.
   j. Key the text in the cells as indicated in figure 21.29.
   k. Add border lines as indicated in figure 21.29.
2. Save the document and name it c21sa03.
3. Print c21sa03.
4. Close c21sa03.

Figure 21.29

| PETERSBURG SCHOOL DISTRICT | | | |
|---|---|---|---|
| **Technology Study Question #6** | | | |
| **How will technology change your work environment?** | **H.S.** | **M.S.** | **E.S.** |
| 1. Improved access to centralized database. | 1 | 2 | 2 |
| 2. Telephone lines for voice and data use in classroom. | 3 | 2 | 1 |
| 3. Increased student access to information. | 4 | 3 | 2 |
| 4. Better communication among peers. | 4 | 4 | 3 |
| 5. Develop and implement a technology classroom model. | 5 | 2 | 4 |
| 6. Technology to meet individual learning styles. | 4 | 4 | 3 |
| 7. Elimination of textbook as primary delivery system. | 5 | 2 | 3 |
| 8. Developing buildings as community learning/resource centers. | 6 | 4 | 5 |

## Assessment 4

1.  At a clear document screen, create the memo shown in figure 21.30 by completing the following steps:
    a.  Key the headings and the first paragraph of the memo shown in figure 21.30.
    b.  With the insertion point a double space below the first paragraph of the memo, create a table with 4 columns and 5 rows (5x4).
    c.  Select the cells in the first row, then change the alignment to center.
    d.  Select cells B2 through D5, then change the alignment to right.
    e.  Key the text in the cells as indicated. (Do not apply any special formatting to the text. This will be done with Table AutoFormat.)
    f.  Position the insertion point in any cell in the table, then apply the *List 8* formatting at the Table AutoFormat dialog box.
    g.  Center the table horizontally.
    h.  Position the insertion point in cell D2, then insert the formula **=C2-B2**.
    i.  Position the insertion point in cell D3, then insert the formula **=C3-B3**.
    j.  Position the insertion point in cell D4, then insert the formula **=C4-B4**.
    k.  Position the insertion point in cell D5, then insert the formula **=C5-B5**.
2.  After completing the table, move the insertion point a double space below the table, then key the rest of the memo.
3.  Save the document and name it c21sa04.
4.  Print c21sa04.
5.  Close c21sa04.

Figure 21.30

DATE:     January 14, 1997

TO:       Beverly Chou-Matheson, Vice President

FROM:     Stephanie Lunden, Chair, Friends of the Hospital

SUBJECT:  FUND-RAISING EVENTS FOR 1996


During 1996, four major fund-raising events were sponsored by the
Friends of the Hospital volunteer group.  These fund-raising events
were very successful due to the time donated by members of Friends
of the Hospital as well as other community and hospital volunteers.
The following table shows the expenditures, revenue, and profit for
each event.

| Event | Costs | Revenue | Net Profit |
|---|---|---|---|
| Silent Auction | $10,230.50 | $27,340.35 | |
| Tree Festival | 30,459.18 | 99,004.50 | |
| Fun Run Marathon | 9,340.74 | 45,120.80 | |
| Health Fair | 21,450.30 | 32,195.28 | |

As you can see from the table, the Tree Festival is our most
popular fund raiser.  This was the fourth year for the Tree
Festival and each year the profits have doubled.  The Health Fair
raised the least amount of money.  At our next Friends of the
Hospital meeting, we will discuss whether or not to participate in
the Health Fair this year.

xx:c21sa04

## Assessment 5

1. At a clear document screen, create the table shown in figure 21.31 by completing the following steps:
   a. Press the Enter key, then create a table with 4 columns and 8 rows (8x4).
   b. Drag the table column marker between the 1-inch mark and the 2-inch mark to the 2-inch mark on the Ruler.
   c. Merge the cells in the first row.
   d. Select the first two rows, then change the alignment to center and change the font to 14-point Century Gothic Bold.
   e. Select cells B3 through D8, then change the alignment to right.
   f. Select cells A3 through D8, then change the font to 12-point Century Gothic.
   g. Key the text in the cells as shown in figure 21.31. (Press Ctrl + Tab before keying the states in the first column.)
   h. Insert the formula =C3-B3 in cell D3. Insert the appropriate formula in cells D4, D5, D6, D7, and D8 to subtract This Year numbers from Last Year numbers.
   i. Insert border lines and shading as shown in figure 21.31.
2. Save the document and name it c21sa05.
3. Print c21sa05.
4. Close c21sa05.

Figure 21.31

## S & D CORPORATION
### Sales in Selected States

| State | Last Year | This Year | Difference |
|-------|-----------|-----------|------------|
| Washington | $1,304,293.90 | $1,540,394.23 | |
| Oregon | 1,450,340.24 | 1,550,345.98 | |
| Idaho | 990,435.33 | 998,320.45 | |
| California | 3,340,288.45 | 3,445,230.50 | |
| Nevada | 1,032,483.78 | 1,224,889.34 | |
| Texas | 2,553,294.50 | 2,654,340.08 | |

# Creating Charts 22

Upon successful completion of chapter 22, you will be able to enhance and improve the clarity of data by creating a chart with the data.

In chapter 21 you learned to create data in tables. While this does an adequate job of representing data, a chart can be created from data in a table that provides a more visual presentation of the data.

A chart is sometimes referred to as a *graph* and is a picture of numeric data. A chart can be created with data in a table or data in a spreadsheet created in other programs such as Microsoft Excel. In this chapter, you will be creating charts from data in a table.

Charts are created with the Microsoft Graph application. Microsoft Graph is called an *applet*, which is a small application designed to work with Windows programs and contains Object Linking and Embedding (OLE) capability. In this chapter, you will learn how to use Microsoft Graph, Version 3.0b. This is the version that is shipped with Word for Windows, Version 6. If you are using Word for Windows as part of Microsoft Office, the Microsoft Graph application may be version 5.0. This version, though similar to version 3.0b, does contain differences. Before beginning this chapter, check to see what version of Microsoft Graph is available to you by completing the following steps:

1. At a clear document screen, click on the Insert Chart button on the Standard toolbar (fourth button from the *right).*
2. At the Microsoft Graph window, choose Help.
3. At the Help drop-down menu, choose About.
4. The version of Microsoft Graph is displayed in the At the About Microsoft Graph dialog box.
5. Choose OK or press Enter.
6. At the Microsoft Graph window, choose File, then Exit and Return to (document name).
7. At the question asking if you want to update the graph, choose No.
8. Close the document without saving changes.

Microsoft Graph lets you create a variety of charts, including bar and column charts, pie charts, area charts, line charts, and scatter charts. Charts are created in color on the screen. Unless you are using a color printer, however, the chart prints in black and shades of gray. The quality of the printed chart depends on the printer you are using.

## ■ Creating a Chart

A chart is created using data in a table. For example, the data shown in the table in figure 22.1 can be created as a chart.

To insert the data shown in the table in figure 22.1 into a 3-D Column chart (the default), you would complete the following steps:

1. Select the entire table.
2. Click on the Insert Chart button on the Standard toolbar.
3. At the Microsoft Graph window shown in figure 22.2, choose File, then Exit and Return to (document name).
4. At the question asking if you want to update the graph, choose Yes.

**Figure 22.1**
*Table*

| Salesperson | January | February |
|-------------|---------|----------|
| A. Perez    | 20,405  | 19,340   |
| J. White    | 28,966  | 29,485   |
| L. Ching    | 41,309  | 25,340   |

When you choose Yes, a chart is inserted in the document below the table. The chart appears as shown in figure 22.3.

**Figure 22.2**
*Microsoft Graph Window*

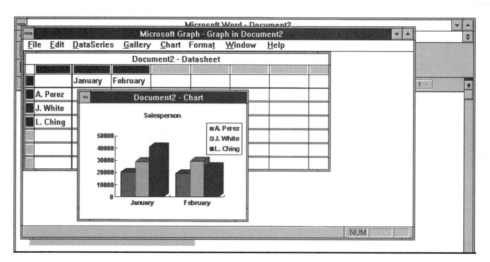

**Figure 22.3**
*Chart Based on Table*

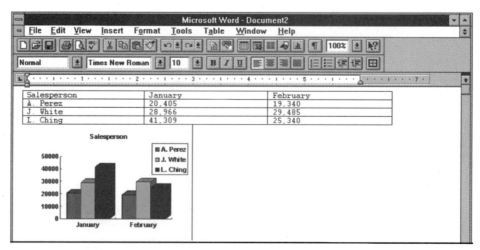

You can display the Microsoft Graph window shown in figure 22.2 by selecting a table, then clicking on the Insert Chart button on the Standard toolbar or by completing the following steps:

1. Choose Insert, then Object.
2. At the Insert Object dialog box with the Create New tab selected, select Microsoft Graph in the Object Type list box.
3. Choose OK or press Enter.

By default, Microsoft Graph charts the data in an orientation referred to as Series in Rows. The text in the first row of the table is the *category names*. Text in the left column is the *series names*. Graph uses the series names as labels for the legend. The legend is the box that labels the different colors used by each series of markers.

In a chart, the left side of the chart displays the values and is referred to as the z-axis. The z-axis is generally marked like a ruler and is broken into units by marks called *ticks*. Next to each tick mark is the amount of the value at that particular point on the axis. The values in the chart in figure 22.3 are broken into tick marks by ten thousands beginning with zero and continuing to 50,000. The values for the z-axis will vary depending on the data in the table.

The series names that display in the left column of the datasheet are the y-axis and are used to create the legend for the chart.

The x-axis is the bottom of the chart. The names of items in the chart generally display along the x-axis. In the chart shown in figure 22.3, the bars are identified along the x-axis as *January* and *February*.

At the Microsoft Graph window, the chart is displayed over the datasheet. The datasheet contains the text in cells as created in the table in the document. By default, the chart is active. To make the datasheet active, click anywhere in the datasheet. To make the chart active, click anywhere in the chart.

## Updating a Chart

At the Microsoft Graph window, you can exit by choosing File, then Exit and Return to (document name). Use the Update option from the File drop-down menu if you make changes to the datasheet in the Microsoft Graph window and want the chart in the document to reflect the changes. Use the Set as Default Chart option from the File drop-down menu if you want the current chart to become the default chart.

## Deleting a Chart

A chart inserted in the document screen can be deleted. To delete the chart, select the entire chart, then press the Delete key.

## ■ Sizing and Framing a Chart

When you choose Exit and Return to (document name) at the Microsoft Graph window, the chart is inserted in the document and displays with sizing handles. You can change the size of the chart by dragging sizing handles.

You can also size the chart by selecting the chart, then choosing Format, then Picture. This displays the Picture dialog box. At the Picture dialog box you can crop the chart, scale the chart, or change the width and height of the chart. You learned about these options in chapter 18.

A chart can be framed like other graphic elements in a document. To frame a chart, change to the Page Layout viewing mode, select the chart, then choose Insert, Frame. When a chart is framed it can be moved in the document. You can also customize the frame at the Frame dialog box.

# ■ Changing the Chart Type

In Microsoft Graph, you can create seven different types of charts. Figure 22.4 shows an illustration and explanation of each type.

Figure 22.4
Types of Charts

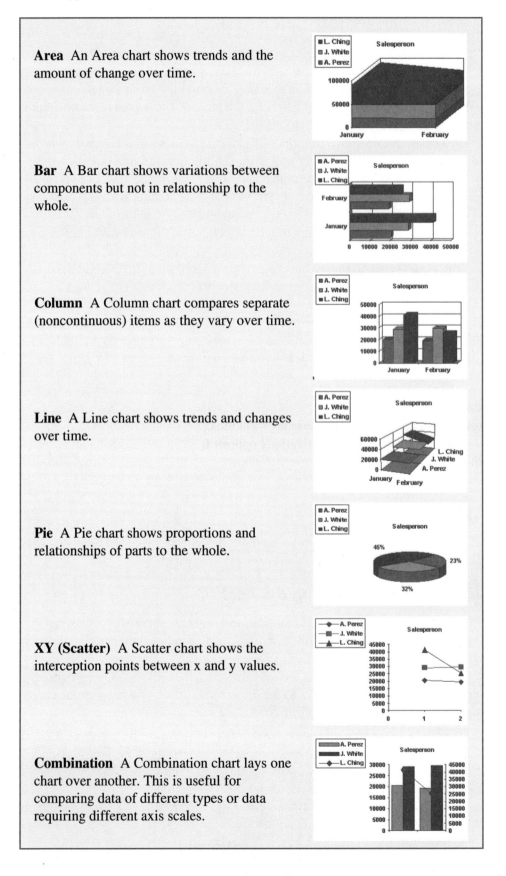

**Area**  An Area chart shows trends and the amount of change over time.

**Bar**  A Bar chart shows variations between components but not in relationship to the whole.

**Column**  A Column chart compares separate (noncontinuous) items as they vary over time.

**Line**  A Line chart shows trends and changes over time.

**Pie**  A Pie chart shows proportions and relationships of parts to the whole.

**XY (Scatter)**  A Scatter chart shows the interception points between x and y values.

**Combination**  A Combination chart lays one chart over another. This is useful for comparing data of different types or data requiring different axis scales.

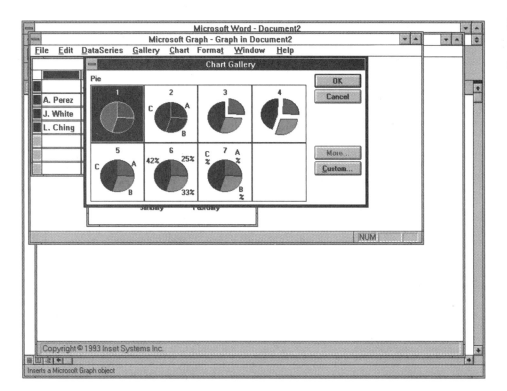

**Figure 22.5**
Pie Chart Gallery

In addition to the seven chart types, Microsoft Graph also includes 3-dimensional chart types for Area, Bar, Column, Line, and Pie charts. The seven chart types as well as the 3-dimensional chart options are available from the Gallery drop-down menu at the Microsoft Graph window.

Microsoft Graph provides variations on each chart containing different combinations of enhancements. With these variations, you can choose a chart with different enhancements or formatting without having to customize the chart yourself. Choose a chart type from the Gallery drop-down menu to display the chart variation options.

For example, to display the various options for a Pie chart for the chart shown in figure 22.3, then choose one of the options, you would complete the following steps:

1. Open Microsoft Graph for the chart shown in figure 22.3.
2. Choose Gallery from the Microsoft Graph menu bar, then choose Pie. This displays the Chart Gallery dialog box with Pie chart options as shown in figure 22.5.
3. To choose a different Pie chart, click on the desired Pie chart or press the left or right arrow key until the desired Pie chart is selected, then choose OK.

You would follow similar steps to display chart variations for the other types of charts including the 3-D options.

# Editing the Datasheet

At the Microsoft Graph window, the datasheet is displayed behind the chart. If you create a chart based on a table, the information in the table is displayed in the datasheet. Changes can be made to the text in the datasheet. To do this, make the datasheet active by clicking on any visible part of the datasheet.

A datasheet is similar to a table. You can move the insertion point to cells within the datasheet, selecting the cell contents, then make changes. In a datasheet, the mouse pointer displays as a thick crossbar. To select a cell with the mouse, position the crossbar in the desired cell, then click the left mouse button. To select multiple cells, drag the crossbar across the cells. To select a row or column, click on the row or column header. A column header is the black box that displays at the left side of the column. A row header is the black box that displays at the top of the row.To select all cells in the datasheet, click in the blank square at the top left corner where row and column headings intersect.

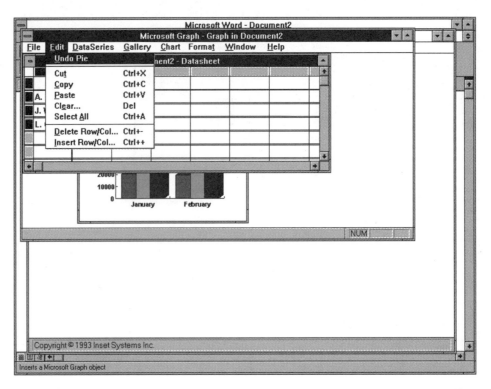

**Figure 22.6**
*Edit Drop-Down Menu*

With options from the Edit drop-down menu shown in figure 22.6, you can cut or copy a cell or selected cells, then paste the cell or cells in a different location in the datasheet. You can clear the data and/or formatting in a cell with the Clear option. Use Select All to select all cells in the datasheet. Delete a row or column (or selected rows or columns) with the Delete Row/Col option. Insert a row or column (or selected rows or columns) with the Insert Row/Col option from the Edit drop-down menu.

## Changing the Data Series

By default, Microsoft Graph uses a default orientation for data called Series in Rows. At this orientation, text in the first row of the datasheet becomes the category names that appear below the x-axis (the horizontal axis). Text in the left column becomes the series names, which Graph uses as labels for the legend.

The orientation of a chart can be changed from Series in Rows to Series in Columns. When the orientation is changed to Series in Columns, Microsoft Graph takes the category names (the x-axis labels) from the left column of the datasheet and the series names (legend labels) from the top row of the datasheet.

To change the chart orientation, display Microsoft Graph for the chart, choose DataSeries, then Series in Columns. If the data series was changed to Series in Columns for the chart in figure 22.3, it would display as shown in figure 22.7.

## Adding Elements to the Chart

When a chart is created by Microsoft Graph, many chart elements are added by default. For example, a title is given to the chart (the contents of the first cell in the first row), and the category names on the x-axis are included along with the series names that create the legend label. In addition to these elements, you can also include other elements such as data labels, arrows, and gridlines.

To add (or delete) elements from a chart, choose the Chart option from the Microsoft Graph menu bar. This displays a drop-down menu as shown in figure 22.8.

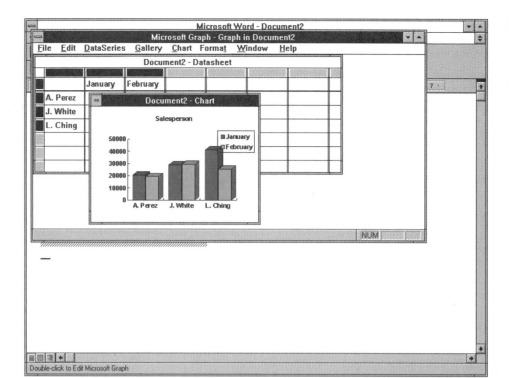

*Figure 22.7*
*Chart with Series in*
*Column Orientation*

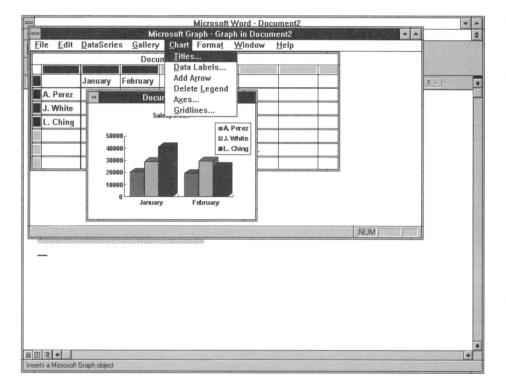

*Figure 22.8*
*Chart Drop-Down*
*Menu*

## Adding Titles

By default, Microsoft Graph includes a title for the chart. The title is the text that is inserted in the first cell of the first row in the table. A title can also be included for the value (z-axis), series (y-axis), or category (x-axis). For example, to add the title, *Gross Sales*, to the value (z-axis) to the chart in figure 22.3, you would complete the following steps:

1. Display Microsoft Graph for the chart.
2. Choose Chart, then Titles.

3. At the Chart Titles dialog box shown in figure 22.9, choose <u>V</u>alue (Z) Axis.
4. Key **Gross Sales**. (You will not be able to see the letters as you key them.)
5. After keying the title for the value, click outside the selected title. (This will display the entire title.)

After adding a title to the value (z-axis), choose <u>F</u>ile, then E<u>x</u>it and Return to (document name). When Word asks if you want to update the chart, choose <u>Y</u>es. You would complete similar steps to add a title to the series (y-axis) or category (x-axis).

When additional elements are added to a chart, the chart can become quite full and elements may overlap. If elements in a chart overlap, an element can be selected and then moved. To select an element, position the arrow pointer on a portion of the element, then click the left mouse button. Position the arrow pointer in the selected element, hold down the left mouse button, drag the element to the desired location, then release the mouse button.

## Adding Data Labels

Labels can be added to elements in a chart, such as values and percents. The type of labels that can be added depends on the type of chart. To add a data label, choose <u>C</u>hart from the Microsoft Graph menu bar, then choose <u>D</u>ata Labels. At the Data Labels dialog box, choose the desired label, then choose OK or press Enter. For example, to create a label for the values in the chart in figure 22.3, you would complete the following steps:

1. Display Microsoft Graph for the chart.
2. Choose <u>C</u>hart, then <u>D</u>ata Labels.
3. At the Data Labels dialog box, choose Show <u>V</u>alue.
4. Choose OK or press Enter.

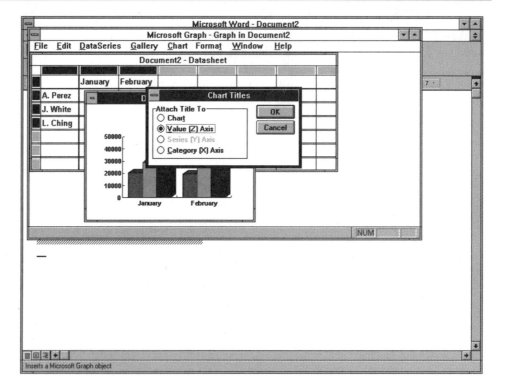

*Figure 22.9*
*Chart Titles Dialog*
*Box*

## Adding an Arrow

An arrow can be added to a chart for emphasis. To add an arrow, choose Chart from the Microsoft Graph menu bar, then choose Add Arrow. You may want to move this arrow to a specific location in the chart. To do this, position the arrow pointer anywhere on the arrow, hold down the left mouse button, drag the outline of the arrow to the desired location, then release the mouse button. When an arrow is added to the chart, the Add Arrow option in the Chart drop-down menu turns into Delete Arrow.

## Adding/Deleting a Legend

By default a legend is created with a chart. This legend can be removed from the chart by choosing Chart from the menu bar, then Delete Legend. If a legend has been deleted, the Delete Legend option turns into Add Legend.

## Adding/Deleting Axes Labels

The category name (x-axis), series name (y-axis), and values (z-axis) are displayed for a chart by default. To remove one or all of these names, choose Chart, then Axes. At the 3-D Axes dialog box, remove the X from axes names you do not want displayed in the chart.

## Adding Gridlines

Gridlines can be added to a chart for the category, series, and value. Depending on the chart, some but not all of these options may be available. To add gridlines, choose Chart, then Gridlines. At the Gridlines dialog box shown in figure 22.10, insert an X in those options for which you want gridlines.

If major and minor gridlines are added to the category and value for the chart in figure 22.3, it will display as shown in figure 22.11.

## ▉ Formatting Chart Elements

While in Microsoft Graph, elements in a chart, such as the title or legend, can be selected and then moved or formatted. To select a chart element, position the arrow pointer on the element, then click the left mouse button. When a chart element is selected, small squares display around the element.

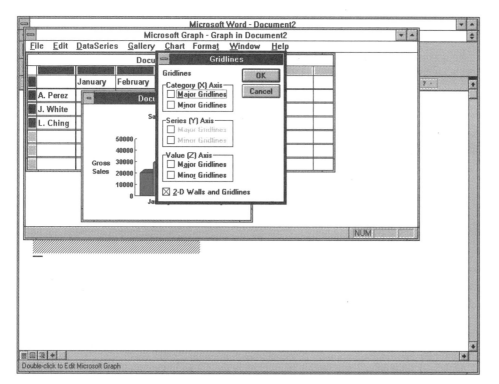

*Figure 22.10*
*Gridlines Dialog Box*

*Figure 22.11*
*Chart with Gridlines*

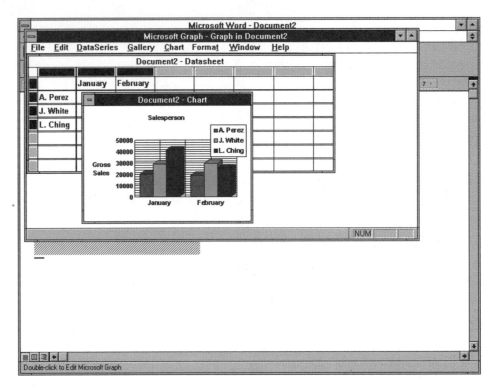

To move a chart element, select the element, position the arrow pointer in the element, hold down the left mouse button, drag the element to the desired position, then release the mouse button.

The entire chart can also be selected while in Microsoft Graph. To select the chart, position the arrow pointer outside the chart but inside the chart window, then click the left mouse button.

A selected element in a chart or a selected chart can be formatted. Formatting can include adding a pattern, changing background and foreground colors of the selected element or chart, and changing the font.

To format an element in a chart or the chart, select the element or chart, then choose the Format option on the Microsoft Graph menu bar. This causes the Format drop-down menu to display as shown in figure 22.12.

Some of the formatting options at the Format drop-down menu may display dimmed. The dimmed options are not available for the currently selected element or the selected chart. The available options depend on what is selected.

## Adding a Pattern

A border and/or pattern can be added to a selected element or a selected table at the Area Patterns dialog box shown in figure 22.13. The options in this dialog box will vary depending on what element is selected. For example, if a title in a chart is selected, the Area Patterns dialog box displays as shown in figure 22.13. If the tick marks along the bottom of a chart are selected, the Axis Patterns dialog box displays with options for changing the border and pattern as well as changing the tick mark type.

With options at the Area Patterns dialog box, you can add a border to the selected element or table, add a pattern, and change the background and foreground color to the pattern. For example, to add a pattern and change the background color of the pattern for the entire chart, you would complete the following steps:

1. Display Microsoft Graph for the chart.
2. Select the chart. To do this, position the arrow pointer anywhere outside the chart but inside the chart window, then click the left mouse button. (Check to make sure the small squares display around the chart.)
3. Choose Format, Patterns.

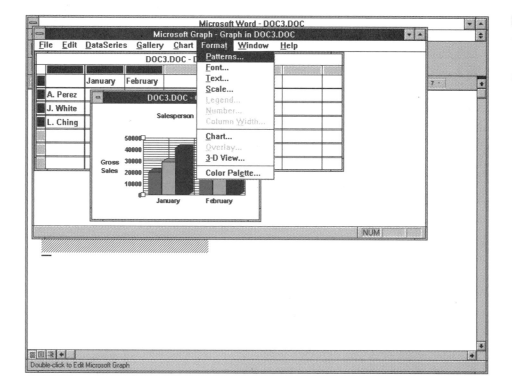

**Figure 22.12**
*Format Drop-Down Menu*

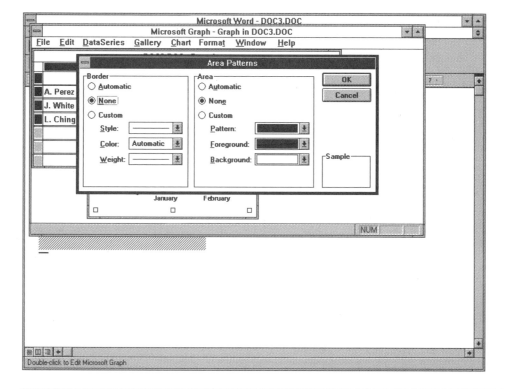

**Figure 22.13**
*Area Patterns Dialog Box*

4. At the Area Patterns dialog box, click on the down-pointing arrow to the right of the Pattern text box, then click on the fifth pattern option that displays in the drop-down menu.

5. Click on the down-pointing arrow to the right of the Background text box, then click on the light blue (aqua) color option.

6. Choose OK or press Enter.

The pattern is added to the chart (excluding the title). You would complete similar steps to add a pattern to other elements in the chart, such as the title. A border can be added to an element, such as the title, with options in the Border section of the Area Patterns dialog box.

## Changing the Font

Microsoft Graph uses a default font for chart elements. More than likely, this default font is 8-point Arial. (This may vary depending on the printer you are using.) The font for chart elements can be changed at the Chart Fonts dialog box, shown in figure 22.14. To display this dialog box, display Microsoft Graph for the chart, select a chart element, then choose Format. At the Format drop-down menu, choose Font.

## Customizing Chart Elements

With the remaining options from the Format drop-down menu, you can format text in the datasheet, the legend, change orientation of text, and much more.

If values are selected, such as the numbers in the vertical axis, the Text option will let you change the orientation of the text. For example, you can change the orientation of the text from horizontal to vertical.

Microsoft Graph determines the values used in the vertical axis based on the data in the table. With the Scale option, you can specify the minimum and maximum numbers used for the vertical axis as well as specify the major and minor units of value for the axis.

By default, Microsoft Graph automatically determines the location of the legend. If you want to position the legend in a different location in the chart, select the legend, choose Format, then choose Legend. At the Legend dialog box, specify if you want the legend positioned at the bottom, top, right, corner, or left side of the chart.

You can specify the formatting for numbers in a cell in the datasheet. To do this, make the datasheet active, position the insertion point in the cell or selected cells, then choose Format, Number. At the Number dialog box, select a numbering format in the Number Format list box. You can also specify formatting for the date and time with options in this list box.

The width of columns in the datasheet is determined by Word. You can specify a column width for a column in the datasheet. To do this, make the datasheet active, position the insertion point in a

*Figure 22.14*
*Chart Fonts Dialog*
*Box*

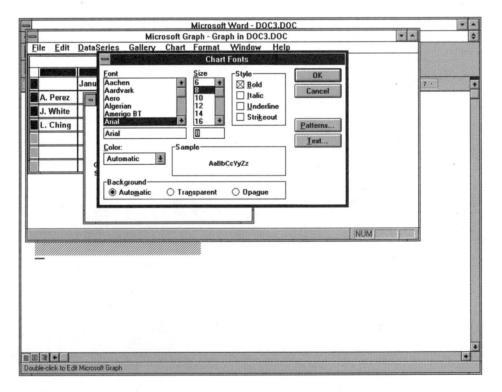

cell in the column to be changed, then choose Format, Column Width. At the Column Width dialog box, enter the number of spaces desired for the column in the Column width text box.

Choose Chart from the Format drop-down menu if you want to change the chart type or customize the gap between bars/columns, or change the depth of a 3-D chart.

With options from the Format 3-D View Dialog box you can change the elevation and rotation of bars/columns. To display the Format 3-D View dialog box, choose Format, then 3-D View.

Microsoft Graph provides 16 colors that can be applied to chart elements. You can blend colors to create your own colors. To do this, choose Format, then Color Palette. This displays the Palette dialog box. At this dialog box, select the color you want to change, then choose Edit. At the custom palette that displays, increase or decrease numbers to change the hue and intensity of the color. When all changes are made, choose OK. The custom color replaces the color selected. To return to the original color, choose Default at the Color Palette dialog box.

# CHAPTER SUMMARY

- In this chapter you created charts from data in a table. Charts are created with the Microsoft Graph application.
- Microsoft Graph lets you create a variety of charts, including bar and column charts, pie charts, area charts, line charts, and scatter charts.
- By default, Microsoft Graph charts the data as Series in Rows. The text in the first row of the table is the *category names*. Text in the left column is the *series names*.
- The left side of the chart displays the values and is referred to as the z-axis. It is generally marked like a ruler and is broken into units by marks called *ticks*.
- The series names that display in the left column of the datasheet are the y-axis and are used to create the legend for the chart.
- The x-axis is the bottom of the chart. The names of items in the chart generally display along the x-axis.
- At the Microsoft Graph window, the chart is displayed over the datasheet. The datasheet contains the text in cells as created in the table in the document.
- Use the Update option from the File drop-down menu if you make changes to the datasheet in the Microsoft Graph window and want the chart in the document to reflect the changes.
- To delete a chart, select the entire chart, then press the Delete key.
- When the chart is first inserted in the document, it displays with sizing handles.
- A chart can be framed like other graphic elements in a document.
- Three-dimensional chart options are available for Area, Bar, Column, Line, and Pie charts.
- Choose a chart type from the Gallery drop-down menu to display the chart variation options.
- If you create a chart based on a table, the information in the table is displayed in the datasheet. Changes can be made to the text in the datasheet. To do this, make the datasheet active by clicking on any visible part of the datasheet.
- The orientation of a chart can be changed from Series in Rows to Series in Columns by choosing DataSeries, then Series in Columns.
- To add or delete elements such as titles, labels, arrows, legends, or gridlines, choose the Chart option from the Microsoft Graph menu bar.
- Elements in a chart, such as the title or legend, can be selected, then moved or formatted.
- Formatting of elements can include adding a pattern, changing background and foreground colors of the selected element or chart, and changing the font. These options are available from the Format drop-down menu.
- With the additional options from the Format drop-down menu, you can format text in the datasheet, the legend, change orientation of text, and much more.

| | Mouse | Keyboard |
|---|---|---|
| Display Microsoft Graph window | Select the table, click on the Insert Chart button on the Standard toolbar; or Insert, Object, then with Create New tab selected, select Microsoft Graph | Select the table, Insert, Object, then with Create New tab selected, select Microsoft Graph |
| Exit Microsoft Graph window | File, then Exit and Return to (document name) | File, then Exit and Return to (document name) |
| Gallery drop-down menu | At the Microsoft Graph window, choose Gallery | At the Microsoft Graph window, choose Gallery |

## CHECK YOUR UNDERSTANDING

**True/False:** Circle the letter T if the statement is true; circle the letter F if the statement is false.

T    F    1.   A chart can be created with data in a table or data in a spreadsheet.

T    F    2.   Microsoft Graph is designed to work with Windows programs and contains OLE, which stands for Object Labels and Elements.

T    F    3.   If you do not have a color printer, the charts will display in black and white on the screen.

T    F    4.   The series names, used to create the legend for the chart, display on the y-axis.

T    F    5.   By default, the chart is displayed over the datasheet at the Microsoft Graph window.

T    F    6.   A chart can be framed by drawing a square around it with the arrow pointer.

T    F    7.   Microsoft Graph uses a default orientation for data called Series in Rows.

T    F    8.   Select a legend in order to add formatting by double-clicking on the legend.

T    F    9.   The default font for charts is generally 12-point Courier.

T    F   10.   Return the chart to the original colors by choosing Default at the Color Palette dialog box.

**Completion:** In the space provided, indicate the correct term, command, or number.

1.   To display the Microsoft Graph window, do this, then click on the Insert Chart button on the Standard toolbar.     _____

2.   You can also display the Microsoft Graph window by choosing this from the Insert menu.     _____

3.   In the default orientation, the *category names* is this text.     _____

4.   This axis is generally marked like a ruler.     _____

5.   At the Microsoft Graph window, use this option if you want the chart in the document to reflect changes made.     _____

6.   Change the size of the chart by dragging these.     _____

7.   Choose a chart type from this drop-down menu.     _____

8.   Changes can be made to the text in the datasheet just as you would to text in this form.     _____

9.   Items such as titles, data labels, arrows, and legends are also called these.     _____

10.   To select an entire chart, position the arrow pointer here.     _____

## Exercise 1

1. Open table02.
2. Save the document with Save As and name it c22ex01.
3. Create a 3-D Column chart for the table by completing the following steps:
   a. Position the insertion point in any cell in the table, then press Alt + 5 (on the numeric keypad with the Num Lock off) to select the entire table.
   b. Click on the Insert Chart button on the Standard toolbar.
   c. At the Microsoft Graph window, choose File, then Exit and Return to C22EX01.DOC.
   d. At the question asking if you want to update the graph, choose Yes.
4. Save the document again with the same name (c22ex01).
5. Print c22ex01. (The table and the chart will print.)
6. Close c22ex01.

## Exercise 2

1. Open c22ex01.
2. Save the document with Save As and name it c22ex02.
3. Change the size of the chart by completing the following steps:
   a. Change to the Page Layout viewing mode.
   b. Change the Zoom to Whole Page. (You can do this with the Zoom Control button on the Standard toolbar.)
   c. Click on the chart to select it.
   d. Drag the middle sizing handle at the right side of the chart to the right approximately 1 inch.
   e. Drag the middle sizing handle at the bottom of the chart down approximately 1 inch.
   f. Change the Zoom back to 100%.
4. Save the document again with the same name (c22ex02).
5. Print c22ex02. (The table and the chart will print.)
6. Close c22ex02.

## Exercise 3

1. Open c22ex02.
2. Save the document with Save As and name it c22ex03.
3. Frame the chart, then move it by completing the following steps:
   a. Change the Zoom to Whole Page.
   b. Click on the chart to select it.
   c. Insert a frame around the chart by choosing Insert, Frame.
   d. With the frame around the chart, position the arrow pointer inside the chart, drag the outline of the frame to the horizontal and vertical middle of the page, then release the mouse button.
   e. With the chart still selected, change the size of the chart by completing the following steps:
      (1) Choose Format, Picture.
      (2) At the Picture dialog box, click on the up- or down-pointing triangle to the right of the Width text box in the Size section until *5.5"* displays in the text box.
      (3) Click on the up- or down-pointing triangle to the right of the Height text box in the Size section until *3.5"* displays in the text box.
      (4) Choose OK or press Enter.
   f. Select the table (the table, not the chart) including the blank line (paragraph mark) below the table, then press Delete.
   g. If necessary, reposition the chart so it displays in the middle of the page.

    h. Deselect the chart.

    i. Change the Zoom to 100%.

4. Save the document again with the same name (c22ex03).

5. Print c22ex03.

6. Close c22ex03.

## Exercise 4

1. Open c22ex03.

2. Save the document with Save As and name it c22ex04.

3. Change the type of chart to a Bar chart by completing the following steps:

    a. Change the Zoom to Whole Page.

    b. Position the arrow pointer in the chart, then double-click the left mouse button. (This displays Microsoft Graph for the chart.)

    c. Choose Gallery from the Microsoft Graph menu bar, then choose Bar.

    d. At the Chart Gallery dialog box, make sure the first chart option is selected (displays with a black background), then choose OK or press Enter.

    e. At the Microsoft Graph window, choose File, then Exit and Return to C22EX04.DOC.

    f. At the question asking if you want to update the chart, choose Yes.

    g. Deselect the chart.

    h. Change the Zoom to 100%.

4. Save the document again with the same name (c22ex04).

5. Print c22ex04.

6. Close c22ex04.

## Exercise 5

1. Open table03.

2. Save the document with Save As and name it c22ex05.

3. Create a Bar chart for the table by completing the following steps:

    a. Select the entire table.

    b. Click on the Insert Chart button on the Standard toolbar.

    c. Choose Gallery from the Microsoft Graph menu bar, then choose Bar.

    d. At the Chart Gallery dialog box, click on the sixth option.

    e. Choose OK or press Enter.

    f. At the Microsoft Graph window, choose File, then Exit and Return to C22EX05.DOC.

    g. At the question asking if you want to update the chart, choose Yes.

    h. Change to the Page Layout viewing mode.

    i. Change the Zoom to Whole Page.

    j. Select the chart, insert a frame around it, then move the chart to the horizontal and vertical middle of the page.

    k. With the chart still selected, change the size of the chart by completing the following steps:

        (1) Choose Format, Picture.

        (2) At the Picture dialog box, click on the up-pointing triangle to the right of the Width text box in the Size section until *4.8"* displays in the text box.

        (3) Click on the up-pointing triangle to the right of the Height text box in the Size section until *3.2"* displays in the text box.

        (4) Choose OK or press Enter.

    l. Select the table, including the line (paragraph mark) below the table, then press the Delete key.

    m. If necessary, reposition the chart so it displays in the middle of the page.

    n. Deselect the chart.

    o. Change the Zoom to 100%.

4. Save the document again with the same name (c22ex05).
5. Print c22ex05.
6. Close c22ex05.

## Exercise 6

1. Open c22ex03.
2. Save the document with Save As and name it c22ex06.
3. Change the contents of certain cells in the datasheet by completing the following steps:
   a. Change the Zoom to Whole Page.
   b. Double-click on the chart. (This displays Microsoft Graph for the chart.)
   c. Position the arrow pointer in any portion of the datasheet (behind the chart), then click the left mouse button. (This makes the datasheet active.)
   d. The insertion point (displays as a crossbar) should be located in the cell containing the numbers *121398*. Key **110780** in this cell. (When you key the number, the previous number is automatically deleted.)
   e. Position the crossbar in the cell containing the number *145238*, then click the left mouse button. (This makes the cell active).
   f. Key **132469**. (This replaces the previous number.)
   g. Position the crossbar in the cell containing the number *64120*, then click the left mouse button. (This makes the cell active.)
   h. Key **78573**.
   i. Make the chart active. To do this, position the arrow pointer in any portion of the chart, then click the left mouse button.
   j. Choose File, then Exit and Return to C22EX06.DOC.
   k. At the update question, choose Yes.
   l. Deselect the chart.
   m. Change the Zoom to 100%.
4. Save the document again with the same name (c22ex06).
5. Print c22ex06.
6. Close c22ex06.

## Exercise 7

1. Open c22ex05.
2. Save the document with Save As and name it c22ex07.
3. Change the orientation to Series in Columns by completing the following steps:
   a. Change the Zoom to Whole Page.
   b. Double-click on the chart.
   c. At the Microsoft Graph window, choose DataSeries.
   d. From the drop-down menu that displays, choose Series in Columns.
   e. Choose File, then Exit and Return to C22EX07.DOC.
   f. At the update question, choose Yes.
   g. Deselect the chart.
   h. Change the Zoom to 100%.
4. Save the document again with the same name (c22ex07).
5. Print c22ex07.
6. Close c22ex07.

## Exercise 8

1. Open c22ex03.
2. Save the document with Save As and name it c22ex08.
3. Add a title to the value (z-axis) and move the legend for the chart by completing the following steps:
   a. Change the Zoom to Whole Page.

b. Double-click on the chart.
c. At the Microsoft Graph window, choose Chart.
d. At the drop-down menu, choose Titles.
e. At the Titles dialog box, choose Value (Z) Axis.
f. Choose OK or press Enter.
g. Key **Net Sales**. (You will not be able to see the letters as you key them.)
h. Click outside the selected title. (This will display the *Net Sales* title.)
i. Move the legend from the right side of the chart to the upper left corner of the chart by completing the following steps:
  (1) Position the arrow pointer in the legend, then click the left mouse button. (This selects the legend.)
  (2) Position the arrow pointer inside the legend, hold down the left mouse button, drag the outline of the legend to the upper left corner of the chart, then release the mouse button.
j. Choose File, then Exit and Return to C22EX08.DOC.
k. At the update question, choose Yes.
l. Deselect the chart.
m. Change the Zoom to 100%.
4. Save the document again with the same name (c22ex08).
5. Print c22ex08.
6. Close c22ex08.

## Exercise 9

1. Open table04.
2. Save the document with Save As and name it c22ex09.
3. Create a Pie chart with data labels by completing the following steps:
   a. Select the entire table.
   b. Click on the Insert Chart button on the Standard toolbar.
   c. At the Microsoft Graph window, choose DataSeries, then Series in Columns.
   d. Choose Gallery, then Pie.
   e. At the Chart Gallery make sure the first option is selected (displays with black background), then choose OK or press Enter.
   f. Choose Chart, then Data Labels.
   g. At the Data labels dialog box, choose Show Percent.
   h. Choose OK or press Enter.
   i. Select the legend, then move it to the upper left corner of the chart.
   j. Select the current title, *Category*, then key **Donation Dollars**. (You will not see all the letters when you key the title.)
   k. Deselect the title.
   l. Choose File, then Exit and Return to C22EX09.DOC.
   m. At the update question, choose Yes.
   n. Change to the Page Layout viewing mode.
   o. Change the Zoom to Whole Page.
   p. Select the chart, then insert a frame around it.
   q. Drag the chart to the middle of the page.
   r. Change the width of the chart to 5 inches and the height to 3.3 inches.
   s. Select the table (including the line below it), then delete the table.
   t. If necessary, reposition the chart in the middle of the page.
   u. Deselect the chart.
   v. Change the Zoom to 100%.
4. Save the document again with the same name (c22ex09).
5. Print c22ex09.
6. Close c22ex09.

## Exercise 10

1. Open c22ex09.
2. Save the document with Save As and name it c22ex10.
3. Delete the legend, then add a data label by completing the following steps:
    a. Change the Zoom to Whole Page.
    b. Double-click on the chart.
    c. At the Microsoft Graph window, choose Chart, then Delete Legend.
    d. Choose Chart, then Data Labels.
    e. At the Data Labels dialog box, choose Show Label And Percent.
    f. Choose OK or press Enter.
    g. Exit Microsoft Graph, saving the changes.
    h. Deselect the chart.
    i. Change the Zoom to 100%.
4. Save the document again with the same name (c22ex10).
5. Print c22ex10.
6. Close c22ex10.

## Exercise 11

1. Open c22ex04.
2. Save the document with Save As and name it c22ex11.
3. Add gridlines to the chart by completing the following steps:
    a. Change the Zoom to Whole Page.
    b. Double-click on the chart.
    c. At the Microsoft Graph window, choose Chart, then Gridlines.
    d. At the Gridlines dialog box, insert an X in the two check boxes in the Category (X) Axis section of the dialog box and the two check boxes in the Value (Y) Axis section.
    e. Choose OK or press Enter.
    f. Select the legend, then move it up slightly and away from the bars.
    g. Exit Microsoft Graph, saving the changes.
    h. Deselect the chart.
    i. Change the Zoom to 100%.
4. Save the document again with the same name (c22ex11).
5. Print c22ex11.
6. Close c22ex11.

## Exercise 12

1. Open c22ex03.
2. Save the document with Save As and name it c22ex12.
3. Add a pattern and change the color behind the bars in the chart and add a border to the chart title, value (Z) Axis, and the legend by completing the following steps:
    a. Change the Zoom to Whole Page.
    b. Double-click on the chart.
    c. At the Microsoft Graph window, select the portion of the chart containing the bars. To do this, position the tip of the arrow pointer immediately above one of the lower bars, then click the left mouse button. (This should select all the bars in the chart.)
    d. Choose Format, then Patterns.
    e. At the Area Patterns dialog box, click on the down-pointing arrow to the right of the Pattern text box, then click on the second pattern from the bottom that displays in the drop-down menu.
    f. Click on the down-pointing arrow to the right of the Background text box, then click on the light blue (aqua) color option.
    g. Choose OK or press Enter.

h. Select the chart title. To do this, position the tip of the arrow pointer on the chart title, *State*, then click the left mouse button.
i. Add a border to the chart title by completing the following steps:
   (1) Choose Forma*t*, then *P*atterns.
   (2) At the Area Patterns dialog box, click on the down-pointing arrow to the right of the *W*eight text box, then click on the second line weight option from the bottom of the drop-down menu.
   (3) Choose OK or press Enter.
j. Select the legend, move the legend up to the upper right corner, then add a border to the legend by completing steps 3i(1) through 3i(3).
k. Exit Microsoft Graph, saving the changes.
l. Deselect the chart.
m. Change the Zoom to 100%.

4. Save the document again with the same name (c22ex12).
5. Print c22ex12.
6. Close c22ex12.

## Exercise 13

1. Open c22ex07.
2. Save the document with Save as and name it c22ex13.
3. Change the font of the title and the legend of the chart by completing the following steps:
   a. Change the Zoom to Whole Page.
   b. Double-click on the chart.
   c. At the Microsoft Graph window, change the font of the title to 14-point Times New Roman by completing the following steps:
      (1) Click on the title, *Stock*.
      (2) Choose Forma*t*, then *F*ont.
      (3) At the Chart Fonts dialog box, choose Times New Roman in the *F*ont list box and 14 in the *S*ize list box.
      (4) Choose OK or press Enter.
   d. Select the legend, then move it to the upper right corner of the chart.
   e. Change the font of the legend to 8-point Times New Roman by completing steps similar to those in 3c(1) through 3c(4).
   f. Exit Microsoft Graph, saving the changes.
   g. Deselect the chart.
   h. Change the Zoom to 100%.

4. Save the document again with the same name (c22ex13).
5. Print c22ex13.
6. Close c22ex13.

# Exercise 14

1. At a clear document screen, key the headings and the first paragraph of the memo shown in figure 22.15.
2. With the insertion point positioned a double space below the first paragraph in the memo, create the table as shown in figure 22.15. (Do not add the gridlines to the table. These are shown in figure 22.15 only as a reference.) After creating the table, press Enter twice.
3. Create a Bar chart for the table, and change the position of the legend and the title by completing the following steps:
   a. Select the entire table.
   b. Click on the Insert Chart button on the Standard toolbar.
   c. At the Microsoft Graph window, change the chart type by completing the following steps:
      (1) Choose Gallery, then 3-D Column.
      (2) At the Chart Gallery, click on the eighth option.
      (3) Choose OK or press Enter.
   d. Change the rotation of the bars by completing the following steps:
      (1) Position the arrow pointer immediately above one of the lower bars, then click the left mouse button. (This selects the bars.)
      (2) Choose Format, then 3-D View.
      (3) At the Format 3-D View dialog box, choose Rotation, then key **40**.
      (4) Choose OK or press Enter.
   e. Change the position of the legend by completing the following steps:
      (1) Select the legend.
      (2) Choose Format, then Legend.
      (3) At the Legend dialog box, choose Corner.
      (4) Choose OK or press Enter.
   f. Change the title by completing the following steps:
      (1) Select the title.
      (2) Key **Software Training**.
      (3) Deselect the title.
   g. Exit Microsoft Graph, saving the changes.
   h. Change to the Page Layout viewing mode.
   i. Insert a frame around the chart.
   j. Move the chart down approximately 0.5 inches, then to the right until it is in the middle of the document.
   k. Select the table (including the line below the table), then delete it.
   l. If necessary reposition the chart.
   m. Press the Enter key until the insertion point is approximately a double space below the chart.
   n. Key the paragraph and the initials and document name in figure 22.15 below the table.
4. Save the document and name it c22ex14.
5. Print c22ex14.
6. Close c22ex14.

Figure 22.15

```
DATE:      (current date)

TO:        Brenda Hogue, Director

FROM:      Scott Sideres, Administrative Assistant

SUBJECT: EMPLOYEE TRAINING SURVEY


All employee training surveys have been collected.  I have analyzed
the section of the survey dealing with training needs.  The chart
below shows the percentage of people requesting training on the
specified software.
```

| Software | Percentage |
|---|---|
| Word Processing | 78 |
| Spreadsheet | 34 |
| Patient Assessment | 21 |
| Database | 45 |

```
As you can see by the chart, word processing is the software most
requested by employees for training.  I will finish analyzing the
rest of the survey by the end of next week.

xx:c22ex14
```

## SKILL ASSESSMENTS

### Assessment 1

1. Open table05.
2. Save the document with Save As and name it c22sa01.
3. Create a chart with the table with the following elements:
   a. Select the table, then display the Microsoft Graph window.
   b. At the Microsoft Graph window, display the Chart Gallery for 3-D Column charts, then choose the fourth option.
   c. Select the legend, then change the position to Left.
   d. Select the title, then change the font to 12-point Arial.
   e. Exit Microsoft Graph, saving the changes.
   f. Change to the Page Layout viewing mode.
   g. Change the Zoom to Whole Page.
   h. Insert a frame around the chart then drag the chart to the middle of the page.
   i. Change the width of the chart to 5 inches and the height to 3.3 inches.
   j. Select the table (and the line below the table), then delete the table.
   k. If necessary, reposition the chart.
   l. Deselect the chart.
   m. Change the Zoom to 100%.
4. Save the document again with the same name (c22sa01).
5. Print c22sa01.
6. Close c22sa01.

## Assessment 2

1. At a clear document screen, create the table shown in figure 22.16. (Do not include the gridlines. These gridlines are shown only as a reference.)
2. After creating the table, move the insertion point below the table, then press the Enter key twice.
3. Select the entire table, then create a chart with the table with the following specifications:
   a. At the Microsoft Graph window, change to a Bar chart (you determine the chart type at the Chart Gallery).
   b. Add data labels for the value.
   c. Move the legend to a more desirable location in the chart.
   d. Exit Microsoft Graph, saving the changes.
   e. Change to the Page Layout viewing mode.
   f. Change the Zoom to Whole Page.
   g. Select the chart, then insert a frame.
   h. Drag the chart to the middle of the page.
   i. Change the width of the chart to 4.8 inches and the height to 3.2 inches.
   j. Select the table (and the line below the table), then delete the table.
   k. If necessary, reposition the chart.
   l. Deselect the chart.
   m. Change the Zoom to 100%.
4. Save the document and name it c22sa02.
5. Print c22sa02.
6. Close c22sa02.

Figure 22.16

| Quarterly Investments | Gross Amount |
|---|---|
| First Qtr. | 130239 |
| Second Qtr. | 143204 |
| Third Qtr. | 198432 |
| Fourth Qtr. | 132864 |

## Assessment 3

1. Open table06.
2. Save the document with Save As and name it c22sa03.
3. Create a chart with the table with the following elements:
   a. At the Microsoft Graph window, change the DataSeries to Series in Columns.
   b. Display the Chart Gallery for Line charts, then choose the fifth option.
   c. Select the legend, then delete it.
   d. Create a title by completing the following steps:
      (1) Choose Chart, then Titles.
      (2) At the Attach Title dialog box, choose OK or press Enter.
      (3) Key **Population Growth - 1960 to 1990**.
      (4) Deselect the title.
   e. Exit Microsoft Graph, saving the changes.
   f. Change to the Page Layout viewing mode.
   g. Change the Zoom to Whole Page.
   h. Select the chart, then insert a frame.
   i. Drag the chart to the middle of the page.
   j. Change the width of the chart to 5 inches and the height to 3.3 inches.
   k. Select the table (and the line below the table), then delete the table.

    l.  Deselect the chart.

    m. If necessary, reposition the chart.

    n.  Change the Zoom to 100%.

4.  Save the document again with the same name (c22sa03).

5.  Print c22sa03.

6.  Close c22sa03.

## Assessment 4

1.  At a clear document screen, key the headings and the first paragraph of the memo shown in figure 22.17.

2.  With the insertion point a double space below the first paragraph of text in the memo, create the table as shown in figure 22.17. (Do not add the gridlines.) After creating the table, move the insertion point below the table, then press Enter twice.

3.  Create a Pie chart for the table with the following elements:

    a.  At the Microsoft Graph window, change the <u>D</u>ataSeries to Series in <u>C</u>olumns.

    b.  Change to a Pie chart (you determine the chart type at the Chart Gallery).

    c.  Move the legend to the left side.

    d.  Add data labels for the percents.

    e.  Change the font of the title to 12-point Times New Roman Bold.

    f.  Add a border around the title.

    g.  Exit Microsoft Graph, saving the changes.

    h.  Change to the Page Layout viewing mode.

    i.  Insert a frame around the chart.

    j.  Move the chart down about 0.25 inches and to the right until it is in the middle of the document.

    k.  Select the table (including the line below the table), then delete it.

    l.  If necessary, reposition the chart.

    m. Press the Enter key until the insertion point is approximately a double space below the chart.

    n.  Key the paragraph and the initials and document name below the table as shown in figure 22.17.

4.  Save the document and name it c22sa04.

5.  Print c22sa04.

6.  Close c22sa04.

Figure 22.17

```
DATE:     (current date)

TO:       Lee Hunter, Editor

FROM:     Paula Diaz, Investment Coordinator

SUBJECT: INVESTMENT ASSETS


The charts presented in last month's newsletter to investors looked
great.  Presenting data in a chart has much more visual impact on
readers than listing it in a table.  I would like the following pie
chart included in the investment section of the newsletter.
```

| Invested Assets | Percentage |
|---|---|
| Mortgage Loans | 36 |
| Bonds | 28 |
| Business Loans | 23 |
| Real Estate | 10 |
| Other | 3 |

```
There may be additional pie charts I would like added to the
newsletter.  As soon as I have computed the percentages and created
the charts, I will send them to your office.

xx:c22sa04
```

# Formatting Text into Columns 23

Upon successful completion of chapter 23, you will be able to create business documents, such as newsletters, agendas, and resumes, with different column styles.

When preparing a document containing text, an important point to consider is the readability of the document. Readability refers to the ease with which a person can read and understand groups of words. The line length of text in a document can enhance or detract from the readability of text. If the line length is too long, the reader may lose his or her place on the line and have a difficult time moving to the next line below. To improve the readability of some documents, such as newsletters or reports, you may want to set the text in columns.

Text can be set in two different types of columns in Word. One type, called *newspaper columns* (also referred to as *snaking columns*), is commonly used for text in newspapers, newsletters, and magazines. The other type, called *side-by-side columns* (also referred to as *parallel columns*), is used for text that you want kept aligned horizontally.

Newspaper columns contain text that flows up and down in the document. When the first column on the page is filled with text, the insertion point moves to the top of the next column on the same page. When the last column on the page is filled with text, the insertion point moves to the beginning of the first column on the next page.

Side-by-side columns contain text that is grouped across the page in rows. The next row begins below the longest column entry of the previous row. In Word, the Tables feature is used to create side-by-side columns.

## Creating Newspaper Columns

Newspaper columns contain text that flows up and down in the document as shown in figure 23.1. When the first column on the page is filled with text, the insertion point moves to the top of the next column on the same page.

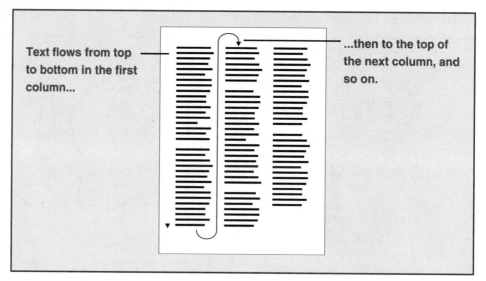

**Figure 23.1**
*Newspaper
Columns*

**Text flows from top
to bottom in the first
column...**

**...then to the top of
the next column, and
so on.**

Newspaper columns can be created with the Columns button on the Standard toolbar or with options from the Columns dialog box. Columns of equal width are created with the Columns button on the Standard toolbar. To create columns of unequal width, use the Columns dialog box. The formatting for newspaper columns can be established before the text is keyed or it can be applied to existing text. Keying text first and then formatting it into newspaper columns is generally faster.

A document can include as many columns as there is room for on the page. Word determines how many columns can be included on the page based on the page width, the margin widths, and the size and spacing of the columns. Columns must be at least 0.5 inches in width.

Changes in columns affect the entire document or the section of the document in which the insertion point is positioned. If you want to create different numbers or styles of columns in a document, divide the document into sections.

There are three ways to insert section breaks into a document. One way is to use the Break dialog box. (To display this dialog box, choose Insert, Break.) Another way is to use the Columns dialog box and tell Word to format text into columns forward in the document from the location of the insertion point. The third way is to select the text first, then apply column formatting.

## Creating Newspaper Columns with the Columns Button

The Columns button on the Standard toolbar is the sixth button from the right. When you position the arrow pointer on the Columns button and hold down the left mouse button (or click the left mouse button), a grid displays as shown in figure 23.2.

**Figure 23.2**
*Columns Grid*

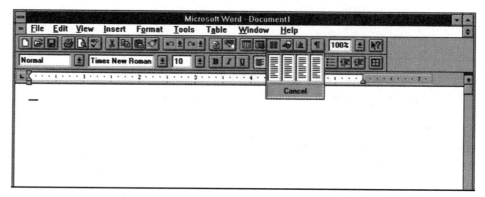

To format text in a document into two newspaper columns, you would complete the following steps:

1. Open the document.
2. Position the arrow pointer on the Columns button on the Standard toolbar, hold down the left mouse button, drag the mouse down and to the right until two columns display with a blue background on the Columns grid (and *2 Columns* displays below the grid), then release the mouse button.

All text in the document is formatted into two columns. If a document contains a title and you want that title to span both columns, you would complete the following steps:

1. Position the insertion point at the left margin where the first line of text displays that will begin the columns.
2. Choose Insert, then Break. This displays the Break dialog box.
3. At the Break dialog box, choose Continuous.
4. Choose OK or press Enter.
5. Position the insertion point below the section break, then format the text into columns.

In addition to the method just described, you could also format the text in a document into columns and not the title by selecting the text in the document *except* the title, then using the Columns button on the Standard toolbar to create the columns. A third method is explained in the next section on creating columns with options from the Columns dialog box.

In the Normal viewing mode, text will display in a single column at the left side of the document screen. If you want to view columns as they will appear when printed, change to the Page Layout viewing mode.

## Creating Newspaper Columns with the Columns Dialog Box

The Columns dialog box can be used to create newspaper columns that are equal or unequal in width. To display the Columns dialog box shown in figure 23.3, choose Format, then Columns.

If you are creating columns of equal width, key the number of columns desired for the document in the Number of Columns text box. You can also click on the up-pointing triangle to the right of the Number of Columns text box until the desired number displays.

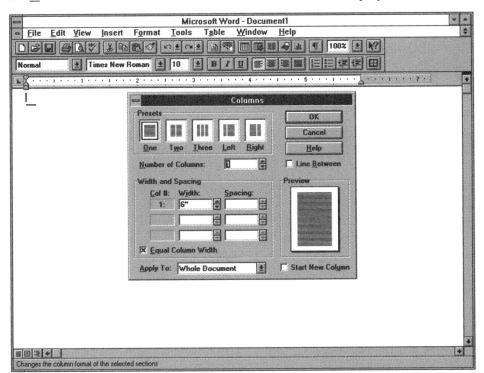

*Figure 23.3*
*Columns Dialog box*

You can also use options in the Presets section of the dialog box to specify the number of columns. By default, the One option is selected in the Presets section. Choose the Two option if you want two columns of text in a document or choose Three if you want three. If you choose the Left option, the right column of text will be twice as wide as the left column of text. Choose the Right option if the want the left column twice as wide. The options contain a preview box showing what the columns will look like.

Word automatically determines column widths for the number of columns specified. By default, the Equal Column Width option contains an X. At this setting, column widths are the same. If you want to enter your own column widths or change the amount of space between columns, specify the number of columns desired, then choose Equal Column Width to remove the X from the check box. When the X is removed, column measurements display in black below the Col #, Width, and Spacing options. To change the measurements of the columns, click on the up- or down-pointing triangles to the right of the width and spacing options until the desired measurements display in the text box. If you are using the keyboard, press the Tab key until the column or spacing measurement you want to change is selected, then key the new measurement.

The dialog box only has room to display measurements for three columns. If you specify more than three columns, a vertical scroll bar displays to the left of the column numbers. To view other column measurements, click on the down-pointing arrow at the bottom of the scroll bar.

By default, columns are separated by 0.5 inches of space. The amount of space between columns can be increased or decreased with the Spacing option. At this option, you can key a new measurement for the amount of spacing between columns or you can click on the up- or down-pointing triangle after the text box to increase or decrease the measurement.

As an example of how to use the Columns dialog box, you would complete the following steps to create two newspaper columns with 0.3 inches of space between columns and the width of the first column set at 2.5 inches and the width of the second column set at 3.2 inches:

1. Open the document containing text you want to format into columns.
2. Choose Format, Columns.
3. At the Columns dialog box, click on the up-pointing arrow to the right of the Number of Columns text box until *2* displays in the text box.
4. Choose Equal Column Width. (This removes the X from the check box.)
5. Click on the down-pointing arrow to the right of the column 1 Width text box until *2.5"* displays in the text box.
6. Click on the down-pointing arrow to the right of the column 1 Spacing text box until *0.3"* displays in the text box. (The measurement *3.2"* will display in the Width text box to the right of column 2.)
7. Choose OK or press Enter.

By default, column formatting is applied to the whole document. With the Apply To option at the bottom of the Columns dialog box, you can change this from *Whole Document* to *This Point Forward*. At the *This Point Forward* option, the column formatting is applied to text from the location of the insertion point to the end of the document.

A line that sets off the columns and adds visual separation can be inserted between columns. To insert a line between columns, choose Line Between at the Columns dialog box. The line between columns is the length of the longest column in the section. The line(s) can be seen in the Page Layout viewing mode or in Print Preview.

The Start New Column option lets you specify where to begin a new column of text. If you choose Start New Column, you must make sure that *This Point Forward* is selected in the Apply To option or the new column instruction is ignored.

When you enter column settings in the Columns dialog box, an example of how the columns will appear is shown in the Preview box in the lower right corner of the dialog box.

## Inserting a Column and/or Page Break

When formatting text into columns, Word automatically breaks the columns to fit the page. At times, a column break may appear in an undesirable location. For example, a heading may appear at the bottom of the column, while the text after the heading begins at the top of the next column. You can insert a column break into a document to control where columns end and begin on the page.

To insert a column break, position the insertion point where you want the new column to begin, then press Ctrl + Shift + Enter. In addition, you can also insert a column break by completing the following steps:

1. Position the insertion point at the location where the new column is to begin.
2. Choose Insert, Break.
3. At the Break dialog box, choose Column Break.
4. Choose OK or press Enter.

If you insert a column break on the last column on a page, the column begins on the next page. If you want a column that is not the last column on the page to begin on the next page, insert a page break. To do this, press Ctrl + Enter. You can also insert a page break by completing the following steps:

1. Position the insertion point at the location in the text where you want the new page to begin.
2. Choose Insert, Break.
3. At the Break dialog box, choose Page Break.
4. Choose OK or press Enter.

Go To Exercise 4

## ◼ *Editing Text in Columns*

To edit text formatted into columns, move the insertion point with the mouse or insertion point movement keys and commands either within columns or between columns.

### Moving the Insertion Point Within Columns

To move the insertion point in a document using the mouse, position the arrow pointer where desired, then click the left button. If you are using the keyboard, the insertion point movement keys—up, down, left, and right arrows—cause the insertion point to move in the direction indicated. If you press the up or down arrow key, the insertion point moves up or down within the column. If the insertion point is located on the last line of a column on a page, the down arrow will cause the insertion point to move to the beginning in the same column on the next page. If the insertion point is located on the beginning of a line of text in columns, pressing the up arrow key will cause the insertion point to move to the end of the same column on the previous page.

The left and right arrow keys move the insertion point in the direction indicated within the column. When the insertion point gets to the end of the line within the column, it moves down to the beginning of the next line within the same column.

### Moving the Insertion Point Between Columns

You can use the mouse or the keyboard to move the insertion point between columns. If you are using the mouse, position the I-beam pointer where desired, then click the left button. If you are using the keyboard, press Alt + up arrow to move the insertion point to the top of the previous column, or press Alt + down arrow to move the insertion point to the top of the next column.

Go To Exercise 5

## ■Removing Column Formatting

If a document contains text formatted into columns, the column formatting can be removed with the Columns button on the Standard toolbar or at the Columns dialog box. To remove column formatting using the Columns button, you would complete the following steps:

1. Position the insertion point in the section containing columns, or select the text in columns.
2. Click on the Columns button on the Standard toolbar.
3. Click on the first column in the Columns grid.

To remove column formatting using the Columns dialog box, you would complete the following steps:

1. Position the insertion point in the section containing columns, or select the text in columns.
2. Choose Format, Columns.
3. At the Columns dialog box, choose One in the Presets section.
4. Choose OK or press Enter.

## ■Changing Column Width and Spacing

The width of and spacing between text formatted into columns can be changed with the column marker on the horizontal ruler. The horizontal ruler is displayed when the viewing mode is Page Layout. The horizontal ruler and the column marker are identified in figure 23.4.

To change the width (and also the spacing) of columns of text in a document using the column marker on the horizontal ruler, you would complete the following steps:

*Figure 23.4*
*Column Marker on*
*the Horizontal Ruler*

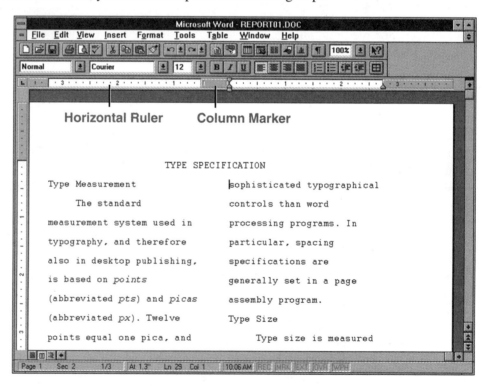

1. Position the arrow pointer on the left or right edge of the column marker on the horizontal ruler until it turns into a double-headed arrow pointing left and right.
2. Hold down the left mouse button, drag the column marker to the left or right to make the column of text wider or thinner, then release the mouse button.

If the columns are of equal width, changing the width of one column changes the width of all columns. If the columns are of unequal width, changing the width of a column only changes that column.

If you hold down the Alt key, then drag the column marker, Word displays the measurements for the columns and the space between columns on the horizontal ruler. The column measurements display in the white section of the horizontal ruler and the measurements for the spaces between columns display in the gray section.

## Balancing Columns on a Page

In a document containing text formatted into columns, Word automatically lines up (balances) the last line of text at the bottom of each column. On the last page of a document, the text is often not balanced between columns. Text in the first column may flow to the end of the page, while the text in the second column may end far short of the end of the page. Columns can be balanced by inserting a section break at the end of the text by completing the following steps:

1. Position the insertion point at the end of the text in the last column of the section you want to balance.
2. Choose Insert, Break.
3. At the Break dialog box, choose Continuous.
4. Choose OK or press Enter.

Figure 23.5 shows the last page of a document containing unbalanced columns and a page where the columns have been balanced.

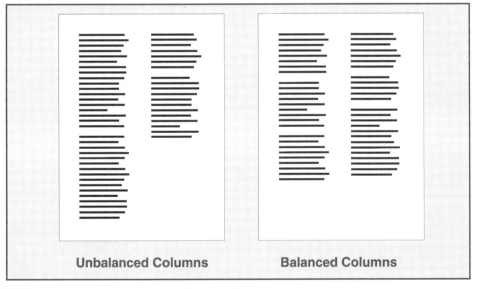

**Unbalanced Columns**    **Balanced Columns**

*Figure 23.5*
*Unbalanced and Balanced Columns*

## Creating Side-by-Side Columns

Side-by-side columns contain text in paragraphs that are horizontally aligned as shown in figure 23.6. Such text is read one paragraph at a time from left to right. With Word, you can format this type of column using the Tables feature. Side-by-side columns are often used in an agenda, itinerary, resume, script, or address list.

Figure 23.6
Parallel Columns

Side-by-side columns are created by inserting a table into a document using either the Insert Table button on the Standard toolbar or the Insert Table dialog box. (*Refer to chapter 21 for a review of creating and formatting tables.*)

## CHAPTER SUMMARY

- Setting text in columns may improve the readability of some documents such as newsletters or reports.
- The two different types of columns that can be created in Word are *newspaper columns* (also called *snaking columns*) and *side-by-side columns* (also called *parallel columns*).
- Newspaper columns of equal width can be created with the Columns button on the Standard toolbar or with options from the Columns dialog box. To create columns of unequal width, use the Columns dialog box.
- Keying text first and then formatting it into newspaper columns is generally faster, but the formatting can be established before the text is keyed.
- By default, columns formatting is applied to the whole document.
- In the Normal viewing mode, text will display in a single column at the left side of the document screen. Change to the Page Layout viewing mode to view columns as they will appear when printed.
- Options at the Columns dialog box let you change the spacing between columns, apply columns formatting from the point of the insertion point forward, insert a line between columns, or start a new column.
- To move the insertion point in a document containing columns using the mouse, position the arrow pointer where desired, then click the left button. To move the insertion point with the keyboard, use the arrow keys.
- Column formatting can be removed with the Columns button on the Standard toolbar or at the Columns dialog box.
- The width of and spacing between text formatted into columns can be changed with the column marker on the horizontal ruler.
- Word automatically lines up (balances) the last line of text at the bottom of each column. The last page of columns can be balanced by inserting a section break at the end of the text.
- Side-by-side columns contain text in paragraphs that are horizontally aligned.
- Create side-by-side columns by inserting a table into a document using either the Insert Table button on the Standard toolbar or the Insert Table dialog box as described in chapter 21.

| | Mouse | Keyboard |
|---|---|---|
| Display Columns dialog box | Format, Columns | Format, Columns |
| Insert a column break | Insert, Break, Column Break | CTRL + SHIFT + ENTER |
| Insert a page break | Insert, Break, Page Break | CTRL + ENTER |
| Insert a section break | Insert, Break, Continuous | Insert, Break, Continuous |
| Move insertion point between columns | Position I-beam pointer where desired, click left button | ALT + ↑ (top of previous column) ALT + ↓ (top of next column) |

## CHECK YOUR UNDERSTANDING

**True/False:** Circle the letter T if the statement is true; circle the letter F if the statement is false.

T   F   1. Newspaper columns contain text that is grouped across the page in rows.

T   F   2. Formatting text into newspaper columns after the text has been keyed is usually quicker than formatting first.

T   F   3. No more than ten columns can be created with Word's columns feature.

T   F   4. Change to the Page Layout viewing mode to view columns as they will appear when printed.

T   F   5. If you choose the Right option at the Columns dialog box, the left column will be twice as wide as the right.

T   F   6. When you enter column settings in the Columns dialog box, an example of how the columns will appear is shown in the Preview box.

T   F   7. In a document with columns, Alt + down arrow moves the insertion point to the top of the previous column.

T   F   8. The best way to remove column formatting is to delete all the paragraph markers in the document.

T   F   9. Side-by-side columns are often used for address lists.

T   F   10. Side-by-side columns are created by inserting a table into a document.

**Completion:** In the space provided at the right, indicate the correct term, command, or number.

1. This type of column contains text that flows up and down in the document.                                    _____

2. This is the minimum width for a column.                                    _____

3. The Columns button on the Standard toolbar is this number of buttons from the right.                                    _____

4. To create different styles of columns in a document, divide the document into these.                                    _____

5. Create columns of unequal width here.                                    _____

6. Columns are separated by this amount of space by default.                                    _____

7. To insert a vertical line between columns, choose this at the Columns dialog box.                                    _____

8. Insert this (or these) into a document to control where columns end and begin on the page.                                    _____

9. Use this on the horizontal ruler to change the width of columns.                                    _____

10. To balance all columns on the last page of text, insert this at the end of the text.                                    _____

## Exercise 1

1. Open report01.
2. Save the document with Save As and name it c23ex01.
3. Change to the Page Layout viewing mode.
4. Select the title, then change the font to 14-point Times New Roman Bold.
5. Select the text in the document from the beginning of the heading *Type Measurement* to the end of the document (this is all text except the title and the blank line below the title). With the text selected, make the following changes:
   a. Change the font to 11-point Times New Roman.
   b. Display the Tabs dialog box, then set a left tab at 0.25 inches.
   c. Format the text into two newspaper columns by positioning the arrow pointer on the Columns button on the Standard toolbar, holding down the left mouse button, dragging the mouse down and to the right until two columns display with a blue background on the Columns grid (and *2 Columns* displays below the grid), then releasing the mouse button.
   d. Deselect the text.
6. Save the document again with the same name (c23ex01).
7. Print c23ex01. (Page breaks may display in undesirable locations. Do not make changes to the page breaks. This document will be used in a later exercise.)
8. Close c23ex01.

## Exercise 2

1. Open report02.
2. Save the document with Save As and name it c23ex02.
3. Select the entire document, then make the following changes:
   a. Change the font to 10-point Times New Roman.
   b. Display the Tabs dialog box, then set a left tab at 0.2 inches.
   c. Deselect the text.
4. Format the text (except the title) into three newspaper columns by completing the following steps:
   a. Position the insertion point at the left margin of the line that begins the text of the report (at the left margin where the sentence begins, "The term *structured publication...*").
   b. Choose Format, Columns.
   c. At the Columns dialog box, click on the up-pointing triangle to the right of the Number of Columns text box until *3* displays in the text box.
   d. Choose Apply To at the bottom of the Columns dialog box, then, from the drop-down list that displays, choose *This Point Forward*.
   e. Choose OK or press Enter.
5. Position the insertion point at the beginning of the document, then automatically hyphenate text in the document.
6. Save the document again with the same name (c23ex02).
7. Print c23ex02.
8. Close c23ex02.

## Exercise 3

1. Open report02.
2. Copy a portion of the report into a new document, then save the new document by completing the following steps:
   a. Select the report from the beginning of the report through the paragraph after the *Running Heads/Feet* section (right before the section that begins with the heading *Page Numbers (Folios)*).

b. Click on the Copy button on the Standard toolbar.

c. Click on the New button on the Standard toolbar.

d. At the clear document screen, click on the Paste button on the Standard toolbar.

e. Save the document and name it c23ex03.

f. Make report02 the active document, then close it. (This should display c23ex03 in the document screen.)

3. With c23ex03 open, make the following changes:

a. Set the title, *STRUCTURED PUBLICATIONS,* in 14-point Arial Bold.

b. Select the text from the beginning of the first paragraph below the title to the end of the document, then make the following changes:

(1) Change the font to 12-point Times New Roman.

(2) Display the Tabs dialog box, then set a left tab at 0.25 inches.

(3) Press Ctrl + 1 to change to single line spacing.

(4) Deselect the text.

4. Insert a hard return above and below the following headings in the document:

*TEMPLATE ELEMENTS*

*Column Grid*

*STANDING ELEMENTS*

*Running Heads/Feet*

5. Format the text of the report into uneven newspaper columns with a line between by completing the following steps:

a. Change to the Page Layout viewing mode.

b. Position the insertion point at the left margin of the first paragraph below the title of the report.

c. Choose Format, Columns.

d. At the Columns dialog box, choose Apply To at the bottom of the Columns dialog box, then, from the drop-down list that displays, choose *This Point Forward.*

e. Choose Left in the Presets section of the Columns dialog box.

f. Choose Line Between.

g. Choose OK or press Enter.

6. Save the document again with the same name (c23ex03). (Check the document. The heading *TEMPLATE ELEMENTS* should begin the second column on the page and the text should fit on one page.)

7. Print c23ex03.

8. Close c23ex03.

## Exercise 4

1. Open c23ex03.

2. Save the document with Save As and name it c23ex04.

3. Make the following changes to the report:

a. Select the report from the beginning of the first paragraph below the title to the end of the report, then click on the Justify button on the Formatting toolbar.

b. Position the insertion point at the beginning of the first paragraph below the title, then automatically hyphenate the text in the document. (This should move the heading *TEMPLATE ELEMENTS* from the top of the second column to the bottom of the first column.)

c. Insert a column break at the heading *TEMPLATE ELEMENTS* by completing the following steps:

(1) Position the insertion point immediately left of the *T* in *TEMPLATE ELEMENTS.* (This heading is located at the bottom of the first column.)

(2) Choose Insert, Break.

(3) At the Break dialog box, choose Column Break.

(4) Choose OK or press Enter.

4. Save the document again with the same name (c23ex04).
5. Print c23ex04.
6. Close c23ex04.

## Exercise 5

1. Open c23ex01.
2. Save the document with Save As and name it c23ex05.
3. Make the following changes to the report:
    a. Select the title, *TYPE SPECIFICATION*, then change the font to 18-point Times New Roman Bold.
    b. Select the heading, *Type Measurement*, *Type Size*, and *Type Style* individually, then change the font to 14-point Times New Roman Bold and the alignment to center.
    c. Select the last four paragraphs of text in the document, then insert bullets.
4. Save the document again with the same name (c23ex05).
5. Print c23ex05.
6. Close c23ex05.

## Exercise 6

1. Open c23ex05.
2. Save the document with Save As and name it c23ex06.
3. Make the following changes to the document:
    a. Select the title, *TYPE SPECIFICATION*, then change the font to 14-point Times New Roman Bold.
    b. Select the document except the title and the blank line below, then press Ctrl + 1 to change to single spacing. Deselect the text.
    c. Position the insertion point anywhere in the heading *Type Measurement,* then change the spacing between columns using the column marker on the horizontal ruler by completing the following steps:
        (1) Position the arrow pointer at the left side of the column marker on the horizontal ruler until it turns into a double-headed arrow pointing left and right.
        (2) Hold down the left mouse button and then the Alt key.
        (3) Drag the mouse to the right until the measurement inside the column marker displays as *0.25".*
        (4) Release the mouse button and then the Alt key.
    d. Change the spacing after the heading *Type Measurement* to 6 points by completing the following steps:
        (1) Position the insertion point anywhere in the heading *Type Measurement.*
        (2) Choose F̲ormat, P̲aragraph.
        (3) At the Paragraph dialog box, make sure the I̲ndents and Spacing tab is selected, then click once on the up-pointing triangle after the Aft̲er text box in the Spacing section of the dialog box. This should change the spacing measurement to *6 pt.*
        (4) Choose OK or press Enter.
    e. Position the insertion point anywhere in the heading *Type Size*, then change the spacing *before* and *after* the paragraph to 6 points. (Follow steps similar to those in 3d(2) through 3d(4).)
    f. Position the insertion point at the beginning of the heading *Type Style,* then insert a column break. (This moves the *Type Style* heading to the beginning of the second column.)
    g. With the insertion point still positioned at the beginning of the heading *Type Style*, change the spacing *after* the paragraph to 6 points.
4. Save the document again with the same name (c23ex06).
5. Print c23ex06.
6. Close c23ex06.

## Exercise 7

1. Open c23ex02.
2. Save the document with Save As and name it c23ex07.
3. Make the following changes to the report:
   a. Change the width of the spacing between columns by completing the following steps:
      (1) Change to the Page Layout viewing mode.
      (2) Position the arrow pointer at the left side of the first column marker from the left on the horizontal ruler until it turns into a double-headed arrow pointing left and right.
      (3) Hold down the left mouse button and then the Alt key.
      (4) Drag the mouse to the right until the measurement inside the column marker displays approximately as *0.28"*.
      (5) Release the mouse button and then the Alt key.
   b. Position the insertion point immediately right of the period at the end of the report (page 3), then insert a continuous break to balance the columns on the third page by completing the following steps:
      (1) Choose Insert, Break.
      (2) At the Break dialog box, choose Continuous.
      (3) Choose OK or press Enter.
4. Save the document again with the same name (c23ex07).
5. Print c23ex07.
6. Close c23ex07.

## Exercise 8

1. At a clear document screen, create the heading for the newsletter shown in figure 23.7 by completing the following steps:
   a. Press the Enter key once, then move the insertion point back up to the first line.
   b. Change the font to 18-point Arial Bold.
   c. Key **Petersburg School District**.
   d. Click on the Borders button on the Standard toolbar. (This turns on the display of the Borders toolbar.)
   e. Change the Line Style to 2 1/4-point double line.
   f. Click on the Bottom Border button on the Borders dialog box. (This inserts the double line shown in figure 23.7.)
   g. Press the down arrow key on the keyboard.
   h. Click on the Align Right button on the Formatting toolbar.
   i. Change the font to 14-point Arial Bold.
   j. Key **April Newsletter**, then press Enter.
   k. Key **Jon Struebing, Editor**, then press Enter.
   l. Click on the Align Left button on the Formatting toolbar.
   m. Press Ctrl + spacebar to remove the font formatting.
   n. Press the Enter key twice.
2. Insert the document named *news01.doc* into the current document. (Use the File option from the Insert menu to do this.)
3. Make the following changes to the document:
   a. Select the text from *Recreation Program* to the end of the document, then change the font to 12-point Times New Roman.
   b. Select the headings *Recreation Program*, *Sixth-Grade Camp*, and *Library News* individually, then change the font to 14-point Times New Roman Bold.
   c. Position the insertion point at the beginning of *Recreation Program,* then format the text into two newspaper columns except the title. (Hint: Change the Apply To option at the Columns dialog box to *This Point Forward*.)

    d.  Insert the picture *sports.wmf* at the beginning of the paragraph that starts *Lewis County Parks and Recreation...*, by completing the following steps:

      (1)  Position the insertion point at the beginning of the paragraph that starts *Lewis County Parks and Recreation....*

      (2)  Choose Insert, Picture.

      (3)  At the Insert Picture dialog box, select *sports.wmf*. (Click on the down-pointing arrow at the bottom of the vertical scroll bar or press the down arrow key until this document is visible, then select the document.)

      (4)  Choose OK or press Enter.

      (5)  Select the picture.

      (6)  Choose Format, Picture.

      (7)  At the Picture dialog box, change the Width to *1.3"* and the Height to *1.2"* (in the Size section).

      (8)  Choose OK or press Enter to close the Picture dialog box.

      (9)  Frame the picture.

    e.  Position the insertion point at the beginning of the paragraph that starts *Young people are invited to...*, then insert the picture *books.wmf* by completing steps similar to those in 3d(1) through 3d(9) except change the width to *1.3"* and the height to *0.8"*.

  4.  Save the document and name it c23ex08.

  5.  Print c23ex08.

  6.  Close c23ex08.

---

**Figure 23.7**

# Petersburg School District

**April Newsletter**
**Jon Struebing, Editor**

## Exercise 9

  1.  At a clear document screen, create the resume shown in figure 23.8 as side-by-side columns by completing the following steps:

    a.  Press the Enter key once, then move the insertion point back up to the first line.

    b.  Change the font to 18-point Arial Bold, then key **TERRY HAMILTON**.

    c.  Display the Borders toolbar, change the Line Style to a 6-point line, then click on the Bottom Border button on the Borders toolbar.

    d.  Press the down arrow key to move the insertion point below the 6-point line.

    e.  Change the paragraph alignment to right and the font to 14-point Arial Bold.

    f.  Key the address and telephone number as shown in figure 23.8. Press the Enter key to end the lines as shown in the figure.

    g.  After keying the telephone number, press the Enter key twice, then change the paragraph alignment to left.

    h.  Create a table with two columns and five rows.

    i.  Change the width of the first column to 2 inches and the width of the second column to 4 inches.

    j.  Select the first column, then change the font to 12-point Arial Bold.

    k.  Select the second column, then change the font to 12-point Times New Roman.

    l.  Key the text shown in figure 23.8. When you have completed keying text in the second column, press the Enter key once. (This separates the rows by a blank line.)

    m.  Change the top and bottom margins to 0.8 inches.

  2.  Save the resume document and name it c23ex09.

  3.  Print c23ex09.

  4.  Close c23ex09.

Figure 23.8

# TERRY HAMILTON

**7645 Freedom Drive Southeast
Petersburg, ND 76321
(501) 555-4329**

OBJECTIVE

A position as a medical secretary in a company that provides opportunity for growth and advancement.

EDUCATION

Lewis County Community College: Associates of Arts and Sciences, Medical Secretary, June 1996

Rollins High School: Honor Graduate, 1994

SKILLS

| | |
|---|---|
| Keyboarding (80+ wpm) | Desktop publishing |
| Medical terminology | Word processing |
| Medical procedures | Machine transcription |
| Accounting | 10-key calculator |
| Database management | Spreadsheet |
| Employee training | Supervision |

EMPLOYMENT

Medical Secretary, Petersburg Medical Clinic, 400 Fourth Street, Petersburg, ND 76321. Duties included answering the telephone, taking messages, scheduling appointments, filing manually and electronically, and transcribing and preparing medical documents.

Assistant Manager, Lowell Pharmacy, 905 Raymond Street, Petersburg, ND 76321. Duties included supervising employees, training new employees, taking inventory, customer service, sales, and operating cash register.

Food Server, Marlene's Cafe, 210 South Third Street, Petersburg, ND 76321. Duties included customer service, hosting birthday parties, cooking, operating cash register and drive-through window, and taking and filling customer orders.

ORGANIZATIONS

Vice-President, Student Government, Rollins High School, 1993-1994

Treasurer, Student Government, Rollins High School, 1992-1993

Member, Phi Beta Lambda, 1991-1994

## Assessment 1

1. Open report03.
2. Save the document with Save As and name it c23sa01.
3. Make the following changes to the report:
   a. Insert an additional hard return between the title *CHAPTER 1: DEVELOPMENT OF TECHNOLOGY, 1900 - 1950* and the heading *World War I.*
   b. Select the text from the beginning of the title *CHAPTER 2: DEVELOPMENT OF TECHNOLOGY, 1950 - 1960* to the end of the document, then delete the text.
   c. Select the text from the heading *World War I* to the end of the document, then make the following changes:
      (1) Change the font to 12-point Times New Roman.
      (2) Display the Tabs dialog box, then set a left tab at 0.25 inches.
      (3) Format the selected text into two newspaper columns.
   d. Set the title, *CHAPTER 1: DEVELOPMENT OF TECHNOLOGY, 1900 - 1950*, and the headings *World War I* and *World War II* in 14-point Times New Roman.
4. Save the document again with the same name (c23sa01).
5. Print c23sa01.
6. Close c23sa01.

## Assessment 2

1. Open report06.
2. Save the document with Save As and name it c23sa02.
3. Make the following changes to the report:
   a. Select the report from the first paragraph below the title to the end of the report, then make the following changes:
      (1) Change the font to 12-point Times New Roman.
      (2) Display the Tabs dialog box, then set a left tab at 0.25 inches.
      (3) Format the selected text into two evenly spaced newspaper columns with a line between.
      (4) Deselect the text.
   b. Change to the Page Layout viewing mode.
   c. Select the title, *CHOOSING BINDING,* then set it in 14-point Arial Bold, and change the alignment to Center.
   d. Select the headings within the body of the report and change the font to 14-point Times New Roman Bold and change the paragraph alignment to center.
   e. Position the insertion point after the last period at the end of the document, then insert a continuous section break.
4. Save the document again with the same name (c23sa02).
5. Print c23sa02.
6. Close c23sa02.

## Assessment 3

1. Open c23sa02.
2. Save the document with Save As and name it c23sa03.
3. Make the following changes to the document:
   a. Position the insertion point anywhere within the text formatted in columns, display the Columns dialog box, then remove the X in the Line Between option.
   b. Delete the text in the document from the paragraph that begins *Case binding (also called edition binding)...* to the end of the document.
   c. Delete the blank line above the heading *Saddle and Side Stitching,* then change the spacing above and below the paragraph containing the heading to 6 points. Complete similar steps for the headings *Mechanical Binding* and *Book Binding.*

d. Change the heading *Saddle and Side Stitching* to *Saddle Stitching*.

e. Insert the picture *books.wmf* in the document with the following specifications:

    (1) Change the width of the picture to 2.5 inches and the height to 1.4 inches.

    (2) Frame the picture then format the frame so the horizontal and vertical positions are centered relative to the page.

4. Save the document again with the same name (c23sa03).

5. Print c23sa03.

6. Close c23sa03.

## Assessment 4

1. At a clear document screen, create the document shown in figure 23.9 as side-by-side columns with the following specifications:

a. Center the title, *OCTOBER SPORTS ACTIVITIES*, and set it in 14-point Arial Bold.

b. With the insertion point a triple space below the title, create a table with three columns and eight rows. Make the following changes to the table:

    (1) Change the width of the first column to 1 inch, the second column to 1.5 inches, and the third column to 3.5 inches.

    (2) Select the entire table, then change the font to 12-point Arial.

    (3) Select the first row, then change the alignment to center and turn on bold.

c. Key the text in the cells as shown in figure 23.9. After keying the text in the last column, press the Enter key once. (This separates the rows by a blank line.)

2. After keying the text in the cells, save the document and name it c23sa04.

3. Print c23sa04.

4. Close c23sa04.

**Figure 23.9**

### OCTOBER SPORTS ACTIVITIES

| Day | Time | Activity |
|---|---|---|
| October 1 | 3:30 - 6:00 p.m. | Junior Varsity Football, Cedar Middle School vs. Lakeview Middle School |
| October 3 | 6:00 - 8:30 p.m. | Ninth Grade Volleyball Jamboree, Oakridge Middle School |
| October 4 | 7:00 - 10:00 p.m. | Varsity Football Game, Meeker High School vs. Rollins High School |
| October 14 | 3:30 - 5:30 p.m. | Varsity Tennis Tournament, Meeker High School vs. Roosevelt High School |
| October 15 | 3:30 - 6:00 p.m. | Junior Varsity Football, Lakeview Middle School vs. Ewing Middle School |
| October 18 | 7:00 - 10:00 p.m. | Varsity Football Game, Rollins High School vs. Roosevelt High School |
| October 22 | 3:30 - 6:00 p.m. | Varsity Tennis Tournament, Meeker High School vs. Rollins High School |

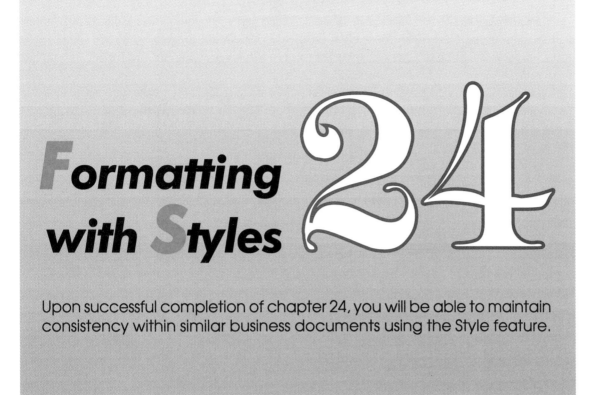

# Formatting with Styles 24

Upon successful completion of chapter 24, you will be able to maintain consistency within similar business documents using the Style feature.

Some documents, such as company newsletters, reports, or brochures, may be created on a regular basis. These documents should maintain a consistency in formatting each time they are created. For example, a newsletter should maintain a consistency from issue to issue, and a company report should contain consistent formatting each time one is created.

Formatting that is applied to a variety of documents on a regular basis or that maintains a consistency within a publication can be applied to text using a *style*. In Word, a style is a set of formatting instructions saved with a name in order to use them over and over.

One real benefit of styles is that when the formatting instructions contained within a style are changed, all the text to which the style has been applied is automatically updated. For example, suppose for subheadings in a newsletter you create a style that sets text in 18-point Arial Bold. After applying the style to several subheadings in the document, you decide that the subheadings would look better if they are set in 14-point Times New Roman Bold instead. To change all the subheadings at once in the document, you change the formatting instructions stored in the style. All subheadings with the style applied are automatically changed to 14-point Times New Roman Bold.

Styles are created for a particular document and are saved with the document. Each time the document is opened, the styles are available.

## Formatting Text with Styles

As you learned in an earlier chapter, a Word document, by default, is based on the Normal template document. Within a normal template document, a Normal style is applied to text by default. This Normal style sets text in the default font (this may vary depending on what you have selected or what printer you are using), uses left alignment and single spacing, and turns on the Widow/Orphan control. In addition to this Normal style, other predesigned styles are available in a document based on the Normal template document. These styles can be displayed by clicking on the down-pointing arrow to the right of the Style button on the Formatting toolbar.

Other template documents also contain predesigned styles. If you choose a different template document from the New dialog box, click on the down-pointing arrow to the right of the Style button on the Formatting toolbar to display the names of styles available for that particular template document.

Styles can be changed and/or applied to text in three ways. The quickest way to apply styles to text in a document is with Word's AutoFormat feature. The advantage to using AutoFormat is that Word automatically applies the styles without you having to select them. The disadvantage is that you have less control over the styles that are applied.

Another method you can use to apply styles is to select a new template at the Style Gallery dialog box. The advantage to this is that you can preview your document as it will appear if formatted with various templates, and then apply the desired template. The disadvantage is that you have less control over the selection of styles.

A third method for applying styles to text is to make changes to those styles available in the template upon which your document is based. The advantage to this method is that you can format a document any way you want by creating and selecting styles. The disadvantage is that you have to create and/or select a style for each element in the document you want formatted.

## Formatting with AutoFormat

Word provides a variety of predesigned styles in the Normal template document that can be applied to text in a document. With this feature, called AutoFormat, Word goes through a document paragraph by paragraph and applies appropriate styles. For example, Word changes the font and size for heading text and adds bullets to listed items. The formatting is done automatically; all you do is sit back and watch Word do the work.

A document can be formatted with the AutoFormat button on the Standard toolbar; the shortcut command, Ctrl + K; or with the AutoFormat option from the Format drop-down menu. To use the AutoFormat button on the Standard toolbar or the shortcut command to automatically format a document, you would complete the following steps:

1. Open the document you want to automatically format.
2. Click on the AutoFormat button on the Standard toolbar (the tenth button from the right); or press Ctrl + K.

To format a document with the AutoFormat option from the Format drop-down menu, you would complete the following steps:

1. Open the document you want to automatically format.
2. Choose Format, AutoFormat.
3. At the AutoFormat dialog box containing the message *Word will automatically format (document name)*, choose OK or press Enter.
4. After Word automatically applies the styles, the AutoFormat dialog box displays with the message *Formatting completed. You can now: • Accept or reject all changes. • Review and reject individual changes. • Choose a custom look with Style Gallery.* At this message, choose Accept or press Enter.

Figure 24.1 shows the report01 document with formatting applied with the AutoFormat feature. When AutoFormat applies styles to a document, it also makes corrections as follows:

- Uses formatting rules to find and format headings, body text, lists, superscript, subscript, addresses, and letter closings.
- Replaces straight quotes and apostrophes with typesetting quotation marks.
- Deletes extra paragraph marks.
- Replaces (c) with ©, (R) with ®, and (TM) with ™.
- Replaces horizontal spaces inserted with the space bar or the Tab key with indents.
- Replaces hyphens, asterisks, or other characters used to list items with a bullet (•).

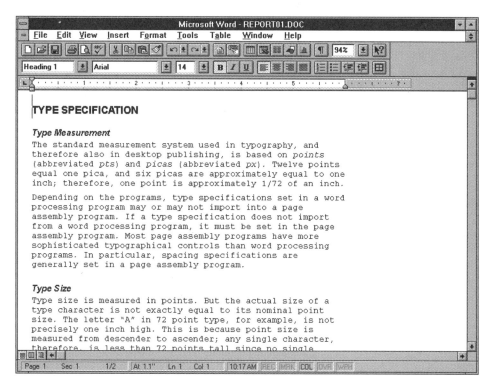

Figure 24.1
Document
Formatted with
AutoFormat

If, after automatically formatting a document you want to undo the changes, immediately choose one of the following:

- Click on the Undo button on the Standard toolbar.
- Choose Edit, then Undo AutoFormat.
- Press Ctrl + Z.

### Reviewing/Rejecting Formatting Changes

If you use the AutoFormat option from the Format drop-down menu to automatically format the document, you can review and then accept or reject changes. To do this, you would complete the following steps:

1.  Open the document you want to automatically format.
2.  Choose Format, AutoFormat.
3.  At the AutoFormat dialog box containing the message *Word will automatically format (document name)*, choose OK or press Enter.
4.  After Word automatically applies the styles, the AutoFormat dialog box displays with the message *Formatting completed. You can now: • Accept or reject all changes. • Review and reject individual changes. • Choose a custom look with Style Gallery.* At this message, choose Review Changes.
5.  At the Review AutoFormat Changes dialog box shown in figure 24.2, accept or reject the changes.
6.  When all formatting has been reviewed, Word inserts a dialog box with the message *Microsoft Word reached the end of the document. Do you want to continue searching from the beginning of the document?*. At this message, choose OK or press Enter.
7.  At the Review AutoFormat Changes dialog box, choose Cancel.
8.  At the next dialog box, choose Accept.

Figure 24.2
Review AutoFormat
Changes Dialog
Box

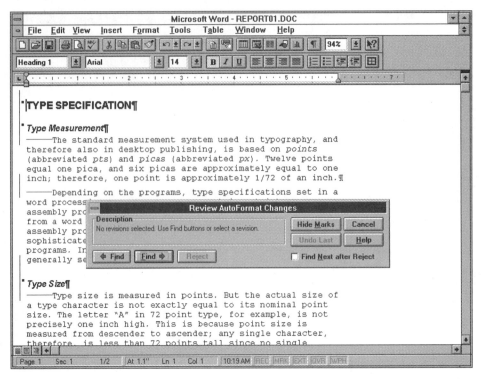

When Word displays the document for review, temporary revision marks are displayed. Revision marks are described in figure 24.3.

Figure 24.3
AutoFormat
Revision Marks

| This revision mark | Means |
| --- | --- |
| Blue paragraph mark | a style was applied to the paragraph. |
| Red paragraph mark | the paragraph mark was deleted. |
| Red strikethrough character (-) | text or spaces were deleted. |
| Underline (_) | the underline character (displays in blue) was added. |
| Vertical bar in left margin | text or formatting was changed in that line. |

As you review changes in a document, Word selects text with formatting applied. If you want to reject the formatting, choose Reject, then choose Find to find the next formatting. If you want to leave the formatting as displayed, choose Find to find the next formatting. If you want to find the previous formatting, choose Find. If you want Word to automatically find the next formatting when you choose Reject, choose the Find Next after Reject. This inserts an X in the check box. To hide the revision marks in a document, choose Hide Marks.

If the Review AutoFormat Changes dialog box is in the way of text you want to see in the document, position the arrow pointer in the title bar of the dialog box, hold down the left mouse button, drag the outline of the dialog box to a new location, then release the mouse button.

### Changing AutoFormat Options

Word follows certain rules when formatting text with AutoFormat. You can make changes to these rules. To do this, choose Tools, then Options. At the Options dialog box, choose the AutoFormat tab. This causes the Options dialog box to display as shown in figure 24.4.

At the Options dialog box with the AutoFormat tab selected, remove the X from a check box if you do not want the option active, or insert an X if you do want the option active. For example, if you do not want AutoFormat to replace asterisks you have used for a list in a document with bullets, choose the Bullet Characters with Bullets option to remove the X.

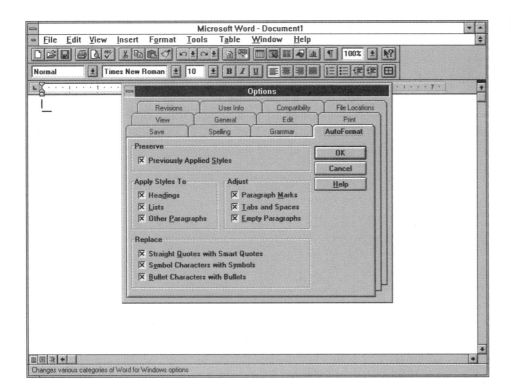

*Figure 24.4*
*Options Dialog Box*
*with AutoFormat*
*Tab Selected*

## Formatting Text with the Style Gallery

As you learned in an earlier chapter, each document is based on a template, with the Normal template document the default. The styles applied to text with AutoFormat are the styles available with the Normal template document. Word also provides predesigned styles with other template documents. You can use the Style Gallery dialog box to apply styles from other templates to the current document. This provides you with a large number of predesigned styles for formatting text.

To display the Style Gallery dialog box shown in figure 24.5, choose Format, then Style Gallery.

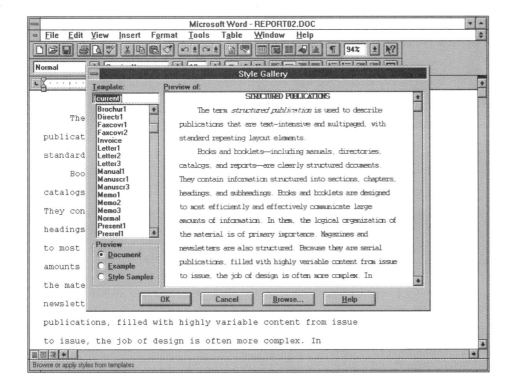

*Figure 24.5*
*Style Gallery Dialog*
*Box*

At the Style Gallery dialog box, the template documents are displayed in the <u>T</u>emplate list box. These are the same template documents that you learned about in chapter 17. The open document is displayed in the <u>P</u>review of section of the dialog box. With this section, you can choose templates from the <u>T</u>emplate list box and see how the formatting is applied to the open document.

At the bottom of the Style Gallery dialog box, the <u>D</u>ocument option is selected in the Preview section. If you choose <u>E</u>xample from the Preview section, Word will insert a sample document in the <u>P</u>review of section that displays the formatting applied to the document. Choosing <u>S</u>tyle Samples will cause the styles to display in the <u>P</u>review of section of the dialog box rather than the document or sample document.

As an example of how to use the Style Gallery dialog box to apply styles to a document, you would complete the following steps to format the letter01 document with styles from the *Letter2* template:

1. Open letter01.
2. Choose F<u>o</u>rmat, Style <u>G</u>allery.
3. At the Style Gallery dialog box, choose *Letter2* in the <u>T</u>emplate list box. To do this with the mouse, click on *Letter2*. If you are using the keyboard, press Alt + T, then press the down arrow key until *Letter2* is selected.
4. Choose OK or press Enter.

## Applying Standard Styles

As you learned earlier in this chapter, Word provides predesigned or standard styles for each template document. You can apply these standard styles to text in a document. You can do this with the AutoFormat feature or you can apply styles individually with the Style button on the Formatting toolbar or at the Style dialog box.

To apply a style with the Style button on the Formatting toolbar, position the insertion point in the paragraph to which you want the style applied, or select the text, then click on the down-pointing arrow to the right of the Style button (the first button on the left). This causes a drop-down list to display as shown in figure 24.6. Click on the desired style in the list to apply the style to the text in the document.

**Figure 24.6**
*Style Drop-Down List*

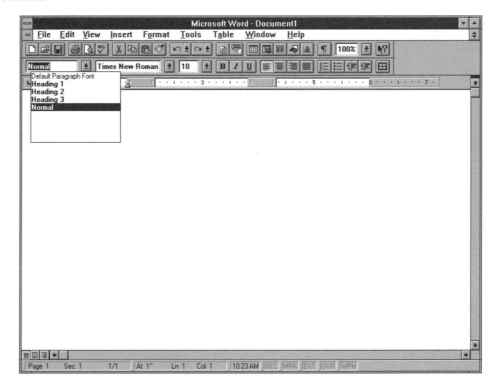

As an example of how to apply a style using the Style button, you would complete the following steps to apply the *Heading 1* style to the title of the report01 document:

1. Open report01.
2. Position the insertion point anywhere in the title, *TYPE SPECIFICATION*.
3. Click on the down-pointing arrow to the right of the Style button on the Formatting toolbar.
4. Click on *Heading 1* in the drop-down list.

When you click on *Heading 1* in the drop-down list, the list is removed from the screen and the style is applied to the title. This style sets the text in 14-point Arial Bold, changes the paragraph alignment to left, and changes the spacing after the title. The style name displays in the Style button on the Formatting toolbar. In addition, Arial displays in the Font button, 14 displays in the Size button, and the Bold button is active. This helps you identify the formatting that is applied to text with the *Heading 1* style.

The Style drop-down list only displays a few styles. Generally, the *Heading 1, Heading 2, Heading 3,* and *Normal* styles display in the list. (Your list may vary.) Word provides many more predesigned styles that you can use to format text in a document. You can display the list of styles available with Word at the Style dialog box shown in figure 24.7. To display the Style dialog box, choose Format, then Style.

To display the entire list of styles provided by Word, choose List at the Style dialog box, then choose *All Styles* in the drop-down list. To do this with the mouse, click on the down-pointing arrow to the right of the List box, then click on *All Styles*. If you are using the keyboard, press Alt + L, then press the down arrow key until *All Styles* is selected. When you choose *All Styles*, the list of styles in the Styles list box displays as shown in figure 24.8. The list is longer than the list box. In the Styles list box, paragraph styles are displayed in bold text and character styles are displayed in normal text.

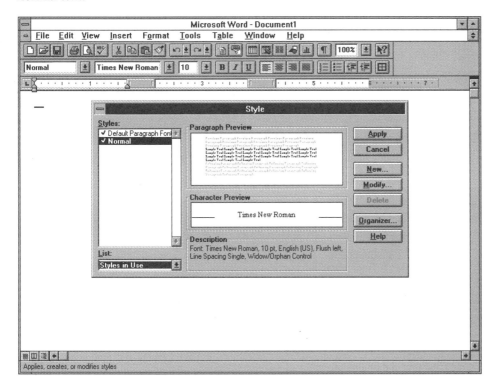

*Figure 24.7*
*Style Dialog Box*

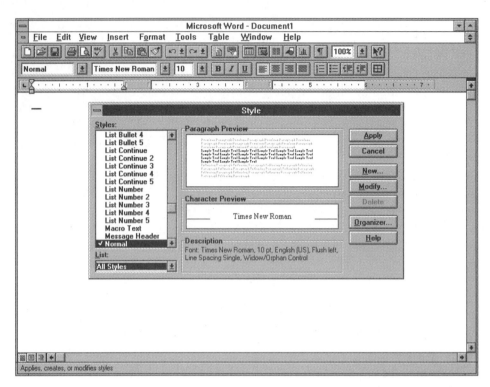

Figure 24.8
Style Dialog Box
with All Styles
Displayed

At the right side of the Style dialog box, the Paragraph Preview box displays an example of how the selected style will format text. The Character Preview box displays the font used to format text. A description of the style is displayed in the Description section of the dialog box.

As an example of how to apply a style at the Style dialog box, you would complete the following steps to apply the *Title* style to the title, *TYPE SPECIFICATION*, in the report01 document:

1. Open report01.
2. Position the insertion point anywhere in the title, *TYPE SPECIFICATION*.
3. Choose F̲ormat, S̲tyle.
4. At the Style dialog box, choose L̲ist, then choose *All Styles*. To do this with the mouse, click on the down-pointing arrow to the right of the L̲ist box, then click on *All Styles*. If you are using the keyboard, press Alt + L, then press the down arrow key until *All Styles* is selected.
5. Select *Title* in the S̲tyles list box. To do this with the mouse, click on the down-pointing arrow at the bottom of the S̲tyles list box scroll bar until *Title* is visible, then click on *Title*. If you are using the keyboard, press the down arrow key until *Title* is selected.
6. Choose A̲pply.

In addition to applying predesigned styles with the Style button on the Formatting toolbar and the Style dialog box, you can use shortcut commands to apply some styles. Figure 24.9 displays the style and the shortcut command you can use to apply the style.

Figure 24.9
Style Shortcut
Commands

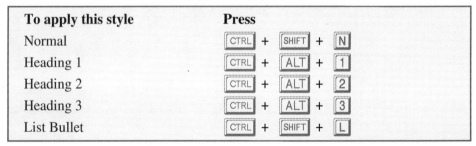

| To apply this style | Press |
| --- | --- |
| Normal | CTRL + SHIFT + N |
| Heading 1 | CTRL + ALT + 1 |
| Heading 2 | CTRL + ALT + 2 |
| Heading 3 | CTRL + ALT + 3 |
| List Bullet | CTRL + SHIFT + L |

If you are using the keyboard, you can make the Style button on the Formatting toolbar active by pressing Ctrl + Shift + S. With the Style button active, press the down arrow to display the Style drop-down list.

# Creating Styles

If all the styles predesigned by Word do not contain the formatting you desire, you can create your own style. Two types of styles can be created: *character* and *paragraph*. Character styles include options available at the Font dialog box such as font; font size; and font style, such as bold, underlining, and italics. Only character formatting is stored in a character style. Character styles are applied to selected text or the word where the insertion point is positioned.

A paragraph style includes character and paragraph formatting such as tabs, indents, borders, shading, etc. Paragraph styles are applied to selected paragraphs or the paragraph where the insertion point is positioned.

A style can be created in two ways. You can either apply the desired formatting instructions to a paragraph, then save those instructions in a style, or you can specify the formatting instructions for a particular style without applying them to text. The first method is useful when you want to see how text appears when certain formatting instructions are applied to it. The second method is often used when you know the particular format that you want to use for certain paragraphs.

When you create your own style, you must give the style a name. When naming a style, avoid using the names already used by Word. The list of style names will display in the Styles list box at the Style dialog box if *All Styles* is selected in the List box. When naming a style, try to name it something that gives you an idea what the style will accomplish. Consider the following when naming a style:

- A style name can contain a maximum of 253 characters.
- A style name can contain spaces and commas.
- A style name is case-sensitive. Uppercase and lowercase letters can be used.
- Do not use the backslash (\), braces ({ }), or a semicolon (;) when naming a style.

## Creating a Style by Example

A style can be easily created by formatting text first, then using the Style button on the Formatting toolbar or the Style dialog box to create the style. As an example of how to create a style by example using the Formatting toolbar, you would complete the following steps to create a style named *Indent* that indents text 0.75 inches from the left and right margins:

1. Key a paragraph of text.
2. Display the Paragraph dialog box, then change the left and right indents to 0.75 inches.
3. With the insertion point positioned in the paragraph containing the indents, click on the down-pointing arrow to the right of the Style button on the Formatting toolbar.
4. Make sure the *Normal* style is selected in the drop-down list. If not, select the *Normal* style.
5. With *Normal* selected, key **Indent**, then press Enter.

This creates the Indent style and also displays *Indent* in the Style button. The Indent style is visible in the Style drop-down list from the Formatting toolbar as well as at the Style dialog box.

A style can also be created by example using the Style dialog box. For example, to create a style by example named *Indent 2* that indents text 0.75 inches from the left and the right margins using the Style dialog box, you would complete the following steps:

1. Key a paragraph of text.
2. Display the Paragraph dialog box, then change the left and right indents to 0.75 inches.
3. With the insertion point positioned in the paragraph containing the indents, choose Format, then Style.
4. At the Style dialog box, choose New.
5. At the New Style dialog box, key **Indent 2** in the Name text box. (The insertion point is automatically positioned in the Name text box when the dialog box is displayed.)
6. Choose OK or press Enter.
7. At the Style dialog box, choose Close.

Go To Exercise 7

## Creating a Style Using the Style Dialog Box

A style can be created before you use it rather than creating it by example. To do this, you use options from the Style dialog box shown in figure 24.7. The Style dialog box can be used to create a style by applying the desired formatting instructions to text or by entering the specific formats without applying them to text. To create a style at the Style dialog box, you would complete the following steps:

1.  Choose Format, then Style.
2.  At the Style dialog box, choose New.
3.  At the New Style dialog box, key a name for the style in the Name text box.
4.  At the New Style dialog box, specify whether you are creating a paragraph or character style. Do this with the Style Type option.
5.  Choose Format, then choose the desired formatting option.
6.  When all formatting has been selected, make sure the correct formatting displays in the Description section of the dialog box, then choose OK or press Enter.
7.  At the Style dialog box, choose Close.

At the New Style dialog box, a variety of formatting can be selected. When you choose Format at the New Style dialog box, a drop-down list displays with the options shown in figure 24.10. Figure 24.10 displays the option as well as what formatting can be selected.

*Figure 24.10*
*Style Formatting*
*Options*

| Choose this | To select this type of formatting |
| --- | --- |
| Font | Font, style, size, color, superscript, subscript, and character spacing. |
| Paragraph | Paragraph alignment, indentations, spacing, and line spacing. (Not available for character styles.) |
| Tabs | Tab stop measurements, alignment, leaders, or clear tabs. |
| Border | Border location, color, style, and shading. (Not available for character styles.) |
| Language | Language that the spell checker, thesaurus, and grammar checker use for the current paragraph. |
| Numbering | Bulleted and Numbered paragraphs in various styles. (Not available for character styles.) |

As an example of how to create a style at the Style dialog box, you would complete the following steps to create a style named *Head 1* that changes the paragraph alignment to center and sets the text in 14-point Times New Roman Bold:

1.  Choose Format, then Style.
2.  At the Style dialog box, choose New.
3.  At the New Style dialog box, key **Head 1** in the Name text box.
4.  Change the paragraph alignment to center by completing the following steps:
    a.  Choose Format.
    b.  At the drop-down menu that displays, choose Paragraph.
    c.  At the Paragraph dialog box, choose Alignment, then Centered.
    d.  Choose OK or press Enter to close the Paragraph dialog box.
5.  Change the font to 14-point Times New Roman Bold by completing the following steps:
    a.  Choose Format.
    b.  At the drop-down menu that displays, choose Font.

6. Make sure the correct formatting displays in the Description section of the dialog box, then choose OK or press Enter to close the New Style dialog box.

7. At the Style dialog box, choose Close.

Go To
Exercise
8

## ■ *A*pplying a *S*tyle

A paragraph style can be applied to the paragraph where the insertion point is positioned or selected paragraphs. A character style can be applied to the word where the insertion point is located or to selected text.

A style can be applied using the Style button on the Formatting toolbar or the Style dialog box. To apply a style using the Formatting toolbar, you would complete the following steps:

1. Position the insertion point in the paragraph to which you want the style applied, or select the text.
2. Click on the down-pointing arrow to the right of the Style button.
3. At the drop-down list of styles, click on the desired style.

To apply a style using the Style dialog box, you would complete the following steps:

1. Position the insertion point in the paragraph to which you want the style applied, or select the text.
2. Choose F<u>o</u>rmat, then <u>S</u>tyle.
3. At the Style dialog box, select the desired style in the <u>S</u>tyles list box. (To view the entire list of styles offered by Word, choose <u>L</u>ist, then *All Styles*.)
4. Choose <u>A</u>pply.

Go To
Exercise
9

## ■ *A*ssigning a *S*hortcut *K*ey to a *S*tyle

A style can be quickly applied in a document if a shortcut key has been assigned to the style. You can use the letters A through Z, numbers 0 through 9, the Delete and Insert keys, combined with the Ctrl, Alt, and Shift keys to create a shortcut key combination. Word has already assigned shortcut key combinations to many features. If you assign a shortcut key combination to a style that is already used by Word, the message *Currently Assigned to (name of feature)* displays. When this happens, choose another shortcut key combination.

To create a shortcut key combination for a style, you would complete the following steps:

1. Open the document containing the style to which you want to assign a shortcut key combination.
2. Choose F<u>o</u>rmat, then <u>S</u>tyle.
3. At the Style dialog box, select the style for which you want to assign a shortcut key combination in the <u>S</u>tyles list box.
4. Choose <u>M</u>odify.
5. At the Modify Style dialog box, choose Shortcut <u>K</u>ey.
6. At the Customize dialog box with the <u>K</u>eyboard tab selected as shown in figure 24.11, press the shortcut key combination in the Press <u>N</u>ew Shortcut Key text box.
7. Choose <u>A</u>ssign.
8. Choose Close to close the Customize dialog box.
9. At the Modify Style dialog box, choose OK or press Enter.
10. At the Style dialog box, choose Close.

Go To
Exercise
10

Figure 24.11
Customize Dialog
Box with Keyboard
Tab Selected

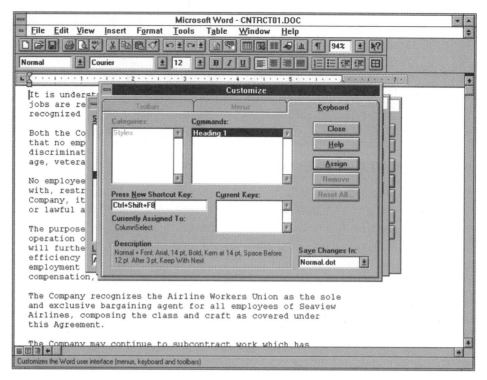

To apply a style assigned to a shortcut key combination, you would complete the following steps:

1. Select the paragraph or text to which you want the style applied.
2. Press the shortcut key combination.

To remove a shortcut key combination from a style, you would complete the following steps:

1. Open the document containing the style with the shortcut key combination.
2. Choose Format, then Style.
3. At the Style dialog box, select the style with the shortcut key combination that you want removed in the Styles list box.
4. Choose Modify.
5. At the Modify Style dialog box, choose Shortcut Key.
6. At the Customize dialog box with the Keyboard tab selected, choose the shortcut key you want to remove in the Current Keys list box.
7. Choose Remove.
8. Choose Close to close the Customize dialog box.
9. At the Modify Style dialog box, choose OK or press Enter.
10. At the Style dialog box, choose Close.

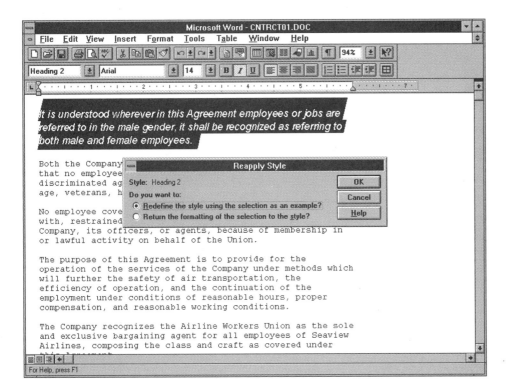

Figure 24.12
Reapply Style
Dialog Box

## Redefining a Style

Once a style has been created, you can redefine the style by changing the formatting instructions that it contains either with the Formatting toolbar or the Style dialog box. When you redefine a style by changing the formatting instructions, all text to which that style has been applied is changed accordingly.

To redefine a style using the Formatting toolbar, you would complete the following steps:

1. Open the document containing a style you want to redefine.
2. Reformat text with the formatting instructions you want changed in the style.
3. Select the text.
4. Click on the down-pointing arrow to the right of the Style button.
5. At the drop-down list of styles, click on the style name you want to redefine.
6. Word displays the Reapply Style dialog box shown in figure 24.12, asking if you want to redefine the style using the selection as an example. At this dialog box, choose OK or press Enter.

You can also redefine a style at the Style dialog box. To redefine a style at the Style dialog box, you would complete the following steps:

1. Open the document containing the style you want to redefine.
2. Choose Format, then Style.
3. At the Style dialog box, select the style name you want to redefine in the Styles list box.
4. Choose Modify.
5. At the Modify Style dialog box shown in figure 24.13, add or delete formatting options by choosing Format, then the appropriate option.
6. When all changes have been made, choose OK or press Enter to close the Modify Style dialog box.
7. At the Style dialog box, choose Close.

**Figure 24.13**
*Modify Style Dialog*
*Box*

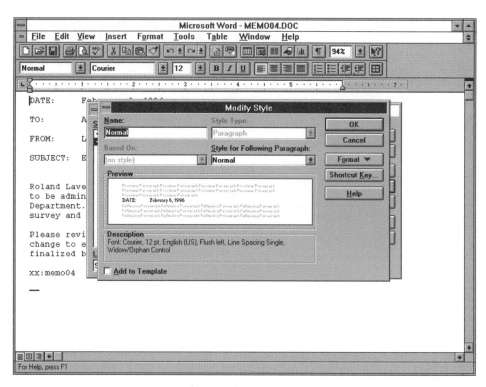

As an example of how to redefine a style, you would complete the following steps to change the font to 18-point Arial Bold for the *Head 1* style:

1. Open the document containing the *Head 1* style.
2. Choose Format, then Style.
3. At the Style dialog box, select *Head 1* in the Styles list box.
4. Choose Modify.
5. At the Modify Style dialog box, change the font to 18-point Arial Bold by completing the following steps:
   a. Choose Format.
   b. At the drop-down menu that displays, choose Font.
   c. At the Font dialog box, choose *Arial* in the Font list box, *Bold* in the Font Style list box, and *18* in the Size list box.
   d. Choose OK or press Enter to close the Font dialog box.
6. At the Modify Style dialog box, choose OK or press Enter.
7. At the Style dialog box, choose Close.

Go To
Exercise
13

## ■ Removing a Style from Text

You may apply a style to text in a document and then change your mind and wish to remove the style. If you decide to remove the style immediately after applying it (before performing some other action), click on the Undo button on the Standard toolbar. You can also choose Edit, Undo Style; or press Ctrl + Z. When a style is removed, the style that was previously applied to the text is applied once again (usually this is the Normal style).

You can also remove a style from text by applying a new style. Only one style can be applied at a time to the same text. For example, if you applied the *Heading 1* style to text and then later decide you want to remove it, position the insertion point in the text containing the *Heading 1* style, then apply the *Normal* style.

Go To
Exercise
14

# ■ Renaming a Style

As you create more and more styles in a particular document, you may find that you need to rename existing styles to avoid duplicating style names. When a style is renamed, the formatting instructions contained within the style remain the same. Any text to which the style has been applied reflects the new name. You can rename styles that you create as often as needed, but you cannot rename Word's standard styles.

To rename a style, you would complete the following steps:

1. Open the document containing the style you want to rename.
2. Choose Format, then Style.
3. At the Style dialog box, select the style you want to rename in the Styles list box.
4. Choose Modify.
5. At the Modify Style dialog box, key the new name for the style.
6. Choose OK or press Enter to return to the Style dialog box.
7. At the Style dialog box, choose Close.

In addition to renaming a style, you can add an *alias* to the style. An alias is an optional name that is shorter than the style name. With an alias, you can more quickly apply a style.

To add an alias to a style name, you would complete the following steps:

1. Open the document containing the style to which you want to add an alias.
2. Choose Format, then Style.
3. At the Style dialog box, select the style name to which you want to add an alias in the Styles list box.
4. Choose Modify.
5. At the Modify Style dialog box, key a comma after the current style name, then key the alias name.
6. Choose OK or press Enter to return to the Style dialog box.
7. At the Style dialog box, choose Close.

# ■ Deleting a Style

A style can be deleted in a document and any style to which that style is applied is returned to the Normal style. To delete a style, you would complete the following steps:

1. Open the document containing the style you want to delete.
2. Choose Format, then Style.
3. At the Style dialog box, select the style name you want to delete in the Styles list box.
4. Choose Delete.
5. At the message asking if you want to delete the style, choose Yes.
6. Choose Close to close the Style dialog box.

You can delete several styles at once at the Organizer dialog box. To do this, you would complete the following steps:

1. Open the document containing the styles you want to delete.
2. Choose Format, then Style.
3. At the Style dialog box, choose Organizer.
4. At the Organizer dialog box, select the style names you want deleted in the In list box at the left side of the dialog box.
5. Choose Delete.
6. At the question asking if you want to delete the first style, choose Yes to All. This tells Word to delete all selected styles.
7. Choose Close to close the Organizer dialog box.

Go To
Exercise
16

You can delete styles that you create but you cannot delete Word's standard styles.

## CHAPTER SUMMARY

- Formatting that is applied to a variety of documents on a regular basis or that maintains a consistency within a publication can be applied to text using a *style*. A style is a set of formatting instructions saved with a name in order to use them over and over.
- When the formatting instructions contained within a style are changed, all the text to which the style has been applied is automatically updated.
- Styles are created for a particular document and are saved with the document.
- In addition to the Normal style that is applied to text by default, other predesigned styles are available in a document based on the Normal template document. Other template documents also contain predesigned styles.
- Styles can be changed and/or applied to text in three ways:
  1. Use Word's AutoFormat feature.
  2. Select a new template at the Style Gallery dialog box.
  3. Make changes to styles available in the template upon which your document is based.
- If you use the AutoFormat option from the Format drop-down menu to automatically format the document, you can review and then accept or reject changes.
- At the Style Gallery dialog box you can see the effects of styles on the open document in the Preview section.
- To display the entire list of styles provided by Word, choose List at the Style dialog box, then choose *All Styles* in the drop-down list.
- In addition to applying predesigned styles with the Style button on the Formatting toolbar and the Style dialog box, you can use shortcut commands.
- A new style can be created in two ways: apply the desired formatting instructions to a paragraph, then save those instructions in a style; or specify the formatting instructions for a style without applying them to text.
- A character style is applied to the word where the insertion point is located or to selected text. A paragraph style is applied to the paragraph where the insertion point is located or to selected paragraphs.
- A style can be applied using the Style button on the Formatting toolbar or the Style dialog box.
- A style can be quickly applied in a document if a shortcut key has been assigned to the style. Assign a shortcut key at the Style dialog box.
- You can redefine a style by changing the formatting instructions that it contains either with the Formatting toolbar or the Style dialog box.
- You can delete a style from a document or rename a style at the Style dialog box.
- You can remove a style from text by applying a new style, since only one style can be applied at a time to the same text.

## COMMANDS REVIEW

|  | Mouse | Keyboard |
|---|---|---|
| Display predesigned Normal template document styles | Click on down-pointing arrow to right of Style button on Formatting toolbar | |
| Format a document with AutoFormat | Click on AutoFormat button on Standard toolbar; or choose Format, AutoFormat, choose OK or press Enter | CTRL + K |
| Undo AutoFormat changes | Immediately click on the Undo button on Standard toolbar; or choose Edit, Undo AutoFormat | CTRL + Z |
| Display Style Gallery dialog box | Click on Format, then Style Gallery | Choose Format, then Style Gallery |
| Display Style dialog box | Click on Format, then Style | Choose Format, then Style |

Shortcut commands for applying some styles:

| | |
|---|---|
| Normal | CTRL + SHIFT + N |
| Heading 1 | CTRL + ALT + 1 |
| Heading 2 | CTRL + ALT + 2 |
| Heading 3 | CTRL + ALT + 3 |
| List Bullet | CTRL + SHIFT + L |

## CHECK YOUR UNDERSTANDING

**True/False:** Circle the letter T if the statement is true; circle the letter F if the statement is false.

T F 1. Using styles helps maintain consistent formatting within similar business documents.

T F 2. One advantage of using styles is that when formatting within a style is changed, the text to which it has been applied changes also.

T F 3. The default style uses right alignment, single spacing, and turns on Widow/Orphan control.

T F 4. The most time-consuming way to apply styles to text is with Word's AutoFormat feature.

T F 5. One of the corrections that AutoFormat makes when it applies styles to a document is to replace with a bullet any characters used to list items.

T F 6. When a style is applied to a document using AutoFormat, all aspects of the style must be accepted.

T F 7. You can create a new style by applying desired formatting to a paragraph, then saving those instructions in a style.

T F 8. A paragraph style can be applied to a paragraph or to selected paragraphs.

T F 9. When assigning a shortcut key to a style, any combination of letters or numbers combined with the Ctrl, Alt, and Shift keys will work.

T F 10. Once a style has been created, the only way to change the style is to rename it and create it again.

**Completion:** In the space provided at the right, indicate the correct term, command, or number.

1. This is a set of formatting instructions saved with a name in order to use them repeatedly. _____

2. By default, a Word document is based on this template document. _____

3. The predesigned styles based on the default template document are displayed by clicking here on the Formatting toolbar. _____

4. Use this shortcut command to format a document. _____

5. When a document to which formatting has been applied is displayed for review, a strikethrough character means this. _____

6. Use this dialog box to apply styles from other templates besides the default template. _____

7. Choose this at the Style dialog box to display all the available styles. _____

8. This is the shortcut command to apply the List Bullet style. _____

9. Create a new style at this dialog box. _____

10. Delete several styles at once at this dialog box. _____

## AT THE COMPUTER

### Exercise 1

1. Open report06.
2. Save the document with Save As and name it c24ex01.
3. Automatically format the document by clicking on the AutoFormat button on the Standard toolbar (the tenth button from the right).
4. Save the document again with the same name (c24ex01).
5. Print c24ex01.
6. Close c24ex01.

### Exercise 2

1. Open report01.
2. Save the document with Save As and name it c24ex02.
3. Format the document with the AutoFormat feature and reject some formatting by completing the following steps:
   a. Choose Format, AutoFormat.
   b. At the AutoFormat dialog box containing the message *Word will automatically format C24EX02.DOC*, choose OK or press Enter.
   c. After Word automatically applies the styles, the AutoFormat dialog box displays with the message *Formatting completed. You can now: • Accept or reject all changes. • Review and reject individual changes. • Choose a custom look with Style Gallery.* At this message, choose Review Changes.
   d. At the Review AutoFormat Changes dialog box, choose Find three times. (This selects the spaces before the first paragraph of text.)
   e. With the spaces before the first paragraph of text selected, choose Reject. (This leaves the spaces before the paragraph rather than omitting the spaces.)
   f. Continue choosing Find until the spaces before the next paragraph of text are selected, then choose Reject. Continue in this manner accepting all formatting changes except the omitting of the spaces before paragraphs of text.
   g. When all formatting has been reviewed, Word inserts a dialog box with the message *Microsoft Word reached the end of the document. Do you want to continue searching from the beginning of the document?*. At this message, choose OK or press Enter.
   h. At the Review AutoFormat Changes dialog box, choose Close.
   i. At the AutoFormat dialog box, choose Accept.

4. Save the document again with the same name (c24ex02).
5. Print c24ex02.
6. Close c24ex02.

## Exercise 3

1. Open memo01.
2. Save the document with Save As and name it c24ex03.
3. Format the memo at the Style Gallery by completing the following steps:
   a. Choose Format, Style Gallery.
   b. At the Style Gallery dialog box, select *Memo2* in the Template list box.
   c. Choose OK or press Enter.
   d. At the memo, you may need to properly align the text after the *DATE:, TO:,* and *FROM:* headings (if necessary) by inserting a Tab between the heading and the text.
4. Save the document again with the same name (c24ex03).
5. Print c24ex03.
6. Close c24ex03.

## Exercise 4

1. Open cntrct02.
2. Save the document with Save As and name it c24ex04.
3. Format the contract at the Style Gallery by completing the following steps:
   a. Choose Format, Style Gallery.
   b. At the Style Gallery dialog box, select *Report1* in the Template list box.
   c. Choose OK or press Enter.
4. Save the document again with the same name (c24ex04).
5. Print c24ex04.
6. Close c24ex04.

## Exercise 5

1. Open report01.
2. Save the document with Save As and name it c24ex05.
3. Make the following changes to the report:
   a. Select the entire document, then make the following changes:
      (1) Press Ctrl + 1 to change the line spacing to single.
      (2) Change the font to 12-point Times New Roman.
   b. Position the insertion point at the beginning of the heading *Type Measurement,* then press the Enter key once.
   c. Position the insertion point at the beginning of the heading *Type Size,* then press the Enter key once.
   d. Position the insertion point at the beginning of the heading *Type Style,* then press the Enter key once.
   e. Select the last four paragraphs of text in the report, then add bullets by clicking on the Bullets button on the Formatting toolbar.
4. Format the title and headings in the report, using styles by completing the following steps:
   a. Position the insertion point anywhere within the title, *TYPE SPECIFICATION,* then apply the *Title* style by completing the following steps:
      (1) Choose Format, Style.
      (2) At the Style dialog box, choose List, then choose *All Styles.* To do this with the mouse, click on the down-pointing arrow to the right of the List box, then click on *All Styles.* If you are using the keyboard, press Alt + L, then press the down arrow key until *All Styles* is selected.

      (3)  Select *Title* in the <u>S</u>tyles list box. To do this with the mouse, click on the down-pointing arrow at the bottom of the <u>S</u>tyles list box scroll bar until *Title* is visible, then click on *Title*. If you are using the keyboard, press the down arrow key until *Title* is selected.

      (4)  Choose <u>A</u>pply. (If you are using the mouse, you can just double-click on *Title*.)

  b.  Position the insertion point anywhere within the heading *Type Measurement*, then apply the *Subtitle* style by completing steps similar to those in 4a(1) through 4a(4).

  c.  Position the insertion point anywhere within the heading *Type Size*, then apply the *Subtitle* style by completing steps similar to those in 4a(1) through 4a(4).

  d.  Position the insertion point anywhere within the heading *Type Style*, then apply the *Subtitle* style by completing steps similar to those in 4a(1) through 4a(4).

5.  Save the document again with the same name (c24ex05).

6.  Print c24ex05.

7.  Close c24ex05.

## Exercise 6

1.  Open jobdes01.

2.  Save the document with Save As and name it c24ex06.

3.  Make the following changes to the document:

  a.  Delete the blank line between *JOB DESCRIPTION* and *REGISTERED NURSE*.

  b.  Delete the blank line between *REGISTERED NURSE* and the text below it.

  c.  Position the insertion point anywhere in the title *JOB DESCRIPTION*, then apply the *Heading 1* style by pressing Ctrl + Alt + 1.

  d.  Position the insertion point anywhere in the subtitle *REGISTERED NURSE*, then apply the *Heading 2* style by pressing Ctrl + Alt + 2.

  e.  Select the text in the document (except the title and subtitle), then apply the *List Bullet* style by pressing Ctrl + Shift + L and change to double spacing by pressing Ctrl + 2.

4.  Save the document again with the same name (c24ex06).

5.  Print c24ex06.

6.  Close c24ex06.

## Exercise 7

1.  Open style01.

2.  Save the document with Save As and name it sty01.

3.  Create a style by example named *Title 1* by completing the following steps:

  a.  Position the insertion point anywhere in the title, *TITLE OF DOCUMENT*.

  b.  Click on the down-pointing arrow to the right of the Style button on the Formatting toolbar.

  c.  Make sure the *Normal* style is selected in the drop-down menu. If not, select the *Normal* style.

  d.  Key **Title 1**, then press Enter.

4.  Create a style by example named *Subtitle 1* using the *Subtitle of Document* text by completing steps similar to those in 3a through 3d.

5.  Create a style by example named *Listing 1* by completing the following steps:

  a.  Position the insertion point anywhere within the paragraph of text preceded by the bullet.

  b.  Click on the down-pointing arrow to the right of the Style button on the Formatting toolbar.

  c.  Make sure the *Normal* style is selected in the drop-down menu. If not, select the *Normal* style.

  d.  Key **Listing 1**, then press Enter.

6. Select all the text in the document, then delete it. (This removes the text but keeps the styles you created.)
7. Save the document again with the same name (sty01).
8. Close sty01.

## Exercise 8

1. Open sty01.
2. Create a style using the Style dialog box named *Indent 1* that indents text 0.5 inches and changes the font to 12-point Times New Roman by completing the following steps:
   a. Choose Format, Style.
   b. At the Style dialog box, choose New.
   c. At the New Style dialog box, key **Indent 1** in the Name text box.
   d. Choose Format, then Paragraph.
   e. At the Paragraph dialog box, click on the up-pointing triangle to the right of the Left text box until *0.5"* displays in the text box.
   f. Choose OK or press Enter to close the Paragraph dialog box.
   g. Choose Format, Font.
   h. At the Font dialog box, choose *Times New Roman* in the Font list box, *Regular* in the Font Style list box, and *12* in the Size list box.
   i. Choose OK or press Enter to close the Font dialog box.
   j. Choose OK or press Enter to close the New Style dialog box.
   k. Choose Close to close the Style dialog box.
3. Create a style using the Style dialog box named *Font 1* that changes the font to Times New Roman by completing the following steps:
   a. Choose Format, Style.
   b. At the Style dialog box, choose New.
   c. At the New Style dialog box, key **Font 1** in the Name text box.
   d. Choose Style Type, then choose *Character* from the drop-down list.
   e. Choose Format, then Font.
   f. At the Font dialog box, choose *Times New Roman* in the Font list box, *Regular* in the Font Style list box, and *12* in the Size list box.
   g. Choose OK or press Enter to close the Font dialog box.
   h. Choose OK or press Enter to close the New Style dialog box.
   i. Choose Close to close the Style dialog box.
4. Save the document again with the same name (sty01).
5. Close sty01.

## Exercise 9

1. Open sty01.
2. Save the document with Save As and name it c24ex09.
3. Insert the document named survey01 into the c24ex09 document. (Hint: Use the File option from the Insert drop-down menu to do this.)
4. Apply the *Title 1* style to the title, *TEACHER DEVELOPMENT TOPICS,* by completing the following steps:
   a. Position the insertion point anywhere in the title, *TEACHER DEVELOPMENT TOPICS.*
   b. Click on the down-pointing arrow to the right of the Style button.
   c. Click on *Title 1* in the drop-down menu.
5. Apply the *Subtitle 1* style to the subtitle, *Activities within your Classroom,* by completing steps similar to those in 4a through 4c.
6. Apply the *Font 1* style to text in the document (except the title and subtitle) by completing the following steps:
   a. Select the text in the document (except the title and subtitle).

   b. Click on the down-pointing arrow to the right of the Style button.

   c. Click on *Font 1* in the drop-down menu.

7. Select the lettered paragraphs (a. through d.) below paragraph 1., then apply the *Indent 1* style using the Style dialog box by completing the following steps:

   a. Choose F̲ormat, S̲tyle.

   b. At the Style dialog box, select *Indent 1* in the S̲tyles list box.

   c. Choose A̲pply.

8. Complete steps similar to those in 7a through 7c to apply the *Indent 1* style to the lettered paragraphs below each of the remaining numbered paragraphs.

9. Hang indent the numbered paragraphs. To do this, position the insertion point anywhere within paragraph 1., then press Ctrl + T. Complete similar steps for each of the other numbered paragraphs.

10. Save the document again with the same name (c24ex09).

11. Print c24ex09.

12. Close c24ex09.

## Exercise 10

1. Open sty01.

2. Save the document with Save As and name it sty02.

3. Create the shortcut key combination Alt + 1 for the *Font 1* style by completing the following steps:

   a. Choose F̲ormat, S̲tyle.

   b. At the Style dialog box, select *Font 1* in the S̲tyles list box.

   c. Choose M̲odify.

   d. At the Modify Style dialog box, choose Shortcut K̲ey.

   e. At the Customize dialog box with the K̲eyboard tab selected, press Alt + 1.

   f. Choose A̲ssign.

   g. Choose Close to close the Customize dialog box.

   h. Choose OK to close the Modify Style dialog box.

   i. Choose Close to close the Style dialog box.

4. Create the shortcut key combination Alt + 2 for the *Indent 1* style by completing steps similar to those in 3a through 3i.

5. Create the shortcut key combination Alt + 3 for the *Listing 1* style by completing steps similar to those in 3a through 3i.

6. Create the shortcut key combination Alt + 4 for the *Subtitle 1* style by completing steps similar to those in 3a through 3i.

7. Create the shortcut key combination Alt + 5 for the *Title 1* style by completing steps similar to those in 3a through 3i.

8. Save the document again with the same name (sty02).

9. Close sty02.

## Exercise 11

1. Open sty02.

2. Save the document with Save As and name it c24ex11.

3. Insert the document named report01 into the c24ex11 document.

4. Select the entire document, then change the font to 12-point Times New Roman.

5. Apply the *Title 1* style to the title by completing the following steps:

   a. Position the insertion point anywhere within the title, *TYPE SPECIFICATION*.

   b. Press Alt + 5.

6. Apply the *Subtitle 1* style to the heading *Type Measurement* by positioning the insertion point in *Type Measurement,* then pressing Alt + 4.

7. Apply the *Subtitle 1* style to the heading *Type Size.*

8. Apply the *Subtitle 1* style to the heading *Type Style*.
9. Select the last four paragraphs of text in the document, then apply the *Listing 1* style with the shortcut key combination Alt + 3 and change to double spacing by pressing Ctrl + 2.
10. Save the document again with the same name (c24ex11).
11. Print c24ex11.
12. Close c24ex11.

## Exercise 12

1. Open sty02.
2. Save the document with Save As and name it sty03.
3. Remove the shortcut key combination Alt + 2 by completing the following steps:
   a. Choose Format, Style.
   b. At the Style dialog box, select *Indent 1* in the Styles list box.
   c. Choose Modify.
   d. At the Modify Style dialog box, choose Shortcut Key.
   e. At the Customize dialog box with the Keyboard tab selected, select *Alt + 2* in the Current Keys list box.
   f. Choose Remove.
   g. Choose Close to close the Customize dialog box.
   h. At the Modify Style dialog box, choose OK.
   i. At the Style dialog box, choose Close.
4. Save the document again with the same name (sty03).
5. Close sty03.

## Exercise 13

1. Open c24ex11.
2. Save the document with Save As and name it c24ex13.
3. Redefine the *Title 1* style by completing the following steps:
   a. Select the title, *TYPE SPECIFICATION*.
   b. Change the font to 18-point Arial Bold.
   c. Display the Paragraph dialog box, then change the spacing after the paragraph to 6 points.
   d. With the text still selected, click on the down-pointing arrow to the right of the Style button on the Formatting toolbar..
   e. At the drop-down list of styles, click on *Title 1*.
   f. At the Reapply Style dialog box, choose OK or press Enter.
4. Redefine the *Subtitle 1* style by completing the following steps:
   a. Choose Format, Style.
   b. At the Style dialog box, select *Subtitle 1* in the Styles list box.
   c. Choose Modify.
   d. At the Modify Style dialog box, change the font to 14-point Arial Bold by completing the following steps:
      (1) Choose Format.
      (2) At the drop-down list that displays, choose Font.
      (3) At the Font dialog box, choose *Arial* in the Font list box, *Bold* in the Font Style list box, and *14* in the Size list box.
      (4) Choose OK or press Enter to close the Font dialog box.
   e. At the Modify Style dialog box, change the spacing after the paragraph to 6 points by completing the following steps:
      (1) Choose Format, then Paragraph.
      (2) At the Paragraph dialog box, click once on the up-pointing triangle to the right of the After text box. (This inserts *6 pt* in the text box.)
      (3) Choose OK or press Enter.

    f.  At the Modify Style dialog box, choose OK or press Enter.

    g.  Choose Close to close the Style dialog box.

5.  Save the document again with the same name (c24ex13).

6.  Print c24ex13. (The title should print in 18-point Arial Bold and the three headings should print in 14-point Arial Bold.)

7.  Close c24ex13.

## Exercise 14

1.  Open c24ex11.

2.  Save the document with Save As and name it c24ex14.

3.  Remove the *Title 1* style from the title of the report by completing the following steps:

    a.  Select the title, *TYPE SPECIFICATION*.

    b.  Click on the down-pointing arrow to the right of the Style button.

    c.  Click on Normal at the drop-down list.

4.  With the title still selected, change the font to 18-point Arial Bold, add 12 points of spacing after the paragraph, and then click on the Center button on the Formatting toolbar to center the title.

5.  Redefine the *Subtitle 1* style by completing the following steps:

    a.  Choose Format, Style.

    b.  At the Style dialog box, select *Subtitle 1* in the Styles list box.

    c.  Choose Modify.

    d.  At the Modify Style dialog box, choose Format, then Paragraph.

    e.  At the Paragraph dialog box, change the spacing After to 6 points.

    f.  Choose OK or press Enter to close the Paragraph dialog box.

    g.  At the Modify Style dialog box, choose Format, Font.

    h.  At the Font dialog box, choose *Arial* in the Font list box, *Bold* in the Font Style list box, and *14* in the Size list box.

    i.  Choose OK or press Enter to close the Font dialog box.

    j.  Choose OK or press Enter to close the Modify Style dialog box.

    k.  Choose Close to close the Style dialog box.

6.  Save the document again with the same name (c24ex14).

7.  Print c24ex14.

8.  Close c24ex14.

## Exercise 15

1.  Open sty01.

2.  Save the document with Save As and name it sty04.

3.  Redefine the *Title 1* style by completing the following steps:

    a.  Choose Format, Style.

    b.  At the Style dialog box, select *Title 1* in the Styles list box.

    c.  Choose Modify.

    d.  At the Modify Style dialog box, change the font to 18-point Arial Bold by completing the following steps:

        (1)  Choose Format, then Font.

        (2)  At the Font dialog box, choose *Arial* in the Font list box, *Bold* in the Font Style list box, and *18* in the Size list box.

        (3)  Choose OK or press Enter to close the Font dialog box.

    e.  Choose Format, then Paragraph.

    f.  At the Paragraph dialog box, change the spacing after the paragraph to 12 points.

    g.  Choose OK or press Enter to close the Paragraph dialog box.

    h.  At the Modify Style dialog box, choose OK or press Enter.

    i.  Choose Close to close the Style dialog box.

4. Redefine the *Subtitle 1* style so the font is 14-point Arial Bold and the space after the paragraph is 12 points by completing steps similar to those in 3a through 3i.
5. Redefine the *Font 1* style by completing the following steps:
   a. Key **This is sample text**.
   b. Select *This is sample text*.
   c. Apply the *Font 1* style to the text. (To do this, click on the down-pointing arrow to the right of the Style button on the Formatting toolbar, then click on *Font 1*.)
   d. With the text still selected, change the font to 12-point Century Gothic.
   e. Click on the down-pointing arrow to the right of the Style button.
   f. At the drop-down list of styles, click on *Font 1*.
   g. At the Reapply Style dialog box, choose OK or press Enter.
   h. Deselect the text.
6. Rename the *Font 1* style to *Century G* and add the alias *CG* by completing the following steps:
   a. Choose Format, Style.
   b. At the Style dialog box, select *Font 1* in the Styles list box.
   c. Choose Modify.
   d. At the Modify Style dialog box, key **Century G,CG**.
   e. Choose OK or press Enter.
   f. Choose Close to close the Style dialog box.
7. Select the text in the document, then press the Delete key.
8. Save the document again with the same name (sty04).
9. Close sty04.

## Exercise 16

1. Open sty04.
2. Insert the document named *report02* into the sty04 document.
3. Save the document with Save As and name it c24ex16.
4. Delete a portion of the text in the document by completing the following steps:
   a. Select the text from the third paragraph below the *Page Numbers (Folios)* section (the paragraph that begins *Page-assembly programs...*) to the end of the document.
   b. Press the Delete key.
5. Delete the *Indent 1* style by completing the following steps:
   a. Choose Format, Style.
   b. At the Style dialog box, select *Indent 1* in the Styles list box.
   c. Choose Delete.
   d. At the message asking if you want to delete the style, choose Yes.
   e. Choose Close to close the Style dialog box.
6. Delete the *Listing 1* style.
7. Apply the *Century G, CG* style to the document by completing the following steps:
   a. Select the entire document.
   b. Press Ctrl + Shift + S. (This makes the Style button on the Formatting toolbar active.)
   c. Key **CG**, then press Enter.
8. Apply the *Title 1* style to the title, *STRUCTURED PUBLICATIONS*.
9. Apply the *Subtitle 1* style to the following headings: *TEMPLATE ELEMENTS, Column Grid, STANDING ELEMENTS, Running Heads/Feet*, and *Page Numbers (Folios)*.
10. Save the document again with the same name (c24ex16).
11. Print c24ex16.
12. Close c24ex16.

## Assessment 1

1. Open report03.
2. Save the document with Save As and name it c24sa01.
3. Automatically format the document with the AutoFormat button on the Standard toolbar.
4. Save the document again with the same name (c24sa01).
5. Print c24sa01.
6. Close c24sa01.

## Assessment 2

1. Open notice01.
2. Save the document with Save As and name it c24sa02.
3. Format the document at the Style Gallery with the *Presrel2* template.
4. Save the document again with the same name (c24sa02).
5. Print c24sa02.
6. Close c24sa02.

## Assessment 3

1. Open sty03.
2. Save the document with Save As and name it c24sa03.
3. Key the following text in the document:
   a. Key **PETERSBURG SCHOOL DISTRICT**, then press Enter.
   b. Key **April Newsletter**, then press Enter.
   c. Key **Jon Struebing, Editor**, then press Enter three times.
4. Insert the document named *news01* into the c24sa03 document.
5. Select the entire document, then change the font to 12-point Times New Roman.
6. Apply the *Title 1* style to the following text:
   > PETERSBURG SCHOOL DISTRICT
   > April Newsletter
   > Jon Struebing, Editor
7. Apply the *Subtitle 1* style to the following text:
   > Recreation Program
   > Sixth-Grade Camp
   > Library News
8. Position the insertion point anywhere in the title, *PETERSBURG SCHOOL DISTRICT*, then insert a 2 1/4-point double-line border below the paragraph.
9. Save the document again with the same name (c24sa03).
10. Print c24sa03.
11. Close c24sa03.

# Assessment 4

1. Open c24sa03.
2. Save the document with Save As and name it c24sa04.
3. Make the following changes to the document:
   a. Redefine the *Title 1* style so the font is 16-point Arial Bold and the paragraph alignment is Right.
   b. Redefine the *Subtitle 1* style so the font is 14-point Arial Bold and the space after the paragraph is 6 points.
   c. Change to the Page Layout viewing mode, then insert the picture *spring.wmf* at the beginning of the document with the following specifications:
      (1) Format the picture so the width is 1.2 inches wide and the height is 1.4 inches.
      (2) Frame the picture.
4. After inserting, formatting, and framing the picture, center the text to the right of the picture a little better by positioning the insertion point at the beginning of the title, *PETERSBURG SCHOOL DISTRICT,* then pressing the Enter key once.
5. Move the insertion point to the end of the document, then delete any blank lines. (The document should fit on one page.)
6. Save the document with Save As and name it c24sa04.
7. Print c24sa04.
8. Close c24sa04.

# UNIT 5

## PERFORMANCE ASSESSMENT

In this unit you have learned to enhance the visual display and readability of documents by formatting text into tables, charts, and columns and to maintain formatting consistency in documents using styles.

## Assessment 1

1. At a clear document screen, create the table shown in figure U5.1.
2. Save the document and name it u05pa01.
3. Print u05pa01.
4. Close u05pa01.

*Figure U5.1*

**ST. FRANCIS MEDICAL CLINIC**

| Name | Company | Address |
|------|---------|---------|
| | | |
| | | |
| | | |
| | | |
| | | |
| | | |
| | | |
| | | |
| | | |
| | | |
| | | |
| | | |
| | | |

Community Health Advisory Committee

## Assessment 2

1. At a clear document screen, create the table shown in figure U5.2. (The width of the first column is 2.6 inches and the widths of the second and third columns are 1.7 inches.)
2. After creating the table, insert the formula =*SUM(ABOVE)* to calculate the amounts in the *First Quarter* column and the *Second Quarter* column.
3. Save the document and name it u05pa02.
4. Print u05pa02.
5. Close u05pa02.

**Figure U5.2**

| LIFETIME ANNUITY ASSOCIATION | | |
|---|---|---|
| **BALANCE SHEET** | | |
| Asset | First Quarter | Second Quarter |
| Bonds | $41,320,356.03 | $42,340,659.00 |
| Stocks | 3,453,964.15 | 4,093,288.05 |
| Mortgages | 30,453,881.68 | 33,430,794.40 |
| Real Estate | 9,440,201.50 | 10,559,300.68 |
| Long-Term Investments | 955,220.00 | 998,452.05 |
| Short-Term Investments | 1,009,349.55 | 1,110,452.30 |
| Other Assets | 445,305.05 | 508,455.25 |
| Total Liabilities | | |

## Assessment 3

1. Open table07.
2. Save the document with Save As and name it u05pa03.
3. Create a chart for the table with the following elements:
   a. At the Microsoft Graph window, change to a Bar chart (you determine the chart type at the Chart Gallery).
   b. Make sure the legend is in a desirable location.
   c. Insert a border around the title.
   d. Exit Microsoft Graph saving the changes.
   e. Change to the Page Layout viewing mode.
   f. Change the Zoom to Whole Page.
   g. Select the chart, then insert a frame.
   h. Drag the chart to the middle of the page.
   i. Change the width of the chart to 5 inches and the height to 3.3 inches.
   j. Select the table (and the line below the table), then delete the table.
   k. If necessary, reposition the chart.
   l. Change the Zoom to 100%.
4. Save the document again with the same name (u05pa03).
5. Print u05pa03.
6. Close u05pa03.

# Assessment 4

1. Open table08.
2. Save the document with Save As and name it u05pa04.
3. Create a Pie chart for the table with the following elements:
   a. At the Microsoft Graph window, change the DataSeries to Series in Columns.
   b. Change to a Pie chart (you determine the chart type at the Chart Gallery).
   c. Move the legend to a more desirable location (you determine the location).
   d. Add data labels for the percents.
   e. Exit Microsoft Graph saving the changes.
   f. Change to the Page Layout viewing mode.
   g. Change the Zoom to Whole Page.
   h. Select the chart, then insert a frame.
   i. Drag the chart to the middle of the page.
   j. Change the width of the chart to 5 inches and the height to 3.3 inches.
   k. Select the table (and the line below the table), then delete the table.
   l. If necessary, reposition the chart.
   m. Change the Zoom to 100%.
4. Save the document again with the same name (u05pa04).
5. Print u05pa04.
6. Close u05pa04.

# Assessment 5

1. Open report04.
2. Save the document with Save As and name it u05pa05.
3. Make the following changes to the report:
   a. Select the text from *CHAPTER 2: OFFSET PRINTING* to the end of the document, then delete it.
   b. Select the entire document, then make the following changes:
      (1) Change the font to 11-point Times New Roman.
      (2) Set a left tab at 0.25 inches.
   c. Format the text, except the title, into two evenly spaced columns with the spacing between changed to 0.4 inches and a line inserted between the columns.
   d. Insert a continuous section break at the end of the document to balance the columns on the second page.
4. Save the document again with the same name (u05pa05).
5. Print u05pa05.
6. Close u05pa05.

# Assessment 6

1. Open sty03.
2. Insert the document named *report06* into the *sty03* document.
3. Save the document with Save As and name it u05pa06.
4. Make the following changes to the document:
   a. With the insertion point positioned at the beginning of the document, press the Enter key three times.
   b. Select the entire document, then change the font to 12-point Times New Roman and set a left tab at 0.25 inches.
   c. Change to the Page Layout viewing mode, then insert the picture named *books.wmf* at the beginning of the document.
   d. Frame the picture.
   e. Apply the *Title 1* style to the title, *CHOOSING BINDING*.

f. Apply the *Subtitle 1* style to the following headings:
*Saddle and Side Stitching*
*Mechanical Binding*
*Book Binding*

g. Insert a 2 1/4-point double-line border below the title, *CHOOSING BINDING*.

5. Save the document again with the same name (u05pa06).
6. Print u05pa06.
7. Close u05pa06.

## Assessment 7

1. Delete the following:
   a. Delete all documents created in chapters 16 through 20.
   b. Delete all documents created for unit 4 Performance Assessment.

## COMPOSING ACTIVITIES

The following activities give you the opportunity to practice your writing skills along with demonstrating an understanding of some of the important Word features you have mastered in this unit. In planning the documents, remember to shape the information according to the writing purpose and the audience. Use correct grammar, appropriate word choices, and clear sentence constructions.

### Activity 1

**Situation:** Check the career center at your school, the Employment Security Department in your city, or the local newspaper for a job announcement that interests you. Using the job announcement and the resume you created for exercise 9 in chapter 23 as an example, design a resume for yourself. Save the resume and name it u05act01. Print, then close u05act01.

### Activity 2

**Situation:** You are Mandy Wheeler, administrative assistant in the Finance Department at St. Francis Medical Center. Your supervisor, Deborah Rutledge, has asked you to prepare a table showing equipment expenditures for each department as shown below:

ST. FRANCIS MEDICAL CENTER

Equipment Expenditures

| Department | Amount |
|---|---|
| Intensive Care Unit | 120,459.34 |
| Emergency Room | 205,490.80 |
| Labor and Delivery | 100,439.50 |
| Coronary Care Unit | 550,340.00 |
| Surgical Unit | 830,492.80 |
| Medical Services | 98,400.00 |
| Pediatrics | 78,390.50 |
| **Total Amount** | (Calculate total) |

Create a table with the data and insert a formula to calculate the total. Save this document and name it u05act02. Print, then close u05act02.

# Activity 3

**Situation:** You work for Lifetime Annuity Association and your supervisor has asked you to create a document that shows customers' average household expenditures. Include the following information:

Average Household Expenditures

The pie chart shows how a typical two paycheck household with an average after-tax income of $42,000 spends its annual income. How does your family's spending compare?

Include this information in the pie chart:

| Expenditure | Percent of Income |
|---|---|
| Housing | 29% |
| Transportation | 17% |
| Food | 15% |
| Insurance | 12% |
| Clothing | 8% |
| Health Care | 4% |
| Other | 15% |

Besides the day-to-day living expenses shown in the chart, added unforeseen expenses may also arise. These could include outstanding medical bills, unpaid debts, and additional child care. How long will the proceeds from your current life insurance last once your family pays for these expenses and then begins to pay for the necessities of life?

When determining your family's life insurance needs, you will want to consider if your coverage will be adequate 5, 10, or even 15 years from now. Your family's financial needs may change over the years and inflation will gradually erode the value of your policy.

When creating the document, consider what typeface you will use, where you will place elements on the page, and how you will create the pie chart. Include a title for this document. Save the document and name it u05act03. Print, then close u05act03.

*Note: For this research activity you will need access to the Microsoft Word for Windows User's Guide.*

Answer the following questions about information in the Microsoft Word for Windows User's Guide.

1. In what chapter do you find information on tables? _____

2. What steps would you follow to get on-line instructions on tables?

   _____

   _____

3. On what pages do you find information on changing column widths? _____

4. What steps would you follow to apply a border to the contents of a cell without placing a border around the cell itself? (Hint: See the Troubleshooting section.)

   _____

   _____

5. What steps would you follow to insert text before a table at the beginning of the document?

   _____

   _____

   _____

6. What pages in the user's guide cover charts (graphs)? _____

7. What steps would you follow to get on-line information about creating and editing charts? (Hint: This information is in the Graph section in the chapter.)

   _____

8. Word automatically applies styles to certain features in a document such as headers and footers. On what page in the user's guide are these styles listed? _____

9. How would you quickly apply the same style to several items in a document? (Hint: This information is in the section on Tips for Applying Styles.)

   _____

   _____

10. On what page is the hierarchy of Word styles displayed?

    _____

# Advanced Document Formatting

## UNIT

# 6

*In this unit you will learn to create personalized documents with standard documents; utilize database features for maintaining records; create business forms; and finish multiple-page reports with reference attributes such as indexes and tables of contents, figures, and authorities.*

# Merging Documents 25

Upon successful completion of chapter 25, you will be able to format and merge separate files to create a series of similar business documents, such as personalized form letters, envelopes, and labels.

Word includes a mail merge feature that you can use to create letters, envelopes, labels, and much more, all with personalized information.

Generally, there are two documents that need to be created for merging. One document, which Word calls the *data source*, contains the variable information. The second document contains the standard text along with identifiers showing where variable information (information that changes) is to be inserted. Word refers to this as the *main document*. After these documents are created, they are merged to produce personalized documents such as letters, envelopes, or labels.

A data source is a document that contains variable information about customers, clients, companies, etc. This may include such information as names, addresses, telephone numbers, and products. The variable information included is determined by the person creating the data source. When creating a data source, consider present and future needs.

Text in a data source is inserted in cells in a table. This can be done as you learned in chapter 21 or you can use Word's Mail Merge Helper to help you create the data source.

## Creating a Data Source with Mail Merge Helper

Generally, a merge takes the *data source* and the *main document*. These documents can be created in any order, but you might find it easiest to create the data source first and then the main document.

Before creating a data source, determine what type of correspondence you will be creating and the type of information you will need to insert in the correspondence.

Word provides predetermined field names that can be used when creating the data source. Use these field names if they represent the data you are creating.

Variable information in a data source is saved as a *record*. A record contains all the information for one unit (for example, a person, family, customer, client, or business). A series of fields make one record, and a series of records make a data source.

Word's Mail Merge Helper feature can be used to create a data source. For example, suppose you want to create a data source for customers of your company shown following and name the

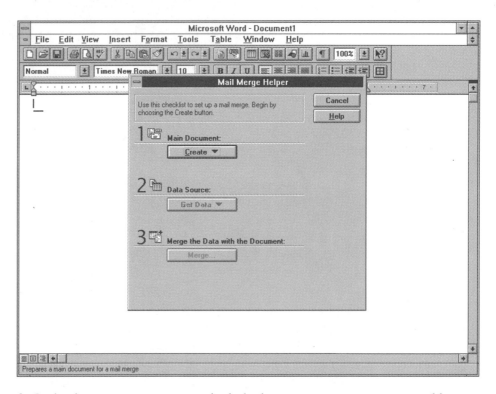

**Figure 25.1**
*Mail Merge Helper
Dialog Box*

data source *custds*. In the data source you want to include the names, company names, addresses, and telephone numbers of your customers.

| Mrs. Sara Kerrick | Mr. Gerald Jorgenson | Ms. Linda White |
|---|---|---|
| Manager | Director | Assistant Manager |
| Rayman Corporation | Baxter Manufacturing | Broadway Builders |
| 209 Tapps Drive | 1203 North 24th Street | 8700 Broadway Avenue |
| Suite 330 | Phoenix, AZ 86342 | Phoenix, AZ 86745 |
| Phoenix, AZ 86744 | (602) 555-9800 | (602) 555-3344 |
| (602) 555-3409 | | |

To create a data source with this information shown above using Mail Merge Helper, you would complete the following steps:

1.  At a clear document screen, choose Tools, Mail Merge.
2.  At the Mail Merge Helper dialog box shown in figure 25.1, choose Create, then from the drop-down list that displays, choose Form Letters.
3.  At the dialog box asking if you want to use the active document or a new document window, choose Active Window.
4.  Choose Get Data, then from the drop-down list that displays, choose Create Data Source.
5.  At the Create Data Source dialog box shown in figure 25.2, the fields provided by Word are shown in the Field Names in Header Row. These fields are needed for the data source except *Country* and *Home Phone*. To remove the *Country* field name, click on the down-pointing arrow on the vertical scroll bar for the Field Names in Header Row list box until *Country* is visible. Select *Country* in the Field Names in Header Row list box, then choose Remove Field Name.
6.  Select *Home Phone* in the Field Names in Header Row list box, then choose Remove Field Name.
7.  Choose OK.
8.  At the Save Data Source dialog box, key **custds**, then choose OK or press Enter.
9.  At the dialog box containing the warning that the data source contains no data, choose Edit Data Source. This displays the Data Form dialog box shown in figure 25.3.

10. At the Data Form dialog box, key the title, *Mrs.*, of the first customer shown on the previous page, then press the Enter key or the Tab key. Continue keying the information in each of the fields identified in the dialog box. Press the Enter key or the Tab key to move to the next field. Press Shift + Tab to move to the preceding field.

11. After entering all the information for Mrs. Sara Kerrick, choose <u>A</u>dd New. This saves the information and displays a blank Data Form dialog box. Continue in this manner until all records have been created.

12. After creating the last record for the data source, choose <u>V</u>iew Source.

13. At the data source document, choose <u>F</u>ile, then <u>S</u>ave.

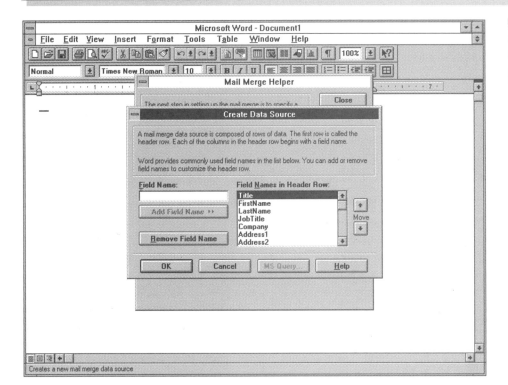

**Figure 25.2**
*Create Data Source Dialog Box*

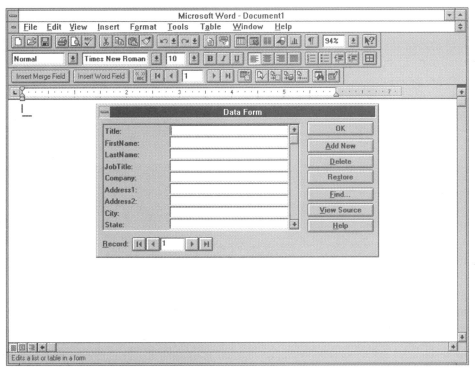

**Figure 25.3**
*Data Form Dialog Box*

Figure 25.4
Example Data
Source Document

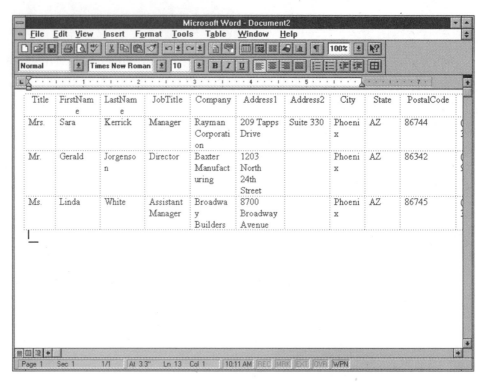

| Title | FirstName | LastName | JobTitle | Company | Address1 | Address2 | City | State | PostalCode |
|---|---|---|---|---|---|---|---|---|---|
| Mrs. | Sara | Kerrick | Manager | Rayman Corporation | 209 Tapps Drive | Suite 330 | Phoenix | AZ | 86744 |
| Mr. | Gerald | Jorgenson | Director | Baxter Manufacturing | 1203 North 24th Street | | Phoenix | AZ | 86342 |
| Ms. | Linda | White | Assistant Manager | Broadway Builders | 8700 Broadway Avenue | | Phoenix | AZ | 86745 |

Figure 25.4 shows an example of how the custds data source document displays when completed. The first row of the table is called the *header row* and identifies the names of the fields. These field names are important in identifying where variable information will be inserted in a main document. Text in the table may wrap as shown in figure 25.4. The text will be inserted properly, however, in the main document.

Some fields in a data source may not contain text. For example, in the second and third records in the custds data source shown in figure 25.4, there is no data for the *Address2* data field.

## Editing a Data Source

A data source document can be edited. For example, you can add additional customers to the data source, correct information for a customer or customers, and delete customers. The simplest method for editing a data source document is to open the data source document in the normal manner. This causes the document to display similar to the data source shown in figure 25.4.

The data source information is inserted in a table. Edit the table using the methods you learned in chapter 21. For example, to edit information for a customer, such as changing the address or correcting misspellings, position the insertion point in the cell containing the information to be changed, then edit the information as required. To add another customer to the data source, insert a row as you learned in chapter 21, then key the information in the appropriate cells in the new row. To insert a row at the end of the table, position the insertion point at the end of the text in the last cell in the last row, then press the Tab key.

To delete a customer from the data source, select then delete the row containing the customer information.

Text in the data source displays in the default font. If you want more text to display on a line rather than wrapping to the next line within the cell, change the format of the text in the data source to a smaller font. For example, to display the text in the data source in 10-point Times New Roman, select the entire table, then change the font. Formatting you apply to the data source is not inserted in the main document.

When all changes have been made to the data source document, save it in the normal manner, then close it. When naming the data source, you may want to add the letters *ds* to the name to identify it as a data source document. For example, you named the data source document shown in figure 25.4 *custds* (for customer data source).

# ■ Creating the Main Document

A main document can be created that includes fields identifying where variable information from the data source is to be inserted. A main document can take on many forms. For example, a main document can be a letter, envelope, or labels.

Before creating the main document, determine what information will remain the same for each document and what information will change (vary). For example, suppose the sales manager of Lifetime Annuity Association wants to introduce a new customer representative to all customers in the Phoenix, Arizona, area. The sales manager determines that a personal letter should be sent to the customers in the custds data source document. Figure 25.5 shows one way this letter can be written and identifies the variable information with parentheses.

```
February 26, 1996



(Name)
(Job Title)
(Company)
(Address)
(City, State Zip)

Dear (Name):

At Lifetime Annuity Association, we are committed to
providing insurance and financial planning services for
employees of our customers.  To provide continuing service
to you, a new customer representative has been hired.  The
new customer representative, Mr. Raymond Miller, began his
employment with Lifetime Annuity Association on February
1.  He comes to our company with over 10 years' experience
in the employee benefits and insurance industry.

Mr. Miller will be in the Phoenix area during the third
week of March.  He would like to schedule a time for a
visit to your company, and will be contacting you by
telephone next week.

Sincerely,



Evelyn Colwell, Manager
Customer Service Department
```

After determining what information you want for the main document, you need to determine what fields from the data source you will need and where they should be inserted in the letter. For example, when you create the main document for the letter shown in figure 25.5, you will use the following fields: *Title, FirstName, LastName, JobTitle, Company, Address1, Address2, City, State*, and *PostalCode*. When the main document is created for the letter shown in figure 25.5, it will look like the letter shown in figure 25.6.

**Figure 25.6**
*Sample Main*
*Document*

February 26, 1996

<<Title>> <<FirstName>> <<LastName>>
<<JobTitle>>
<<Company>>
<<Address1>>
<<Address2>>
<<City>>, <<State>> <<PostalCode>>

Dear <<Title>> <<Last Name>>:

At Lifetime Annuity Association, we are committed to
providing insurance and financial planning services for
employees of our customers.  To provide continuing service
to you, a new customer representative has been hired.  The
new customer representative, Mr. Raymond Miller, began his
employment with Lifetime Annuity Association on February
1.  He comes to our company with over 10 years' experience
in the employee benefits and insurance industry.

Mr. Miller will be in the Phoenix area during the third
week of March.  He would like to schedule a time for a
visit to your company, and will be contacting you by
telephone next week.

Sincerely,


Evelyn Colwell, Manager
Customer Service Department

When creating a main document with the information shown in figure 25.6, you need to identify the data source that will be used for the variable information. In this example the data source document is *custds*. To create the main document shown in figure 25.6, you would complete the following steps:

1. At a clear document screen, choose Tools, Mail Merge.
2. At the Mail Merge Helper dialog box, choose Create (below Main Document).
3. At the drop-down list that displays, choose Form Letters.
4. At the question asking if you want to use the active document window or a new document, choose Active Window.
5. At the Mail Merge Helper dialog box, choose Get Data (below Data Source).
6. At the drop-down list that displays, choose Open Data Source.
7. At the Open Data Source dialog box, select *custds* in the list , then choose OK or press Enter. (You can also double-click on the data source document name.)
8. At the Microsoft Word dialog box telling you that Word found no fields in your main document, choose Edit Main Document.
9. At the clear document screen with the Merge toolbar displayed below the Formatting toolbar, key the letter to the point where the first field is to be inserted, then complete the following steps:
   a. Click on the Insert Merge Field button on the Merge toolbar (first button from the left).

b. From the drop-down menu that displays, click on *Title*.

10. Press the space bar once, then insert the *FirstName* data field by completing steps similar to those in 9a and 9b. Continue in this manner until all data fields have been entered as shown in figure 25.6.

11. After keying the entire main document, save it and name it in the normal manner.

When naming a main document, you may want to add the initials *md* to indicate that it is a main document. For example, you could name the main document in figure 25.6 *custmd* (for customer main document).

Notice that in figure 25.6 there is a space between the fields. Spaces are inserted between fields as if there were text, then, when the variable information is inserted, it is spaced correctly. This is also true for punctuation. Insert punctuation in a main document as you would a normal document. For example, key the comma immediately after the <<City>> field in the address and key the colon (:) immediately after the <<Last Name>> field in the salutation.

The <<Title>> and <<LastName>> fields were used more than once in the main document in figure 25.6. Fields in a main document can be used as often as needed.

#  Merging Files

Once the data source and the main document have been created and saved, they can be merged. Merged documents can be saved in a new document or they can be sent directly to the printer. There are several ways to merge a data source with a main document. A main document and a data source can be merged with buttons on the Merge toolbar or options at the Merge dialog box.

## Merging to a New Document

To merge a main document with a data source to a new document using a button on the Merge toolbar, open the main document, then click on the Merge to New Document button. For example, to merge the *custds* data source with the *custmd* main document to a new document and name the new document *custltrs*, you would complete the following steps:

1. Open custmd.
2. Click on the Merge to New Document button on the Merge toolbar (fifth button from the right).
3. Word merges custmd with custds and creates a personalized letter for each record in the data source. These letters display in the current document screen. Save the document and name it *custltrs*.
4. Print custltrs.
5. Close custltrs.
6. Close custmd.

A main document can also be merged with a data source at the Merge dialog box. To do this, you would complete the following steps:

1. Open a main document.
2. Choose <u>T</u>ools, Mail Me<u>r</u>ge; or click on the Mail Merge Helper button on the Merge toolbar.
3. At the Mail Merge Helper dialog box, choose <u>M</u>erge.
4. At the Merge dialog box shown in figure 25.7, make sure *New Document* displays in the Merge To text box, then choose <u>M</u>erge.
5. Word merges the data source with the main document, then displays the merged forms in a new document. Save this document in the normal manner. Then, if required, print the document.

Figure 25.7
Merge Dialog Box

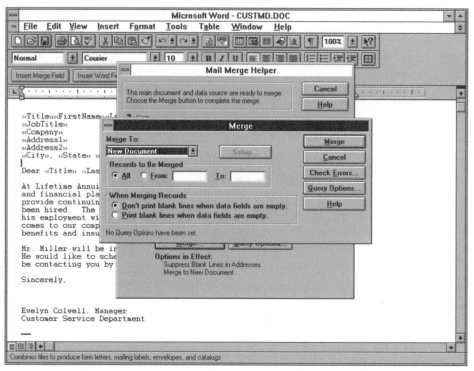

During a merge, if a field contains no data, Word removes the blank line. For example, in the *custds* data source shown in figure 25.4, two records do not contain data for *Address2*. Instead of printing a line with no data, Word removes the blank line. At the Merge dialog box, the *Don't print blank lines when data fields are empty* option is selected. If you do not want the blank line removed, choose the *Print blank lines when data fields are empty* option.

## Merging to the Printer

In the steps in the preceding section, the records in the data source are merged with the main document, then inserted in a new document. You can also merge the records in a data source with a main document and send the merged documents directly to the printer. To do this, open the main document, then click on the Merge to Printer button on the Merge toolbar (the fourth button from the right).

You can also merge a data source with a main document by completing the following steps:

1. Open the main document.
2. Choose Tools, Mail Merge; or click on the Mail Merge Helper button on the Merge toolbar.
3. At the Mail Merge Helper dialog box, choose Merge.
4. At the Merge dialog box, choose Merge To, then select *Printer*. To do this with the mouse, click on the down-pointing arrow to the right of the Merge To text box, then click on *Printer* in the drop-down list. If you are using the keyboard, press Alt + R, then select *Printer*.
5. Choose Merge.

When you choose Merge, the data source is merged with the main document, then sent directly to the printer. Before completing these steps, make sure the printer is turned on.

## Merging Specific Records

By default, Word merges the main document with each record in the data source. With options at the Merge dialog box, you can specify a range of records to be merged. To specify a range of records, you would complete the following steps:

1. Open the main document.
2. Choose <u>T</u>ools, Mail Me<u>r</u>ge; or click on the Mail Merge Helper button on the Merge toolbar.
3. At the Mail Merge Helper dialog box, choose <u>M</u>erge.
4. At the Merge dialog box, choose <u>F</u>rom, then key the record number of the first record in the range.
5. Choose <u>T</u>o, then key the record number of the last record in the range.
6. Choose Merge To, then select *New Document* if you want the records in the range merged to a new document or choose *Printer* if you want the records in the range merged to the printer.
7. Choose <u>M</u>erge.

# ■ *Viewing Merged Records in the Main Document*

When the main document is open, the data fields, such as <<Title>> and <<FirstName>>, display in the document as shown in figure 25.6. With buttons on the Merge toolbar, you can view the main document with the fields merged with the data source.

Click on the View Merged Data button on the Merge toolbar (third from left) to view the main document merged with the first record in the data source. After viewing the main document merged with a record in the data source, click on the View Merged Data button again to return the display to fields. When the View Merged Data button is active, it displays with a lighter gray background than the other buttons on the Merge toolbar.

If you click on the View Merged Data button, Word displays the main document merged with the first record in the data source. If you want to see the main document merged with the next record in the data source, click on the Next Record button on the Merge toolbar. Figure 25.8 identifies the buttons on the Merge toolbar.

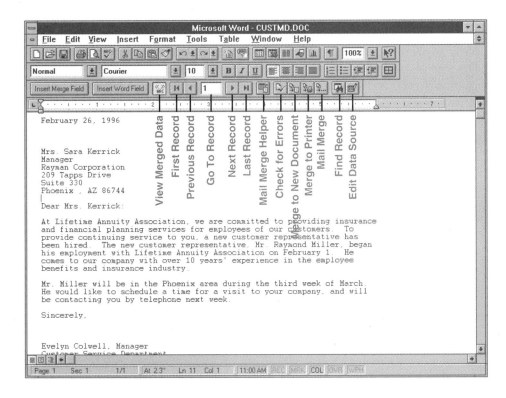

*Figure 25.8*
*Buttons on the*
*Merge Toolbar*

Click on the First Record button to view the document merged with the first record in the data source or click on the Last Record button to view the document merged with the last record in the data source. If you want to view the document merged with a specific record in the data source and you know the number of the record, key that number in the Go To Record box on the Merge toolbar. For example, to see the main document merged with the second record in the data source, you would complete the following steps:

1. Using the mouse, select the current number in the Go To Record box.
2. Key **2**.
3. Press Enter or position the I-beam pointer anywhere in the document screen, then click the left mouse button.

## ■ Finding a Specific Record

In a data source containing a large number of records, you may find the Find Record button useful. Use this button to find a record that matches a specific criterion. When you click on the Find Record button on the Merge toolbar, the Find in Field dialog box shown in figure 25.9 displays.

Key the text for which you are searching in the Find What text box, then select the field in the In Field text box. For example, to search for the record in the *custds* data source document that contains the ZIP Code *86342*, you would complete the following steps:

1. With the *custmd* main document open, click on the Find Record button on the Merge toolbar.
2. At the Find in Field dialog box, key **86342** in the Find What text box.
3. Choose In Field, then select *PostalCode*. To do this with the mouse, click on the down-pointing arrow to the right of the In Field text box, then click on *PostalCode* in the drop-down list. If you are using the keyboard, press Alt + N, then press the down arrow key until *PostalCode* is selected in the drop-down list.
4. Choose Find First.
5. Word searches the records in the data source, then merges the record that matches the text in the Find What text box and displays the merged document.
6. To find the next record that matches the text in the Find What text box, choose Find Next. Continue in this manner until Word displays a message indicating that Word has reached the end of the database. At this message, choose Yes if you want to continue searching the database or choose No if you do not want to continue searching.
7. Choose Close to close the dialog box.

*Figure 25.9*
*Find in Field Dialog*
*Box*

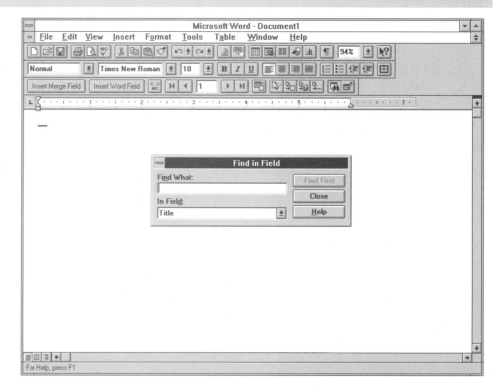

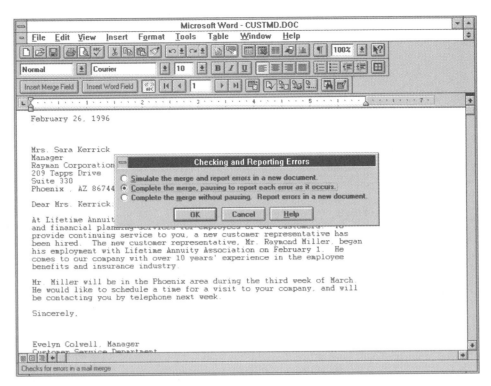

Figure 25.10
*Checking and
Reporting Errors
Dialog Box*

# **C**hecking for **E**rrors

For a merge to operate smoothly, no errors can occur in the main document or the data source. Word includes a helpful feature you can use to check for errors in the main and data source documents. This provides you with the opportunity to correct errors before completing the merge.

To correct errors, open a main document, then click on the Check for Errors button on the Merge toolbar. When you click on the Check for Errors button, the Checking and Reporting Errors dialog box shown in figure 25.10 displays.

The Checking and Reporting Errors dialog box contains three options. You can tell Word to simulate the merge, then report errors in a new document; complete the merge, pausing to report each error as it occurs; or complete the merge without pausing, then reporting errors in a new document. If you are going to merge a main document with a data source containing a large number of records and you expect there may be errors, choose the *Simulate the merge and report errors in a new document* option. The steps to check will vary depending on the options you choose.

Consider the following guidelines and you will reduce or eliminate errors in the merge:

- Field names must be unique, begin with a letter, and contain no spaces. (If you let Word choose the field names for you when creating the data source, this will not be a problem.)
- Field names must be in one row at the beginning of the data source.
- Each field (column) must have a field name.

# **E**diting the **D**ata **S**ource

With the main document displayed, you can edit records in a data source with the Edit Data Source button on the Merge toolbar. When you click on the Edit Data Source button, Word displays the Data Form dialog box containing the information for the record number displayed in the Go To Record box on the Merge toolbar.

With the Data Form dialog box displayed, make changes to the text in the record as required. Press the Tab key to move to the next field; press the Shift + Tab key to move to the previous field.

Use the arrow buttons at the bottom left side of the Data Form dialog box to display the first record, next record, previous record, or last record in the data source.

To delete a record from the data source, display the desired record, then choose Delete. If edit a record and then decide you want to return the record to its original state before editin. choose Restore.

If you want to make edits to the data source, choose View Source. This displays the data source document in the table format. When the data source is displayed, the Database toolbar displays below the Formatting toolbar and above the Ruler (if the Ruler is displayed). Figure 25.11 identifies the buttons on the Database toolbar and what you can perform with each button.

*Figure 25.11*
*Buttons on the*
*Database Toolbar*

| Choose this button | Named | To do this |
|---|---|---|
| | Data Form | display the Data Form dialog box where you can add or delete records or edit existing records. |
| | Manage Fields | display the Manage Fields dialog box where you can add, remove, or rename field names in the header row. |
| | Add New Record | add a new record at the location of the insertion point in the table. |
| | Delete Record | remove a record at the location of the insertion point in the table. |
| | Sort Ascending | sort the records in the table in ascending order on the current field. |
| | Sort Descending | sort the records in the table in descending order on the current field. |
| | Insert Database | display the Database dialog box where you can insert a file containing a database. |
| | Update Fields | update fields in the document. |
| | Find Record | display the Find in Field dialog box where you can search for a specific record. |
| | Mail Merge Main Document | open the main document attached to the current data source. |

With the buttons on the Database toolbar as described in figure 25.11, you can easily manage the data source document. If you want to add or remove field names from the header row in the data source, display the Manage Fields dialog box shown in figure 25.12 by clicking on the Manage Fields button on the Database toolbar.

At the Manage Fields dialog box, you can add a data field to the data source and remove or rename a data field. To add a data field, key the new data field name in the Field Name text box, then choose Add. Word adds the new field name to the end of the list in the Field Names in Header Row list box and adds a new column at the right side of the table in the data source document. Key information in the cells in the new column as needed.

Go To
Exercise
7

In chapter 26, you will learn how to sort data source records in ascending and descending order and also how to select specific records.

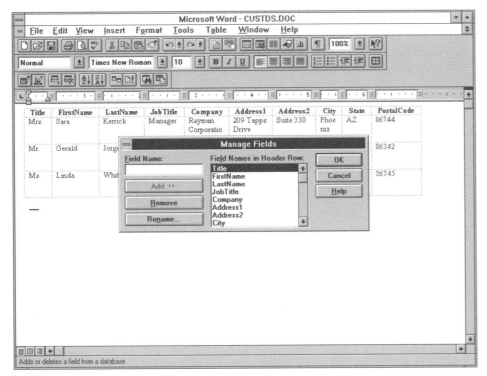

Figure 25.12
Manage Fields
Dialog Box

# Creating a Data Source Manually

In this chapter, you have learned how to use Mail Merge Helper to create a data source. A data source document can also be created manually. If you use Mail Merge Helper to create a data source, Word provides field names you can use when creating the data source and the main document. You can use these field names, or you can create your own. When creating your own field names, consider the following:

- A field name can be a maximum of 40 characters in length.
- A field name must begin with a letter.
- A field name cannot include spaces.
- Either uppercase or lowercase letters can be used.

When creating your own data source, create a table at a clear document screen, key the field names in the first row, called the *header row*, then key the variable information in the cells below the header row. For example, suppose you want to create a data source named *employds* that contains the name, title, and extension number of the 10 employees in your department. To do this, you would complete the following steps:

1. At a clear document screen, create a table with 3 columns and 11 rows.
2. With the insertion point positioned in the first cell in the table (cell A1), key **Name**.
3. Press the Tab key to move the insertion point to the next cell, then key **Title**.
4. Press the Tab key to move the insertion point to the next cell, then key **Extension**.
5. Press the Tab key, then key the name of a person in your department.
6. Press the Tab key, then key the title of the person entered in the previous cell.
7. Press the Tab key, then key the extension number of the person entered in the first cell of the current row.
8. Continue entering the names, titles, and extension numbers of the people in the department.
9. When the table is completed, save the document in the normal manner and name it *employds*.

Go To
Exercise
8

*Figure 25.13*
*Sample Memo Main*
*Document*

```
DATE:        March 12, 1996

TO:          <<Name>>, <<Title>>

FROM:        Hillary Listman, Director of Facilities

SUBJECT:     REMODELING PROJECT


The remodeling schedule for the Human Resources Department
has been prepared.  Preliminary work will begin on April 1
with the major work to begin the end of April.  During the
remodeling, several offices will be moved to different
sections of the center. If your office will be affected,
you will be contacted by Robert Morechild the last week of
March.  The completion date for the remodeling is July 1.
The remodeling will create additional noise and confusion
in your department, but the results will be worth it.

xx:memo
```

After the *employds* data source has been created, it can be merged with a main document. For example, suppose you want to send a memo to all employees of the department telling them about a remodeling project. To do this, you would design a memo like the one shown in figure 25.13 that identifies where the variable information is to be inserted during the merge.

To create the memo shown in figure 25.13 as a main document and specify *employds* as the data source, you would complete the following steps:

1. At a clear document screen, choose <u>T</u>ools, Mail Me<u>r</u>ge.
2. At the Mail Merge Helper dialog box, choose <u>C</u>reate (below Main Document).
3. At the drop-down list that displays, choose Form <u>L</u>etters.
4. At the question asking if you want to use the active document window or a new document, choose <u>A</u>ctive Window.
5. At the Mail Merge Helper dialog box, choose <u>G</u>et Data (below Data Source).
6. At the drop-down list that displays, choose <u>O</u>pen Data Source.
7. At the Open Data Source dialog box, select *employds* in the list, then choose OK or press Enter. (You can also double-click on the data source document name.)
8. At the Microsoft Word dialog box telling you that Word found no fields in your main document, choose Edit <u>M</u>ain Document.
9. At the clear document screen with the Merge toolbar displayed, key the memo to the point where the first field is to be inserted, then complete the following steps:
   a. Click on the Insert Merge Field button on the Merge toolbar (first button from the left).
   b. From the drop-down menu that displays, click on *Name*.
10. Key a comma (,), press the space bar, then insert the *Title* field by following directions similar to those in 9a and 9b.
11. Key the remainder of the memo, then save it in the normal manner.
12. To merge the main document and the records in the data source to a new document, click on the Merge to New Document button on the Merge toolbar.

After saving the merged document, you can print it in the normal manner and then close it. If necessary, save the main document (containing the memo with the fields).

# ■ Merging Envelopes

If you create a letter as a main document and then merge it with a data source, more than likely you will need an envelope properly addressed in which to send the letter. An envelope can be created that contains fields that are then merged with a data source. In this way, you can quickly prepare envelopes. For example, to prepare envelopes for the customers in the data source document named *custds*, you would complete the following steps:

1. At a clear document screen, choose Tools, Mail Merge.
2. At the Mail Merge Helper dialog box, choose Create (below Main Document).
3. At the drop-down list that displays, choose Envelopes.
4. At the question asking if you want to use the active document window or a new document, choose Active Window.
5. At the Mail Merge Helper dialog box, choose Get Data (below Data Source).
6. At the drop-down list that displays, choose Open Data Source.
7. At the Open Data Source dialog box, select *custds* in the list, then choose OK or press Enter. (You can also double-click on the data source document name.)
8. At the Microsoft Word dialog box telling you that Word needs to set up your main document, choose Set Up Main Document.
9. At the Envelope Options dialog box with the Envelope Options tab selected, make sure the correct envelope size is displayed, then choose OK or press Enter.
10. At the Envelope Address dialog box, choose Insert Merge Field, then choose *Title* from the drop-down list. To do this with the mouse, click on the Insert Merge Field button, then click on *Title*. If you are using the keyboard, press Alt + Shift + S. With *Title* selected, press Enter. (This inserts <<Title>> in the Sample Envelope Address section of the dialog box.)
11. Press the space bar once, then insert the <<FirstName>> data field by completing steps similar to those in step 10.
12. Continue entering the fields in the Sample Envelope Address section of the dialog box until all necessary fields are entered. When you are done, the Envelope Address dialog box should look like figure 25.14.
13. To add a POSTNET bar code to the envelope, choose Insert Postal Bar Code. This causes the Insert Postal Bar Code dialog box to display. At this dialog box, insert the *PostalCode* field in the Merge Field with ZIP Code text box. To do this with the mouse, click on the down-pointing arrow to the right of the text box, click on the down-pointing arrow on the vertical scroll bar until *PostalCode* is visible, then click on *PostalCode*. If you are using the keyboard, press the space bar to display the drop-down list, then press the down arrow key until *PostalCode* is selected. Choose OK or press Enter.
14. After all fields have been inserted in the Sample Envelope Address section of the Envelope Address dialog box, and a POSTNET bar code has been added, if desired, choose OK.
15. At the Mail Merge Helper dialog box, choose Merge.
16. At the Merge dialog box, choose Merge.

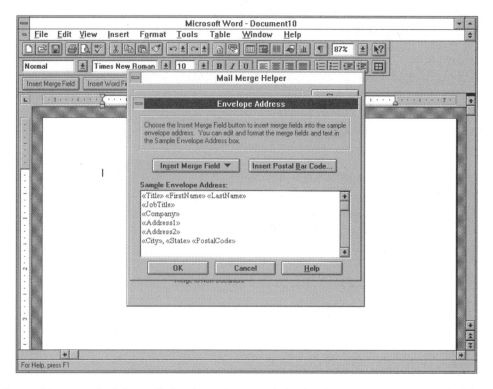

Figure 25.14
Envelope Address
Dialog Box with
Data Fields

When you choose <u>M</u>erge at the Merge dialog box, the records in the data source are merged with the envelope, then the merged envelopes are inserted in a document. Print this document in the normal manner. If you want to send the merged envelopes directly to the printer, change the Me<u>r</u>ge To option at the Merge dialog box to *Printer*, then choose <u>M</u>erge.

If you want to save the merged envelopes, save the document in the normal manner, then close it. This displays the envelope main document. If you think you will need this main envelope document in the future, save it with a name that includes the letters *md* to identify it as a main document.

At the Envelope Address dialog box, you can also identify a FIM-A for the envelope. To do this, choose Insert Postal <u>B</u>ar Code, specify the *PostalCode* field in the Merge Field with <u>Z</u>IP Code text box, then choose <u>F</u>IM-A Courtesy Reply Mail.

## ■ *M*erging *M*ailing *L*abels

Mailing labels can be created for records in a data source in much the same way that you create envelopes. For example, to create mailing labels for Avery 5164 shipping labels using the records in the *custds* data source document, you would complete the following steps:

1. At a clear document screen, choose <u>T</u>ools, Mail Merge.
2. At the Mail Merge Helper dialog box, choose <u>C</u>reate (below Main Document).
3. At the drop-down list that displays, choose <u>M</u>ailing Labels.
4. At the question asking if you want to use the active document window or a new document, choose <u>A</u>ctive Window.
5. At the Mail Merge Helper dialog box, choose <u>G</u>et Data (below Data Source).
6. At the drop-down list that displays, choose <u>O</u>pen Data Source.
7. At the Open Data Source dialog box, select *custds* in the list, then choose OK or press Enter. (You can also double-click on the data source document name.)
8. At the Microsoft Word dialog box telling you that Word needs to set up your main document, choose <u>S</u>et Up Main Document.
9. At the Label Options dialog box, choose Product <u>N</u>umber, then *5164 - Shipping*, then choose OK or press Enter.

10. At the Create Labels dialog box, choose Insert Merge Field, then choose *Title* from the drop-down list. To do this with the mouse, click on the Insert Merge Field button, then click on *Title*. If you are using the keyboard, press Alt + Shift + S. With *Title* selected, press Enter. (This inserts <<Title>> in the Sample Label box.)

11. Press the space bar once, then insert the <<FirstName>> data field by completing steps similar to those in step 10.

12. Continue entering the fields in the Sample Label box until all necessary fields are entered.

13. To add a POSTNET bar code to the label, choose Insert Postal Bar Code. At the Insert Postal Bar Code dialog box, insert the *PostalCode* field in the Merge Field with ZIP Code text box.

14. After all fields have been inserted in the Sample Label box of the Create Labels dialog box, choose OK.

15. At the Mail Merge Helper dialog box, choose Merge.

16. At the Merge dialog box, choose Merge.

When you choose Merge at the Merge dialog box, the records in the data source are merged with the mailing label, then the merged labels are inserted in the document screen. Print this document in the normal manner. If you want to send the merged labels directly to the printer, change the Merge To option at the Merge dialog box to *Printer*, then choose Merge.

If you want to save the merged labels, save the document in the normal manner, then close it. This displays the label main document. If you think you will need this label main document in the future, save it with a name that includes the letters *md* to identify it as a main document.

## Creating Lists with Merge

When merging form letters, envelopes, or mailing labels, a new form is created for each record. For example, if there are eight records in the data source that is merged with a form letter, eight letters are created. If there are twenty records in a data source that is merged with a mailing label, twenty labels are created. In some situations, you may want merged information to remain on the same page. This is useful, for example, when creating a list such as a directory or address list.

A merge document can be created that inserts records on the same page by using the Catalog option from the Create drop-down list at the Mail Merge Helper dialog box. For example, suppose you want to create a list of the employees in a company by name, department, and extension. The first step is to create the data source. This can be created with Mail Merge Helper, or it can be created at a clear document screen by creating a table. In this example, the data source contains three fields: *Name*, *Department*, and *Extension*. After the data source is created, the next step is to create the main document and link it to the data source by completing the following steps:

1. At a clear document screen, choose Tools, Mail Merge.
2. At the Mail Merge Helper dialog box, choose Create (below Main Document).
3. At the drop-down list that displays, choose Catalog.
4. At the question asking if you want to use the active document window or a new document, choose Active Window.
5. At the Mail Merge Helper dialog box, choose Get Data (below Data Source).
6. At the drop-down list that displays, choose Open Data Source.
7. At the Open Data Source dialog box, select the name of the data source, then choose OK or press Enter. (You can also double-click on the data source document name.)
8. At the Microsoft Word dialog box telling you that Word found no fields in your main document, choose Edit Main Document.
9. At the clear document screen, complete the following steps:

> a. Set a left tab at 0.5 inches, 2.5 inches, and 5 inches.
> b. Press the Tab key to move the insertion point to the first tab stop.
> c. Insert the *Name* field by clicking on the Insert Merge Field button on the Merge toolbar, then clicking on *Name*.
> d. Press the Tab key, then insert the *Department* field.
> e. Press the Tab key, then insert the *Extension* field.
> f. Click on the Merge to New Document button on the Merge toolbar.
> 10. Save the merged list document in the normal manner, then print it.

After printing the merged list document, close the document. This displays the main document. If you will need this document in the future, save it. When naming the document, you may want to add the letters *md* to identify it as a main document.

## Inputting Text During a Merge

Word's Merge feature contains a large number of Word fields that can be inserted in a main document. In this chapter, you will learn about the *Fill-in* field, which is used for information that is input at the keyboard during a merge. For more information on the other Word fields, please refer to the Word for Windows User's Guide.

Situations may arise in which you do not need to keep all variable information in a data source. For example, there may be variable information that changes on a regular basis such as a customer's monthly balance, a product price, etc. Word lets you input variable information with the keyboard into a document during the merge.

A Fill-in field is inserted in a main document by clicking on the Insert Word Field button on the Merge toolbar, then clicking on Fill-in in the drop-down list. A document can contain any number of Fill-in fields. By default, a Fill-in field does not display in the main document. To turn on the display of the Fill-in field, press Alt + F9. This displays the Fill-in field and also changes the display of other data fields. For example, with the display of fields turned on, the <<Title>> field will display as { MERGEFIELD Title }.

As an example of how to insert a Fill-in field in a main document, suppose you want to add a specific date to the last paragraph in the letter shown in figure 25.6. Instead of the last paragraph stating *He would like to schedule a time for a visit to your company, and will be contacting you by telephone next week*, you would like it to display as follows:

He would like to schedule a time for a visit to your company on { **FILLIN "Insert date."** }. He will contact you by telephone next week.

To edit the *custmd* so the last paragraph displays as above and includes the Fill-in field, you would complete the following steps:

> 1. Open custmd.
> 2. Position the insertion point immediately left of the comma (,) after the word *company* in the last paragraph.
> 3. Delete the comma, press the space bar, then insert the Fill-in field by completing the following steps:
>    a. Press Alt + F9. (This turns on the display of fields.)
>    b. Click on the Insert Word Field button on the Merge toolbar.
>    c. At the drop-down menu that displays, click on Fill-in.
>    d. At the Insert Word Field: Fill-in dialog box shown in figure 25.15, key **Insert date.**
>    e. Choose OK or press Enter.
>    f. At the Microsoft Word dialog box with *Insert date.* displayed in the upper left corner, choose OK or press Enter.
> 4. Key a period. Then edit the last sentence in the paragraph so it displays as *He will contact you by telephone next week.*
> 5. Save the main document in the normal manner.

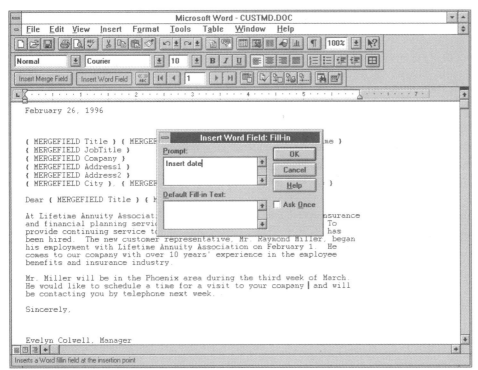

Figure 25.15
Insert Word Field:
Fill-in Dialog Box

After inserting the Fill-in field, save the main document (with the same name or a new name). To merge the main document with the data source, click on the Merge to New Document button on the Merge toolbar or the Merge to Printer button. When Word merges the main document with the first record in the data source, the Microsoft Word dialog box with *Insert date.* in the upper left corner displays in the document screen as shown in figure 25.16.

Key the date for the first record in the data source, then click on the OK button. If you are using the keyboard, key the date, press the Tab key to make the OK button active, then press Enter.

Word displays the dialog box again. Key the date for the second record in the data source, then click on OK; or press the Tab key, then press Enter. Continue in this manner until the date has been entered for each record in the data source. Word then completes the merge.

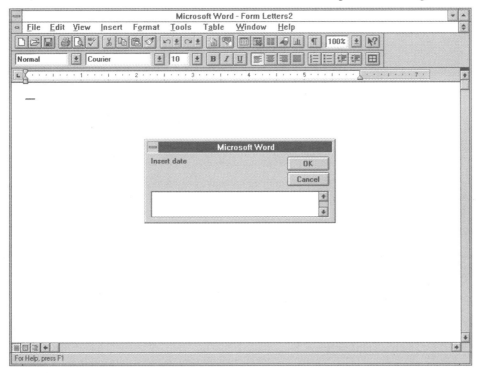

Figure 25.16
Microsoft Word
Dialog Box with Fill-in Prompt

- Word includes a mail merge feature that you can use to create letters, envelopes, labels, and much more, all with personalized information.
- Two different documents are usually required for merging. The *data source* document contains the variable information. The *main document* contains the standard text along with identifiers showing where variable information is to be inserted.
- Text in a data source is inserted in cells in a table. Or, you can use Word's Mail Merge Helper to assist you in creating the data source.
- At the Mail Merge Helper, Word provides predetermined field names that can be used when creating the data source.
- Variable information in a data source is saved as a *record*. A record contains all the information for one unit. A series of fields make one record, and a series of records make a data source.
- You can add names, correct information, or delete names from a data source document. Edit the data source by opening the document in the normal manner and then editing the table using methods described in chapter 21.
- After determining what information you want in the main document, you need to determine what fields from the data source you will need and where they should be inserted in the main document.
- When creating a main document, you need to identify what data source will be used for the variable information. This is done at the Mail Merge Helper dialog box.
- Once the data source and the main document have been created and saved, they can be merged. Merged documents can be saved in a new document or sent directly to the printer.
- With options at the Merge dialog box, you can specify a range of records to be merged.
- When the main document is open, you can use buttons on the Merge toolbar to view how the document will look after merging with the first record, the next record, the last record, or a specific record from the data source.
- Use the Find Record button on the Merge toolbar to locate a specific record in a data source.
- With the Check for Errors button on the Merge toolbar you can check the data source and the main document for errors before merging.
- With the Edit Data Source button on the Merge toolbar, you can edit records in a data source. With buttons on the Database toolbar, you can easily manage the data source document.
- You can manually create a data source by creating a table, keying the field names in the first row, called the header row, then keying the variable information in the cells below the header row.
- An envelope can be created that contains data fields that are then merged with a data source. Mailing labels can be created for records in a data source in much the same way.
- A merge document can be created that inserts records on the same page by using the Catalog option from the Create drop-down list at the Mail Merge Helper dialog box.
- Word lets you input variable information with the keyboard into a document during the merge. To do this, a Fill-in field is inserted in a main document by clicking on the Insert Word Field button on the Merge toolbar, then clicking on Fill-in in the drop-down list.

## COMMANDS REVIEW

| | Mouse | Keyboard |
|---|---|---|
| Display Mail Merge Helper dialog box | Tools, Mail Merge | Tools, Mail Merge |

**True/False:** Circle the letter T if the statement is true; circle the letter F if the statement is false.

T  F  1.  Two documents usually must be created for merging.
T  F  2.  A main document is a document that contains variable information about customers, etc.
T  F  3.  Text in a data source is inserted in cells in a table.
T  F  4.  A record contains all the information for one unit.
T  F  5.  A series of fields make a record.
T  F  6.  The easiest way to edit a data source is to rekey each record.
T  F  7.  FirstName, JobTitle, and Address1 are examples of field names.
T  F  8.  Begin merging by opening the data source.
T  F  9.  During a merge, if a field contains no data, Word removes the blank line by default.
T  F  10. By clicking on the Check for Errors button on the Merge toolbar, Word will check all text in merged documents for misspelled words.

**Completion:** In the space provided, indicate the correct term, command, or number.

1.  At the _____ dialog box, predetermined fields are provided by Word.
2.  The first row of a data source table is called a(n) _____ and identifies the names of the fields.
3.  Before creating the main document, determine what information will remain the same and what information will _____.
4.  When creating a main document, you need to identify what _____ will be used for the variable information.
5.  The data source and the main document can be merged to a new document or to the _____.
6.  Click on the _____ button on the Merge toolbar to view the main document merged with the first record in the data source.
7.  Click on the _____ button on the Merge toolbar to begin searching for a specific record in a data source.
8.  With the main document displayed, you can edit records in a data source with the _____ button on the Merge toolbar.
9.  When manually creating your own data source, first create a(n) _____ at a clear document screen.
10. To begin creating envelopes or mailing labels for the names and addresses in a source document, choose _____ at the Mail Merge Helper dialog box.
11. So that merged information remains on the same page, choose the _____ option from the Create drop-down list at the Mail Merge Helper dialog box.
12. A field that is used for information that is input at the keyboard during a merge is called a(n) _____ field.

## AT THE COMPUTER

### Exercise 1

1.  At a clear document screen, create a data source named *mpcustds* containing the information shown in figure 25.17 by completing the following steps:
    a.  Choose Tools, Mail Merge.
    b.  At the Mail Merge Helper dialog box, choose Create, then from the drop-down list that displays, choose Form Letters.
    c.  At the dialog box asking if you want to use the active document or a new document window, choose Active Window.

d. Choose <u>G</u>et Data, then from the drop-down list that displays, choose <u>C</u>reate Data Source.

e. At the Create Data Source dialog box, select *JobTitle* in the Field <u>N</u>ames in Header Row list box, then choose <u>R</u>emove Field Name.

f. Select *Company* in the Field <u>N</u>ames in Header Row list box, then choose <u>R</u>emove Field Name.

g. Select *Address2* in the Field <u>N</u>ames in Header Row list box, then choose <u>R</u>emove Field Name.

h. Select *Country* in the Field <u>N</u>ames in Header Row list box, then choose <u>R</u>emove Field Name.

i. Select *HomePhone* in the Field <u>N</u>ames in Header Row list box, then choose <u>R</u>emove Field Name.

j. Select *WorkPhone* in the Field <u>N</u>ames in Header Row list box, then choose <u>R</u>emove Field Name.

k. Choose OK.

l. At the Save Data Source dialog box, key **mpcustds**, then choose OK or press Enter.

m. At the dialog box containing the warning that the data source contains no data, choose Edit <u>D</u>ata Source.

n. At the Data Form dialog box, key **Mr. and Mrs.** in the *Title* field, then press the Enter key or the Tab key.

o. Continue keying the information in figure 25.17 for the customers Mr. and Mrs. Dennis Haynes in the appropriate fields. Press the Enter key or the Tab key to move to the next field. Press Shift + Tab to move to the preceding field.

p. After entering all the information for Mr. and Mrs. Haynes, choose <u>A</u>dd New. This saves the information and displays a blank Data Form dialog box. Continue in this manner until all records shown in figure 25.17 have been created. (This figure continues on the next page.)

q. After creating the last record for the data source, choose <u>V</u>iew Source.

r. At the data source document, choose <u>F</u>ile, then <u>S</u>ave.

2. Print mpcustds.

3. Close mpcustds.

4. Close the clear document screen without saving the changes.

**Figure 25.17**

```
Title          =    Mr. and Mrs.
FirstName      =    Dennis
LastName       =    Haynes
Address1       =    1810 23rd Avenue
City           =    Seattle
State          =    WA
PostalCode     =    98221

Title          =    Ms.
FirstName      =    Deborah
LastName       =    Burke
Address1       =    17420 Vander Road
City           =    Federal Way
State          =    WA
PostalCode     =    98045
```

```
Title          =    Mr.
FirstName      =    Kevin
LastName       =    Jergens
Address1       =    10605 Lakeside Drive
City           =    Seattle
State          =    WA
PostalCode     =    98188

Title          =    Mr. and Mrs.
FirstName      =    Lloyd
LastName       =    Rienhart
Address1       =    818 Vista Drive
City           =    Redmond
State          =    WA
PostalCode     =    98013

Title          =    Dr.
FirstName      =    Janice
LastName       =    Crivello
Address1       =    9905 West 50th Street
City           =    Seattle
State          =    WA
PostalCode     =    98041
```

## Exercise 2

1. At a clear document screen, create the main document shown in figure 25.18 and name it mpcustmd by completing the following steps:
   a. Choose Tools, Mail Merge.
   b. At the Mail Merge Helper dialog box, choose Create (below Main Document).
   c. At the drop-down list that displays, choose Form Letters.
   d. At the question asking if you want to use the active document window or a new document, choose Active Window.
   e. At the Mail Merge Helper dialog box, choose Get Data (below Data Source).
   f. At the drop-down list that displays, choose Open Data Source.
   g. At the Open Data Source dialog box, select *mpcustds* in the list, then choose OK or press Enter. (You can also double-click on *mpcustds*.)
   h. At the Microsoft Word dialog box telling you that Word found no fields in your main document, choose Edit Main Document.
   i. At the clear document screen with the Merge toolbar displayed below the Formatting toolbar, key the letter shown in figure 25.18 to the point where the first field is to be inserted, then complete the following steps:
      (1) Click on the Insert Merge Field button on the Merge toolbar (first button from the left).
      (2) From the drop-down menu that displays, click on *Title*.
   j. Press the space bar once, then insert the *FirstName* data field by completing steps similar to those in 1i(1) and 1i(2). Continue in this manner until all data fields have been entered as shown in figure 25.18.
   k. After keying the entire main document, choose File, then Save.
   l. At the Save As dialog box, key **mpcustmd**.
   m. Choose OK or press Enter.
2. Print mpcustmd.
3. Close mpcustmd.

Figure 25.18

(current date)


<<Title>> <<FirstName>> <<LastName>>
<<Address1>>
<<City>>, <<State>> <<PostalCode>>

Dear <<Title>> <<LastName>>:

We would like to introduce you to a great way to earn free travel
to Alaska, Hawaii, Europe, Asia, and hundreds of other places.
Because you are a valued MilesPlus member, you have been
preapproved for the First Choice credit card with a credit line of
$3,000.  This is the only credit card that offers you the ability
to earn one MilesPlus mile for every purchase dollar you charge.

You can use your First Choice card for all kinds of purchases at
over 10 million locations throughout the world.  Every purchase you
make brings you closer to your next free flight to Seaview Airlines
destinations.  You can also enjoy a 30-day, interest-free grace
period on your purchases when you pay your previous balance in full
by the due date.

Take advantage of this special opportunity to earn more miles and
fantastic free travel by accepting your preapproved First Choice
card today.

Sincerely,



Walter Chamberlin
Marketing Manager

xx:mpcustmd

## Exercise 3

1. Merge mpcustmd with mpcustds by completing the following steps:
   a. Open mpcustmd.
   b. Click on the Merge to New Document button on the Merge toolbar (fifth button from the right).
   c. When the main document is merged with the data source, save the document and name it c25ex03.
2. Print c25ex03.
3. Close c25ex03.
4. Close mpcustmd without saving the changes.

# Exercise 4

1. Merge the third through the fifth records in the mpcustds document with the mpcustmd document at the printer by completing the following steps:
   a. Open mpcustmd.
   b. Choose Tools, Mail Merge; or click on the Mail Merge Helper button on the Merge toolbar.
   c. At the Mail Merge Helper dialog box, choose Merge.
   d. At the Merge dialog box, choose From, then key **3**.
   e. Choose To, then key **5**.
   f. Choose Merge To, then select *Printer*.
   g. Choose Merge.
   h. At the Print dialog box, choose OK or press Enter.
2. Close mpcustmd without saving the changes.

# Exercise 5

1. At a clear document screen, create the letter shown in figure 25.19 and attach it to the mpcustds document by completing the following steps:
   a. Choose Tools, Mail Merge.
   b. At the Mail Merge Helper dialog box, choose Create (below Main Document).
   c. At the drop-down list that displays, choose Form Letters.
   d. At the question asking if you want to use the active document window or a new document, choose Active Window.
   e. At the Mail Merge Helper dialog box, choose Get Data (below Data Source).
   f. At the drop-down list that displays, choose Open Data Source.
   g. At the Open Data Source dialog box, select *mpcustds* in the list, then choose OK or press Enter. (You can also double-click on *mpcustds*.)
   h. At the Microsoft Word dialog box telling you that Word found no fields in your main document, choose Edit Main Document.
   i. At the clear document screen with the Merge toolbar displayed below the Formatting toolbar, key the letter shown in figure 25.19. Insert the fields as indicated. (Use the Insert Merge Field button to do this.)
   j. After keying the entire main document, choose File, Save.
   k. At the Save As dialog box, key **mpltr2md**.
   l. Choose OK or press Enter.
2. Position the insertion point at the beginning of the document, then click on the View Merged Data button on the Merge toolbar to view the main document merged with the first record in the data source.
3. Click on the Next Record button on the Merge toolbar to view the main document merged with the second record in the data source.
4. Click on the Last Record button on the Merge toolbar to view the main document merged with the last record in the data source.
5. Find the record in the data source that contains the last name *Rienhart* by completing the following steps:
   a. Click on the Find Record button on the Merge toolbar.
   b. At the Find in Field dialog box, key **Rienhart** in the Find What text box.
   c. Choose In Field, then select *LastName*.
   d. Choose Find First.
   e. Word searches the records in the data source, then merges the main document with the record containing the name *Rienhart*. Choose Find Next.
   f. At the message indicating that Word has reached the end of the database, choose No.
   g. Choose Close to close the dialog box.

6. Click on the View Merged Data button on the Merge toolbar. (This redisplays the main document with the fields.)
7. Print mpltr2md.
8. Close mpltr2md without saving the changes.

Figure 25.19

```
(current date)



<<Title>> <<FirstName>> <<LastName>>
<<Address1>>
<<City>>, <<State>> <<PostalCode>>

Dear <<Title>> <<LastName>>:

A few weeks ago, we shared with you the exciting news that you are
preapproved for the First Choice credit card.  This card offers you
the ability to earn one MilesPlus mile for every purchase dollar
you charge.

Now is the time to take us up on this incredible offer.  Just
accept your preapproved First Choice card and we will credit your
MilesPlus account with 5,000 bonus miles after your First Choice
account has been opened.

All you need to do to accept your First Choice card is to mail your
enclosed Acceptance Form in the postage-paid envelope provided or
call our toll-free number, 1-800-555-8900.  In addition to the
miles you will earn, you will also enjoy cash advances available 24
hours a day, traveler's message service, and toll-free customer
service.

Sincerely,



Walter Chamberlin
Marketing Manager

xx:mpltr2md

Enclosures
```

## Exercise 6

1. Open mpltr2md.
2. Check for errors in the main document and data source document by completing the following steps:
   a. Click on the Check for Errors button on the Merge toolbar.
   b. At the Checking and Reporting dialog box, make sure *Complete the merge, pausing to report each error as it occurs* is selected, then choose OK or press Enter.

c. If Word finds any errors, make the necessary corrections. If no errors are found, the main document is merged with the data source and the merged document is displayed in the document screen.
3. Save the merged document and name it c25ex06.
4. Print c25ex06.
5. Close c25ex06.
6. Close mpltr2md saving the changes (if any were made).

## Exercise 7

1. Edit the mpcustmd document by completing the following steps:
   a. Open mpcustmd.
   b. Click on the Edit Data Source button on the Merge toolbar.
   c. At the Data Form dialog box, click once on the button to the right of the Record text box containing the right-pointing triangle at the left side of the dialog box. (This displays the second record in the data source containing the name *Deborah Burke*.
   d. Press the Tab key until *17420 Vander Road* is selected, then key **4133 Monta Vista**.
   e. Press the Tab key to select *Federal Way*, then key **Auburn**.
   f. Press the Tab key until *98045* is selected, then key **98023**.
   g. Click on <u>V</u>iew Source. (This displays the data source document.)
   h. At the data source document, click on the Add New Record button (third button from left) on the Database toolbar.
   i. With the insertion point positioned in the first cell of the new row, key the text below after *Title* (shown below), then press the Tab key. Continue keying the text as indicated below:

   | | | |
   |---|---|---|
   | *Title* | = | Mrs. |
   | *FirstName* | = | Tammy |
   | *LastName* | = | Houston |
   | *Address1* | = | 7903 South 122nd |
   | *City* | = | Federal Way |
   | *State* | = | WA |
   | *PostalCode* | = | 98045 |

   j. Add a new field to the data source and add information to the field by completing the following steps:
      (1) Click on the Manage Fields button (second button from left) on the Database toolbar.
      (2) At the Manage Fields dialog box, key **Company**.
      (3) Choose <u>A</u>dd.
      (4) Choose OK or press Enter.
      (5) Position the arrow pointer in the cell below the *Company* field in the row containing the name *Dennis Haynes*, click the left mouse button (this positions the insertion point in the cell), then key **Design Creations**.
      (6) Position the arrow pointer in the cell below the *Company* field in the row containing the name *Deborah Burke*, click the left mouse button, then key **Auburn Wood Products**.
      (7) Position the arrow pointer in the cell below the *Company* field in the row containing the name *Kevin Jergens*, then key **Northwest Services**.
   k. Save the data source document with the same name (mpcustds).
   l. Close mpcustds.
   m. At the mpcustmd document, insert the <<Company>> field above the <<Address1>> field. (Use the Insert Merge Field button on the Merge toolbar to do this.)
   n. Click on the Merge to New Document button on the Merge toolbar.
2. Save the merged document and name it c25ex07.
3. Print c25ex07.
4. Close c25ex07.
5. Close mpcustmd and save the changes.

## Exercise 8

1.  At a clear document screen, create a data source manually with the information shown in figure 25.20 by completing the following steps:
    a.  Create a table with 3 columns and 7 rows.
    b.  With the insertion point positioned in the first cell in the table (cell A1), key **NameAdd**.
    c.  Press the Tab key to move the insertion point to the next cell, then key **Salutation**.
    d.  Press the Tab key to move the insertion point to the next cell, then key **PIN**.
    e.  Press the Tab key, then key **Ms. Cathy Hudson**. Press the Enter key, then key **9013 Myers Road**. Press the Enter key, then key **Pittsburgh, PA 19044**.
    f.  Press the Tab key, then key **Ms. Hudson**.
    g.  Press the Tab key, then key **23661**.
    h.  Press the Tab key, then key the name and address for the second person shown in figure 25.20.
    i.  Continue entering the names and addresses, salutations, and personal identification numbers (PIN) for the people shown in figure 25.20.
2.  When the table is completed, save the document and name it nacustds.
3.  Print nacustds.
4.  Close nacustds.

---

**Figure 25.20**

```
NameAdd          =     Ms. Cathy Hudson
                       9013 Myers Road
                       Pittsburgh, PA 19044
Salutation       =     Ms. Hudson
PIN              =     23661


NameAdd          =     Mr. Brad Martelli
                       11918 64th Street
                       Bethel Park, PA 19076
Salutation       =     Mr. Martelli
PIN              =     10392


NameAdd          =     Ms. Mary Jo Webb
                       15110 Meridian Street
                       Monroeville, PA 19089
Salutation       =     Ms. Webb
PIN              =     43029


NameAdd          =     Dr. David Barclay
                       6423 36th Avenue
                       Pittsburgh, PA 19065
Salutation       =     Dr. Barclay
PIN              =     45320


NameAdd          =     Ms. Carol Fuller
                       14223 132nd Avenue
                       Pittsburgh, PA 19058
Salutation       =     Ms. Fuller
PIN              =     90342


NameAdd          =     Mr. Robert Keohane
                       1209 Alder Road
                       Bethel Park, PA 19076
Salutation       =     Mr. Keohane
PIN              =     34998
```

# Exercise 9

1. At a clear document screen, create the main document shown in figure 25.21 by completing the following steps:
   a. Choose Tools, Mail Merge.
   b. At the Mail Merge Helper dialog box, choose Create (below Main Document).
   c. At the drop-down list that displays, choose Form Letters.
   d. At the question asking if you want to use the active document window or a new document, choose Active Window.
   e. At the Mail Merge Helper dialog box, choose Get Data (below Data Source).
   f. At the drop-down list that displays, choose Open Data Source.
   g. At the Open Data Source dialog box, select *nacustds* in the list, then choose OK or press Enter. (You can also double-click on *nacustds*.)
   h. At the Microsoft Word dialog box telling you that Word found no fields in your main document, choose Edit Main Document.
   i. At the clear document screen with the Merge toolbar displayed, key the letter shown in figure 25.21. Use the Insert Merge Field button on the Merge toolbar to insert the fields.
   j. When the letter is completed, save it and name it nacustmd.
2. With nacustmd still open in the document screen, complete the following steps:
   a. Click on the Check for Errors button on the Merge toolbar.
   b. At the Checking and Reporting dialog box, make sure *Complete the merge, pausing to report each error as it occurs* is selected, then choose OK or press Enter.
   c. If Word finds any errors, make the necessary corrections. If no errors are found, the main document is merged with the data source and the merged document is displayed in the document screen.
3. Save the merged document and name it c25ex09.
4. Print c25ex09.
5. Close c25ex09.
6. Close nacustmd saving the changes (if any were made).

Figure 25.21

(current date)


<<NameAdd>>

Dear <<Salutation>>:

We have just made it easier for you to use Northeast Annuities'
Automated Telephone Service.  With your new Personal Identification
Number (PIN), you can easily transfer funds or reallocate premiums.

Your new PIN is <<PIN>>.  With this PIN, you can receive Northeast
Annuities performance information, unit values, accumulation
totals, and automated services.  Only you and our automated
telephone system know what your PIN is, so all your requests will
be secure and entirely confidential.  If you need help or more
information, just call us at 1-800-555-2005.

We hope you will agree that our "new" Automated Telephone Service
is an improvement over the old one.  We are enclosing a brochure
for more details.

Very truly yours,



Sheryl Omoto
Vice President

xx:nacustmd

Enclosure

## Exercise 10

1. At a clear document screen, create a main document for envelopes with the nacustds data source document attached by completing the following steps:
   a. Choose Tools, Mail Merge.
   b. At the Mail Merge Helper dialog box, choose Create (below Main Document).
   c. At the drop-down list that displays, choose Envelopes.
   d. At the question asking if you want to use the active document window or a new document, choose Active Window.
   e. At the Mail Merge Helper dialog box, choose Get Data (below Data Source).
   f. At the drop-down list that displays, choose Open Data Source.
   g. At the Open Data Source dialog box, select *nacustds* in the list, then choose OK or press Enter. (You can also double-click on *nacustds*.)
   h. At the Microsoft Word dialog box telling you that Word needs to set up your main document, choose Set Up Main Document.

i. At the Envelope Options dialog box with the Envelope Options tab selected, make sure the correct envelope size is displayed, then choose OK or press Enter.

j. At the Envelope Address dialog box, choose Insert Merge Field, then choose *NameAdd* from the drop-down list. To do this with the mouse, click on the Insert Merge Field button, then click on *NameAdd*. If you are using the keyboard, press Alt + Shift + S. With *NameAdd* selected press Enter. (This inserts <<NameAdd>> in the Sample Envelope Address section of the dialog box.)

k. Choose OK to close the Envelope Address dialog box.

l. At the Mail Merge Helper dialog box, choose Merge.

m. At the Merge dialog box, make sure *New Document* displays in the Merge To text box, then choose Merge.

2. Save the merged document and name it c25ex10.

3. Print c25ex10.

4. Close c25ex10.

5. At the envelope main document, save it and name it naenvmd.

6. Close naenvmd.

## Exercise 11

1. At a clear document screen, create mailing labels for Avery 5163 shipping labels using the records in the *mpcustds* data source document by completing the following steps:

a. Choose Tools, Mail Merge.

b. At the Mail Merge Helper dialog box, choose Create (below Main Document).

c. At the drop-down list that displays, choose Mailing Labels.

d. At the question asking if you want to use the active document window or a new document, choose Active Window.

e. At the Mail Merge Helper dialog box, choose Get Data (below Data Source).

f. At the drop-down list that displays, choose Open Data Source.

g. At the Open Data Source dialog box, select *mpcustds* in the list, then choose OK or press Enter. (You can also double-click on *mpcustds*.)

h. At the Microsoft Word dialog box telling you that Word needs to set up your main document, choose Set Up Main Document.

i. At the Label Options dialog box, choose Product Number, then *5163 - Shipping*, then choose OK or press Enter.

j. At the Create Labels dialog box, choose Insert Merge Field, then choose *Title* from the drop-down list. To do this with the mouse, click on the Insert Merge Field button, then click on *Title*. If you are using the keyboard, press Alt + Shift + S. With *Title* selected, press Enter. (This inserts <<Title>> in the Sample Label box.)

k. Press the space bar once, then insert the <<FirstName>> field by completing steps similar to those in step j.

l. Continue entering the data fields in the Sample Label box until all necessary fields are entered.

m. To add a POSTNET bar code to the label, choose Insert Postal Bar Code. At the Insert Postal Bar Code dialog box, insert the *PostalCode* field in the Merge Field with ZIP Code text box, then choose OK.

n. At the Create Labels dialog box, choose OK.

o. At the Mail Merge Helper dialog box, choose Merge.

p. At the Merge dialog box, make sure *New Document* displays in the Merge To text box, then choose Merge.

2. Save the merged document and name it c25ex11.

3. Print c25ex11

4. Close c25ex11.

5. At the labels main document, save it and name it mplblmd.

6. Close mplblmd.

# Exercise 12

1. At a clear document screen, create a list containing the names, addresses, and PINs for the customers in the *nacustds* data source document by completing the following steps:
   a. Choose Tools, Mail Merge.
   b. At the Mail Merge Helper dialog box, choose Create (below Main Document).
   c. At the drop-down list that displays, choose Catalog.
   d. At the question asking if you want to use the active document window or a new document, choose Active Window.
   e. At the Mail Merge Helper dialog box, choose Get Data (below Data Source).
   f. At the drop-down list that displays, choose Open Data Source.
   g. At the Open Data Source dialog box, select *nacustds*, then choose OK or press Enter. (You can also double-click on *nacustds*.)
   h. At the Microsoft Word dialog box telling you that Word found no fields in your main document, choose Edit Main Document.
   i. At the clear document screen, complete the following steps:
      (1) Insert the *NameAdd* field by clicking on the Insert Merge Field button on the Merge toolbar, then clicking on *NameAdd*.
      (2) Press the Tab key four times, then insert the *PIN* field.
      (3) Press the Enter key twice.
   j. Click on the Merge to New Document button on the Merge toolbar.
2. At the merged document, complete the following steps:
   a. Position the insertion point at the beginning of the document.
   b. Press the Enter key three times.
   c. Move the insertion point back to the beginning of the document.
   d. Turn on bold, then key **Customer**.
   e. Press the Tab key seven times.
   f. Key **PIN**.
3. Save the merged list document and name it c25ex12.
4. Print c25ex12.
5. Close c25ex12.
6. Save the list main document and name it nalistmd.
7. Close nalistmd.

# Exercise 13

1. Edit the mpltr2md main document so it includes Fill-in fields by completing the following steps:
   a. Open mpltr2md.
   b. Change the third paragraph in the document to the paragraph shown in figure 25.22. Insert the first Fill-in field by completing the following steps:
      (1) Press Alt + F9. (This turns on the display of fields.)
      (2) Click on the Insert Word Field button on the Merge toolbar.
      (3) At the drop-down menu that displays, click on *Fill-in*.
      (4) At the Insert Word Field: Fill-in dialog box, key **Insert rep name.**
      (5) Choose OK or press Enter.
      (6) At the Microsoft Word dialog box with *Insert rep name.* displayed in the upper left corner, choose OK.
   c. Complete steps similar to those in 1b(2) through 1b(6) to insert the second Fill-in field.
   d. Press Alt + F9 to turn off the display of fields.
2. When the paragraph is completed, save the document with Save As and name it mpltr3md.
3. Merge the main document with the data source by completing the following steps:
   a. Click on the Merge to New Document button on the Merge toolbar.

b. When Word merges the main document with the first record, a dialog box displays with the message *Insert rep name.* At this dialog box, key **Charles Noland**, then click on OK.

c. At the dialog box with the message *Insert phone number.*, key **(206) 555-3443**, then click on OK.

d. At the dialog box with the message *Insert rep name.*, key **Denise Nickel** (this replaces Charles Noland), then click on OK.

e. At the dialog box with the message *Insert phone number.*, key **(206) 555-3430**, then click on OK.

f. At the dialog box with the message *Insert rep name.*, key **Andrew Christie**, then click on OK.

g. At the dialog box with the message *Insert phone number.*, key **(206) 555-3456**, then click on OK.

h. At the dialog box with the message *Insert rep name.*, key **Nicole Gelmann**, then click on OK.

i. At the dialog box with the message *Insert phone number.*, key **(206) 555-3422**, then click on OK.

j. At the dialog box with the message *Insert rep name.*, key **Angie Yuan**, then click on OK.

k. At the dialog box with the message *Insert phone number.*, key **(206) 555-3470**, then click on OK.

l. At the dialog box with the message *Insert rep name.*, key **Michael Valenti**, then click on OK.

m. At the dialog box with the message *Insert phone number.*, key **(206) 555-3488**, then click on OK.

4. Save the merged document and name it c25ex13.
5. Print c25ex13.
6. Close c25ex13.
7. Close mpltr3md and save the changes.

**Figure 25.22**

```
All you need to do to accept your First Choice card is to mail your
enclosed Acceptance Form in the postage-paid envelope provided or
call our service representative, { FILLIN "Insert rep name." }, at
{ FILLIN "Insert phone number." }.  In addition to the miles you
will earn, you will also enjoy cash advances available 24 hours a
day, traveler's message service, and toll-free customer service.
```

## SKILL ASSESSMENTS

### Assessment 1

1. Look at the letter in figure 25.24 and the information in figure 25.23. Determine the fields you need for the main document and the data source. Create the data source and name it seprtds. Create the main document shown in figure 25.24, then merge it with seprtds to a new document. (Use Mail Merge Helper to do this.)
2. Save the merged document and name it c25sa01.
3. Print c25sa01.
4. Close c25sa01.
5. Save the main document and name it seprtmd.
6. Close seprtmd.

**Figure 25.23**

```
Mr. and Mrs. Charles Vuong
10421 Fifth Avenue
Petersburg, ND 76322

Ms. Julie Combs
309 Fawcett Drive
Petersburg, ND 76322

Mr. John Stahl
4707 North Oakes
Apartment 4C
Petersburg, ND 76322

Mr. and Mrs. Darrell Wren
21883 South 43rd
Petersburg, ND 76322

Mrs. Rhonda Visell
5404 North Foster
Apartment 206
Petersburg, ND 76322
```

Figure 25.24

(current date)


Name
Address
City, State Zip

Dear (Name):

The results of the parent self-study are attached.  As you read
through the information, you will find there are several areas that
will become a focus for change.  Your input was extremely valuable
and is being used to develop our student learning improvement plan
and to apply for a legislative student learning improvement grant.

A concern that was mentioned repeatedly in the survey was the lack
of computers.  The reason new schools have access to the networking
systems and computers is that it is built into the entire new
school package that is impacted by state matching funds.  One of
the levy components is computer technology to bring existing
schools in line with the technology currently experienced in new
buildings.  We hope that the voter registration drive currently
under way will impact the number of voters going to the polls in
November.

Thank you for your input and for being an integral partner with us
in your child(ren)'s education.  If you would like to discuss the
results further or have additional comments, please give me a call.

Sincerely,



Kathryn Rosell, Principal
Stewart Elementary School

xx:seprtmd

Attachment

## Assessment 2

1. Create an envelope main document for the records in the seprtds data source.
2. Merge the envelope main document with seprtds to a new document.
3. Save the merged document and name it c25sa02.
4. Print c25sa02.
5. Close c25sa02.
6. Save the envelope main document and name it seenvmd.
7. Close seenvmd.

## Assessment 3

1. Create a mailing label main document for the records in the seprtds data source. (Use the 5163 - Shipping mailing labels.)
2. Merge the mailing labels main document with seprtds to a new document.
3. Save the merged document and name it c25sa03.
4. Print c25sa03.
5. Close c25sa03.
6. Save the label main document and name it selblmd.
7. Close selblmd.

## Assessment 4

1. Open nacustmd.
2. Edit nacustmd so it includes Fill-in fields in the first paragraph as shown in figure 25.25.
3. Save the edited main document with Save As and name it naltr2md.
4. Merge the records to a new document. At the dialog boxes asking for the customer number, key the following:

   | Record 1 | = | NA-345 |
   | Record 2 | = | NA-221 |
   | Record 3 | = | NA-430 |
   | Record 4 | = | NA-900 |
   | Record 5 | = | NA-784 |
   | Record 6 | = | NA-663 |

5. Save the merged document and name it c25sa04.
6. Print c25sa04.
7. Close c25sa04.
8. Close naltr2md, saving the changes.

**Figure 25.25**

We have just made it easier for you to use Northeast Annuities' Automated Telephone Service. With your new Personal Identification Number (PIN), together with your customer number, { **FILLIN "Insert customer number."** }, you can easily transfer funds or reallocate premiums.

# Sorting and Selecting 26

Upon successful completion of chapter 26, you will be able to sort information in a properly prepared document and select records from a data source.

Word is a word processing program that includes some basic database functions. Database programs include features that let you alphabetize information or arrange numbers numerically. In addition, with a database program, you can select specific records from a larger file.

In Word, you can sort text in paragraphs, text in rows in tables, or records in a data source. Sorting can be done alphabetically, numerically, or by date. You can also select specific records from a data source to be merged with a main document.

Word can perform the three types of sorts shown in figure 26.1.

**Alphanumeric:** In an alphanumeric sort, Word arranges the text in the following order: special symbols such as @ and # first, numbers second, and letters third. You can tell Word to sort text in all uppercase letters first, followed by words beginning with uppercase letters, then words beginning with lowercase letters.

**Numeric:** In a numeric sort, Word arranges the text in numeric order and ignores any alphabetic text. Only the numbers 0 through 9 and symbols pertaining to numbers (such as $, %, -, (), a decimal point, and a comma) are recognized.

**Date:** In a date sort, Word sorts dates that are expressed in common date format, such as 04-03-96; 04/03/96; April 3, 1996; or 3 April 1996. Word does not sort dates that include abbreviated month names without periods. Dates expressed as a month, day, or year by themselves are also not sorted.

*Figure 26.1*
*Types of Sorts*

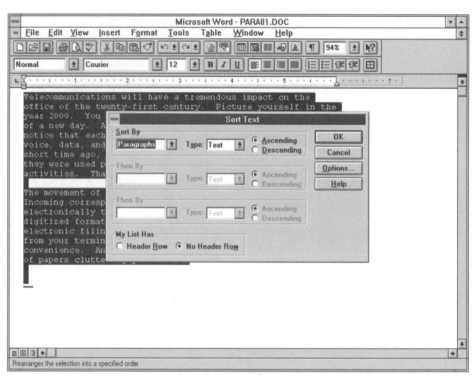

Figure 26.2
Sort Text Dialog
Box

# Sorting Text in Paragraphs

Text arranged in paragraphs can be sorted by the first character of the paragraph. This character can be a number, a symbol (such as $ or #), or a letter. The paragraphs to be sorted can be keyed at the left margin or indented with the Tab key. Unless you select paragraphs to be sorted, Word sorts the entire document.

Paragraphs can be sorted either alphanumerically, numerically, or by date. In an alphanumeric sort, punctuation marks or special symbols are sorted first, followed by numbers, and then text. If you sort paragraphs either alphanumerically or numerically, dates are treated as regular numbers.

To sort text in paragraphs, you would follow these basic steps:

1. Open the document containing the paragraphs to be sorted. (If the document contains text you do not want sorted with the paragraphs, select the paragraphs you want to sort.)
2. Choose Table, Sort Text.
3. At the Sort Text dialog box shown in figure 26.2, make sure *Paragraphs* displays in the Sort By text box and the Ascending option is selected.
4. Choose OK or press Enter.

The Sort By option at the Sort Text dialog box has a default setting of *Paragraphs*. This default setting changes depending on the text in the document. For example, if you are sorting a table, the Sort By option has a default setting of *Column 1*. If you are sorting only the first word of each paragraph in the document, leave the Sort By option at the default of *Paragraphs*.

The Type option at the Sort Text dialog box has a default setting of *Text*. This can be changed to *Number* or *Date*. Figure 26.1 specifies how Word will sort numbers and dates.

When Word sorts paragraphs that are separated by a double space (two hard returns), the hard returns are removed and inserted at the beginning of the document. If you want the sorted text separated by hard returns, you will need to insert the hard returns by positioning the insertion point where you want the hard return, then pressing the Enter key.

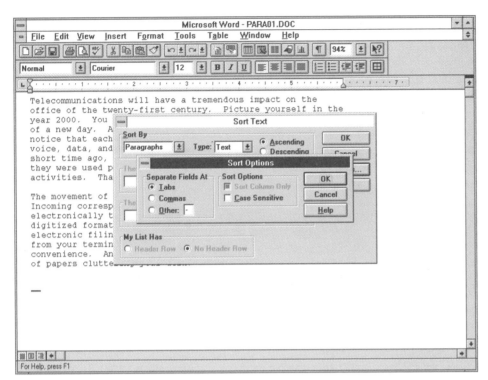

Figure 26.3
*Sort Options Dialog
Box*

## Changing Sort Options

The Sort By options will also vary depending on the options at the Sort Options dialog box shown in figure 26.3. To display the Sort Options dialog box, open a document containing text to be sorted, then choose Table, Sort Text. At the Sort Text dialog box, choose Options.

The Separate Fields At section of the dialog box contains three options. The first option, Tabs, is selected by default. At this setting, Word assumes that text to be sorted is divided by tabs. This can be changed to Commas or Other. With the Other setting, you can specify the character that divides text to be sorted. For example, suppose a document contains first and last names in paragraphs separated by a space and you want to sort by the last name. To do this, you would choose Other at the Sort Options dialog box, then press the space bar. (This inserts a space, which is not visible, in the Other text box.) If names are separated by a comma, choose Commas as the separator.

The Sort Options dialog box contains two options in the Sort Options section. The first option, Sort Column Only, sorts only the selected column. This option is dimmed unless a column of text is selected. If an X appears in the Case Sensitive option, Word will sort text so that a word whose first letter is a capital letter is sorted before any word whose first letter is the same letter in lowercase. This option is available only if *Text* is selected in the Type text box at the Sort Text dialog box.

When you change options at the Sort Options dialog box, the options available with Sort By at the Sort Text dialog box will vary. For example, if you choose Other at the Sort Options dialog box, then press the space bar, the options for Sort By at the Sort Text dialog box will include *Word 1, Word 2, Word 3*, etc.

## ◼ *Sorting Text in Columns*

Text arranged in columns with tabs between the columns can be sorted alphabetically or numerically. Text in columns must be separated with tabs. When sorting text in columns, Word sorts by *fields*. Text keyed at the left margin is considered *Field 1*, text keyed at the first tab stop is considered *Field 2,* and so on. As an example of how to sort columns, you would complete the following steps to sort the first column of text shown in figure 26.4 (keyed at the first tab stop, not the left margin) alphabetically by last name:

1. With the columns displayed in the document screen, select the text in all three columns, except the headings.
2. Choose T<u>a</u>ble, Sor<u>t</u> Text.
3. At the Sort Text dialog box, choose <u>O</u>ptions.
4. At the Sort Options dialog box, make sure <u>T</u>abs is selected in the Separate Fields At section of the dialog box. (If not, choose <u>T</u>abs.)
5. Choose OK or press Enter to close the Sort Options dialog box.
6. At the Sort Text dialog box, choose <u>S</u>ort By. At the drop-down list that displays, choose *Field 2*. (Field 2 is the first tab stop.)
7. Make sure <u>A</u>scending is selected.
8. Choose OK or press Enter.

Figure 26.4
*Columns*

| Employee | School | Ext. |
|----------|--------|------|
| Sinclair, Rodney | Rollins H.S. | 3201 |
| Rosello, Kathryn | Overman E.S. | 1023 |
| McKenzie, Douglas | Oakridge M.S. | 2213 |
| Carl-Rivera, Martha | Rollins H.S. | 3205 |
| Burnett, Russel | Overman E.S. | 1239 |
| Kingsley, Rhonda | Rollins H.S. | 3340 |

With columns of text such as that shown in figure 26.4, only one tab may be inserted between columns. If you press the Tab key more than once between columns, Word recognizes each tab as a separate column. In this case, the field number you specify may correspond to an empty column rather than the desired column.

## Sorting on More Than One Field

When sorting text, you can sort on more than one field. For example, in the text shown in the columns in figure 26.4, you can sort the text alphabetically by school name and then tell Word to sort the last names alphabetically within the school names. To do this, you would complete the following steps:

1. With the columns displayed in the document screen, select the text in all three columns, except the headings.
2. Choose T<u>a</u>ble, Sor<u>t</u> Text.
3. At the Sort Text dialog box, choose <u>O</u>ptions.
4. At the Sort Options dialog box, make sure <u>T</u>abs is selected in the Separate Fields At section of the dialog box. (If not, choose <u>T</u>abs.)
5. Choose OK or press Enter to close the Sort Options dialog box.
6. At the Sort Text dialog box, choose <u>S</u>ort By. At the drop-down list that displays, choose *Field 3*. (Field 3 is the second tab stop.)
7. Choose <u>T</u>hen By, then choose *Field 2* from the drop-down list.
8. Make sure <u>A</u>scending is selected.
9. Choose OK or press Enter.

Word sorts the second column of text (Field 3) alphabetically by school name. Word then sorts the names in the first column of text (Field 2) by last name. This results in the columns displaying as shown in figure 26.5.

| Employee | School | Ext. |
|---|---|---|
| McKenzie, Douglas | Oakridge M.S. | 2213 |
| Burnett, Russel | Overman E.S. | 1239 |
| Rosello, Kathryn | Overman E.S. | 1023 |
| Carl-Rivera, Martha | Rollins H.S. | 3205 |
| Kingsley, Rhonda | Rollins H.S. | 3340 |
| Sinclair, Rodney | Rollins H.S. | 3201 |

**Figure 26.5**
*Sorted Columns*

Notice that the school names in the second column in figure 26.5 are alphabetized and that the last names *within* the school names are alphabetized. For example, *Burnett* is sorted before *Rosello* within *Overman E.S.*

## Specifying a Header Row

The Sort Text dialog box contains the option Header Row in the My Text Has section. If a document contains only columns of text with headings, you can use this option to tell Word to sort all text except for the headings of the columns. For example, to sort the columns of text in figure 26.4 alphabetically by the school name using the Header Row option, you would complete the following steps:

1. With the columns displayed in the document screen, position the insertion point anywhere within the document.
2. Choose Table, Sort Text.
3. At the Sort Text dialog box, choose Header Row in the My List Has section of the dialog box.
4. Choose Options.
5. At the Sort Options dialog box, make sure Tabs is selected in the Separate Fields At section of the dialog box.
6. Choose OK or press Enter to close the Sort Options dialog box.
7. At the Sort Text dialog box, choose Sort By. At the drop-down list that displays, choose *School*.
8. If the Then By text box contains any text, choose Then By, then select *(none)* at the drop-down list.
9. Make sure Ascending is selected.
10. Choose OK or press Enter.

# Sorting Text in Tables

Sorting text in columns within tables is very similar to sorting columns of text separated by tabs. The same principles that apply to sorting columns of text also apply to sorting text within table columns.

If a table contains a header row, you can tell Word to not include the header row when sorting by choosing Header Row at the Sort dialog box. (The Sort Text dialog box becomes the Sort dialog box when sorting a table.) You can also select the cells in the table except the header row and then complete the sort.

If Header Row is selected at the Sort dialog box, the information in the header row becomes the Sort By options. For example, in the table shown in figure 26.6, if Header Row is selected, the Sort By options are *Salesperson, January Sales,* and *February Sales.*

As an example of how to sort text in a table, you would complete the following steps to sort the text numerically in the second column in the table displayed in figure 26.6:

Go To
Exercise
7

1. With the table displayed in the document screen, position the insertion point anywhere within the table.
2. Choose Table, Sort.
3. At the Sort dialog box, choose Header Row in the My List Has section of the dialog box.
4. Choose Sort By. At the drop-down list that displays, choose *January Sales*.
5. Choose Type, then choose *Number* from the drop-down list.
6. Make sure Ascending is selected.
7. Choose OK or press Enter.

**Figure 26.6**
*Table*

| Salesperson | January Sales | February Sales |
|---|---|---|
| Hazelton, Arthur | 130,230.35 | 145,302.45 |
| Blake, Cathy | 99,435.05 | 100,234.23 |
| Charette, Jean | 210,320.43 | 223,100.55 |
| Engelmann, Susan | 245,344.10 | 260,450.25 |

Go To
Exercise
8

In the steps above, you selected Header Row at the Sort dialog box. You can also sort text in a table by first selecting the cells you want sorted, then displaying the Sort dialog box.

## Sorting Records in a Data Source

In chapter 25 you learned how to create a data source document. When a data source document is opened from a main document, the Database toolbar displays below the Formatting toolbar. You can sort records in a data source with the Sort Ascending and Sort Descending buttons on the Database toolbar. In addition to sorting with the buttons on the Database toolbar, you can sort a data source as you learned in the previous section of this chapter, "Sorting Text in Tables." This is because a data source is set up in a table.

As an example of how to use the Sort Ascending and the Sort Descending buttons, you would complete the following steps to sort the records in the mpcustds document that is attached to the mpcustmd document alphabetically by last name:

1. Open mpcustmd.
2. Click on the Edit Data Source button on the Merge toolbar.
3. At the Data Form dialog box, choose View Source.
4. With the data source document displayed, position the insertion point in any cell in the *LastName* column.
5. Click on the Sort Ascending button on the Database toolbar.

Go To
Exercise
9

To sort the records alphabetically in descending order by last name, you would position the insertion point in any cell in the *LastName* column, then click on the Sort Descending button on the Database toolbar.

You can also sort text in a data source like a normal table. For example, to sort the records in the mpcustds document alphabetically by city, you would complete the following steps:

1. Open mpcustds.
2. Position the insertion point in any cell in the table.
3. Choose Table, Sort.
4. At the Sort dialog box, choose Header Row in the My List Has section of the dialog box.
5. Choose Sort By. At the drop-down list that displays, choose *City*.
6. Make sure *Text* displays in the Type text box and Ascending is selected.
7. Choose OK or press Enter.

Go To
Exercise
10

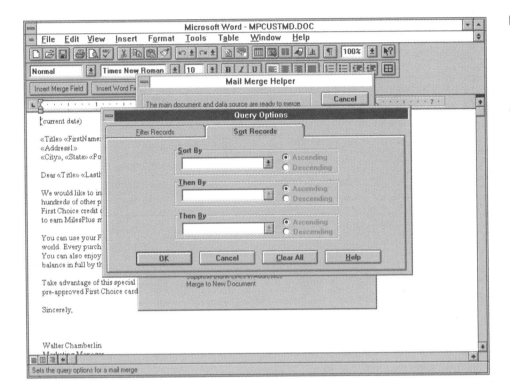

Figure 26.7
*Query Options
Dialog Box with Sort
Records Tab
Selected*

## Sorting at the Query Options Dialog Box

In addition to the two methods just described for sorting records in a data source, you can also sort records at the Query Options dialog box with the Sort Records tab selected. For example, to sort records alphabetically by city in the mpcustds data source document that is attached to the mpcustmd main document, you would complete the following steps:

1. Open mpcustmd.
2. Click on the Mail Merge button on the Merge toolbar.
3. At the Merge dialog box, choose Query Options.
4. At the Query Options dialog box, choose the Sort Records tab.
5. At the Query Options dialog box with the Sort Records tab selected as shown in figure 26.7, choose Sort By, then choose *City* from the drop-down menu.
6. Make sure Ascending is selected.
7. Choose OK or press Enter.
8. At the Merge dialog box, choose Merge if you want to merge the main document with the data source to a new document or choose Close to close the Merge dialog box.

Go To
Exercise
11

# ▇ *Selecting Records*

If you have created a main document and a data source document to create personalized form letters, there may be situations that arise where you want to merge the main document with specific records in the data source. For example, you may want to send the letter to customers with a specific ZIP Code or who live within a certain city.

With options from the Query Options dialog box with the Filter Records tab selected, you can select records for merging with the main document. For example, to specify only those records with the city Federal Way in the mpcustds data source document attached to the mpcustmd main document, you would complete the following steps:

Figure 26.8
Query Options
Dialog Box with
Filter Records Tab
Selected

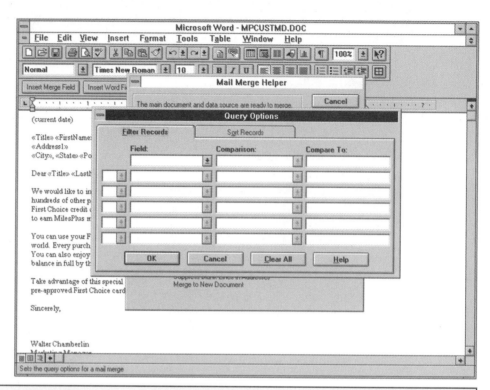

1. Open mpcustmd.
2. Click on the Mail Merge button on the Merge toolbar.
3. At the Merge dialog box, choose Query Options.
4. At the Query Options dialog box, make sure the Filter Records tab is selected. (The dialog box will display as shown in figure 26.8.)
5. Insert *City* in the Field text box. To do this with the mouse, click on the down-pointing arrow to the right of the Field text box, click on the down-pointing arrow at the bottom of the vertical scroll bar until *City* is displayed, then click on *City*. If you are using the keyboard, press the space bar to display the drop-down list, press the down arrow key until *City* is selected, then press Enter. (When *City* is inserted in the Field text box, Word inserts *Equal to* in the Comparison text box and positions the insertion point in the Compare To text box.)
6. With the insertion point positioned in the Compare To text box, key **Federal Way**.
7. Choose OK or press Enter.
8. At the Merge dialog box, choose Merge if you want to merge the main document with the data source to a new document or choose Close to close the Merge dialog box.

When you select a field from the Field drop-down list, Word automatically inserts *Equal to* in the Comparison text box. There are other comparisons you can make. Clicking on the down-pointing arrow to the right of the Comparison text box causes a drop-down list to display with these additional options: *Not Equal to, Less than, Greater than, Less than or Equal, Greater than or Equal, is Blank*, and *is Not Blank*. Use one of these options to create a select equation. For example, you could select all customers with a ZIP Code higher than 90543 by choosing *PostalCode* from the Field drop-down list, choosing *Greater than* from the Comparison drop-down list, and keying **90543** in the Compare To text box.

Go To
Exercise
12

When a field is selected from the Field drop-down list, Word automatically inserts *And* in the first box at the left side of the dialog box. This can be changed, if needed, to *Or*. With the *And* and *Or* options, you can specify more than one condition for selecting records. For example, you could select all records from the city of Seattle with the ZIP Code 98221 in the mpcustds data source attached to the mpcustmd document. To do this, you would complete the following steps:

1. Open mpcustmd.
2. Click on the Mail Merge button on the Merge toolbar.
3. At the Merge dialog box, choose Query Options.
4. At the Query Options dialog box, make sure the Filter Records tab is selected.
5. Insert *City* in the Field text box. To do this with the mouse, click on the down-pointing arrow to the right of the Field text box, click on the down-pointing arrow at the bottom of the vertical scroll bar until *City* is displayed, then click on *City*. If you are using the keyboard, press the space bar to display the drop-down list, press the down arrow key until *City* is selected, then press Enter. (When *City* is inserted in the Field text box, Word inserts *Equal to* in the Comparison text box and positions the insertion point in the Compare To text box.)
6. With the insertion point positioned in the Compare To text box, key **Seattle**.
7. Insert *PostalCode* in the second Field text box (the one below the box containing *City*). To do this, complete steps similar to those listed in step 5 above.
8. With the insertion point positioned in the second Compare To text box (the one below the box containing *Seattle*), key **98221**.
9. Choose OK or press Enter.
10. At the Merge dialog box, choose Merge if you want to merge the main document with the data source to a new document or choose Close to close the Merge dialog box.

If you want to clear the current options at the Query Options dialog box with the Filter Records tab selected, choose Clear All. This clears any text from text boxes and leaves the dialog box on the screen. Choose Cancel if you want to close the Query Options dialog box without specifying any records.

Go To
Exercise
13

## CHAPTER SUMMARY

- Although Word is a word processing program, it includes some basic database functions. Database programs include features that let you alphabetize information or arrange numbers numerically.
- Word lets you sort text in paragraphs, text in table rows, or records in a data source. You can also select specific records from a data source to be merged with a main document.
- Word can perform these three types of sorts: alphanumeric, numeric, and date.
- Text arranged in paragraphs can be sorted by the first character of the paragraph at the Sort Text dialog box.
- The Sort By option at the Sort Text dialog box has a default setting of *Paragraphs*. This Default setting changes depending on the text in the document and options specified at the Sort Options dialog box.
- Text arranged in columns with tabs between the columns can be sorted alphabetically or numerically. Text keyed at the left margin is considered *Field 1*, text keyed at the first tab stop is considered *Field 2*, and so on.
- When sorting text, you can sort on more than one field.
- Use the option Header Row in the My Text Has section of the Sort Text dialog box to tell Word to sort all text in columns except for the headings of the columns.
- Sorting text in columns within tables is very similar to sorting columns of text separated by tabs.
- You can sort records in a data source the same way you sort text in a table, or you can use the Sort Ascending and Sort Descending buttons on the Database toolbar.
- Records can also be sorted at the Query Options dialog box with the Sort Records tab selected.
- With options from the Query Options dialog box with the Filter Records tab selected, you can select records for merging with the main document.

|  | **Mouse** | **Keyboard** |
|---|---|---|
| Display Sort Text dialog box | Table, Sort Text | Table, Sort Text |
| Display Sort Options dialog box | Table, Sort Text, Options | Table, Sort Text, Options |

## CHECK YOUR UNDERSTANDING

**True/False:** Circle the letter T if the statement is true; circle the letter F if the statement is false.

**T  F  1.** Word is a database program that includes some word processing functions.

**T  F  2.** Text arranged in paragraphs can be sorted only if the first character is a letter.

**T  F  3.** Word sorts the entire document unless you select paragraphs to be sorted.

**T  F  4.** When Word sorts paragraphs that are separated by a double space, the hard returns are moved to the beginning of the document.

**T  F  5.** When keying text in columns that may be sorted later, use the default tab settings.

**T  F  6.** You can only sort on one field at a time.

**T  F  7.** Sorting text in columns within tables is very similar to sorting paragraphs.

**T  F  8.** To alphabetically sort records in a data source, click on the Sort Ascending button on the Database toolbar.

**T  F  9.** When selecting records from a data source at the appropriate dialog box, be sure the Filter Records tab is selected.

**T  F  10.** With the *And* and *Or* options, you can specify more than one condition for selecting records.

**Completion:** In the space provided at the right, indicate the correct term, command, or number.

1. With the sorting feature, you can sort text in paragraphs, records in a data source, or this type of text.  _____

2. These three types of sorts can be performed by Word's sort feature: alphanumeric, numeric, and this.  _____

3. Sort text in paragraphs at this dialog box.  _____

4. This is the default selection at the Separate Fields At section of the Sort Options dialog box.  _____

5. When sorting columns, text keyed at the first tab stop is considered to be this field number.  _____

6. Choose this option at the Sort Text dialog box to tell Word not to include the column headings in the sort.  _____

7. When a data source document is opened from a main document, the Database toolbar displays here.  _____

8. You can sort records in a data source as you would a table, or using the Database toolbar, or at this dialog box.  _____

9. Select specific records from a data source to be merged with the main document from this dialog box.  _____

10. To complete the last step to select all customers from a data source that have a balance higher than $500, key **500** at this text box.  _____

## Exercise 1

1. Open biblio01.
2. Save the document with Save As and name it c26ex01.
3. Sort the paragraphs alphabetically by the last name by completing the following steps:
   a. Choose Table, Sort Text.
   b. At the Sort Text dialog box, make sure *Paragraphs* displays in the Sort By text box and the Ascending option is selected.
   c. Choose OK or press Enter.
   d. Deselect the text.
   e. Delete the hard returns at the beginning of the document.
   f. Position the insertion point immediately left of the letter *F* in *Fischer,* then press the Enter key.
   g. Position the insertion point immediately left of the letter *M* in *Makalena,* then press the Enter key.
   h. Position the insertion point immediately left of the letter *S* in *Salas,* then press the Enter key.
4. Save the document again with the same name (c26ex01).
5. Print c26ex01.
6. Close c26ex01.

## Exercise 2

1. At a clear document screen, key the text shown in figure 26.9. Begin each line of text at the left margin.
2. After keying the text, save the document and name it c26ex02.
3. With c26ex02 still open in the document screen, sort the text alphabetically by first name by completing the following steps:
   a. Choose Table, Sort Text.
   b. At the Sort Text dialog box, make sure *Paragraphs* displays in the Sort By text box and the Ascending option is selected.
   c. Choose OK or press Enter.
   d. Deselect the text.
4. Save the document again with the same name (c26ex02).
5. Print c26ex02.
6. With c26ex02 still displayed in the document screen, sort the text by the last name (second word) by completing the following steps:
   a. Choose Table, Sort Text.
   b. At the Sort Text dialog box, choose Options.
   c. At the Sort Options dialog box, choose Other, then press the space bar.
   d. Choose OK or press Enter.
   e. At the Sort Text dialog box, choose Sort By, then *Word 2*.
   f. Make sure the Ascending option is selected.
   g. Choose OK or press Enter.
   h. Deselect the text.
7. Save the document again with the same name (c26ex02).
8. Print c26ex02.
9. Close c26ex02.

```
Rafael Ohala, Labor and Delivery
Rosemary Stratten, Emergency Room
Benjamin Moon, Intensive Care Unit
Sandra Ellerbe, Medical Services
Joan Harris-Lee, Surgical Unit
Alyce Arevalo, Pediatrics
Lisa Murray, Coronary Care Unit
```

## Exercise 3

1. At a clear document screen, create the document shown in figure 26.10 by completing the following steps:
   a. Set left tabs at 0.5 inches, 2.5 inches, and 5 inches.
   b. Key the text in columns as shown in figure 26.10. Press the Tab key before keying each entry in the first column.
2. Save the document and name it c26ex03.
3. With c26ex03 still displayed in the document screen, sort the first column alphabetically by last name by completing the following steps:
   a. Select the text in all three columns except the headings.
   b. Choose Table, Sort Text.
   c. At the Sort Text dialog box, choose Options.
   d. At the Sort Options dialog box, make sure Tabs is selected in the Separate Fields At section of the dialog box. (If not, choose Tabs.)
   e. Choose OK or press Enter to close the Sort Options dialog box.
   f. At the Sort Text dialog box, choose Sort By. At the drop-down list that displays, choose *Field 2*. (Field 2 is the first tab stop.)
   g. Make sure Ascending is selected.
   h. Choose OK or press Enter.
   i. Deselect the text.
4. Save the document again with the same name (c26ex03).
5. Print c26ex03.
6. With c26ex03 still open in the document screen, sort the third column of text numerically by completing the following steps:
   a. Select the text in all three columns except the headings.
   b. Choose Table, Sort Text.
   c. At the Sort Text dialog box, choose Options.
   d. At the Sort Options dialog box, make sure Tabs is selected in the Separate Fields At section of the dialog box. (If not, choose Tabs.)
   e. Choose OK or press Enter to close the Sort Options dialog box.
   f. At the Sort Text dialog box, choose Sort By. At the drop-down list that displays, choose *Field 4*. (Field 4 is the third tab stop.)
   g. Make sure *Number* displays in the Type text box. (If not, choose Type, then choose *Number* from the drop-down list.)
   h. Make sure Ascending is selected.
   i. Choose OK or press Enter.
   j. Deselect the text.
7. Save the document again with the same name (c26ex03).
8. Print c26ex03.
9. Close c26ex03.

Figure 26.10

| Employee | Department | Ext. |
|----------|------------|------|
| Levine, Kenneth | Administration | 1200 |
| Hogue, Brenda | Training & Education | 4320 |
| Greerson, Leslie | Human Resources | 2099 |
| Jackson, Mariah | Administration | 2056 |
| Aversen, Leah | Training & Education | 2114 |
| Pauline Coffey | Training & Education | 2443 |
| Lavell, Roland | Administration | 2190 |
| Adams, Joan | Human Resources | 3105 |

## Exercise 4

1. At a clear document screen, create the document shown in figure 26.11. (Set left tabs for the columns, including the first column. Press the Tab key before keying each entry in the first column.)
2. Save the document and name it c26ex04.
3. With c26ex04 still displayed in the document screen, sort the second column by date by completing the following steps:
   a. Select the text in all three columns except the title.
   b. Choose Table, Sort Text.
   c. At the Sort Text dialog box, choose Options.
   d. At the Sort Options dialog box, make sure Tabs is selected in the Separate Fields At section of the dialog box. (If not, choose Tabs.)
   e. Choose OK or press Enter to close the Sort Options dialog box.
   f. At the Sort Text dialog box, choose Sort By. At the drop-down list that displays, choose *Field 3*. (Field 3 is the second tab stop.)
   g. Make sure *Date* appears in the Type text box and Ascending is selected.
   h. Choose OK or press Enter.
   i. Deselect the text.
4. Save the document again with the same name (c26ex04).
5. Print c26ex04.
6. Close c26ex04.

Figure 26.11

**TRAINING SCHEDULE**

| | | |
|---|---|---|
| Recordkeeping | 04/09/96 | 1:00 - 3:00 p.m. |
| Word Processing | 03/12/96 | 9:00 - 11:00 a.m. |
| Database | 06/06/96 | 1:30 - 3:30 p.m. |
| Spreadsheet | 02/15/96 | 2:00 - 3:30 p.m. |

## Exercise 5

1. Open c26ex03.
2. Save the document with Save As and name it c26ex05.
3. Sort the text in columns alphabetically by department, then alphabetically by last name by completing the following steps:
   a. Select the text in all three columns, except the headings.
   b. Choose Table, Sort Text.
   c. At the Sort Text dialog box, choose Options.
   d. At the Sort Options dialog box, make sure Tabs is selected in the Separate Fields At section of the dialog box. (If not, choose Tabs.)

e. Choose OK or press Enter to close the Sort Options dialog box.
f. At the Sort Text dialog box, choose Sort By. At the drop-down list that displays, choose *Field 3*. (Field 3 is the second tab stop.)
g. Choose Then By, then choose *Field 2* from the drop-down list.
h. Make sure Ascending is selected.
i. Choose OK or press Enter.
j. Deselect the text.
4. Save the document again with the same name (c26ex05).
5. Print c26ex05.
6. Close c26ex05.

## Exercise 6

1. Open c26ex03.
2. Save the document with Save As and name it c26ex06.
3. Sort the third column of text numerically by the extension number by completing the following steps:
   a. With the columns displayed in the document screen, position the insertion point anywhere within the document.
   b. Choose Table, Sort Text.
   c. At the Sort Text dialog box, choose Header Row in the My List Has section of the dialog box.
   d. Choose Options.
   e. At the Sort Options dialog box, make sure Tabs is selected in the Separate Fields At section of the dialog box. (If not, choose Tabs.)
   f. Choose OK or press Enter to close the Sort Options dialog box.
   g. At the Sort Text dialog box, choose Sort By. At the drop-down list that displays, choose *Ext.*
   h. Make sure Ascending is selected.
   i. Choose OK or press Enter.
   j. Deselect the text.
4. Save the document again with the same name (c26ex06).
5. Print c26ex06.
6. Close c26ex06.

## Exercise 7

1. Open table03.
2. Save the document with Save As and name it c26ex07.
3. Sort the text alphabetically in the first column by completing the following steps:
   a. Position the insertion point anywhere within the table.
   b. Choose Table, Sort.
   c. At the Sort dialog box, choose Header Row in the My List Has section of the dialog box.
   d. Choose Sort By. At the drop-down list that displays, choose *Stock*.
   e. Make sure Ascending is selected.
   f. Choose OK or press Enter.
4. Save the document again with the same name (c26ex07).
5. Print c26ex07.
6. Close c26ex07.

## Exercise 8

1. Open c26ex07.
2. Save the document with Save As and name it c26ex08.
3. Sort the numbers in the second column in descending order by completing the following steps:

a. Select all the cells in the table except the cells in the first row.
b. Choose Table, Sort.
c. At the Sort dialog box, choose Sort By. At the drop-down list that displays, choose *Column 2*.
d. Choose Descending.
e. Choose OK or press Enter.
4. With the insertion point positioned anywhere in the table, display the Table AutoFormat dialog box, then apply the *Classic 2* format.
5. Save the document again with the same name (c26ex08).
6. Print c26ex08.
7. Close c26ex08.

## Exercise 9

1. Sort the records in the nacustds document that is attached to the nacustmd document numerically by PIN number by completing the following steps:
   a. Open nacustmd.
   b. Click on the Edit Data Source button on the Merge toolbar.
   c. At the Data Form dialog box, choose View Source.
   d. With the data source document displayed, position the insertion point in any cell in the *PIN* column.
   e. Click on the Sort Ascending button on the Database toolbar.
   f. Deselect the text.
2. Print the sorted data source by clicking on the Print button on the Standard toolbar.
3. Close nacustds without saving the changes.
4. Close nacustmd without saving the changes.

## Exercise 10

1. Sort the records in the mpcustds document numerically by ZIP Code by completing the following steps:
   a. Open mpcustds.
   b. Position the insertion point in any cell in the table.
   c. Choose Table, Sort.
   d. At the Sort dialog box, choose Header Row in the My List Has section of the dialog box. (This option may already be selected.)
   e. Choose Sort By. At the drop-down list that displays, choose *PostalCode*.
   f. Make sure *Number* displays in the Type text box.
   g. Make sure Ascending is selected. (If not, choose Ascending.)
   h. Choose OK or press Enter.
   i. Deselect the text.
2. Print mpcustds.
3. Close mpcustds without saving the changes.

## Exercise 11

1. Sort the records alphabetically by *LastName* in the mpcustds data source document attached to the mpcustmd main document by completing the following steps:
   a. Open mpcustmd.
   b. Click on the Mail Merge button on the Merge toolbar.
   c. At the Merge dialog box, choose Query Options.
   d. At the Query Options dialog box, choose the Sort Records tab.
   e. At the Query Options dialog box with the Sort Records tab selected, choose Sort By, then choose *LastName* from the drop-down list.
   f. Make sure Ascending is selected.

g. Choose OK or press Enter.

h. At the Merge dialog box, choose Close.

i. Click on the Edit Data Source button on the Merge toolbar.

j. At the Data Form dialog box, choose <u>V</u>iew Source.

2. With the data source document displayed, click on the Print button on the Standard toolbar.

3. Close mpcustds without saving the changes.

4. Close mpcustmd without saving the changes.

## Exercise 12

1. Select the records with a PIN higher than 30000 in the nacustds data source document attached to the nacustmd main document, then merge the records to a new document by completing the following steps:

    a. Open nacustmd.

    b. Click on the Mail Merge button on the Merge toolbar.

    c. At the Merge dialog box, choose <u>Q</u>uery Options.

    d. At the Query Options dialog box, make sure the <u>F</u>ilter Records tab is selected.

    e. Insert *PIN* in the Field text box. To do this with the mouse, click on the down-pointing arrow to the right of the Field text box, click on the down-pointing arrow at the bottom of the vertical scroll bar until *PIN* is displayed, then click on *PIN*. If you are using the keyboard, press the space bar to display the drop-down list, press the down arrow key until *PIN* is selected, then press Enter. (When *PIN* is inserted in the Field text box, Word inserts *Equal to* in the Comparison text box and positions the insertion point in the Compare To text box.)

    f. With the insertion point positioned in the Compare To text box, key **30000**.

    g. Insert *Greater than* in the Comparison text box. To do this with the mouse, click on the down-pointing arrow to the right of the first Comparison text box, then click on *Greater than*. If you are using the keyboard, press Shift + Tab to select *Greater than* in the Comparison text box, press the space bar, press the down arrow key until *Greater than* is selected, then press Enter.

    h. Choose OK or press Enter.

    i. At the Merge dialog box, make sure *New Document* displays in the Me<u>r</u>ge To text box, then choose <u>M</u>erge.

2. Save the merged document and name it c26ex12.

3. Print c26ex12.

4. Close c26ex12.

5. Close nacustmd without saving the changes.

## Exercise 13

1. Select the records in the mpcustds data source document attached to the mpcustmd main document that contain the city Redmond or Federal Way by completing the following steps:

    a. Open mpcustmd.

    b. Click on the Mail Merge button on the Merge toolbar.

    c. At the Merge dialog box, choose <u>Q</u>uery Options.

    d. At the Query Options dialog box, make sure the <u>F</u>ilter Records tab is selected.

    e. Insert *City* in the Field text box. To do this with the mouse, click on the down-pointing arrow to the right of the Field text box, click on the down-pointing arrow at the bottom of the vertical scroll bar until *City* is displayed, then click on *City*. If you are using the keyboard, press the space bar to display the drop-down list, press the down arrow key until *City* is selected, then press Enter.

    f. With the insertion point positioned in the Compare To text box, key **Redmond**.

    g. Click on the down-pointing arrow to the right of the text containing the word *And* (at the left side of the dialog box). From the drop-down list that displays, click on *Or*.

h. Insert *City* in the second Field text box (the one below the box containing *City*). To do this, complete steps similar to those listed in step 1e above.

i. With the insertion point positioned in the second Compare To text box (the one below the box containing *Redmond*), key **Federal Way**.

j. Choose OK or press Enter.

k. At the Merge dialog box, make sure *New Document* displays in the Me<u>r</u>ge To text box, then choose <u>M</u>erge.

2. Save the merged document and name it c26ex13.
3. Print c26ex13.
4. Close c26ex13.
5. Close mpcustmd without saving the changes.

## SKILL ASSESSMENTS

### Assessment 1

1. At a clear document screen, create the document shown in figure 26.12.
2. Save the document and name it c26sa01.
3. Sort the names (not the titles) alphabetically by last name.
4. Save the sorted document again with the same name (c26sa01).
5. Print c26sa01.
6. Close c26sa01.

**Figure 26.12**

```
PETERSBURG SCHOOL DISTRICT


Dorothy Warner, Superintendent
David O'Shea, Assistant Superintendent
Damion Japhet, Curriculum/Instruction Specialist
Donna Schmitt, Support Services Specialist
Alex Perozzo, Information Specialist
Jon Struebing, Newsletter Editor
Karen Delano, Assistant Newsletter Editor
```

### Assessment 2

1. At a clear document screen, create the document shown in figure 26.13. (Set tabs for each column of text in the document.)
2. Save the document and name it c26sa02.
3. Sort the first column of text alphabetically by last name. (*Hint: Select the columns of text but not the title, subtitle, and headings.*)
4. Print c26sa02.
5. Sort the columns of text by the date of hire in the third column.
6. Print c26sa02.
7. Sort the columns of text alphabetically by the department name and then alphabetically by last name.
8. Save the document again with the same name (c26sa02).
9. Print c26sa02.
10. Close c26sa02.

Figure 26.13

**LIFETIME ANNUITIES ASSOCIATION**

**New Employees**

| Employee | Department | Hire Date |
|----------|------------|-----------|
| Neiman, Randy | Human Resources | 05/23/96 |
| Groux, Diana | Accounting | 04/23/96 |
| Alegado, Jose | Human Resources | 03/11/96 |
| Langaard, Ann | Security | 01/22/96 |
| Morrell, Paula | Accounting | 02/20/96 |
| Poynter, Chris | Human Resources | 06/20/96 |
| Roberts, Jay | Security | 05/15/96 |

## Assessment 3

1. Open table02.
2. Save the document with Save As and name it c26sa03.
3. Sort the text in the first column of the table alphabetically.
4. Print c26sa03.
5. Sort the text in the second column of the table numerically in ascending order.
6. Display the Table AutoFormat dialog box and apply a table formatting of your choosing to the table.
7. Save the document again with the same name (c26sa03).
8. Print c26sa03.
9. Close c26sa03.

## Assessment 4

1. Create a main document for envelopes that has the mpcustds data source document attached, then merge the envelope with those records in mpcustds with a ZIP Code higher than *98100*. Merge to a new document. (*Hint: Begin at the Mail Merge Helper dialog box.*)
2. Save the merged document and name it c26sa04.
3. Print c26sa04.
4. Close c26sa04.
5. Close the envelope main document without saving the changes.

# Creating Outlines 27

Upon successful completion of chapter 27, you will be able to enhance the formatting and organization of business reports with Word's outlining feature.

Word's outlining feature will format headings within a document as well as let you view formatted headings and body text in a document. With the outlining feature you can quickly see an overview of a document by collapsing parts of a document so that only the headings show. With headings collapsed, you can perform such editing functions as moving or deleting sections of a document.

## Creating an Outline

To create an outline, you identify particular headings and subheadings within a document as certain heading levels. Switch to the Outline view to assign particular heading levels to text. You can also enter text and edit text while working in Outline view. To change to the Outline view, click on the Outline View button at the left side of the horizontal scroll bar, or choose View, then Outline. Figure 27.1 shows the report01 document in Outline view with heading levels applied to the title and headings in the document.

In Figure 27.1, the title, *TYPE SPECIFICATION*, has been identified as a first-level heading, the subheading *Type Measurement* identified as a second-level heading, and the paragraphs following as normal text.

When a document contains headings and text that have been formatted in the Outline view, each paragraph is identified as a particular heading level or as normal text. Paragraphs are identified by *paragraph selection symbols* that appear in the selection bar at the left side of the screen. Figure 27.2 describes the three outline selection symbols and what they indicate.

Figure 27.1
*Document in
Outline View*

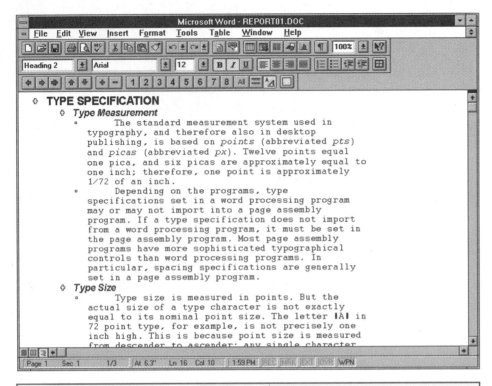

Figure 27.2
*Outline Selection
Symbols*

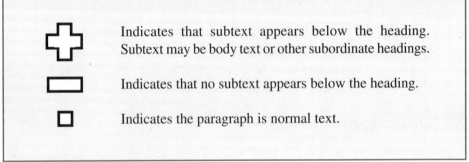

The outline selection symbols can be used to select text in the document. To do this, position the arrow pointer on an outline selection symbol next to text you want to select until it turns into a four-headed arrow, then click the left mouse button. For example, to select a paragraph of text in Outline view, you would complete the following steps:

1. Position the arrow pointer on the ☐ symbol that displays before the paragraph you want to select until it turns into a four-headed arrow.
2. Click the left mouse button.

# ■ *Assigning Headings*

When a document is displayed in Outline view, the Outline toolbar displays below the Formatting toolbar as shown in figure 27.1. Use buttons on this toolbar to assign various heading levels and outline numbers to paragraphs.

When you initially display a document in Outline view, each paragraph is identified as a normal text paragraph. To identify certain paragraphs as heading levels, use the arrow buttons at the left side of the Outline toolbar. These buttons and their keyboard equivalents are described in figure 27.3 along with the other buttons on the Outline toolbar.

| Button | Name | Keyboard Command | Action |
|---|---|---|---|
| ◄ | Promote | ALT + SHIFT + ← | Promotes heading (and its body text) by one level; promotes body text to the heading level of the preceding heading. |
| ► | Demote | ALT + SHIFT + → | Demotes heading by one level; demotes body text to the heading level below the preceding heading. |
| ⇒ | Demote to Body Text | ALT + SHIFT + 5 | Demotes heading to body text. |
| ▲ | Move Up | (None) | Moves selected paragraph(s) before first visible paragraph that precedes selected paragraph(s). |
| ▼ | Move Down | (None) | Moves selected paragraph(s) after first visible paragraph that follows selected paragraph(s). |
| + | Expand | ALT + SHIFT + − (or - key on keypad) | Expands first heading level below currently selected heading. |
| − | Collapse | ALT + SHIFT + + (or + key on keypad) | Collapses body text into heading then collapses lowest heading levels into higher heading levels. |
| | Show Headings 1 through 8 | ALT + SHIFT + # | Displays all headings and text through lowest level button chosen. |
| All | All | ALT + SHIFT + A | Displays all text if some collapsed; displays only headings if all text already expanded. |

Figure 27.3
*Outline Toolbar Buttons*

| Button | Name | Keyboard Command | Action |
|--------|------|------------------|--------|
| ☰ | Show First Line Only | (None) | Switches between displaying all body text or only first line of each paragraph. |
| ᴬ/A | Show Formatting | (None) | Displays outline with or without character formatting. |
| ▢ | Master Document View | (None) | Changes to master document view or back to outline view. Displays Master Document toolbar to right of Outline toolbar. |

To change a paragraph that is identified as normal text to a first-level heading, you would complete the following steps:

1. Position the insertion point on any character in the text (or select the text).
2. Click on the Promote button on the Outline toolbar; or press Alt + Shift + left arrow.

This applies the *Heading 1* style to the paragraph. The *Heading 1* style is a style that has been predefined by Word. This style displays in the Style button on the Formatting toolbar. (First button at left side.) The *Heading 1* style sets the text in 14-point Arial Bold.

To change a paragraph to a second-level heading, position the insertion point anywhere within the text, then click on the Demote button or press Alt + Shift + right arrow. This applies the *Heading 2* style to the text. The *Heading 2* style sets text in 12-point Arial Bold Italic and indents the text 0.5 inches. Figure 27.4 shows the formatting that is applied for each heading level.

*Figure 27.4*
*Heading Formatting*

| | |
|---|---|
| Heading 1 | 14-point Arial Bold |
| Heading 2 | 12-point Arial Bold Italic; indented 0.5 inches from left margin |
| Heading 3 | 12-point Times New Roman Bold; indented 1 inch from left margin |
| Heading 4 | 12-point Times New Roman Bold Italic; indented 1.5 inches from left margin |
| Heading 5 | 11-point Arial; indented 2 inches from left margin |
| Heading 6 | 11-point Arial Italic; indented 2.5 inches from left margin |
| Heading 7 | 10-point Arial; indented 3 inches from left margin |
| Heading 8 | 10-point Arial Italic; indented 3.5 inches from left margin |
| Heading 9 | 9-point Arial Italic; indented 4 inches from left margin |

You can also promote or demote a heading in the Outline view by dragging the heading symbol to the left or right 0.5 inches. For example, to demote text identified as a Heading 1 to Heading 2, you would complete the following steps:

1. Position the arrow pointer on the plus symbol before the Heading 1 text until it turns into a four-headed arrow.
2. Hold down the left mouse button, drag the mouse to the right until a gray vertical line displays down the screen, then release the mouse button.

To promote a heading, complete similar steps. For example, to promote a Heading 2 to a Heading 1, you would complete the following steps:

1. Position the arrow pointer on the plus symbol before the Heading 2 text until it turns into a four-headed arrow.
2. Hold down the left mouse button, drag the mouse to the left until a gray vertical bar displays with a small square attached, then release the mouse button.

To demote a heading, position the insertion point in the heading text, then click on the Demote to Text button on the Outline toolbar; or press Alt + Shift + 5 (on the numeric keypad). If you use the keyboard command, make sure Num Lock is turned off.

## Collapsing and Expanding Outline Headings

The real benefit of working in the Outline view is the ability to see a condensed outline of your document without all of the text in between headings or subheadings. Word lets you collapse a heading level in an outline. This causes any text or subsequent lower heading levels to disappear temporarily. When heading levels are collapsed, viewing the outline of a document is much easier. For example, when an outline is collapsed, you can see an overview of the entire document and move quickly around in the document. You can also move headings and their subordinate headings to new locations in the outline.

The ability to collapse and expand headings in an outline gives you great flexibility in using Word's outline feature. One popular use of this capability is to move quickly from one portion of a document to another. For example, if you are working at the beginning of a lengthy document and you wish to move to a particular section, but you cannot remember the name of the heading in that section or the page number on which it is located, you can switch to the Outline view, collapse the entire outline, position the insertion point in the desired heading, then expand the outline.

Another popular use of the collapse and expand feature is in maintaining consistency between various headings. While creating a particular heading, you may need to refer to the previous heading. To do this, switch to the Outline view, collapse the outline, and the previous heading is visible.

To collapse the entire outline, click on the Show Heading button number that corresponds to the number of headings desired. For example, if a document contains three heading levels, clicking on the Show Heading 2 button on the Outline toolbar will collapse the outline so only heading 1 and heading 2 text are displayed.

The first time you click on the All button on the Outline toolbar, the document collapses and only heading text is displayed, not body text. Click on the All button again and the document expands to show all heading levels and body text. If you are using the keyboard, press Alt + Shift + A. If you click on the All button or press Alt + Shift + A for the document shown in figure 27.1, the document would display as shown in figure 27.5. When a heading is collapsed, a gray horizontal line displays beneath it.

Figure 27.5
Collapsed Outline

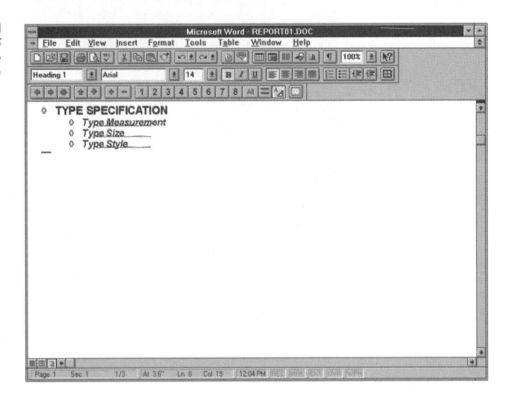

To collapse all of the text beneath a particular heading (including the text following any subsequent headings), position the insertion point within the heading, then click on the Collapse button on the Outline toolbar. If you are using the keyboard, press the gray minus key on the numeric keypad or press Alt + Shift + - (hyphen) to collapse the text below the heading. To make the text appear again, click on the Expand button on the Outline toolbar; press the gray plus key on the numeric keypad; or press Alt + Shift + plus symbol. For example, if you collapsed the first second-level heading shown in the document in figure 27.1, the document would display as shown in figure 27.6.

Figure 27.6
Collapsed Second-
Level Heading

# ■Organizing an Outline

Collapsing and expanding headings within an outline are only part of the versatility offered by Word's outline feature. It also offers you the ability to rearrange an entire document by reorganizing an outline. Whole sections of a document can quickly be rearranged by moving the headings at the beginning of those sections. The text that is collapsed beneath the headings is moved at the same time.

For example, to move a second-level heading below other second-level headings, you would collapse the outline, select the second-level heading to be moved, then click on the Move Down button on the Outline toolbar until the second-level heading is in the desired position. For example, to move the second-level heading *Type Measurement* below the second-level heading *Type Size* in the document shown in figure 27.1, you would complete the following steps:

1. Click on the All button on the Outline toolbar or press Alt + Shift + A to collapse the outline.
2. Position the arrow pointer in the selection bar to the left of the plus symbol before *Type Measurement* until it turns into an arrow pointing up and to the left, then click the left mouse button. (This selects *Type Measurement*.)
3. Click on the Move Down button on the Outline toolbar.

If headings are collapsed, you only need to select the heading and move it to the desired location. Any subsequent text that is hidden is moved automatically.

You can also move headings in a document by completing the following steps:

1. Position the arrow pointer on the plus symbol before the desired heading until it turns into a four-headed arrow.
2. Hold down the mouse button, drag the heading to the desired location, then release the mouse button.

As you drag the mouse, a gray horizontal line displays in the document with an arrow attached. Use this horizontal line to help you move the heading to the desired location.

# ■Numbering an Outline

Headings in an outline can be automatically numbered with options from the Heading Numbering dialog box. If headings in an outline are moved, inserted, or deleted, the headings are automatically renumbered by Word. Heading numbers become part of the document and display in the Normal and Page Layout viewing modes as well as the Outline view.

To number headings in an outline, you would complete the following steps:

1. Open the document containing text formatted with outlining.
2. Click on the Outline View button to the left of the horizontal scroll bar or choose View, then Outline to change to the Outline viewing mode.
3. With the insertion point positioned anywhere within the document, choose Format, then Heading Numbering.
4. At the Heading Numbering dialog box shown in figure 27.7, choose the desired numbering style, then choose OK or press Enter.

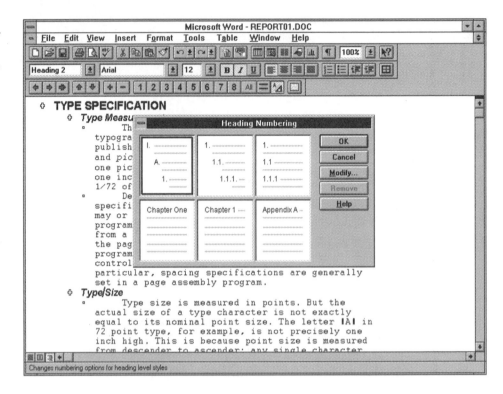

## CHAPTER SUMMARY

- In Word's outlining feature you can format headings within a document as well as view formatted headings and body text in a document.

- To create an outline, first identify particular headings and subheadings within a document as certain heading levels. The Outline view is used to assign particular heading levels to text.

- When a document contains headings and text that have been formatted in the Outline view, the paragraphs are identified by one of the *paragraph selection symbols* that appear in the selection bar at the left side of the screen.

- The outline selection symbols can be used to select text in the document.

- When a document is displayed in Outline view, the Outline toolbar displays below the Formatting toolbar. Use buttons on the Outline toolbar to assign various level headings to paragraphs.

- When a paragraph is identified as a first-level heading, the Heading 1 style is applied to that paragraph. This style sets the text in 14-point Arial Bold.

- Heading 2 style is applied to a paragraph identified as a second-level heading. This style sets text in 12-point Arial Bold Italic and indents the text 0.5 inches.

- The advantage of working in the Outline view is the ability to see a condensed outline of your document without all of the text in between headings or subheadings.

- Another benefit of working in the Outline view is in maintaining consistency between various headings.

- Word's outline feature offers you the ability to rearrange an entire document by rearranging an outline.

- Headings in an outline can be automatically numbered with options from the Heading Numbering dialog box. If headings in an outline are moved, inserted, or deleted, the headings are automatically renumbered.

|  | **Mouse** | **Keyboard** |
|---|---|---|
| Change to Outline view | Click on Outline view button at left side of horizontal scroll bar; or choose View, Outline | View, Outline |

## CHECK YOUR UNDERSTANDING

**Matching:** Choose the term from the first list that best matches the description in the second list. Terms may be chosen more than once.

- A. Outline view
- B. paragraph selection symbols
- C. normal text
- D. Outline toolbar
- E. Heading Numbering dialog box
- F. Alt + Shift + right arrow
- G. Alt + Shift + left arrow
- H. Heading 1
- I. Heading 2
- J. Collapse
- K. Expand
- L. Move Down

1. Paragraphs are first displayed as this in Outline view. _____
2. Keyboard command that changes a paragraph of normal text to a second-level heading. _____
3. 12-point Arial Bold Italic. _____
4. Outline toolbar button used to rearrange sections of a document. _____
5. Used to assign particular heading levels to text. _____
6. Indents paragraph 0.5 inches from left margin. _____
7. Text temporarily disappears. _____
8. Appear(s) in the selection bar at the left side of the screen. _____
9. Click on this Outline toolbar button to make collapsed text appear. _____
10. 14-point Arial Bold. _____

## AT THE COMPUTER

### Exercise 1

1. Open report01.
2. Save the document with Save As and name it c27ex01.
3. Change to the Outline viewing mode by choosing View, then Outline; or clicking on the View Outline button to the left of the horizontal scroll bar.
4. Promote and demote heading levels by completing the following steps:
   a. Position the insertion point anywhere in the title, *TYPE SPECIFICATION*, then click on the Promote button on the Outline toolbar, or press Alt + Shift + left arrow. (*Heading 1* will display in the Style button on the Formatting toolbar.)
   b. Position the insertion point anywhere in the subheading *Type Measurement*, then click on the Demote button on the Outline toolbar, or press Alt + Shift + right arrow. (*Heading 2* will display in the Style button on the Formatting toolbar.)

    c. Position the insertion point on the subheading *Type Size*, then click on the Promote button or press Alt + Shift + left arrow. (*Heading 2* will display in the Style button on the Formatting toolbar.)

    d. Position the insertion point on the subheading *Type Style*, then click on the Promote button or press Alt + Shift + left arrow. (*Heading 2* will display in the Style button on the Formatting toolbar.)

5. Change the view back to Normal by choosing <u>V</u>iew, then <u>N</u>ormal or clicking on the Normal View button to the left of the horizontal scroll bar.

6. Center align the title, *TYPE SPECIFICATION*.

7. Select the last four paragraphs of text in the document, then add bullets.

8. Save the document again with the same name (c27ex01).

9. Print c27ex01.

10. Close c27ex01.

## Exercise 2

1. Open report06.

2. Save the document with Save As and name it c27ex02.

3. Change to the Outline viewing mode by choosing <u>V</u>iew, <u>O</u>utline or clicking on the Outline View button to the left of the horizontal scroll bar.

4. Promote the title, *CHOOSING BINDING*, to a Heading 1 level by completing the following steps:

    a. Position the insertion point on the square symbol before *CHOOSING BINDING* until it turns into a four-headed arrow.

    b. Hold down the left mouse button, drag the mouse to the left until a gray vertical line displays down the screen, then release the mouse button.

5. Demote the heading *Saddle and Side Stitching* to a Heading 2 level by completing the following steps:

    a. Position the insertion point on the square symbol before *Saddle and Side Stitching* until it turns into a four-headed arrow.

    b. Hold down the left mouse button, drag the mouse to the right until a gray vertical line displays down the screen (the first gray line), then release the mouse button.

6. Promote the heading *Mechanical Binding* to a Heading 2 level by completing the following steps:

    a. Position the insertion point on the square symbol before *Mechanical Binding* until it turns into a four-headed arrow.

    b. Hold down the left mouse button, drag the mouse to the left until the first gray vertical bar displays, then release the mouse button.

7. Promote the heading *Book Binding* to a Heading 2 level by completing steps similar to those in 6a and 6b.

8. Change the viewing mode back to Normal by choosing <u>V</u>iew, then <u>N</u>ormal or clicking on the Normal View button to the left of the horizontal scroll bar.

9. Select the three numbered paragraphs, 1), 2), and 3), then press Ctrl + T to hang indent the text.

10. Save the document again with the same name (c27ex02).

11. Print c27ex02.

12. Close c27ex02.

## Exercise 3

1. Open c27ex01.

2. Save the document with Save As and name it c27ex03.

3. Change to the Outline viewing mode.

4. Collapse the entire outline by clicking on the All button on the Outline toolbar.

5. With the outline collapsed, select the heading *Type Size*, then delete it. (This deletes the heading and all text below the heading.)
6. Change to the Normal viewing mode.
7. Save the document again with the same name (c27ex03).
8. Print c27ex03.
9. Close c27ex03.

## Exercise 4

1. Open c27ex02.
2. Save the document with Save As and name it c27ex04.
3. Make the following changes to the document:
    a. Change to the Outline viewing mode.
    b. Position the insertion point anywhere in the title, *CHOOSING BINDING*, then click on the Collapse button on the Outline toolbar. (This collapses the document so only the title and headings display.)
    c. Click on the Expand button to expand the display of the document.
    d. With the insertion point still positioned anywhere in the title, *CHOOSING BINDING*, click on the Show Heading 1 button on the Outline toolbar. (This displays only the title.)
    e. Click on the Show Heading 2 button on the Outline toolbar. (This displays the title and headings.)
    f. Click on the Expand button on the Outline toolbar.
    g. Click on the Show First Line Only button on the Outline toolbar. (This displays only the first line of each paragraph.)
    h. Click on the Show First Line Only button to deactivate it.
    i. Click on the Collapse button on the Outline toolbar. (This displays only the title and headings in the document.)
    j. Select the heading *Mechanical Binding,* then delete it.
    k. Click on the All button on the Outline toolbar to display the document.
    l. Change to the Normal viewing mode.
4. Save the document again with the same name (c27ex04).
5. Print c27ex04.
6. Close c27ex04.

## Exercise 5

1. Open report04.
2. Save the document with Save As and name it c27ex05.
3. Make the following changes to the document:
    a. Change to the Outline viewing mode.
    b. Promote or demote the following titles, headings, or subheadings as identified below:

| | | |
|---|---|---|
| *CHAPTER 1: FINISHED PUBLICATIONS* | = | *Heading 1* |
| *LASER PRINTOUTS* | = | *Heading 2* |
| *Time and Cost Considerations* | = | *Heading 3* |
| *REPRODUCTION QUALITY* | = | *Heading 2* |
| *Color* | = | *Heading 3* |
| *CHAPTER 2: OFFSET PRINTING* | = | *Heading 1* |
| *IMAGESETTING* | = | *Heading 2* |
| *WYSIWYG* | = | *Heading 3* |
| *Output Options* | = | *Heading 3* |
| *METAL-PLATE OFFSET PRINTING* | = | *Heading 2* |
| *Preparing Mechanicals* | = | *Heading 3* |
| *Pasteup* | = | *Heading 3* |

 c. Save the document again with the same name (c27ex05).

 d. Click on the Show Heading 3 button on the Outline toolbar.

 e. Move *REPRODUCTION QUALITY* (and the heading below it) above *LASER PRINTOUTS* by completing the following steps:

  (1) Position the insertion point on the plus symbol before the heading *REPRODUCTION QUALITY* until it turns into a four-headed arrow, then click the left mouse button.

  (2) Click twice on the Move Up button on the Outline toolbar.

 f. Move the heading *IMAGESETTING* (and all subheadings below it) below *METAL-PLATE OFFSET PRINTING* and the subheadings below it by completing the following steps:

  (1) Position the arrow pointer on the plus symbol immediately left of the heading *IMAGESETTING* until it turns into a four-headed arrow.

  (2) Hold down the left mouse button, drag the mouse down until the gray horizontal line with the arrow attached is positioned below *Pasteup*, then release the mouse button.

  (3) Deselect the text.

4. Save the document again with the same name (c27ex05).

5. Print c27ex05. (Only the outline will print.)

6. Close c27ex05.

## Exercise 6

1. Open c27ex05.

2. Save the document with Save As and name it c27ex06.

3. Make the following changes to the document:

 a. Click on the Show Heading 3 button on the Outline toolbar.

 b. Add numbering by completing the following steps:

  (1) Choose Format, Heading Numbering.

  (2) At the Heading Numbering dialog box, make sure the first option is selected (displays with a blue border), then choose OK or press Enter.

 c. Move the title *CHAPTER 1: FINISHED PUBLICATIONS* (and all the headings and subheadings below it) below the title *CHAPTER 2: OFFSET PRINTING* (and all the headings and subheadings below it).

 d. Change the chapter numbers in the titles to match the automatic numbers.

4. Save the document again with the same name (c27ex06).

5. With the document still collapsed to display only heading levels, print the document.

6. Close c27ex06.

## Assessment 1

1. Open report03.
2. Save the document with Save As and name it c27sa01.
3. Make the following changes to the document:
   a. Change to the Outline viewing mode.
   b. Promote or demote the following titles, headings, or subheadings as identified below:

   | | | |
   |---|---|---|
   | *CHAPTER 1: DEVELOPMENT OF* | | |
   | *TECHNOLOGY, 1900 - 1950* | = | *Heading 1* |
   | *World War I* | = | *Heading 2* |
   | *World War II* | = | *Heading 2* |
   | *CHAPTER 2: DEVELOPMENT OF* | | |
   | *TECHNOLOGY, 1950 - 1960* | = | *Heading 1* |
   | *Korean War* | = | *Heading 2* |
   | *Cold War and Vietnam* | = | *Heading 2* |

   c. Collapse the outline so only the two heading levels are displayed.
4. Save the document again with the same name (c27sa01).
5. Print c27sa01. (This will print the collapsed outline, not the entire document.)
6. Close c27sa01.

## Assessment 2

1. Open report05.
2. Save the document with Save As and name it c27sa02.
3. Make the following changes to the document:
   a. Change to the Outline viewing mode.
   b. Change the two chapter titles to Heading 1 and change the headings within the document to Heading 2.
   c. Collapse the outline so only two heading levels show.
   d. Move the first chapter title and the headings below it after the second chapter title and the headings below it.
   e. Renumber the chapters (chapter 4 becomes 3 and chapter 3 becomes 4).
   f. Move the section on *Specialty Inks* below the section on *Special Effects*.
4. With the outline still collapsed, save the document again with the same name (c27sa02).
5. Print c27sa02.
6. Close c27sa02.

## Assessment 3

1. Open c27sa02.
2. Save the document with Save As and name it c27sa03.
3. Make the following changes to the document:
   a. Change to the Outline viewing mode.
   b. Add numbering to the outline.
   c. Delete the section on *Special Effects*.
4. Save the document again with the same name (c27sa03).
5. Print c27sa03.
6. Close c27sa03.

# Creating Fill-in Forms 28

Upon successful completion of chapter 28, you will be able to create a variety of business forms with text boxes, check boxes, and drop-down lists.

Many businesses use preprinted forms that are generally filled in by hand or with a typewriter. These forms require additional storage space and also cost the company money. With Word's form feature, you can create your own forms, eliminating the need for preprinted forms.

In this chapter, you will learn how to create a template document for a form that includes text boxes, check boxes, and pull-down lists. You will learn how to save the form as a protected document and then open the form and key information in the fill-in boxes. You will create basic form documents in this chapter. For ideas on creating advanced forms, please refer to the Word for Windows User's Guide.

In chapter 25, you learned how to create Fill-in fields in a main document. The main document containing fill-in fields also required a data source for other variable information. Creating a form does not require a main document or a data source. The form is created as a template document that contains fill-in fields. Information is keyed in the fields when a document is opened based on the form template.

## Creating a Form

In Word, a *form* is a protected document that includes fields where information is entered. A form document contains *form fields* that are locations in the document where one of three actions is performed: text is entered, a check box is turned on or off, or information is selected from a drop-down list.

There are three basic steps that are completed when creating a form:

1. Create a form document based on a template and build the structure of the form.
2. Insert form fields where information is to be entered at the keyboard.
3. Save the form as a protected document.

## Creating the Form Template

A form is created as a template so that when someone fills in the form they are working on a copy of the form, not the original. The original is the template document that is saved as a protected document. In this way, a form can be used over and over again without changing the original form. When a form is created from the template form document that has been protected, information can only be keyed in the fields designated when the form was created.

As an example of how to create a protected form document, look at the form shown in figure 28.1.

*Figure 28.1*
*Example Form*

### TRI-STATE AUTOMOBILE PROTECTOR POLICY

Policy Number: ▓▓▓▓          Date Issued: ▓▓▓▓

Personal ☐          Business ☐

Name of Insured: ▓▓▓▓

Address of Insured: ▓▓▓▓

Car: ▓▓▓▓          Year: ▓▓▓▓

Make: ▓▓▓▓          Model: ▓▓▓▓

Coverage: ▓▓▓▓

☐ Bodily Injury
☐ Property Damage
☐ Automobile Personal Injury Protection
☐ Underinsured Motorist Coverage (BI)
☐ Underinsured Motorist Coverage (PD)

A form can be created that contains fields for text, such as the fields *Policy Number:, Date Issued:*, etc.; as check boxes, such as the boxes after *Personal* and *Business*; or as a drop-down list (not used in the form example). You will learn about drop-down lists later in this chapter.

To create the form shown in figure 28.1 as a template document based on the Normal template document and name it xxxauto.dot (where the *xxx* are your initials), you would complete the following steps:

1. Choose File, New.
2. At the New dialog box, select *Normal* in the Template list box.
3. Choose Template in the New section of the dialog box.
4. Choose OK or press Enter.
5. At the document screen, key the beginning portion of the form shown in figure 28.1 up to the colon after *Policy Number:*. After keying the colon, press the space bar twice, then insert a form field where the policy number will be keyed by completing the following steps:
   a. Choose Insert, Form Field.

b. At the Form Field dialog box shown in figure 28.2, make sure Text is selected in the Type section, then choose OK or press Enter. (The form field displays as a shaded area in the document screen.)

6. After inserting the form field, press the Tab key four times, then key **Date Issued:**.

7. Press the space bar twice, then insert a text form field by completing steps 5a and 5b above.

8. Press the Enter key twice, key **Personal**, then press the space bar twice.

9. Insert the check box form field by completing the following steps:

   a. Choose Insert, Form Field.

   b. At the Form Field dialog box, choose Check Box.

   c. Choose OK or press Enter.

10. Continue keying the document adding text and check box form fields as needed.

11. After the form is completed, protect the document by completing the following steps:

    a. Choose Tools, Protect Document.

    b. At the Protect Document dialog box shown in figure 28.3, choose Forms.

    c. Choose OK or press Enter.

12. Save the document with Save As and name it xxxauto.dot. (Use your initials in place of the *xxx*.)

13. Close xxxauto.dot.

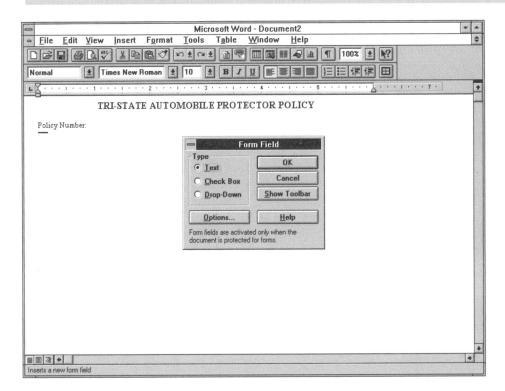

*Figure 28.2*
*Form Field Dialog Box*

Figure 28.3
Protect Document
Dialog Box

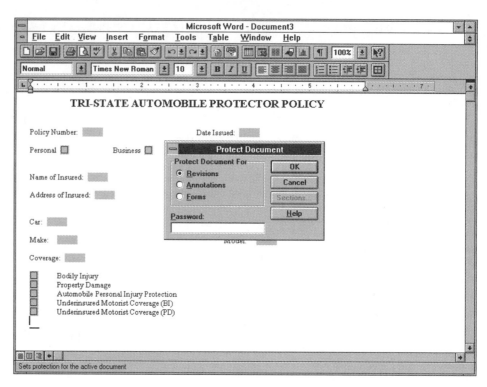

Word provides a Forms toolbar with buttons you can use to easily insert a text box, check box, or other form fields into a form template document. To display the Forms toolbar shown in figure 28.4, choose Show Toolbar at the Form Field dialog box.

Figure 28.4
Forms Toolbar

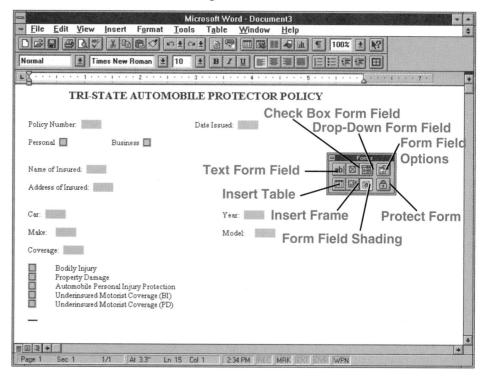

You can also turn on the display of the Forms toolbar by completing the following steps:

1. Choose View, Toolbars.
2. At the Toolbars dialog box, select *Forms* in the Toolbars list box. To do this with the mouse, click in the check box before the *Forms* option. If you are using the keyboard, press the down arrow key until *Forms* is selected, then press the space bar.
3. Choose OK or press Enter.

Complete the same steps listed above to turn off the display of the Forms toolbar. You can also turn off the display of the Forms toolbar by clicking on the document control button in the upper left corner of the Forms toolbar. (This is the button containing a hyphen.)

## Filling in a Form Document

After a template form document is created, protected, and saved, the template can be used to create a personalized form document. When you open a form template document that has been protected, the insertion point is automatically inserted in the first form field. Key the information for the form field, then press the Tab key or the Enter key to move the insertion point to the next form field. You can move the insertion point to a preceding form field by pressing Shift + Tab. To fill in a check box form field, move the insertion point to the check box, then key X or press the space bar. Complete the same steps to remove an X from a check box form field.

As an example of how to fill in a form template, you would complete the following steps to create a form with the *xxxauto.dot* template document:

1. Choose File, New.
2. At the New dialog box, select *Xxxauto* (where your initials are displayed instead of the *Xxx*).
3. Choose OK or press Enter.
4. Word displays the form document with the insertion point positioned in the first form field after *Policy Number:*. Key a number for the policy, then press the Tab key or the Enter key to move to the next form field.
5. With the insertion point positioned in the form field after *Date Issued:*, key the current date, then press the Tab key or the Enter key.
6. With the insertion point positioned in the check box after *Personal*, press the Tab key or the Enter key. (This leaves the check box blank.)
7. With the insertion point positioned in the check box after *Business*, key the letter **X** or press the space bar. (This inserts an X in the check box.)
8. Continue filling in the form as required.
9. When the form is completed, save the document in the normal manner.

## Printing a Form

After the form fields in a form document have been filled in, the form can be printed in the normal manner. In some situations, you may want to print just the data (not the entire form) or print the form and not the fill-in data.

If you are using a preprinted form that is inserted in the printer, you will want to print just the data. Word will print the data in the same location on the page as it appears in the form document. To print just the data in a form, you would complete the following steps:

1. Open the form document with all data entered in the form fields.
2. Choose Tools, Options.
3. At the Options dialog box, choose the Print tab.
4. At the Options dialog box with the Print tab selected, choose Print Data Only for Forms in the Options for Current Document Only section. (This inserts an X in the check box.)
5. Choose OK or press Enter.
6. Click on the Print button on the Standard toolbar.

After printing only the data, complete the steps above to remove the X from the Print Data Only for Forms check box.

To print only the form without the data, you would complete the following steps:

1. Choose File, New.
2. At the New dialog box, select the desired template document in the Template list box, then choose OK or press Enter.
3. With the form document displayed in the document screen, click on the Print button on the Standard toolbar.
4. Close the document.

## ■ Editing a Form Template

When a form template is created and then protected the text in the template cannot be changed. If you need to make changes to a form template, you must open the template document, unprotect the document, then make the changes. After making the changes, protect the document again.

For example, to edit the *xxxauto.dot* form template, you would complete the following steps:

1. Choose File, Open.
2. At the Open dialog box, choose Drives, then choose the drive where the *template* subdirectory is located. (If you are working on a hard-drive system, the *template* subdirectory is probably located on the *c:* drive. If you are using a network system, check with your instructor to determine where the *template* subdirectory is located.)
3. Choose *template* in the Directories list box. (If the *template* subdirectory is not visible, check with your instructor to determine where the *template* subdirectory is located.)
4. Choose List Files of Type, then from the drop-down list that displays, choose *All Files (*.*)*.
5. Select *xxxauto.dot* in the File Name list box. (Depending on your first initial, you may need to scroll through the list to find the document.)
6. With *xxxauto.dot* selected, choose OK or press Enter.
7. With the xxxauto.dot form template displayed in the document screen, unprotect the document by choosing Tools, Unprotect Document.
8. Make any needed changes to the document.
9. Protect the document again by choosing Tools, Protect Document.
10. Save the document with the same name (xxxauto.dot).
11. Close xxxauto.dot.

# ■ Customizing Form Field Options

A drop-down list, text box, or check box form field is inserted in a document with default options. You can change these default options for each form field. Options at the Drop-Down Form Field Options dialog box can be used to create form fields with drop-down lists.

## Creating Form Fields with Drop-Down Lists

When creating form fields for a form document, there may be some fields where you want the person entering the information to choose from specific options, rather than keying the data. To do this, you need to create a form field with a drop-down list.

For example, suppose there are three types of auto insurance policies for people to choose from in the form shown in figure 28.1. The types are *Safe Driver Policy*, *Fleet Policy*, and *High-Risk Policy*. These three choices can be added as a drop-down list in the form field. To do this, you would open the xxxauto.dot form template, then create the form field by completing the following steps:

1. Choose File, Open.
2. At the Open dialog box, choose Drives, then choose the drive where the *template* subdirectory is located. (If you are working on a hard-drive system, the *template* subdirectory is probably located on the *c:* drive. If you are using a network system, check with your instructor to determine where the *template* subdirectory is located.)
3. Choose *template* in the Directories list box. (If the *template* subdirectory is not visible, check with your instructor to determine where the *template* subdirectory is located.)
4. Choose List Files of Type, then from the drop-down list that displays, choose *All Files (\*.\*)*.
5. Select *xxxauto.dot* in the File Name list box. (Depending on your first initial, you may need to scroll through the list to find the document.)
6. With *xxxauto.dot* selected, choose OK or press Enter.
7. With the xxxauto.dot form template displayed in the document screen, unprotect the document by choosing Tools, Unprotect Document.
8. Position the insertion point between *Personal* and *Name of Insured:*, then key **Type of Insurance:**.
9. Press the space bar twice, then choose Insert, Form Field.
10. At the Form Field dialog box, choose Drop-Down.
11. Choose Options.
12. At the Drop-Down Form Field Options dialog box shown in figure 28.5, key **Safe Driver Policy** in the Drop-Down Item text box.
13. Choose Add.
14. Key **Fleet Policy** in the Drop-Down Item text box.
15. Choose Add.
16. Key **High-Risk Policy** in the Drop-Down Item text box.
17. Choose Add.
18. Choose OK or press Enter.
19. Save the document with the same name (xxxauto.dot).

Figure 28.5
*Drop-Down Form
Field Options Dialog
Box*

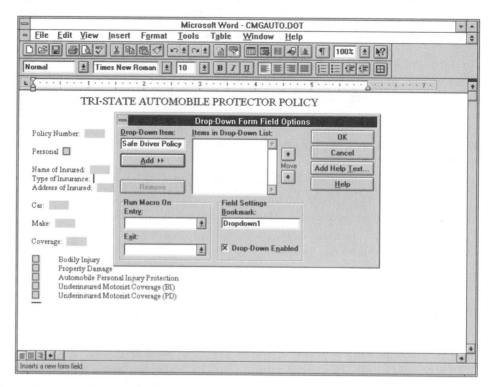

When the form document is protected, a drop-down form field displays as a gray box with a down-pointing arrow at the right side of the box.

At the Form Field Options dialog box, you can remove drop-down items by selecting the item to be removed in the Items in Drop-Down List list box, then choosing Remove.

When filling in a form field in a form template document that contains a drop-down list, position the insertion point in the drop-down form field, then complete one of the following steps:

- Click on the down-pointing arrow at the right side of the form field.
- Press F4.
- Press Alt + down arrow key.

When you choose one of the methods above, a drop-down list displays with the choices for the form field. Click on the desired choice, or press the up or down arrow key to select the desired choice, then press the Enter key.

## Changing Text Form Field Options

To change options for a text form field, choose Options at the Form Field text box with the Text option selected, and the Text Form Field Options dialog box shown in figure 28.6 displays in the document screen.

At the Text Form Field Options dialog box, you can change the type of text that is to be inserted in the form field. The default setting at the Type text box is *Regular Text*. This can be changed to *Number*, *Date*, *Current Date*, *Current Time*, or *Calculation*.

If you change the Type option, Word will display an error message if the correct type of information is not entered in the form field. For example, if you change the form field type to *Number* in the Type text box, only a number can be entered in the form field. If something other than a number is entered, Word displays an error message, the entry is selected, and the insertion point stays in the form field until a number is entered.

If a particular text form field will generally need the same information, key that information in the Default Text text box. This default text will display in the form field. If you want to leave the default text in the form document, just press the Tab key or the Enter key when filling in the form. If you want to change the default text, key text over the default text when filling in the form.

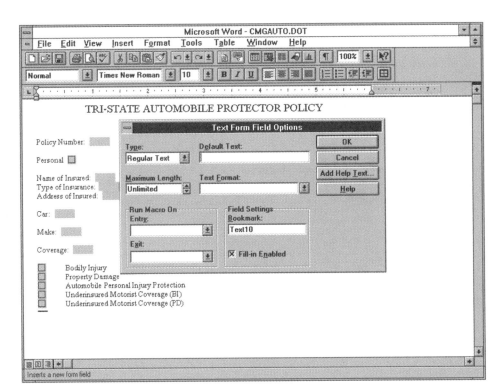

Figure 28.6
Text Form Field
Options Dialog Box

With the <u>M</u>aximum Length option at the Text Form Field Options dialog box, you can specify an exact measurement for a form field. This option has a setting of *Unlimited* by default.

Formatting options for text in a form field can be applied with options at the Text <u>F</u>ormat text box. For example, if you want text to display in all uppercase letters, choose Text <u>F</u>ormat, then choose *Uppercase* from the drop-down list. When you key text in the form field while filling in the form, the text is converted to uppercase letters as soon as you press the Tab key or Enter key. The Text <u>F</u>ormat options will vary depending on what is selected in the Type text box.

## Changing Check Box Form Field Options

Check box form field options can be changed at the Check Box Form Field Options dialog box shown in figure 28.7. To display this dialog box, choose <u>O</u>ptions at the Form Field text box with the <u>C</u>heck Box option selected.

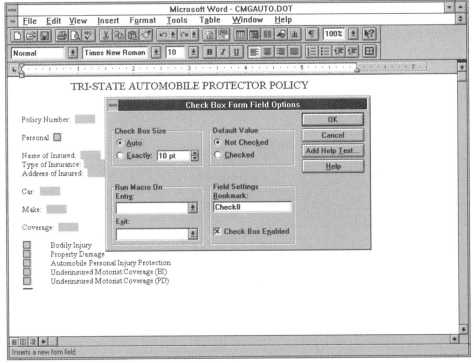

Figure 28.7
Check Box Form
Field Options Dialog
Box

By default, Word inserts a check box in a form template document in the same size as the adjacent text. This is because Auto is selected at the Check Box Form Field Options dialog box. If you want to specify an exact size for the check box, choose Exactly, then key the desired point measurement in the Exactly text box.

A form field check box is empty by default. If you want the check box to be checked by default, display the Check Box Form Field Options dialog box, then choose Checked in the Default Value section.

## ■ Creating Tables in a Form Template

A table can be very useful when creating a form with form fields. A table can be customized to create a business form such as an invoice and a purchase order. Figure 28.8 shows an example of a form created with the table feature.

Figure 28.8
Sample Form

```
ST. FRANCIS MEDICAL CENTER
300 Blue Ridge Boulevard
Kansas City, MO 63009
(816) 555-2000
```

Department: ▓▓▓▓   Name: ▓▓▓▓

Purpose: ▓▓▓▓   Date: ▓▓▓▓

| Item | Description | Qty | Price |
|------|-------------|-----|-------|
|      |             |     |       |

Create the form shown in figure 28.8 in the same manner as the form shown in figure 28.1. For example, to create the form shown in figure 28.8 as a template document based on the *Normal* template document and named *xxxinv.dot* (where the *xxx* are your initials), you would complete the following steps:

1. Choose File, New.
2. At the New dialog box, select *Normal* in the Template list box.
3. Choose Template in the New section of the dialog box.
4. Choose OK or press Enter.
5. At the document screen, change the font to 12-point Courier New.
6. Create a table with 4 columns and 12 rows. Make the following changes to the table:
   a. Merge cells A1, B1, C1, and D1.
   b. Add border lines to the table as shown in the figure.
   c. Select cells A2, B2, C2, and D2, then change the alignment to center and turn on bold.

d. Select cells A3 through A12, then change the alignment to center.

e. Select cells C3 through D12, then change the alignment to right.

7. After creating the table, position the insertion point in cell A1, press the Enter key, press Ctrl + Tab, then key ***ST. FRANCIS MEDICAL CENTER***. Continue keying the text in cell A1 as shown in figure 28.8. Press Ctrl + Tab to move the insertion point to a tab stop.

8. Before creating the first form field, turn on the display of the Forms toolbar by completing the following steps:

   a. Choose View, Toolbars.

   b. At the Toolbars dialog box, select *Forms* in the Toolbars list box. To do this with the mouse, click in the check box before the *Forms* option. If you are using the keyboard, press the down arrow key until *Forms* is selected, then press the space bar.

   c. Choose OK or press Enter.

9. Insert form fields where you see the shaded areas in the form by completing the following steps:

   a. Position the insertion point where you want the form field inserted.

   b. Click on the Text Form Field button on the Forms toolbar.

10. After the table is completed, protect the document by completing the following steps:

    a. Choose Tools, Protect Document.

    b. At the Protect Document dialog box, choose Forms.

    c. Choose OK or press Enter.

11. Save the document with Save As and name it xxxinv.dot. (Use your initials in place of the *xxx*.)

12. Close xxxinv.dot.

## CHAPTER SUMMARY

- You can create your own forms with Word's form feature, thus eliminating the need for preprinted forms.

- A form is created as a template document that contains fill-in fields. Information based on the form template is keyed in the fields when a document is opened.

- A form document contains *form fields* where one of three actions is performed: text is entered, a check box is turned on or off, or information is selected from a drop-down list.

- Three basic steps are involved in creating a form:
  1. Create a form document based on a template and build the structure of the form.
  2. Insert form fields where information is to be entered at the keyboard.
  3. Save the form as a protected document.

- Create a template document by choosing Template at the New dialog box.

- Word provides a Forms toolbar with buttons you can use to easily insert a text box, check box, or other form field into a form template document.

- After a template form document is created, protected, and saved, the template can be used to create a personalized form document.

- After the form fields have been filled in, the form can be printed in the normal manner, or you can print just the data from the Options dialog box with the Print tab selected.

- When a form template is created and then protected, the text in the template cannot be changed. To edit a template document, you must open the document, unprotect it, make the needed changes, then protect the document again.

- Options at the Drop Down Form Field Options dialog box can be used to create form fields with drop-down lists.
- Change options for a text form field at the Text Form Field Options dialog box.
- Check Box form field options can be changed at the Check Box Form Field Options dialog box.
- A table can be customized to create a business form such as an invoice or a purchase order.

## COMMANDS REVIEW

|  | **Mouse** | **Keyboard** |
|---|---|---|
| Display New dialog box | File, New | File, New |
| Display Form Field dialog box | Insert, Form Field | Insert, Form Field |

## CHECK YOUR UNDERSTANDING

**True/False:** Circle the letter T if the statement is true; circle the letter F if the statement is false.

T F 1. A template document is similar to a data source and is always merged with a main document.

T F 2. When filling in a form that has been protected, information can only be keyed in the fields designated when the form was created.

T F 3. To bring to the screen a template form document that has been created, protected, and saved, display the New dialog box.

T F 4. A protected document can be edited by changing the view to Page Layout.

T F 5. An error message will display if the wrong type of data is entered in a form field.

T F 6. The default setting for the Maximum Length option at the Text Form Field Options dialog box is 24.

T F 7. Word inserts a check box in a form template document in the same size as the adjacent text by default.

T F 8. To use a customized table to create a template document, begin at the New dialog box.

T F 9. A form field check box is checked by default.

**Completion:** In the space provided at the right, indicate the correct term, command, or number.

1. A fill-in form can include text boxes, check boxes, or these. _____

2. This is the third basic step performed when creating a form document. _____

3. Begin creating a template document at this dialog box. _____

4. To display the Forms toolbar, choose this at the Form Field dialog box. _____

5. To protect a document, first choose this from the Standard toolbar. _____

6. If you want the user to fill in a form by choosing from specific options, create this type of form field. _____

7. The default setting for a text form field can be changed to *Number, Date, Current Time, Calculation,* or this. _____

8. If you want text to display in all uppercase letters, first choose this at the Text Form Field Options dialog box. _____

9. Display the Forms toolbar by first choosing this on the Standard toolbar. _____

10. A table can be customized to create a business form such as an invoice or this. _____

## Exercise 1

1. Create the form shown in figure 28.9 as a template document named *xxxc28x1.dot* by completing the following steps:
   a. Choose File, New.
   b. At the New dialog box, select *Normal* in the Template list box.
   c. Choose Template in the New section of the dialog box.
   d. Choose OK or press Enter.
   e. At the document screen, change the default font to 12-point Courier New by completing the following steps:
      (1) Choose Format, Font.
      (2) At the Font dialog box, choose *Courier New* in the Font list box and choose *12* in the Size list box.
      (3) Choose Default.
      (4) At the question asking if you want to change the default font, choose Yes.
   f. Key the beginning portion of the form shown in figure 28.9 up to the colon after *Name:*. After keying the colon, press the space bar twice, then insert a form field where the name will be keyed by completing the following steps:
      (1) Choose Insert, Form Field.
      (2) At the Form Field dialog box, make sure Text is selected in the Type section, then choose OK or press Enter. (The form field displays as a shaded area in the document screen.)
   g. After inserting the form field, press the Enter key, then create the remaining text and text form fields as shown in figure 28.9. To create the check boxes after Yes and No, complete the following steps:
      (1) Turn on the display of the Forms toolbar by completing the following steps:
         (a) Choose View, Toolbars.
         (b) At the Toolbars dialog box, click in the check box before *Forms* in the Toolbars list box.
         (c) Choose OK or press Enter.
      (2) With the insertion point positioned where the check box is to be inserted, click on the Check Box Form Field button on the Forms toolbar.
   h. After the form is completed, protect the document by clicking on the Protect Form button on the Forms toolbar.
   i. Turn off the display of the Forms toolbar by clicking on the document control button in the upper left corner of the toolbar (the button containing a hyphen).
2. Save the document and name it xxxc28x1.dot. (Use your initials in place of the xxx.)
3. Print xxxc28x1.dot.
4. Close xxxc28x1.dot.

Figure 28.9

**LIFETIME ANNUITY INSURANCE APPLICATION**

FIRST APPLICANT

Name:
Address:
Date of Birth:
Occupation:

SECOND APPLICANT

Name:
Address:
Date of Birth:
Occupation:

1.  During the past 3 years, have you for any reason consulted a
    doctor or been hospitalized?

    First Applicant:              Second Applicant:
    Yes ☐   No ☐                  Yes ☐   No ☐

2.  Have you ever been treated for or advised that you had any of
    the following:  heart, lung, nervous, kidney, or liver
    disorder; high blood pressure; drug abuse including alcohol;
    cancer or tumor; AIDS or any disorder of your immune system;
    diabetes?

    First Applicant:              Second Applicant:
    Yes ☐   No ☐                  Yes ☐   No ☐

These answers are true and complete to the best of my knowledge and
belief.  To determine my insurability, I authorize any health care
provider or insurance company to give any information about me or
my physical or mental health.

FIRST APPLICANT'S SIGNATURE      SECOND APPLICANT'S SIGNATURE

_____          _____

## Exercise 2

1.  Create a form with the xxxc28x1.dot form template by completing the following steps:
    a.  Choose File, New.
    b.  At the New dialog box, select *Xxxc28x1* in the Template list box (where your initials are
        displayed instead of the *Xxx*).
    c.  Choose OK or press Enter.
    d.  Word displays the form document with the insertion point positioned in the first form
        field after *Name:*. Key the name **Dennis Utley** (as shown in figure 28.10), then press the
        Tab key or the Enter key to move to the next form field.

e. Fill in the remaining text and check box form fields as shown in figure 28.10. Press the Tab key or the Enter key to move the insertion point to the next form field. Press Shift + Tab to move the insertion point to the preceding form field.

f. When the form is completed, save the document and name it c28ex02.

2. Print c28ex02.

3. Close c28ex02.

**Figure 28.10**

### LIFETIME ANNUITY INSURANCE APPLICATION

FIRST APPLICANT

Name:  Dennis Utley
Address:  11315 Lomas Drive, Seattle, WA 98123
Date of Birth:  02/23/59
Occupation:  Accountant

SECOND APPLICANT

Name:  Geneva Utley
Address:  11315 Lomas Drive, Seattle, WA 98123
Date of Birth:  09/04/62
Occupation:  Social Worker

1.  During the past 3 years, have you for any reason consulted a doctor or been hospitalized?

    First Applicant:          Second Applicant:
    Yes  ☐    No  ☒          Yes  ☐    No  ☒

2.  Have you ever been treated for or advised that you had any of the following:  heart, lung, nervous, kidney, or liver disorder; high blood pressure; drug abuse including alcohol; cancer or tumor; AIDS or any disorder of your immune system; diabetes?

    First Applicant:          Second Applicant:
    Yes  ☐    No  ☒          Yes  ☐    No  ☒

These answers are true and complete to the best of my knowledge and belief.  To determine my insurability, I authorize any health care provider or insurance company to give any information about me or my physical or mental health.

FIRST APPLICANT'S SIGNATURE     SECOND APPLICANT'S SIGNATURE

_____     _____

## Exercise 3

1. Open c28ex02.
2. Print only the data in the form fields by completing the following steps:
   a. Choose Tools, Options.
   b. At the Options dialog box, choose the Print tab.
   c. At the Options dialog box with the Print tab selected, choose Print Data Only for Forms in the Options for Current Document Only section. (This inserts an X in the check box.)
   d. Choose OK or press Enter.
   e. Click on the Print button on the Standard toolbar.
3. After printing, remove the X from the Print Data Only for Forms option by completing the following steps:
   a. Choose Tools, Options.
   b. At the Options dialog box with the Print tab selected, choose Print Data Only for Forms in the Options for Current Document Only section. (This removes the X in the check box.)
   c. Choose OK or press Enter.
4. Close c28ex02 without saving the changes.

## Exercise 4

1. Add the text shown in figure 28.11 to the xxxc28x1.dot form template by completing the following steps:
   a. Choose File, Open.
   b. At the Open dialog box, choose Drives, then choose the drive where the *template* subdirectory is located. (If you are working on a hard-drive system, the *template* subdirectory is probably located on the *c:* drive. If you are using a network system, check with your instructor to determine where the *template* subdirectory is located.
   c. Choose *template* in the Directories list box. (If the *template* subdirectory is not visible, check with your instructor to determine where the *template* subdirectory is located.)
   d. Choose List Files of Type, then from the drop-down list that displays, choose *All Files (*.*)*.
   e. Select *xxxc28x1.dot* in the File Name list box. (Depending on your first initial, you may need to scroll through the list to find the document.)
   f. With *xxxc28x1.dot* selected, choose OK or press Enter.
   g. With the *xxxc28x1.dot* form template displayed in the document screen, unprotect the document by choosing Tools, Unprotect Document.
   h. Add the paragraph and the check boxes shown in figure 28.11 to the form (below the paragraph numbered with 2. and the Yes and No check boxes.)
   i. Protect the document again by completing the following steps:
      (1) Choose Tools, Protect Document.
      (2) At the Protect Document dialog box, choose Forms.
      (3) Choose OK or press Enter.
   j. Save the document with the same name (xxxc28x1.dot).
2. Print xxxc28x1.dot.
3. Close xxxc28x1.dot.
4. Return the drive back to the drive where your student data disk is located by completing the following steps:
   a. Choose File, Open.
   b. At the Open dialog box, choose Drives, then choose *a:* (or *b:*, depending on where your disk is located).
   c. Choose List of Files of Type, then choose *Word Documents (*.doc)* from the drop-down list.
   d. Choose Cancel.

**Figure 28.11**

3.  During the past 3 years, have you for any reason been denied
    life insurance by any other insurance company?

    First Applicant:          Second Applicant:
    Yes ☐    No ☐             Yes ☐    No ☐

## Exercise 5

1.  Create the form shown in figure 28.12 as a template document named *xxxc28x5.dot* by
    completing the following steps:
    a.  Choose File, New.
    b.  At the New dialog box, select *Normal* in the Template list box.
    c.  Choose Template in the New section of the dialog box.
    d.  Choose OK or press Enter.
    e.  At the document screen, change the default font to 12-point Courier New. (For help on
        how to do this, see exercise 1, step 1e.)
    f.  Key the title of the form, *APPLICATION FOR PREFERRED INSURANCE,* centered
        and bolded. Press the Enter key twice, then return the paragraph alignment back to left.
        Key **Date:**, press the space bar twice, then insert a text form field that inserts the current
        date by completing the following steps:
        (1) Choose Insert, Form Field.
        (2) At the Form Field text box, choose Text, then Options.
        (3) At the Text Form Field Options dialog box, choose Type, then select *Current Date*
            from the drop-down list. To do this with the mouse, click on the down-pointing arrow
            to the right of the Type text box, then click on *Current Date*. If you are using the
            keyboard, press Alt + P, then press the down arrow key until *Current Date* is selected.
        (4) Choose OK or press Enter.
    g.  Press the Enter key twice, key **Name:,** press the space bar twice, then create the form
        field. Do the same for **Address:** and **Date of Birth:**.
    h.  Key **Social Security Number:**, press the space bar twice, then create a text form field
        that allows a maximum of 11 characters (the number required for the Social Security
        number including the hyphens) by completing the following steps:
        (1) With the insertion point positioned two spaces after *Social Security Number:*, choose
            Insert, Form Field.
        (2) At the Form Field dialog box, choose Text, then Options.
        (3) At the Text Form Field Options dialog box, choose Maximum Length, then enter **11** in
            the text box. To do this with the mouse, click on the up-pointing triangle after the
            Maximum Length text box until *11* displays in the text box. If you are using the
            keyboard, press Alt + M, then key **11**.
        (4) Choose OK or press Enter.
    i.  Press the Enter key twice, key **Gender:**, then press the space bar twice. Create the text
        and check boxes after *Gender:* as shown in the figure.
    j.  Press the Enter key twice, key **Nonprofit Employer:**, press the space bar twice, then
        create a text box with three choices by completing the following steps:
        (1) Choose Insert, Form Field.
        (2) At the Form Field dialog box, choose Drop-Down.
        (3) Choose Options.
        (4) At the Drop-Down Form Field Options dialog box, key **College** in the Drop-Down
            Item text box.
        (5) Choose Add.

(6) Key **Public School** in the <u>D</u>rop-Down Item text box.

(7) Choose <u>A</u>dd.

(8) Key **Private School** in the <u>D</u>rop-Down Item text box.

(9) Choose <u>A</u>dd.

(10) Choose OK or press Enter.

k. Press the Enter key twice, key **How are premiums to be paid?**, press the space bar twice, then create a text form field with the choices *Annually, Semiannually,* and *Quarterly* by completing steps similar to those in 1j(1) through 1j(10).

l. Continue creating the remainder of the form. Create the text form fields and check boxes as shown in figure 28.12.

m. After the form is completed, protect the document.

2. Save the document and name it xxxc28x5.dot. (Use your initials in place of the xxx.)

3. Print xxxc28x5.dot.

4. Close xxxc28x5.dot.

---

**Figure 28.12**

### APPLICATION FOR PREFERRED INSURANCE

Date:

Name:

Address:

Date of Birth:

Social Security Number:

Gender:    Female ☐        Male ☐

Nonprofit Employer:

How are premiums to be paid?

1.  Will this insurance replace any existing insurance or annuity?
    Yes ☐    No ☐

2.  Within the past 3 years has your driver's license been suspended, revoked, or have you been convicted for driving under the influence of alcohol or drugs?
    Yes ☐    No ☐

3.  Do you have any intention of traveling or residing outside the United States or Canada within the next 12 months?
    Yes ☐    No ☐

Signature of proposed insured:

_____    Date _____

## Exercise 6

1. Create a form with the xxxc28x5.dot form template by completing the following steps:
   a. Choose File, New.
   b. At the New dialog box, select *Xxxc28x5* (where your initials are displayed instead of the *Xxx*).
   c. Choose OK or press Enter.
   d. Word displays the form document with the insertion point positioned in the *Name:* form field. Fill in the text and check boxes as shown in figure 28.13. (Press the Tab key or Enter key to move the insertion point to the next form field. Press Shift + Tab to move the insertion point to the preceding form field.) To fill in the form fields with drop-down lists, complete the following steps:
      (1) With the insertion point in the drop-down list form field, click on the down-pointing arrow at the right side of the text box.
      (2) Click on the desired option in the drop-down list.
2. When the form is completed, save the document and name it c28ex06.
3. Print c28ex06.
4. Close c28ex06.

Figure 28.13

**APPLICATION FOR PREFERRED INSURANCE**

Date:  (current date)

Name:  Jennifer Reynolds

Address:  2309 North Cascade, Renton, WA 98051

Date of Birth:  12/18/63

Social Security Number:  411-23-6800

Gender:  Female  ⊠          Male  ☐

Nonprofit Employer:  Public School

How are premiums to be paid?  Quarterly

1. Will this insurance replace any existing insurance or annuity?
   Yes  ⊠    No  ☐

2. Within the past 3 years has your driver's license been suspended, revoked, or have you been convicted for driving under the influence of alcohol or drugs?
   Yes  ☐    No  ⊠

3. Do you have any intention of traveling or residing outside the United States or Canada within the next 12 months?
   Yes  ☐    No  ⊠


Signature of proposed insured:

_____    Date _____

## Exercise 7

1. Create the form shown in figure 28.14 as a template document based on the Normal template document and named *xxxc28x7.dot* (where the *xxx* are your initials), by completing the following steps:

   a. Choose File, New.

   b. At the New dialog box, select *Normal* in the Template list box.

   c. Choose Template in the New section of the dialog box.

   d. Choose OK or press Enter.

   e. At the document screen, change the default font to 12-point Courier New.

   f. Create a table with 4 columns and 12 rows. Make the following changes to the table:

   (1) Change the width of the first, third, and fourth columns to 1 inch; change the width of the second column to 3 inches.

   (2) Merge cells A1, B1, C1, and D1.

   (3) Add border lines to the table as shown in the figure.

   (4) Select cells A2, B2, C2, and D2, then change the alignment to center and turn on bold.

   (5) Select cells A3 through A12, then change the alignment to center.

   (6) Select cells C3 through C12, then change the alignment to right.

   (7) Select cells D3 through D12, then change the alignment to center.

   g. After creating the table, position the insertion point in cell A1, press Ctrl + Tab, then key **GOOD SAMARITAN HOSPITAL**. Continue keying the text in cell A1 as shown in figure 28.14. Press Ctrl + Tab to move the insertion point to a tab stop within a cell. Before inserting the first text form field, turn on the display of the Forms toolbar. Insert form fields where you see the shaded areas in the form by completing the following steps:

   (1) Position the insertion point where you want the form field inserted.

   (2) Click on the Text Form Field button on the Forms toolbar.

   h. After the table is completed, protect the document by clicking on the Protect Form button on the Forms toolbar.

   i. Turn off the display of the Forms toolbar.

2. Save the document and name it xxxc28x7.dot. (Use your initials in place of the *xxx*.)

3. Print xxxc28x7.dot.

4. Close xxxc28x7.dot.

Figure 28.14

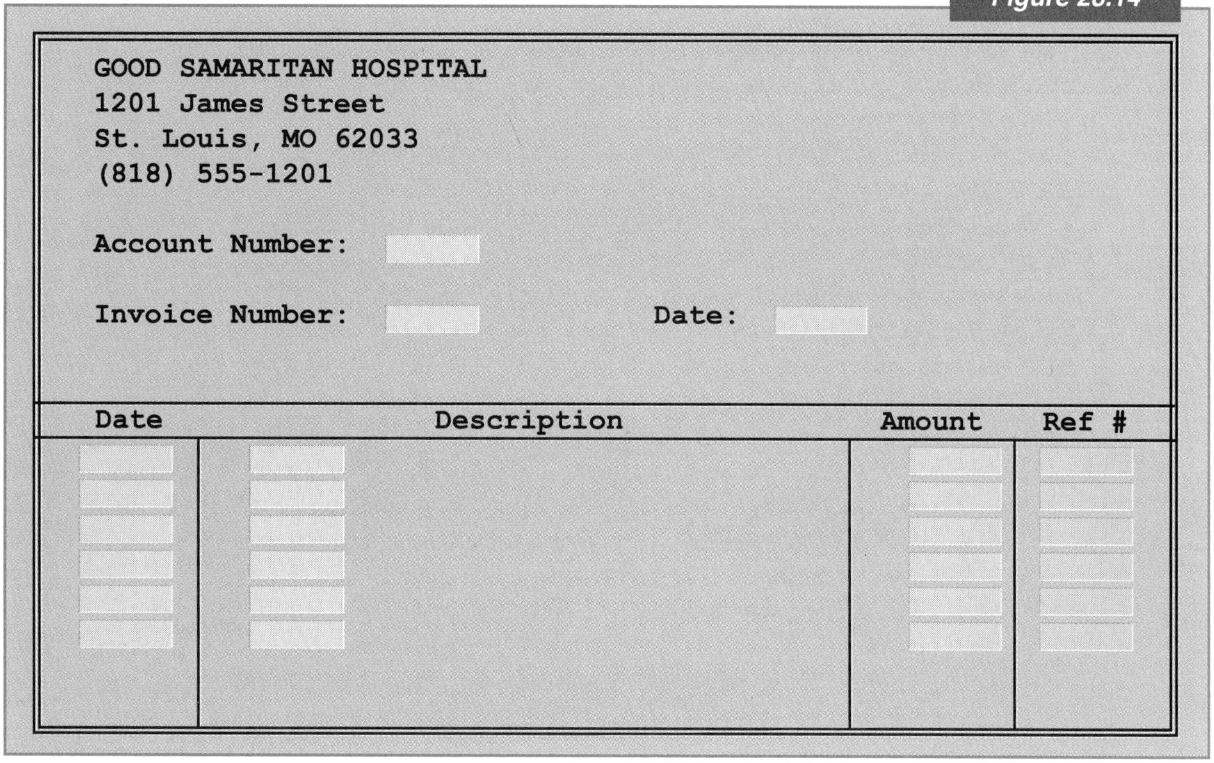

GOOD SAMARITAN HOSPITAL
1201 James Street
St. Louis, MO 62033
(818) 555-1201

Account Number:

Invoice Number:                          Date:

| Date | Description | Amount | Ref # |
|------|-------------|--------|-------|

## Exercise 8

1. Create a form with the xxxc28x7.dot form template by completing the following steps:
   a. Choose File, New.
   b. At the New dialog box, select *Xxxc28x7* in the Template list box (where your initials are displayed instead of the *Xxx*).
   c. Choose OK or press Enter.
   d. Word displays the form document with the insertion point positioned in the first form field. Fill in the text and check boxes as shown in figure 28.15. (Press the Tab key or Enter key to move the insertion point to the next form field. Press Shift + Tab to move the insertion point to the preceding form field.)
2. When the form is completed, save the document and name it c28ex08.
3. Print c28ex08.
4. Close c28ex08.

Figure 28.15

```
GOOD SAMARITAN HOSPITAL
1201 James Street
St. Louis, MO 62033
(818) 555-1201


Account Number:  3423-001


Invoice Number:  342        Date:  04/30/96
```

| Date | Description | Amount | Ref # |
|---|---|---|---|
| 04/16/96 | Bed linens | $984.50 | 5403 |
| 04/24/96 | Hospital slippers | 204.00 | 9422 |
| 04/26/96 | Hospital gowns | 750.25 | 6645 |

## SKILL ASSESSMENTS

### Assessment 1

1. Create the form shown in figure 28.16 as a template document named *xxx28sa1.dot*. Insert text form fields and check box form fields in the document as shown in figure 28.16.
2. Save the document and name it xxx28sa1.dot. (Use your initials in place of the *xxx*.)
3. Print xxx28sa1.dot.
4. Close xxx28sa1.dot.

Figure 28.16

ST. FRANCIS MEDICAL CENTER

APPLICATION FOR FUNDING

Project Title: [   ]

Department Applying: [   ]

Facility: ☐ SFH ☐ LC ☐ SCC

Contact Person(s): [   ]

Check the statement(s) that best describe(s) how this proposal will meet the eligibility criteria:

☐ Improved patient care outcomes

☐ Cost reduction

☐ Improved customer satisfaction

☐ Reduced outcome variation

☐ Compliance with quality standards

_____          _____
Signature                            Date

_____          _____
Department                           Extension

## Assessment 2

1. Create a form with the xxx28sa1.dot form template. Insert the following information in the form:
   Project Title:  Quality Improvement Project
   Department Applying:  Pediatrics
   Facility: (check SFH)
   Contact Person(s):  Alyce Arevalo
   Check all the statements describing the proposal except the second statement.
2. When the form is completed, save the document and name it c28sa02.
3. Print c28sa02.
4. Close c28sa02.

## Assessment 3

1. Create the table form shown in figure 28.17 as a template document named *xxx28sa3.dot*. Customize the table as shown in figure 28.17. Insert text form fields and check box form fields in the table shown in the figure.
2. Save the document and name it xxx28sa3.dot. (Use your initials in place of the *xxx*.)
3. Print xxx28sa3.dot.
4. Close xxx28sa3.dot.

Figure 28.17

# LIFETIME ANNUITY

## PROFESSIONAL LIABILITY INSURANCE APPLICATION

Name:

Address:

County:          SSN:          DOB:

Type of Deduction:
☐ Flat
☐ Participating

Deduction Amount:
☐ None          ☐ $2,500
☐ $1,000        ☐ $5,000

Check if this insurance is to be part of a program.
☐ AANA          ☐ AAOMS          ☐ APTA-PPS          ☐ None

Check your specific professional occupation.

☐ Chiropractor
☐ Dental Anesthesiologist
☐ Dental Hygienist
☐ Dietitian/Nutritionist
☐ Laboratory Director
☐ Medical Office Assistant

☐ Medical Technician
☐ Nurse
☐ Nurse Practitioner
☐ Occupational Therapist
☐ Optometrist
☐ Paramedic/EMT

Signature:          Date:

## Assessment 4

1. Create a form with the xxx28sa3.dot form template. Insert the following information in the form:

   Name:  Steven Katori
   Address:  11502 South 32nd Street, Bellevue, WA 98049
   County:  King
   SSN:  230-52-9812
   DOB:  11/20/60
   Type of Deduction: (check Flat)
   Deduction Amount:  (check $1,000)
   Part of insurance program? (check None)
   Occupation: (check Nurse Practitioner)

2. When the form is completed, save the document and name it c28sa04.
3. Print c28sa04.
4. Close c28sa04.

## Assessment 5

1. Delete the form template documents created in this chapter by completing the following steps:

   a. Display the Open dialog box.
   b. At the Open dialog box, choose Find File.
   c. At the Search dialog box, choose File Name, then choose *Document Templates (*.dot)* from the drop-down list.
   d. Choose Location, then key **c:\winword\template**. (Check with your instructor to determine if this is the location of template documents for your system. If not, ask for specific directions on displaying the subdirectory containing template documents.)
   e. Choose OK or press Enter.
   f. At the Find File dialog box, select the template documents that begin with your initials in the Listed Files list box.
   g. Choose Commands, then Delete.
   h. At the question asking if you want to delete the documents, choose Yes.
   i. Choose Close.

# Creating Tables and Indexes

**29**

Upon successful completion of chapter 29, you will be able to mark information in a document to be included in a table of contents, index, table of figures, or table of authorities and then compile the table or list.

A book, textbook, report, or manuscript often includes sections such as a table of contents, index, and table of figures in the document. Creating these sections can be tedious when done manually. With Word, these functions can be automated to create the sections quickly and easily.

## Creating a Table of Contents

A table of contents appears at the beginning of a book, manuscript, or report and contains headings and subheadings with page numbers. Figure 29.1 shows an example of a table of contents.

**TABLE OF CONTENTS**

*Figure 29.1*
*Table of Contents*

Text to be included in a table of contents can be identified by applying a heading style or text can be marked as a field entry. The advantage to using styles to mark text for a table of contents is that it is quick and easy. The disadvantage is that the headings in the document will display with the formatting applied by the style.

The advantage to marking headings for a table of contents as a field entry is that no formatting is applied to the heading in the document. The disadvantage is that it takes more time to mark headings.

## Marking Table of Contents Entries as Styles

A table of contents can be created by applying heading styles to text to be included in the table of contents. When creating a table of contents, there are two steps involved:

> 1. Apply the appropriate styles to the text that will be included in the table of contents.
> 2. Compile the table of contents in the document.

Word automatically includes text that is formatted with a heading style in a table of contents. In chapters 24 and 27 you learned that Word contains nine heading styles that can be applied to text. If you have already applied these styles to create an outline, the same headings are included in the table of contents. If the styles have not previously been applied, you can apply them with the Style button on the Formatting toolbar, or with buttons on the Outline toolbar in the Outline viewing mode.

As an example of how to apply styles for a table of contents, you would complete the following steps to apply styles to the title and headings in the report01 document:

> 1. Open report01.
> 2. Position the insertion point on any character in the title, *TYPE SPECIFICATION*, click on the down-pointing arrow to the right of the Style button on the Formatting toolbar, then click on *Heading 1*.
> 3. Position the insertion point on any character in the heading *Type Measurement*, click on the down-pointing arrow to the right of the Style button on the Formatting toolbar, then click on *Heading 2*.
> 4. Position the insertion point on any character in the heading *Type Size*, click on the down-pointing arrow to the right of the Style button on the Formatting toolbar, then click on *Heading 2*.
> 5. Position the insertion point on any character in the heading *Type Style*, click on the down-pointing arrow to the right of the Style button on the Formatting toolbar, then click on *Heading 2*.

## Compiling a Table of Contents

After the necessary heading styles have been applied to text that you want to include in the table of contents, the next step is to compile the table of contents. To do this, position the insertion point where you want the table to appear, display the Index and Tables dialog box with the Table of Contents tab selected, make any desired changes, then choose OK.

For example, to compile a table of contents for report01 that contains the title and headings marked with heading styles, you would complete the following steps:

> 1. With report01 open in the document screen and the title and headings marked, position the insertion point at the beginning of the document, then press the Enter key once.
> 2. Position the insertion point at the beginning of the document.
> 3. Key **TABLE OF CONTENTS**, centered and bolded.
> 4. Press the Enter key, then return the paragraph alignment back to left.
> 5. With the insertion point positioned at the left margin, choose Insert, then Index and Tables.
> 6. At the Index and Tables dialog box, choose the Table of Contents tab.
> 7. With the Index and Tables dialog box with the Table of Contents tab selected as shown in figure 29.2, choose the desired formatting in the Formats list box. (The Preview box displays how the table of contents will appear in the document.)
> 8. Choose OK or press Enter.

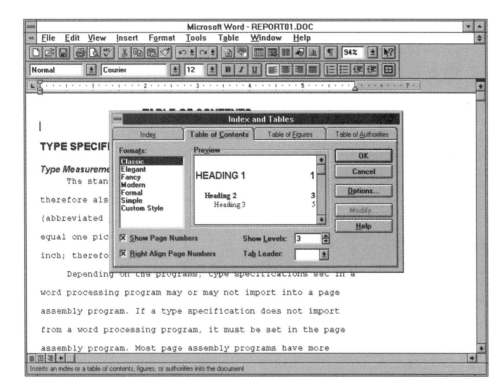

Word compiles the table of contents and then inserts it at the location of the insertion point with the formatting selected at the Index and Tables dialog box.

At the Index and Tables dialog box with the Table of Contents tab selected, you can choose from a variety of preformatted tables. These formats are displayed in the Formats list box in the dialog box. When a format is selected, a preview displays in the Preview box. The check boxes at the bottom let you specify how much of the formatting you want applied to text in the table of contents. The page number displays after the text or aligned at the right margin depending on the formatting selected. The number of levels displayed depends on the number of heading levels specified in the document.

Tab leaders can be added to guide the reader's eyes from the table of contents heading to the page number. To add leaders, choose Tab Leader, then choose the desired leader character from the drop-down list. If leaders are added, the Preview box displays the leaders. Some formats provide leaders.

If you want the table of contents to print on a page separate from the document text, insert a section break that begins a new page between the table of contents and the title of the document. If the beginning of the text in the document, rather than the table of contents, should be numbered as page 1, change the starting page number for the section. For example, to add a section break that begins a new page and change the beginning page number to 1 for the second section of the report01 document, you would complete the following steps:

1. Open report01.
2. Position the insertion point between the table of contents and the title of the document, then insert a section break by completing the following steps:
   a. Choose Insert, Break.
   b. At the Break dialog box, choose Next Page.
   c. Choose OK or press Enter.
3. Position the insertion point below the section break, then insert page numbering and begin page numbering at 1 by completing the following steps:
   a. Choose Insert, Page Numbers.

b.  At the Page Numbers dialog box, change the Position and/or Alignment options if necessary, then choose Format.

c.  At the Page Number Format dialog box, choose Start At. (This inserts 1 in the Start At text box.)

d.  Choose OK or press Enter to close the Page Number Format dialog box.

e.  At the Page Numbers dialog box, choose OK or press Enter.

A table of contents is generally numbered with lowercase Roman numerals. If you want page numbering to appear on the table of contents page, position the insertion point anywhere in the table of contents, then complete the following steps:

1.  Choose Insert, Page Numbers.
2.  At the Page Numbers dialog box, choose Format.
3.  At the Page Number Format dialog box, choose Number Format, then choose *i, ii, iii, ...* from the drop-down list.
4.  Choose OK or press Enter to close the Page Number Format dialog box.
5.  Choose OK or press Enter to close the Page Numbers dialog box.

## Marking Table of Contents Entries as Fields

If you do not want style formatting to be applied to the title, headings, or subheadings in a document but you do want to create a table of contents for the document, mark text for the table as fields. When text is marked for a table of contents, a field code is inserted in the document. To be able to see this field code, click on the Show/Hide button on the Standard toolbar to turn on the display of nonprinting characters. Before compiling the table of contents, turn off the display of nonprinting characters.

As an example of how to mark text for a table of contents, you would complete the following steps to mark the title, *TYPE SPECIFICATION*, as a field:

1.  Open report01.
2.  Click on the Show/Hide button on the Standard toolbar to turn on the display of nonprinting characters.
3.  Position the insertion point at the beginning of the title, *TYPE SPECIFICATION*.
4.  Choose Insert, Field.
5.  At the Field dialog box shown in figure 29.3, select *Index and Tables* in the Categories list box.
6.  Select *TC* in the Field Names list box.
7.  Choose Field Codes, then position the insertion point a space after *TC* in the text box. To do this with the mouse, position the I-beam pointer inside the Field Codes text box to the right of the *TC,* then click the left mouse button. If you are using the keyboard, press Alt + F, then press the right arrow key once.
8.  **Key "TYPE SPECIFICATION"\l1.** (The first character after the backslash is a lowercase L [representing level] and the second character is the number 1.)
9.  Choose OK or press Enter.

The field code *{ TC "TYPE SPECIFICATION"\l1 }* is inserted at the beginning of the document title. The backslash and the lowercase L are referred to as a *switch.* This switch tells Word that the character after the switch is the heading level for the table of contents. If you were marking a heading for level 2 in the table of contents, you would enter a *2* after the \l switch.

After marking text for a table of contents, compile the table of contents as described earlier in this chapter.

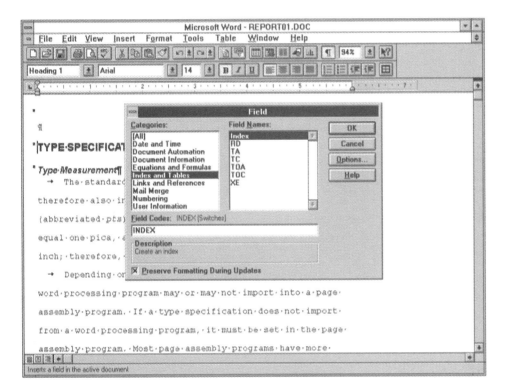

Figure 29.3
Field Dialog Box

## Updating or Replacing a Table of Contents

If you make changes to a document after compiling a table of contents, you can either update the existing table of contents or replace the table of contents with a new one.

To update the current table of contents, you would complete the following steps:

1. Position the insertion point anywhere within the current table of contents. (This causes the table of contents to display with a gray background.)
2. Press F9. (This is the Update Field key.)
3. At the Update Table of Contents dialog box shown in figure 29.4, choose Update Page Numbers Only if the only changes occur to the page numbers, or choose Update Entire Table if changes were made to headings or subheadings within the table.
4. Choose OK or press Enter.

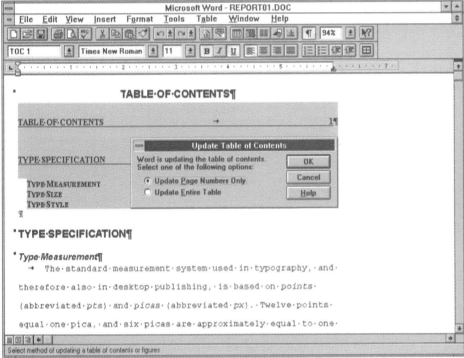

Figure 29.4
Update Table of Contents Dialog Box

If you make extensive changes to the document, you may want to replace the entire table of contents. To do this, you would complete the following steps:

1. Position the insertion point anywhere within the current table of contents. (This causes the table of contents to display with a gray background.)
2. Choose Insert, then Index and Tables.
3. At the Index and Tables dialog box, make sure the Table of Contents tab is selected.
4. Choose OK or press Enter.
5. At the prompt asking if you want to replace the existing table of contents, choose Yes.

Go To Exercise 3

## Deleting a Table of Contents

A table of contents that has been compiled in a document can be deleted. To do this, select the entire table of contents in the normal manner, then press the Delete key.

When the insertion point is positioned on any character in the table of contents, the entire table of contents displays with a gray background. This does not select the table. To delete the table, you must select it in the normal manner using either the mouse or the keyboard.

# Creating an Index

An index is a list of topics contained in a publication, and the pages where those topics are discussed. Word lets you automate the process of creating an index in a manner similar to that used for creating a table of contents. When creating an index, you mark a word or words that you want included in the index. Creating an index takes some thought and consideration. The author of the book, manuscript, or report must determine the main entries desired and what subentries will be listed under main entries. An index may include such things as the main idea of a document, the main subject of a chapter or section, variations of a heading or subheading, and abbreviations.

Figure 29.5 shows an example of an index.

**Figure 29.5**
*Index*

### INDEX

**A**
Alignment, 12,16
ASCII, 22, 24, 35
    data processing, 41
    word processing, 39

**B**
Backmatter, 120
    page numbering, 123
Balance, 67-69
Banners, 145

**C**
Callouts, 78
Captions, 156
Color, 192-195
    ink for offset printing, 193
    process color, 195

**D**
Databases, 124-130
    fields, 124
    records, 124
Directional flow, 70-71

## Marking Text for an Index

A selected word or words can be marked for inclusion in an index. Before marking words for an index, determine what main entries and subentries are to be included in the index. Selected text is marked as an index entry at the Mark Index Entry text box. To mark text for an index, you would complete the following steps:

1. Select the word or words.
2. Choose Insert, Index and Tables.
3. At the Index and Tables dialog box, choose the Index tab.
4. At the Index and Tables dialog box with the Index tab selected as shown in figure 29.6, choose Mark Entry.
5. At the Mark Index Entry dialog box shown in figure 29.7, the selected word(s) appears in the Main Entry text box. Make any necessary changes to the dialog box, then choose Mark. (When you choose Mark, Word automatically turns on the display of nonprinting characters and displays the index field code.)
6. Choose Close to close the Mark Index Entry dialog box.

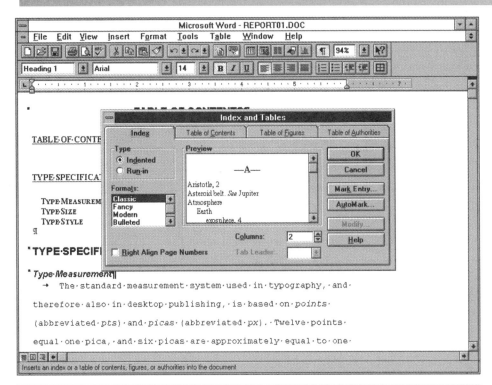

*Figure 29.6*
*Index and Tables*
*Dialog Box with*
*Index Tab Selected*

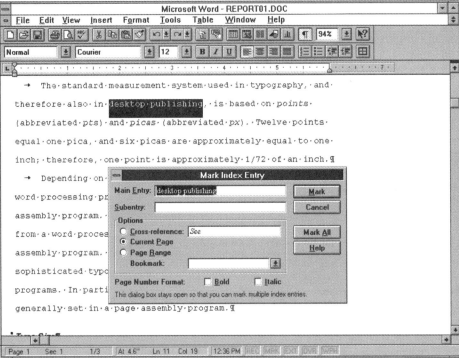

*Figure 29.7*
*Mark Index Entry*
*Dialog Box*

At the Mark Index Entry dialog box, the selected word or words display in the Main Entry text box. If the text is a main entry, leave this as displayed. If, however, the selected text is a subentry, key the main entry in the Main Entry text box, select Subentry, then key the selected text in the Subentry text box. For example, suppose a publication includes the terms *Page layout* and *Portrait*. The words *Page layout* are to be marked as a main entry for the index and *Portrait* is to be marked as a subentry below *Page layout*. To mark these words for an index, you would complete the following steps:

1. Select *Page layout*.
2. Choose Insert, Index and Tables.
3. At the Index and Tables dialog box, make sure the Index tab is selected, then choose Mark Entry.
4. At the Mark Index Entry dialog box, choose Mark.
5. With the Mark Index Entry dialog box still displayed on the screen, click in the document to make the document active, then select *Portrait*.
6. Click on the Mark Index Entry dialog box title bar to make it active.
7. Select *Portrait* in the Main Entry text box, then key **Page layout**.
8. Choose Subentry, then key **Portrait**.
9. Choose Mark.
10. Choose Close.

The main entry and subentry do not have to be the same as the selected text. You can select text for an index, type the text you want to display in the Main Entry or Subentry text box, then choose Mark.

At the Mark Index Entry dialog box, you can apply bold and/or italic formatting to the page numbers that will appear in the index. To apply formatting, choose Bold and/or Italic to insert an X in the check box.

The Options section of the Mark Index Entry dialog box contains several options, with Current Page the default. At this setting, the current page number will be listed in the index for the main and/or subentry. If you choose Cross-reference, you would key the text you want to use as a cross-reference for the index entry in the Cross-reference text box. For example, you could mark the word *Monospaced* and cross reference it to *Typefaces*.

Choose the Mark All button at the Mark Index Entry dialog box to mark all occurrences of the text in the document as index entries. Word marks only those entries whose uppercase and lowercase letters exactly match the index entry.

Some index entries will appear on consecutive pages. If you want Word to reference a range of pages rather than singular pages, you must select the range of pages and then assign a bookmark to the selected text. For example, suppose the word *Typeface* appears on pages 1 through 5 of a publication. To create a bookmark named *Font* for the range and then reference the range of pages for *Typeface*, you would complete the following steps:

1. Select pages 1 through 5.
2. Choose Edit, Bookmark.
3. At the Bookmark dialog box, key **Font**. (A bookmark name can be up to 20 characters in length.)
4. Choose OK or press Enter.
5. Select *Typeface* anywhere within the range of pages in the bookmark.
6. Choose Insert, Index and Tables.
7. At the Index and Tables dialog box, make sure the Index tab is selected, then choose Mark Entry.

8. At the Mark Index Entry dialog box, with *Typeface* in the Main <u>E</u>ntry text box, choose Page <u>R</u>ange Bookmark.

9. With the insertion point positioned in the Page <u>R</u>ange Bookmark text box, key **Font**.

10. Choose <u>M</u>ark.

11. Choose Close.

When the index is created, Word searches the pages included in the bookmark and displays them as a range. For example, if the word *Typeface* appeared on all five pages in the range, the index entry would appear as *Typeface; 1-5*. (The format may vary depending on the format you choose for the index.)

## Compiling an Index

After all necessary text has been marked as a main entry or subentry for the index, the next step is to compile the index. An index should appear at the end of a document, generally on a page by itself. To compile the index, you would follow these steps:

1. Position the insertion point at the end of the document.
2. Insert a page break.
3. With the insertion point positioned below the page break, key **INDEX**, centered and bolded.
4. Press the Enter key.
5. With the insertion point positioned at the left margin, choose <u>I</u>nsert, then Inde<u>x</u> and Tables.
6. At the Index and Tables dialog box, choose the Inde<u>x</u> tab.
7. With the Index and Tables dialog box with the Inde<u>x</u> tab selected, select the desired formatting, then choose OK or press Enter.

Word compiles the index, then inserts it at the location of the insertion point with the formatting selected at the Index and Tables dialog box. Word also inserts a section break above and below the index text.

At the Index and Tables dialog box with the Inde<u>x</u> tab selected, you can specify how the index entries will appear. In the Type section, the In<u>d</u>ented option is selected by default. At this setting, subentries will appear indented below main entries. If you choose Ru<u>n</u>-in, subentries will display on the same line as main entries.

Word provides seven formatting choices in the Forma<u>t</u>s list box. When you select an option from this list, the Pre<u>v</u>iew box displays how the index will appear in the document.

By default, numbers are right aligned in the index. If you do not want numbers right aligned, choose <u>R</u>ight Align Page Numbers to remove the X from the check box.

The C<u>o</u>lumns option has a default setting of *2*. At this setting, the index will display in two newspaper columns. This number can be increased or decreased.

The Ta<u>b</u> Leader option is dimmed for all formats except *Formal*. If you choose *Formal* from the Forma<u>t</u>s list box, the Ta<u>b</u> Leader option displays in black. The default tab leader character is a period. To change to a different character, click on the down-pointing arrow to the right of the text box, then click on the desired character.

## Creating a Concordance File

Words that appear frequently in a document can be saved as a concordance file. This saves you from having to mark each reference in a document. A concordance file is a regular Word document containing a single, two-column table with no text outside the table. In the first column of the table, you enter words you want to index. In the second column, you enter the main entry and subentry that should appear in the index. To create a subentry, separate each main entry from a subentry by a colon.

As an example of how to create a concordance file, you would complete the following steps to create a file with *Typeface* as a main entry and *Portrait* and *Landscape* as subentries under the index, main entry *Typeface:*

1. At a clear document screen, choose Ta̲ble, I̲nsert Table.
2. At the Insert Table dialog box, choose OK or press Enter. (This inserts a table in the document containing two rows and two columns.)
3. Key **Typeface** in the first cell (cell A1).
4. Press the Tab key, then key **Typeface** in the first cell of the second column (cell B1). (This tells Word to mark every occurrence of *Typeface* in the document as the main entry, *Typeface.*)
5. Press the Tab key, then key **Portrait** in the second cell of the first column.
6. Press the Tab key, then key **Typeface:Portrait** in the second cell of the second column.
7. Press the Tab key, then key **Landscape** in the third cell of the first column.
8. Press the Tab key, then key **Typeface:Landscape** in the third cell of the second column.
9. Save the document in the normal manner. (You may want to include the letters *cf* as part of the name to identify it as a concordance file.)

After a concordance file has been created, it can be used to quickly mark text for an index in a document. To do this, you would complete the following steps:

1. Open the document containing text you want marked for the index using the concordance file.
2. Choose I̲nsert, Inde̲x and Tables.
3. At the Index and Tables dialog box, choose Au̲toMark.
4. At the Open Index AutoMark File dialog box shown in figure 29.8, select the concordance file name in the File N̲ame list box.
5. Choose OK or press Enter.

*Figure 29.8*
*Open Index*
*AutoMark File*
*Dialog Box*

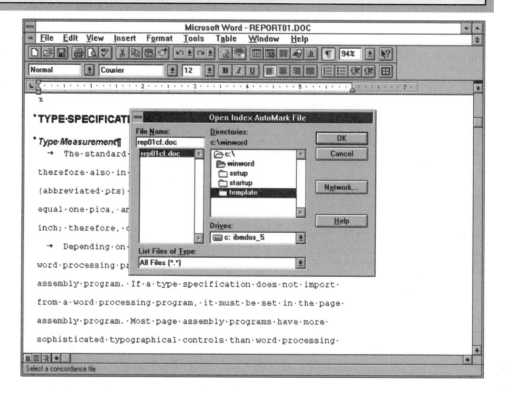

Word turns on the display of nonprinting characters, searches through the document for text that matches the text in the concordance file, then marks it accordingly. After marking text for the index compile the index for the document as described earlier.

## Updating or Replacing an Index

If you make changes to a document after inserting an index, you can either update the existing index or replace the index with a new one. To update an index, position the insertion point anywhere within the index (displays with a gray background), then press F9.

Replace an index in the same manner as replacing a table of contents. For example, to replace an index, you would complete the following steps:

1. Position the insertion point anywhere within the current index. (This causes the index to display with a gray background.)
2. Choose Insert, then Index and Tables.
3. At the Index and Tables dialog box, make sure the Index tab is selected.
4. Choose OK or press Enter.
5. At the prompt asking if you want to replace the existing index, choose Yes.

## Deleting an Index

An index that has been compiled in a document can be deleted. An index is deleted in the same manner as a table of contents. To delete an index, select the entire index using either the mouse or the keyboard, then press the Delete key.

## Creating a Table of Figures

A document that contains figures should include a list (table) of figures so the reader can quickly locate a specific figure. Figure 29.9 shows an example of a table of figures.

**TABLE OF FIGURES**

FIGURE 1 SCANNED LINE ART .................................................................. 3
FIGURE 2 DIGITAL HALFTONE MATRIX ................................................ 8
FIGURE 3 BAR CHARTS ............................................................................. 12
FIGURE 4 LINE CHARTS ............................................................................ 15
FIGURE 5 DETAIL VS. WEIGHT ............................................................... 18

*Figure 29.9*
*Table of Figures*

A table of figures can be created using a variety of methods. The easiest method is to mark figure names as captions, then use the caption names to create the table of figures.

## Creating Captions

There are a variety of methods you can use to create a caption for text. One method you can use to create a caption for text is to complete the following steps:

1. Select the text.
2. Choose Insert, Caption.
3. At the Caption dialog box shown in figure 29.10, make sure *Figure 1* displays in the Caption text box and the insertion point is positioned after *Figure 1*, then key the name for the caption.
4. Choose OK or press Enter.

Word inserts *Figure 1 (caption name)* below the selected text.

Figure 29.10
Caption Dialog Box

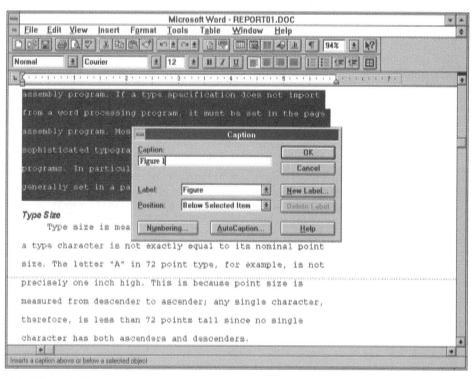

## Compiling a Table of Figures

Once figures have been marked as captions in a document, a table of figures can be compiled and inserted in the document. A table of figures is compiled in a document in a manner similar to a table of contents. A table of figures generally displays at the beginning of the document, after the table of contents.

To compile a table of figures in a document containing figures marked as captions, you would complete the following steps:

1. Open the document containing figures marked as captions.
2. Position the insertion point at the beginning of the document, then insert a section break that begins a new page. (If the document contains a table of contents, position the insertion point between the table of contents and the title of the document.)
3. Move the insertion point above the section break, then key **TABLE OF FIGURES**, bolded and centered.
4. Press the Enter key, then change the paragraph alignment back to left.
5. Choose Insert, Index and Tables.
6. At the Index and Tables dialog box, choose the Table of Figures tab.
7. At the Index and Tables dialog box with the Table of Figures tab selected as shown in figure 29.11, make any necessary changes, then choose OK or press Enter.

The options at the Index and Tables dialog box with the Table of Figures tab selected are similar to those options available at the dialog box with the Table of Contents tab selected. For example, you can choose a format for the table of figures from the Formats list box, change the alignment of the page number, or add leaders before page numbers.

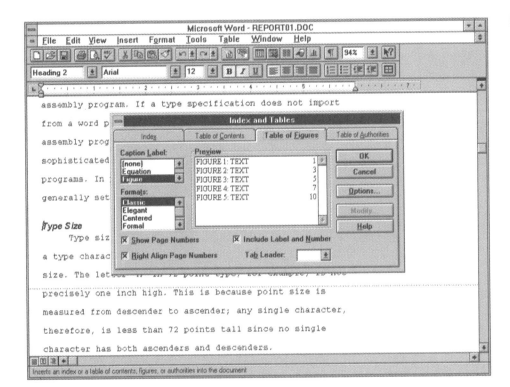

## Updating or Replacing a Table of Figures

A table of figures can be updated in the same manner as updating a table of contents. To update a table of figures, you would complete the following steps:

1. Position the insertion point anywhere within the current table of figures. (This causes the table of figures to display with a gray background.)
2. Press F9. (This is the Update Field key.)
3. At the Update Table of Figures dialog box, choose Update Page Numbers Only if the only changes occur to the page numbers, or choose Update Entire Table if changes were made to caption names in the document.
4. Choose OK or press Enter.

If you make extensive changes to the document, you may want to replace the entire table of figures. To do this, you would complete the following steps:

1. Position the insertion point anywhere within the current table of figures.
2. Choose Insert, then Index and Tables.
3. At the Index and Tables dialog box, make sure the Table of Figures tab is selected.
4. Choose OK or press Enter.
5. At the prompt asking if you want to replace the existing table of figures, choose Yes.

## Deleting a Table of Figures

A table of figures that has been compiled in a document can be deleted. A table of figures is deleted in the same manner as a table of contents. To delete a table of figures, select the entire table of figures using either the mouse or the keyboard, then press the Delete key.

# ■ Creating a Table of Authorities

A table of authorities is a list of citations identifying the pages where the citations appear in a legal brief or other legal document. Word provides many common categories under which citations can be organized. Word includes Cases, Statutes, Other Authorities, Rules, Treatises, Regulations, and Constitutional Provisions. Within each category, Word alphabetizes the citations. Figure 29.12 shows an example of a table of authorities.

*Figure 29.12*
*Table of Authorities*

---

**TABLE OF AUTHORITIES**

### CASES

Mansfield v. Rydell, 72 Wn.2d 200, 433 P.2d 723 (1983) ......................... 3
State v. Fletcher, 73 Wn.2d 332, 124 P.2d 503 (1981) ............................... 5
Yang v. Buchwald, 21 Wn.2d 385, 233 P.2d 609 (1991) .......................... 7

### STATUTES

RCW 8.12.230(2) ........................................................................................ 4
RCW 6.23.590 ............................................................................................ 7
RCW 5.23.103(3) ..................................................................................... 10

---

Some thought goes into planning a table of authorities. Before marking any text in a legal brief, you need to determine what section headings you want and what should be contained in the sections.

When marking text for a table of authorities, you need to find the first occurrence of the citation, mark it as a full citation with the complete name, then specify a short citation. To mark a citation for a table of authorities, you would complete the following steps:

1. Select the first occurrence of the citation.
2. Choose Insert, Index and Tables.
3. At the Index and Tables dialog box, select the Table of Authorities tab.
4. At the Index and Tables dialog box with the Table of Authorities tab selected, choose Mark Citation.
5. At the Mark Citation dialog box shown in figure 29.13, edit and format the text in the Selected Text box as you want it to appear in the table of authorities. Edit and format the text in the Short Citation text box so it matches the short citation you want Word to search for in the document.
6. Choose Category, then select the category that applies to the citation from the drop-down list.
7. Choose Mark to mark the selected citation or choose Mark All if you want Word to mark all long and short citations in the document that match those displayed in the Mark Citation dialog box.
8. The Mark Citation dialog box remains in the document screen so you can mark other citations. To find the next citation in a document, choose Next Citation. (This causes Word to search through the document for the next occurrence of text commonly found in a citation such as *in re* or *v.*)
9. Select the text for the next citation, then complete steps 5 through 7.
10. After marking all citations, choose Close.

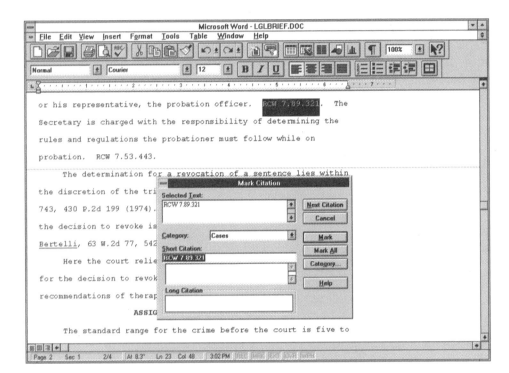

**Figure 29.13**
*Mark Citation Dialog Box*

## Compiling a Table of Authorities

Once citations have been marked in a document, the table of authorities can be compiled and inserted in the document. A table of authorities is compiled in a document in a manner similar to a table of contents or figures. A table of authorities generally displays at the beginning of the document.

To compile a table of authorities in a document containing text marked as citations, you would complete the following steps:

1.  Position the insertion point at the beginning of the document, then press the Enter key twice.
2.  Position the insertion point at the beginning of the title of the document, then insert a section break that begins a new page.
3.  Position the insertion point at the beginning of the document, then key **TABLE OF AUTHORITIES**, centered and bolded.
4.  Press the Enter key, then change the paragraph alignment back to left.
5.  Choose Insert, then Index and Tables.
6.  At the Index and Tables dialog box, choose the Table of Authorities tab.
7.  With the Index and Tables dialog box with the Table of Authorities tab selected, choose the desired formatting.
8.  Choose OK or press Enter.

If you want the table of authorities to print on a page separate from the document text, insert a section break that begins a new page between the table of authorities and the title of the document. If the beginning of the text in the document, rather than the table of authorities, should be numbered as page 1, change the starting page number for the section.

The Index and Tables dialog box with the Table of Authorities tab selected contains options for formatting a table of authorities. The Use Passim option is active by default (the check box contains an X). When it is active, Word replaces five or more page references to the same authority with *passim*. With the X in the Keep Original Formatting check box, Word will retain the formatting of the citation as it appears in the document. Choose the Tab Leader option if you want to change the leader character.

By default, Word compiles all categories for the table of authorities. If you want to compile citations for a specific category, select that category from the Category drop-down list.

## Updating or Replacing a Table of Authorities

A table of authorities can be updated in the same manner as updating a table of contents or figures. To update a table of authorities, you would complete the following steps:

> 1. Position the insertion point anywhere within the current table of authorities. (This causes the table of authorities to display with a gray background.)
> 2. Press F9. (This is the Update Field key.)
> 3. At the Update Table of Authorities dialog box, choose Update Page Numbers Only if the only changes occur to the page numbers, or choose Update Entire Table if changes were made to citations in the document.
> 4. Choose OK or press Enter.

If you make extensive changes to the document, you may want to replace the entire table of authorities. To do this, you would complete the following steps:

> 1. Position the insertion point anywhere within the current table of authorities.
> 2. Choose Insert, then Index and Tables.
> 3. At the Index and Tables dialog box, make sure the Table of Authorities tab is selected.
> 4. Choose OK or press Enter.
> 5. At the prompt asking if you want to replace the existing table of authorities, choose Yes.

## Deleting a Table of Authorities

A table of authorities that has been compiled in a document can be deleted. A table of authorities is deleted in the same manner as a table of contents. To delete a table of authorities, select the entire table of authorities using either the mouse or the keyboard, then press the Delete key.

## CHAPTER SUMMARY

- Creating sections of a long document such as a table of contents, index, and table of figures can be automated with Word.
- Text to be included in a table of contents can be identified by applying a heading style, or text can be marked as a field entry.
- Two steps are involved in creating a table of contents: apply the appropriate styles to the text that will be included, and compile the table of contents in the document.
- To compile the table of contents, position the insertion point where you want it to appear, display the Index and Tables dialog box with the Table of Contents tab selected, make any desired changes, then choose OK.
- At the Index and Tables dialog box, you can choose from a variety of preformatted tables.
- If you want the table of contents to print on a page separate from the document text, insert a section break that begins a new page between the table of contents and the title of the document. You may need to adjust the page numbering also.
- If you make changes to a document after compiling a table of contents, you can either update the existing table of contents or replace it. An index, a table of figures, or a table of authorities can be updated in the same manner.
- To delete a table of contents, select the entire table of contents, then press the Delete key. Delete an index, a table of figures, or a table of authorities in the same manner.

- An index is a list of topics contained in a publication, and the pages where those topics are discussed. Word lets you automate the process of creating an index in a manner similar to that used for creating a table of contents.
- Mark text for an index at the Index and Tables dialog box with the Index tab selected.
- After all necessary text has been marked as a main entry or subentry for the index, the next step is to compile the index so that it appears at the end of a document on a page by itself.
- Word provides seven formatting choices for an index in the Formats list box at the Index and Tables dialog box.
- Words that appear frequently in a document can be saved as a concordance file so that you need not mark each reference in a document.
- A concordance file is a regular document containing a two-column table created at the Insert Table dialog box.
- A table of figures can be created using a variety of methods. The easiest method is to mark figure names as captions, then use the caption names to create the table of figures.
- A table of figures is compiled in a document in a manner similar to a table of contents and generally displays at the beginning of the document, after the table of contents.
- A table of authorities is a list of citations identifying the pages where the citations appear in a legal brief or other legal document.
- When marking text for a table of authorities, you need to find the first occurrence of the citation, mark it as a full citation with the complete name, then specify a short citation at the Index and Tables dialog box.
- A table of authorities is compiled in a document in a manner similar to a table of contents or figures. A table of authorities generally displays at the beginning of the document.

## COMMANDS REVIEW

|  | Mouse | Keyboard |
|---|---|---|
| Display Index and Tables dialog box | Insert, Index and Tables | Insert, Index and Tables |
| Display Insert Table dialog box | Table, Insert Table | Table, Insert Table |

**Matching:** Choose the term from the first list that best matches the description in the second list. Terms may be chosen more than once.

| | | | |
|---|---|---|---|
| A. | Table of Contents | G. | Insert Table dialog box |
| B. | Index | H. | Fields |
| C. | Table of Figures | I. | Compiling |
| D. | Table of Authorities | J. | Captions |
| E. | Concordance file | K. | Main entries |
| F. | Index and Tables dialog box | L. | Subentries |

1. Helps save time when marking text for an index.     _____
2. Identifies citations in a legal brief.     _____
3. Generally placed at the end of a document.     _____
4. The next step in creating a table of contents after applying the necessary heading styles.     _____
5. If included in a document, it usually follows the Table of Contents.     _____
6. To use a concordance file to quickly mark text for an index, choose AutoMark at this dialog box.     _____
7. The easiest way to create a table of figures is to use these.     _____
8. If you do not want style formatting applied in a document, mark text for the table of contents as these.     _____
9. Choose a preformatted table of contents at this dialog box.     _____
10. To delete this, select as you would normal text then press the Delete key.     _____

## AT THE COMPUTER

### Exercise 1

1. Open report02.
2. Save the document with Save As and name it c29ex01.
3. Select the entire document, then change the font to 12-point Times New Roman.
4. Apply heading styles to the title, headings, and subheadings by completing the following steps:
   a. With the insertion point positioned at the beginning of the document, press the Enter key once. (This adds room for the table of contents you will be inserting later.)
   b. Position the insertion point on any character in the title, *STRUCTURED PUBLICATIONS*, click on the down-pointing arrow to the right of the Style button on the Formatting toolbar, then click on *Heading 1*.
   c. Position the insertion point on any character in the heading *TEMPLATE ELEMENTS*, click on the down-pointing arrow to the right of the Style button on the Formatting toolbar, then click on *Heading 2*.
   d. Position the insertion point on any character in the subheading *Column Grid*, click on the down-pointing arrow to the right of the Style button on the Formatting toolbar, then click on *Heading 3*.
   e. Complete steps similar to those in 4c or 4d to apply the styles to the headings and subheadings identified below:

   | | | |
   |---|---|---|
   | *STANDING ELEMENTS* | = | *Heading 2* |
   | *Running Heads/Feet* | = | *Heading 3* |
   | *Page Numbers (Folios)* | = | *Heading 3* |
   | *SERIAL ELEMENTS* | = | *Heading 2* |

5. Position the insertion point immediately left of the *S* in *STRUCTURED PUBLICATIONS,* then insert a section break by completing the following steps:
   a. Choose Insert, Break.
   b. At the Break dialog box, choose Next Page.
   c. Choose OK or press Enter.
6. With the insertion point positioned below the section break, insert page numbering and change the beginning number to 1 by completing the following steps:
   a. Choose Insert, Page Numbers.
   b. At the Page Numbers dialog box, choose Alignment, then choose *Center* from the drop-down list.
   c. Choose Format.
   d. At the Page Number Format dialog box, choose Start At. (This inserts *1* in the Start At text box.)
   e. Choose OK or press Enter to close the Page Number Format dialog box.
   f. At the Page Numbers dialog box, choose OK or press Enter.
7. Compile and insert a table of contents at the beginning of the document by completing the following steps:
   a. Position the insertion point at the beginning of the document.
   b. Key **TABLE OF CONTENTS**, centered and bolded.
   c. Press the Enter key once, then change the paragraph alignment back to left and make sure Bold is turned off.
   d. Choose Insert, then Index and Tables.
   e. At the Index and Tables dialog box, choose the Table of Contents tab.
   f. With the Index and Tables dialog box with the Table of Contents tab selected, select *Formal* in the Formats list box.
   g. Choose OK or press Enter.
8. Select the title, *TABLE OF CONTENTS*, then change the font to 14-point Times New Roman Bold.
9. Insert page numbering in the Table of Contents page by completing the following steps:
   a. With the insertion point positioned in the Table of Contents page, choose Insert, Page Numbers.
   b. At the Page Numbers dialog box, choose Format.
   c. At the Page Number Format dialog box, choose Number Format, then choose *i, ii, iii, ...* from the drop-down list.
   d. Choose Start At. (This inserts *1* in the Start At text box.)
   e. Choose OK or press Enter.
   f. At the Page Numbers dialog box, choose OK or press Enter.
10. Check the page breaks in the document and, if necessary, make adjustments to the page breaks.
11. Save the document again with the same name (c29ex01).
12. Print the table of contents page. (Check with your instructor to see if you should print the entire document.)
13. Close c29ex01.

## Exercise 2

1. Open report03.
2. Save the document with Save As and name it c29ex02.
3. Mark the title, headings, and subheadings as fields for a table of contents by completing the following steps:
   a. With the insertion point positioned at the beginning of the document, press the Enter key once. (This adds room for the table of contents you will be inserting later.)
   b. Position the insertion point at the beginning of the title, *CHAPTER 1: DEVELOPMENT OF TECHNOLOGY, 1900 - 1950*, then mark it as a field for the table of contents by completing the following steps:

(1) Choose <u>I</u>nsert, Fi<u>e</u>ld.

(2) At the Field dialog box, select *Index and Tables* in the <u>C</u>ategories list box.

(3) Select *TC* in the Field <u>N</u>ames list box.

(4) Choose <u>F</u>ield Codes, then position the insertion point a space after *TC* in the text box. To do this with the mouse, position the I-beam pointer inside the <u>F</u>ield Codes text box to the right of the *TC*, then click the left mouse button. If you are using the keyboard, press Alt + F, then press the right arrow key once.

(5) Key **"CHAPTER 1: DEVELOPMENT OF TECHNOLOGY, 1900 - 1950"\l1**. (The first character after the backslash is a lowercase L and the second character is the number 1.)

(6) Choose OK or press Enter.

c. Position the insertion point at the beginning of the heading *World War I*, then mark it as a field for the table of contents by completing the following steps:

(1) Click on the Show/Hide button on the Standard toolbar to turn on the display of nonprinting characters.

(2) Choose <u>I</u>nsert, Fi<u>e</u>ld.

(3) At the Field dialog box, select *Index and Tables* in the <u>C</u>ategories list box.

(4) Select *TC* in the Field <u>N</u>ames list box.

(5) Choose <u>F</u>ield Codes, then position the insertion point a space after *TC* in the text box. To do this with the mouse, position the I-beam pointer inside the <u>F</u>ield Codes text box to the right of the *TC*, then click the left mouse button. If you are using the keyboard, press Alt + F, then press the right arrow key once.

(6) Key **"World War I"\l2**. (The first character after the backslash is a lowercase L and the second character is the number 2.)

(7) Choose OK or press Enter.

d. Complete steps similar to those in 4b or 4c to mark the following text as a field with the specified level:

| | | |
|---|---|---|
| World War II | = | Level 2 |
| CHAPTER 2: DEVELOPMENT OF | | |
| TECHNOLOGY, 1950 - 1960 | = | Level 1 |
| Korean War | = | Level 2 |
| Cold War and Vietnam | = | Level 2 |

e. Click on the Show/Hide button on the Standard toolbar to turn off the display of nonprinting characters.

4. Position the insertion point immediately left of the *C* in *CHAPTER 1,* then insert a section break that begins a new page. (Hint: Refer to exercise 1, step 5.)

5. With the insertion point positioned below the section break, insert page numbering at the bottom center of each page of the section and change the starting number to 1. (Hint: Refer to exercise 1, step 6.)

6. Compile and insert a table of contents at the beginning of the document by completing the following steps:

a. Position the insertion point at the beginning of the document.

b. **Key TABLE OF CONTENTS**, centered and bolded.

c. Press the Enter key once, then change the paragraph alignment back to left and make sure Bold is turned off.

d. Choose <u>I</u>nsert, then Inde<u>x</u> and Tables.

e. At the Index and Tables dialog box, choose the Table of <u>C</u>ontents tab.

f. With the Index and Tables dialog box with the Table of <u>C</u>ontents tab selected, select *Elegant* in the Forma<u>t</u>s list box.

g. Choose <u>O</u>ptions.

h. At the Table of Contents Options dialog box, choose Table <u>E</u>ntry Fields.

i. Choose OK or press Enter.

    j.  Choose OK or press Enter to close the Index and Tables dialog box.

7.  Insert page numbering on the Table of Contents page at the bottom center. (Hint: Refer to exercise 1, step 9.)

8.  Select the title, *TABLE OF CONTENTS*, then change the font to 14-point Times New Roman.

9.  Check the page breaks in the document and, if necessary, adjust the page breaks.

10.  Save the document again with the same name (c29ex02).

11.  Print the table of contents page. (Check with your instructor to see if you should print the entire document.)

12.  Close c29ex02.

## Exercise 3

1.  Open c29ex02.

2.  Save the document with Save As and name it c29ex03.

3.  Insert a page break at the beginning of the title, *CHAPTER 2: DEVELOPMENT OF TECHNOLOGY, 1950 - 1960*. (This title is located on page 2.)

4.  Update the table of contents by completing the following steps:

    a.  Position the insertion point anywhere within the current table of contents. (This causes the table of contents to display with a gray background.)

    b.  Press F9. (This is the Update Field key.)

    c.  At the Update Table of Contents dialog box, make sure Update Page Numbers Only is selected, then choose OK or press Enter.

5.  Save the document again with the same name (c29ex03).

6.  Print the table of contents page. (Check with your instructor to see if you should print the entire document.)

7.  Close c29ex03.

## Exercise 4

1.  Open report01.

2.  Save the document with Save As and name it c29ex04.

3.  Make the following changes to the document:

    a.  Number pages at the bottom center of each page.

    b.  Select the entire document, then change the font to 12-point Times New Roman.

    c.  Select the last four paragraphs (lines) of text in the document, then insert bullets.

4.  Mark the word *Type* (in the heading *Type Measurement*) for the index as a main entry and mark *Measurement* as a subentry with *Type* as the main entry by completing the following steps:

    a.  Select *Type* (in the heading *Type Measurement*).

    b.  Choose Insert, Index and Tables.

    c.  At the Index and Tables dialog box, select the Index tab.

    d.  Choose Mark Entry.

    e.  At the Mark Index Entry dialog box, choose Mark.

    f.  With the Mark Index Entry dialog box still displayed on the screen, click in the document to make the document active, then select *Measurement* (in the heading *Type Measurement*).

    g.  Click on the Mark Index Entry dialog box title bar to make it active.

    h.  Select *Measurement* in the Main Entry text box, then key **Type**.

    i.  Choose Subentry, then key **measurement**.

    j.  Choose Mark All.

    k.  With the Mark Index Entry dialog box still displayed, complete steps similar to those in 4f through 4j to mark the *first* occurrence of the following words as main entries or subentries for the index:

In the first paragraph in the Type Measurement section:

| | | |
|---|---|---|
| *points* | = | main entry (change to *Points*) |
| *picas* | = | main entry (change to *Picas*) |

In the second paragraph in the Type Measurement section:

| | | |
|---|---|---|
| *specification* | = | subentry (main entry = *Type*) |

In the first paragraph in the *Type Size* section:

| | | |
|---|---|---|
| *size* | = | subentry (main entry = *Type*) |

In the third paragraph in the Type Size section:

| | | |
|---|---|---|
| *display* | = | subentry (main entry = *Type*) |
| *fonts* | = | main entry (change to *Fonts*) |
| *non-PostScript* | = | subentry (main entry = *Fonts*) |
| *PostScript* | = | subentry (main entry = *Fonts*) |

In the first paragraph in the Type Style section:

| | | |
|---|---|---|
| *style* | = | subentry (main entry = *Type*) |
| *letterforms* | = | main entry (change to *Letterforms*) |

In the second paragraph in the Type Style section:

| | | |
|---|---|---|
| *bold* | = | subentry (main entry = *Letterforms*) |

In the third paragraph in the Type Style section:

| | | |
|---|---|---|
| *italic* | = | subentry (main entry = *Letterforms*) |

    l. Click on the Show/Hide button on the Standard toolbar to turn off the display of nonprinting characters.

5. Set the title, *TYPE SPECIFICATION*, and the headings, *Type Measurement*, *Type Size*, and *Type Style*, in 14-point Times New Roman Bold.
6. Save the document again with the same name (c29ex04).
7. Close c29ex04.

## Exercise 5

1. Open c29ex04.
2. Save the document with Save As and name it c29ex05.
3. Compile and insert the index for the document by completing the following steps:
   a. Position the insertion point at the end of the document.
   b. Insert a page break.
   c. With the insertion point positioned below the page break, key **INDEX**, centered and bolded.
   d. Press the Enter key, then change the paragraph alignment back to left and make sure Bold is turned off.
   e. Choose Insert, then Index and Tables.
   f. At the Index and Tables dialog box, choose the Index tab.
   g. With the Index and Tables dialog box with the Index tab selected, make sure *Classic* is selected in the Formats list box, then choose OK or press Enter.
4. Save the document again with the same name (c29ex05).
5. Print the index (last page). (Check with your instructor to see if you should print the entire document.)
6. Close c29ex05.

## Exercise 6

1. At a clear document screen, create the text shown in figure 29.14 as a concordance file by completing the following steps:
   a. Choose Table, Insert Table.
   b. At the Insert Table dialog box, choose OK or press Enter. (This inserts a table in the document containing two rows and two columns.)
   c. Key the text in the cells as shown in figure 29.14.
2. Save the document and name it c29cf.
3. Print c29cf. (The gridlines will not print. They were inserted in the figure as a visual aid.)
4. Close c29cf.

**Figure 29.14**

| World War I | World War I |
|---|---|
| Technology | Technology |
| technology | Technology |
| teletypewriters | Technology:teletypewriter |
| motion pictures | Technology:motion picture |
| television | Technology:television |
| Radio Corporation of America | Radio Corporation of America |
| coaxial cable | Coaxial cable |
| telephone | Technology:telephone |
| Communications Act of 1934 | Communications Act of 1934 |
| World War II | World War II |
| radar system | Technology:radar system |
| computer | Computer |
| Atanasoff Berry Computer | Computer:Atanasoff Berry Computer |
| Korean War | Korean War |
| Columbia Broadcasting System | Columbia Broadcasting System |
| Cold War | Cold War |
| Vietnam | Vietnam |
| artificial satellite | Technology:artificial satellite |
| Communications Satellite Act of 1962 | Communications Satellite Act of 1962 |

## Exercise 7

1. Open report03.
2. Save the document with Save As and name it c29ex07.
3. Mark text for the index using the concordance file by completing the following steps:
   a. Choose Insert, Index and Tables.
   b. At the Index and Tables dialog box, choose AutoMark.
   c. At the Open Index AutoMark File dialog box, select *c29cf.doc* in the File Name list box.
   d. Choose OK or press Enter.
4. Compile and insert the index in the document by completing the following steps:
   a. Position the insertion point at the end of the document.
   b. Insert a page break.
   c. With the insertion point positioned below the page break, key **INDEX** bolded and centered.
   d. Press the Enter key, then return the paragraph alignment to left and make sure Bold is turned off.
   e. Choose Insert, then Index and Tables.
   f. At the Index and Tables dialog box, choose the Index tab.
   g. With the Index and Tables dialog box with the Index tab selected, choose *Formal* in the Formats list box, then choose OK or press Enter.
   h. Click on the Show/Hide button on the Standard toolbar to turn off the display of nonprinting characters.
5. Check the page breaks in the document and, if necessary, adjust the page breaks.
6. Save the document again with the same name (c29ex07).
7. Print the index (last page). (Check with your instructor to see if you should print the entire document.)
8. Close c29ex07.

## Exercise 8

1. Open c29ex07.
2. Save the document with Save As and name it c29ex08.
3. Insert a page break at the beginning of the title, *CHAPTER 2: DEVELOPMENT OF TECHNOLOGY, 1950 - 1960*.
4. Update the index by completing the following steps:
   a. Position the insertion point on any character in the index.
   b. Press F9.
5. Save the document again with the same name (c29ex08).
6. Print the index. (Check with your instructor to see if you should print the entire document.)
7. Close c29ex08.

## Exercise 9

1. Open report07.
2. Save the document with Save As and name it c29ex09.
3. Add the caption *Figure 1 Basic Hardware* to the bulleted text and the lines above and below the bulleted text that displays in the middle of page 2 by completing the following steps:
   a. Move the insertion point to the middle of page 2, then select the lines and the bulleted text between the two lines.
   b. Choose Insert, Caption.
   c. At the Caption dialog box, press the space bar once, then key **Basic Hardware**. (The insertion point is automatically positioned in the Caption text box, immediately after *Figure 1*.)
   d. Choose OK or press Enter.
4. Complete steps similar to those in 3a through 3d to create the caption *Figure 2 Input Devices* for the bulleted text at the bottom of the second page (the line below the bulleted text may display at the top of the third page). (Be sure to include the lines above and below the bulleted items.)
5. Complete steps similar to those in 3a through 3d to create the caption *Figure 3 Output Devices* for the bulleted text on the third page. (Be sure to include the lines above and below the bulleted text.)
6. Compile and insert a table of figures at the beginning of the document by completing the following steps:
   a. Position the insertion point at the beginning of the document, press the Enter key, then insert a page break.
   b. Move the insertion point above the page break, then key **TABLE OF FIGURES** bolded and centered.
   c. Press the Enter key, then change the paragraph alignment back to left and make sure Bold is turned off.
   d. Choose Insert, Index and Tables.
   e. At the Index and Tables dialog box, choose the Table of Figures tab.
   f. At the Index and Tables dialog box with the Table of Figures tab selected, choose *Formal* in the Formats list box.
   g. Choose OK or press Enter.
7. Check the page breaks in the document and, if necessary, adjust the page breaks.
8. Save the document again with the same name (c29ex09).
9. Print the table of figures page. (Check with your instructor to see if you should print the entire document.)
10. Close c29ex09.

## Exercise 10

1. Open lglbrief.
2. Save the document with Save As and name it c29ex10.
3. Mark *RCW 7.89.321* as a statute citation by completing the following steps:
   a. Select *RCW 7.89.321*. (This citation is located toward the end of the second page. Hint: Use the Find feature to help you locate this citation.)
   b. Choose Insert, Index and Tables.
   c. At the Index and Tables dialog box, select the Table of Authorities tab.
   d. At the Index and Tables dialog box with the Table of Authorities tab selected, choose Mark Citation.
   e. At the Mark Citation dialog box, choose Category (at the left side of the dialog box), then select *Statutes* from the drop-down list.
   f. Choose Mark All.
   g. Choose Close.
4. Complete steps similar to those in 3a through 3g to mark *RCW 7.53.443* as a statute citation. (This citation is located at the end of the second page.)
5. Complete steps similar to those in 3a through 3g to mark *RCW 7.72A.432(2)* as a statute citation (you may need to use the keyboard to select the citation). (This citation is located in the middle of the third page.)
6. Complete steps similar to those in 3a through 3g to mark *RCW 7.42A.429(1)* as a statute citation (you may need to use the keyboard to select the citation). (This citation is located in the middle of the third page.)
7. Mark *State v. Connors, 73 W.2d 743, 430 P.2d 199 (1974)* as a case citation by completing the following steps:
   a. Select the *State v. Connors, 73 W.2d 743, 430 P.2d 199 (1974)*. (This citation is located at the beginning of the third page. Hint: Use the Find feature to help you locate this citation.)
   b. Choose Insert, Index and Tables.
   c. At the Index and Tables dialog box, with the Table of Authorities tab selected, choose Mark Citation.
   d. At the Mark Citation dialog box, choose Category (at the left side of the dialog box), then select *Cases* from the drop-down list.
   e. Choose Short Citation, delete the text in the box then key **State v. Connors**.
   f. Choose Mark All.
   g. Choose Close.
8. Complete steps similar to those in 7a through 7g to mark *State v. Bertelli, 63 W.2d 77, 542 P.2d 751 (1971)*. Enter *State v. Bertelli* as the short citation. (This citation is located toward the top of the third page.)
9. Complete steps similar to those in 7a through 7g to mark *State v. Landers, 103 W.2d 432, 893 P.2d 2 (1984)*. Enter *State v. Landers* as the short citation. (This citation is located in the middle of the third page.)
10. Turn on page numbering and compile the table of authorities by completing the following steps:
    a. Position the insertion point at the beginning of the document, then press the Enter key once.
    b. Position the insertion point immediately left of the *S* in *STATEMENT OF CASE,* then insert a section break that begins a new page.
    c. With the insertion point positioned below the section break, turn on page numbering at the bottom center of each page and change the starting number to 1.
    d. Position the insertion point above the section break, then key **TABLE OF AUTHORITIES**, centered and bolded.

e. Press the Enter key, then change the paragraph alignment back to left and make sure Bold is turned off.
f. Choose Insert, then Index and Tables.
g. At the Index and Tables dialog box, choose the Table of Authorities tab.
h. At the Index and Tables dialog box with the Table of Authorities tab selected, choose *Formal* in the Formats list box.
i. Choose OK or press Enter.

11. With the insertion point positioned anywhere in the table of authorities, turn on page numbering at the bottom center of each page and change the numbering format to lowercase Roman numerals.
12. Save the document again with the same name (c29ex10).
13. Print the table of authorities. (Check with your instructor to see if you should print the entire document.)
14. Close c29ex10.

## SKILL ASSESSMENTS

### Assessment 1

1. Open report04.
2. Save the document with Save As and name it c29sa01.
3. Make the following changes to the document:
   a. Mark titles, headings, and subheadings for a table of contents.
   b. Number the pages at the bottom center of each page.
   c. Compile the table of contents. (Include a title for the table of contents.)
   d. Number the table of contents page at the bottom center of the page. (Change the number to a lowercase Roman numeral.)
4. Save the document again with the same name (c29sa01).
5. Print the table of contents page. (Check with your instructor to see if you should print the entire document.)
6. Close c29sa01.

### Assessment 2

1. At a clear document screen, create the text shown in figure 29.15 as a concordance file.
2. Save the document and name it c29sacf.
3. Print c29sacf.
4. Close c29sacf.
5. Open c29sa01.
6. Save the document with Save As and name it c29sa02.
7. Mark text for an index using the concordance file, c29sacf.doc.
8. Compile the index at the end of the document.
9. Save the document again with the same name (c29sa02).
10. Print the index. (Check with your instructor to see if you should print the entire document.)
11. Close c29sa02.

### Assessment 3

1. Open c29sa02.
2. Save the document with Save As and name it c29sa03.
3. Insert a page break at the beginning of the title, *CHAPTER 2: OFFSET PRINTING*.
4. Update the table of contents and the index.
5. Save the document again with the same name (c29sa03).
6. Print the table of contents and then the index. (Check with your instructor to see if you should print the entire document.)
7. Close c29sa03.

Figure 29.15

| | |
|---|---|
| FINISHED PUBLICATIONS | Finished publications |
| printing | Printing |
| Laser | Printing:laser |
| laser | Printing:laser |
| toner | Toner |
| print engine | Print engine |
| raster-image processor | Raster-image processor |
| throughput | Throughput |
| REPRODUCTION QUALITY | Reproduction quality |
| resolution | Resolution |
| dpi | Resolution:dpi |
| offset | Printing:offset |
| Color | Printing:color |
| color | Printing:color |
| imagesetter | Imagesetter |
| WYSIWYG | WYSIWYG |
| Output | Output |
| output | Output |
| positive | Output:positive |
| negative | Output:negative |
| OFFSET | Printing:offset |
| METAL-PLATE | Printing:metal plate |
| metal plates | Printing:metal plate |
| Metal plates | Printing:metal plate |
| halftones | Printing:halftones |
| reverses | Printing:reverses |
| surprints | Printing:surprints |
| mechanicals | Mechanicals |
| flats | Flats |
| stripping | Stripping |
| crop marks | Crop marks |
| bleed | Bleed |
| fold lines | Fold lines |
| registration marks | Registration marks |
| Pasteup | Pasteup |
| pasteup | Pasteup |
| Rubber cement | Rubber cement |
| Wax | Wax |

# UNIT 6

# PERFORMANCE ASSESSMENT

In this unit you have learned to create personalized documents with standard documents; utilize database features for maintaining records; create business forms; and finish multiple-page reports with reference attributes such as indexes and tables of contents, figures, and authorities.

## Assessment 1

1. Look at the letter in figure U6.2 and the information in figure U6.1. Determine the fields you need for the main document and the data source. Create the data source and name it omsccds. Create a main document with the text shown in figure U6.2, then merge it with omsccds to a new document. (Use Mail Merge Helper to do this.)
2. Save the merged document and name it u06pa01.
3. Print u06pa01.
4. Close u06pa01.
5. Save the main document and name it omsccmd.
6. Close omsccmd.

**Figure U6.1**

```
Ms. Shirlene Riggs
4928 North Linden Drive
Petersburg, ND 76324
child's name: Erica

Mr. and Mrs. Darrell Street
5637 South 122nd Avenue
Petersburg, ND 76322
child's name: Tyrone

Mr. and Mrs. Gerald Currie
16115 58th Avenue
Apartment 302
Petersburg, ND 76324
child's name: Brett
```

```
Mr. Marvin Antonetti
14013 North 26th
Petersburg, ND 76324
child's name: Angela


Mrs. Sharon Bergen
1244 Wilkes Street
Apartment 2B
Petersburg, ND 76322
child's name: Kelly
```

```
October 7, 1996



Name
Address
City, State Zip

Dear (Name):

Your child, (child's name), has been invited to be one of a group
of Oakridge Middle School students to experience the Petersburg
Challenge Course on Wednesday, October 23, 1996.  We will leave the
school about 8:00 a.m. and return at 2:15 p.m.

The Challenge Course is a series of physical obstacles and
activities where group and individual tasks are conducted under
careful supervision.  The sequence of manageable challenges
requires adult leaders and students to develop skills of goal
setting, group problem solving, communication with others, and
applying oneself with total commitment.  In the process
participants learn to reflect upon their experiences and gain
insight into personal and social behaviors and attitudes which they
can readily apply to different life situations.

Have (child's name) dress appropriately for the weather of the day.
A sack lunch will be needed along with something to drink (no
bottles).  Please return the attached parent consent form by
October 17, 1996.


Sincerely,



Douglas McKenzie, Principal
Oakridge Middle School

xx:omsccmd

Attachment
```

## Assessment 2

1. Create a main document for envelopes that has the omsccds data source document attached then merge the envelope main document with those records in omsccds with the ZIP Code *76324*. Merge to a new document. (*Hint: Begin at the Mail Merge Helper dialog box.*)
2. Save the merged document and name it u06pa02.
3. Print u06pa02.
4. Close u06pa02.
5. Close the envelope main document without saving the changes.

## Assessment 3

1. Open report02.
2. Save the document with Save As and name it u06pa03.
3. Make the following changes to the document:
   a. Change to the Outline viewing mode.
   b. Apply Heading 1, Heading 2, and Heading 3 styles to the title, headings, and subheadings in the document.
   c. Collapse the outline so only three heading levels are displayed.
   d. Move the *TEMPLATE ELEMENTS* and the subheading below it after *SERIAL ELEMENTS*.
4. With the outline still collapsed, save the document again with the same name (u06pa03).
5. Print u06pa03.
6. Close u06pa03.

## Assessment 4

1. Create the table form shown in figure U6.3 as a template document named *xxxu6pa4.dot*. Customize the table as shown in figure U6.3. Insert text form fields in the table shown in the figure.
2. Save the document with Save As and name it xxxu6pa4.dot. (Use your initials in place of the *xxx*.) (*Hint: Protect the template document before you save it.*)
3. Print xxxu6pa4.dot.
4. Close xxxu6pa4.dot.

```
MOUNTAIN COMMUNITY COLLEGE
500 Silverdale Drive
Colorado Springs, CO 87422
(719) 555-3100


Name:                              Date:


Department:
```

| Description | Qty. | Cost |
|---|---|---|
| | | |

## Assessment 5

1. Create a form with the xxxu6pa4.dot form template. Insert the following information in the form:

   Name:  Jay Burris
   Date:  (key the current date)
   Department:  Public Relations

   Description:  Transfer Brochure
   Qty.:  400
   Cost: $225.00

   Description:  Technology Degree Brochure
   Qty.:  250
   Cost:  179.50

   Description:  College Newsletter
   Qty.:  2,000
   Cost:  150.50

2. When the form is completed, save the document and name it u06pa05.
3. Print u06pa05.
4. Close u06pa05.

## Assessment 6

1. At a clear document screen, create the text shown in figure U6.4 as a concordance file.
2. Save the document and name it u06cf.
3. Print u06cf.
4. Close u06cf.
5. Open report05.

6. Save the document with Save As and name it u06pa06.
7. Mark text for an index using the concordance file u06cf.doc.
8. Compile the index at the end of the document.
9. Mark titles, headings, and subheadings for a table of contents.
10. Compile the table of contents at the beginning of the document.
11. Save the document again with the same name (u06pa06).
12. Print the table of contents and the index. (Check with your instructor to see if you should print the entire document.)
13. Close u06pa06.

| paper | Paper |
|---|---|
| stock | Paper:stock |
| color | Paper:color |
| inks | Ink |
| finish | Finish |
| opacity | Opacity |
| thickness | Paper:thickness |
| Grades | Paper:grade |
| grade | Paper:grade |
| Book | Paper:book |
| vellum | Paper:vellum |
| Writing | Paper:writing |
| weight | Paper:weight |
| linen | Paper:linen |
| laid | Paper:laid |
| parchment | Paper:parchment |
| Cover | Paper:cover |
| premixed | Ink:premixed |
| High-gloss | Ink:high-gloss |
| high-gloss | Ink:high-gloss |
| Fluorescent | Ink:fluorescent |
| Thermography | Thermography |
| Engraving | Engraving |
| engraving | Engraving |
| Foil leaf stamping | Foil leaf stamping |
| metal die | Metal die |

## Assessment 7

1. Delete the following:
   a. All documents created in chapters 21 through 24.
   b. All documents created for the unit 5 Performance Assessment.

## COMPOSING ACTIVITIES

The following activities give you the opportunity to practice your writing skills along with demonstrating an understanding of some of the important Word features you have mastered in this unit. In planning the documents, remember to shape the information according to the writing purpose and the audience. Use correct grammar, appropriate word choices, and clear sentence constructions.

## Activity 1

**Situation:** You are Arnold Kiehn, volunteer coordinator for St. Francis Medical Center. Compose a letter to the new volunteers listed below thanking them for their interest in volunteering at St. Francis Medical Center and invite them to a volunteer orientation on Tuesday, October 15, 1996, from 7:00 p.m. to 8:30 p.m. During this orientation, volunteers will learn more about volunteer positions available in the hospital, the duties performed by volunteers, and the time commitment required of volunteers. Create a data source with the names and addresses below that is attached to the main document, which is the letter to the volunteers. After creating the data source and the main document, merge the data source with the main document. You determine the names for the data source document and the main document. Save the merged document as u06act01. Print then close u06act01.

Mr. Lester Schneider
1720 South Oak Street
Kansas City, MO 63065

Mrs. Helen Hegland
6712 21st Avenue
Gladstone, MO 64229

Ms. Mona Krueger
3213 80th Avenue
Gladstone, MO 64229

Mr. Lewis Robbins
906 Union Drive
Kansas City, MO 63043

Mrs. Carla Simoneau
1311 Warner Street
Raytown, MO 64120

Mr. Ray Elkins
31004 107th South
Kansas City, MO 63031

## Activity 2

**Situation:** You are an administrative assistant at St. Francis Medical Center and you have been asked by your supervisor to create a directory with the information displayed below. Include an appropriate title and column headings. After creating the directory, sort the text alphabetically by last name. Save the document and name it u06act02. Print u06act02. Open u06act02, sort the text numerically by extension, then save the document with the same name. Print then close u06act02.

| | | |
|---|---|---|
| St. Germaine, Allison | President | 2005 |
| Aversen, Leah | Vice President | 2012 |
| Jackson, Mariah | Vice President | 2056 |
| Chaou-Matheson, Beverly | Vice President | 2190 |
| Levine, Kenneth | Vice President | 2089 |
| Greerson, Leslie | Director | 2971 |
| Hogue, Brenda | Director | 2702 |
| Listmann, Hillary | Director | 2864 |
| Moon, Benjamin | Director | 2311 |
| Stratten, Rosemary | Director | 2788 |
| Ohala, Rafael | Director | 2622 |
| Murray, Lisa | Director | 2541 |
| Harris-Lee, Joan | Director | 2482 |
| Ellerbe, Sandra | Director | 2766 |
| Arevalo, Alyce | Director | 2515 |

## Activity 3

**Situation:** You are an administrative assistant in the vocational department at Mountain Community College. You have been asked by your supervisor to create a fill-in form template for advisory committees that contains the information on the next page (you determine the layout of the form and the types of form fields used):

ADVISORY COMMITTEE MEMBER APPLICATION

Committee Requested:  Science, Social Studies, Arts, or
        Health and Fitness

Name:
Company Address:
Telephone:
Job Title:
Years of Experience:
Gender: Male or Female
Ethnic Origin (optional): American Indian/Alaska Native,
        Hispanic, Black, Asian/Pacific Islander, Caucasian, Other

After creating the form template, save the template document as xxxadv.dot. Use the xxxadv.dot form template to create a filled-in form. You make up information to fill in the form fields. After the form is filled in, save it and name it u06act03. Print then close u06act03.

## RESEARCH ACTIVITY

*Note: For this research activity you will need access to the Microsoft Word User's Guide.*

Answer the following questions about information in the Word for Windows User's guide.

1. On what pages do you find information on checking errors in a main document and data source?                                                   _____

2. If a merge field in the main document doesn't match one of the field names from the data source, what dialog box does Word display? _____

3. What chapter covers advanced mail merge techniques?                    _____

4. On what pages can you find information on specifying multiple rules for selecting records?
_____

5. What types of documents does the user's guide show as examples of what can be created with the mail merge catalog option?
_____

6. What pages cover information on merging to electronic mail and fax systems? _____

7. What kind of formatting cannot be applied to a document in the Outline viewing mode?
_____

8. On what pages do you find information on selecting text in the Outline viewing mode?
_____

9. What steps would you complete to change the order of items in a drop-down list?

_____

_____

_____

10. When a document is protected, what changes does Word make to the document?

_____

_____

_____

11. What steps would you complete to prevent a section of a document from being protected?

_____

_____

_____

12. On what pages do you find information on tips for laying out a grid-type form? _____

13. A concordance file can be created using either a two-column table or this. _____

14. What can you do to speed up the creation of a concordance file?

_____

_____

15. What steps would you complete to update or display a table of figures using a shortcut menu?

_____

_____

16. If you add text to a legal document, additional citations can be marked by selecting the original long citation and then pressing this shortcut command.

_____

# Appendix A • Using the Mouse

Word for Windows can be operated using a keyboard or it can be operated with the keyboard and a special piece of equipment called a *mouse*. A mouse is a small device that sits on a flat surface next to the computer. It is operated with one hand and works best if sitting on a mouse pad. The mouse may have two or three buttons on top, which are pressed to execute specific functions and commands.

To use the mouse, rest it on a flat surface or a mouse pad and put your hand over it with your palm resting on top of the mouse. As you move the mouse on the flat surface, a corresponding icon moves on the screen.

## ■ Understanding Mouse Terms

When using the mouse, there are three terms you should understand—click, double-click, and drag. *Click* means to press a button on the mouse quickly, then release it. *Double-click* means to press the button twice in quick succession. The term *drag* means to hold down a button, move the mouse pointer to a specific location, then release the button.

## ■ Using the Mouse Pointer

The mouse pointer will change appearance depending on the function being performed or where the pointer is positioned. The mouse pointer may appear as one of the following images:

I

The mouse pointer appears as an I-beam (called the *I-beam pointer*) in the document screen and can be used to move the insertion point or select text.

The mouse pointer appears as an arrow pointing up and to the left (called the *arrow pointer*) when it is moved to the Title bar, Menu bar, or one of the toolbars at the top of the screen or when a dialog box is displayed. For example, to open a new document with the mouse, you would move the I-beam pointer to the File option on the Menu bar. When the I-beam pointer is moved to the Menu bar, it turns into an arrow pointer. To choose the File option on the Menu bar, position the tip of the arrow on File, then click the left mouse button. In the File drop-down menu, the mouse pointer also displays as an arrow pointer. You can choose options from the drop-down menu by positioning the tip of the arrow pointer on the desired option, then clicking the left mouse button.

The mouse pointer becomes a double-headed arrow (either pointing left and right or pointing up and down) when performing certain functions such as changing the size of a picture or sizing a frame.

In certain situations, such as moving a picture or frame, the mouse pointer becomes a four-headed arrow. The four-headed arrow means that you can move the object left, right, up, or down.

When Word is processing a request, or when the Word program is being loaded, the mouse pointer appears as an hourglass. This image means "please wait." When the process is completed, the mouse pointer returns to an I-beam pointer or an arrow pointer.

The mouse pointer displays as a hand with a pointing index finger in certain functions such as Help and indicates that there is more information available about the item.

# Appendix B • Formatting Disks

Before a disk can be used to save Word documents, it must be formatted. (If you are using the student data disk that comes with this textbook, the disk has already been formatted. Do not format it again since formatting erases everything on the disk.)

Formatting is a process that prepares the surface of a disk for receiving data from the particular disk operating system that is being used. A disk can be formatted using the Format command from the Disk Operating System (DOS).

During the formatting process, any information on the disk is erased. Before formatting, make sure you do not have anything on the disk that you want to save.

Complete the following steps to format a disk:

1. Turn on the computer.
2. At the *C:\>* prompt, key **format a:,** then press Enter.
3. The message *Insert new diskette for drive A: and press Enter when ready ...* appears on the screen. Insert a blank disk in drive a, close the disk drive door, then press Enter.
4. When you press Enter, the formatting process begins and the disk light comes on. Do not remove the disk as the disk is being formatted.
5. When the disk is formatted, you will see the message *Format another (Y/N)?*. If you do not want to format another disk, key an **N**, then press Enter. The *C:\>* appears on the screen. (Depending on the version of DOS you are using, you may see the message *Volume label (11 characters, Enter for none)?*. At this message, press Enter or key your name, then press Enter.)
6. Take out the disk and turn off the computer.

# Appendix C • Choosing Commands

In Word for Windows, 6.0, there are several methods that can be used to choose commands. A command is an instruction that tells Word for Windows to do something. You can choose a command with one of the following methods:

- Click on a toolbar button with the mouse.
- Choose a command from a menu.
- Use shortcut keys.
- Use a shortcut menu.

## ■ Choosing Commands on Toolbars

Word for Windows provides several toolbars containing buttons for common tasks. Generally, two toolbars are visible on the screen (unless your system has been customized). The toolbar directly below the Menu bar is called the Standard toolbar. The toolbar below the Standard toolbar is called the Formatting toolbar. To choose a command from a toolbar, position the tip of the arrow pointer on a button, then click the left mouse button. For example, to print the document currently displayed in the document screen, click on the Print button on the Standard toolbar.

## ■ Choosing Commands on the Menu Bar

The Menu bar at the top of the Word screen contains a variety of options you can use to format a Word document or complete file management tasks. Word features are grouped logically into options, which display on the Menu bar. For example, features to work with Word files (documents) are grouped in the File option. Either the mouse or the keyboard can be used to make choices from the Menu bar or choose options from a dialog box.

To use the mouse to make a choice from the Menu bar, move the I-beam pointer to the Menu bar. This causes the I-beam pointer to display as an arrow pointer. Position the tip of the arrow pointer on the desired option, then click the left mouse button.

To use the keyboard, press the Alt key or press F10 to make the Menu bar active. Options on the Menu bar display with an underline below one of the letters. To choose an option from the Menu bar, key the underlined letter of the desired option, or press the left or right arrow keys to move to the option desired, then press Enter. This causes a drop-down menu to display.

For example, to display the File drop-down menu shown in figure C.1 using the mouse, position the arrow pointer on File on the Menu bar, then click the left mouse button. To display the File drop-down menu with the keyboard, press the Alt key or F10, then key the letter F for File.

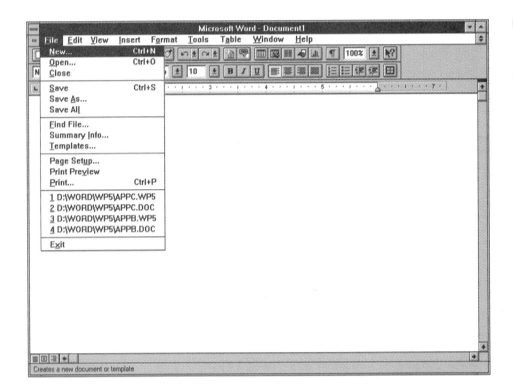

Figure C.1
File Drop-Down
Menu

# ■ Choosing Commands from Drop-Down Menus

To choose a command from a drop-down menu with the mouse, position the arrow pointer on the desired option, then click the left mouse button. You can also position the arrow pointer on the desired option on the Menu bar (such as File), hold down the left mouse button, drag the arrow pointer to the desired option, then release the mouse button. When you position the arrow pointer on an option and hold down the left mouse button, a drop-down menu appears. As you drag the arrow pointer down the menu, the various options in the menu will be selected.

To make a selection from the drop-down menu with the keyboard, key the underlined letter of the desired option. Once the drop-down menu is displayed, you do not need to hold down the Alt key with the underlined letter.

Some menu options may be gray shaded (dimmed). When an option is dimmed, that option is currently not available. For example, if you choose the Edit option from the Menu bar, the Edit drop-down menu displays with several dimmed options including Cut and Copy. If text is selected before the Edit drop-down menu is displayed, these options are not dimmed because they are available.

Some menu options are preceded by a check mark. The check mark indicates that the option is currently active. To make an option inactive (turn it off) using the mouse, position the arrow pointer on the option, then click the left mouse button. To make an option inactive (turn it off) with the keyboard, key the underlined letter of the option.

If an option from a drop-down menu displays followed by ellipses (...), a dialog box will display when that option is chosen. A dialog box provides a variety of options to let you specify how a command is to be carried out. For example, if you choose File, then Print, the Print dialog box shown in figure C.2 displays.

Figure C.2
Print Dialog Box

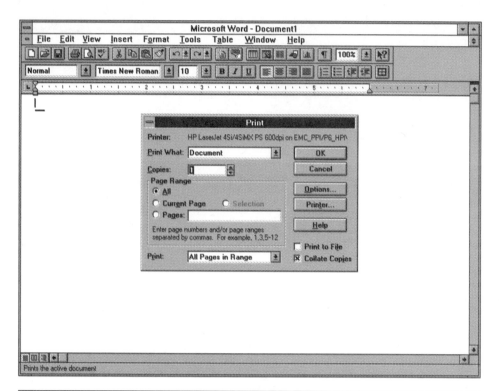

Figure C.3
Font Dialog Box

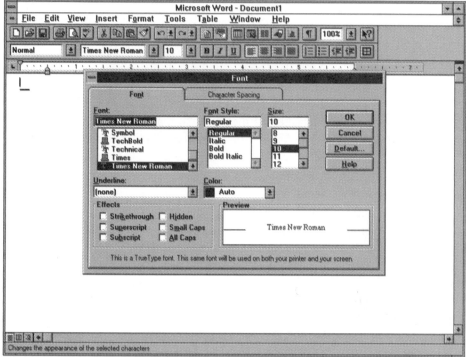

Or, if you choose Format, then Font from the Menu bar, the Font dialog box shown in figure C.3 displays.

Some dialog boxes provide a set of options. These options are contained on separate tabs. For example, the Font dialog box shown in figure C.3 contains a tab at the top of the dialog box with the word Font on it. To the right of that tab is another tab with the words Character Spacing. The tab that displays in the front is the active tab. To make a tab active using the mouse, position the arrow pointer on the desired tab, then click the left mouse button. If you are using the keyboard, press Ctrl + Tab or press Alt + the underlined letter on the desired tab. For example, to change the tab to Character Spacing in the Font dialog box, click on Character Spacing, or press Ctrl + Tab, or press Alt + R.

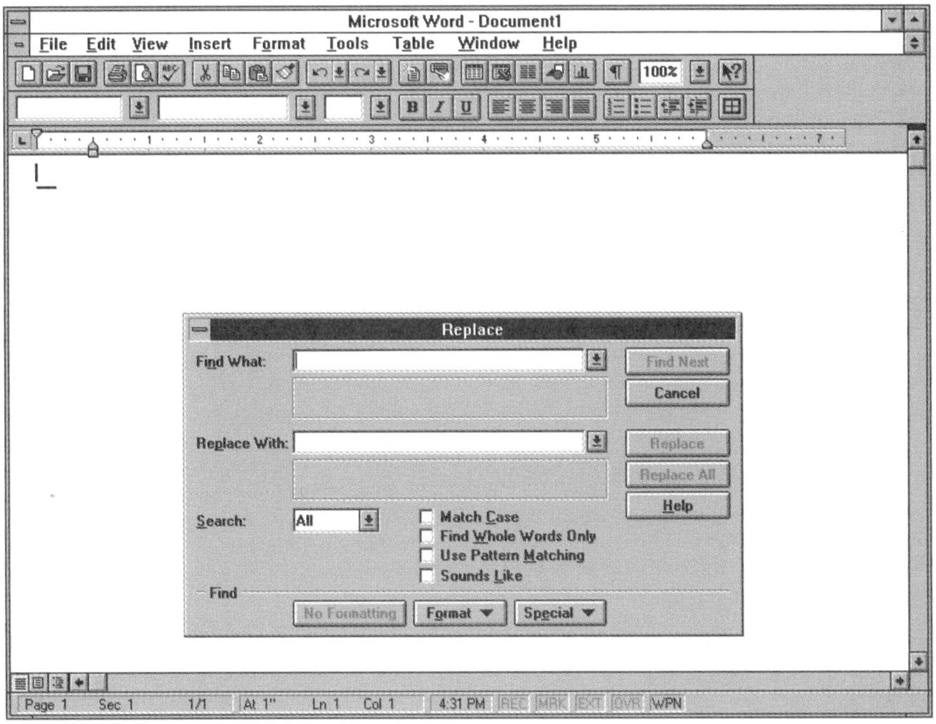

Figure C.4
Replace Dialog Box

To choose options from a dialog box with the mouse, position the arrow pointer on the desired option, then click the left mouse button. If you are using the keyboard, press the Tab key to move the insertion point forward from option to option. Press Shift + Tab to move the insertion point backward from option to option. You can also hold down the Alt key, then press the underlined letter of the desired option.

When an option is selected, it will display either in reverse video (white letters on a blue background) or surrounded by a dashed box called a *marquee*.

A dialog box contains one or more of the following elements: text boxes, list boxes, check boxes, option buttons, spin boxes, and command buttons.

## Text Boxes

Some options in a dialog box require text to be entered. For example, the boxes to the right of the Find What and Replace With options at the Replace dialog box shown in figure C.4 are text boxes.

In a text box, you key text or edit existing text. Edit text in a text box in the same manner as normal text. Use the left and right arrow keys on the keyboard to move the insertion point without deleting text and use the Delete key or Backspace key to delete text.

Figure C.5
Open Dialog Box

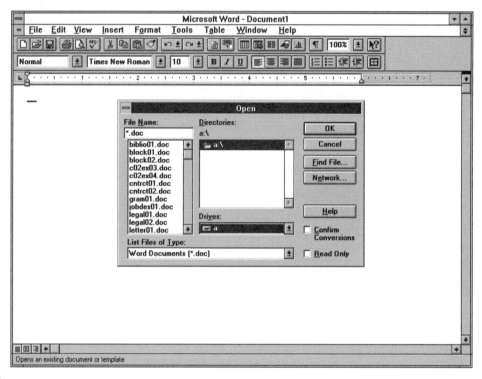

## List Boxes

Some dialog boxes such as the Open dialog box shown in figure C.5 may contain a list box. The list of files below the File Name text box are contained in a list box. To make a selection from a list box with the mouse, move the arrow pointer to the desired option, then click the left mouse button.

Some list boxes may contain a scroll bar. This scroll bar can be used to move through the list if the list is longer than the box. To move down through the list, position the arrow pointer on the down scroll arrow and hold down the left mouse button. To scroll up through the list, position the arrow pointer on the up scroll arrow and hold down the left mouse button. You can also move the arrow pointer above the scroll box and click the left mouse button to scroll up the list or move the arrow pointer below the scroll box and click the left mouse button to move down the list.

To make a selection from a list using the keyboard, move the insertion point into the box by holding down the Alt key and pressing the underlined letter of the desired option. For some options, you may also need to press the Tab key. For example, in the Open dialog box, the File Name option is selected by default. To move the cursor into the list of documents, press the Tab key. To move to a specific option in a list box, press the up or down arrow keys.

In some dialog boxes where there is not enough room for a list box, lists of options are inserted in a drop-down list box. Options that contain a drop-down list box display with a down-pointing arrow. For example, the Underline option at the Font dialog box contains a drop-down list. To display the list, click on the down-pointing arrow. If you are using the keyboard, press Alt + U.

## Check Boxes

Some dialog boxes contain options preceded by a box. An X may or may not appear in the boxes. The Font dialog box shown in figure C.3 displays a variety of check boxes within the Effects section. If an X appears in the box, the option is active (turned on). If there is no X in the check box, the option is inactive (turned off). Any number of check boxes can be active. For example, in the Font dialog box, you can insert an X in any or all of the boxes in the Effects section and these options will be active.

To make a check box active or inactive with the mouse, position the tip of the arrow pointer in the check box, then click the left mouse button. If you are using the keyboard, press Alt + the underlined letter of the desired option.

## Option Buttons

In the Print dialog box shown in figure C.2, the options in the Page Range section are preceded by option buttons. Only one option button can be selected at any time. When an option button is selected, a dark circle displays in the button.

To select an option button with the mouse, position the tip of the arrow pointer inside the option button, then click the left mouse button. To make a selection with the keyboard, hold down the Alt key, then press the underlined letter of the desired option.

## Spin Boxes

Some options in a dialog box contain measurements or numbers that can be increased or decreased. These options are generally located in a spin box. For example, the Paragraph dialog box shown in figure C.6 contains a variety of spin boxes including Left, Right, Before, and After. To increase a number in a spin box, position the tip of the arrow pointer on the up-pointing triangle to the right of the box, then click the left mouse button. To decrease the number, click on the down-pointing triangle. If you are using the keyboard, press Alt + the underlined letter of the desired option, then press the up arrow key to increase the number or the down arrow key to decrease the number.

## Command Buttons

In the Replace dialog box shown in figure C.4, the boxes at the right side of the dialog box are called *command buttons*. A command button is used to execute or cancel a command. Some command buttons display with ellipses (...). A command button that displays with ellipses will open another dialog box.

The default command button will display with the marquee. It can be changed with the mouse by positioning the tip of the arrow pointer on the desired command button, then clicking the left mouse button. To change the active command button with the keyboard, press the Tab key until the desired command button contains the marquee, then press the Enter key.

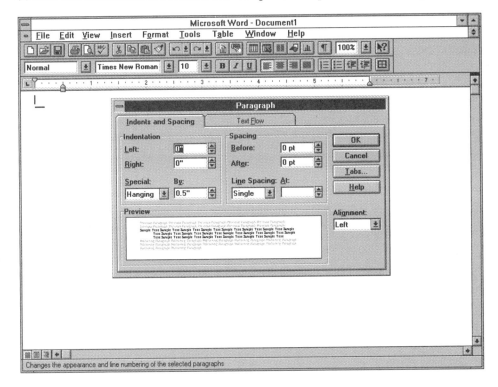

*Figure C.6*
*Paragraph Dialog*
*Box*

## ■ *Choosing Commands with Shortcut Keys*

At the left side of a drop-down menu is a list of options. At the right side, shortcut keys for specific options are displayed. For example, the shortcut keys to save a document are Ctrl + S and are displayed to the right of the <u>S</u>ave option of the File drop-down menu shown in figure C.1.

To use shortcut keys to choose a command, hold down the Ctrl key, key the letter for the command, then release the Ctrl key.

## ■ *Choosing Commands with Shortcut Menus*

Word for Windows includes shortcut menus that contain commands related to the item you are working with. A shortcut menu appears right where you are working in the document. To display a shortcut menu, click the right mouse button or press Shift + F10.

For example, if the insertion point is positioned in a paragraph of text, clicking the right mouse button or pressing Shift + F10 will cause the shortcut menu shown in figure C.7 to display in the document screen.

To select an option from a shortcut menu with the mouse, click on the desired option. If you are using the keyboard, press the up or down arrow key until the desired option is selected, then press the Enter key.

To close a shortcut menu without choosing an option, click anywhere outside the shortcut menu or press the Esc key.

*Figure C.7*
*Shortcut Menu*

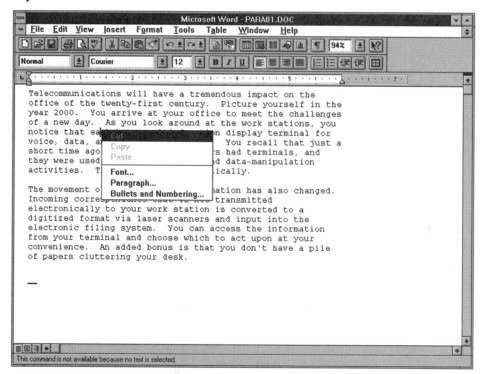

# Appendix D • Formatting Business Documents

There are many memorandum and business letter styles. This appendix includes one memorandum and two business letter styles.

At the end of a memorandum or business letter, the initials of the person keying the document appear. In exercises in this textbook, insert your initials where you see the *xx* at the end of a document. The name of the document is included after the initials.

Both business letters in this appendix were created with standard punctuation. Standard punctuation includes a colon after the salutation and a comma after the complimentary close.

A business letter can be printed on letterhead stationery, or the company name and address can be keyed at the top of the letter. For the examples in this text, assume that all business letters you create will be printed on letterhead stationery.

*1-inch top margin*

```
DATE:      September 28, 1996
                ds
TO:        Adam Mukai, Vice President
                ds
FROM:      Carol Jenovich, Director
                ds
SUBJECT:   NEW EMPLOYEES
                ts
Two new employees have been hired to work in the Human Resources
Department.  Lola Henderson will begin work on October 1 and Daniel
Schriver will begin October 14.
                ds
Ms. Henderson has worked for three years as an administrative
assistant for another company.  Due to her previous experience, she
was hired as a program assistant.
                ds
Mr. Schriver has just completed a one-year training program at Gulf
Community College.  He was hired as an Administrative Assistant I.
                ds
I would like to introduce you to the new employees.  Please
schedule a time for a short visit.
                ds
xx:memo
```

Traditional Memo Style

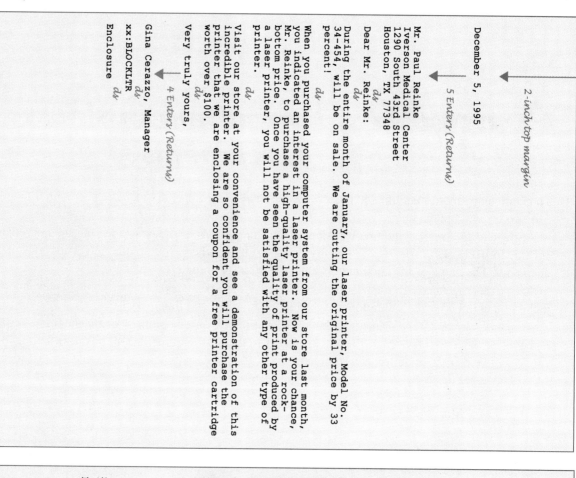

2-inch top margin

December 5, 1995

5 Enters (Returns)

Mr. Paul Reinke
Iverson Medical Center
1290 South 43rd Street
Houston, TX 77348
*ds*

Dear Mr. Reinke:
*ds*

During the entire month of January, our laser printer, Model No. 34-454, will be on sale. We are cutting the original price by 33 percent!
*ds*

When you purchased your computer system from our store last month, you indicated an interest in a laser printer. Now is your chance, Mr. Reinke, to purchase a high-quality laser printer at a rock-bottom price. Once you have seen the quality of print produced by a laser printer, you will not be satisfied with any other type of printer.
*ds*

Visit our store at your convenience and see a demonstration of this incredible printer. We are so confident you will purchase the printer that we are enclosing a coupon for a free printer cartridge worth over $100.
*ds*

Very truly yours,
*4 Enters (Returns)*
*ds*

Gina Cerazzo, Manager
*ds*
xx:BLOCKLTR
Enclosure
*ds*

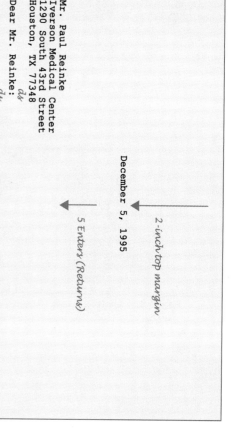

2-inch top margin

December 5, 1995

5 Enters (Returns)

Mr. Paul Reinke
Iverson Medical Center
1290 South 43rd Street
Houston, TX 77348
*ds*

Dear Mr. Reinke:
*ds*

During the entire month of January, our laser printer, Model No. 34-454, will be on sale. We are cutting the original price by 33 percent!
*ds*

When you purchased your computer system from our store last month, you indicated an interest in a laser printer. Now is your chance, Mr. Reinke, to purchase a high-quality laser printer at a rock-bottom price. Once you have seen the quality of print produced by a laser printer, you will not be satisfied with any other type of printer.
*ds*

Visit our store at your convenience and see a demonstration of this incredible printer. We are so confident you will purchase the printer that we are enclosing a coupon for a free printer cartridge worth over $100.
*ds*

Very truly yours,
*ds*
HOUSTON COMPUTING
*4 Enters (Returns)*
*ds*

Gina Cerazzo, Manager
*ds*
xx:BLOCKLTR
Enclosure

# Appendix E • Proofreaders' Marks

| Proofreaders' Mark | | Example | Revised |
|---|---|---|---|
| # | Insert space | lettertothe | letter to the |
| ℒ | Delete | the commands is | the command is |
| lc / | Lowercase | he is Branch Manager | he is branch manager |
| cap or uc ≡ | Uppercase | Margaret simpson | Margaret Simpson |
| # | New paragraph | The new product | The new product |
| no # | No paragraph | the meeting. | the meeting. Bring the |
| | | Bring the | |
| ∧ | Insert | pens clips | pens, and clips |
| ⊙ | Insert period | a global search | a global search. |
| ⊐ | Move right | With the papers | With the papers |
| ⊏ | Move left | access the code | access the code |
| ⊐⊏ | Center | Chapter Six | Chapter Six |
| ∪ | Transpose | It is raesonable | It is reasonable |
| sp | Spell out | 475 Mill Ave. | 475 Mill Avenue |
| … | Stet (do not delete) | I am very pleased | I am very pleased |
| ⌒ | Close up | regret fully | regretfully |
| ss | Single-space | The margin top ss is 1 inch. | The margin top is 1 inch. |
| ds | Double-space | Paper length is set for 11 inches. | Paper length is set for 11 inches. |
| ts | Triple-space | Use options from the File drop-down menu | Use options from the File drop-down menu |
| bf | Boldface | Boldface type provides emphasis. | **Boldface** type provides emphasis. |
| ital | Italics | Use italics for terms to be defined. | Use *italics* for terms to be defined. |

# *A*ppendix *F* • *W*ord *T*oolbars

## *S*tandard

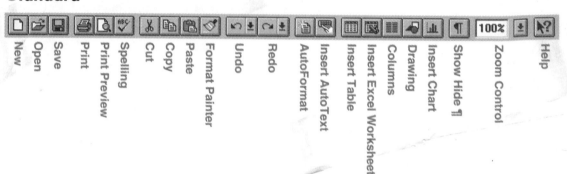

New
Open
Save
Print
Print Preview
Spelling
Cut
Copy
Paste
Format Painter
Undo
Redo
AutoFormat
Insert AutoText
Insert Table
Insert Excel Worksheet
Columns
Drawing
Insert Chart
Show Hide ¶
Zoom Control
Help

## *F*ormatting

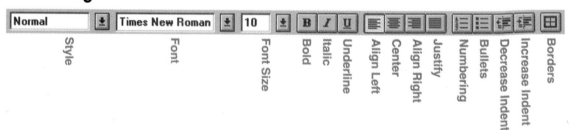

Style
Font
Font Size
Bold
Italic
Underline
Align Left
Center
Align Right
Justify
Numbering
Bullets
Decrease Indent
Increase Indent
Borders

# *B*orders

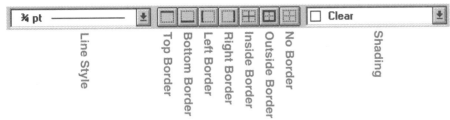

Line Style

Top Border
Bottom Border
Left Border
Right Border
Inside Border
Outside Border
No Border

Shading

# *D*atadase

Data Form
Manage Fields
Add New Record
Delete Record
Sort Ascending
Sort Descending
Insert Database
Update Fields
Find Record
Mail Merge Main Document

# Drawing

- Line
- Rectangle
- Ellipse
- Arc
- Freeform
- Text Box
- Callout
- Format Callout
- Fill Color
- Line Color
- Line Style
- Select Drawing Objects
- Bring to Front
- Send to Back
- Bring in Front of Text
- Send Behind Text
- Group
- Ungroup
- Flip Horizontal
- Flip Vertical
- Rotate Right
- Reshape
- Snap to Grid
- Align Drawing Objects
- Create Picture
- Insert Frame

# Forms

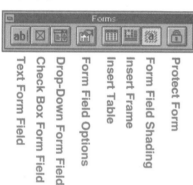

- Text Form Field
- Check Box Form Field
- Drop-Down Form Field
- Form Field Options
- Insert Table
- Insert Frame
- Form Field Shading
- Protect Form

# Microsoft

- Microsoft Ex
- Microsoft PowerPoint
- Microsoft Mail
- Microsoft Access
- Microsoft FoxPro
- Microsoft Project
- Microsoft Schedule+
- Microsoft Publisher

# Appendix G • ClipArt Images

1stplace.wmf

anchor.wmf

artist.wmf

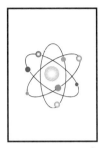
atomengy.wmf

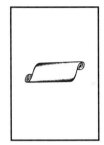
banner.wmf

bearmrkt.wmf

bird.wmf

books.wmf

bullmrkt.wmf

buttrfly.wmf

cat.wmf

celtic.wmf

checkmrk.wmf

cityscpe.wmf

coffee.wmf

compass.wmf

computer.wmf

conductr.wmf

confiden.wmf

continen.wmf

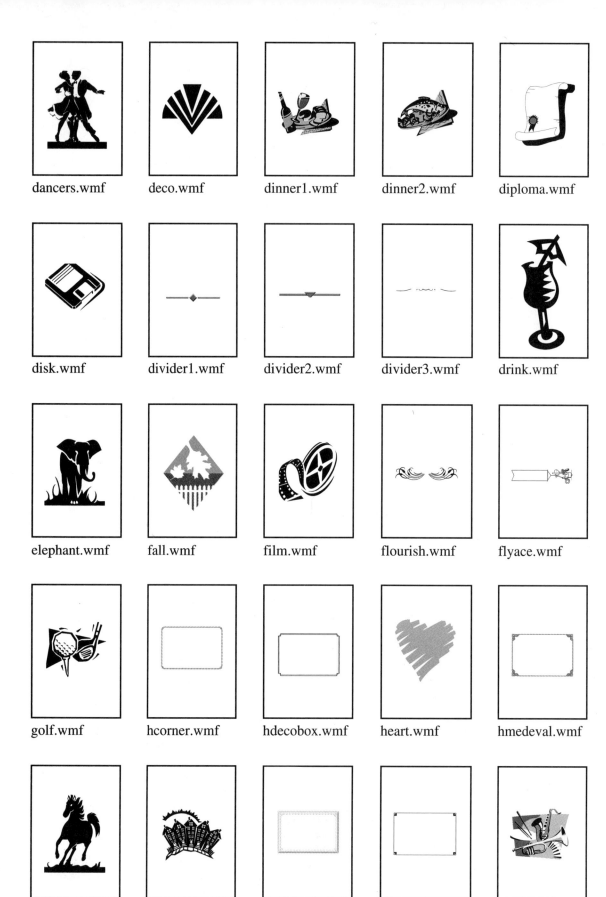

dancers.wmf    deco.wmf    dinner1.wmf    dinner2.wmf    diploma.wmf

disk.wmf    divider1.wmf    divider2.wmf    divider3.wmf    drink.wmf

elephant.wmf    fall.wmf    film.wmf    flourish.wmf    flyace.wmf

golf.wmf    hcorner.wmf    hdecobox.wmf    heart.wmf    hmedeval.wmf

horse.wmf    houses.wmf    hplaque.wmf    hpresbox.wmf    jazz.wmf

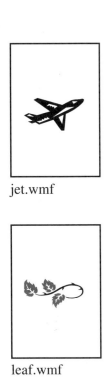

jet.wmf

label1.wmf

label2.wmf

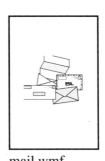

lblkdiam.wmf

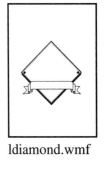

ldiamond.wmf

leaf.wmf

lightblb.wmf

luggage.wmf

mail.wmf

math.wmf

medstaff.wmf

motorcrs.wmf

movie.wmf

nosmoke.wmf

notes.wmf

nouveau1.wmf

nouveau2.wmf

nouvflwr.wmf

office.wmf

ornamnt1.wmf

ornamnt2.wmf

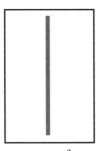

ornamnt3.wmf

ornate.wmf

party.wmf

pharmacy.wmf

realest.wmf

recycle.wmf

sail.wmf

scales.wmf

server.wmf

speaker.wmf

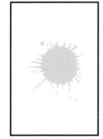

splat.wmf

sports.wmf

spring.wmf

summer.wmf

tennis.wmf

theatre.wmf

wheelchr.wmf

# Index

### Standard Toolbar

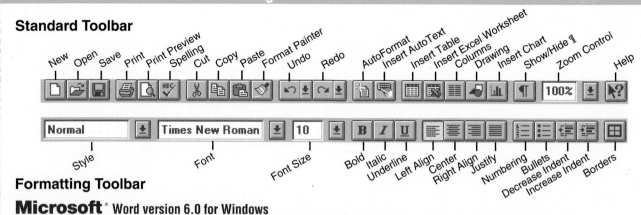

### Formatting Toolbar

**Microsoft**® Word version 6.0 for Windows

## Word Keyboard Shortcuts

### Paragraph Formatting

| | |
|---|---|
| Center | Ctrl+E |
| Right Align | Ctrl+R |
| Left Align | Ctrl+L |
| Justify | Ctrl+J |
| Increase Indent | Ctrl+M |
| Decrease Indent | Ctrl+Shift+M |
| Hanging Indent | Ctrl+T |
| Remove Hanging Indent | Ctrl+Shift+T |
| Open/Close Space Before | Ctrl+0 (zero) |
| Single-space Lines | Ctrl+1 |
| Double-space Lines | Ctrl+2 |
| Apply Style | Ctrl+Shift+S |
| Reset to Style | Ctrl+Q |

### Character Formatting

| | |
|---|---|
| Bold | Ctrl+B |
| Italic | Ctrl+I |
| Continuous Underline | Ctrl+U |
| Word Underline | Ctrl+Shift+W |
| Double Underline | Ctrl+Shift+D |
| Subscript | Ctrl+= |
| Superscript | Ctrl+Shift+= |
| All Caps | Ctrl+Shift+A |
| Small Caps | Ctrl+Shift+K |
| Font | Ctrl+D |
| Point Size | Ctrl+Shift+P |
| Hidden | Ctrl+Shift+H |
| Reset Character | Ctrl+Shift+Z, or Ctrl+Spacebar |

### Other Actions

| | |
|---|---|
| Cut | Ctrl+X |
| Copy | Ctrl+C |
| Paste | Ctrl+V |
| Repeat | Ctrl+Y or F4 |
| Cancel | Esc |
| New Line | Shift+Enter |
| New Page | Ctrl+enter |
| New Column/Split Table | Ctrl+Shift+Enter |
| Optional Hyphen | Ctrl+Hyphen |
| Nonbreaking Hyphen | Ctrl+Shift+Hyphen |
| Nonbreaking Space | Ctrl+Shift+Spacebar |
| Tab Character (table) | Ctrl+Tab |
| Show Nonprinting Characters | Ctrl+Shift+* |

**Microsoft**® Word version 6.0 for Windows

For complete help on keyboard shortcuts, double-click the Help button and type **Keyboard shortcuts**

## Word Function Keys

**F1**

Help
Context Help

**F2**

Move
Copy

**F3**

AutoText
Change Case

Cut to Spike
Insert Spike

**F4**

Repeat Command
Repeat Find/Go To
Quit Word
Close Document

**F5**

Go To
Go Back
Restore App Window
Restore Doc Window
Edit Bookmark

**F6**

Next Pane
Previous Pane
Next Window
Previous Window

key only
SHIFT+
ALT+
CTRL+
CTRL+SHIFT+

**F7**

Spelling
Thesaurus

Move Doc Window

**F8**

Extend Selection
Shrink Selection

Size Doc Window

**F9**

Update Field
Toggle Field Code
Toggle All Field Codes
Insert Field
Unlink Field
Do Field Click

**F10**

Menu Bar
Shortcut Menu
Max App Window
Max Doc Window

**F11**

Next Field
Previous Field
Go To Annotation Text
Lock Field
Unlock Field

**F12**

Save As
Save

Open
Print

key only
SHIFT+
ALT+
CTRL+
CTRL+SHIFT+
ALT+SHIFT+

**Microsoft**® Word version 6.0 for Windows

For complete help on keyboard shortcuts, double-click the Help button and type **Keyboard shortcuts**